Henry Parry Liddon

Explanatory analysis of St. Paul's Epistle to the Romans

Henry Parry Liddon
Explanatory analysis of St. Paul's Epistle to the Romans
ISBN/EAN: 9783337729806

Printed in Europe, USA, Canada, Australia, Japan

Cover: Foto ©ninafisch / pixelio.de

More available books at **www.hansebooks.com**

EXPLANATORY ANALYSIS

OF

PAUL'S EPISTLE TO THE ROMANS

BY

H. P. LIDDON, D.D., D.C.L., LL.D.

LATE CANON AND CHANCELLOR OF ST. PAUL'S
IRELAND PROFESSOR OF EXEGESIS IN THE UNIVERSITY OF OXFORD 1870-1882

LONDON
LONGMANS, GREEN, AND CO.
AND NEW YORK: 15 EAST 16th STREET
1893

ADVERTISEMENT

THE following 'Notice' was prefixed to the unpublished copies of the Analysis of the Epistle to the Romans which the late Dr. Liddon caused to be printed for distribution in 1876.

NOTICE.

A few words may be due to any into whose hands this Analysis may chance to fall.

It is composed of a series of papers which were distributed to Students who attended the Author's Lectures in 1875-76. These papers were designed to furnish a clue to the sequence of the Apostle's teaching in his greatest Epistle; and also to supply a skeleton, around which more detailed information and illustrations might be grouped in private study.

The writer has largely followed the suggestions of Meyer, wherever the theological or untheological crotchets of that great scholar have not impaired the value of his opinion.

This Analysis is *not* published, for two reasons among others. The scale of the earlier chapters does not correspond with that of the later; and the writer is not without some anxiety as to the explanation which has been given of Rom. vii. 14-25.

CH. CH. H. P. L.
June 19, 1876.

After 1876, Dr. Liddon rewrote the Analysis of the earlier chapters on a greatly enlarged scale, made considerable additions and alterations throughout, and modified his view of Rom. vii. 14–25. The present edition is printed in part (capp. i.–v. 11) from a manuscript dated Feb. 1878, in part from an interleaved copy of the earlier issue dated Oct. 1880. The book is simply Dr. Liddon's: it was by him intended for publication: and the work of the editor has scarcely gone beyond the verification and correction of references.

Dr. Liddon's literary executors desire to express their thanks to Mr. Campbell Dodgson, late scholar of New College, and the Rev. J. O. Nash, of Pusey House, for labour devoted to the verification of references; also to the Rev. G. A. Cooke, Fellow of Magdalen College, for revision of the Hebrew quotations.

SEXAGESIMA, 1892.

HEADS OF ANALYSIS OF THE EPISTLE

INTRODUCTION (i. 1-17).
    A. Apostolical Salutation (1-7).
    B. The Apostle's interest in the Roman Church explained (8-17). This explanation concludes by stating the leading Proposition of the Epistle (16 b-17). Man becomes righteous before GOD by faith in Jesus Christ.

DOGMATIC PART (i. 17 –xi. 36).
    Division I (i. 18—v. 21). Justification by faith considered in itself and objectively. Its place in human nature and religious history.
        (A) Man's need of righteousness universal (i. 18—iii. 20).
        (B) Righteousness received by faith through Christ's Atoning Death (iii. 21-30).
        (C) This Righteousness by faith in Christ anticipated in the O. T. (iii. 31—iv. 25).
        (D) Happiness of the justified, and grounds of their encouragement under trials (v. 1-11).
        (E) Comparison of Christ, the Author of Righteousness and of man's true life, with Adam, the author of sin and death (v. 12-21).
    Division II (vi—viii). Justification considered subjectively and in its effects upon life and conduct. Moral consequences of justification.
        (A) The Life of Justification and sin (vi. 1-14).
        (B) The Life of Justification and the Mosaic Law (vi. 15—vii. 25).
        (C) The Life of Justification and the work of the Holy Spirit (viii).
    Division III (appendix). Relation of the Jewish people to Justification by faith (ix—xi).
        (A) Introduction. The Apostle's sorrow at the condition of Israel (ix. 1-5).
        (B) Israel's failure in the light of GOD's Attributes (ix. 6-29).
        (C) Israel's failure in the light of man's responsibility (ix. 30 – x. 21).
        (D) Israel's failure in the light of a happier future (xi. 1-32).
        (E) Concluding Doxology (xi. 33-36).

PRACTICAL PART (xii. 1—xv. 13).
    Division I. General moral obligations (xii, xiii).
        (A) In their application to the Christian—
            (1) As possessing an animal and spiritual nature (xii. 1, 2).
            (2) As a member of the Body of Christ (xii. 3-8).
            (3) As a member of human society at large (xii. 9-21).
            (4) As living under a (pagan) civil government (xiii. 1-7).
        (B) Considered as animated by two great motives in particular (xiii. 8-14).
    Division II. Particular questions solved (xiv. 1—xv. 13).
        (A) The questions stated (xiv. 1-5).
        (B) Principles to which they are referred for solution (xiv. 6—xv. 13).

EPILOGUE (xv. 14-33). The tone of parts of the Epistle justified.

CONCLUSION (xvi).

SPECIAL TABULAR ANALYSIS OF APOSTOLICAL SALUTATION, I. 1–7.

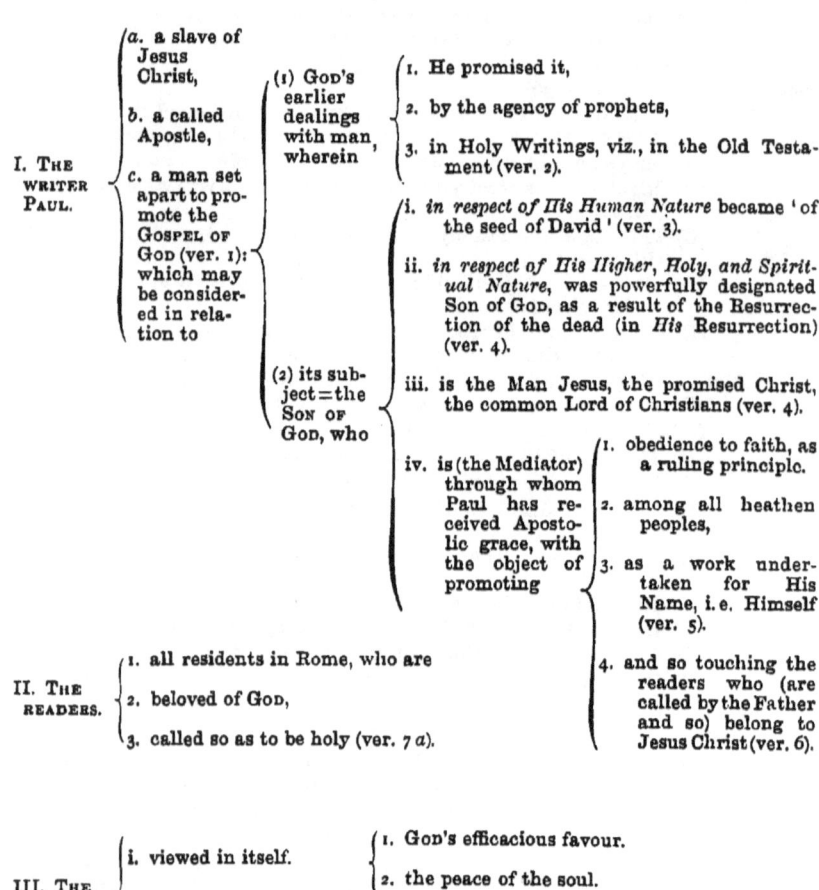

ST. PAUL'S
EPISTLE TO THE ROMANS.

INTRODUCTORY PORTION OF THE EPISTLE.
Chap. I. 1-17.
A.
The Apostolical Salutation. 1-7.

[*Obs.* As in Gal. i. 1 sqq.; Tit. i. 1 sqq., the Apostle enlarges his salutation by appended relative clauses, in which the main ideas of the Epistle are, to a certain extent, anticipated. The salutation itself is contained in vers. 1 and 7. But the intermediate verses are not parenthetical; the structure is continuous. So at Col. iii. 12-14. Winer, *Grammar of N. T. Greek*, p. 707 (ed. Moulton, 3rd edit., Clark, Edin. 1882).]

I. The writer of the Epistle.
  1. The writer of the Epistle, describes himself as
     a. a slave of Jesus Christ (δοῦλος Ἰησ. Χρ.),
     b. a (divinely) celled Apostle (κλητὸς ἀπόστολος),
     c. a man separated from his fellows for a special work (ἀφωρισμένος εἰς κ.τ.λ.) (ver. 1).

[*Obs.* 1. The description δοῦλος Ἰησοῦ Χριστοῦ corresponds to עֶבֶד יְהוָה, which is used (1) of worshippers of GOD generally, as in Neh. i. 10; Ezra v. 11; Ps. xxxiv. 23; cxiii. 1; cxxxiv. 1; cxxxvi. 22; Is. liv. 17; lxiii. 17, &c. (2) Of persons entrusted with some special work or office, as of Abraham, Ps. cv. 6, 42; of Moses, Josh. i. 1; of Joshua, Josh. xxiv. 29; Judges ii. 8; of Job, Job i. 8; of David, Ps. xviii. 1; xxxvi. 1; lxxviii. 70; lxxxix. 4, 21; of Isaiah, Is. xx. 3; of Eliakim, Is. xxii. 20; of prophets, Amos iii. 7; Jer. vii. 25; xxv. 4; xxvi. 5; xxxv. 15; xliv. 4; Daniel ix. 6; Ezra ix. 11; of Zerubbabel, Hag. ii. 23, and in a special sense, in Isaiah's later writings, of Messiah. Here the Apostle uses the term in the second sense; he was a slave who bore office in the kingdom of Jesus Christ: the specific form of his service is defined in the next clause as ἀπόστολος. He had voluntarily surrendered his liberty; yet he belonged to Christ as purchased with Christ's Blood. In Gal. i. 10 he opposes his condition as Χριστοῦ δοῦλος to that of pleasers of men, Col. iv. 12. This is the earliest Epistle in which the word occurs at the beginning; it is also found in Phil., Tit., S. James, 2 Pet., S. Jude.]

[*Obs.* 2. In κλητὸς ἀπόστολος the specific form of S. Paul's δουλεία is given. In the New Testament ἀπόστολος means (1) a man taught by Christ Himself, and sent forth by Him to teach His Gospel. Thus it belongs properly to the Twelve, Luke vi. 13, Acts i. 26, whose office is termed ἡ ἀποστολή Acts i. 25. In a wider sense (2) it is used of a Christian teacher, not immediately instructed by Jesus Christ, as S. Barnabas, Acts xiv. 4. (In Rom. xvi. 7 this sense is at least doubtful.) S. Paul claims to be an Apostle in the first and highest sense ; Christ Himself, exalted in glory, had taught and sent him ; Acts ix. 6, 15 ; xxvi. 16 ; and as to his doctrine, οὐδὲ γὰρ ἐγὼ παρὰ ἀνθρώπου παρέλαβον αὐτό, οὔτε ἐδιδάχθην, ἀλλὰ δι' ἀποκαλύψεως Ἰησ. Χρ. Gal. i. 12. κλητός completes the title ; S. Paul was a divinely-called Apostle. A divine call was essential to the ἀποστολή : and it marked S. Paul off from self-appointed teachers, Acts xxii. 21 ἐγὼ εἰς ἔθνη μακρὰν ἐξαποστελῶ σε : xxvi. 17 εἰς οὓς νῦν σε ἀποστέλλω. It was by no act of his own, or through accidental circumstances, that he became what he was, οὐχ αὑτὸς ζητήσας εὗρεν, ἀλλὰ κληθεὶς παρεγένετο S. Chrys.]

[*Obs.* 3. ἀφωρισμένος. S. Paul was definitely separated from his friends and countrymen by the call and ordination to the Apostolate, Acts xiii. 2 ἀφορίσατε δή μοι κ.τ.λ. He is probably thinking of Lev. xx. 26 הִבְדִּיל, and of the words of our Lord, ἐξαιρούμενός σε ἐκ τοῦ λαοῦ καὶ τῶν ἐθνῶν, εἰς οὓς νῦν σε ἀποστέλλω Acts xxvi. 17. In Gal. i. 15 he goes further : ὁ ἀφορίσας με ἐκ κοιλίας μητρός μου, points to the act in the Divine Mind which preceded the call, not to the historical fact of separation from kinsmen, &c., which followed it, as here. The προορισμός of Paul, as of all the elect, was indeed prior to birth (Jer. i. 5), nay it was from all eternity (Eph. i. 5, 11) ; it must not be confounded with the more specific separation that took place in time.]

2. His *life-work*,—the propagation of the Gospel of GOD, εἰς εὐαγγέλιον Θεοῦ. This Gospel of GOD he more specifically describes by

(i) its relation to earlier religious history. It was

    a. promised by GOD in preceding ages,

    b. by the agency of GOD's prophets,

    c. in Sacred Scriptures.

(ii) Its subject is THE SON OF GOD (περὶ τοῦ Υἱοῦ αὐτοῦ), Who

    a. in respect of His Manhood (κατὰ σάρκα) was born of the race of David ;

    b. in respect of His Holy, superhuman Being (κατὰ Πνεῦμα Ἁγιωσύνης), was decisively marked out as the SON OF GOD, as a result of His Resurrection ;

    c. is known by the

        a. human name

        b. official designation   of   Jesus Christ our Lord ;

        c. title of authority

    d. conveys from GOD the Father to the writer (δι' οὗ ἐλάβομεν) whatever graces and powers He has received.

Introductory: ch. I, *vv.* 1–7.

[*Obs.* 1. (ver. 1.) The Apostle was a man set apart εἰς εὐαγγέλιον Θεοῦ. For the phrase, cf. 2 Cor. ii. 12 ἐλθὼν δὲ εἰς τὴν Τρῳάδα εἰς τὸ εὐαγγέλιον τοῦ Χριστοῦ. The Gospel was to be the aim of his whole thought and life. In 2 Cor. x. 14 he speaks of it as the scene or sphere of his activity: ἄχρι γὰρ καὶ ὑμῶν ἐφθάσαμεν ἐν τῷ εὐαγγελίῳ τοῦ Χριστοῦ. εἰς may = 'in order to propagate the Gospel.' εὐαγγέλιον, which meant from Homer to Plutarch, the *reward for* bringing a good message or *sacrifice* for a good message, came in later writers to mean the *message itself;* cf. Cremer, *Bibl. Theol. Lex.* (ed. 1889, p. 30), s.v. The New Testament use is opposed neither to the formation of the word from εὐάγγελος, nor to the *usus loquendi*. εὐαγγέλιον is in the New Testament the correlative of ἐπαγγελία; ἐπαγγελία is the promise of salvation, εὐαγγέλιον the good news whereby this promise is fulfilled. Acts xiii. 32 ἡμεῖς ὑμᾶς εὐαγγελιζόμεθα τὴν πρὸς τοὺς Πατέρας ἐπαγγελίαν γενομένην, ὅτι ταύτην ὁ Θεὸς ἐκπεπλήρωκεν. Eph. iii. 6 εἶναι τὰ ἔθνη . . . . . . συμμέτοχα τῆς ἐπαγγελίας ἐν Χριστῷ Ἰησοῦ διὰ τοῦ εὐαγγελίου. The εὐαγγέλιον is here not merely the (*transitive*) 'proclamation of salvation' (so Theodoret τὸ κήρυγμα), but the good news itself; cf. Rom. xv. 16; 1 Thess. ii. 2, 8, 9; 1 S. Pet. iv. 17. It is the fulness of grace and truth which GOD has given to the world in Christ, and with the communication of which the Apostles were charged. The art. is omitted before εὐαγγέλιον, because there is only one εὐαγγέλιον Θεοῦ, and the word is virtually a proper name, when followed by the *gen.* Θεοῦ. Winer, *Gr. N. T.*, p. 155. Θεοῦ seems here to be *gen. originis*, as Christ is the substance of the εὐαγγέλιον, cf. vers. 3, 4.]

[*Obs.* 2. (ver. 2.) The Gospel was first announced by Christ and His Apostles. But it was not absolutely new. It had been promised by GOD in distant bygone ages. For προεπηγγείλατο, see 2 Cor. ix. 5. Of this previous announcement of the εὐαγγέλιον GOD's prophets had been the organs. Moses and David were among these προφῆται. They had foretold the coming of Christ, Acts xiii. 22; His works, and His sufferings and death, and resurrection, Acts iii. 18, 21; iv. 25; 1 Cor. xv. 3; 1 S. Pet. i. 11; the remission of sins through faith in Christ, Acts x. 43; the blessings destined for the heathen, Acts xv. 15 sqq.; the happiness of good Christians hereafter, Tit. i. 2. Thus 'In vetere [testamento] novum latet, et in novo vetus patet' S. Aug. *Quaest.* 73 *in Exod.* Their words are preserved ἐν γραφαῖς ἁγίαις, i. e. Sacred Writings of the Jews. These are generally called αἱ γραφαί and ἡ γραφή—the Books or Writings κατ' ἐξοχήν: S. John v. 39; Rom. iv. 3. Without the art., however, γραφαὶ ἅγιαι could only mean Sacred Books of the Old Testament; ἁγίαις shows sufficiently what books must be meant. Comp. Rom. xvi. 26, where γραφαὶ προφητικαί are necessarily *the* prophetical writings. The Apostle's object in this statement may have been incidentally to meet the charge of novelty which was urged against his teaching (S. Chrys. *in loc.*), but chiefly that the greatness and majesty of the Gospel, as present to the Divine Mind in bygone ages, might be impressed on his readers.]

[*Obs.* 3. (ver. 3) περὶ τοῦ Υἱοῦ αὐτοῦ may be connected with ὁ προεπηγγείλατο (Theodoret, Tholuck, Fritzsche), but is more naturally taken with εὐαγγέλιον, ver. 1; Winer, *Gr. N. T.*, p. 233. This complete phrase, εὐαγγέλιον περὶ τοῦ Υἱοῦ, which occurs here only, explains εὐαγγέλιον τοῦ Χριστοῦ, as *gen. obj.*, the Gospel about Christ, not that which He preached. The Son of GOD was a title of Messiah, Ps. ii. 7, 12; Luke i. 35; S. Matt. iv. 3; S. Luke xxii. 70;

S. John i. 50. 'But,' observes Meyer, 'ὁ υἱὸς τοῦ Θεοῦ is not by any means to be taken merely as a designation of Messiah: it is always used of Christ by the Apostle, from the standpoint of the knowledge which God had given him by revelation (Gal. i. 16) of the pre-existent Sonship (viii. 3, 32; υἱὸς ἴδιος Gal. iv. 4; Col. i. 13 sqq.; Phil. ii. 6 sqq.).' Thus it is equivalent to υἱὸς μονογενὴς παρὰ πατρός S. John i. 14. For [the theory of] a modification in S. Paul's conviction there is no ground: the υἱὸς τοῦ Θεοῦ is 'He who had proceeded out of the essence of the Father like Him in substance,' Meyer.]

[*Obs.* 4. (vers. 3, 6.) The Son of God considered in respect of His visible and lower nature κατὰ σάρκα. σάρξ is here used without ethical significance, as the material of the human frame, from which however the ψυχή is inseparable. Christ was not, morally, σαρκικός (vii. 14), or ψυχικός (1 Cor. ii. 14), although His bodily nature made Him capable of temptation, Heb. ii. 18; iv. 15(Meyer). He had a σῶμα τῆς σαρκός Col. i. 22, but only in appearance a *sinful* one, ἐν ὁμοιώματι σαρκὸς ἁμαρτίας Rom. viii. 3. σάρξ refers *generally* to our Lord's Humanity, which is there more specifically described as being ἐκ σπέρματος Δαβίδ. In respect of this nature he came to be (γενομένου, comp. Gal. iv. 4) of the race of David, as Messiah was to be, Jer. xxiii. 15; Ps. cxxxii. 11; S. Matt. xxii. 42; S. John vii. 42. Of our Lord's supernatural birth of a Virgin Mother S. Paul says nothing; it was sufficient for his present purpose to describe Him as truly man and a descendant of David, i. e. as Messias. On the Davidic descent of the Mother of our Lord, see Dr. Mill, *On the Mythical Interp. of the Gospels*, pp. 208-211 (Cambr. 1861).]

[*Obs.* 5. (ver. 4 a.) The Son of God considered in respect of His superhuman being, κατὰ πνεῦμα ἁγιωσύνης. It is impossible to mistake the antithetical relation of κατὰ πνεῦμα ἁγιωσύνης to κατὰ σάρκα, and πνεῦμα ἁγιωσύνης cannot be well explained (1) of the Holy Ghost, because this destroys the antithesis between two elements in the Being of Christ, and does violence to κατά: nor (2) of Christ's Human πνεῦμα, the higher element of His ψυχή, because thus the solemn force of ἁγιωσύνης is missed. πνεῦμα ἁγιωσύνης translates רוּחַ הַקֹּדֶשׁ i. e. quite generally the Divine Nature of Christ, which is referred to more generally as πνεῦμα, and then specifically and in concrete personality as Υἱὸς Θεοῦ. The essential nature of God is called πνεῦμα in S. John iv. 24, while in 1 Tim. iii. 16 πνεῦμα, and in Heb. ix. 14 πνεῦμα αἰώνιον, stand for the Divine Nature in Christ; cf. [S. Clem. Rom.] *Ep. ii. ad Cor.* ix. 5 Χριστὸς ὁ Κύριος, ὢν μὲν τὸ πρῶτον πνεῦμα, ἐγένετο σάρξ.

In respect of this Divine Nature, thus conceived of indefinitely, He was designated (ὁρισθέντος), with decisive emphasis, ἐν δυνάμει, as the Son of God, as a consequence of His Resurrection. The Resurrection furnished the ὁρισμός: it made His Divine Sonship plain to the apprehension of believing men. Observe the contrast between ὁρισθέντος and γενομένου. He *became* man; He *was* already the Son of God before the creation of the world, and was sent into it, Rom. viii. 3; Gal. iv. 4. But the humiliations of His Life and His Passion made necessary some act whereby His true and eternal Being might be made plain to mankind. Accordingly the Resurrection was the transition to His manifested δόξα; in the Resurrection as well as before all worlds, Heb. i. 2, the words were fulfilled, 'Thou art my Son, this Day have I begotten Thee,' Acts xiii. 33. ἐκ is used rather than διά with ἀναστάσεως to mark that it was *in virtue of* the Resurrection that Christ's Divinity was thus marked out: but the ὁρισμός did not simply *date* from the ἀνάστασις, it *resulted* from that event; cf. Meyer *in loc.* ἀνάστασις νεκρῶν, not ἀνάστασις ἐκ νεκρῶν : 'Resurrection *of* the Dead' is the general category of which the personal rising of Jesus was the first and greatest instance. This bearing of the Resurrection on Christ's Divine Sonship explains 1 Cor. xv. 14 'If Christ be not risen, our preaching is vain.' The Messiah was announced to rise by prophecy: Acts ii. 24 sq.; xiii. 32 sq.; xvii. 2, 3; xxvi. 22 sqq. Had He not risen, He would not have been recognised as Son of God, in the sense of the Messianic predictions. This, as well as the fact that He rose by His own power [S. John x. 18] gives His Resurrection a significance, which does not belong to that of Lazarus, S. John xi. 44, and others, S. Matt. xvii. 3; xxvii. 53, who were not defined by it to be superhuman beings. The efficacy of the designation is expressed by ἐν δυνάμει, which, as at Col. i. 29. 2 Thess. i. 11, and like בַּכֹּחַ Ps. xxix. 4, is here used adverbially and qualifies ὁρισθέντος.]

[*Obs.* 6. The clause Ἰησοῦ Χριστοῦ τοῦ Κυρίου ἡμῶν is in apposition with περὶ τοῦ Υἱοῦ αὐτοῦ ver. 3. It describes Him by His Human Name, His official title, and His theandric relation to His people. Placed immediately before the clause which follows, it suggests the graces and the high dignity of the Apostolical ministry which He has instituted, as Mediator (δι' οὗ) with the Father. ἐλάβομεν refers only to S. Paul's personal reception of the Apostolate, and not to that of the other Apostles; it is the *plural of the category* (Meyer), but the following ἐν πᾶσι τοῖς ἔθνεσιν shows that S. Paul was thinking of himself alone.]

3. His *powers and commission.*

   a. Grace. Χάρις (*generic*). God's gifts in the widest sense, illumination, conversion, guidance, perseverance, &c.

   b. Apostolic Mission (ἀποστολή), of which he notes
{ the *purpose*—to make men *obedient* to Faith,
  the *range*—among all nations,
  the *motive*—to do something for His Name, i.e. Himself.

   c. Immediate practical reference. His mission to *all* heathen brings him into contact with his readers—ἐν οἷς ἐστὲ καὶ ὑμεῖς κλητοὶ Ἰησοῦ Χριστοῦ— among which, heathen, also you, called servants of Jesus Christ, are.

[*Obs.* 1. (ver. 5.) χάριν καὶ ἀποστολήν, not hendiadys, for 'the Grace of the Apostolate' (S. Chrys.). This construction arbitrarily blends into one two elements which separately yield a very satisfactory sense. S. Aug. understands by χάρις the general grace of Redemption, by ἀποστολή the specific apostolical office: 'Gratiam cum omnibus fidelibus accepit, apostolatum non cum omnibus.' Perhaps καί is best taken epexegetically: 'Grace, and indeed particularly the Apostolate.' But the two seem to be combined in Rom. xv. 15 sqq.; Gal. i. 15; ii. 7 9; Eph. iii. 2, 8.]

[*Obs*. 2. (ver. 5.) The *purpose* of the ἀποστολή is εἰς ὑπακοὴν πίστεως where πίστεως is not a *gen. subj*., 'the obedience which faith produces,' but a *gen. obj*. 'the obedience which is due to faith.' Hence πίστις might denote the object of faith, rather than the act or habit, this objective sense, although rare, not being foreign to the N. T.; e.g. Acts vi. 7 ὑπήκουον τῇ πίστει: Gal. i. 23 εὐαγγελίζεται τὴν πίστιν. For the use of ὑπακοή with a *gen. obj*., cf. 2 Cor. x. 5 ἡ ὑπακοὴ τοῦ Χριστοῦ: 1 S. Pet. i. 22 ἡ ὑπακοὴ τῆς ἀληθείας: and compare Rom. x. 16 οὐ πάντες ὑπήκουσαν τῷ εὐαγγελίῳ. The phrase ὑπακοὴ πίστεως occurs again Rom. xvi. 26. If πίστις, as being without the art., here and in Rom. xvi. 26, is understood subjectively, the phrase implies the obedience of the soul, not to a new truth, but to a new grace or virtue which controls it. The *range* of this ὑπακοή was to be ἐν πᾶσι τοῖς ἔθνεσιν, i.e. not all nations generally, inclusive of the Jews, but (see Gal. i. 16; ii. 8; Acts ix. 15; xxvi. 17 sqq., in accordance with S. Paul's office as ἀπόστολος τῶν ἐθνῶν, and the prominence assigned to it in this Epistle, i. 13; xi. 13; xv. 16) all non-Israelite nations, to which class the Romans belonged. The majority of the Roman Church must have consisted of converts from heathenism. The *motive* of this work is to achieve something on behalf of the Name of Jesus; ὑπὲρ τοῦ ὀνόματος αὐτοῦ. The name is the Person as revealed in human language. His Name describes and so it stands for Himself: cf. 2 Cor. v. 20 Ὑπὲρ Χριστοῦ οὖν πρεσβεύομεν. Christ was to be served, by making His Name known among the heathen; Acts ix. 15 σκεῦος ἐκλογῆς μοι ἐστὶν οὗτος, τοῦ βαστάσαι τὸ ὄνομά μου ἐνώπιον ἐθνῶν καὶ βασιλέων: xv. 26; xxi. 13, the Name of Jesus would be known and honoured when the heathen were brought to the true Faith.]

[*Obs*. 3. (ver. 6.) κλητοὶ Ἰησοῦ Χριστοῦ (not *gen. causae*, but *gen. possess*.), 'who through being called by the Father belong to Jesus Christ.' The κλῆσις of the soul is assigned to the Father by S. Paul: Rom. viii. 30; ix. 24: 1 Cor. i. 9; vii. 15, 17; 1 Thess. ii. 12; 2 Thess. ii. 14; 2 Tim. i. 9.]

[*Obs*. 4. The whole sentence εἰς ὑπακοὴν πίστεως ἐν πᾶσι τοῖς ἔθνεσιν ὑπὲρ τοῦ ὀνόματος αὐτοῦ is Hebrew rendered literally into Greek. It answers to לְהַשְׁמִיעַ הָאֱמוּנָה בְּכָל הַגּוֹיִם עַל שְׁמוֹ. A Greek would have written: ἵνα ὑπακούωσι δι' ἐμοῦ πάντα τὰ ἔθνη τῇ πίστει, κ.τ.λ. *Obs*. 2.]

II. The readers of the Epistle, viewed according to their

  (1) present outward circumstances—They are resident Christians in Rome;

  (2) relation to GOD—They are beloved by Him;

  (3) religious destiny—They are called to a consecrated life.

[*Obs*. 1. (ver. 7.) The phrase πᾶσι τοῖς οὖσιν ἐν Ῥώμῃ ἀγαπητοῖς Θεοῦ, κλητοῖς ἁγίοις, stands instead of τῇ ἐκκλησίᾳ or τοῖς πιστεύσασι εἰς Χριστόν, apparently with the object of expressing more fully the relation in which Christians stand towards God through the redemptive work of Christ. The collective Roman Church is addressed as at Phil. i. 1; Eph. i. 1; Col. i. 1; but no such inference can be drawn hence as that the Roman Church was not yet sufficiently organized to be properly called an ἐκκλησία; whatever may have been really the case.]

[*Obs.* 2. Christians are ἀγαπητοὶ Θεοῦ, inasmuch as in their vocation, conversion, and many subsequent graces they have had rich proof of GOD's love. Those who are reconciled to GOD in Christ τῷ ἠγαπημένῳ (Eph. i. 6) are special objects of His Love, Rom. v. 8 sqq.; viii. 39; Col. iii. 12. Cf. also 1 S. John iv. 10.]

[*Obs.* 3. They are also called (as) saints whatever they may become afterwards. Their κλῆσις out of the world of men has involved, not merely a separation from it, but consecration to GOD. The word ἅγιος, like קָדוֹשׁ, implies (1) separation from what is merely natural and earthly, and then (2) consecration to GOD. This double sense of separation and consecration is implied in the case of Israel in such passages as Lev. xi. 44; xix. 2; Exod. xix. 5 sqq.; and Christian ἁγιότης in the New Testament corresponds, in implying consecration as well as separation. Cf. Eph. i. 4 καθὼς ἐξελέξατο ἡμᾶς ... εἶναι ἡμᾶς ἁγίους καὶ ἀμώμους κατενώπιον αὐτοῦ ἐν ἀγάπῃ. That this ἁγιότης is to be understood in a Christian theocratic sense, corresponding to that of קָדֵשׁ and not of personal moral sanctification, appears from the fact that all the Roman Christians *as* Christians are ἅγιοι. For this sense see 1 Cor. vii. 14 ἡγίασται γὰρ ὁ ἀνὴρ ὁ ἄπιστος ἐν τῇ γυναικί, καὶ ἡγίασται ἡ γυνὴ ἡ ἄπιστος ἐν τῷ ἀνδρί.]

III. The substance of the greeting—

1. Blessings invoked on the readers.

{ Grace. χάρις. GOD's operative favour.
{ Peace. εἰρήνη. Repose of the soul in GOD.

2. Source of these Blessings—

{ GOD the Father and
{ Our Lord Jesus Christ.

[*Obs.* 1. χάρις represents the general epistolary χαίρειν of the Greeks (Acts xv. 23; James i. 1). For this the Apostle substitutes the more direct χάρις. It corresponds to חֵן, i. e. good-will, favour, which on the part of GOD contains implicitly all active blessings which He has to bestow. εἰρήνη is = שָׁלוֹם, peace, the great Hebrew blessing (Ps. lxxxv. 8; cxxii. 6; Luke xix. 42) and greeting (שָׁלוֹם לְךָ Judges xix. 20; S. Luke xxiv. 36). It was especially used to allay anxiety, Gen. xliii. 23, שָׁלוֹם לָכֶם, S. John xx. 19, 26. In the Old Testament the word often had predominant reference to external circumstances, in the New Testament to internal and spiritual, S. Matt. x. 12. In the Old Testament the Hebrew sense of safety predominates in the New Testament the Greek sense of peace. In S. John xiv our Lord distinguishes between His own gift of peace and that of the world: in Eph. ii. 15, the εἰρήνη between Jew and Gentile, effected by the abolition of Jewish ordinances on the cross, is in question. Here χάρις and εἰρήνη describe the entire inward work of Christ. χάρις is the seed, εἰρήνη the flower. The germ of the Christian life is GOD's grace, preventive and effectual, and its fruit is an inward tranquillity which is independent of circumstances.

The Father is especially ὁ χαρισάμενος, the Son, ὁ εἰρηνοποιός through the work of the Spirit.]

[*Obs.* 2. The *gen.* Κυρίου Ἰησοῦ Χριστοῦ is not dependent upon πατρός so as to stand parallel with ἡμῶν, as if the Apostle meant 'GOD the Father, of us and of the Lord Jesus Christ.' Κυρίου Ἰησοῦ Χριστοῦ depends on ἀπό, and must be co-ordinated with Θεοῦ πατρός: cf. Gal. i. 3. Hence the remark of the Greek Fathers that in this juxtaposition of the Names of GOD the Father and Christ, the Godhead of Christ, and His oneness of substance with the Father is clearly implied. Comp. 1 Cor. i. 3 ; 2 Cor. i. 2 ; Eph. i. 2 ; Phil. i. 2 ; 1 Thess. i. 1 ; 2 Thess. i. 1 sqq. ; 1 Tim. i. 2 ; 2 Tim. i. 2 ; Tit. i. 4 ; Philemon 3. Against the theory of making ἡμῶν and Κυρίου Ἰησοῦ Χριστοῦ depend both on πατρός, lies the fact that Scripture never speaks of '*our and* Christ's' Father, Tit. i. 4 ; 2 Tim. i. 2. Meyer will not allow that the formal equalisation of GOD and Christ in this text proves the divine nature of Christ, because 'the different predicates πατρός and Κυρίου imply the different conceptions of the *causa principalis* and *medians*.' This, however, begs a large question, viz. that these admittedly different conceptions necessarily place the *causa medians* wholly without the area of the Godhead. No created being can impart (as distinct from announcing) χάριν καὶ εἰρήνην. In Gal. i. 1, the Father like Christ is described as the 'mediator' of the Apostolate, διὰ Ἰησοῦ Χριστοῦ καὶ Θεοῦ πατρός.]

B.

Interest of the Apostle in the Roman Church, forming an Introduction to the great Thesis of his Epistle. 8–17.

[*Obs.* This *captatio benevolentiae* by which the Apostle would secure the sympathies of his readers, is not a rhetorical artifice, but springs naturally out of his instinctively sympathetic character. As also in Phil. i. 3 sqq. ; Col. 1. 3 sqq. The three proofs of his interest widen and heighten as he proceeds.]

I. Proofs of the Apostle's warm interest in the Roman Church (8–10).

Proof 1. He *thanks* GOD through Jesus Christ for the world-wide celebrity of the faith of the Roman Church (ver. 8).

[*Obs.* 1. This is introduced by πρῶτον μέν, to which no δεύτερον δέ corresponds in the apodosis. The construction was interrupted, because the second proof of his interest in the Roman Church was not distinct from, but a proof and confirmation of the first: cf. v. 9. Other such anacolutha occur in Rom. iii. 2 ; 1 Cor. xi. 18 sqq. Winer, *Gr. N. T.*, pp. 720, 721.]

[*Obs.* 2. The Apostle calls GOD *his* GOD (τῷ Θεῷ μου) on account of GOD's individualising love towards each reconciled soul. Each such soul feels GOD to be his, as if He belonged to no other, Acts vii. 32 ; Phil. iv. 19. The Apostle thanks his GOD, διὰ Ἰησοῦ Χριστοῦ : it is only through the mediating agency of Jesus Christ that thanksgiving or prayer can reach the Father. διὰ Ἰησοῦ Χριστοῦ is used of our Lord's mediatorial action in all its forms, Rom. ii. 16 ; v. 1 ; 2 Cor. i. 5. Winer, *Gr. N. T.*, p. 473. So, 'By Whom and with Whom in the unity of the Holy Ghost, all honour and glory be unto Thee, O Father Almighty,' Communion Service.]

Introductory: ch. I, *vv.* 8–17.

[*Obs.* 3. Origen observes on πάντων, that S. Paul was satisfied with the world-wide reputation of the faith of *all* the members of the Roman Church. Observe how cautiously he writes to Churches, a section of whose members he is obliged to censure ; 1 Cor. i. 4, he thanks GOD, ἐπὶ τῇ χάριτι τοῦ Θεοῦ τῇ δοθείσῃ to the Corinthians ; cf. too Col. i. 4, where he does not attribute the faith and love, in the Colossian Church, for which he thanks GOD, to all its members. It is by Christians that the faith of the Roman Church καταγγέλλεται; among non-Christians, Roman Christianity, so say the Jews, πανταχοῦ ἀντιλέγεται Acts xxviii. 22. The expression ἐν ὅλῳ τῷ κόσμῳ means 'Apostolic Christendom,' it is, strictly taken, hyperbolical : he had said six years before of the Thessalonians that their faith ἐν παντὶ τόπῳ ... ἐξελήλυθεν 1 Thess. i. 8. The language of S. Paul was often echoed, in succeeding ages, by the Fathers ; S. Cyprian, *epp.* 59. 14 ; 60. 2 (Hartel) ; S. Jerome, *Apolog. contr. Rufin.* 3. 12 (ed. Vallars.) 'Scito romanam fidem, apostolicâ voce laudatam, istiusmodi praestigias non recipere ; etiamsi angelus aliter annuntiet, quam semel praedicatum est, Pauli auctoritate munitam, non posse mutari.']

Proof 2. He calls upon GOD, whom he serves in the very sanctuary of his soul in labour for the Gospel, to attest the truth of his assertion that he *incessantly* mentions the Roman Christians in his prayers (ver. 9).

[*Obs.* 1. This statement is a proof (cf. γάρ) of the assurance conveyed in ver. 8. One who incessantly interceded for the Roman Church would be morally certain to thank GOD, when his prayers were heard. The stress lies on ἀδιαλείπτως: the Apostle practises what he had enjoined, ἀδιαλείπτως προσεύχεσθε 1 Thess. v. 17, but he mentions it here to illustrate, not his moral consistency, but his profound and unaffected interest in the Roman Church. As S. Chrys. says *in loc.* : τὸ ἐν εὐχαῖς ἔχειν ἀδιαλείπτως, ἐννόησον πόσης ἐστὶ διαθέσεως καὶ φιλίας. Cf. 2 Tim. i. 3 ; Eph. i. 16 ; 1 Thess. i. 2 ; iii. 10.]

[*Obs.* 2. The solemn adjuration, μάρτυς γάρ μου ἐστὶν ὁ Θεός is rendered necessary by the natural surprise of his readers at the Apostle's taking such deep interest in a Church which he had never visited. For other such oaths introducing an assertion, see 2 Cor. i. 23 ἐγὼ δὲ μάρτυρα τὸν Θεὸν ἐπικαλοῦμαι ἐπὶ τὴν ἐμὴν ψυχήν, ὅτι φειδόμενος ὑμῶν οὐκ ἦλθον εἰς Κόρινθον : xi. 31. after enumerating his infirmities, he adds, ὁ Θεὸς καὶ πατὴρ τοῦ Κυρίου ἡμῶν Ἰησοῦ Χριστοῦ οἶδεν, ὁ ὢν εὐλογητὸς εἰς τοὺς αἰῶνας, ὅτι οὐ ψεύδομαι : Phil. i. 8 μάρτυς γάρ μου ἐστὶν ὁ Θεὸς ὡς ἐπιποθῶ πάντας ὑμᾶς ἐν σπλάγχνοις Ἰησοῦ Χριστοῦ. The appeal to GOD is explained by the difficulties which the readers might have in accepting the statement which follows it. Such appeals are not to be confused with the levity of language condemned by the Third Commandment. In the present passage the appeal is strengthened by the words ᾧ λατρεύω, κ.τ.λ. The Apostle's life is a λατρεία, i. e. *religious* service, not merely or chiefly external, but offered in his inmost being, ἐν τῷ πνεύματί μου : while the outer sphere in which this λατρεία displays itself is ἐν τῷ εὐαγγελίῳ τοῦ Υἱοῦ αὐτοῦ, by preaching, defending, and in every way promoting it. With ἐν τῷ πνεύματι compare 2 Tim. i. 3 ᾧ λατρεύω ... ἐν καθαρᾷ συνειδήσει and Heb. xii. 28.]

[*Obs.* 3. ὡς seems to be used in ver. 9 not as a substitute for and equivalent to ὅτι, = that, but as expressing the *manner in which* something is to be understood, = how. Not merely the fact of the Apostle's incessant prayers for the Romans, but the *mode* of their being offered, were witnessed by GOD: Phil. i. 8; 2 Cor. vii. 15; Acts x. 28. For μνείαν ποιεῖσθαι, as used of naming before GOD the subjects of intercessory prayer, cf. Eph. i. 16; Phil. i. 3; 1 Thess. i. 2.]

Proof 3. He explains that the particular petition which he always associates with his prayer for the Roman Christians, is that God would, in His own time and way, enable him to visit Rome (ver. 10).

[*Obs.* 1. This statement enhances the proof of interest in the Roman Church which had been created by ver. 9, as ver. 9 had enhanced that resulting from ver. 8. The drift of the μνεία (ver. 9) is here more precisely defined; πάντοτε ... δεόμενος. ἐπί, which is to be referred to the notion of a definition of time, indicates the form of an action which takes place. ἐπὶ προσευχῶν 1 Thess. i. 2; Eph. i. 16. Winer refers it to the *local* sense of ἐπί, with a gen. of that to which something else attaches itself, 'with, [or in] my prayers;' *Gr. N. T.*, p. 470.]

[*Obs.* 2. εἴπως ἤδη ποτέ, 'if perhaps after awhile at some time or other.' ἤδη = already, and thus (comparing a time long delayed with the present) at length (Meyer). εἴπως expresses the hesitation of the Apostle in making the definite request, and ποτέ the shrinking from any attempt to specify a time for its accomplishment. εὐοδοῦσθαι mid. (1) to make a prosperous journey, but (2) generally *to prosper*, corresponding to הִצְלִיחַ from צָלַח Ps. i. 3. Ecclus. xxxviii. 14; 2 Macc. x. 7; 3 S. John 2; 1 Cor. xvi. 2. The Apostle conditions this prayer for being prospered to come to Rome, by ἐν τῷ θελήματι τοῦ Θεοῦ,—apart from which will he cannot anticipate this or any other project for the future.]

II. Motives for the longing (ἐπιποθῶ γὰρ ἰδεῖν ὑμᾶς) which leads him to make this specific prayer. (11–16.)

Motive 1. His purpose of imparting to the Romans some χάρισμα πνευματικόν, which may have a twofold effect in

a. strengthening *their* Christian life, εἰς τὸ στηριχθῆναι ὑμᾶς.

b. the simultaneous encouragement of the Apostle and his readers, by the sense of their common faith (11, 12).

[*Obs.* 1. (ver. 11.) For ἰδεῖν as expressing by implication personal presence, see Acts xix. 21; xxviii. 20. The χάρισμα which S. Paul wishes to impart to the Romans is πνευματικόν, not as belonging to the human spirit, but as a product of the activity of the Divine πνεῦμα whose organ the Apostle is. 1 Cor. xii. 4 διαιρέσεις δὲ χαρισμάτων εἰσί, τὸ δὲ αὐτὸ πνεῦμα. The word χάρισμα points to some definite endowment or faculty, more distinctly than, e.g. εὐλογία πνευματική in Eph. i. 3. What the χάρισμα here alluded to is, we can only conjecture: its object is the confirmation of the life and faith of the Roman Church, εἰς τὸ στηριχθῆναι. Cf. Acts xvi. 5 αἱ ἐκκλησίαι ἐστερεοῦντο τῇ πίστει: Rom. xvi. 25 τῷ δὲ δυναμένῳ ὑμᾶς στηρίξαι ... ᾧ ἡ δόξα: 1 Thess. iii. 2 ἐπέμψαμεν Τιμόθεον ... εἰς τὸ στηρίξαι ὑμᾶς, καὶ παρακαλέσαι ὑμᾶς περὶ τῆς πίστεως ὑμῶν. The pressure of adverse circumstances and human weakness always threatened Christian faith and life with disintegration: hence the Apostle's anxiety. The idea of 'Confirmation,'—whether it be or be not glanced at in the χάρισμα of this passage,—is to establish the baptismal grace by a reinforcement from above.]

[*Obs.* 2. In ver. 12 a modifying explanation (τοῦτο δέ ἐστιν) of the Apostle's object in desiring to visit Rome, as expressed in εἰς τὸ στηριχθῆναι ὑμᾶς, is introduced. The Roman Christians would not be the only gainers by his visit; he himself expected to profit by it spiritually. The Apostle alone is the subject of ουμπαρακληθῆναι; that the readers are not is clear from ἐν ὑμῖν, which would be superfluous if it only meant *in animis vestris*. ἐν ἀλλήλοις does not differ from ἀλλήλων; but ὑμῶν τε καὶ ἐμοῦ enter more readily into direct dependence on πίστεως than ὑμῖν τε καὶ ἐμοί would. The παράκλησις which he hopes to share is one of the accompaniments of the primary meaning of the word, 'talking to with a view to producing an effect,'—viz. admonition, or consolation, or encouragement. See Cremer, *in voc.* παρακαλεῖν, p. 474. Here one of the two last would be meant. Even the Apostle, the organ of so many great spiritual graces, was dependent upon those to whom he ministered for courage and confidence; his gifts and work react upon himself. So in the holy Body—the Church—the eye cannot say to the hand, or the head to the feet, χρείαν ὑμῶν οὐκ ἔχω 1 Cor. xii. 21. The ἡ ἐν ἀλλήλοις πίστις is the one faith which lives both in the Apostle and the Roman Christians; its quasi-objective character is suggested by this phrase better than it would be by ἡ ἀλλήλων πίστις. In ὑμῶν τε καὶ ἐμοῦ the Apostle, with the delicacy of true humility, puts the Romans before himself.]

Motive 2. He longs to have some spiritual fruit (καρπόν) among the Romans, as among the other peoples of Heathendom (13).

[*Obs.* 1. Before stating the second motive he encounters a tacit objection.

Obj. Why, if these were his feelings, had he not visited Rome before the present time?

Answ. He had often intended (πολλάκις προεθέμην) to do so, but had been prevented by circumstances up to the present date (ἐκωλύθην ἄχρι τοῦ δεῦρο). (13 a.)]

[*Obs.* 2. (ver. 13.) The formula οὐ θέλω δὲ ὑμᾶς ἀγνοεῖν is used by the Apostle to introduce a statement upon which he lays particular stress; xi. 25; 1 Cor. x. 1; xii. 1; 2 Cor. i. 8; 1 Thess. iv. 13. In Phil. i. 12 γινώσκειν δὲ ὑμᾶς βούλομαι. The Roman Christians might have heard of S. Paul's intentions from Aquila and Priscilla. The clause καὶ ἐκωλύθην ἄχρι τοῦ δεῦρο is parenthetical, ἵνα καρπόν κ.τ.λ. depending on προεθέμην. δεῦρο here only in New

Testament is used of time, though often elsewhere in later Greek. S. Paul's plans were thwarted sometimes by Satan, 1 Thess. ii. 18; sometimes by the restraining action of the Holy Spirit, Acts xvi. 6, 7; sometimes by his own hesitation to intrude on the field of labour assigned to others, Rom. xv. 22; 2 Cor. x. 15. Here the cause of the ἐκωλύθην is probably stated at xv. 22, 23, as found in the requirements of the many places in which Christ was unknown: διὸ καὶ τὰ πολλὰ ἐνεκοπτόμην τοῦ ἐλθεῖν πρὸς ὑμᾶς.]

[*Obs.* 3. By καρπόν we must understand a spiritual result of apostolical toil; the Apostle thinks of himself as a husbandman, ὁ φυτεύων 1 Cor. iii. 7, who sows the seed of the Faith in the soil of human hearts, or in the great field of Heathendom. Individual souls reconciled to GOD in Christ are the Apostle's καρπός,—a harvest gathered in for Christ, yet also for himself, since he has no other object than Christ's glory. In the same way the Philippians will secure S. Paul's καύχημα εἰς ἡμέραν Χριστοῦ Phil. ii. 16; and the Thessalonians are ἡ δόξα ἡμῶν καὶ ἡ χαρά 1 Thess. ii. 20. The Lat. *fructus* is used similarly, Cicero, *Cat. Maj.* xviii. 62. There is no necessity for straining σχῶ to mean 'acquire': the Apostle is thinking of the time when, his toil being over, he would *possess* the spiritual fruit. καὶ ἐν ὑμῖν καθὼς καὶ ἐν is written hastily for ἐν ὑμῖν καθὼς καὶ ἐν, or for καὶ ἐν ὑμῖν καθὼς ἐν. 'Geminavit per aliquam cogitandi celeritatem καί comparativum,' Fritzsche. In ἐν τοῖς λοιποῖς ἔθνεσιν he is thinking of the Lycaonians, Acts xiv. 6 sqq., the Macedonians, Acts xvi. 12, the Athenians, Acts xvii. 34.]

Motive 3. His conviction that, as Christ's Apostle, he owes the faith (ὀφειλέτης εἰμί) to the whole heathen world, without regard to differences of nationality or of culture. Thus he is eager, according to his powers (τὸ κατ᾽ ἐμὲ πρόθυμον), to preach the gospel to the citizens of Rome also (14, 15).

[*Obs.* 1. In ver. 14 the prayer to visit Rome is referred to a general principle, viz. his Apostolic obligations to all the peoples of Heathendom. For the exhaustive description of all nations by dividing them into Hellenes and Barbarians, see Hor. *Ep.* i. 2, 7 'Graecia barbariae lento collisa duello.' Sen. *de Ira*, iii. 2. Liv. xxxi. 29 'cum barbaris aeternum omnibus Graecis bellum est, eritque; natura enim quae perpetua est non mutabilibus in diem causis, hostes sunt.' Thucyd. i. 3. The Hellenes included the Jews among the βάρβαροι, as the Hellenized Jew Philo does [see Q. *Liber sit*, cc. 11, 12 (T. ii. p. 455. ed. Mangey) and the Christian Justin Martyr, *Apol.* i. 5, 46]. But the New Testament writers would have conceived of the Ἰουδαῖοι as contrasting with and independent of the ἔθνη altogether, iii. 29; ix. 24, and therefore as not falling under either head of the division, especially as S. Paul was not an ὀφειλέτης to the Jews, Gal. ii. 7. Before the Apostle's day Greek culture had become prevalent at Rome; and the Romans associated themselves with the Hellenes, in opposition to the barbarians. S. Paul would probably therefore, from his instinctive courtesy, have thought of the Romans as 'Hellenes': cf. Cic. *de Fin.* ii. 15, 49, where Greece and Italy are opposed to 'barbaria,' although Greek authors (Polyb. v. 104, ix. 37. 5) and Plautus

Introductory: ch. I, *vv.* 8-17.

(*Mil. Glor.* ii. 2. 58; *Poen.* iii. 2. 21) included Romans among barbarians. The second division into σοφοί and ἀνόητοι is not coincident with the first; some of the Hellenes would be ἀνόητοι.]

[*Obs.* 2. For ὀφειλέτης see Acts xxvi. 17 sqq. for our Lord's words, εἰς οὓς νῦν σε ἀποστέλλω: Gal. ii. 7 πεπίστευμαι τὸ εὐαγγέλιον τῆς ἀκροβυστίας: 1 Cor. ix. 16 ἀνάγκη γάρ μοι ἐπίκειται· οὐαὶ δέ μοι ἐστίν, ἐὰν μὴ εὐαγγελίζωμαι: 2 Cor. iv. 5. The δι' οὗ ἐλάβομεν χάριν καὶ ἀποστολήν (ver. 5) implied a moral obligation or debt to be discharged—viz. the employment of the grace of the Apostolate in the conversion of heathen nations·]

[*Obs.* 3. In ver. 15 οὕτω has an inferential force, Acts vii. 8; 1 Cor. xiv. 25 = 'in consequence.' S. Paul's sense of duty towards the Romans was a consequence of the debt which he owed to the whole of heathendom. τὸ κατ' ἐμὲ πρόθυμον is taken (1) τὸ κατ' ἐμέ, πρόθυμον, 'so far as I am concerned there is eagerness,' πρόθυμον being subject and ἐστί supplied, or (2) τό is connected with πρόθυμον and κατ' ἐμέ taken as = μου, τὸ πρόθυμόν μου [ἐστίν] κ.τ.λ., 'my earnest inclination is,' &c., or (3) τὸ κατ' ἐμέ is treated as subject, and πρόθυμον as predicate. 'All that depends on my efforts is ready.' Meyer adopts (3) 'the inclination on my part is to preach,' &c. So Winer, *Gk. N. T.* p. 289 [but he adopts (2) p. 294]. The words τὸ κατ' ἐμέ express his sense of dependence upon God, and are in antithesis to ἐν τῷ θελήματι τοῦ Θεοῦ ver. 10.]

[*Obs.* 4. καὶ ὑμῖν τοῖς ἐν Ῥώμῃ. He is addressing members of the Church in Rome, with whom, however, he associates in thought for the moment their heathen fellow-citizens. If he owed the Gospel to the heathen world, he owed it especially to Rome, the ἐπιτομὴ τῆς οἰκουμένης, Athenaeus *Deipnos.* I. p. 20 B. But the magnificence of Rome leads him to think of the work which he is proposing to take in hand. If he might shrink from putting himself forward, he is not ashamed of the Gospel.]

Motive 4. His sense of the greatness of his work, stated *negatively*, as not being ashamed of the Gospel of Christ (ver. 16 a).

[*Obs.* This motive is a reason (γάρ) for the preceding πρόθυμον . . . . εὐαγγελίσασθαι. The negative form of his statement is to be accounted for (1) by his sense of the impression produced among unbelievers by the Doctrine of the Cross. ὁ λόγος γὰρ ὁ τοῦ σταυροῦ τοῖς μὲν ἀπολλυμένοις μωρία ἐστίν 1 Cor. i. 18; 2 Tim. i. 8; and (2) by the indignities to which he had been exposed in Athens (σπερμολόγος Acts xvii. 18), in Corinth, and in Ephesus. It might have been supposed that with his practical experience of the minds of men he would see in the Gospel something intrinsically worthless, through which no honour could be gained, and by the continued advocacy of which a clever man could only bring discredit and contempt upon himself. Cf. 2 Tim. i. 12 δι' ἣν αἰτίαν καὶ ταῦτα πάσχω, καὶ οὐκ ἐπαισχύνομαι, οἶδα γὰρ ᾧ πεπίστευκα. ἐπαισχύνομαι, like αἰσχύνομαι, with acc. of the object: cf. Meyer.]

§ 1st Reason (γάρ) for Motive 4 (ver. 16 b). The Gospel is

calculated to provoke not shame but enthusiasm on account of it. For it is

> i. in itself—a Power from GOD (δύναμις Θεοῦ).
> ii. in its purpose—working for the salvation of man (εἰς σωτηρίαν).
> iii. in its range—destined for every believing human being (παντὶ τῷ πιστεύοντι) with due recognition of the prior claim of the Jews, as the covenant-people (Ἰουδαίῳ τε πρῶτον καὶ Ἕλληνι) (ver. 16).

[*Obs.* 1. The words δύναμις Θεοῦ εἰς σωτηρίαν παντὶ τῷ πιστεύοντι are the fullest and deepest definition of the Gospel. See Origen *in loc.* By εὐαγγέλιον the Apostle means, not the proclamation of the good news, from heaven, but as in vers. 1, 9, the good news itself. Of this he says that it is (1) in itself δύναμις Θεοῦ (gen. origin) a Power going forth from GOD, into the human world. Such δύναμις may be destructive, Matt. x. 28 τὸν δυνάμενον καὶ ψυχὴν καὶ σῶμα ἀπολέσαι ἐν γεέννῃ : its character is here determined by the context. The δύναμις from GOD manifested in the Gospel is seen in its results upon the characters and lives of men, in this world and upon their destiny hereafter. Hence,

[*Obs.* 2. The Gospel is (2) in its purpose εἰς σωτηρίαν. The σωτηρία here meant is not social or political, but that eternal σωτηρία which was always associated with the promise of a Messiah. In classical Greek the word stands for prosperity, happiness ; cf. τοῦ κοινοῦ ἡ σωτηρία Thuc. ii. 60. 4. The Hebrew יְשׁוּעָה combines both meanings. In the New Testament (excepting Acts vii. 25 ; xxvii. 34 ; Heb. xi. 7, where it is used in the general sense as = salvation ; and Rev. vii. 10 ἡ σωτηρία τῷ Θεῷ ἡμῶν : xii. 10 ; xix. 1, where it expresses an ascription of praise like הוֹשִׁיעָה־נָּא Ps. cxviii. 25) it means salvation from sin here and from eternal death hereafter. Cf. S. Luke i. 71, 77. It is contrasted with θάνατος, 2 Cor. vii. 10 ; with ὀργή, 1 Thess. v. 9 ; S. John iv. 22 ; with ἀπώλεια, Phil. i. 28. Our Lord is κέρας σωτηρίας S. Luke i. 69 ; He has won σωτηρία αἰώνιος Heb. v. 9 ; the preaching of His Apostles is ὁ λόγος τῆς σωτηρίας ταύτης Acts xiii. 26 ; the Gospel is τὸ εὐαγγέλιον τῆς σωτηρίας ὑμῶν Eph. i. 13 ; the Christian life, ὁδὸς σωτηρίας Acts xvi. 17 ; the span of each man's life, ἡμέρα σωτηρίας 2 Cor. vi. 2. Cf. Is. xlix. 8. In its completeness it is still future, and is an object of hope ; 2 Thess. ii. 13 ; 1 Thess. v. 8 ἐλπίδα σωτηρίας : Heb. i. 14 κληρονομεῖν σωτηρίαν : ix. 28 ὀφθήσεται τοῖς αὐτοῦ ἀπεκδεχομένοις εἰς σωτηρίαν : 1 S. Pet. i. 5 ; Rom. xiii. 11 νῦν γὰρ ἐγγύτερον ἡμῶν ἡ σωτηρία, ἢ ὅτε ἐπιστεύσαμεν. Thus σωτηρία includes the whole of Christ's redemptive work in the soul of man, which begins in justification and sanctification here, and is completed in endless happiness hereafter. See Cremer, Lexicon *s. v.* and σώζειν, pp. 827 and 824.]

[*Obs.* 3. The Gospel is (3), in point of range, destined παντὶ τῷ πιστεύοντι. This παντί is resolved into Ἰουδαίῳ τε πρῶτον καὶ Ἕλληνι. As from the Greek point of view, mankind is divided into Ἕλληνες and βάρβαροι (ver. 14), so from the Jewish point of view they are Ἰουδαῖοι and Ἕλληνες. Every man who was

Introductory: ch. I, *vv.* 8-17.

not a Jew was, since the date of Antiochus Epiphanes, an Ἕλλην Acts xiv. 1, 1 Cor. x. 32, i. e. a heathen—the foremost race of which, in Jewish eyes, is put for the whole of heathendom. The Gospel is destined for every human being; but among the races of men, the Jews have a first claim to consideration. πρῶτον refers, not merely or chiefly to the fact that in the order of time the Gospel was to be preached *first* to the Jews (S. Chrys. *in loc.*), but to the promises, in virtue of which this order was observed, and which gave the Jews a prior right to it. They are the children of the Kingdom, S. Matt. viii. 12. Cf. Rom. iii. 1; ix. 1 seq.; xi. 16; xv. 9. But, for them, as for all others, faith was an indispensable condition for making the Gospel εἰς σωτηρίαν: hence πιστεύοντι. This introduces the Thesis of the Epistle, which is a reason for the immediately preceding statement.]

§ 2nd Reason (dependent on 1st reason) for Motive 4. In the Gospel the Righteousness which God gives is disclosed as being from first to last dependent on faith in man (ver. 17).

[*Obs.* This is a justification (γάρ) of the immediately preceding (ver. 16) statement that the Gospel is a δύναμις Θεοῦ εἰς σωτηρίαν. Man can only be saved by being as he should be according to the Law of his Creator, and this is only possible if God gives him the moral endowment by which he becomes so, viz. δικαιοσύνη, and which he must receive by that effort of his intellectual and moral being, which is called πίστις.]

Thesis of the Epistle (ver. 17).

In the Gospel the Righteousness which God gives (δικαιοσύνη Θεοῦ) is revealed as depending on Faith, and as producing the faith on which it depends (ἐκ πίστεως εἰς πίστιν).

[*Obs.* 1. δικαιοσύνη is that relationship to δίκη or Right which fulfils its claims; which makes a moral being what he should be. As rights imply a person, δικαιοσύνη always has reference either to God or to man, whether other men or the agent. Δίκη is in pagan language Right (as apprehended by established usage,—the best available criterion), and so personified as the daughter of Zeus and Themis; this abstract divinity is mentioned Acts xxviii. 4. The conception is also treated as personified in Wisd. i. 8 οὐδὲ παροδεύσῃ αὐτὸν ἡ δίκη. Elsewhere δίκη appears in the LXX only in its narrower post-Homeric sense of judgment; and thus it is used to translate רִיב Psalm ix. 4, and דִּין Lev. xxvi. 25; Deut. xxxii. 41; Ezek. xxv. 12. In the New Testament we find δίκην αἰτεῖν κατά τινος 'to demand justice,' Acts xxv. 15; δίκην ὑπέχειν Jude 7, 'to render justice,' of those who undergo punishment so as to maintain the Right violated by them, and δίκην τίνειν 2 Thess. i. 9, 'to give satisfaction,' to pay the debt of right by being punished. The δίκαιος then is the moral being who fulfils all the claims of Right; who is as he should be. In Homer the δίκαιος is the man who does his duty towards gods and men; Nägelsbach (*Nachhomerische Theologie*, pp. 237 ff., says that in the Ethics of Homer there is no separation of the spheres of rights, of morals and of religion. In post-Homeric Greek, δίκαιος refers [mainly] to the sphere of social life. The σώφρων who keeps within the limits marked out for him by the rights of others is the δίκαιος, and thus δίκαιος is used when we might expect σώφρων. The δίκαιος remembers that he will die; he brings his life and conduct into correspondence with the true conditions of his being and so is hardly distinguishable from the εὐσεβής. Hence the word was employed by the LXX to translate צדק (Fuerst 'rectum esse, planum esse'), in a state conformable to right, i. e. to God, as revealed in the Moral Law. צדק means conformity to the Jewish Law on the ground that the Law is a revelation of Right; and thus it is translated by δικαιοσύνη.

The principle of δικαιοσύνη then is always the same, viz. conformity to Right, but the actual moral attainments which it represents vary with the varying conceptions of δίκη, and with the subjects to which it is attributed. A rough practical definition of its current meaning in Pagan society occurs in Plat. Rep. iv. 433 *a* τὸ τὰ αὑτοῦ πράττειν καὶ μὴ πολυπραγμονεῖν δικαιοσύνη ἐστίν. As applied to God it describes His perfect correspondence with the necessary and eternal Laws of His moral nature, Ps. l. 6; Rom. iii. 5. He is the true standard of Absolute Right to Himself, as to all other moral beings. The Biblical sense of δικαιοσύνη, therefore, is that conformity to Right which God enjoins and of which He is the standard. Thus the Christian is ὁ κατὰ Θεὸν κτισθεὶς ἐν δικαιοσύνῃ Eph. iv. 24. He is to seek first of all God's kingdom, and τὴν δικαιοσύνην αὐτοῦ S. Matt. vi. 33, and to remember that human passions δικαιοσύνην Θεοῦ οὐ κατεργάζεται S. James i. 20. In these two cases Θεοῦ is apparently a genitive *qualitatis*; and the phrase describes that Righteousness of which God is the standard and which He expects at the hands of Christians.

δικαιοσύνη, however, is presented to us in the New Testament under two leading aspects, as a standard or principle of human conduct, and as a gift from God to man, in virtue of which man may tranquilly await God's judgment.

a. It is frequently viewed as a standard or ideal of human conduct, or as good human conduct itself: Matt. iii. 15 πληρῶσαι πᾶσαν δικαιοσύνην: Acts x. 35 ἐργάζεσθαι δικαιοσύνην: Heb. xi. 33; S. James i. 20. The expression ποιεῖν δικαιοσύνην is peculiar to S. John: 1 S. John iii. 10; Rev. xxii. 11. Thus it is also treated as if it were an abstract force or principle, of which the organs of human life should be the weapons or instruments, ὅπλα δικαιοσύνης Rom. vi. 13; as being enslaved to it, δοῦλα τῇ δικαιοσύνῃ Rom. vi. 19; and from which sinners are fatally emancipated, ἐλεύθεροι ἦτε τῇ δικαιοσύνῃ Rom. vi. 20. Yet it is fertile and productive, as if instinct with the life of a parent or a plant, so 2 Cor. ix. 10 γεννήματα τῆς δικαιοσύνης: Phil. i. 11 καρπὸν δικαιοσύνης. It is the sphere in which God is to be served, S. Luke i. 75; and it is a breastplate, which protects the soul against the assaults of Evil, Eph. vi. 14 τὸν θώρακα τῆς δικαιοσύνης. It excites the hunger and thirst of holy souls, οἱ πεινῶντες καὶ διψῶντες τὴν δικαιοσύνην S. Matt. v. 6; Christ's disciples are to seek it first of all things, S. Matt. vi. 33.

b. But it is often considered as a gift from God to man, Rom. v. 16 τὸ δώρημα . . . τὸ χάρισμα, and ver. 17 ἡ δωρεὰ τῆς δικαιοσύνης, so that by it, many

Introductory : ch. I, vv. 8-17.

δίκαιοι κατασταθήσονται, ver. 19. Indeed in the dogmatic language of S. Paul δικαιοσύνη Θεοῦ means the Righteousness which GOD bestows on Man, Rom. i. 17; iii. 5, 21, 22, 25, 26; x. 3; 2 Cor. v. 21. This appears, partly from the passages which attribute Justification to GOD; (Rom. iii. 30, ὃς δικαιώσει τὴν περιτομὴν : iv. 5 ὁ δικαιῶν τὸν ἀσεβῆ : viii. 33 Θεὸς ὁ δικαιῶν :) and partly from the expansion of the expression in Phil. iii. 9 into ἡ ἐκ Θεοῦ δικαιοσύνη. By nature all men are ἄδικοι, and as such ὑπόδικοι τῷ Θεῷ Rom. iii. 19. From this condition man cannot free himself by any efforts of his own; he cannot really obey the Law; he can only recover his true relation to GOD and to himself by partaking in that true δικαιοσύνη which GOD gives us, out of His free grace, in Christ, Who (1) by His Atoning Death, expiated the guilt of the race which He represented, and (2) by His Spirit, enables fallen man ἐνδύσασθαι τὸν καινὸν ἄνθρωπον, τὸν κατὰ Θεὸν κτισθέντα ἐν δικαιοσύνῃ Eph. iv. 24. For the Holy Spirit, by Whom ἡ ἀγάπη τοῦ Θεοῦ ἐκκέχυται ἐν ταῖς καρδίαις ἡμῶν Rom. v. 5, does thereby purify and strengthen the will and work a true δικαιοσύνη within us. The δικαιοσύνη then which GOD gives includes these two elements; acquittal of the guilt of sin, or justification in the narrower sense of the word, and the communication of a new moral life, ἵνα τὸ δικαίωμα τοῦ νόμου πληρωθῇ ἐν ἡμῖν Rom. viii. 4. These two sides of the gift of δικαιοσύνη can only be separated in thought; in fact, they are inseparable. Man is actually and inwardly freed from the guilt of sin at the moment when that sanctifying grace, which is the Holy Ghost Himself, streams into man's heart; and each effort flows directly from the action of faith directed upon GOD's redeeming mercy in Christ. The δικαιοσύνη which is *objectively* won by Christ for the whole human family, becomes *subjective* to each individual man by *faith*; the δικαιοσύνη Θεοῦ becomes a δικαιοσύνη ἐνώπιον τοῦ Θεοῦ for the individual, *by faith*.

Opposed to this δικαιοσύνη Θεοῦ is Phil. iii. 9 ἡ ἐμὴ δικαιοσύνη ἡ ἐκ τοῦ νόμου. This imperfect and false righteousness is thus contrasted with the true, (1) as being a man's own work in himself. It is ἐμή and ἰδία, not Θεοῦ; the fruit of private and personal effort, and not GOD's gracious gift. Thus Rom. x. 3, the Jews ἀγνοοῦντες τὴν τοῦ Θεοῦ δικαιοσύνην καὶ τὴν ἰδίαν δικαιοσύνην ζητοῦντες στῆσαι, τῇ δικαιοσύνῃ τοῦ Θεοῦ οὐχ ὑπετάγησαν : (2) as being a product of the Jewish Law. It is ἡ ἐκ τοῦ νόμου, not ἐκ πίστεως. But a real righteousness under the law was, according to the law itself, impossible. For it could only be achieved by an exact obedience : Rom. x. 5 Μωσῆς γὰρ γράφει τὴν δικαιοσύνην τὴν ἐκ τοῦ νόμου, Ὅτι ὁ ποιήσας αὐτὰ ἄνθρωπος ζήσεται ἐν αὐτοῖς. And hence it followed that Gal. iii. 11 ἐν νόμῳ οὐδεὶς δικαιοῦται παρὰ τῷ Θεῷ. The righteousness which was attained was, when judged by a divine standard, worthless, as being imperfect, both in its motives and in its range. This incapacity of the legal system to produce real Righteousness was implied in the gift of the Gospel, which, when received by faith, does ensure the gift of Righteousness and Life : Gal. iii. 21 εἰ γὰρ ἐδόθη νόμος ὁ δυνάμενος ζωοποιῆσαι, ὄντως ἂν ἐκ νόμου ἦν ἡ δικαιοσύνη.

To this false righteousness, worked out by man's natural powers under the system of the Law, is opposed the freely-given Righteousness of GOD, received by faith in Jesus Christ. This true Righteousness is one, not two, or more. The maxim 'justitia alia justificationis, sanctificationis alia' is not S. Paul's. S. Paul knows nothing of an external Righteousness which is reckoned without being given to man; and the Righteousness which

C

faith receives is not external only but internal, not imputed only but imparted to the believer. Justification and sanctification may be distinguished by the student, as are the arterial and nervous systems in the human body; but in the living soul they are coincident and inseparable.]

[*Obs.* 2. In the Gospel the δικαιοσύνη Θεοῦ is being revealed, ἀποκαλύπτεται. It has for ages been a μυστήριον hidden (xvi. 25) in the Eternal Counsels, though darkly hinted at in the Old Testament, Rom. iv. 3 sqq. The Apostles are unveiling it by their preaching (1) the ἀπολύτρωσις from sin effected by Christ's Atoning Death, which implies His *obedientia activa*, of which His Death was the climax, and His Divinity, which imparted to His Death its immeasurable value, and (2) the need and power of faith in the recipient of this divinely-imparted Righteousness.]

[*Obs.* 3. The expression ἐκ πίστεως εἰς πίστιν may be variously taken as it is connected with ἀποκαλύπτεται or with δικαιοσύνη. The first construction is natural and that of many fathers. Thus (1) ἐκ πίστεως is [referred to] the faith of the Apostle, or of the preachers of the Gospel, and εἰς πίστιν to that of the hearers; so Sedulius, 'ex fide praedicantium in fidem credentium.' Or (2) ἐκ πίστεως refers to the imperfect faith of the Jewish Church, and εἰς πίστιν to the complete faith of the Gospel; so Tertullian, 'ex fide legis in fidem evangelii.' To this the objection lies in ἐν αὐτῷ: ἐκ πίστεως too is within the range of the Gospel. The Apostle in this epistle only discusses a δικαιοσύνη which the Gospel reveals. Or (3) ἐκ πίστεως is the imperfect faith which first receives the Gospel, and εἰς πίστιν the stronger faith which is the fruit and reward of its reception: cf. Ps. lxxxiv. 7 They will go from strength to strength; 2 Cor. iii. 18 μεταμορφούμεθα ἀπὸ δόξης εἰς δόξαν. This does not suit the connection. The Apostle is not discussing the progress of the Divine Life in Man, but he is insisting on the fact that in the Gospel a new way is opened to attain the δικαιοσύνη Θεοῦ, viz. the way of faith. Thus (4) it seems best to take ἐκ πίστεως as denoting the starting-point of man's receiving δικαιοσύνη Θεοῦ, and εἰς πίστιν as pointing to the permanent condition of its reception. (In this case the abstract εἰς πίστιν is practically equivalent to the concrete εἰς τὸν πιστεύοντα. So Oecumenius, *in loc.*: ἀπὸ πίστεως ἄρχεται καὶ εἰς τὸν πιστεύσαντα λήγει.) The Righteousness of GOD in Man dates from the act of faith which receives Jesus Christ, and tends to produce faith, εἰς πίστιν, as a condition of its being continuously imparted. It is only given to the man who continues to believe. Hence the δικαιοσύνη Θεοῦ is also called ἡ κατὰ πίστιν δικαιοσύνη Heb. xi. 7, and δικαιοσύνη τῆς πίστεως Rom. iv. 11, or πίστεως ib. 13, and δικαιοσύνη ἡ ἐκ πίστεως Rom. ix. 30; ἡ ἐκ πίστεως δικαιοσύνη Rom. x. 6.

1. πίστις is used in the LXX. to translate אֱמוּנָה, firmness, constancy (from אָמֵן, to hold trustworthy, Hiph. of אָמַן, unusual except in participle, to support). The Hebrew substantive always has the passive sense of trustworthiness, constancy, and is rendered in the LXX. by ἀλήθεια, or by πίστις in this same passive sense. But constancy under suffering would in an Israelite imply belief in GOD; men 'endured as seeing Him that is invisible.' Thus the passive meaning of the word suggested the active; and this is already the case in Hab. ii. 4, where

even אֱמוּנָה seems to hover between the active and passive meanings; and S. Paul quotes the LXX rendering because he understands πίστις in the former of these. See Lightfoot, *Galatians*, pp. 154 ff., ed. 1890.

2. The Greek word itself seems to have had originally an active sense, and to have gradually acquired the passive, which, except in Hab. ii. 4, it always bears in the Old Testament, although in the Apocrypha the active sense seems to be reasserting itself, Ecclus. xlvi. 15; xlix. 10; 1 Macc. ii. 52, quoted by Lightfoot, *ubi supr.* While the passive sense is found in Rom. iii. 3 τὴν πίστιν τοῦ Θεοῦ, the fidelity of GOD, the active sense is the usual one, especially in S. Paul's writings. He uses πίστις, πιστεύειν to describe an act or state of living adhesion on the part of the human soul to the way of salvation revealed by GOD.

3. S. Paul then uses faith in the sense of being persuaded that something out of the range of experience is true, on the ground that GOD, where wisdom and goodness make it impossible that He should deceive or be deceived, has revealed it. πιστεύειν is used in the popular sense of holding to be true, being persuaded of the truth of something, in such passages as Rom. vi. 8 πιστεύομεν ὅτι καὶ συζήσομεν: Rom. x. 9 ἐὰν πιστεύσῃς ἐν τῇ καρδίᾳ σου, ὅτι ὁ θεὸς ἤγειρεν αὐτὸν ἐκ νεκρῶν, σωθήσῃ; and a half-formed persuasion is described in 1 Cor. xi. 18 καὶ μέρος τι πιστεύω. In these passages we have before us a conviction which does not depend upon grounds of ocular demonstration, or of sensuous experience. Where the grounds of a conviction are *per se* irresistible, the result is not faith but scientific knowledge; and faith differs from this in that it always implies the presence of a moral factor, which atones for the deficiency of evidence, mathematically speaking, and makes the act of belief a criterion of the moral condition of the believer. This contrast between belief and science, in the strictly modern sense of the latter word, is expressed by S. Paul, 2 Cor. v. 7 διὰ πίστεως περιπατοῦμεν οὐ διὰ εἴδους. In the same way, Rom. iv. 18, Abraham, παρ' ἐλπίδα ἐπ' ἐλπίδι ἐπίστευσεν, believed in the truth of what GOD had told him to expect, in spite of natural expectations founded upon experience to the contrary. This accords with the definition of faith in Heb. xi. 1, as an ἐλπιζομένων ὑπόστασις, πραγμάτων ἔλεγχος οὐ βλεπομένων; faith, by reason of the moral ingredient in it, does amount to proof, and yields substantial support to the [expectation].

4. Thus it is that faith always supposes a witness to its object, and so it differs from οἴεσθαι, νομίζειν, κ.τ.λ. This witness must produce credentials, whether miracles or character or both; 'the works that I do bear witness of me.' Miracles do not warrant a creed, but they do certificate a teacher who announces it, and who, on the strength of them, is believed as to matters beyond the province of experience. Such a teacher, and his doctrine, are a necessary condition of faith, Rom. x. 17 πίστις ἐξ ἀκοῆς; and ver. 14 πῶς δὲ πιστεύσουσιν οὗ οὐκ ἤκουσαν; πῶς δὲ ἀκούσουσι χωρὶς κηρύσσοντος. And the production of faith is graphically described in Acts xxviii. 23, 24, where S. Paul, in Rome, ἐξετίθετο διαμαρτυρόμενος τὴν βασιλείαν τοῦ Θεοῦ, πείθων τε αὐτοὺς τὰ περὶ τοῦ Ἰησοῦ . . . . καὶ οἱ μὲν ἐπείθοντο τοῖς λεγομένοις, οἱ δὲ ἠπίστουν. Faith is thus an act partly of the intelligence and partly of the will, to which the soul is moved by the

words of an authoritative teacher, whether spoken or written, but which it may fail or refuse to engage in. The teacher is believed because he is held to represent GOD; hence the phrases πιστεύειν εἰς Θεόν : ἐπὶ Θεόν, Rom. x. 14; iv. 5. 24, in which the believing act is represented as moving towards or as resting upon GOD, and which thus are equivalent to πιστεύειν Θεῷ.

5. Of the particular truths which are more immediately apprehended by justifying faith it will be time to speak hereafter. Here let it be noted that such faith is not, in S. Paul's mind, a bare holding either the Atoning Work of Christ or any other truths of Revelation for true: it is a loving and soul-constraining self-surrender to them, so that they are grasped by the moral no less than by the intellectual man. The mere apprehension, which is divorced from all will and love, would not be called πίστις by S. Paul at all; it was the travesty of his πίστις, which his antinomian followers advocated, and which S. James condemned as νεκρά (ii. 17). S. Paul would probably have at the best termed it γνῶσις and have contrasted it disparagingly with ἀγάπη. With S. Paul, justifying faith is always *practically* inseparable from hope and love; it is ὑπόστασις ἐλπιζομένων (Heb. xi. 1) and it is δι' ἀγάπης ἐνεργουμένη (Gal. v. 6). It may be parted from them in our ideas; but it is bound up with them in the living fact; and thus the faith which justifies (Rom. iii. 28), was rightly described by the schoolmen as a 'fides formata charitate.' Love is its *forma*, its vivifying and plastic principle; and accordingly it brings man into a vital communion with Christ, fills him with devotion to GOD, and by uniting him with the Crucified Saviour, now living in Glory, cleanses him from his sins, and gives him a real share in the righteousness of the Saviour which is communicated to him.

On this subject Luther uses language which is sometimes, but incorrectly, attributed to S. Paul. Luther understands by faith, in some of the most characteristic passages of his Commentary on the Galatians, the bare act of apprehending Christ: he urges that, if charity be also needful, the sinner will despair; he is almost indignant with the text in which S. Paul says that if he had all faith so that he could remove mountains, and had not charity, he is nothing. Probably, by this language Luther meant at bottom to say that the justifying power of faith lies not in itself, but only in Christ whom it embraces; and Luther saw in love a trace of human effort or merit, instead of a gift of the Redeemer through preventive grace. And so he was betrayed into the language which has so often been quoted and which would have shocked the great Apostle whom he undertook to interpret, 'Esto peccator et pecca fortiter, sed fortius fide et gaude in Christo,' Luther, *Epistt.* (Jena, 1556), tom. 1, pp. 345, 6. For such faith love was not necessary; such faith rendered man perfectly acceptable to GOD, without sanctifying him; to such faith Christ's righteousness was an external object—the justified believer might still be impure. Instead of a morally renovating and vital principle, placing man in real communion with Christ, and securing a real *communication* of his righteousness, we have a bare apprehension of it, resulting in an imputation of righteousness which is not really communicated at all.

Luther saw that there was a great deal of language in Scripture which this theory of faith would not cover, and which was more or less distinctly opposed to it. Hence the distinction between the instrumental faith which justifies, and the faith which is a source of good works and which works by charity. The latter kind of faith is described by Luther in glowing terms in his preface to the Epistle to the Romans, 'Faith,' he says, 'is a Divine work within us, which changes us, makes us to be born again out of God, destroys the old Adam, and transforms us as it were into other men, in heart, in feeling, in every faculty, and communicates to us the Holy Spirit. This faith is something living and efficacious; so that it is impossible that it should not always work good. Faith does not first ask whether good works are to be done; but before it enquires about the matter it has already wrought many good works and is ever busy in working.' It would be impossible to state the Pauline idea of faith more fully; but then this was the only faith to which S. Paul allowed any justifying power. The conception of a twofold faith, one only apprehensive and justifying, and the other loving, practical and sanctifying, has no basis in S. Paul, and is the creation of a theory which has seen its day.]

§ Accordance of the Thesis with Hab. ii. 4, which promises life to the man whose Righteousness depends on faith,

Heb. וְצַדִּיק בֶּאֱמוּנָתוֹ יִחְיֶה

LXX ὁ δὲ δίκαιος μοῦ ἐκ πίστεως ζήσεται.

[*Obs.* 1. This is the second line of the prophecy respecting the ungodly power of the Chaldaeans, which follows the Divine answer to Habakkuk's cry for light. The fundamental thought of all that follows is contained in ii. 4, viz., that the presumptuous and proud, notwithstanding appearances, will not continue, but the just alone will live. By the man puffed up עֻפְּלָה, is meant the Chaldaean; his soul is not straight within him, and this portends moral and ultimately material ruin. In contrast to him is the צַדִּיק the typical Israelite, or the prophet himself, who desires to satisfy the claims of God according to the terms of the Old Testament revelation. He, the righteous, through his faith, will live. בֶּאֱמוּנָתוֹ belongs not to צַדִּיק but to יִחְיֶה. אֱמוּנָה here does not mean an 'honourable character or fidelity to conviction'(Hitzig). Derived from אָמַן it means (1) *firmness*, Ex. xvii. 12, then (2) in God, faithfulness to His promises, Deut. xxxii. 4; Ps. xxxiii. 4; lxxxix. 33, and (3) in man, fidelity in word and deed, Jer. vii. 28; ix. 3; Ps. xxxvii. 3; and (4) *in his relation to God* firm confidence in Him. That in Hab. ii. 4, אֱמוּנָה refers to a relation between man and God is clear from the context; the prophet is waiting for a promised [vision], preceded by a period of suffering. It was not Habakkuk's integrity towards man, but his faith in God which was imperilled. The אמונה of the just is opposed to the pride of the Chaldaean who exalts himself above God, and thus it must mean not integrity but some quality antithetical to pride,—humble, trustful, submissive. Hence the Jewish intt. and LXX render it by faith. See Keil, *in loc.* Dr. Pusey, *Minor Prophets,* in loc.]

[*Obs.* 2. The LXX have changed the suffix and rendered ἐκ πίστεώς μου instead of αὐτοῦ or ἑαυτοῦ (so Aquila and other Greek verses). They have thus missed the sense. S. Paul omits the erroneous μου of the LXX without restoring the αὐτοῦ.]

[*Obs.* 3. In Gal. iii. 12, the verse is quoted to show that the law cannot secure justification; ἐκ πίστεως is antithetical to ὁ ποιήσας. In Heb. x. 38 as a reason for patient faithfulness to Christ, under the pressure of persecutions which tempted to apostacy. Here, although the Hebrew does not bear it out, S. Paul seems to connect ἐκ πίστεως not with ζήσεται but with ὁ δίκαιος. The man whose Righteousness is that of faith shall live. The purpose of his appeal to the passage is to confirm from the Old Testament the revelation, not of *the life ἐκ πίστεως*, but of *the righteousness ἐκ πίστεως*.]

DOGMATIC PORTION OF THE EPISTLE.

Division I.   Chap. I. 18—V. 21.

The ΔΙΚΑΙΟΣΥΝΗ ΘΕΟΥ ΕΚ ΠΙΣΤΕΩΣ CONSIDERED OBJECTIVELY, WITH REFERENCE TO THE FACTS OF HUMAN NATURE AND RELIGIOUS HISTORY.

A.

All men need this δικαιοσύνη Θεοῦ. I. 18—III. 20.

[*Obs.* The argument of this section may be thus stated :—

Major premiss.   Whosoever sins, incurs τὸ κρῖμα τοῦ Θεοῦ, from which he can only be delivered by the δικαιοσύνη Θεοῦ (ii. 1-16).

Minor premiss.   But the heathen, although taught by Nature and Conscience (i. 18-32), and the Jews, although possessing the Mosaic Law (ii. 17-iii. 8), have sinned by falling short of, or contradicting, their respective standards of δικαιοσύνη.

Concl.   Therefore, as the Old Testament had already proclaimed, ὑπόδικος γίνεται πᾶς ὁ κόσμος τῷ Θεῷ (iii. 19), and accordingly needs His δικαιοσύνη (iii. 9-20).]

§ 1.

(Minor premiss, part 1.) *The Heathen Nations, taught by Nature and Conscience, have failed to attain* δικαιοσύνη (I. 18-32).

[*Obs.* That the heathen have failed to attain δικαιοσύνη, or, in other words, are sinners, needing God's Righteousness, is shown from a review of the downward moral course of the heathen world. In it too, as in the Gospel, there is an ἀποκάλυψις, but an ἀποκάλυψις ὀργῆς, and not δικαιοσύνης Θεοῦ. This is stated generally in ver. 18.]

Proposition. The moral history of heathendom is a revelation of God's Wrath against all impiety and unrighteousness of men who repress, by their unrighteousness, the promptings of truth [as taught by nature and conscience].

[*Obs.* 1. This verse is a reason (γάρ) for δικαιοσύνη in ver. 17. That πίστις is the condition of an ἀποκάλυψις τῆς δικαιοσύνης is shown by the fact that where πίστις does not exist as in heathendom, there is an ἀποκάλυψις, not of Divine Righteousness, but of Divine Wrath. ὀργὴ Θεοῦ is antithetical to δικαιοσύνη Θεοῦ, and ἀπ' οὐρανοῦ to ἐν εὐαγγελίῳ.]

[*Obs.* 2. ὀργή primarily denotes force or impulse of the soul; ὀργάω is used of [swelling or maturing] plants, or of brute animal impulses. In Attic Greek it means, not the affection itself, but its expression in roused feeling. When used of God it is opposed to ἔλεος, Rom. ix. 22, and means God's wrath against *sin*, the effect of which is to exclude from redemption, Heb. iii. 11, iv. 3; 1 Thess. v. 9. Hence it is contrasted in its effects with δικαιοῦν, Rom. v. 9, and its manifestation in the imputation and punishment of sin is implied in Rom. ii. 5 ἡμέρα ὀργῆς: Rom. iv. 15 νόμος ὀργὴν κατεργάζεται: Rom. iii. 5 ὁ ἐπιφέρων τὴν ὀργήν, said of God; ix. 22 θέλων ὁ Θεὸς ἐνδείξασθαι τὴν ὀργήν, *ib.* σκεύη ὀργῆς: Eph. ii. 3 τέκνα ὀργῆς: 1 Thess. ii. 16 ἔφθασε ἐπ' αὐτοὺς ἡ ὀργὴ εἰς τέλος. The anthropopathic expression ὀργὴ Θεοῦ—the disposition of the Personal God towards moral evil—is the reverse side of His love. He could not love goodness if He were not angry with evil. Lactantius, *De Ira Dei*, v. 9 'Si Deus non irascitur impiis et injustis, nec pios utique justosque diligit, ... In rebus enim divinis aut in utramque partem moveri necesse est aut in neutram.' Lactantius will not allow that God's ὀργή exists only *effectu*, and not *affectu*; it is, he urges, a real affection in the Divine Being which is roused by moral evil. Tertullian in the same sense writes against Marcion, who in his attack upon the Old Testament had feigned a 'Deus bonus' who was incapable of anger. See Tert. *Contr. Marcion.* i. 26 'Stupidissimus ergo qui non offenditur facto quod non amat fieri; . . . si offenditur, debet irasci, si irascitur, debet ulcisci.' *De Anima*, c. 16 'Indignabitur Deus rationaliter, quibus scilicet debet; et concupiscet Deus rationaliter quae digna sunt ipso.' The dread of anthropomorphism led to more cautious language in the great fathers. S. Aug. *Enchiridion*, c. 10 'Ex humanis motibus translato vocabulo, vindicta ejus quae nonnisi justa est, irae nomen accepit.' *Civ. Dei*, xv. 25, God's anger is 'judicium quo irrogatur poena peccato.' Meyer denounces this as a rationalising interchange of ideas. See Suicer, s. v. ὀργή, Petavius, *Dogm. Theol.* 'De Deo,' iii. 2. 14–16. For anger in man, see Bp. Butler, Eighth Sermon *on Resentment*, where he shows that a sense of injury, as distinct from pain or loss, is its proper object.]

[*Obs.* 3. The revelation of the wrath of God, which is here in question, is actually taking place (ἀποκαλύπτεται) in the heathen world. It is seen in the punishment of unfaithfulness to natural light, which will presently be described: cf. παρέδωκεν αὐτούς (vers. 24, 28). That it is not a revelation of wrath in the Gospel which is in question is clear from the contrast between ἀπ' οὐρανοῦ ver. 18, and ἐν αὐτῷ in ver. 17, although some interpreters would repeat ἐν αὐτῷ in ver. 18. This ἀποκάλυψις of Divine wrath in heathen history is said to be ἀπ' οὐρανοῦ in order to point to the source of the punishment of the heathen. It did not come from any natural agency, but from heaven, the dwelling-place and throne of God, S. Matt. vi. 9. It is possible that the phrase is partly determined by the image of the lightning; but it contrasts with ἐν εὐαγγελίῳ, wherein the Divine δικαιοσύνη is revealed, as suggesting a revelation, obvious not merely to the conscience of the believing Christian, but also to the ordinary observer of the course of human events.]

[*Obs.* 4. The object of GOD's ὀργή is man's irreligiousness (ἀσέβεια, 2 Pet. ii. 5; 2 Tim. ii. 16), and immorality (ἀδικία), cf. ver. 29, or failure to satisfy the rights of GOD as defined by man's present moral standard. It is not merely the presence of wickedness under this twofold aspect which provokes the Divine ὀργή, but the fact that those who are guilty of it possess a certain measure of *religious* truth (ἀλήθειαν), which they *hold down* (κατέχουσι) so as to prevent its producing its natural effects upon conduct in their immorality (ἐν ἀδικίᾳ). On κατέχειν as = to hinder, Vulg. *detinere*, cf. 2 Thess. ii. 6; S. Luke iv. 42; 1 Macc. vi. 27. The sense of *possess* (1 Cor. vii. 30; xv. 2; 2 Cor. vi. 10), 'who hold the truth in unrighteousness,' is contradicted by ver. 21, where the continued possession of truth is negatived by ἐματαιώθησαν. ἐν ἀδικίᾳ is here instrumental; it was by ἀδικία that the truth was held down. Observe the Apostolic theory as to the place of heathendom in man's religious development. It is not a natural stage of development through which man must pass to monotheism, but it is *unnatural*; it arises from and is a product of sin against previously-possessed natural light.]

a.

Neglect and abuse of natural light by the heathen peoples, issuing in ignorance, folly, and idolatry (vers. 19–23).

1. A limited knowledge of GOD in heathendom—(τὸ γνωστὸν τοῦ Θεοῦ) (ver. 19–20) derived from

    a. The light of conscience (φανερὸν ἐν αὐτοῖς). This inner φανέρωσις of GOD has been made by Himself; but its ground (γάρ) is found in

    b. the witness of external Nature. In Nature

    (1) the unseen truths about GOD (τὰ ἀόρατα αὐτοῦ) more precisely defined as His everlasting power and divinity (ἥ τε ἀΐδιος αὐτοῦ δύναμις καὶ θειότης)

    (2) are seen (καθορᾶται) through being *mentally* discerned (νοούμενα),

    (3) by means of His works (τοῖς ποιήμασι),

    (4) ever since the creation of the world (ἀπὸ κτίσεως κόσμου).

    c. the result being that the heathen are inexcusable ἀναπολογήτους (ver. 20).

[*Obs.* 1. ver. 19 explains the assertion in ver. 18 τὴν ἀλήθειαν ἐν ἀδικίᾳ κατεχόντων. If the heathen had repressed the truth out of ignorance they would be excusable. But they had a knowledge of GOD, and they repressed truth out of immorality. This proof of their knowledge shows why they are ἀναπολόγη-τοι (ver. 20); διότι = propterea quod.]

[*Obs.* 2. The phrase τὸ γνωστὸν τοῦ Θεοῦ must, according to the invariable New Testament and LXX use, mean *that which is known*, not *that which may be known about* GOD. The latter would be the classical sense (cf. Meyer). But γνωστός = known in S. Luke ii. 44; John xviii. 15; Acts i. 19, xv. 18. xxviii. 22. And S. Paul is speaking of an objective body of knowledge which becomes subjective in the φανέρωσις, Winer, *Gr. N. T.* p. 295. This knowledge becomes manifest in their consciousness; ἐν αὐτοῖς does not mean 'among them,' since νοούμενα καθορᾶται point to an internal manifestation. On this manifestation of truth through nature to conscience, see Acts xiv. 17, where, at Lystra, S. Paul, after remarking that GOD had permitted the heathen nations to go in their own way, adds καί τοί γε οὐκ ἀμάρτυρον ἑαυτὸν ἀφῆκεν, ἀγαθοποιῶν. The witness was yielded by rain and the succession of seasons of the year. At Athens, Acts xvii. 26, he points to the creation of man, ἐξ ἑνὸς αἵματος, and to the epochs and frontiers of each national development as incitements to seek GOD—ver. 27 κάτοιγε οὐ μακρὰν ἀπὸ ἑνὸς ἑκάστου ἡμῶν ὑπάρχοντα. And yet, 1 Cor. i. 21 ἐν τῇ σοφίᾳ τοῦ Θεοῦ, οὐκ ἔγνω ὁ κόσμος διὰ τῆς σοφίας τὸν Θεόν: as a matter of fact heathen philosophy failed to *know* Him who had revealed Himself in part through nature to conscience. [In regard to the universality of some conception of God] Aristotle had observed, *De Coelo*, i. 3 (270 b. 5) πάντες ἄνθρωποι περὶ θεῶν ἔχουσι ὑπόληψιν. Xen. *Mem.* iv. 4. 19 παρὰ πᾶσιν ἀνθρώποις πρῶτον νομίζεται θεοὺς σέβειν.]

[*Obs.* 3. The revelation of GOD in conscience is explained by reference (γάρ) to external nature. The first impression which nature yields as to its Author is His power—δύναμις. The many invisible attributes of GOD (τὰ ἀόρατα αὐτοῦ), more precisely GOD's everlasting power and divinity, may be learnt from nature. θειότης, divinity, that which GOD is, as a Being possessed of Divine attributes; not θεότης, the being GOD, Col. ii. 9. Under θειότης all GOD's other attributes—wisdom, goodness, &c.—are included. These truths about GOD are seen, through being mentally perceived; the νοῦς, as distinct from the senses of man, must see GOD in nature; καθορᾶται cannot refer to any action of the bodily senses. With ἀόρατα it forms an oxymoron, with which compare Arist. *De Mundo*, 6 (399 b. 22) ἀθεώρητος ἀπ' αὐτῶν τῶν ἔργων θεωρεῖται [ὁ θεός]. This revelation of GOD in nature dates from the creation; in ἀπὸ κτίσεως κόσμου, κτίσις must mean *creatio*, not *res creata*, because in the latter case τοῖς ποιήμασι νοούμενα would be superfluous. The ποιήματα are GOD's productions as Creator; ποίημα corresponds to מַעֲשֶׂה, Eccles. iii. 11, vii. 14, but does not mean GOD's acts in governing the world, to which ἀπὸ κτίσεως κόσμου would not apply.]

[*Obs.* 4. On the responsibility of this knowledge of GOD through nature and conscience, see Tertull. *Apolog.* c. 17: 'Quod colimus [nos], Deus unus est, qui totam molem istam cum omni instrumento elementorum, corporum, spirituum, verbo quo jussit, ratione quâ disposuit, virtute quâ potuit, de nihilo expressit in ornamentum majestatis suae, unde et Graeci nomen mundo κόσμον accommodaverunt. Invisibilis est, etsi videtur; incomprehensibilis, etsi per gratiam repraesentatur; inaestimabilis etsi humanis sensibus aestimatur.... Hoc est quod Deum aestimari facit, dum aestimari non capit.

Ita eum vis magnitudinis et notum hominibus objecit et ignotum. Et haec est summa delicti nolentium recognoscere quem ignorare non possunt.' On the way in which nature witnesses to GOD, see Luthardt, *Fundamental Truths of Christianity* (3rd ed.), p. 44 sqq. On the function of reason in discerning this witness, see Christlieb, *Modern Doubt and Christian Belief*, p. 70 sqq. On the 'Dispensation of Paganism,' see Newman, *Arians*, i. §§ 3-5 (p. 83, 3rd ed.)].

2. How this natural knowledge of GOD has been lost in heathendom (ver. 21–23).

Stage 1. Practical Indifference to known truth. The natural knowledge of GOD was not acted on. He was neither praised on account of His perfections, so far as they were known (οὐχ ὡς Θεὸν ἐδόξασαν), nor thanked for the blessings which were seen to be due to Him (ἢ εὐχαρίστησαν) (ver. 21).

Stage 2. Intrinsically worthless speculation about GOD. The ideas and reflections which the heathen formed for themselves respecting the Deity, corresponded to nothing in fact: they were reduced to emptiness (ἐματαιώθησαν ἐν τοῖς διαλογίσμοις) (ver. 21).

Stage 3. Disappearance of the idea of GOD, as revealed in nature and conscience, from the minds of men. The whole inner being (καρδία) was darkened, it had become incapable of discerning truth (ἀσύνετος) through the ματαιότης of its speculative folly (ver. 21).

Stage 4. A Pride of Philosophy coinciding with abandonment to spiritual and moral folly (φάσκοντες εἶναι σοφοὶ ἐμωράνθησαν) (ver. 22).

Stage 5. Fetichism. The majesty of the Imperishable GOD exchanged for something shaped like the image of (a) perishable man or (b) of the lower creatures (ver. 23).

[*Obs.* 1. ver. 21. *Stage of practical indifference to known truth.* διότι connects the clause εἰς τὸ ἀναπολογήτους εἶναι with the following account of heathen degradation. The heathen originally possessed such knowledge of GOD as could be derived from conscience and nature (γνόντες τὸν Θεόν). This knowledge was a true knowledge so far as it went; but like all religious truth, it could only be retained on condition of being acted on. The heathen originally knew GOD as a Being of infinite Perfections; his θειότης (ver. 20) as well as His Power were known to them from nature. Yet did they not glorify Him as GOD,—the correlative moral act to their knowledge of His Nature. They knew too that He had given them all that they were and had, yet did they not *thank* Him for His gifts. The debt of adoration due to GOD, on account of man's natural knowledge of Him is exhausted by the words δοξάζειν and εὐχαριστεῖν.]

[Obs. 2. *Stage of worthless speculation about GOD.* The heathen were reduced to being mere triflers in their thoughts about GOD. Although they did not praise and thank Him, they could not but think of Him; only thought about GOD without the practical safeguards of devotion, becomes empty and fruitless. Hence their ματαιότης· ματαιοῦσθαι corresponds to הִסְכִּיל to become foolish, or to הֶבֶל [cf. 2 Kings xvii. 15; Job xxvii. 12]. The meaning is that there was nothing in fact to correspond to the διαλογισμοί of the heathen. In Eph. iv. 17 the heathen are said περιπατεῖν ἐν ματαιότητι τοῦ νοὸς αὐτῶν. For 'vanity,' emptiness, as a characteristic of heathenism, see Jer. ii. 5; 2 Kings xvii. 15; Ps. xciv. 11. At Lystra the Apostles beg the heathen multitude ἀπὸ τούτων τῶν ματαίων ἐπιστρέφειν ἐπὶ τὸν Θεὸν τὸν ζῶντα Acts xiv. 15. In the New Testament διαλογισμοί are always πονηροί, κακοί, whether thoughts, S. Matt. xv. 19; or reasonings, S. Luke v. 22; or doubts, S. Luke xxiv. 38. Here 'thoughts.']

[Obs. 3. ver. 21. *Stage of the disappearance of the idea of GOD from the heathen mind.* The καρδία, לֵב, is the centre of the soul's life,—of will, of thought, and of emotion. Delitzsch, *Bibl. Psych.* pp. 292 ff. E. T. It is darkened, because the empty speculations had rendered it ἀσύνετος, i.e. incapable of understanding what is true and right. Winer seems to think ἀσύνετος a proleptic use of the *adjectiva effectus*, but in reality *less* is implied by ἀσύνετος than by ἐσκοτίσθη, Winer, *Gr. N. T.*, p. 779. Compare Eph. iv. 18, for the heathen πώρωσις τῆς καρδίας as the cause of ἄγνοια; and Eph. v. 17 for the contrast between ἄφρονες and συνιέντες τί τὸ θέλημα τοῦ Κυρίου. The passage is based on Wisd. xi. 15. The whole representation is seemingly condensed from Wisd. xiii.–xv.]

[Obs. 4. ver. 22. *Stage of a false conceit of wisdom coincident with abandonment to spiritual and moral folly.* The claim to wisdom was often repeated and was unfounded: φάσκειν, *dictitare*, to make unfounded assertions, Acts xxiv. 9; xxv. 19; Rev. ii. 2. For ἐμωράνθησαν, cf. 1 Cor. i. 20 οὐχὶ ἐμώρανεν ὁ Θεὸς τὴν σοφίαν τοῦ κόσμου τούτου, 1 Cor. iii. 18–20.]

[Obs. 5. ver. 23. *Stage of Fetichism.* The δόξα τοῦ Θεοῦ is the כְּבוֹד יְהוָֹה, the Glory or Perfection of GOD—His θειότης. δόξα applied to a person is the *manifestation* of excellence. The Shekinah was the visibly displayed יהוה כבוד, 1 Kings viii. 11, the glory (ἡ δόξα) of the Lord filled the house. S. John xi. 40 ἐὰν πιστεύσῃς ὄψῃ τὴν δόξαν τοῦ Θεοῦ. The particular effulgence or glory of GOD here meant is that displayed on the face of, although distinct from, nature. GOD is ἄφθαρτος:—His ἀφθαρσία is the result of His unchangeableness. See Pearson, *Min. Theol. Works*, I. 92 (Oxford 1844). Aristotle, *Phys.* V. 1. (225 a. 17), defines φθορά as ἡ ἐξ ὑποκειμένου εἰς οὐχ ὑποκείμενον, φθορὰ ἁπλῶς μὲν ἡ ἐκ τῆς οὐσίας εἰς τὸ μὴ εἶναι. For ἄφθαρτος as a Divine attribute, see 1 Tim. i. 17; 1 Tim. vi. 16 μόνος ἔχων ἀθανασίαν, Ps. cii. 26, 27, 'The heavens shall perish, but Thou remainest; and they all shall wax old as doth a garment, and as a vesture shalt Thou change them and they shall be changed, but Thou art the same and Thy years shall not fail.' The heathen ought to have made τὴν δόξαν τοῦ Θεοῦ, manifested to them in the revelation of nature, an object of worship. Instead of that they chose what was shaped like an image of a perishable man for this purpose. ἀλλάσσειν τι ἐν τινὶ is a vivid phrase based on Ps. cv. 20, LXX ἠλλάξαντο τὴν δόξαν αὐτῶν ἐν ὁμοιώματι μόσχου. ἐν ὁμοιώματι for εἰς ὁμοίωμα according to the usual substitution of ἐν for εἰς when translating בְּ. ὁμοίωμα εἰκόνος—the ὁμοίωμα of the heathen deity was a likeness—not an absolute copy—of a statue of a man. It was the likeness found in the image of that which it represents. In ἀνθρώπου S. Paul is thinking of the Hellenic form of idolatry; in πετεινὰ κ.τ.λ. of the Egyptian. On the Egyptian worship of animals (Wisd. xiii. 10 ἀπεικάσματα ζῴων) see Döllinger, *Gentile and Jew*, vol. i. p. 454 E. T.; Philo, *Leg. ad Caium*, pp. 566, 570 (ed. Mangey).

b.

Punishment of the Heathen for their neglect and abuse of the natural knowledge of GOD, as seen in their abandonment to the *moral* consequences of this unfaithfulness (24–32).

[*Obs.* In this punishment three stages are marked, each introduced by παρέδωκεν (vers. 24, 26, 28), and παρέδωκεν cannot safely be paraphrased by εἴασε (S. Chrys. and others) as if it described a mere permission. This paraphrase was undoubtedly intended to screen GOD, from any blasphemous imputation of being the cause of moral evil. But the language will not bear it; and the dreaded consequence of construing the language literally does not follow. GOD as Creator had established a *nexus* between moral acts, involving the consequence of one crime upon another,—parallel to the consequence of one virtue upon another. 'To him that hath shall be given; from him that hath not shall be taken away even that which he seemeth to have.' As each grace which is corresponded to, is rewarded by a higher grace; so each vice, which is accepted by the will, leads to a deeper vice beyond itself. 'Das ist der Fluch des Bösen, dass es ewig Böses zeugt.' To abandon *voluntarily* the true idea of GOD is to fall necessarily under the empire of material nature, with all its dominant instincts and desires. Hence in the Old Testament idolatry is consistently described as fornication; nothing short of a faithful hold upon the truth of GOD's nature will keep man from sinking beneath the debasements of a life of sensuality. παρέδωκεν, therefore, implies something more than permission. namely, GOD's original appointment in the laws of interconnection between one moral act and another, which are a part of His original design for the moral world, and in strict accordance with the essential and necessary sanctity of His Nature.]

Stage 1. παρέδωκεν εἰς ἀκαθαρσίαν. Impurity of life, generally, springing up in the field of their natural ἐπιθυμίαι and leading to mutual corporeal degradation (ver. 24).

§ Reasons for this dreadful παρέδωκεν (25).

Reason 1. The heathen exchanged the Divine Reality for a lie (ψεῦδος), viz. the false gods.

Reason 2. The heathen generally paid worship and ritual service to the creature, i. e. neglecting the Creator (ver. 25).

[*Obs.* 1. ver. 24. ἀκαθαρσία—*spurcitia*, impurity arising from indulged lusts. In Gal. v. 19 it is the third of the ἔργα τῆς σαρκός. In Eph. iv. 19 the heathen ἀπηλγηκότες ἑαυτοὺς παρέδωκαν τῇ ἀσελγείᾳ εἰς ἐργασίαν ἀκαθαρσίας πάσης ἐν πλεονεξίᾳ. Col. iii. 5 νεκρώσατε οὖν τὰ μέλη ὑμῶν τὰ ἐπὶ τῆς γῆς, πορνείαν, ἀκαθαρσίαν. τοῦ ἀτιμάζεσθαι is gen. of precise definition. The ἀκαθαρσία consists in their bodies being reciprocally dishonoured. ἀτιμάζεσθαι passive, not middle, see Meyer.]

[*Obs.* 2. The reasons for the deliverance to ἀκαθαρσία are restated; the Apostle feeling that the severity of the Divine Judgment requires the repetition. οἵτινες, in that they, *quippe qui*: for this causal use, introducing the motive which determined God to give the heathen up, see Rom. vi. 2; 2 Cor. viii. 10; Gal. v. 4; S. Matt. vii. 15. The expression τὴν ἀλήθειαν τοῦ Θεοῦ seems to harmonize with τὴν δόξαν τοῦ Θεοῦ in ver. 23: hence Θεοῦ is a *gen. subj.*, the truth which comes from God. But practically it is the truth about him, so that in meaning it is ὁ ἀληθινὸς Θεός. This the heathen exchanged for a ψεῦδος. An idol is a concrete lie. שֶׁקֶר means ψεῦδος as often as idols, Is. xliv. 20; Jer. iii. 10; xiii. 25. Cf. 1 Thess. i. 9 ἐπεστρέψατε πρὸς τὸν Θεὸν ἀπὸ τῶν εἰδώλων, δουλεύειν Θεῷ ζῶντι καὶ ἀληθινῷ, and Gal. iv. 8, where he implies the same antithesis in speaking of the heathen φύσει μὴ ὄντες θεοί. Cf. 1 Cor. viii. 4.]

[*Obs.* 3. The general cultus of creatures is indicated by ἐσεβάσθησαν. σεβάζομαι here an ἅπ. λεγ. in New Testament for the usual σέβομαι. It means, to treat with pious reverence. ἐλάτρευσαν points to sacrificial and ritual service. This worship was offered to the creature, before the Creator, 'prae creatore'; the context showing that the preference of the creature was not merely relative, but that it *excluded* the latter. The heathen did not, in fact, worship the Creator at all. The preposition παρά with the accusative is often used for מִן in this comparative sense. Here the sense is substantially expressed by S. Cyprian, *Test.* iii. 10, 'relicto creatore,' and S. Hilary, *De Trin.* xii. 3, 'praeterito creatore'; Jer. ii. 27, 'They have turned their back on Me and not their face.']

[*Obs.* 4. For doxologies, offered to God by deeply moved piety as acts of reparation for some wrong done Him in thought or act, see xi. 36; Gal. i. 5; 2 Cor. xi. 31; Eph. i. 3; iii. 21. Such doxologies are common among the Orientals, especially the Mahommedans, under such circumstances.]

Stage 2. παρέδωκεν εἰς πάθη ἀτιμίας παρὰ φύσιν (ver. 26). Sensual degradation, assuming in both sexes unnatural forms:

    a. crime of θήλειαι—described generally as changing τὴν φυσικὴν χρῆσιν εἰς τὴν παρὰ φύσιν.

Dogmatic : ch. I, *vv.* 18-32.

b. crime of ἄρρενες—described more particularly
{ 1. *negatively*, as ἀφέντες τὴν φυσικὴν χρῆσιν τῆς θηλείας.
{ 2. *positively.*

in the stage of
{ i. ὄρεξις.   It is a brutal ἐξεκαύθησαν.
{ ii. completed action (κατεργάζεσθαι). It is ἀσχημοσύνη.
{ iii. penal result (ἀντιμισθία). That which was in accordance with natural order (ἣν ἔδει), viz. the loss of the natural knowledge of GOD.

[*Obs.* 1. In the expression describing the sensual degradation of the heathen ἀτιμίας is a *gen. qualitatis* : cf. πνεῦμα ἁγιωσύνης ver. 4. The words θήλειαι and ἄρρενες are selected to give prominence to the animal idea of sex, instead of the higher human idea of man and woman : by φυσικὴν χρῆσιν is meant the use of the sexual organs appointed by GOD in nature.]

[*Obs.* 2. For the degradation of heathen females by unnatural sins, see Martial, *Epigram.* Lib. i. 90. 5 ; Lucian, *Dialog.* v. *in Meretric.* 2, on the vice λεσβιάζειν. Cf. the ἑταιριστρίαι in Plato, *Symp.* p. 191 E. They were also called τριβάδες.]

[*Obs.* 3. In describing the degradation of heathen males by unnatural sins, ἐξεκαύθησαν is used by the Apostle as stronger than the simple form: cf. πυροῦσθαι 1 Cor. vii. 9. κατεργάζεσθαι is used of *perfected* action, whether evil (ii. 9, vii. 8, xv. 17 sqq.) or good (v. 3, xv. 18); Phil. ii. 12). For ἀσχημοσύνην, see Gen. xxxiv. 7 ; Rev. xvi. 15. It is the opposite of εὐσχημοσύνην, xiii. 13. With the article it means 'the well-known shame' which characterised pagan society. The πλάνη referred to is the wandering from GOD as known in nature and conscience to idols ; and the ἀντιμισθία ἐν ἑαυτοῖς, the hateful and unnatural desires just described. πλάνη seems to mean wilful and corrupting delusion, 1 Thess. ii. 3 and 2 Pet. ii. 18, iii. 17 ; S. Jude 11. ἀντιμισθία is not found in Greek writers or LXX : but cf. 2 Cor. vi. 13 ; 2 [Clem. Rom.] *ad Cor.* 1. ἣν ἔδει : the necessity referred to is implied in the moral order of the world as ruled by the Creator. On the prevalence of παιδεραστία in antiquity, see Döllinger, *Gentile and Jew,* Bk. IX. i. 2. § 33 : 'In very truth the whole of society was infected by it, and people inhaled the pestilence with the air they breathed. . . . The erotic sayings or discourses of philosophers contributed to fan the evil flame.' Seneca, the contemporary of S. Paul, writes : 'Transeo puerorum infelicium greges, quos post transacta convivia aliae cubiculi contumeliae exspectant : transeo agmina exoletorum per nationes coloresque descripta' *Epp.* xv. 3 (95) § 24. Suetonius describes the infamous proceedings of the Emperor Nero, Suet. *Ner.* cc. 28, 29. In the *Amores,* attributed to Lucian (*Dial.* xxxviii. § 51, ed. Dindorf), this vice is considered the privilege of philosophers. S. Justin Martyr denounces its universality and publicity (*Apol.* i. 27). Clem. Alexand. *Pedagog.* iii. 3. 21 (Dindorf). Tatian, *Orat. ad Graecos.* c. 25.]

Stage 3. παρέδωκεν εἰς ἀδόκιμον νοῦν. An active mental disposition (νοῦν) towards intellectual and moral truth, which must be pronounced reprobate, according to any *objective* standard.

a. Measure of this νοῦς ἀδόκιμος corresponds (καθώς) with their contemptuous rejection of the natural knowledge of GOD, which ought to have been brought to an ἐπιγνῶναι,—a penetrating and living knowledge of Him.

b. Practical outcome of this νοῦς ἀδόκιμος. It leads in action to their doing what cannot be deemed seemly, τὰ μὴ καθήκοντα.

[*Obs.* 1. The measure of the refusal of the heathen to retain GOD in their knowledge was the measure of His giving them over to a mind about religious and moral truth that was really reprobate. καθώς implies this correspondence; it is not used in a causal sense. The heathen did not think GOD worth (οὐκ ἐδοκίμασαν) retaining in their knowledge. Cf. 1 Thess. ii. 4; 1 Cor. xvi. 3; 2 Cor. viii. 22. The fuller, deeper knowledge, ἐπίγνωσις, 1 Cor. xiii. 12; Phil. i. 9, would have resulted from faithful use of the teaching of nature and conscience about God. Their unfaithfulness to light was punished by a proportionate moral darkness expressed by ἀδόκιμον νοῦν. Their mind, and its collective powers of thinking and willing, (cf. νοῦς in Delitzsch, *Bibl. Psych.* p. 211, E. T.) is rejected on trial (ἀδόκιμος), not indeed in their own estimate, but when tested by the absolute standard of right and truth. For ἀδόκιμος see 1 Cor. ix. 27; 2 Cor. xiii. 5, 6, 7; 2 Tim. iii. 8; Tit. i. 16; Heb. vi. 8, and observe the paronomasia between οὐκ ἐδοκίμασαν and ἀδόκιμον. ἀδόκιμος cannot mean 'incapable of judging' since the word is not derived from δοκιμάζω.]

[*Obs.* 2. The infinitive clause ποιεῖν κ.τ.λ. is epexegetical: the ἀδόκιμος νοῦς shows itself in the habitual commission of sin, without hesitation or regret. The word καθήκοντα describes acts suited to a moral standard, or a given position. Cf. Ex. v. 13 τὰ ἔργα τὰ καθήκοντα, of the tasks appointed to the Israelites; Acts xxii. 22 οὐ γὰρ καθῆκεν αὐτὸν ζῆν, of what befits the moral order of the Divine Government as understood by the speakers; 2 Macc. vi. 4 τὰ μὴ καθήκοντα ἔνδον εἰσφερόντων, of objects incompatible with the sanctity of the Jewish Temple. Here τὰ μὴ καθήκοντα, what cannot be thought to be suitable to moral right; the negative expression is correlative to ἀδόκιμος νοῦς. τὰ μὴ καθήκοντα, like τὰ μὴ δέοντα, ἃ μὴ δεῖ, 1 Tim. v. 13, Tit. i. 11, expresses a moral estimate; while τὰ οὐκ ἀνήκοντα Eph. v. 4 describes an objectively existing class of things. Cf. Winer, *Gr. N. T.*, p. 603.]

§ Twenty-one illustrations of the general ποιεῖν τὰ μὴ καθήκοντα—which practically results from the νοῦς ἀδόκιμος (29-31).

The heathen of S. Paul's time are described as

I. Having been filled with (πεπληρωμένους) four governing forms of evil:

1. ἀδικίᾳ, disregard of all rights, human as well as Divine.
2. πονηρίᾳ, absence of all principle; moral rottenness.

Dogmatic: ch. I, vv. 18–32.

   3. πλεονεξίᾳ, selfish greed, whether to acquire wealth, or to gratify lust.
   4. κακίᾳ, the lack of all that constitutes human excellence.

II. Full of (μεστούς) bitter anti-social sins:

1. in act or feeling (abstract)
   1. φθόνου, envy [which leads to]
   2. φόνου, murder, [and]
   3. ἔριδος, party-strife, [and attains its ends by]
   4. δόλου, deceit, [and exhibits itself generally in]
   5. κακοηθείας, malignity of judgment.

2. in language (concrete)
   1. ψιθυριστάς, secret detractors, 'delatores.'
   2. καταλάλους, defamers, in public as well as private.
   3. both of which classes are specially θεοστυγεῖς, hateful to GOD.

III. Sinners, by self-assertion, or pride. Of these there are three kinds in a descending climax:
   1. ὑβριστάς, men who, in their pride, insult others, by word or deed.
   2. ὑπερηφάνους, men who, in their pride, look down upon others, but without openly insulting them.
   3. ἀλαζόνας, men who, in their pride, swagger about themselves, but without reference to other men.

IV. Sinners of six kinds against natural principles on which society is based:
   1. ἐφευρετὰς κακῶν, inventors of new vices, luxuries, tortures.
   2. γονεῦσιν ἀπειθεῖς, men wanting in natural dutifulness.
   3. ἀσυνέτους, men wanting in moral intelligence of right and wrong.
   4. ἀσυνθέτους, men wanting in faithfulness to engagements.
   5. ἀστόργους, men wanting in natural love of kinsfolk.
   6. ἀνελεήμονας, men wanting in natural pity for the suffering.

[*Obs.* 1. General forms of evil which fill the heathen mind and govern public life. πεπληρωμένους, this passive verb is used with a genitive, Rom. xv. 14; Luke ii. 40; Acts xiii. 52; 2 Tim. i. 4; with a dative, 2 Cor. vii. 4; with an accusative, Phil. i. 11; Col. i. 9. The verb suggests a date in human history when the case was otherwise, and so differs from μεστούς which describes the matter of fact without any retrospect. It is from having been filled with the general principles of evil, that the heathen are now full of sins against their brother men in detail. (1) Of these words ἀδικία is the most general. It is opposed to δικαιοσύνη in Rom. iii. 5; vi. 3. It is used with ἀσέβεια in i. 18; hence ἀδικία refers to the violated claims of GOD as well as man. 2 Tim. ii. 19 Let every one that nameth the name of the Lord ἀποστήτω ἀπ' ἀδικίας. 1 S. John v. 17 πᾶσα ἀδικία ἁμαρτία ἐστίν. Cf. Cremer, s. v. p. 300. (2) πονηρία, *physically* of a bad nature, καρπῶν, ὀφθαλμῶν, cf. Jer. xxiv. 8, *morally* of utter worthlessness, arising from lack of principle. In 1 Cor. v. 8, it is joined with κακία to complete the antithesis with εἰλικρινείᾳ καὶ ἀληθείᾳ. Its *general* sense of moral worthlessness appears in Plat. *Theaetet.* 176 B—C, *Sophistes* 228 D νόσος τῆς ψυχῆς. It bears the specific sense of *maliciousness* in Mark vii. 22 ὀφθαλμὸς πονηρός, Matt. xxii. 18. Cf. the conduct of the Pharisees and Herodians, Luke xi. 39. πονηρός in LXX generally translates יָרַע which signifies, first of all, that which is physically offensive. (3) πλεονεξία includes (a) covetousness and (b) impure desires, unregulated ὄρεξις, 1 Thess. iv. 6 πλεονεκτεῖν. On the lust of possession as characteristic of Roman policy, cf. for a foreign estimate, Tacit. *Agricol.* 30, Cicero, *in Verrem*, iii. 89 'Lugent omnes provinciae, queruntur omnes liberi populi, regna denique jam omnia de nostris cupiditatibus et injuriis expostulant, locus intra oceanum jam nullus est ... quo non per haec tempora nostrorum hominum libido iniquitasque pervaserit. Sustinere jam populus Romanus non vim, non arma, non bellum, sed luctum, lachrymas, quaerimonias non potest.' *Pro Lege Manil.* 22 'Difficile est dictu Quirites quanto in odio simus apud exteras nationes, propter eorum, quos ad eas per hos annos cum imperio misimus, injurias ac libidines. Quod enim fanum putatis in illis terris nostris magistratibus religiosum, quam civitatem sanctam, quam domum satis clausam ac munitam fuisse?' Compare Juvenal's question, *Sat.* i. 87 'Et quando uberior vitiorum copia, quando, Major avaritiae patuit sinus?' On the sensual sense of πλεονεξία, see Seneca, *De beneficiis*, i. 9; iii. 16; Juvenal, *Sat.* vi. 293. (4) κακία, badness, in the sense of *moral inefficiency*. Opposed to ἀρετή in both the physical and moral sense; cf. Plat. *Rep.* i. 348 C; ix. 580 B; *Cratylus* 386 D; Arist. *Eth. Nic.* vii. 11; Wisd. v. 13, 14. It is synonymous with ἀνανδρία. As ἀρετή indicates the possession of the qualities which characterize a subject, κακία designates their absence. In this general sense, Gen. vi. 5; Acts viii. 22; 1 Cor. xiv. 20. It means specifically *malevolence* in Tit. iii. 3; Col. iii. 8; Eph. iv. 31, and evil in the sense of misfortune in S. Matt. vi. 34. Here it is used in the general sense.]

[*Obs.* 2. Five sins against fellow men, ver. 29. μεστούς, used of things in S. John xix. 29; xxi. 11; S. James iii. 8, and tropically of the human mind as filled with good and evil impulses, S. Matt. xxiii. 28; 2 S. Pet. ii. 14; S. James iii. 17; Rom. xv. 14. (1) φθόνου and φόνου are placed in juxtaposition, on account of the paronomasia: so in the list of ἔργα τῆς σαρκός Gal. v. 21. But they are also connected as cause and effect; Wisd. ii. 24 'Through envy of the devil came death into the world.' In 1 S. John iii. 12, 15, the φθόνος of Cain is the cause of the murder of Abel. (2) φόνος here means not the act of murder (which is incompatible with μεστούς), but the thought or design; cf. Acts ix. 1 Σαῦλος ἔτι ἐμπνέων ἀπειλῆς καὶ φόνου. (3) ἔρις too is an ethical result of φθόνος, with which it is closely associated in 1 Tim. vi. 4, as among the results of Ephesian false teaching; and in Phil. i. 15, as the motives of some early preachers of Christianity in

Rome. (4) δόλος suggests Juv. *Sat.* iii. 41 'Quid Romae faciam? mentiri nescio.' (5) κακοήθεια, Vulg. *malignitas*, malicious disposition accustomed ἐπὶ τὸ χεῖρον ὑπολαμβάνειν τὰ πάντα Arist. *Rhet.* ii. 13. (1389 b. 20.)]

[*Obs.* 3. Two classes of sinners against fellow men, ver. 30. (1) ψιθυρισταί, secret slanderers, 'susurrones ... qui ut inviso homini noceant quae ei probro sint crimina tanquam in aurem alicui insusurrant;' Fritzsche. (2) καταλάλους means detractors generally, but *not exclusively public* ones, as Theophylact and others suggest, in order perhaps to create an adequate antithesis to ψιθυρισταί. As regards the character of Rome for ill-natured gossip, cf. Cicero, *Pro Flacco*, 3 'In maledicentissima civitate'; *Pro Caelio*, 16 'At fuit fama. Quotus quisque istam effugere potest in tam maledica civitate?' Probably S. Paul is thinking of the *delatores*. Tacitus, *Ann.* vi. 7 'Quod maximè exitiale tulere illa tempora, cum primores senatûs infimas etiam delationes exercerent; alii propalam, alii per occultum: neque discerneres alienos a conjunctis, amicos ab ignotis, quid recens, aut vetustate obscurum, perinde in foro, in convivio, quaqua de re locuti incusabantur, ut quis praevenire, et reum destinare properat, pars ad subsidium sui, plures infecti quasi valetudine et contactu.' (3) θεοστυγεῖς hated by GOD; θεοστύγεις would be GOD-haters. Either would be possible; Meyer decides for the first, which is that of the Vulg. *Deo odibiles*, as being according to the *usus loquendi*. GOD-hating would be better expressed by μισόθεος, Aesch. *Ag.* 1090, like φιλόθεος. The word expresses the attitude of the Divine mind towards all the preceding classes of sinners, quâ they are sinners.]

[*Obs.* 4. The self-assertion of Heathenism is expressed by three terms which follow in a descending climax. The worst are (1) the ὑβρισταί; the *insolent*, 'qui prae superbiâ non solum contemnant alios, sed etiam contumeliose tractant'; in 1 Tim. i. 13, S. Paul says that he was a ὑβριστής as well as a blasphemer and a persecutor before his conversion. On the insolence of Roman life, see Cicero, *Ad Quintum fratrem*, Ep. i. 1. 9 'Romae—ubi tanta arrogantia est, tam immoderata libertas, tam infinita hominum licentia.' Next come (2) the ὑπερήφανοι, who, from an imaginary superiority, look down upon others; cf. Theophrastus, *Charact.* xxiv. 1. They will characterize the last days, 2 Tim. iii. 2; are opposed to the ταπεινοί, Prov. iii. 34, quoted in S. James iv. 6; 1 S. Pet. v. 5; their confusion described in the Magnificat, S. Luke i. 51. (3) Last are the ἀλάζονες, *vani ostentatores*, (ἄλη, *circumvagatio*) 'swaggerers, but without any design of insulting others.' Theophrastus, *Charact.* xxiii. 1. Aristotle describes the ἀλάζων (*Eth. Nic.* iv. (7) 2) as προσποιητικὸς τῶν ἐνδόξων καὶ μὴ ὑπαρχόντων, καὶ μειζόνων ἢ ὑπάρχει—ἕνεκα δόξης καὶ τιμῆς. *Magn. Moral.* i. c. 33. § 28. Josephus (*Ant.* viii. 10. 4) calls Rehoboam an ἀλάζων. They too will be among the men of the last days, 2 Tim. iii. 2. On the passage, see Tittmann, *Syn. N. T.*, pp. 72-77. Polybius speaks of an ἔμφυτος ἀλαζονεία among the Aetolians, *Hist.* iv. 3. 1.]

[*Obs.* 5. In the list of six kinds of sinners against the principles on which human society is based, the positive and general ἐφευρεταὶ κακῶν introduces five classes described regularly, with the privative α. For ἀσπόνδους in text. rec. there is no sufficient authority. (1) The ἐφευρεταί (ἅπ. λεγ. in New Testament) κακῶν, are devisers of evil things, whether new refinements in vicious pleasure, or new cruelties and tortures. Cf. 2 Macc. vii. 31 where the youngest of the seven brothers addresses Antiochus Epiphanes, σὺ δὲ πάσης κακίας εὑρετὴς γενόμενος; Philo, *In Flacc.* p. 975 (Mangey) ὁ καινῶν ἀδικημάτων εὑρετής; Tac. *Ann.* iv. 11 'Sejanus, facinorum omnium repertor.' Virgil, *Aen.* ii. 164 'Scelerumque inventor Ulixes.' Sallust, *Hist.* 'Ep. Mith.' 7 'Persen, apud Samothracas Deos receptum in fidem, callidi ac repertores perfidiae, quia pacto vitam dederant, insomniis occidere.' (2) The γονεῦσιν ἀπειθεῖς sin against the *natural* law of parental jurisdiction over children, as well as the Divine. They will be found in the last times, 2 Tim. iii. 2. (3) The ἀσύνετοι here are void of moral or religious intelligence (cf. ver. 21 καὶ ἐσκοτίσθη ἡ ἀσύνετος αὐτῶν καρδία); they have no moral insight when acting or omitting to act; Ecclus. xv. 7 ἀσύνετος = בָּזָה. (4) ἀσυνθέτους follows ἀσυνέτους as a paronomasia; ἅπ. λεγ. in New Testament, but cf. Jer. iii. 7 ἡ ἀσύνθετος Ἰούδα. This faithlessness to engagements was specially characteristic of social relations under the Empire. (5) ἀστόργους, without the affection of natural love; στοργή is 'amor in necessarios.' This will mark the last times, 2 Tim. iii. 3. See Tac. *Vit. Agricolae*, 43, for the bitter comments on Domitian's association with the wife and daughter of Agricola, as his heir. Domitian was flattered; but, says Tacitus, 'tam caeca et corrupta mens assiduis adulationibus erat, ut nesciret a *bono* patre non scribi haeredem nisi malum principem.' (6) ἀνελεήμονας (ἅπ. λεγ. in New Testament), the unpitying, Prov. v. 9; xii. 10 τὰ δὲ σπλάγχνα τῶν ἀσεβῶν ἀνελεήμονα, Ecclus. xiii. 12; Wisd. xii. 5; xix. 1.]

[*Obs.* 6. On the general question of the debasement of morals in the heathen world in S. Paul's time, see Neander's *Denkwürdigkeiten*, Bk. I. p. 143. seq. (ed. 1825), qu. by Tholuck. Also Seneca, *De Ira*, ii. 8 'Omnia sceleribus ac vitiis plena sunt. Plus committitur quam quod possit coercitione sanari. Certatur ingenti quodam nequitiae certamine; major quotidie peccandi cupiditas, minor verecundia est. Expulso melioris aequiorisque respectu, quocunque visum est, libido se impingit: nec furtiva jam scelera sunt; praeter oculos eunt. Adeoque in publicum missa nequitia est, et in omnium pectoribus evaluit, ut *innocentia non rara sed nulla est*. Numquid enim singuli aut pauci rupere legem? Undique, velut signo dato, ad fas nefasque miscendum coorti sunt.' Cf. also Pausanias, *Graeciae Descriptio*, viii. c. 2.]

[*Obs.* 7. Other lists of sins or sinners in S. Paul's writings are 2 Cor. xii. 20 (abstract), a list of eight *sins* against charity which the Apostle fears that he will find at Corinth. Gal. v. 19 (abstract), a list of seventeen ἔργα τῆς σαρκός in contrast to the καρπὸς τοῦ πνεύματος which consists in nine graces. Eph. v. 3 (abstract), six sinful subjects which are to be banished from Christian conversation, as τὰ οὐκ ἀνήκοντα. 1 Tim. i. 9 (concrete), sinners of fourteen kinds, arranged with a view to the order of the Decalogue, as falling under the sentence of the Divine Law. 2 Tim. iii. 2–5 (concrete), sinners of nineteen kinds who will characterize the ἔσχαται ἡμέραι. Of these four appear in the list of heathen vices in the text.]

c. Climax of the νοῦς ἀδόκιμος. Heathen immorality is wilful opposition to knowledge and conscience.

1. *Knowledge* possessed by the heathen. They all know, as a class, and by discernment (οἵτινες ἐπιγνόντες), the decision of GOD

(δικαίωμα) manifested in their moral consciousness, viz. that men who practise (πράσσουσι) such things as are described above, are worthy of [eternal] death.

2. *Conduct* of the heathen. They

   (1) not only do (ποιοῦσι) the acts in question,
   (2) but are also, morally, in agreement with others who practise the sins (πράσσουσι) habitually (ver. 32).

[*Obs*. 1. The climax of the νοῦς ἀδόκιμος is reached by the classes before referred to, but on *account of their* acting against light and knowledge. οἵτινες—' of such a moral character that they,' quippe qui. It is not the specification of a new reason as in ver. 25. ἐπιγνόντες—not merely γνόντες: the heathen have a higher knowledge gained by reflecting on the lessons of nature; cf. ver. 28 ἐν τῇ ἐπιγνώσει.]

[*Obs*. 2. τὸ δικαίωμα τοῦ Θεοῦ. The decision or natural law in accordance with rights which GOD, as Legislator and Judge, has made. This decision is manifested to the heathen in their moral consciousness. δικαίωμα is the result or product of δικαιοῦν; it is the art whereby a δίκαιον or a δίκαιος is recognised or constituted. Thus the word δικαίωμα may mean, (1) an *enactment* in accordance with right as, (*a*) a legal ordinance, S. Luke i. 6; Heb. ix. 10. (*b*) a moral requirement, ii. 26 τὰ δικαιώματα τοῦ νόμου; viii. 4 τὸ δικαίωμα τοῦ νόμου. (*c*) a decision or sentence, *as here*; but not in Rom. v. 16. (2) An *act* in accordance with *right*: Rom. v. 18 δι' ἑνὸς δικαιώματος. Rev. xv. 4, the δικαιώματα of GOD; xix. 8, of the saints in glory.—In accordance with the meaning of the word in this passage is its use of charters and other legal instruments in the time of the lower Empire; see Du Cange, *Gloss. med. et inf. Graec.* s.v. In Arist. *Eth. Nic.* v. 10, it is defined as τὸ ἐπανόρθωμα τοῦ ἀδικήματος, in which the idea of an act involving legal rectification of wrong seems to predominate... The Divine δικαίωμα or sentence manifest in the heathen conscience is that gross immorality deserves θάνατος, i.e. death beyond the grave. Cf. Aesch. *Eum*. 259-265 :—

> ὄψει δὲ κεἴ τις ἄλλος ἥλιτεν βροτῶν
> ἢ Θεὸν ἢ ξένον τιν' οὐκ εὐσεβῶν ἢ τοκέας φίλους,
> ἔχονθ' ἕκαστον τῆς δίκης ἐπάξια
> μέγας γὰρ "Αιδης ἐστὶν εὔθυνος βροτῶν
> ἔνερθε χθονός,
> δελτογράφῳ δὲ πάντ' ἐπωπᾷ φρενί.

The heathen presentiment of punishment in Hades involves a truth to which S. Paul here calls attention :—viz. that sinners deserve eternal death, 2 Thess. i. 8, although the heathen apprehended this under forms associated with their own mythology. Cf. Plat. *Rep.* p. 330 D. It is no mere temporal death which is in question, as in Ex. xix. 12; xxi. 15, 16, 17; but that of which physical death is the shadow, S. James i. 15. So in ii. 8, 9; vi. 16, 21, 23; viii. 13. This δικαίωμα is apprehended by the moral sense.]

[*Obs*. 3. The *conduct* of the heathen, who knew by reflection GOD's sentence of death upon wilful sinners, involves deliberate rejection of light for which they are responsible. For (1) the heathen *do the acts* which entail this sentence (ποιοῦσι). (2) Not only so. They are in moral agreement (συνευδοκοῦσι) with those who practise (πράσσουσι) these things habitually. ποιεῖν is to produce an act which may be often repeated ; πράσσειν to engage in a course of conduct. συνευδοκεῖν is to consent in moral judgment; it is used by our Lord of the Jews, S. Luke xi. 48 συνευδοκεῖτε τοῖς ἔργοις τῶν πατέρων ὑμῶν, and S. Paul was συνευδοκῶν at the martyrdom of S. Stephen, Acts viii. 1 ; xxii. 20 ; cf. 1 Cor. vii. 12 ; 1 Macc. i. 57 ; 2 Macc. xi. 24. The man who morally consents to evil in others, is worse than the agent, because he cannot plead the force of passion or temptation. Of this Eli had been an example, 1 Sam. ii. 29. Cf. Seneca, *Epp.* xvi. 2 (97). § 3 referring to the money which was received by judges in order to hush up some gross crimes, observes, 'Minus crimine, quam absolutione peccatum est.' S. Paul, however, hints at something more than conspiracy with or connivance at evil ;—the heathen of his time actively sympathised with those who practised it. The injustice and greed of Roman policy, the envy, malignity, and murder, which characterised the court life, the secret informers and scandalous gossip of the capital ; the unbearable pride which was insolent, contemptuous and ridiculously vain by turns ; the vice which was so ingenious in its discoveries, and so defiant of the elementary principles of dutifulness, common moral sense, honour, natural affection, and human pity,—all this was yet in harmony with and approved by the mass of heathen opinion. What more could be said to show that the triumph of the νοῦς ἀδόκιμος—and the failure to attain δικαιοσύνη—was complete ?]

§ 2.

[*Major premiss, see above* p. 23.] *Whosoever sins incurs* τὸ κρῖμα τοῦ Θεοῦ (*from which he can only be delivered by the* δικαιοσύνη Θεοῦ). II. 1–16.

[*Obs.* This general proposition, although applicable to Jews and heathen alike, is especially addressed (ii. 1) to the Jews who had peculiar temptations to forget it. The Apostle supposes (ver. 1) a (Jewish) reader to be condemning the Gentile sins which he has just described, and this affords him an opportunity for making an appeal to conscience in passing, which naturally introduces the general proposition beyond (ver. 2).]

§ *Passing warning to the* (*Jewish*) *readers.* II. 1.

By reason of those very heathen sins the reader, be he who he may, who condemns them is himself without excuse before the Justice of God.

Reason 1. γάρ. In passing judgment on another, he utterly condemns himself.

Dogmatic: ch. II, vv. 1-16.

Reason 2. (for reason 1. γάρ.) He himself, the critic, practises the very things which he condemns.

[Obs. 1. διό must refer to the foregoing picture of heathen sin (i. 18-32), there being no grammatical authority for its proleptic use. The (Jewish) reader is naturally shocked at the sins of the heathen. But this moral judgment, whether expressed in words or not, does really leave the man who forms it without excuse before the Justice of GOD. By ἄνθρωπε is meant more particularly the Jewish reader; the Jew however is only named at ver. 17. So the heathen are at first referred to as ἀνθρώπων (i. 18), and the more direct reference to them is only made at a later stage in the paragraph, although the word ἔθνη is not used. For the reproachful use of the vocative ἄνθρωπε see ix. 20; S. Luke xii. 14.]

[Obs. 2. ἀναπολόγητος used only here and at i. 20 to which it carries us back. There it is applied to the heathen who are convicted of guilty ignorance of GOD by those works of His which exhibit His attributes and which lie spread out before their eyes. Here, to the individual (Jewish) reader who feels or expresses a natural abhorrence at the gross sins of the heathen, The Jews were much given to self-righteous condemnation of the Gentiles as rejected by GOD; but this distinctive fault of the Jew only becomes fully prominent at ver. 17. By κρίνειν is here meant the condemning action of the moral faculty, as at S. Matt. vii. 1. Observe the double contrast between κρίνειν and the stronger κατακρίνειν, and between τὸν ἕτερον and σεαυτόν. For this last 1 Cor. x. 24-29; Gal. vi. 4; Phil. ii. 4. ἐν ᾧ may = (1) for that, ἐν τούτῳ ὅτι, or (2) in the point concerning which, xiv. 21. The critic practised the same sins (τὰ αὐτά), not in all their details and particulars, but in their governing principles. Cf. our Lord's rebuke to the Jews about the adulterous woman, S. John viii. 7. Thus thoughtless hero-worship given to bad men might be in principle an illustration of the heathen συνευδοκεῖν τοῖς πράσσουσι Rom. i. 32.]

Proposition. The κρίμα τοῦ Θεοῦ is (1) *regulated* by the standard of moral truth, κατὰ ἀλήθειαν, and (2) *visited* upon those who practise such sins as the heathen, (whether they be Jews or Heathen). ver. 2.

[Obs. 1. ver. 2. By οἴδαμεν the Apostle associates his readers with himself in the recognition of a truth patent to their common sense, iii. 19 'We know that whatsoever the law saith it saith to them that are under the law'; 1 Cor. viii. 4 'We know that an idol is nothing in the world': or to their religious faith, Rom. vii. 14 'We know that the law is spiritual'; viii. 28 'We know that all things work together for good to them that love GOD.' Here natural thought and Divine revelation teach the same lesson about the Judgment of GOD. τοῦ Θεοῦ is emphatic after τὸ κρῖμα, in opposition to ἄνθρωπε ὁ κρίνων, ver. 1.]

[Obs. 2. κατὰ ἀλήθειαν expresses the standard of GOD's Judgment, Winer, *Gr. N. T.* p. 501. ἀλήθεια means reality, fact, as opposed to κατὰ προσωποληψίαν ver. 11; κατ' ὄψιν S. John vii. 24; κατὰ τὴν σάρκα S. John viii. 15; cf. S. John

viii. 16 ἡ κρίσις ἡ ἐμὴ ἀληθινή ἐστιν. ἐπὶ πράσσοντας expresses its objects. The Jews thought that the heathen (as ἁμαρτωλοί Tob. xiii. 6 רְשָׁעִים) were alone its objects; they themselves, as Jews, were יְשָׁרִים, Dan. xi. 17. But it was not race, but personal conduct, which determined the Divine Judgment. The position of ἐστί is emphatic.]

The proposition established—

(A) by an appeal to the conscience (of the critic, ver. 1) respecting his secret reasons for doubting whether the τὸ κρῖμα τοῦ Θεοῦ will touch *him*.

a. calculated trust in theocratic privilege. Does he calculate (λογίζῃ) that, while he does the very acts (ποιῶν) of the conduct for which he condemns others, he personally (σύ) as being in some privileged position, will escape utterly from the range of the Divine Judgment? (ver. 3.)

[*Obs.* 1. The case here is slightly stronger than that of the critic in ver. 1. It is that of a man who ποιεῖ as well as πράσσει, and yet counts upon escape from judgment. Observe how τοῦτο emphatically prepared for the clause, ὅτι σύ, κ.τ.λ., describing the substance of the calculation. ἐκφεύξασθαι means not acquittal before the Judge, but escape from His power, 1 Thess. v. 3 οὐ μὴ ἐκφύγωσι: Heb. ii. 3 πῶς ἡμεῖς ἐκφευξόμεθα; 2 Macc. vi. 26.]

[*Obs.* 2. The emphasis lies on σύ with especial reference to the Jew's confidence in his theocratic position, as a safeguard against punishment due to his personal sins, S. Matt. iii. 9 πατέρα ἔχομεν τὸν Ἀβραάμ, S. Luke iii. 8. The Jews believed themselves to be οἱ υἱοὶ τῆς βασιλείας S. Matt. viii. 12, and that the race of Abraham would be exempted from judgment, S. Justin Mart. *dial. cum Tryph.* cc. 44, 125; Eisenmenger, *Entdecktes Judenthum*, Theil ii. k. 4, pp. 293-295.]

b. contemptuous estimate of the Divine Mercy as though it were merely easy goodnatured indifference to sin. Or, dismissing the calculations ver. 3, does he think cheaply (καταφρονεῖς) of the wealth of

GOD's { goodness towards all His creatures, χρηστότης,
displayed even towards sinners, as ἀνοχή,
and delaying punishment after long provocation, μακροθυμία?

[*Obs.* 1. ἤ draws attention away from the explanation first proposed and suggests another, vi. 3; 1 Cor. ix. 6, etc., Meyer. The καταφρονεῖν implies the contempt which arises from measuring the Divine goodness by easy temper in man.]

[*Obs.* 2. πλοῦτος is often used by S. Paul metaphorically in connection with the Attributes and Gifts of GOD. So ix. 23 τὸν πλοῦτον τῆς δόξης: xi. 33 ὦ βάθος πλούτου καὶ σοφίας καὶ γνώσεως: Eph. i. 7 τὸ πλοῦτος τῆς χάριτος: ver. 18 ὁ πλοῦτος τῆς δόξης τῆς κληρονομίας. The expression is specially characteristic of the Epp. of the First imprisonment. Cf. in addition to the last passages, Eph. ii. 7; iii. 8, 16; Phil. iv. 19; Col. i. 27; ii. 2. It is used by Greek authors, Plat. *Euthyphro*, p. 12 A. It is a vivid expression of the idea of abundance and vastness. The χρηστότης of GOD is His goodness; 'benignitas Dei ad beneficiendum hominibus potius parata quam ad puniendum.' Tittmann, *Syn.* p. 195 (ed. 1829). It differs from χάρις, in that the latter always suggests preeminently the idea that its objects *deserve* nothing,—an idea not necessarily implied in χρηστότης. The Divine χρηστότης becomes manifest in benefits bestowed on man, S. Luke vi. 35, specially in the Incarnation. Tit. iii. 4 where ἡ χρηστότης ... ἐπεφάνη. ἀνοχή, GOD's forbearance with sin and sinners, is still χρηστότης face to face with moral evil and modifying itself accordingly. Cf. iii. 26 ἐν τῇ ἀνοχῇ τοῦ Θεοῦ, S. Matt. xvii. 17. When these sins are persevered in, the ἀνοχή of a moment becomes prolonged into μακροθυμία, which is still χρηστότης face to face with moral evil for long periods of time, and so delaying the merited punishment. Observe the gradation in the three aspects of the Attribute: for the last, see ix. 22 ὁ Θεὸς ... ἤνεγκεν ἐν πολλῇ μακροθυμίᾳ σκεύη ὀργῆς, 1 Tim. i. 16; 1 S. Pet. iii. 20. Compare Pearson, *Minor Theological Works*, i. p. 75, on the 'benignitas Dei' as 'bonitas Divina quatenus in Deo est per modum affectus' constantly impelling Him to benefit and bless His creatures. Also Tertull. *Adv. Marcion.* ii. 4, for a fine passage on the goodness of GOD.]

In this καταφρονεῖν the Apostle detects—

(i) tragic *ignorance* of the true action of this attribute of the Divine Nature upon the human soul. The goodness of GOD is designed to be an impelling force towards repentance.

[*Obs.* ἀγνοῶν denotes the simple fact of ignorance, for which however the καταφρονῶν is responsible. It does not mean voluntary ignorance *at the time*. As here ἄγει is used of the *moral leading* of the Attribute of χρηστότης, so in viii. 14 the sons of GOD are defined to be ὅσοι Πνεύματι Θεοῦ ἄγονται. The same relation of this Attribute to the moral life of man is expressed in 2 S. Pet. iii. 9 GOD μακροθυμεῖ εἰς ὑμᾶς, μὴ βουλόμενός τινας ἀπολέσθαι ἀλλὰ πάντας εἰς μετάνοιαν χωρῆσαι.]

(ii) disastrous preparation of misery for a coming time.

  a. its *measure*.—It is proportioned (κατά) to the despiser's hardness and impenitent heart.
  b. its *growth*.—It is gradually accumulated, like a fortune, to the despiser's destruction.
  c. its *character*.—It is the Wrath of GOD, which breaks out into penal woe on a given day, described as THE DAY

{ 1. of wrath, ὀργῆς,
  2. of unveiling, ἀποκαλύψεως,
  3. of the Righteous Judgment, δικαιοκρισίας, } τοῦ Θεοῦ.

[*Obs.* 1. For κατά of the rule or measure, with accus., see Winer, *Gr. N. T.* p. 501, and ver. 2 κατὰ ἀλήθειαν. σκληρότης, duritia, *tropol.* contumacia, Deut. ix. 27, here only in N. T. But we find σκληρός (from σκέλλω, σκλῆναι, for קָשֶׁה, in LXX) = asper, severus, S. Matt. xxv. 24; σκληροκαρδία, obdurate mind, S. Matt. xix. 8, S. Mark x. 5 (a *vox biblica*); and σκληροτράχηλος, hard-necked, *hartnäckig*, only in Acts vii. 51 N. T. and Ex. xxxiii. 3, 5; xxxiv. 9, LXX קָשֵׁה עֹרֶף, not classical.]

[*Obs.* 2. θησαυρίζεις glances at τοῦ πλούτου τῆς χρηστότητος αὐτοῦ. The treasure of wrath is substituted by the impenitent for the wealth of the Divine goodness. σεαυτῷ, dat. incommodi. For the idea of a 'treasure of evil,' see Deut. xxxii. 33-35; Prov. i. 18; ii. 7; Amos iii. 10; Micah vi. 10; S. James v. 3, and classical authors apud Wetstein.]

[*Obs.* 3. The Day of Judgment is (1) ἡμέρα ὀργῆς, gen. of external relations applied to designations in time. It is the day on which God's wrath against sin will manifest itself in the punishment of sinners. 'Dies irae' —the great hymn of Thomas de Celano—was suggested by this expression of the Apostle. In ὀργὴν ἐν ἡμέρᾳ ὀργῆς, observe (1) the emphatic repetition of ὀργῆς after ὀργήν in order to accentuate the idea, and (2) the brachylogy, 'wrath *which will break forth* on the day of wrath'; cf. 1 Thess. iv. 7 and other exx., Winer, *Gr. N. T.* p. 519. (2) ἀποκαλύψεως. It is a Day of Revelation, of τὰ κρυπτὰ τῶν ἀνθρώπων, ver. 16, but especially of the just judgment of God, which is at present veiled from human eyes. (3) δικαιοκρισίας, only here in New Testament, probably made by S. Paul: though found in an unknown translation of Hos. vi. 5, *Test. xii patriarchs*, iii. 3. 15 (Fabricius, pp. 547, 581); [S. Justin Martyr], *Quaest. Gentil.* c. 28. Cf. S. Jude 6 κρίσις μεγάλης ἡμέρας.]

[*Obs.* 4. On the *Day* of Judgment see Pearson, *Creed*, Art. 7. In the Old Testament יוֹם עֶבְרָה, day of wrath, Ezek. xxii. 24; יוֹם אַף, day of indignation, Zeph. iii. 11; יוֹם נוֹרָא, day to be feared, Joel ii. 11; iii. 14: prophetic descriptions of this 'day' occur in Amos v. 18-20; Joel ii. 1-5; Zeph. i. 14-18; Is. xiii. 9-13; Acts xvii. 31, 'God hath appointed a Day in which He will judge the world in righteousness by that Man whom He hath ordained.' Cf. ἐν ἡμέρᾳ ὅτε, κ.τ.λ. This Future Judgment, at a fixed time known only to the Father, is quite consistent with the fact that God is always judging us.]

(B) by a statement of the principles which will govern the δικαιοκρισία τοῦ Θεοῦ (ver. 5) (6-16).

Principle, I. κατὰ τὰ ἔργα. God will render to each man that which corresponds to his deeds (6-8).

1. To those whose—
   a. Rule of life is to persevere in doing good, καθ' ὑπομονὴν ἔργου ἀγαθοῦ:
   b. Object in life is to obtain hereafter a glorious, honoured and imperishable existence τοῖς δόξαν καὶ τιμὴν καὶ ἀφθαρσίαν ζητοῦσι:
GOD will give Eternal Life (ζωὴν αἰώνιον) (ver. 7).

2. To those who—
   a. (viewed as a class) belong to the category of selfish intriguers (τοῖς δὲ ἐξ ἐριθείας):
   b. (viewed as the servants of a governing motive) obey,
      (i) *not* the Truth (τῇ ἀληθείᾳ),
      (ii) *but* immorality (τῇ ἀδικίᾳ),
there will be [ἔσται sc.] GOD's

Anger {in its tranquil judicial form of ὀργή,
       {in its outward self-manifestation as θυμός (ver. 8).

[*Obs.* 1. ver. 6 κατὰ τὰ ἔργα αὐτοῦ. GOD's award to every man (ἑκάστῳ) hereafter will be in accordance with his conduct, and not, as the Jews thought, with his theocratic position. Cf. S. Matt. xvi. 27 ἀποδώσει ἑκάστῳ κατὰ τὴν πρᾶξιν αὐτοῦ: S. Matt. xxv. 31-46; 2 Cor. v. 10, we must all appear before Christ's seat of judgment, ἵνα κομίσηται ἕκαστος τὰ διὰ τοῦ σώματος πρὸς ἃ ἔπραξεν, εἴτε ἀγαθὸν εἴτε κακόν: Gal. vi. 5 ἕκαστος γὰρ τὸ ἴδιον φορτίον βαστάσει: ver. 7 ὃ γὰρ ἐὰν σπείρῃ ἄνθρωπος τοῦτο καὶ θερίσει: Eph. vi. 8 ἐάν τι ἕκαστος ποιήσῃ ἀγαθὸν τοῦτο κομιεῖται παρὰ τοῦ Κυρίου: Col. iii. 24 ἀπὸ Κυρίου ἀπολήψεσθε τὴν ἀνταπόδοσιν τῆς κληρονομίας: Rev. ii. 23 δώσω ὑμῖν ἑκάστῳ κατὰ τὰ ἔργα ὑμῶν: xx. 12 ἐκρίθησαν οἱ νεκροὶ . . . κατὰ τὰ ἔργα αὐτῶν: xxii. 12 ὁ μισθός μου μετ' ἐμοῦ, ἀποδοῦναι ἑκάστῳ ὡς τὸ ἔργον αὐτοῦ ἔσται. This law, that moral action is the standard by which all men will be judged at the last day, is here stated broadly, and without reference (1) to the worthlessness of ἔργα νόμου before GOD, or (2) to the justifying faith which receives a δικαιοσύνη that issues in ἔργα ἀγαθά.

[*Obs.* 2. καθ' ὑπομονήν, the principle or standard by which the search after δόξα is guided. ἔργου ἀγαθοῦ is a gen. of the object to which ὑπομονή refers, 1 Thess. i. 3. The blessedness of the future salvation is described as in these several ways the reverse of the condition of Christians in this life, (1) δόξα, brilliancy of light. 2 Cor. iv. 17 βάρος δόξης: Matt. xiii. 43 τότε οἱ δίκαιοι ἐκλάμψουσιν ὡς ὁ ἥλιος ἐν τῇ βασιλείᾳ τοῦ πατρὸς αὐτῶν: 2 Cor. iii. 18 ἡμεῖς πάντες ἀνακεκαλυμμένῳ προσώπῳ τὴν δόξαν Κυρίου κατοπτριζόμενοι τὴν αὐτὴν εἰκόνα μεταμορφούμεθα ἀπὸ δόξης εἰς δόξαν: Rom. viii. 18 ὁ τὴν μέλλουσαν δόξαν ἀποκαλυφθῆναι εἰς ἡμᾶς. (2) τιμήν, the honour involved in it as the prize of victory, 1 Cor. ix. 25; Phil. iii. 14; 2 Tim. iv. 8; 1 S. Pet. v. 4, and the being associated with the inheritance and reign of Christ, viii. 17; 2 Tim. ii. 12. This τιμή is veiled in this life. (3) ἀφθαρσίαν. Its imperishableness, 1 Cor. xv. 53;

Rev. xxi. 4; 1 S. Pet. i. 4; all these are included in ζωὴ αἰώνιος which is here *eternal life in the future world:* (cf. ἀποδώσει), as also v. 21; vi. 22; Gal. vi. 8.]

[*Obs.* 3. With ver. 8 the construction changes: instead of ἀποδώσει with acc. we have nominatives with ἔσται. ἐριθείας from ἔριθος, a hired artisan, a spinner; (1) mercenary greed, or (2) partisan intrigue. The latter always in New Testament. The incessant plotting for material earthly advantage or superiority, as distinct from the repose of a soul, satisfied with and at peace with GOD, is what is meant. Origen, *in loc.*, says of the οἱ ἐκ τῆς ἐριθείας, 'quidquid libuerit pro lege defendunt.' The word is thus extended to partisanship in Phil. i. 17; S. James iii. 14, 16. ἐκ with gen. of the class or category, not of the source. The Jewish ἐριθεία was constantly opposing its self-seeking spirit to the Gospel, Acts xiii. 45; xviii. 12; Gal. iv. 17; vi. 12; 1 Thess. ii. 14. The ἀλήθεια which is not obeyed is the Gospel, Gal. iii. 1; v. 7; 2 Thess. ii. 6-10, it is contrasted with ἀδικία which is obeyed. Each revealed truth and immorality is represented as a soul-governing principle received by the will, vi. 12, 16, 19; vii. 14, 23. ὀργὴ καὶ θυμός, cf. i. 18, and for the distinction between them, Tittmann, *Syn.* p. 131 'quum θυμός proprie ipsum animum denotet ... ad omnem animi vehementiorem impetum transfertur ... ὀργή autem ipsam iram cum studio ulciscendi denotat.' Thus θυμός is the manifestation of ὀργή. Rev. xvi. 19 θυμὸς τῆς ὀργῆς, aestus irae; cf. 1 Thess. i. 10 τῆς ὀργῆς τῆς ἐρχομένης.]

Principle, II. οὐ προσωπολημψία παρὰ τῷ Θεῷ (ver. 11), GOD will take no account of outward distinctions between man and man (9-11).

1. There will be—

a. outward calamity, θλῖψις,	upon every soul belonging to a man who brings evil to pass, κατεργαζομένου,	of the Jew first and also of the Greek (ver. 9).
b. and inward source of oppression, στενοχωρία,		

2. There will be—

a. radiancy, δόξα,	to every man who works at (ἐργαζομένῳ) what is good,	to the Jew first and also to the Greek (ver. 10).
b. honour, τιμή,		
c. eternal repose εἰρήνη,		

[*Obs.* 1. θλῖψις, properly pressure, hence in biblical Greek, affliction, angustiae; LXX for צָרָה used with ἀνάγκη and διωγμός. στενοχωρία angustia loci; Is. viii. 22, metaph. grave pressure of calamity, viii. 35; 2 Cor. vi. 4. The words seem to correspond to Is. xxx. 6 צָרָה וְצוּקָה—the one more to material pressure or pain, 2 Thess. i. 6, 7. Opposed to ἄνεσις, ἀνάπαυσις, ἀνάψυξις, the other to inner oppression of the soul. The contrast is apparent in 2 Cor. iv. 8 θλιβόμενοι ἀλλ' οὐ στενοχωρούμενοι. ἐπὶ πᾶσαν ψυχήν = כָּל־נֶפֶשׁ, although a Hebrew idiom, Rom. xiii. 1; Acts ii. 43; iv. 23; vii. 14; S. James

i. 21 ; Heb. x. 39 ; S. Luke xii. 47, is yet used here not redundantly, but to express the seat of feeling. ἐργάζεσθαι, working at good, involves δόξα, τιμή, κ.τ.λ.; κατεργάζεσθαι, bringing evil to pass, leads to θλῖψις and στενοχωρία, cf. i. 27 ; vii. 8, 13. εἰρήνη, LXX for שָׁלוֹם, welfare, as inseparable from peace. It is another aspect of the ἀφθαρσία and ζωὴ αἰώνιος of ver. 7.]

[*Obs*. 2. The ἀπροσωποληψία of GOD is implied in πᾶσαν ψυχήν ver. 9, παντί ver. 10, and the repeated phrase 'of' or 'to' the 'Jew first and also the Greek,' vers. 9. 10. The insertion of πρῶτον before τε ... καί gives the sense of 'especially,' Winer, *Gr. N. T.* p. 721. This phrase occurs at i. 16. The use of πρῶτον there, and in ver. 10 shows that it is not ironical in ver. 9. As the people of revelation, with its promises and threatenings, the Jews precede the heathen, as the recipients of punishment or of reward. The first Ἰουδαίου τε πρῶτον counteracts the Jewish conceit of exemption from punishment.]

[*Obs*. 3. προσωποληψία (Tisch. προσωπολημψία) is a word of Hellenistic manufacture. πρόσωπον, the face, that which meets the eye, is used by LXX to translate both פָּנִים and אַפִּים. The noun προσωποληψία is based on the Hebrew נָשָׂא פָנִים, LXX πρόσωπόν τινος λαμβάνειν—θαυμάζειν (Gen. xix. 21), δέχεσθαι (Gen. xxxii. 21). It means such a regard to outward circumstances, to wealth, position, reputation, as blinds the judgment to questions of right, truth and duty. The extreme form of προσωποληψία was that of judges who received presents from persons who appeared before them ; whence נָשָׂא פָנִים came to mean to be partial (Lev. xix. 15 ; Deut. x. 17) and the substantive מַשָּׂא פָנִים, 'partiality.' In the New Testament the word is always used in a bad sense. GOD is not προσωπολήπτης Acts x. 34 ; Eph. vi. 9 ; Col. iii. 25 ; Gal. ii. 6 πρόσωπον Θεὸς ἀνθρώπου οὐ λαμβάνει : S. Luke xx. 21 ; S. Matt. xxii. 16 ; S. Mark xii. 14 ; 2 Cor. x. 7 ; S. Jude 16 θαυμάζοντες πρόσωπα ὠφελείας χάριν. The idea of προσωποληψία, as the sacrifice of objective justice to something else which met the eye of the judge, is familiar to the ancients, although the word is unclassical. The symbolic expression of the idea was the bandage over the eyes of the statues of Justitia.]

Principle, III. GOD's judgment of men will be relative to their varying opportunities in life (ver. 12).

Thus—

1. The *Heathen* who have sinned, without the advantage of a Revealed Law (ἀνόμως), will also perish, by the sentence of GOD, as being unfaithful to the light of nature, but without any reference to Revealed Law (ἀνόμως).

2. The Jews, who have sinned, in the midst of a system of Revealed Law (ἐν νόμῳ), will be judged by this Revealed Law (διὰ νόμου), as if it were the author of their condemnation (ver. 12).

[*Obs*. 1. Ver. 12 is a reason (γάρ) for the statement that there is no προσωποληψία with GOD. His ἀπροσωποληψία is seen in the condemnation of the heathen to eternal ruin, for their transgression of what they knew of His law, by the light of nature. ἀνόμως without the guidance of the Revealed Law; opposed to ἐν νόμῳ, where the Law is conceived of as an atmosphere of moral truth within which the Jew lives and acts. ἀπολοῦνται expresses the antithesis to σωτηρία i. 16; ζήσεται i. 17; ζωὴ αἰώνιος ii. 7; δόξα, τιμή, εἰρήνη ii. 10. It must be referred, not to any natural necessity, but, as the context implies, to the sentence of GOD at the last Judgment. It corresponds with the milder κριθήσονται, which here however expresses all that is necessary to describe the impartiality of the Divine Judge. The Jew who, having the guidance of revealed law, should commit the same sins as the heathen, would be sentenced to a punishment proportioned in its severity to the light which he had abused.]

[*Obs.* 2. νόμος is here used of the Mosaic law, without the article, as if it were a proper name. This is frequent in the Apocrypha, and of particular laws in classical writers. Cf. ii. 23; iii. 31; iv. 13, 14, 15; v. 13, 20; vii. 1; x. 4; xiii. 8; 1 Cor. ix. 20; Gal. ii. 21; iii. 11, 18, 21; iv. 5, etc.]

Objection 1. (to 2 in ver. 12.) Will not the privileged position of the Jew, as an ἀκροατὴς νόμου, of itself make him δίκαιος παρὰ τῷ Θεῷ and so screen him from condemnation?

Resp. No. The Divine Rule is that the ποιηταὶ νόμου will be adjudged righteous (at the last day, ver. 16).

[*Obs.* 1. The Jews are called ἀκροαταὶ νόμου with reference to the public reading of the Thorah on the sabbath, S. John xii. 34; Acts xv. 21 Μωσῆς ... κατὰ πᾶν σάββατον ἀναγινωσκόμενος: 2 Cor. iii. 14, for the veiling of the Jewish heart during this reading, Joseph. *Ant.* v. 1. 26; 2. 7. The *substantive* is more forcible than the *participle*: it means 'those whose business it is to hear,' whether they listen to any purpose or not. Among the Greeks ἀκούοντες or ἀκροαταί were applied to students, Polyb. *Hist.* i. 13. 6; ix. 1. 2. The word is in vivid antithesis to ποιηταί.]

[*Obs.* 2. παρὰ τῷ Θεῷ. The Divine standard of δικαιοσύνη is contrasted tacitly with the Jewish. παρά is here used as ἐνώπιον at iii. 20. Not privileged knowledge, but conscientious obedience to the Divine Law is the condition of being declared righteous by GOD. δικαιόω is (1) to justify, make one who was unrighteous, righteous. Cf. Ps. lxxiii. 13 ματαίως ἐδικαίωσα τὴν καρδίαν μου, where it = זִכָּה, to purify. So iii. 23 δικαιούμενοι δωρεὰν τῇ ἐκείνου χάριτι: iv. 5 ἐπὶ τὸν δικαιοῦντα τὸν ἀσεβῆ: Gal. iii. 8 ἐκ πίστεως δικαιοῖ τὰ ἔθνη ὁ Θεός. (2) To account righteous in the judicial sense, i.e. acquit = הִצְדִּיק, Ex. xxiii. 7 οὐ δικαιώσεις τὸν ἀσεβῆ ἕνεκεν δώρων, 1 Kings viii. 32; so Prov. xvii. 15; Ps. li. 6; 1 Cor. iv. 4. I know nothing against myself, ἀλλ᾽ οὐκ ἐν τούτῳ δεδικαίωμαι. It is opposed to καταδικάζειν in this sense, which is that of the present passage. This verse is not contradictory of iii. 20 ἐξ ἔργων νόμου οὐ δικαιωθήσεται πᾶσα σὰρξ ἐνώπιον αὐτοῦ, because that passage describes the actual fact, this the antecedent and general Divine rule.]

Objection 2. (arising out of resp. to obj. 1.) If it be the general rule

Dogmatic: ch. II, vv. 1-16.

of GOD's judgment that οἱ ποιηταὶ νόμου δικαιωθήσονται, what is the application of this rule to the heathen, who live, sin, and die, without the pale of the Mosaic Law, ἀνόμως ἀπολοῦνται? (ver. 12).

Resp. The general rule does apply, in its degree, to the heathen. For although they possess a something which cannot be considered Revealed Law (ἔθνη τὰ μὴ νόμον ἔχοντες) they do, by natural guidance, and without cultivation (φύσει) carry out certain precepts or principles of the Revealed Law (τὰ τοῦ νόμου ποιοῦσι). Thus, while they cannot be thought of as possessing the Revealed Law, their moral nature is to them what the Revealed Law of Sinai is to the Jews (ver. 14).

[*Obs.* 1. The parenthesis includes vers. 14, 15 according to Meyer and Lachmann: Winer would begin with ver. 13 (*Gr. N. T.* p. 707), on the ground that the three verses constitute a group of thoughts complete in itself. But ἐν ἡμέρᾳ connects itself as easily with δικαιωθήσονται in ver. 13 as with κριθήσονται in ver. 12: and the relation of ver. 13 to 12 is more intimate than that of ver. 14 to 13.]

[*Obs.* 2. Remark (1) the contrast between ἔθνη ... ἔχοντα and οὗτοι ... ἔχοντες in the two clauses; as the Apostle advances the abstract impersonal conception of heathendom is resolved into the individual men who compose it. (2) The contrast between τὰ μὴ νόμον ἔχοντα, possessing only an analogon to the Revealed Law, and νόμον μὴ ἔχοντες, not possessing the real Revealed Law. On φύσις here, as signifying the original outfit of natural powers given to man at his birth, and independent of subsequent training, see Meyer *in loc.* For this sense of the expression, Arist. *Nic. Eth.* iii. (5) 15 τοῖς μὲν διὰ φύσιν αἰσχροῖς οὐδεὶς ἐπιτιμᾷ ... οὐδεὶς γὰρ ἂν ὀνειδίσειε τυφλῷ φύσει. In *Nic. Eth.* v. (7), the distinction between φυσικόν and νομικόν, this last being only human positive law, is thus stated : φυσικὸν μὲν τὸ πανταχοῦ τὴν αὐτὴν ἔχον δύναμιν καὶ οὐ τῷ δοκεῖν ἢ μή. Νομικὸν δέ, ὃ ἐξ ἀρχῆς μὲν οὐδὲν διαφέρει οὕτως ἢ ἄλλως, ὅταν δὲ θῶνται, διαφέρει ... οἷον τὸ θύειν Βρασίδᾳ. Cic. *pro Caecina*, 27 'Ita justus et bonus vir est, ut natura non disciplina consultus esse videatur.' τὰ τοῦ νόμου, not τὸν νόμον: the heathen only fulfil certain parts of the Revealed Law—precepts belonging to it. In doing this, however, they become a moral standard of a certain value to themselves—just as the Revealed Law is a standard to the Jews. For the phrase ἑαυτοῖς εἰσὶ νόμος, compare Arist. *Nic. Eth.* 4. (8) 10 ὁ δὴ χαρίεις καὶ ἐλευθέριος οὕτως ἕξει, οἷον νόμος ὢν ἑαυτῷ.]

[*Obs.* 3. On the unwritten laws of nature, see Xen. *Memorab.* iv. 4. 19 ἀγράφους τινὰς οἶσθα, ἔφη, ὦ Ἱππία, νόμους; τούς γ' ἐν πάσῃ, ἔφη, χώρᾳ κατὰ ταὐτὰ νομιζομένους. Since men could not meet together to vote these laws, or, if they did, could not be expected to agree, θεοὺς οἶμαι τοὺς νόμους τούτους τοῖς ἀνθρώποις θεῖναι: Soph. *Oed. Tyr.* 863 sqq.

ὧν νόμοι πρόκεινται
ὑψίποδες, οὐρανίαν | δι' αἰθέρα τεκνωθέντες,

ὧν Ὄλυμπος | πατὴρ μόνος, οὐδέ νιν
θνατὰ φύσις ἀνέρων ἔτικτεν....

Cf. Dion. Halicar. iii. 23. 474. Philo Jud. speaks of the νόμος καὶ θεσμὸς ἄγραφος, *De Abrah.* vol. ii. p. 388, *De v. Mosis,* i. p. 627, where he says that the νόμος ἔμψυχός τε καὶ λογικός long preceded the work of the lawgiver.]

[*Obs.* 4. The words ὅταν γὰρ ἔθνη ... φύσει τὰ τοῦ νόμου ποιῇ were employed by Pelagius to show that man can obey God's law without God's grace. In reply S. Augustine, *de Spir. et Litera,* c. 46, explains that by ἔθνη are meant heathen, who have been already converted to the Christian faith, or who fulfil the law through some special and extraordinary supply of grace. On ver. 10, S. Chrysostom had understood under Hellenes, the pre-Christian heathen, Melchizedeck, Job, and Ἕλληνας τοὺς θεοσεβοῦντας, τοὺς τῷ φυσικῷ πειθομένους νόμῳ. The objection to S. Augustine's reply is that it is opposed to the context, which makes his limitation of ἔθνη impossible. The broad answer to Pelagius is that his use of the passage (1) ignores what is said about the heathen in i. 18-32 ; (2) is inconsistent with the whole drift of the Apostle's argument that all men, whether heathens or Jews, need the δικαιοσύνη τοῦ Θεοῦ : (3) overlooks the force of τὰ τοῦ νόμου ποιῇ—as if it meant to fulfil the law. It really means a partial and relative obedience such as was possible in a state of nature, but falling far short of δικαιοσύνη.]

§ Proof that the Heathen ἑαυτοῖς εἰσὶ νόμος (ver. 14).

[*Obs.* οἵτινες is logical ; it may be resolved into γάρ, 'for that they,' quippe qui, i. 25.]

This is observable—

1. *By their actions,* the Heathen give external proof that the conduct which corresponds to the law (τὸ ἔργον τοῦ νόμου) is written as a code upon their hearts.

2. *In their moral consciousness,* the Heathen find a concurrent testimony (συμμαρτυρούσης) that this natural rule of conduct does supply them with the major premiss of the syllogism of conscience.

3. *In their secret moral judgments,* as between man and man, the Heathen condemn or acquit each other by appealing to this unwritten rule of conduct (ver. 15).

[*Obs.* 1. Direct evidence of better heathen conduct. That ἐνδείκνυνται refers to the outward evidence of this law in the heathen heart is gathered from τὰ τοῦ νόμου ποιῇ ver. 14, and from the preposition in συμμαρτυρούσης, which expresses not simply attestation, but the concordance between the inner evidence of conscience, and the outer evidence of conduct. See Meyer, *in loc.* note 1. τὸ ἔργον τοῦ νόμου, the conduct which corresponds to the law ; cf. ἁμαρτήματα νόμου Wisd. ii. 12, the sins which violate the law. ἔργον is collective ; it comprises the ἔργα τοῦ νόμου, iii. 20,

28 ; ix. 32, etc. ; the practical upshot of the Mosaic Law is what the expression means, as distinct from any one of its particular precepts. γραπτόν = γεγραμμένον : the word is chosen with reference to the written Law of Moses, Heb. viii. 10. The essential contents of the law are shown to be written upon the hearts of the better heathen by their conduct. Observe how this sentence balances the description at i. 28–32. There were heathen and heathen.]

[*Obs.* 2. Concurrent witness of the heathen conscience. In συμμαρτυρούσης the σύν points out the relation between the consciousness of the better heathen and their outer conduct. Not only does this law govern their actions very largely, but they *know* it. συνείδησις is here the faculty by which man recognises the natural law within him ; and this law is not the conscience, but that which regulates its consciousness,—the major premiss of its decisions. In this passage, says Delitzsch, *Bibl. Psych.* p. 163, E. T. the Apostle places conscience in a relation to the inner natural law, which resembles that of prophecy to the Jewish Thorah. As prophecy, which has been strikingly called the conscience of the Israelitish state, testifies to the Thorah, and places the circumstances and conduct of Israel in the light of the Thorah, from time to time,—thus conscience gives witness to that inner law in man in his own sight (συμμαρτυρεῖ), impels and directs man to act according to that law, (the so-called precedent conscience) judges his doings according to this law and reflects his actions and his circumstances in the light of this law (the subsequent conscience).]

[*Obs.* 3. The λογισμοί, reasoned thoughts, which necessarily arise from the apprehension of the internal law by the συνείδησις of men, either condemn or excuse the acts which pass before it. *Whose* acts? The man's own (says Delitzsch, *Bibl. Psych.* p. 164, E. T.) ; he is reflecting upon his individual conduct, or his state as a whole. Those of others, (says Meyer, *in loc.*) the accusations and vindications are conceived to be carried on between heathen and heathen, μεταξὺ ἀλλήλων. Observe the contrast between αὐτῶν τῆς συνειδήσεως and μεταξὺ ἀλλήλων : the latter expression occuring here only in S. Paul, to contrast the mutual judgment of the thoughts of different men, with the personal and individual tendency of conscience. ἀλλήλων must be referred to ἔθνη not to λογισμοί, as is plain from its necessary antithetical correspondence with αὐτῶν. Although Meyer seems to keep closer to the text the current interpretation refers λογισμοί to the acts of the man himself, and connects this clause with that which follows on the day of judgment. Thus S. Cyril Jerus. *Catech.* xv. c. 25 ἐκ τῆς συνειδήσεώς σου κρινῇ μεταξὺ τῶν λογισμῶν κατηγορούντων ἢ καὶ ἀπολογουμένων ἐν ἡμέρᾳ ὅταν, κ.τ.λ : Tertull. *de Testim. An.* c. 6 'Merito igitur omnis anima et rea et testis est ; in tantum et rea erroris, in quantum et testis veritatis. Et stabit ante aulas Dei in die judicii, nihil habens dicere.']

§ This correspondence between the sentence of God and the opportunities enjoyed by men, will be made manifest on the Day when—

GOD will judge
- i. (*subject-matter of His judgment*) the secret side of human conduct (τὰ κρυπτὰ τῶν ἀνθρώπων).
- ii. (*standard of His judgment*) according to the tenor of the Gospel as taught by the Apostle (κατὰ τὸ εὐαγγέλιόν μου).
- iii. (*Minister of His judgment*) by the agency of Jesus Christ (ver. 16).

[Obs. 1. ἐν ἡμέρᾳ defines the time when δικαιωθήσονται, ver. 13, will take place; and this day is further defined by the clause ὅτε κρινεῖ. 'Εν ἡμέρᾳ is not 'on every day, on which GOD causes the gospel to be preached'; κρινεῖ is future. Cf. ὃς ἀποδώσει ver. 6; κριθήσονται ver. 12; δικαιωθήσονται ver. 13. GOD is always judging men; but this is not the sense of the text. For ἐν ἡμέρᾳ, see further 1 Cor. i. 8; v. 5; 2 Cor. i. 14.]

[Obs. 2. τὰ κρυπτὰ τῶν ἀνθρώπων, all in the outer or inner life of a man which does not come to the knowledge of other men;—thoughts, feelings, acts, motives—advantages or disadvantages, 1 Cor. iv. 5 φωτίσει τὰ κρυπτὰ τοῦ σκότους, καὶ φανερώσει τὰς βουλὰς τῶν καρδιῶν: Ecclus. i. 30; S. Luke xii. 2 οὐδὲν κρυπτὸν ὃ οὐ γνωσθήσεται: 1 Cor. xiv. 25; 2 Cor. iv. 2 τὰ κρυπτὰ τῆς αἰσχύνης.]

[Obs. 3. κατὰ τὸ εὐαγγέλιόν μου. This can hardly mean that the assertion that GOD will judge the secrets of men by the agency of Jesus Christ was in accordance with the *Apostle's* gospel, as well as that of others. For no other teacher questioned the doctrine, and the μου would be meaningless. The accent lies on κατά. The Divine judgment would be in correspondence with the *truths taught by* the Apostle. The correspondence of the Divine sentence, on the one hand, with the secret Predestination of GOD, on the other its being κατὰ τὰ ἔργα, viii. 4; 2 Cor. v. 10; Eph. v. 5; 1 Cor. vi. 9, &c. is what he means.

μου is antithetical, not to the gospel of other Apostles, but of false and Judaising teachers in xvi. 25; 2 Tim. ii. 8.]

[Obs. 4. That our Lord is the Minister of the Judgment, cf. S. John v. 22 τὴν κρίσιν πᾶσαν δέδωκεν τῷ Υἱῷ: Acts x. 42 ὁ ὡρισμένος ὑπὸ τοῦ Θεοῦ κριτὴς ζώντων καὶ νεκρῶν: xvii. 31 ἐν ἀνδρὶ ᾧ ὥρισεν: 1 Cor. iv. 5; 2 Cor. v. 10: Pearson, *On the Creed*, art. vii.]

§ 3.

[*Minor premiss.* Part ii. see above p. 23.] *The Jewish people, although entrusted with the Law revealed to Moses, have failed to attain* δικαιοσύνη (ii. 17–iii. 8).

[*Obs.* The argument of this paragraph may be stated thus:—
Maj. Those who enjoy great religious privileges and yet sin flagrantly, have not attained δικαιοσύνη.
Min. But the Jews make loud claims to the possession of such privileges (17-20) and yet do sin flagrantly (21-24).
Concl. Therefore, the Jews have not attained to δικαιοσύνη.]

Dogmatic: chs. II, v. 17—III, v. 8.

I. Religious position and consequent responsibility of the Jew, measured—

(i) by positive features, defining his unique relation to GOD (vers. 17, 18).

    1. his *theocratic* name, of 'Jew.'
    2. his *confidence* in (the possession of) the Divine Law.
    3. his *exulting boast* in God (as the Guardian of Israel) (ver. 17).
    4. his *knowledge* of The Will (of the Most Holy).
    5. his superior *moral insight* which approvingly recognizes true excellence and which is due to his having been instructed out of the Sacred Law (ver. 18).

[*Obs.* 1. The protasis of the sentence comprises vers. 17-20, and the apodosis begins with ver. 21. In ver. 17, the true reading is εἰ δέ; the *recept.* ἴδε is merely a copyist's error. As the Apostle proceeds with the protasis, he loses sight of εἰ, ver. 17; he has forgotten it, when he reaches the end of the protasis. Accordingly, he begins the apodosis ver. 21 with οὖν, involving an anacoluthon, due to the vehemence of the Apostle's language. Winer, *Gr. N. T.* p. 711 sqq. The paragraph is suggested by ver. 13; the position that not the hearers but the doers of the law shall be justified is here applied to the Jew, in proof that he cannot, by himself, attain to δικαιοσύνη.]

[*Obs.* 2. The protasis, although dwelling on the privileges of the Jew, refers to *his own* language about them, and in terms of censure, which deepens as he proceeds. (1) εἰ δὲ Ἰουδαῖος ἐπονομάζῃ—'if thou art named Jew'—the theocratic name of honour; a member of the chosen race, as opposed to heathenism, Gal. ii. 15; Rev. ii. 9; iii. 9. Judah the patriarch had a name of religious significance, from הוֹדָה אֶת־יְהֹוָה, Jehovam celebrare, Gen. xxix. 35; so that יְהוּדִי was understood to mean either ὁ ἐξομολογούμενος τῷ Θεῷ Philo, *Alleg.* (ed. Mangey), i. p. 55, or ἡ ἐξομολόγησις τοῦ Θεοῦ Philo, *de plant. Noe*, i. p. 233. ἐπονομάζεσθαι used of *imposing* a name : cf. Meyer. (2) ἐπαναπαύειν is used of reliance on a guarantee, as here of salvation; it answers to נִשְׁעַן עַל, to support oneself on something. Cf. Mic. iii. 11. The Jew relied on the law, as if eternal life resided in *it*, whatever his own relation to it might be in practice; S. John v. 39 ἐν αὐταῖς (see the Old Testament γραφαί) δοκεῖτε ζωὴν αἰώνιον ἔχειν. (3) καυχᾶσαι: for the form see ver. 23; xi. 18; 1 Cor. iv. 7. καυχᾶσθαι in class. with ἐπί or εἰς; with ἐν in Gal. vi. 13; 2 Cor. x. 15, as marking the object in which the καύχησις rests. The Jew boasted in GOD, as the author of the everlasting covenant with Abraham, Gen. xvii. 7; as 'their GOD,' Jeremiah xxxi. 33; 'In the Lord shall all the seed of Israel be justified and shall glory' Is. xlv. 25. Note the climax—Ἰουδαῖος, νόμῳ, Θεῷ. The Jewish καύχησις is baptized by the Apostle in Rom. v. 11 καυχώμενοι ἐν τῷ Θεῷ διὰ τοῦ Κυρίου ἡμῶν Ἰησοῦ Χριστοῦ.]

[*Obs.* 3. (4) The expression τὸ θέλημα is unique; but this use of a substantive with the article is found with dogmatic technical terms, cf. ἡ ὀργή Rom. iii. 5; v. 9; xii. 19. No will could be meant but One; there was no need for adding Θεοῦ. The Jew dwelt on this knowledge, as of itself so precious, as to make corresponding conduct relatively unimportant. (5) By δοκιμάζεις τὰ διαφέροντα is meant. 'Thou approvest things that are excellent,' not 'Thou testest things which are different (a) whether from each other or (b) from the will of GOD.' Cf. Phil. i. 10; 1 Thess. v. 21. The Jew prided himself less on his power of seeing the distinction between right and wrong than on his faculty for doing justice to superior excellence whenever he saw it. This faculty he had trained, by being catechetically instructed in youth out of the Law. κατήχειν used of repeated oral instruction, S. Luke i. 4; Acts xviii. 25; xxi. 21, 24; 1 Cor. xiv. 19; Gal. vi. 6. With κατηχούμενος, cf. ἀκροαταί ver. 13.]

(ii) by current and highly cherished titles, defining the Jews' presumed relation to the Heathen (vers. 19–20 a).

a. He is confident with respect to himself that he is
 guide of the blind—ὁδηγὸς τυφλῶν:
 light of those in darkness—φῶς τῶν ἐν σκότει:
 educator of the senseless—παιδευτὴς ἀφρόνων:
 teacher of babes—διδάσκαλος νηπίων.

[*Obs.* 1. Of these titles, used of themselves by the Rabbinical teachers, the first, ὁδηγὸς τυφλῶν, is referred to by our Lord, who upbraids the Pharisees with being ὁδηγοὶ τυφλοὶ τυφλῶν S. Matt. xv. 14. The second, φῶς τῶν ἐν σκότει, is probably a Rabbinical adaptation of one of the titles of the Messiah; cf. Is. xlix. 6, and S. Luke ii. 32. When Messiah came, His people were to declare His glory among the Gentiles; Is. lxvi. 19, and hence the title was appropriated by individual Jews. The third, παιδευτὴς ἀφρόνων, is referred by Tholuck to the Rabbis who instructed Jewish proselytes, to whom the terms ἄφρονες and νήπιοι seem to have been applied (Selden, *De Jure Nat.* xi. 4, p. 162, ed. 1640) like νεόφυτοι and νήπιοι to young Christians. But this reference is doubtful: διδάσκαλος νηπίων, a teacher of them who are wanting in the first elements of spiritual wisdom; obs. the contrast between νήπιος and σοφός in 1 Cor. iii. 1.]

[*Obs.* 2. In these titles the Jew contrasts himself with the heathen. The Jew conceives himself to be a source of moral and intellectual truth; he is an ὁδηγός and παιδευτής; he is φῶς and a δ.δάσκαλος. The heathen is spiritually blind, and without spiritual understanding: he is in darkness and his mind is as undeveloped, for religious purposes, as a child's. The moral and intellectual elements of the description alternate. On the Jewish estimate of the heathen world, see Eisenmenger, *Entdecktes Judenthum*, part ii, pp. 206–208.]

§ Reason for the Jew's confidence—

He possesses the law, in which γνῶσις and ἀλήθεια have received the expression or form (μόρφωσιν) which befits their nature (ver. 20 b).

[*Obs.* 1. μόρφωσις occurs only here and in 2 Tim. iii. 5 ἔχοντες μόρφωσιν εὐσεβείας, τὴν δὲ δύναμιν αὐτῆς ἠρνημένοι (the verb μορφόω occurs in Gal. iv. 19), μόρφωσις means in that passage form without substance, 'Scheinbild': but here it can only be taken in the sense of *formandi ratio*, τύπος, exemplar. The Thorah was for the Jew the real expression of all moral truth, the form in which it became incorporate; its substance thrown into such shape as to become matter of intellectual cognizance; cf. Is. xliv. 13. LXX; Ecclus. xxiv. 23. That S. Paul could not find in the Thorah only the form or appearance, as distinct from the substance of truth, see iii. 21, 31.]

[*Obs.* 2. The religious privileges of Israel, here referred to as they existed in the minds of the Rabbinical order and with scarcely veiled censure on the emphasis laid on them, are treated with profound sympathy in ix. 3-5. Thus S. Paul is following our Lord's judgment on the claim to be σπέρμα Ἀβραάμ in S. John viii. 33-42.]

II. The sin of the Jew viewed (vers. 21-24).

(i) in itself—
  1. as being against knowledge and, moreover, knowledge pressed as binding on the consciences of others
    a. generally, ὁ οὖν διδάσκων κ.τ.λ. (ver. 21);
    b. specifically, as e.g.
      . 1. thieving, on the part of preachers of the eighth commandment (ver. 21).
      2. adultery, on the part of teachers of the seventh commandment (ver. 22).
  2. as conflicting with strong religious professions. Thus,
    The Jew professed the utmost dread of physical contact with an idol.
    Yet, upon occasion, he would enrich himself by the plunder of a Pagan temple (ver. 22).

(ii) in its consequences—
  a. The Jew's transgression of the law, which is the subject of his 'boast,' brings its Divine author into dishonour among the heathen (ver. 23). For
  b. Isaiah's reference to the dishonour of the Name of GOD, through the reduction of the Jews to slavery by their heathen conquerors, may well describe the dishonour which is done to Him in the minds of the Heathen through Jewish sin (ver. 24).

[*Obs.* 1. (ver. 21.) For this contrast between teaching and personal practice, cf. Ps. l. 16, 39 'But unto the ungodly said GOD, Why dost thou teach my law?' S. Ign. *Eph.* 15; *Aboth Nathan* 29, quoted by Wetstein. Aba Saul the son of Nani said: 'The disciples of the wise are fourfold: first there is he who teaches others but teaches not himself.' Seneca, *De Vita Beata* 18 'Aliter inquit loqueris, et aliter vivis. Hoc Platoni objectum est, objectum Epicuro, objectum Zenoni. Omnes enim isti dicebant non quemadmodum ipsi viverent, sed quemadmodum vivendum esset': Seneca, *Ep.* cviii. 36 'Nullos autem pejus mereri de omnibus mortalibus judico, quam qui philosophiam velut aliquod artificium venale didicerunt, qui aliter vivunt quam vivendum esse praecipiunt.' So 'video meliora proboque deteriora sequor.']

[*Obs.* 2. (ver. 21.) For thefts by preachers of the eighth commandment see Koheleth R. viii. 4, quoted by Wetstein, 'The disciple said to a certain master, Rabbi thou sayest to me, that a man may not take hay, yet thou takest it. Mayest thou then do that which is forbidden to me?' Compare the picture of the 'vir bonus omne forum quem spectat et omne tribunal' in Hor. *Epist.* i. 16. 57, and whose secret prayer is—

' Da mihi fallere, da justo sanctoque videri
Noctem peccatis et fraudibus objice nubem.'

Josephus mentions a case of theft by four Jews, not long before this date at Rome, who applied to their own uses some consecrated gifts destined for the temple by a proselyte Fulvia, *Ant.* xviii. 3. 5.]

[*Obs.* 3. (ver. 22.) In the Talmud Rabbis Akiba and Eleasar are accused of adultery (Tholuck *in loc.*). λέγεις is used as = to give a judicial decision, S. Matt. xv. 5; S. Mark vii. 11.]

[*Obs.* 4. (ver. 22.) On βδελυσσόμενος τὰ εἴδωλα, see Deut. vii. 26 LXX οὐκ εἰσοίσεις βδέλυγμα εἰς τὸν οἶκόν σου. The feeling became intense after the captivity: idols were always referred to as βδελύγματα, תוֹעֵבוֹת, 1 Macc. i. 54; vi. 7. On the occasion of Pilate's bringing to Jerusalem the military standards which were adorned with the representation of the emperor, multitudes of the Jews went to meet him at Caesarea. During five days they were refused an audience; and when Pilate appeared he ordered them to withdraw on pain of death. They threw themselves on the ground and exposed their necks, preferring to die rather than that the law should be violated by the entrance of idols into the city, Joseph. *Antiq.* xviii. c. 3. 1; *De Bell. Jud.* ii. 9. 4. The reference in ἱεροσυλεῖς is best explained of robbery of heathen temples: the Jew who dreaded contact with idols resigned himself to it when something was to be got. That Jews were ἱερόσυλοι may be inferred from the speech of the town-clerk at Ephesus, Acts xix. 37; Joseph. *Ant.* iv. 8. 10. Delitzsch *in loc.* quotes *Aboda Zara* 53ᵃ, where the case of Jewish לסטים (λῃσταί), who should have stolen a Pagan idol is noticed. The words have been referred (*a*) to thefts in the Jewish temple, whether of offered money or of sacrifices, and (*b*) to general profanity, as involved in robbing GOD of the glory which is due to Him.]

[*Obs.* 5. ver. 23 is an answer to the four reproachful questions, vers. 21, 22. according to Meyer. But the interrogative punctuation of ver. 23 is more probable; and, in this case, the verse is an all-including question which presses the particulars specified in the preceding verses upon the conscience with collective force. The robbery of gold and silver from pagan idols is disallowed, Deut. xvii. 25, so that this would be a form of the τὸ ἀτιμάζειν τοῦ Θεοῦ. But the full meaning of this 'dishonour' is illustrated by the quotation in ver. 24.]

Dogmatic: chs. II, v. 17—III, v. 8.

[*Obs.* 6. (ver. 24.) The quotation of Is. lii. 5 is intended to show that the Jews were an occasion of dishonour to the name of GOD,

Heb. וְתָמִיד כָּל־הַיּוֹם שְׁמִי מִנֹּאָץ

[and continually all the day My name is blasphemed],

LXX δι' ὑμᾶς διὰ παντὸς τὸ ὄνομά μου βλασφημεῖται ἐν τοῖς ἔθνεσιν.
There is nothing in the present Hebrew text corresponding to δι' ὑμᾶς and ἐν τοῖς ἔθνεσιν. The pagans uttered wild blasphemies against GOD; the occasion of their doing so was the captive people of Israel among them. S. Paul is at liberty to neglect the primary historical sense of the passage, as he does not quote it as a fulfilled prophecy: the passage will bear a sense in its LXX form which illustrates his present meaning.]

[*Obs.* 7. In ver. 24 γάρ is not found either in the Hebrew or LXX; it is introduced by S. Paul to show how ver. 24 justifies the τὸν θεὸν ἀτιμάζεις of ver. 23. That the Apostle is quoting from the Old Testament is only indicated by καθὼς γέγραπται at the close of his quotation.]

III. Jewish objections to this conclusion considered. ii. 25-iii. 8.

Objection I. *from the efficacy of circumcision.* Does not circumcision place the Jew in a religious position, which is thus rendered secure independently of his personal conduct?

Resp. No. The advantage (ὠφελεῖ) conferred by circumcision is conditional. It is only secured, when the Law is carried into practice (πράσσῃς) by the circumcised person. The circumcised Jew who is a παραβάτης νόμου might just as well be uncircumcised (ver. 25).

From this it follows, (οὖν ver. 26)—

1. That an uncircumcised heathen who observes the moral precepts (δικαιώματα) of the Law, will at the last day, be reckoned before GOD as a circumcised Jew (ver. 26).

2. That—further,—such a heathen, uncircumcised in virtue of his birth, but obedient to the Law, will be the (tacit) condemnation of the Jew, who with his scriptures and his circumcision, transgresses the law (ver. 27).

Proof that 2. (ver. 27) is accordant with the Old Testament revelation.

Reason 1. from the *falsehood* of the popular and externalised conception of what is meant by a 'Jew' and 'circumcision,' in the Sacred Language—

(a) a 'Jew' is not one whose *external life only* (ἐν τῷ φανερῷ) corresponds to the word.

(b) 'circumcision' is not merely a wound on the flesh visible to the senses.

Hence the mere Jew by birth who has received legal circumcision is not ensured against condemnation.

Reason 2. from the spiritual reality which the words imply.

(a) the true Jew is such in his inner life of service and praise—ὁ ἐν τῷ κρυπτῷ.

(b) the true circumcision (also ἐν τῷ κρυπτῷ) has for
(i) its seat, the centre of man's inmost being—καρδίαν:
(ii) its creative power—the Holy Spirit, not the letter of the Jewish Thorah (ἐν πνεύματι οὐ γράμματι):
(iii) its result — that which commands if not the praise of men, yet the approval of GOD.

[*Obs.* 1. In ver. 25 γάρ corroborates the conclusion arrived at in vers. 23, 24, by meeting a tacit objection from the supposed spiritual insurance effected by circumcision. The advantage of circumcision consisted in the admitting to all the blessings and promises conferred by GOD on the people of the covenant. The privileges however depended on the observance of the Law as their condition, Gen. xvii. 1 'I am the Almighty God; walk before Me and be thou perfect.' Lev. xviii. 5; Deut. xxvii. 26; Gal. v. 3. In the event of (ἐάν, Winer, *Gr. N. T.* p. 366) a Jew's transgressing the Law, his circumcision becomes עָרְלָה, ἀκροβυστία, thereby γέγονεν describes the moral result which takes place:—a present of the completed action.]

[*Obs.* 2. Circumcision (מוּלָה from מוּל, περιτομή from περιτέμνω τινά, praecido alicui praeputium), the distinctive sign of the Old Covenant, אוֹת־בְּרִית, Gen. xvii. 11, the privileges and obligations of which it signified. Circumcision implied (1) that every member of *the race* which guarded the Revelation made a sacrifice of his body, rejecting the impurities of heathen life; but (2) it implied *no* propitiation of the Divine justice; nor (3) did it establish any *personal* relationship between GOD and the recipient of the ordinance; nor (4) was it a 'means of grace,' like a Christian Sacrament. It was a *signum merum*, not a *signum efficax*. It only effected admission to the fellowship of the covenant people of those who were qualified, either by birth as Israelites, or by later incorporation with the national union of Israel. Thus while on the one hand it required *no antecedent moral conditions* in the recipient in order to its due reception, it did bind the Israelites who received it to blameless obedience, Gen. xvii. 1. Hence the expression 'circumcision of heart,' (meaning purification of the inmost being, affections and will, disposing man to listen to GOD and to obey Him, Deut. x. 16; xxx. 6), and 'uncircumcision of heart,' in other words unmortified desires and consequent insensibility to the voice of GOD, Lev. xxvi. 41; Jer. ix. 25. The uncircumcised state is ἀκροβυστία, an Alexandrian provincialism for ἀκροποσθία, Heb. עָרְלָה.... As to its historical origin, the custom seems to have been one of immemorial antiquity among some nations of Western Asia and Africa. It is not probable that the usage spread from a single centre: Diodorus found it among the Troglodytes, and in modern times it has been found among the South Sea islanders. The theory of its Egyptian origin rests only on Hdt. ii. 104; for its Egyptian practice see Philo, *De Circumcis*. ii. 210. Herodotus' statement that the Phoenicians and Syrians of Palestine received circumcision from the Egyptians, is based on a misapprehension; see the full discussion in Oehler, *Theol. d. Alt. Test*. §§ 87, 88. 'Josh. v. 9 and Jer. ix. 24 sqq. prove nothing for, Ezek. xxxi. 18; xxxii. 19 nothing against it. This investment of a preexisting custom with a new religious significance by making it the sign of GOD's covenant with Abraham is analogous to the later elevation of Jewish baptisms into the Christian Sacrament, &c. For the subject, see further Winer, *Bibl. Realwoerterbuch*, art. Beschneidung; Oehler, *ubi supra*; Smith's *Bible Dict.* art. Circumcision.]

[*Obs*. 3. In ver. 26 the Apostle means by δικαιώματα the moral enactments in accordance with right made by the Mosaic law, cf. on Rom. i. 32. The uncircumcised Gentiles do obey these, in obeying the moral law of nature, cf. ver. 14. In εἰς περιτομήν, εἰς is used of the result, as in ix. 8; Acts xix. 27. The αὐτοῦ after ἀκροβυστία is suggested by the concrete noun ἀκρόβυστος latent in the previous abstract ἀκροβυστία: so S. Luke xxiii. 51; S. John viii. 44; Winer, *Gr. N. T.* p. 181 sqq. The sense is given in 1 Cor. vii. 19 ἡ περιτομὴ οὐδέν ἐστιν, καὶ ἡ ἀκροβυστία οὐδέν ἐστιν, ἀλλὰ τήρησις ἐντολῶν Θεοῦ.]

[*Obs*. 4. In ver. 27 the Apostle makes an advance upon the question in ver. 26. The opposition between περιτομή and ἀκροβυστία is more sharply defined. The ἡ ἐκ φύσεως ἀκροβυστία means those persons, who, from having been born heathens, are uncircumcised. ἐκ φύσεως is here used as φύσει Ἰουδαῖος Gal. ii. 15; τῶν κατὰ φύσιν κλάδων Rom. xi. 21; ἐκ τῆς κατὰ φύσιν ἀγριελαίου Rom. xi. 24. τὸν νόμον τελοῦσα = executing the law, S. James ii. 8 εἰ μέντοι νόμον τελεῖτε βασιλικόν. It implies a more energetic form of obedience than φυλάσσειν and τηρεῖν νόμον. This obedient ἀκροβυστία is a περιτομὴ ἐν πνεύματι. It *will judge* by the force of tacit contrast the disobedient but circumcised Jew. For this form of κρίνειν, as meaning the indirect and silent condemnation, cf. our Lord's saying about the men of Nineveh and the men of His own generation, S. Matt. xii. 41, 42, and the judicial significance of Noah's making the ark with respect to the men of his day, Heb. xi. 7. In διὰ γράμματος καὶ περιτομῆς, διά denotes the surrounding circumstances of an action; here those *in spite of which* it took place. So iv. 11 τῶν πιστευόντων δι' ἀκροβυστίας: viii. 25 δι' ὑπομονῆς ἀπεκδεχόμεθα: xiv. 20 τῷ διὰ προσκόμματος ἐσθίοντι: 2 Cor. ii. 4 ἔγραψα ὑμῖν διὰ πολλῶν δακρύων: Winer, *Gr. N. T.* p. 475. Observe that here γράμμα is not as in ver. 29 used *depreciatingly* as if merely in *contrast* with πνεῦμα: it refers to the sacred origin of the Law, as written with the finger of GOD, as in Exod. xxxi. 18.]

[*Obs*. 5. (vers. 28, 29.) The *religious* sense of the sacred word Ἰουδαῖος ver. 17, and περιτομή ver. 25, is insisted on. First, *negatively*. Neither word is satisfied by the *external* circumstances which it suggests; ἐν τῷ φανερῷ is contrasted with ἐν τῷ κρυπτῷ in S. Matt. vi. 6. The difference between the apparent and the real Israel is insisted on in ix. 6 οὐ πάντες οἱ ἐξ Ἰσραὴλ οὗτοι Ἰσραήλ: S. John i. 48 ἀληθῶς Ἰσραηλίτης said of Nathanael; Gal. vi. 16 ἐπὶ τὸν Ἰσραὴλ τοῦ Θεοῦ of the Christian church. In the second clause of ver. 28 ἐν σαρκί more precisely defines ἐν τῷ φανερῷ as applied to circumcision. Secondly, *positively*. Each word implies something internal. With ὁ ἐν τῷ κρυπτῷ Ἰουδαῖος, compare 1 S. Pet. iii. 4 ὁ κρυπτὸς τῆς καρδίας ἄνθρωπος. The true Jew is he whose inner life corresponds to the idea of his theocratic position. The true circumcision is (1) seated in the heart. With περιτομὴ καρδίας, cf. Lev. xxvi. 41 LXX ἡ καρδία αὐτῶν ἡ ἀπερίτμητος: Deut. x. 16 περιτεμεῖσθε τὴν σκληροκαρδίαν ὑμῶν: Jer. iv. 4 'Circumcise yourselves unto the Lord, and cut off the foreskins of your heart, ye men of Judah'; ix. 26 for the contrast πάντα τὰ ἔθνη ἀπερίτμητα σαρκί, καὶ πᾶς οἶκος Ἰσραὴλ ἀπερίτμητοι καρδίας αὐτῶν: Acts vii. 51 ἀπερίτμητοι τῇ καρδίᾳ καὶ τοῖς ὠσίν. Philo Judaeus calls circumcision σύμβολον ἡδονῶν ἐκτομῆς. This, in which the Jews were wanting, is (Col. ii. 11) περιτομὴ ἀχειροποίητος. It is 'the true circumcision of the Spirit that our hearts and all our members being mortified from all worldly and carnal lusts, we may in all things obey GOD's blessed will,' Collect for Circumcision. So Phil. iii. 3 ἡμεῖς (we Christians) γάρ ἐσμεν ἡ περιτομή, οἱ ἐν πνεύματι Θεῷ λατρεύοντες, καὶ καυχώμενοι ἐν Χριστῷ Ἰησοῦ, καὶ οὐκ ἐν σαρκὶ πεποιθότες. Hence (2) ἐν πνεύματι, in the Holy Spirit, as the power in which the circumcised heart is founded, just as the circumcision of the flesh is based in the literal directions of the Thorah, ἐν γράμματι. Πνεῦμα here is the Divine Spirit Himself, as distinct from the 'spirit of the law' or 'the principle of the new life in man,' or any influence or tendency which is due to His agency. For this contrast see vii. 6; 2 Cor. iii. 6, which make it certain that πνεῦμα here cannot mean the spirit in man. οὗ cannot be referred to Ἰουδαῖος, without difficulty; it refers to the whole description of the true Jew and the true circumcision in ver. 29, 'of which state of things the praise,' &c. The circumcised heart is beyond the province of sense. On the Divine award of praise, cf. 1 Cor. iv. 5 τότε ὁ ἔπαινος γενήσεται ἑκάστῳ ἀπὸ τοῦ Θεοῦ, and Rom. ii. 13 οὐ γὰρ ἀκροαταὶ νόμου δίκαιοι παρὰ τῷ Θεῷ. . . . The passage 25-29 is further illustrated in iv. 9 sqq.]

Obj. II. *from the apparent drift of the answer to Obj.* I. based (οὖν) *on* ii. 28, 29. *If the true Jew and the true circumcision be wholly* internal, *the literal Jew and the literal circumcision of the Old Testament imply no religious superiority or advantage whatever.* iii. 1.

[*Obs.* 1. The Apostle puts the objection as if it were his own, but for the moment he places himself at the point of view of a Jewish disputant, and speaks his language. It arises naturally out of the preceding assertion of the *spiritual* and internal character of the 'Jew' and 'circumcision' in the sense of Scripture.]

[*Obs.* 2. τὸ περισσόν = 'religious superiority' of the Jew, i.e. as contrasted with the heathen, περισσόν as in Eccles. vi. 11. ὠφέλεια = religious advantage of circumcision to the Jew; cf. ὠφελεῖ ii. 25. As a believer in the Old Testament the Apostle could not deny that to be a Jew and to be circumcised, even in the bare literal sense, was represented as religiously advantageous; and yet his arguments seemed to have destroyed the advantage. If not, wherein did it consist? He had to justify himself to his own principles.]

Dogmatic: chs. II, *v.* 17—III, *v.* 8.   59

Resp. This is a mistake. The circumcised Jews, as such, have many prerogatives. The *first* is that to them as the covenant people were committed the prophetic utterances about Messiah (ver. 2).

[*Obs.* 1. πολύ refers to both τὸ περισσόν and ἡ ὠφέλεια; and κατὰ πάντα τρόπον cannot be regarded as only hyperbolical. It means 'however we look at the matter,' 'in every way.' Had the Apostle continued his reply to Obj. II. the expression would have been justified. He is interrupted by the emergence of Obj. III. at ver. 3.]

[*Obs.* 2. The first prerogative (πρῶτον) of a series (which is not continued here, but which is more fully stated at ix. 4) is that the Jews were entrusted with the Divine λόγια. The indefinite expression τὰ λόγια τοῦ Θεοῦ means any sayings of Divine origin. The LXX translate דָּבָר and אָמְרָה by λόγιον; the expression occurs in Num. xxiv. 16, אִמְרֵי־אֵל, Ps. xii. 7 'The words of the Lord (λόγια Θεοῦ) are pure words'; cxix. 103 'How sweet are Thy words (τὰ λόγιά σου) unto my throat.' In New Testament, Acts vii. 38, Moses ἐδέξατο λόγια ζῶντα δοῦναι ἡμῖν. Twice of truths revealed to Christendom, Heb. v. 12 τίνα τὰ στοιχεῖα τῆς ἀρχῆς τῶν λογίων τοῦ Θεοῦ: 1 Pet. iv. 11 εἴ τις λαλεῖ, ὡς λόγια Θεοῦ. In Ps. xix. 15 λόγια is used of human words. That the λόγια here meant are the promises of a coming Messiah is clear from the reference to the ἀπιστία of the Jews in ver. 3; cf. αἱ ἐπαγγελίαι (ix. 4) to which it corresponds. Reithmeyer gives a wider sense to λόγια, as though including the whole contents of 'the earlier revelation. [Cf. Lightfoot, *Essays on Supernat. Rel.*, pp. 172 ff.] For the construction ἐπιστεύθησαν τὰ λόγια, cf. 1 Cor. ix. 17; Gal. ii. 7; 1 Thess. ii. 4; 1 Tim. i. 11; Tit. i. 3.]

Obj. III. (from the actual state of the Jewish people.) 'The majority of the Jews do not believe in Christ; what then is the advantage of their being entrusted with those λόγια which refer to Him?'

[*Obs.* This objection is supposed to arise at once on the mention of the *first* prerogative of the Jewish people in ver. 2. That only a *portion* of the people disbelieved in Christ—although it was in fact the majority—is guardedly stated, ἠπίστησάν τινες. By τινες the Apostle embodies one feature of his reply in the statement of the objection. The unbelief would only have cancelled the advantages of Israel's being entrusted with the λόγια had it been universal: it was at most partial (τινες). That ἠπίστησαν, ἀπιστία here mean, not unfaithfulness, but unbelief, see iv. 20; xi. 20, 23. The word is in contrast not with ἐπιστεύθησαν but with τὰ λόγια τοῦ Θεοῦ.]

Resp. 1. *Arg. a priori: from the Divine fidelity.* This unbelief of a section of the covenant people *cannot* be supposed to destroy the value of GOD's ancient promise to Israel (ver. 3).

Resp. 2. *Arg. from that confidence as to the event, which faith in David's inspired language would create.* In the event it will be seen, that by fulfilling the Promises of a Coming Messiah, GOD has kept His word; while those Jews who, as members of the covenant people, were bound to believe in the fulfilment of His Promises, are the real ψεῦσται, as being false to Him (ver. 4).

[*Obs.* 1. By τὴν πίστιν τοῦ Θεοῦ is meant 'fides qua Deus promissis stat': cf. ἀληθής ver. 4. That Θεοῦ is a *gen. subjecti* appears, partly from the contrast with ἀπιστία αὐτῶν, and partly by the expansion of what is meant in ver. 4, as well as Θεοῦ δικαιοσύνη in ver. 5. The adj. πιστός is constantly used of GOD in this sense, 1 Cor. i. 9; x. 13; 2 Tim. ii. 13.]

[*Obs.* 2. μὴ γένοιτο, 'may it not be,' an exclamation of abhorrence corresponding to חָלִילָה, Gen. xliv. 17; Josh. xxii. 29, properly 'to profane things,' *ad profana*; hence *absit*, 'be it far from thee.' The Greek formula occurs again in vers. 6, 31; vi. 2, 15; vii. 7, 13; ix. 14; xi. 1, 11; 1 Cor. vi. 15; Gal. ii. 17; iii. 21, &c. It belongs to dialectic discussion. Elsewhere only at S. Luke xx. 16 in its absolute form. γινέσθω, 'let GOD become true'; i.e. let the inevitable result take place. γινέσθω implies φανερούσθω Theophyl. but is not equivalent to it. The Apostle desires what he knows *must* be: so that his exclamation has a future force. ἀληθής is here used of GOD as keeping faith with man; cf. τὴν πίστιν τοῦ Θεοῦ ver. 3. Compare S. John iii. 33; viii. 26. By πᾶς ἄνθρωπος is meant every man who would challenge GOD's πίστις, especially the Jews who are bound to *faith* in the promises of GOD. The phrase occurs Ps. cxvi. 11 LXX, but the Apostle is thinking of the quotation from Ps. li which follows.]

§ This is in accordance with Ps. li. 6, which shows that when GOD's ways are subjected to human criticism, He justifies Himself in the end (ver. 4).

Heb. לְמַעַן תִּצְדַּק בְּדָבְרֶךָ
תִּזְכֶּה בְשָׁפְטֶךָ

LXX ὅπως ἂν δικαιωθῇς ἐν τοῖς λόγοις σου καὶ νικήσῃς ἐν τῷ κρίνεσθαί σε.

[*Obs.* The LXX inaccurately renders תִּזְכֶּה, 'that thou mayest be pure' by νικήσῃς, and בְשָׁפְטֶךָ, Kal, cum judicas, by ἐν τῷ κρίνεσθαί σε, med. 'when thou disputest.' ὅπως, לְמַעַן, is not to be taken as 'in order that,' but 'so that,' in the event of decision, 'thou mayest,' &c. δικαιωθῇς be acknowledged as faultless [in Thy words]: δικαιόω used of acquittal in the forensic sense as at ii. 13 δικαιωθήσονται. It is used of man's judgment of GOD in S. Luke vii. 29, 35, ἐδικαίωσαν τὸν Θεόν. ἐν τοῖς λόγοις σου, 'in that which Thou hast said.' In quoting this the Apostle is thinking of the λόγια τοῦ Θεοῦ ver. 2, which were disbelieved by the ἀπιστία of the Jewish majority. νικήσῃς here only in New Testament, used in the classical sense of winning a law-suit: as opposed to ἡττᾶσθαι. It is equivalent here to δικαιωθῇς in the preceding line. κρίνεσθαι here in the classical sense of 'disputest as a litigant' rather than 'when thou art judged.' Cf. 1 Cor. vi. 6 ἀδελφὸς μετὰ ἀδελφοῦ κρίνεται. Job ix. 3; xiii. 19 LXX. What David felt after his deep sin with Bathsheba, was not less true of Israel in its collective capacity. In the midst of all human sin, whether ἀπιστία or other, GOD's truthfulness remains consistent with itself and becomes eventually more and more manifest.]

Obj. IV. (based on a perverse construction of ver. 4.) If the sin of man (as e.g. the unbelief of the Jews) does but make GOD's Righteousness indisputably clear; then is not GOD *unrighteous*, if He punishes such sin? (ver. 5.)

[*Obs.* It might have seemed a sufficient answer to say that the guilt of a sinful action is not removed, because GOD so overrules it as to make it promote results which the sinner himself never contemplated. GOD would be *righteous*, not *unrighteous* in punishing such an action; since any good which may result from it, is due to its indirect effects, and is traceable not to the will of the sinner but to His own wisdom and goodness. But the Apostle overlooks these more abstract arguments, and meets the objection by pointing out its irreconcileableness with the truth of the Day of Judgment.]

Resp. No. To suppose Him unrighteous is to deny His moral fitness to judge the world. If He punishes unrighteous unbelief, He must, as the Judge of men, be righteous in doing so. That He will judge the world is a truth of faith; and to be Judge of the world and yet to be ἄδικος is a contradiction in terms (ver. 6).

[*Obs.* 1. The objector reads Ps. li. 6 as meaning that David sinned *in order that GOD might be justified*, whereas David means that GOD is not less justified in condemning his sin, than He would have been had no sin been committed at all. Whatever be the perversions of the human will, the Divine Will is always right. But the objector overlooks this. GOD, he argues, is under a certain obligation to the sinner who by his sin establishes GOD's character for Righteousness, and who cannot therefore be righteously punished. Observe the absence of the article before Θεοῦ δικαιοσύνην, such a thing as righteousness on the part of GOD. The well-known attribute would have been τὴν Θεοῦ δικαιοσύνην. Θεοῦ is here gen. subj. with possessive force. συνιστάναι is used here and v. 8 of proving, and so establishing things: then GOD *proves* His love to us by the Death of His Son. τί ἐροῦμεν peculiar to this Epistle, where it either states an objection as here, vi. 1; vii. 7; ix. 14, or winds up an argument as ix. 30.]

[*Obs.* 2. (ver. 6.) The question μὴ ἄδικος ὁ Θεός (ver. 5) awaits a *negative* answer. Winer, *Gr. N. T.*, p. 641 sq. τὴν ὀργήν the (well-known) wrath, v. 9: S. Matt. iii. 7 τῆς μελλούσης ὀργῆς: 1 Thess. i. 10 τῆς ἐρχομένης. See i. 18.—The Apostle is stating an objection with which as an inspired Apostle he has no sympathy. κατὰ ἄνθρωπον used thus, Gal. iii. 15; 1 Cor. ix. 8; 2 Cor. xi. 17.]

[*Obs.* 3. (ver. 6.) ἐπεί, 'for otherwise'; it assigns a reason for μὴ γένοιτο. If GOD, ὁ ἐπιφέρων τὴν ὀργήν, is unrighteous, *how* will he be morally able to judge the world? κρινεῖ is emphatic; it is a future of *ethical possibility*, as Rom. x. 14; S. John vi. 68; S. Matt. xii. 26; Winer, *Gr. N. T.*, p. 348. τὸν κόσμον here not (1) the universe, nor (2) the great society of men quâ alienated from GOD, but (3) all mankind, cf. ver. 19. The Apostle is thinking of Gen. xviii. 25, 'Shall not the Judge of all the earth do right?']

§ Illustrative confirmation of the foregoing argument (vers. 7–8). If GOD is *unrighteous* in punishing the unbelief which He so overrules as to make it promote His glory, then the relation of GOD to the Judgment of the world would yield two absurd consequences.

1. It would make GOD's judgment of *man as a sinner* impossible; if judged, man must be accepted. For GOD's truth would have been glorified by man's falsehood or sin, which, on the plea suggested in ver. 5, GOD would therefore be unjust in punishing (ver. 7).

2. It would encourage men to do evil that good might come, i.e., that GOD might be glorified. This principle of action is injuriously ascribed to Christians; some even accuse them of teaching it. But it would become natural, if GOD were believed to be unrighteous in punishing sin, which He overrules to His own glory. And yet, how deserving of condemnation is such conduct! (ver. 8).

[*Obs.* 1. The vers. 7, 8 are an illustration of the main reply (ver. 6) by which the Apostle meets the objection (ver. 5), 'that GOD cannot take vengeance on Jewish unbelief which in the event redounds to His glory.' The answer (ver. 6) is that this objection would prove too much, even for the Jew; it would make it unjust for GOD to judge the world at all. In some way *all* sin is overruled to the glory of the perfect Moral Being, and therefore, no sin, if the objection be admitted, could be punished. Hence (1) ver. 7 states the plea of any sinner in the day of judgment, who paraphrases, in his own interest, the Jewish objection of ver. 5. The sinner urges that his 'lie,' or sin, has been the occasion of GOD's truth being advanced in the world, and so of the promotion of GOD's glory; and he therefore claims exemption from condemnation. If GOD retains the function of Judge of the world, He must not judge any man as a sinner; since, He has made human sin promote His glory. To this first moral absurdity (2) a second follows in ver. 8. If sin, as thus promoting GOD's glory, cannot be punished justly by GOD, men will naturally sin that GOD's glory may be promoted,—they will do evil, that the highest good may come. . . . The objection to considering ver. 7, 8 as an amplification of the objection stated in ver. 5, is that this construction would oblige us to put all ver. 6 into a parenthesis; thus also (1) destroying the reference of γάρ in ver. 7 to the immediately preceding verse; (2) making the Apostle state an elaborate objection, to only one half of which he replies by the anathema, ὧν τὸ κρῖμα ἔνδικόν ἐστ.ν.]

[*Obs*. 2. The speaker in ver. 7 is not (1) a Jew, since ver. 7 is an answer to the Jewish objection in ver. 5, which it reduces, by a paraphrase, to a moral absurdity; nor (2) a heathen, since τὸν κόσμον ver. 6 includes more than this, but (3) any sinner, at the last, in presence of the Judgment of GOD. This universal sinner uses indeed the terms ἀλήθεια and ψεῦσμα, which refer, taken exactly, to the case of the Jews, ver. 4; but they represent the wider ideas of δικαιοσύνη and ἀδικία, as ver. 5 shows, viz., the *moral truth*, i. e., GOD's Righteousness, and the *moral lie*, i. e., man's immorality which always contains an element of falsehood. The verb ἐπερίσσευσεν is a stronger expression for συνίστησι, ver. 5; the aorist denotes the result, viewed at the day of judgment as a thing of the past; the man's life, though a moral lie, has redounded to GOD's glory. ἔτι—whatever might have been before the ἐπερίσσευσεν—now after that assumed result, τί κρίνομαι κ.τ.λ. κἀγώ, 'I too who have glorified GOD through my ψεῦσμα,'—in contrast with any whose sins have not had this result.]

[*Obs*. 3. In ver. 8, τί must be supplied before μή from ver. 7, 'and why should we not.' Had S. Paul completed the sentence on the plan begun by καὶ μή, he would have said 'and why should we not do evil that good,' &c. But the intervening clause καθὼς βλασφημούμεθα κ.τ.λ. (as it was intended to be) controls the construction to the end of the sentence, so that this original design of it is lost sight of. ὅτι ποιήσωμεν (in direct address) is accordingly joined to λέγειν; ὅτι having a recitative force; and the saying about 'doing evil that good may come' is introduced as the substance of heathen slander, not as the practical immoral result of the Jewish argument in ver. 5. This, however, is what the Apostle originally intended. Winer, *Gr. N. T.*, p. 783. If any word be supplied, it would be λέγωμεν after τί μή (Dr. Vaughan). But this is unnecessary, and indefensible, as the original structure is destroyed by the attractive power of the clause καθὼς βλασφημούμεθα. Of βλασφημεῖν the object is (1) generally GOD, S. Matt. ix. 3; xxvi. 65; S. Mark iii. 28, 29; S. John x. 36; Acts xxvi .11.. (2) Sometimes *holy things*, as Christian doctrine, ἡ διδασκαλία 1 Tim. vi. 1; ὁ λόγος τοῦ Θεοῦ Titus ii. 5; or the Christian Name, S. James ii. 7; or the Christian Life, ἡ ὁδὸς τῆς ἀληθείας 2 S. Pet. ii. 2; or the good intentions of Christians, Rom. xiv. 16; or the Name of GOD, but this means Himself, as ii. 24. (3) Sometimes, as here, men, 1 Cor. x. 30; Tit. iii. 2. The first Christians were charged, it seems, not merely with acting on the principle 'Let us do evil that good may come,' but with teaching it as a maxim of conduct. This accusation was probably made by heathen, who misunderstood S. Paul's teaching on the subject of grace; cf. vi. 1 ἐπιμενοῦμεν τῇ ἁμαρτίᾳ, ἵνα ἡ χάρις πλεονάσῃ; There is no reason for understanding the Judaisers by τινές. Of all who act or teach thus, the Apostle says that their condemnation is just: they are beyond argument, and have on them already the mark of perdition. Yet the practical adoption of this maxim would have been a natural result of accepting the Jewish argument in ver. 5, that because GOD brought the triumph of the Gospel out of Jewish unbelief, therefore this unbelief could not be justly punished by GOD.]

§ *Conclusion* from the foregoing discussion (οὖν II. 25—III. 8) of Jewish objections.

If it be asked by a Jew whether the Jews are placed in a higher position than the Heathen before the Sanctity and Justice of GOD, the answer must be negative (ver. 9).

Reason. (γάρ) The Apostle has already charged both Jews (II. 17–24) and Heathen (I. 18–32) that they are all *under the empire of sin.* And, in the case of the Jews this objection has not been removed by the objections discussed (II. 25—III. 8) (ver. 9).

[*Obs* 1. Meyer confines the retrospective force of οὖν to vers. 6–8, and he understands προεχόμεθα, middle, as having the ordinary sense of putting forward a defensive argument. (προέχεσθαι is used with ἀσπίδα, *Il.* xvii. 355, and so metaphorically, with πρόφασιν, 'to hold forth an excuse.') 'What then follows from the discussion of Obj. IV. (ver. 6-8)? Are we (Jews) making a defence for ourselves?' This, although in accordance with linguistic usage, (1) ignores the absolute position of προεχόμεθα to which Meyer arbitrarily supplies τί, since he does not venture to unite it with τί οὖν in a single question, and (2) it destroys the force of γάρ. That the Apostle had already charged the Jews and Gentiles with being all under sin, is a reason for denying that the Jews have any preeminence in the way of δικαιοσύνη, but it is no reason for denying that they would put forward arguments to defend their position, since the Apostolic προῃτιασάμεθα would be nothing to the Jewish disputant. It is better to render thus, τί οὖν (sc. ἐστί), 'What is the state of the case?' Acts xxi. 22; 1 Cor. xiv. 15, 26; cf. vi. 15; xi. 7; προεχόμεθα (*passive*), 'Are we placed in a better position?' this meaning being exceedingly rare; see Olsh. *in loc.* προέχειν in *act.* often means 'to *prefer*' in classical Greek writers, as well as 'to have the advantage over'; and it must be a passive of the word with the former meaning that we here meet with, 'Are we then preferred by GOD?' Vulg. 'praecellimus eos.' In οὐ πάντως observe displacement of the negative particle; Winer, *Gr. N. T.*, p. 693. Properly it would be πάντως οὐ, 1 Cor. xvi. 12; the effect of the change is to make it 'Not by any means,' cf. 1 Cor. v. 10.]

[*Obs.* 2. ὑφ' ἁμαρτίαν = 'under the empire of sin '—a stronger expression than ἁμαρτωλούς. Cf. vii. 14 πεπραμένος ὑπὸ τὴν ἁμαρτίαν. Gal. iii. 22, The Scripture has concluded τὰ πάντα ὑπὸ ἁμαρτίαν. In Hellenistic Greek ὑπό is not found with the dative; the idea of *rest under* is entirely transferred to the accusative. S. Matt. viii. 9 ὑπὸ ἐξουσίαν: S. Luke xvii. 24 ὑπὸ τὸν οὐρανόν: S. John i. 49 ὑπὸ τὴν συκῆν: Rom. vi. 14, 15 ὑπὸ νόμον, &c. See Dr. Vaughan's note *in loc.* For this moral dependence of man on the power of sin cf. vii. 25 τῇ δὲ σαρκὶ [δουλεύω] νόμῳ ἁμαρτίας, Gal. iii. 22. Scripture hath concluded τὰ πάντα ὑπὸ τὴν ἁμαρτίαν—this general sinfulness was recognised by the heathen; cf. Hesiod's description of the Iron Age, *Op. et dies,* 174 sqq.; Soph. *Ant.* 1023:

ἀνθρώποισι γὰρ
τοῖς πᾶσι κοινόν ἐστι τοὐξαμαρτάνειν.

Eur. *Hipp.* 615:

ἁμαρτεῖν εἰκὸς ἀνθρώπους.

Thuc. iii. 45. 2 πεφύκασι ἅπαντες καὶ ἰδίᾳ καὶ δημοσίᾳ ἁμαρτάνειν, καὶ οὐκ ἔστι νόμος ὅστις ἀπείρξει τούτου: cf. Xen. *Cyrop.* v. 4. 19.]

Dogmatic: ch. III, *vv.* 10-20.   65

§ 4.

This subjection of all men to the empire of sin, and their consequent need of a δικαιοσύνη Θεοῦ, *is proved from the Jewish Scriptures.* (Proof of the whole minor premiss of the syllogism, p. 23) ver. 10-20.

[*Obs.* 1. These quotations are introduced by καθὼς γέγραπται, which occurs fourteen times in the Epistle. It answers to the Talmudic בכתוב, which however is used of quotations from the Kethubim, as כמו שנאמר is used when the Thorah and the Nebiim are quoted. The Apostle does not observe this distinction.]

[*Obs.* 2. 'The recitative ὅτι (ver. 10) introduces quotations from Scripture very various in character, which, after the Jewish manner, are arranged in immediate succession. They are taken from the LXX, though for the most part with variations,' Meyer.]

These Old Testament quotations illustrate

1. The *general* state of mankind as ὑφ᾽ ἁμαρτίαν (ver. 10-12).

Ps. xiv. 1-3 is quoted as describing human wickedness, viewed—

a. in its negative aspects. There is an entire absence in the world of
   i. correspondence between human conduct and the rule of right. There exists no δίκαιος.
   ii. moral intelligence as to the chiefest concerns and true conduct of men. There exists not ὁ συνιῶν.
   iii. thought and endeavour directed towards GOD. There exists not the ἐκζητῶν τὸν Θεόν (ver. 11).

b. in its *positive* aspects of
   i. general apostacy from truth and virtue, πάντες ἐξέκλιναν.
   ii. general demoralisation,—uselessness and corruption, ἅμα ἠχρειώθησαν.

c. in its practical result
   i. the absence of practical goodness is universal. There exists not a ποιῶν χρηστότητα.
   ii. so universal, as not to admit of a solitary exception οὐκ ἔστιν ἕως ἑνός (ver. 12).

Ps. xiv. 1-3, Heb.
[הִשְׁחִיתוּ הִתְעִיבוּ עֲלִילָה]
אֵין עֹשֵׂה־טוֹב
2. [יְהוָה מִשָּׁמַיִם הִשְׁקִיף עַל־בְּנֵי־אָדָם
לִרְאוֹת] הֲיֵשׁ מַשְׂכִּיל
דֹּרֵשׁ אֶת־אֱלֹהִים
3. הַכֹּל סָר יַחְדָּו נֶאֱלָחוּ
אֵין עֹשֵׂה טוֹב אֵין גַּם־אֶחָד

F

LXX [διεφθόρησαν καὶ ἐβδελύχθησαν ἐν ἐπιτηδεύμασιν]
     οὐκ ἔστιν ποιῶν χρηστότητα, οὐκ ἔστιν ἕως ἑνός.
  2. [Κύριος ἐκ τοῦ οὐρανοῦ διέκυψεν ἐπὶ τοὺς υἱοὺς τῶν ἀνθρώπων,
     τοῦ ἰδεῖν] εἰ ἔστιν συνιῶν
     ἢ ἐκζητῶν τὸν Θεόν.
  3. πάντες ἐξέκλιναν, ἅμα ἠχρειώθησαν
     οὐκ ἔστιν ποιῶν χρηστότητα, οὐκ ἔστιν ἕως ἑνός.

[*Obs*. 1. Of these verses the Apostle quotes only so much as his immediate purpose requires. He substitutes δίκαιος (ver. 1) for the LXX ποιῶν χρηστότητα, as including that and much more, and with a view to describing ὑφ᾽ ἁμαρτίαν εἶναι as a want of δικαιοσύνη. It is a striking instance of the Apostle's consciousness of possessing an equivalent inspiration, which leads him thus to enlarge for the sake of his own argument, the sense both of the LXX and of its Hebrew original. οὐδὲ εἷς, which he quotes from the LXX, is unrepresented in the Hebrew. In ver. 11, the Apostle so quotes from the LXX, that the negative statement which is only *implied* in the Hebrew and LXX, is expressed by himself *directly*. οὐκ, twice repeated, and the article before συνιῶν and ἐκζητῶν are his own. In ver. 12 he adheres closely to the LXX.]

[*Obs*. 2. ὁ συνιῶν. The inserted article implies a definite person representing the class. Buttmann. *Neutest. Gr.* § 144, 9, ed. 1859. συνιῶν usual in LXX instead of συνιείς, Ps. xxxiii. 15. ὁ συνιῶν is the practically wise man; in the Old Testament goodness is wisdom, and sin is folly. See Gesen. *s. v.* שָׂכַל; the Hiph. which often means to be prudent, has the sense of to be pious here and Dan. xi. 33-35; xii. 3, 10. In ὁ ἐκζητῶν τὸν Θεόν, the description advances a step. Not only is there none who knows God; there is none who makes efforts to know Him, i. 21. Cf. Gesen. *s. v.* דָּרַשׁ.]

[*Obs*. 3. The general declension from natural rectitude is described as from without by ἐξέκλιναν: כּוּר is used absolutely so as to express moral degeneracy here and in Deut. xi. 16; Jer. v. 23; Dan. ix. 11. See Gesen. *s. v.* This degeneracy is more intimately described by ἠχρειώθησαν: they have become useless, corrupt, good-for-nothing, ἀχρεῖοι, S. Matt. xxv. 30. נֶאֱלָחוּ. The Arabic root אלח means to become sour, as milk; the Niphal of this verb is used metaphorically with a moral reference here, Ps. liii. 3; Job xv. 16. Instead of אֵין־גַּם־אֶחָד the LXX translates οὐκ ἔστιν ἕως ἑνός, as though the Hebrew were עַד־אֶחָד, which is the more familiar form of expression. ἕως ἑνός is as far as to one, inclusive.]

[*Obs*. 4. Ps. xiv is David's. In the reprobation of the moral and religious character of the men of the age, which Ps. xiv has in common with Ps. xii, we have a confirmation of the לְדָוִד. Ps. xiv. 7 does not oblige us to come down to the Exile (Delitzsch, *Intr.*). What the Psalmist says in ver. 1-3 applies primarily to Israel, David's immediate neighbours; but at the same time to the heathen, as is evident. He laments the universal corruption which prevails not less in Israel than in the heathen world. Ib. on ver. 3.]

2. *Specific* sins, which characterise all human life:

    a. of the tongue (vers. 13, 14) as

Dogmatic: ch. III, *vv.* 10–20.

1. *full of corruption*, like an open grave, which yawns to receive others, Ps. v. 9.
2. *insidious* in their corrupting influence, like the poison of asps, Ps. cxl. 3.
3. *ruinous* to all charity—issuing in cursing and bitterness, Ps. x. 7.

§ Ps. v. 9 illustrates the corrupting power of sins of the tongue.

Heb. קֶבֶר־פָּתוּחַ גְּרוֹנָם
לְשׁוֹנָם יַחֲלִיקוּן

LXX τάφος ἀνεῳγμένος ὁ λάρυγξ αὐτῶν
ταῖς γλώσσαις αὐτῶν ἐδολιοῦσαν.

A yawning-grave is their throat
[to this] they make smooth their tongue.

[*Obs.* 1. יַחֲלִיקוּן, they make smooth their tongue in order to conceal their real design beneath soft language. הֶחֱלִיק means directly to flatter in Ps. xxxvi. 3; Prov. xxix. 5. ἐδολιοῦσαν, the imperfect implies that the deceit was going on up to the present time. With this Alexandrian form of the 3rd person plural, compare εἴχοσαν S. John xv. 22; παρελάβοσαν 2 Thess. iii. 6.]

[*Obs.* 2. Ps. v is David's, probably belonging to the time of Absalom's rebellion, and written in Jerusalem. It is a morning prayer, corresponding to Ps. iv, which is an evening prayer. The reference to the companions of Absalom in the text is suggested by the prayer which David will make in the front court of the tabernacle, towards the Holy of Holies.]

§ Ps. cxl. 3 illustrates the *insidiousness* of sins of the tongue.

Heb. חֲמַת עַכְשׁוּב תַּחַת שְׂפָתֵימוֹ
LXX ἰὸς ἀσπίδων ὑπὸ τὰ χείλη αὐτῶν.

[*Obs.* The Apostle quotes the LXX exactly. עַכְשׁוּב, an adder, is an ἅπ. λεγ. from עָכַשׁ, to bend, coil. This Psalm is David's; he is complaining of serpent-like enemies who are preparing their plans against him and with whom he will have to fight in open battle. Ps. lviii and lxiv are very similar. The Psalm is probably to be referred to the rebellion of Absalom,—an outbreak of Ephraimitic jealousy, to which the rebellion of Sheba the son of Bichri of Benjamin attached itself. Delitzsch.]

§ Ps. x. 7 illustrates the *uncharitableness* of sins of the tongue.

Heb. אָלָה פִּיהוּ מָלֵא וּמִרְמוֹת וָתֹךְ
LXX οὗ ἀρᾶς τὸ στόμα αὐτοῦ γέμει καὶ πικρίας καὶ δόλου.

[*Obs.* Here the Apostle ὧν τὸ στόμα ἀρᾶς καὶ πικρίας γέμει. Thus he makes the reference of the verse plural by substituting ὧν for οὗ, and omits δόλου. The LXX mistranslates מִרְמוֹת deceit, or craft of all kinds by πικρίας which may represent a different Hebrew text. תֹּךְ too is oppression rather than δόλος. The persons alluded to are heathen, in the two last strophes; but apostates from and persecutors of Israel in the earlier part of the Psalm as here. In Ps. ix on the contrary, with which this is intimately connected, the persecutors are heathen. The Psalm is without a title; the LXX and Vulg. make it one with Ps. ix. It may be Davidic, but the date is uncertain.]

b. of deed (vers. 15–17).

- a. murder, ὀξεῖς ἐκχέαι αἷμα.
- b. oppression, σύντριμμα καὶ ταλαιπωρία.
- c. quarrelsomeness, ὁδὸν εἰρήνης οὐκ ἔγνωσαν.

Is. lix. 7, 8 is freely quoted and shortened from the LXX, as illustrating the sins of deed which characterize unredeemed humanity.

Heb. 7. רַגְלֵיהֶם לָרַע יָרֻצוּ
וִימַהֲרוּ לִשְׁפֹּךְ דָּם [נָקִי]
* * * *
שֹׁד וָשֶׁבֶר בִּמְסִלּוֹתָם
8. דֶּרֶךְ שָׁלוֹם לֹא יָדָעוּ

LXX. 7. οἱ δὲ πόδες αὐτῶν ἐπὶ πονηρίαν τρέχουσιν
ταχινοὶ ἐκχέαι αἷμα [ἀναίτιον]
* * * *
σύντριμμα καὶ ταλαιπωρία ἐν ταῖς ὁδοῖς αὐτῶν,
8. καὶ ὁδὸν εἰρήνης οὐκ ἔγνωσαν.

[Obs. The Apostle condenses the first two lines of the LXX into ὀξεῖς οἱ πόδες αὐτῶν ἐκχέαι αἷμα: the last two he quotes accurately. The verbs יָרֻצוּ and יְמַהֲרוּ depict active pleasure in wickedness; σύντριμμα, distress, as from a fracture. The description of the crimes of some of the Jewish captives in Babylon towards their own countrymen explains *why* God would not have come to the help of His people. The misery and degradation belonging to the last period of the Captivity are seen and described by the prophet as if present to his sight.]

3. The *source* of sin: absence of any fear of God (ver. 18). Ps. xxxvi. 2, quoted as illustrating this principle of all moral ruin.

Heb. [נְאֻם־פֶּשַׁע לָרָשָׁע בְּקֶרֶב לִבִּי]
אֵין־פַּחַד אֱלֹהִים לְנֶגֶד עֵינָיו

[An oracle of transgression hath the ungodly within his heart,]
'There is no fear of God before his eyes.'

LXX [φησὶν ὁ παράνομος τοῦ ἁμαρτάνειν ἐν ἑαυτῷ,]
οὐκ ἔστιν φόβος Θεοῦ ἀπέναντι τῶν ὀφθαλμῶν αὐτοῦ.

[Obs. The Apostle follows the LXX except in writing αὐτῶν for αὐτοῦ. In Ps. xxxvi. as in Pss. xii, xiv, xxxvii, David himself describes the moral corruption of his generation; with this Psalm and liii they form a group. It is a result of 'the inspiration of iniquity' in the heart of the wicked that the fear of God never occurs to him. The wicked has no sense of the sanctity of God which inspires this fear.]

Dogmatic: ch. III, vv. 10-20.

§ *Jewish tacit objection.* 'The foregoing descriptions of sin apply to the heathen; they do not touch Israel.'

Resp. This cannot be allowed. For it is plain both to our faith and our common sense that 'whatever the Old Testament Revelation (ὁ νόμος) contains is addressed especially to those who live under or within its sphere of jurisdiction.' And this fact has a twofold providential design (ἵνα); viz.

Object 1. That no man, whether Jew or Heathen, may plead before GOD anything in favour of his possessing δικαιοσύνη of his own. That every mouth be stopped (ver. 19).

Object 2. That the whole human race (πᾶς ὁ κόσμος) should be placed in the position of owing to GOD the penalty of transgression (ὑπόδικος γένηται τῷ Θεῷ) (ver. 19).

Reasons (διότι, propterea quod) for this aim of the Old Testament Revelation.

Reason 1. Because any true justification before GOD, must be gained by some other means than outward compliance with the Rules of the Law (ἔργα νόμου) (ver. 20).

Reason 2. (*reason* γάρ *for reason* 1.) Because the *true* function of the law is to create an ἐπίγνωσις ἁμαρτίας,—a true inward sense of sin; (the Law reveals personal moral evil which it cannot remove, and thus becomes a παιδαγωγὸς εἰς Χριστόν) (ver. 20).

[*Obs.* 1. For the implied Jewish objection that the stern sayings of the law could not apply to Israel, see Eisenmenger, *Entd. Judenth.*, i. 568 sqq. All the above quotations, even Ps. xiv, really refer originally to Jewish transgressors; but the later Jews had learnt to read the threatenings of their Scriptures as applicable only to the heathen. The Apostle appeals to a principle plain both to faith and to common sense, ii. 2 οἴδαμεν γάρ. ὅσα includes condemnatory as well as other language. ὁ νόμος is here, as the quotations 10-18 show, the Old Testament generally. Thus in 1 Cor. xiv. 21 νόμος is applied by S. Paul to Isaiah; in S. John x. 34 by our Lord to Ps. lxxxii; in S. John xii. 34 to 2 Sam. vii by the people; S. John xv. 25 by our Lord to Ps. xxxv. 19. S. Paul purposely does not say ὅσα οἱ προφῆται (although he only quotes David and Isaiah in vers. 8-10), but ὅσα ὁ νόμος, viz. that 'law' which the Apostle thinks of always as an undivided whole, while yet he is thinking sometimes more of its ritual, sometimes of its moral aspects: cf. Usteri, *Paulinischer Lehrbegriff*, iii. 3 sqq. The Apostle distinguishes the teaching of the law as (1) propositions contained in it, λέγει and (2) propositions proclaimed to man; λέγειν (λόγος) describes the inward aspect of speech, the production of thoughts and the formation of words; λαλεῖν = the outward expression of what is within. By τοῖς ἐν νόμῳ is meant 'those who live within the sphere of the law,' whether Jews or Gentiles; in ii. 12 ἐν νόμῳ ἥμαρτον means the Jews only.]

[*Obs.* 2. The two consequences of this principle are introduced by ἵνα, which may only express a result of what has preceded, but taken with νόμος λαλεῖ is better understood τελικῶς. (1) In the phrase φράσσειν στόμα, 'videtur allusisse Paulus ad forensem consuetudinem, quâ reus, si nequeat sibi objecta repellere, silens sententiam expectat, et quasi ore obstructo obmutescit,' Justiniani. GOD so speaks in the law, as to make it impossible for man to utter any claim to justification on the score of his obedience to it. (2) ὑπόδικος here only in New Testament, LXX, Apocr. punishable, liable to satisfy the claims of δίκη: 'cui merito δίκη debeatur,' Estius. Theodoret τιμωρίαις ὑπεύθυνος. τῷ Θεῷ depends upon ὑπόδικος: GOD is He to whom the penalty incurred by disobedience is due.]

[*Obs.* 3. (ver. 20.) The reasons for the foregoing conclusions are introduced by διότι propterea quod. The object of the law's λαλεῖ ver. 19 is to make *the whole human world* ὑπόδικος τῷ Θεῷ. The Gentiles were, in the judgment of Israel, already so; and the law itself places the Jews also in the same category. And it does this (1) *because*, as a matter of fact, actual righteousness, such as will stand before GOD (ἐνώπιον αὐτοῦ), cannot be secured by outward acts in accordance with the directions of the Old Testament (ἐξ ἔργων νόμου). πᾶσα σάρξ is here substituted for πᾶς ἄνθρωπος or πᾶς ὁ κόσμος, in order to express the ideas of sinfulness and weakness which are inseparable from unredeemed humanity, 1 Cor. i. 20. ἔργα νόμου are outward conduct conformed to the Law, whether ceremonial or moral; there seems no sufficient reason for limiting νόμου to the former. Such ἔργα are without the informing spirit and motives which connect with justifying faith those evangelical ἔργα which necessarily spring from and are the practical side of it. δικαιωθήσεται, 'will be *made* just'; there is no question, in this negative statement, of being *accounted* just. The *fut.* is rather of *moral possibility* than *of time*; and thus it refers to the moment of justification in this life, not to the day of judgment. Throughout the Epistle justification is treated as arising immediately from faith. ἐνώπιον αὐτοῦ marks the distinction of a Divine from a merely human standard of justification. The sentence is repeated almost verbatim, as a reason for the Apostolic εἰς Χριστὸν Ἰησοῦν ἐπιστεύσαμεν in Gal. ii. 16 διότι οὐ δικαιωθήσεται ἐξ ἔργων νόμου πᾶσα σάρξ. It is based on Ps. cxliii. 2 ὅτι οὐ δικαιωθήσεται ἐνώπιόν σου πᾶς ζῶν.]

[*Obs.* 4. (ver. 20.) The reason γάρ why no human being is justified, ἐξ ἔργων νόμου, is that it is not the true function of the law to achieve this justification. The law only creates in the soul an ἐπίγνωσις ἁμαρτίας which it cannot satisfy. Jesus Christ can remove this sense of sin by the gift of δικαιοσύνη to the faith which apprehends Him; and thus the law is a παιδαγωγὸς εἰς Χριστόν Gal. iii. 24. This providential purpose of the law is more fully stated at vii. 7-13. In διὰ νόμου ἐπίγνωσις ἁμαρτίας the *moral* side of the law is more emphasised, as it is this which stimulates the conscience to such ἐπίγνωσις; in ἐξ ἔργων νόμου, all its aspects, ceremonial as well as moral, to which the conduct of a religious Jew would endeavour to correspond.]

Dogmatic: ch. III, *vv.* 21-30.

B[1].

How δικαιοσύνη Θεοῦ is attained by man. III. 21-30.

§ 1.

Accompanying conditions under which δικαιοσύνη Θεοῦ is made patent to mankind (πεφανέρωται) ver. 21-23.

[*Obs.* νυνί is according to Meyer probably *dialectical* rather than *temporal*: 'but under these circumstances' not 'nostris temporibus': vii. 17; 1 Cor. v. 11; xii. 18; xiii. 13. On the other hand is to be considered the common division of the present age of being, αἰὼν οὗτος, into two periods, of which the former is that in which God, εἴασε πάντα τὰ ἔθνη πορεύεσθαι ταῖς ὁδοῖς αὐτῶν Acts xiv. 16, and are thus χρόνοι τῆς ἀγνοίας Acts xvii. 30, and of bondage, Gal. iv. 3, 4, under the law, Rom. vii. 5; Gal. iii. 23 ὑπὸ νόμον ἐφρουρούμεθα. The same contrast between the past and the present is implied in Rom. xvi. 25, 26; Col. i. 21, 26; 1 Tim. ii. 6; 2 Tim. i. 10; Heb. i. 1; 1 S. Pet. i. 20. Perhaps therefore the temporal sense of νῦν, as representing an idea so deeply imbedded in the Apostle's mind and in the whole of the New Testament, as the contrast between the Christian and pre-Christian age, cannot be abandoned in deference to considerations which are mainly linguistic. πεφανέρωται, corresponding to ἀποκαλύπτεται i. 17, is a present of the completed action, 'has been manifested and is now open to view.' The δικαιοσύνη Θεοῦ had been as yet hidden; this is presupposed by the expression πεφανέρωται. δικαιοσύνη Θεοῦ here as in i. 17, the righteousness which God gives to man (Θεοῦ gen. orig.) and by which man is rendered δίκαιος, such as he should be, before God. Not the righteousness quâ Deus justus est, but that quâ nos justos facit, as in ver. 26; iv. 5 sqq.; Gal. iii. 8.]

Condition 1. *Negative relation to the Law.* The Righteousness which God gives, is χωρὶς νόμου. The Law is in no way concerned in securing it (ver. 21).

[*Obs.* In χωρὶς νόμου the Law is used in its widest sense, for the whole Old Testament revelation; while in ὑπὸ τοῦ νόμου the Thorah as distinct from the Prophets is in question. χωρὶς νόμου is opposed to Gal. iii. 11 δικαιοῦσθαι ἐν νόμῳ, Gal. v. 4.]

Condition 2. *Historical relation to the Old Testament.* The Righteousness which God gives is μαρτυρουμένη ὑπὸ τοῦ νόμου καὶ τῶν προφητῶν, i. e. by the whole of the sacred literature of Israel (ver. 21).

[*Obs.* νόμος καὶ προφῆται denote the entire Old Testament, as does νόμος alone in ver. 19. Although the δικαιοσύνη Θεοῦ is manifested to the world χωρὶς νόμου, yet it is not without a justification in the sacred literature of Israel. It is the μυστήριον διὰ γραφῶν προφητικῶν εἰς πάντα τὰ ἔθνη γνωρισθέν xvi. 26. Our Lord said of the Jewish Scriptures, ἐκεῖναί εἰσιν αἱ μαρτυροῦσαι περὶ ἐμοῦ

[1] For A. see p. 23.

S. John v. 39. 'Novum testamentum in vetere latet, vetus in novo patet' S. Aug. The Apostle is probably thinking of all the types, promises, and prophecies of a coming Messiah in the Old Testament, since the δικαιοσύνη Θεοῦ became manifest in and with Christ; cf. Rom. i. 2; iii. 12; Acts x. 43 τούτῳ πάντες οἱ προφῆται μαρτυροῦσιν : Acts xxviii. 23, S. Paul at Rome preaches to the Jews τὰ περὶ τοῦ Ἰησοῦ ἀπό τε τοῦ νόμου Μωσέως καὶ τῶν προφητῶν : S. Luke xxiv. 27. For τοῦ νόμου, see iv. 3-5; x. 6 sqq. On the general subject see Art. vii 'Both in the Old and New Testaments, everlasting life is promised to mankind through Christ.']

Condition 3. *Instrument of appropriation by mankind.* The Righteousness which GOD gives is appropriated by faith which has Jesus Christ for its object, διὰ πίστεως Ἰησοῦ Χριστοῦ (ver. 22).

[*Obs.* δέ is repeated like *aber*, Winer, *Gr. N. T.* p. 553 with the same idea, δικαιοσύνη Θεοῦ which is now more precisely defined, as being secured by the instrumentality of faith. Ἰησοῦ Χριστοῦ is a gen. object. as generally; see Winer, *Gr. N. T.* p. 232; Gal. ii. 16, 20; iii. 22; Eph. iii. 12; iv. 13; Phil. iii. 9; S. James ii. 1. The idea is as well expressed by the gen. as with εἰς and the accusative. The *usus loquendi* is opposed to the theory which makes Χριστοῦ a gen. subject. : 'the faith in GOD which was inculcated by Christ.' Meyer points to the passages where the gen. with πίστις is a thing or an abstract idea, Phil. i. 27; 2 Thess. ii. 13; Acts iii. 16; Col. ii. 12; πίστις Θεοῦ S. Mark xi. 22. This faith is the mediating cause whereby we men take to ourselves the δικαιοσύνη Θεοῦ, and so unite ourselves to it as to become through it holy. Christ has won this δικαιοσύνη Θεοῦ for all mankind by His death upon the Cross: *objectively* it is the result of His obedience unto Death; but it is appropriated *subjectively* by each man through faith, i.e. by an act of the intellect and the will involving free, entire, and unreserved self-surrender to the salvation wrought by GOD in Christ.]

Condition 4. *Range of destined extension among mankind.* The Righteousness which GOD gives is destined for (εἰς) and is actually bestowed upon (ἐπί) all who believe (πάντας τοὺς πιστεύοντας) whatever their nationality or antecedent religious circumstances (ver. 22).

[*Obs.* After the *modus acquisitionis* of the δικαιοσύνη Θεοῦ follows the range of its extension among mankind. This is expressed by the prepositions εἰς and ἐπί; cf. Winer, *Gr. N. T.* p. 521. It is meant for (εἰς) all; and it does extend itself over all (ἐπί) who believe in Jesus Christ. The Apostle loves to use several prepositions with the same noun that its relation to another idea may be completely defined on every side, Gal. i. 1 ἀπό, διά : Col. i. 16 ἐν, διά, εἰς: Rom. xi. 36 ἐκ, διά, εἰς. But this is no mere redundancy of style : each prep. defines a relation which would not otherwise be expressed. The emphasis here lies not upon πιστεύοντας, but upon πάντας, which is presently justified. καὶ ἐπὶ πάντας is wanting in A. B. C. P. ℵ* several versions, and is omitted by Lachmann and Tischendorf, but Meyer observes that a gloss on εἰς πάντας was quite needless, and that the twice repeated πάντας would have occasioned the omission in very early MSS.]

§ Reasons for (γάρ) this destined, universal extension (πάντας ... πάντας, ver. 22) of the Righteousness which GOD gives among mankind (ver. 22 b–23).

Reason I. There is no distinction (διαστολή) between man and man, or race and race, in virtue of which some races, or some men, (e. g. the Jews,) might possibly attain to the δικαιοσύνη Θεοῦ, independently of any faith in Jesus Christ (ver. 22).

[Obs. διαστολή is used of the spiritual advantages of races, x. 12; of the mystic tongues, 1 Cor. xiv. 7.]

Reason II. (for γάρ reason I.) All men have sinned without exception. This historical fact (ἥμαρτον) shows that there is no difference between any in this respect: and that the Righteousness which GOD gives should be extended to all (ver. 23).

[Obs. ἥμαρτον. The aorist points to the sinful acts as things in the past, which have produced the state described by ὑστεροῦνται, κ.τ.λ.]

Reason III. All men, through sin, have come short of that moral glory which GOD gave to our first parents and which He restores in Christ—τῆς δόξης τοῦ Θεοῦ. Hence the universal need for its recovery in the δικαιοσύνη Θεοῦ ἐκ πίστεως (ver. 23). 2

[Obs. The δόξα τοῦ Θεοῦ, effulgent beauty which GOD gives, is generally represented as future, Rom. v. 2; 1 Thess. ii. 12 συνδοξασθῆναι τῷ Χριστῷ, Rom. viii. 17 sqq.; Col. iii. 4. But this is not a decisive reason against its having existed in the past, as ὑστερεῖσθαι with the gen. of its object, having the sense of destitui, Lobeck, *Phryn.* p. 237, might seem to suggest. The glory which GOD gave to unfallen man is described by Bishop Bull as 'certain supernatural gifts and powers, in which his perfection chiefly consisted, and without which his natural powers were of themselves insufficient to the attainment of an heavenly immortality'; 'State of Man before the Fall,' *Works*, vol. ii. p. 52. This original righteousness was indeed forfeited by the fall, Rom. v. 12; 1 Cor. xv. 22, but this forfeiture was confirmed and made permanent by the separate sins (ἥμαρτον) in past time which were the moral consequences of the fall. That τοῦ Θεοῦ is a gen. auctoris is implied in the analogous δικαιοσύνη Θεοῦ. Compare Art. ix 'man is very far gone from original righteousness.' For the use of ὑστερεῖσθαι, see Dr. Vaughan, *in loc.*]

§ 2.

Causes of δικαίωσις, i. e. the communication of δικαιοσύνη Θεοῦ to mankind (vers. 24–26).

[Obs. δικαιούμενοι, being *made* righteous. The part. cannot stand for καὶ δικαιοῦνται: it explains or proves ὑστεροῦνται since they are being made righteous. Winer, *Gr. N. T.* p. 443. The δικαίωσις is represented as depending on the ὑστεροῦνται τῆς δόξης τοῦ Θεοῦ.]

74   *The Epistle to the Romans.*

Cause I. *Efficient (remote).* The unmerited Love and Mercy of GOD (τῇ αὐτοῦ χάριτι) which bestows Righteousness on man in the way of a free gift (δωρεάν) (ver. 24).

[*Obs.* δωρεάν properly an accus. : 'in the way of a gift'; 'Geschenksweise.' LXX for חִנָּם gratis, gratuitously. 1 Macc. x. 33 ; S. Matt. x. 8; 2 Cor. xi. 7 ; 2 Thess. iii. 8; Rev. xxi. 6; xxii. 17 ; Is. lii. 3 δωρεὰν ἄνευ ἀργυρίου. The word implies that nothing, whether it be faith or works, that precedes justification, can avail to deserve it. The χάρις of Almighty GOD is the original source of this free gift : Eph. ii. 8 τῇ γὰρ χάριτί ἐστε σεσωσμένοι διὰ τῆς πίστεως, καὶ τοῦτο οὐκ ἐξ ὑμῶν· Θεοῦ τὸ δῶρον, οὐκ ἐξ ἔργων : Eph. i. 6 ἐχαρίτωσεν ἡμᾶς ἐν τῷ ἠγαπημένῳ : Tit. iii. 5 οὐκ ἐξ ἔργων, τῶν ἐν δικαιοσύνῃ, ὧν ἐποιήσαμεν ἡμεῖς, ἀλλὰ κατὰ τὸν αὐτοῦ ἔλεον ἔσωσεν ἡμᾶς.]

Cause II. *Efficient (meritorious).* The Redemption of man, διὰ τῆς ἀπολυτρώσεως (ver. 24).

a. In whom is this Redemption found? In Christ Jesus, ἐν Χριστῷ Ἰησοῦ. In the Messiah (Christ) who is Jesus (ver. 24).

[*Obs.* ἀπολύτρωσις, prop. the payment of a λύτρον to an enemy with a view to purchasing a captive's liberty, see Plutarch, *Pompeius*, 24 πόλεων αἰχμαλώτων ἀπολυτρώσεις. It is used ten times in the New Testament, once without metaphor, Heb. xi. 35 ; elsewhere of the ransoming of mankind by Christ, whether as accomplished, 1 Cor. i. 30 ἐγενήθη ... ἡμῖν ... ἀπολύτρωσις : Heb. ix. 15 θανάτου γενομένου εἰς ἀπολύτρωσιν : Eph. i. 7 ; Col. i. 14, or as destined to have its full effect hereafter, as in Eph. iv. 30 ἡμέρα ἀπολυτρώσεως. Cf. Eph. i. 14 ; S. Luke xxi. 28. Instead of the verb ἀπολυτρῶν we find ἀγοράζειν, ἐξαγοράζειν, Gal. iii. 13 ; iv. 5 ; 1 Cor. vi. 20 ; 2 S. Pet. ii. 1 ; Rev. v. 9. The enemies who held man captive were (1) sin, S. John viii. 31-36 ; Rom. vii. 14 πεπραμένος ὑπὸ τὴν ἁμαρτίαν, 23 νόμον ... αἰχμαλωτίζοντά με τῷ νόμῳ τῆς ἁμαρτίας, and its consequence a curse of death, Rom. viii. 10 ; Gal. iii. 10, 13, 23, which curse Jesus, by dying, removed, 2 Cor. v. 15, 21. (2) Satan, lord of the realm of darkness (ἐξουσία τοῦ σκότους Col. i. 13, which is also ἐξουσία τοῦ Σατανᾶ Acts xxvi. 18). But the λύτρον was not paid to Satan, whose power was an usurpation, but to GOD Whose eternal and necessary morality also required a satisfaction for sin. Hence the Son of Man gave His life, λύτρον ἀντὶ πολλῶν S. Matt. xx. 28 ; ἑαυτὸν ἀντίλυτρον ὑπὲρ πάντων 1 Tim. ii. 6 ; γενόμενος ὑπὲρ ἡμῶν κατάρα Gal. iii. 13 ; cf. ἁμαρτίαν ἐποίησεν 2 Cor. v. 21 ; and so is ὁ ῥυόμενος ἡμᾶς ἀπὸ τῆς ὀργῆς τῆς ἐρχομένης 1 Thess. i. 10. That which is purchased is (1) ἄφεσις τῶν ἁμαρτιῶν here, Col. i. 14 ; Eph. i. 7 ; Heb. ix. 15 ; and (2) future blessedness, S. Luke xxi. 28 ; Eph. i. 14 ; iv. 30 ; Rom. viii. 23.]

b. By *whom* is this Redeemer set forth? By GOD the Father. He has openly set forth for Himself (προέθετο) as if in the midst of human history, the crucified Redeemer (ver. 25).

[*Obs.* The expression προέθετο may have been suggested by our Lord's reference to the Brasen Serpent, S. John iii. 14. The word refers not to the πρόθεσις in the Eternal Counsels of GOD, but to the historical fact of the Crucifixion, which was not a passing accident, but a public act of the Ruler of the Universe. προτίθεσθαι was used by Greek authors to describe the exposure of dead bodies (Stallbaum ad Plat. *Phaed.* p. 115 E. qu. by Meyer) and Jesus Crucified has been set forth by the Father before the eyes of believing Christendom to the end of time; cf. Gal. iii. 1 οἷς κατ' ὀφθαλμοὺς Ἰησοῦς Χριστὸς προεγράφη ἐν ὑμῖν ἐσταυρωμένος. The preaching of the Apostle carried out the purpose of the Divine προέθετο.]

c. Under what aspect is this Redeemer set forth? Under that of a propitiation, ἱλαστήριον ..... ἐν τῷ αὐτοῦ αἵματι (ver. 25).

[*Obs.* ἱλαστήριον is probably a substantive and not a substantival neuter of ἱλαστήριος, since this adjective does not occur in classical Greek, and only seldom in ecclesiastical Greek. It is 'something that propitiates'; cf. φυλακτήριον, θυσιαστήριον, θυμιατήριον: such words are common in later Greek, as δεητήριον, ἰαματήριον. Winer, *Gr. N. T.*, p. 119. The analogy of δικαστήριον, ἀκροατήριον, φυλακτήριον, καθιστήριον would suggest that ἱλαστήριον is a *nomen loci*, the *place* of expiation. Only Dio Chrys. and a writer of the seventh century are quoted as making it analogous to χαριστήριον, an expiatory *gift*. The LXX use ἱλαστήριον as a translation for כַּפֹּרֶת, Ex. xxv. 18, 19, 20, 21; xxxi. 7; xxxv. 12; xxxvii. 7, 8, 9; Lev. xvi. 2, 13, 14, 15; Numb. vii. 89, and adjectivally τὸ ἱλαστήριον ἐπίθεμα in Exod. xxv. 17; xxxvii. 6, where we are told what is the material of which the כַּפֹּרֶת is made. The LXX also use ἱλαστήριον for the עֲזָרָה or ledge of the altar for burnt offerings, Ezek. xliii. 14, 17, 20, because this too, like the Capporeth, was to be sprinkled with the reconciling blood of the sacrifice. The Capporeth (explained also by Levy, *Chald. Dict.* as a *place* of expiation) was the golden lid which covered the Sacred Ark, and upon which the blood of a bullock and a goat was sprinkled at the yearly feast of expiation. This lid covered not only the Ark, containing the law, but, Exod. xxx. 6, the law itself. The blood of the appointed victims only becomes propitiatory when it is on the Capporeth, Lev. xvii. 11; xvi. 14, 15. Thus ἱλαστήριον, which certainly means the Capporeth, in Heb. ix. 5 Χερουβὶμ δόξης κατασκιάζοντα τὸ ἱλαστήριον is best explained by it here also. According to Ex. xxv. 22, and Lev. xvi. 2 the Capporeth is the central seat of GOD's saving presence on earth and of His gracious revelations to man. The Holy of Holies itself was only the בֵּית־הַכַּפֹּרֶת, the House of the Capporeth, 1 Chron. xxviii. 11; 1 Kings vi. 5. That the Incarnate Christ, sprinkled with His own Blood, should be called ἱλαστήριον, was therefore natural. Meyer understands by the word ἱλαστήριον, expiatorium generally, without any more precise definition of its sense. But he prefers the explanation which defines it by ἱερόν or θῦμα. S. Chrys. takes it as 'expiatory sacrifice'—the antitype of the animal offerings. In 1 S. John ii. 2; iv. 10 Christ is called an ἱλασμός, as it is He by Whom sin is covered and expiated.

Cause III. *Efficient (receptive).* The faith which receives, as might a hand, Christ the ἱλαστήριον ἐν τῷ αὐτοῦ αἵματι as the δικαιοσύνη Θεοῦ.

[*Obs.* 1. τῆς is wanting in C*. D*. F. G. ℵ and several Fathers; A. and Chrys. omit the whole διὰ τῆς πίστεως; Lachm. and Tisch. omit τῆς. Probably the omission of the art. was suggested by διὰ πίστεως ver. 22, and the clause should be retained.]

[*Obs.* 2. ἐν τῷ αὐτοῦ αἵματι, although following διὰ τῆς πίστεως, is not dependent on it, as if 'through faith in His Blood': since in that case τῆς would have been repeated before ἐν τῷ αἵματι, and εἰς with an acc. would have been *more natural* than ἐν, although πίστις or πιστεύειν are used with ἔν τινι in Eph. i. 15, Col. i. 4, 1 Tim. iii. 13, 2 Tim. iii. 15, our Lord Jesus Christ being in all these cases the object *in* which Faith rests. Both expressions here are best regarded as adverbial clauses added to ὅν . . . . ἱλαστήριον. διὰ [τῆς] πίστεως represents the means of subjective appropriation of the ἱλαστήριον; ἐν τῷ αὐτοῦ αἵματι, the objective medium of its exhibition to the world.]

[*Obs.* 3. The relation of the αἷμα τοῦ Χριστοῦ to Christ as the ἱλαστήριον, is to be explained by the relation between the soul and the Blood which is taught in the Jewish Scriptures. (1) Gen. ix. 4-6, where in ver. 4 דָּמוֹ is in apposition to נַפְשׁוֹ, and is paraphrased in LXX ἐν αἵματι ψυχῆς. The blood of beasts may not be eaten, because it is the 'soul' of beasts. In ver. 5 man's blood and man's soul are even more closely associated: the life of man as contained in the blood of man is not to be even touched by beasts or men, under penalty of death. (2) Lev. xvii. 10-14, The eater of blood was to be destroyed, because 'the soul of the flesh (i. e. of the nature living in the flesh נֶפֶשׁ הַבָּשָׂר) is in the blood; and I have given it to you upon the altar to make an atonement for your souls: for the blood, by means of the soul (בַּנֶּפֶשׁ, ב *instrumenti*) is an atonement.' This is mistranslated in A. V. 'The blood maketh an atonement for the soul.' The blood atones by the power of the soul which is resident in it. (3) Deut. xii. 23, Beasts of Sacrifice may be slaughtered and eaten, like the roebuck and the hart, i. e. non-sacrificial beasts, 'only be sure that thou eat not the blood; for *the blood is the soul*, and thou mayest not eat the soul with the flesh. Thou shalt not eat of it; thou shalt pour it upon the earth like water. The eating blood was, on this account, considered sin, 1 Sam. xiv. 32; punished in the prophetic ages, Ezek. xxxiii. 25; and even forbidden by the Apostles, Acts xv. 20-29; xxi. 25. Hence moral qualities are applied to the blood, considered as the soul; Ps. xciv. 21 דָּם נָקִי; and S. Matt. xxiii. 35 αἷμα δίκαιον. This unity of the blood and the soul was implied in Virgil's *Aen.* ix. 349 'purpuream vomit ille animam,' and was taught in Aristotle's treatise *De Anim.* i. 2. 405 b. 5. Tertull. *De Anim.* c. 15. But Scripture nowhere combines spirit (רוּחַ) and blood as a unity; only soul and blood: and it does not confine even the sensuous soul to the blood, so that it is not also in the organs, e. g. of respiration, as נֶפֶשׁ. This language of Scripture is physiologically true, since (1) the efficiency of the body depends on the quantity of the blood; the blood is the basis of physical life; and so far, the soul, as the principle of bodily life, is preeminently in the blood; (2) the blood is also the original material from which, in the embryonic state, the human organism is developed; hence S. John i. 13 says of the sons of GOD, οὐκ ἐξ αἱμάτων, cf. Acts xvii. 26; cf. Delitzsch, *Bibl. Psychol.* pp. 281 ff. In our Lord's case, His Blood had an atoning value, as representing not merely a נֶפֶשׁ or ψυχή, like the sacrificial animals under the law, but as being hypostatically united to πνεῦμα αἰώνιον, His eternal Divinity (see Delitzsch on Heb. ix. 14), which imparts to it such absolute value that it can screen the whole guilty race of man. Hence the language applied to the Blood of Christ. It is περὶ πολλῶν ἐκχυνόμενον εἰς ἄφεσιν ἁμαρτιῶν Matt. xxvi. 28. It is the αἷμα ἴδιον of GOD with which He purchased (περιεποιήσατο) the Church, Acts xx. 28. By it

Christians have τὴν ἀπολύτρωσιν Eph. i. 7, and in it, i.e. in the sphere of its operation, they are brought near (ἐγγὺς ἐγενήθητε) to God, Eph. ii. 13. It is the blood of sprinkling, 1 S. Pet. i. 2, 19; the Precious Blood ὡς ἀμνοῦ ἀμώμου καὶ ἀσπίλου Χριστοῦ (ib.). It is the Blood of Christ's Cross, whereby He has made peace, Col. i. 20; it καθαριεῖ τὴν συνείδησιν ἡμῶν Heb. ix. 14; it καθαρίζει ἀπὸ πάσης ἁμαρτίας 1 S. John i. 7; in it the saved have been washed, τῷ λούσαντι Rev. i. 5; and have whitened their stoles, ἐλεύκαναν Rev. vii. 14; by it Christ has bought them, ἠγόρισας v. 9; and in it Christians have παρρησίαν εἰς τὴν εἴσοδον τῶν ἁγίων Heb. x. 19. As the αἷμα διαθήκης αἰωνίου Heb. xiii. 20, it corresponds antitypically to the blood of the Jewish sacrifices; with it Christ's people are sprinkled ῥαντισμὸν αἵματος 1 Pet. i. 2, and sanctified, ἵνα ἁγιάσῃ διὰ τοῦ ἰδίου αἵματος Heb. xiii. 12; by it they conquer the adversary, Rev. xii. 11. It is the summary of the whole redemptive work of Christ; it implies the Incarnation on the one hand as the secret of its power, and on the other the Resurrection as the warrant of its efficacy. 'Sanguis Christi, Christi Evangelium.']

Cause IV. Final (1) *Ultimately* (εἰς). The manifestation of God's own attribute of Righteousness, εἰς ἔνδειξιν τῆς δικαιοσύνης αὐτοῦ (ver. 25), εἰς τὸ εἶναι αὐτὸν δίκαιον (ver. 26).

Reason for this ἔνδειξις. It was necessary on account of the indulgent overlooking of sins in the pre-Christian ages (διὰ τὴν πάρεσιν τῶν προγεγονότων ἁμαρτιῶν) in virtue of the forbearance (ἐν τῇ ἀνοχῇ) of God, that He should display in Christ's Atoning Death His own unchanged relation to moral evil (ver. 26).

[*Obs.* 1. The clause εἰς ἔνδειξιν depends upon προέθετο, defining its final purpose. It is ἵνα ἐνδείξηται Eph. ii. 7. ἔνδειξις is used for a practical proof of human affection, 2 Cor. viii. 24, and for an intimation of coming destruction, ἀπωλείας Phil. i. 28. In ii. 15 ἐνδείκνυνται is used of the outward practical proof given by the lives of the better heathen that an ideal of conduct in accordance with the Law is written in their hearts. The δικαιοσύνη αὐτοῦ is here, not the Righteousness which God gives, but as the context requires, the Righteousness which is His attribute : cf. ver. 26 εἰς τὸ εἶναι αὐτὸν δίκαιον. Winer says that it is difficult to think that S. Paul wrote δικαιοσύνης αὐτοῦ close to ἐν αἵματι αὐτοῦ, and would read δικαιοσύνης αὐτοῦ, but adds that it is a question for editors, *Gr. N. T.* p. 189.]

[*Obs.* 2. διὰ τὴν πάρεσιν κ.τ.λ. seems to depend on εἰς ἔνδειξιν τῆς δικαιοσύνης αὐτοῦ, rather than on προέθετο. The display of the Attribute of Righteousness in His indignation against sin on the Cross, was rendered needful by God's pretermission of sins in earlier ages, in order to vindicate Him from apparent indifference to moral evil. It must not be translated as if τὴν πάρεσιν τῶν προγεγονότων ἁμαρτιῶν gives the formal cause of justification, which consists in the remission of past sins. For (*a*) διά with *acc*. would thus be taken as equivalent to διά with *gen*. On the inadmissibility of this, see Winer, *Gr. N. T.* p. 497. (*b*) πάρεσις would be taken as ἄφεσις. But ἄφεσις is remissio; πάρεσις praetermissio. πάρεσις occurs here only in Scripture; though παριέναι occurs in Ecclus. xxxiii. 2, and the idea of πάρεσις is expressed by ὑπερβαίνων ἀσεβείας Mich. vii. 18, and ὑπεριδὼν ὁ Θεὸς τοὺς χρόνους τῆς ἀγνοίας Acts xvii. 30. Then pre-Christian sins were not forgiven; they were let go unpunished. Particular acts of sin are hinted at in the form ἁμάρτημα, which only occurs in S. Mark iii. 28, 29; 1 Cor. vi. 18; 2 S. Pet. i. 9. This pretermission, πάρεσις, of sin was the corollary in GOD's active providence to His ἀνοχή, i. e. His χρηστότης face to face with human sin, ii. 4; just as ἄφεσις would have corresponded to His χάρις. In ἐν τῇ ἀνοχῇ, ἐν is used in the sense of the ethical ground or sphere. The bearing of Christ's redemption upon Jewish sins in the pre-Christian ages is referred to in Heb. ix. 15 θανάτου γενομένου εἰς ἀπολύτρωσιν τῶν ἐπὶ τῇ πρώτῃ διαθήκῃ παραβάσεων, where these ancient sins are spoken of, not as a reason for the ἔνδειξις δικαιοσύνης Θεοῦ in the Crucifixion, but as redeemed by it.]

(2) Immediately (πρός) the manifestation of the righteousness which He gives to sinners at this present time, as the justifier of τὸν ἐκ πίστεως Ἰησοῦ (ver. 26).

[*Obs.* 1. πρός resumes, by a parallel clause, the εἰς ἔνδειξιν in ver. 25; but εἰς is exchanged for the nearly equivalent πρός in order to suggest a *more immediate* purpose of the προέθετο. ἐν τῷ νῦν καιρῷ serves to mark its force, and introduces a new element.]

[*Obs.* 2. The closing words εἰς τὸ εἶναι αὐτὸν δίκαιον κ.τ.λ. summarize and explain the whole preceding passage εἰς ἔνδειξιν τῆς δικαιοσύνης κ.τ.λ. εἰς τὸ εἶναι αὐτὸν δίκαιον corresponds to εἰς ἔνδειξιν τῆς δικαιοσύνης τοῦ Θεοῦ: and δικαιοῦντα τὸν ἐκ πίστεως Ἰησοῦ to πρὸς ἔνδειξιν τῆς δικαιοσύνης αὐτοῦ ἐν τῷ νῦν καιρῷ.]

[*Obs.* 3. On the question of Justification, see Waterland, *Summary View of the Doctrine of Justification*, Works, vol. ix. 427. (Oxf. 1823); Bull, *Examen Censurae*, Works, vol. iv. p. 93 sqq.; Bp. Philpotts, *Pastoral Letter to the Clergy of the Diocese of Exeter on the Present State of the Church*, p. 19 (Murray, 1851); Sadler, *Justification of Life* (Bell, 1888).]

[*Obs.* 4.

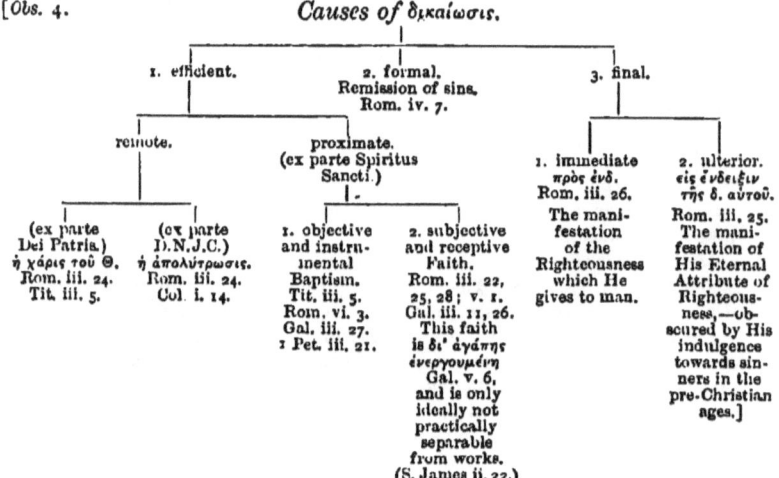

Causes of δικαίωσις.

1. efficient.

remote.

(ex parte Dei Patris.)
ἡ χάρις τοῦ Θ.
Rom. iii. 24.
Tit. iii. 5.

(ex parte D.N.J.C.)
ἡ ἀπολύτρωσις.
Rom. iii. 24.
Col. i. 14.

2. formal.
Remission of sins.
Rom. iv. 7.

proximate.
(ex parte Spiritus Sancti.)

1. objective and instrumental Baptism.
Tit. iii. 5.
Rom. vi. 3.
Gal. iii. 27.
1 Pet. iii. 21.

2. subjective and receptive Faith.
Rom. iii. 22, 25, 28; v. 1.
Gal. iii. 11, 26.
This faith is δι' ἀγάπης ἐνεργουμένη Gal. v. 6, and is only ideally not practically separable from works.
(S. James ii. 22.)

3. final.

1. immediate
πρὸς ἔνδ.
Rom. iii. 26.
The manifestation of the Righteousness which He gives to man.

2. ulterior.
εἰς ἔνδειξιν τῆς δ. αὐτοῦ.
Rom. iii. 25.
The manifestation of His Eternal Attribute of Righteousness,—obscured by His indulgence towards sinners in the pre-Christian ages.]

§ 3.

Inferences (οὖν ver. 27) from the preceding account of δικαίωσις (27-30).

Inference I. The Jew can no longer make his wonted boast (ἡ καύχησις) in his theocratic position. This boast is excluded from consideration by a law whose ποιότης is not works but faith (ver. 27).

Reason. (γάρ) *from the drift of the present argument*: our argument is that a man is justified by faith, apart from works of the law (ver. 28).

[*Obs.* 1. (ver. 27.) The rapid interchange of question and answer in ver. 27 implies the Apostle's sense of the conclusiveness of his argument. In ἡ καύχησις the art. indicates the well-known boasting of the Jews, already referred to in ii. 17 sqq. This boasting is excluded from the sphere of the religious relation to GOD proclaimed by the Apostle. The Apostle assumes that this exclusion must be effected by *some* law, which no longer allows it. What is the quality of this law? διὰ ποίου νόμου; It cannot be the law which requires outward works, since these afford scope for the Jewish καύχησις; it must be a law which is only a law in a wider sense, as *a revelation of the Will of God*, but which requires *faith* as the characteristic act of obedience to it. For this wider sense of νόμος compare ix. 31 νόμος δικαιοσύνης: viii. 2 ὁ νόμος τοῦ πνεύματος : S. James ii. 12 νόμος ἐλευθερίας.]

[*Obs.* 2. (ver. 28.) The clause λογιζόμεθα γάρ κ.τ.λ. gives the reason for διὰ νόμου πίστεως ἐξεκλείσθη ἡ καύχησις ver. 27. λογίζεσθαι, as in ii. 3, of inferential argument: by the plural the Apostle associates himself with his readers, whom he assumes to be following him. The reading οὖν, *textus receptus*, must be abandoned for γάρ in deference to decisive external testimony; although οὖν lends itself to a very tenable construction of the passage. ἄνθρωπον, a 'human being,' is used here like as at ii. 1, 3 and πᾶσαν ψυχὴν ἀνθρώπου ii. 9. The argument applies to every human being as such. For χωρὶς ἔργων νόμου compare ver. 20 ἐξ ἔργων νόμου οὐ δικαιωθήσεται πᾶσα σάρξ, and ver. 21 χωρὶς νόμου δικαιοσύνη Θεοῦ πεφανέρωται. On this verse see Sadler, *Justification of Life*, ch. iii. § 1, especially pp. 106, 107.]

Inference II. GOD is the One GOD of the whole human family, and not of the Jews only (ver. 29).

Reason. This equal relation of the One GOD to the whole human race is implied in His imparting δικαιοσύνη on the same terms of Faith to both Jew and Heathen.

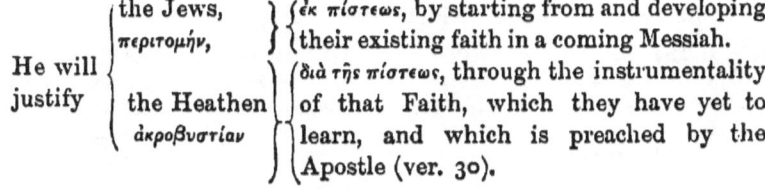

He will justify
{ the Jews, περιτομήν, } { ἐκ πίστεως, by starting from and developing their existing faith in a coming Messiah.
{ the Heathen ἀκροβυστίαν } { διὰ τῆς πίστεως, through the instrumentality of that Faith, which they have yet to learn, and which is preached by the Apostle (ver. 30).

[*Obs.* 1. ἤ, as at ii. 4, introduces an alternative supposition to that which has just been stated in ver. 28. Or, if we are wrong in thinking that a human being is made just apart from works of obedience to the Jewish law, are we to say that God is the God of the Jews only? God must have been only a Jewish God, if He made δικαίωσις depend exclusively upon works of obedience to the Jewish law. In ναὶ καὶ ἐθνῶν the Apostle controverts the Jewish exclusiveness; the equal relation of God to the heathen was implied in the promises to the heathen in the Jewish prophets, and had been expressly revealed to S. Paul himself, Gal. i. 16. εἶναί τινος properly 'to belong to some one,' here as God, Who is the Possession of the human soul, as well as its Maker and Owner.]

[*Obs.* 2. The Unity of God, εἷς ὁ Θεός, which is here connected with His relation to the whole human race, is asserted in 1 Cor. viii. 4, as against heathen polytheism, in Gal. iii. 20, and 1 Tim. ii. 5 in relation to our Lord's mediation, in Eph. iv. 6 as the climax of the unities which are the objects of Christian devotion; in S. James ii. 19 as the subject of intellectual assent, common to men and devils.]

[*Obs.* 3. ἐπείπερ here only in New Testament if the true reading; but A.B.C.D**א* have εἴπερ 'if, at least.' Meyer retains ἐπείπερ 'whereas'; he thinks that it would have been altered on account of its being unfamiliar to the copyists. δικαιώσει, 'future of the rule'; δικαιοῦν is viewed as an act of God which will continue to be thus performed throughout the ages of Christianity, Winer, *Gr. N. T.* p. 350. In ἐκ πίστεως and διὰ τῆς πίστεως Winer cannot allow that the Apostle intended any distinction in sense, since πίστις may with equal propriety be conceived of as the *source* or as the *means* of blessedness, Gal. iii. 8; Eph. ii. 8; *Gr. N. T.* p. 512. He thinks that the use of different prepositions in parallel clauses is solely for the sake of variety. But cf. on ver. 22, and observe the significant insertion of the art. in διὰ τῆς πίστεως. It was the development of the subjective belief of the Jews which would lead to their justification : it was the objective faith of Christendom, of which as yet they knew nothing, which would be the means of justifying the Gentiles.]

C.

The δικαιοσύνη Θεοῦ ἐκ πίστεως is confirmed by the authority of the Old Testament (iii. 31—iv. 25).

General Thesis. The doctrine of Justification by faith is so far from destroying the authority of the Mosaic Law that it establishes this authority by appealing to it for a sanction on its own distinctive characteristics (iii. 31).

[*Obs.* 1. The question 'Do we then make the Law of none effect through the principle of faith?' is a natural inference (οὖν) from what has been said as to δικαίωσις ... ἐκ πίστεως ... χωρὶς ἔργων νόμου. The antithesis of νόμος and πίστις shows that here the Mosaic Law is meant (cf. Acts xxi. 28; Gal. iv. 21). which the objection supposed to be rendered invalid διὰ τῆς πίστεως, by making faith the condition of justification.]

[*Obs.* 2. In the answer νόμον ἱστάνομεν the form ἱστάνομεν has preponderating authority in its favour. The simple ἱστάνω here only in Scripture. 'We make the law stand' in all its old authority: (=βεβαιοῦμεν) Theodoret. S. Paul does not mean that the Law is not abrogated considered as a rule of outward actions performed in order to the attainment of righteousness, Rom. vii. 4; x. 4; 2 Cor. iii. 7; Gal. ii. 19; Gal. iii. 12, since in that sense the Law was destroyed by the Gospel: but this same law, inasmuch as it taught that faith is the receptive condition of δικαιοσύνη, is therefore confirmed in its authority by that Gospel to which it thus witnesses.]

Proof of the Thesis, iii. 31 νόμον ἱστάνομεν διὰ τῆς πίστεως, from the case of Abraham, father of the faithful (iv. 1–25).

§ 1. The question stated (iv. 1–3).

Quest. If δικαιοσύνη ἐκ πίστεως, instead of abrogating, establishes the Law, what religious advantage, (such as righteousness,) can we say that Abraham the typical ancestor of the race has attained to, in accordance with the genius of an external system like that of the Law? (iv. 1).

Resp. No advantage whatever.

Reason 1. (γάρ) *from observing the limited scope of the current Jewish answer in a contrary sense.* The Jewish doctors say that Abraham *has* attained to some advantage, viz. that he 'was justified by outward works.' Supposing this to have been the case, the Apostle admits that Abraham has matter for boasting, καύχημα; he has attained righteousness through his own efforts. But he has not this ground of boasting with respect to GOD, πρὸς τὸν Θεόν, since his justification is, (upon the supposition,) not at all GOD's act but purely his own (ver. 2).

Reason 2. (proof, γάρ, of οὐ πρὸς τὸν Θεόν (ver. 2) in Reason 1) *from the explicit statement of Scripture.* Gen. xv. 6 teaches that what GOD took account of in Abraham was his *faith*, and hence it follows that if he did become righteous ἐξ ἔργων, this is no real ground of glory with respect to GOD, καύχημα πρὸς τὸν Θεόν (ver. 2).

[*Obs.* 1. (ver. 1.) οὖν introduces the proof of iii. 31 to be drawn from the history of Abraham in the form of an inference (Meyer). The Apostle asks a question which implies a negative answer; and this negative answer supplies a corrective to the Jewish misunderstanding of νόμον ἱστάνομεν, while at the same time it introduces Abraham's true relation to the receptive cause of δικαιοσύνη Θεοῦ. The words κατὰ σάρκα are joined to τὸν πατέρα ἡμῶν by A.C.D.E.F.G.ℵ and many Fathers; but while this connection may have been the motive of the transposition, it is really tautologous. The words are better taken with εὑρηκέναι : εὑρίσκειν is used like מָצָא 'to acquire,' 'earn,' S. Luke i. 30; Heb. ix. 12. In κατὰ σάρκα, σάρξ is used as nature, without the higher element of grace which was to be received by faith, κατὰ σάρκα, in a purely human way, by his natural efforts. The words τὸν πατέρα ἡμῶν (προπάτορα, A.B.ℵ, &c. is *probably* a gloss) are significant. Abraham was the typical ancestor of Israel, whether natural or spiritual; his history was to be the spiritual rule for that of his true posterity. If he attained to justification by his own efforts then the Jewish teachers who appealed to the authority of his example were right: if in the way of faith, then the Apostle might claim him as the spiritual ancestor of believing Christendom.]

[*Obs.* 2. (ver. 2.) γάρ justified the negative reply which the question in ver. 1 implies. Abraham attained to no advantage whatever κατὰ σάρκα. If he was justified by works as the Jewish doctors say, this (is in its way a matter of boasting—but it) has no reference to GOD, and is not therefore τί εὑρηκέναι; Observe that εὑρηκέναι in the Apostle's question ver. 1 corresponds to ἐδικαιώθη in the Jewish statement, ver. 2, and κατὰ σάρκα in ver. 1 to ἐξ ἔργων in ver. 2. But this correspondence does not involve equivalence; the expressions in ver. 1 are wider and more generic. In ἐξ ἔργων, ἔργα are products of natural human energy, not of the new element of Divine life received by faith, as in S. James ii. 21 Ἀβραὰμ ὁ πατὴρ ἡμῶν οὐκ ἐξ ἔργων ἐδικαιώθη ἀνενέγκας Ἰσαὰκ τὸν υἱὸν αὐτοῦ ἐπὶ τὸ θυσιαστήριον; The Jews inferred from Gen. xxvi. 5 that Abraham kept the whole law of Moses, Beresch. Rabba, f. 57. 4; Kiddusch. f. 82. 1. καύχημα, *materies gloriandi*, Phil. i. 26; ii. 16, in New Testament (but not in classics) distinguished from καύχησις. πρὸς τὸν Θεόν, with reference to, not ἐνώπιον or 'apud.' ἔχειν καύχημα πρός is explained by its opposite ἔχειν μομφὴν πρός, Col. iii. 13. Abraham, regarded as present (ἔχει, see Winer, *Gr. N. T.* p. 384) may, if justified as the Jews assert, pass for a δίκαιος before men, but he cannot say that he is a δίκαιος with reference to GOD, because GOD, as Scripture testifies, only reckons to him his faith as δικαιοσύνη.]

[*Obs.* 3. In ver. 3 Gen. xv. 6 is quoted as a proof (γάρ) of the words οὐ πρὸς τὸν Θεόν in ver. 2.]

§ Gen. xv. 6, quoted to show that Abraham's faith, not his antecedent works, were placed to his account as δικαιοσύνην by GOD.

Heb. וְהֶאֱמִן בַּיהוָה וַיַּחְשְׁבֶהָ לּוֹ צְדָקָה
LXX καὶ ἐπίστευσεν Ἀβραμ τῷ Θεῷ, καὶ ἐλογίσθη αὐτῷ εἰς δικαιοσύνην.

[*Obs.* 1. The Apostle quotes verbatim from the LXX, only substituting δέ after ἐπίστευσε for καί before it, as does S. James ii. 23, although at Gal. iii. 6 the Apostle omits both. Ἀβραμ does not occur in the Hebrew, and τῷ Θεῷ is substituted for בַּיהוָה. ἐλογίσθη represents the active וַיַּחְשְׁבֶהָ, and he reckoned it.]

[*Obs.* 2. Abraham's faith was conspicuously shown (1) in his leaving his native land and kindred at the call of GOD, Gen. xiii. 1; Acts vii. 2 sqq.; Heb.

xi. 8 πίστει ὑπήκουσεν ἐξελθεῖν. (2) In his believing, in spite of his advanced years, that Sarah would bear him a son whose posterity would be innumerable like the stars of heaven, Gen. xv. 6 as here : cf. Gal. iii. 6 ; and (3) in his willing surrender of the son of promise at the bidding of GOD, Gen. xxii ; Heb. xi. 17-19 πίστει . . . τὸν μονογενῆ προέφερεν . . . τὰς ἐπαγγελίας ἀποδεξάμενος. (The Epistle to the Hebrews adds Abraham's tent-life in the promised land, xi. 9, 10, as a further instance of his personal faith in addition to that which was common to him with the Patriarchs generally, ib. 13-16, while the preternatural birth of Isaac is *there* connected with the faith of Sarah ib. 11, 12.) For Jewish recognition of the faith of Abraham see 1 Macc. ii. 52 ἐν πειρασμῷ εὑρέθη πιστὸς καὶ ἐλογίσθη αὐτῷ εἰς δικαιοσύνην : Philo, *De Abrahamo*, pp. 386, 387, and the beautiful passage ' Quis rerum divinarum haeres,' p. 493, quoted by Tholuck. The act of faith in the promise of an innumerable seed which was reckoned to Abraham for righteousness, did not make so great a demand upon him as the offering up Isaac : yet it was an heroic act of belief and the Apostle describes its difficulty in vers. 18, 19. Perhaps it is selected because it best illustrated the triumph of faith as such ; the believing assent of the mind and will of Abraham to GOD's promise of a posterity did not at once issue in any definite act, such as the leaving his home before, or the offering his son afterwards, although it was ready to do so.

When S. James, before quoting Gen. xv. 6, says that Abraham's faith συνήργει τοῖς ἔργοις αὐτοῦ καὶ ἐκ τῶν ἔργων ἡ πίστις ἐτελειώθη, he is referring to the sacrifice of Isaac, Gen. xxii. 9, 12, as explaining the Divine estimate of faith in Gen. xv. 6. Faith is always capable of works, whether it actually produces them or not.]

[*Obs*. 3. In Gen. xv Abraham gave evidence of his faith in GOD's promise of a posterity by at once obeying GOD's command to 'fetch an heifer three years old' and other animals, and 'divide them in the midst and lay each piece one against another' (vers. 9, 10) and GOD gave evidence that He reckoned Abraham's faith to him for righteousness, by that which followed : ' When the sun went down, and it was dark, behold a smoking furnace, and a burning lamp that passed between those pieces' (ver. 17), and 'in the same day the Lord made a covenant with Abraham.' The Lord reckoned Abraham's faith to him as righteousness by making a covenant with him, by taking him into covenant with himself (Keil, *in loc.*). Abraham's πιστεύειν τῷ Θεῷ did not differ substantially from the πίστις of Christians ; because Abraham's faith had reference to GOD's promise of a posterity which embraced in it the future Messiah, John viii. 56 καὶ εἶδε καὶ ἐχάρη. On the צְדָקָה of the Old Testament, see Kurtz, *History of the Old Covenant*, i. p. 226, Engl. Transl. 'He who in the exercise of his free will comes up to the Divine idea and to the purpose of his existence is righteous. By the fall man lost *this* righteousness, or rather the capacity for attaining it. But as salvation is impossible without righteousness, and as in the eternal counsel of His grace GOD has resolved to save man, *GOD must Himself* restore righteousness to man. . . . Just as, according to the original arrangement, he would have been just who had come up to the requirements of the Divine idea expressed in creation, so now is he righteous who submits to the conditions of the plan of salvation. . . . Of this plan . . . the condition is that man should fall in with the salvation offered him, in as far as it became manifest in each successive stage of development. Thus then a new way in which to obtain righteousness, that of faith, i. e. of a full, free and unconditional surrender of oneself to the idea embodied in the Divine plan of salvation. This faith does not indeed work out salvation, but it is the condition under which salvation becomes ours. Abraham believed, i. e. he wholly surrendered himself to the truth contained in the Divine promise under which at that stage of development salvation appeared, and thus he became just.']

§ 2. Exposition of Gen. xv. 6 (vers. 4–25).

A. Negative import of Gen. xv. 6 (vers. 4–16 a). Agencies which did not contribute to Abraham's justification. He was justified

I. χωρὶς ἔργων (ver. 6). Abraham's previous 'natural' *good conduct* had no share in bringing about his δικαίωσις (vers. 4–8).

(a) *Arg.* from the logical conception of ἐλογίσθη. It implies that a return of some kind is made κατὰ χάριν,—purely in the way of grace or favour. Thus it is sharply opposed to the conception of ἐργάζεσθαι which implies a return for work, κατὰ τὸ ὀφείλημα, according to the measure of debt. Had Abraham been justified by good conduct *previous to his faith in* the Divine Promise, Gen. xv. 6, his δικαιοσύνη would have been described as a debt which was due, not as a grace which was reckoned to him. As it was, he illustrates the general Law, that 'the faith of the man who believes in GOD, the *Justifier* even of the impious, is reckoned to that man for righteousness' (vers. 4–5).

(b) *Arg.* (confirmatory of the preceding (a)) from the general proposition laid down by David, Ps. xxxii. 1–2, in which he congratulates the man whose sins are forgiven him and covered, i. e. not imputed. This, the negative aspect of λογίζεσθαι δικαιοσύνην, must have been the μακαρισμός of believing Abraham, to whom GOD reckoned righteousness without reference to previous conduct (vers. 6–8).

[*Obs.* 1. In vers. 4, 5, an illustration of ver. 3 is supplied, consisting of two categories or general relations of moral life contrasted with each other. There are (1) the ἐργαζόμενος and (2) the μὴ ἐργαζόμενος conceived generally. (1) The ἐργαζόμενος, the man who deals in works, has corresponding wages (ὁ μισθός), which are 'reckoned' to him according to the standard not of grace but of debt. S. Paul assumes from ver. 3 that Abraham's δικαιοσύνη came to him κατὰ χάριν; and hence Abraham cannot have been an ἐργαζόμενος. (2)

The man who cannot be thought of as an ἐργαζόμενος, but who believes (ἐπί) on GOD, the Justifier of the ungodly,—his faith is reckoned as δικαιοσύνη. This was obviously Abraham's case, as described in Gen. xv. But in both verses the language is purposely wider than was needed by the particular case ; Abraham alone is not the μὴ ἐργαζόμενος still less the ἀσεβής of ver. 5. Probably the Apostle is thinking of himself in τῷ ἐργαζομένῳ, such as he was before his conversion, κατὰ δικαιοσύνην τὴν ἐκ νόμου ἄμεμπτος Phil. iii. 6, blameless in his own sight as a fulfiller of the law, and entitled to its rewards as a matter of strict justice. In the μὴ ἐργαζόμενος, he is thinking also of himself ; he does work, but cannot think of himself as an ἐργαζόμενος : looking to his previous life, it is that of an ἀσεβής who needs justification before GOD, and who is justified by believing on Him. πιστεύειν ἐπὶ τὸν Θεόν is not merely *credere Deo*, or *credere Deum*, but *credere in Deum*, expressing not only the direction of faith, but its character, ' credendo amare, credendo diligere, credendo in Eum ire et eius membris incorporari,' Augustine, *in Joann. tr.* xxix. 6.]

[*Obs.* 2 in ver. 2. The quotation from David's Ps. xxxii. 1, 2 is an accessory (καθάπερ) argument. This μακαρισμός congratulation (not blessedness), of the person to whom GOD reckons a δικαιοσύνη χωρὶς ἔργων, is based on the forgiveness of sins. καθάπερ for καθώς, xii. 4 ; 1 Cor. xii. 12 ; 2 Cor. iii. 13, 18 ; viii. 11 ; 1 Thess. ii. 11, &c. μακαρισμός only in ver. 9 and Gal. iv. 15.]

[*Obs.* 3. There is no place in Scripture in which the Righteousness of Jesus Christ is said to be imputed, as distinct from being imparted. When Scripture says that Faith is reckoned to a man for righteousness, it does not thereby say that the Righteousness of Christ is imputed without being imparted. Faith is imputed for righteousness on a common sense and almost a natural principle. Faith is the initial act of all union with GOD or Christ. Accordingly an all-gracious GOD does not wait until the sinner has done such or such good works before He receives him into favour ; He sees the fruit in the germ, He takes the will for the deed ; He sees the career of faith in its earliest beginning. So it was with Abraham ; the event, we may reverently say, justified GOD's εἰς δικαιοσύνην ἐλογίσθη. When Abraham believed GOD's promise of a posterity, GOD accounted his faith as righteousness : and when the day of trial came, it proved to be righteousness, since the same faith which made Abraham believe the promise, made him sacrifice the child of promise. Sadler, *Justification of Life*, (2nd ed.) pp. 60, 61.]

§ Ps. xxxii. 1-2, quoted to show that David confirms the Apostle's account of the δικαιοσύνη of Abraham as being imparted χωρὶς ἔργων.

Heb.
1. אַשְׁרֵי נְשׂוּי־פֶּשַׁע
כְּסוּי חֲטָאָה
2. אַשְׁרֵי אָדָם
לֹא יַחְשֹׁב יְהוָֹה לוֹ עָוֹן

LXX μακάριοι ὧν ἀφέθησαν αἱ ἀνομίαι
καὶ ὧν ἐπεκαλύφθησαν αἱ ἁμαρτίαι
μακάριος ἀνὴρ ᾧ οὐ μὴ λογίσηται Κύριος ἁμαρτίαν.

[*Obs.* 1. The Apostle exactly follows the LXX. Sin is termed פֶּשַׁע, as a breaking loose from GOD; חֲטָאָה, as a deviation from that which is His Will; עָוֺן, as a perverse misdeed. The forgiveness of sins is described by נָשָׂא, as a lifting up and taking away; by כָּפָה, as a covering, so that sin becomes invisible to a Holy GOD; and by לֹא חָשַׁב, as a not-reckoning. Ps. xxxii was written by David at the end of the year's agony which followed his sin with Bathsheba, and in the midst of which he wrote Ps. li. Ps. li was written in the midst of the penitential struggle; Ps. xxxii after the recovery of inward peace. Ps. xxxii was S. Augustine's favourite psalm.]

[*Obs.* 2. In ἀφέθησαν, ἐπεκαλύφθησαν the aorist expresses the completeness of the forgiveness; in οὐ μὴ λογίσηται, the future generally,—without precise definition—as the Day of Judgment 'will certainly not impute.' οὐ μή, 1 Cor. viii. 13; Gal. iv. 30; v. 16; 1 Thess. iv. 15; v. 3.]

II. χωρὶς περιτομῆς. Abraham's Circumcision had no connection with his justification (vers. 9–12).

(a) *Arg. from the order of events in Abraham's life.* At the time when Abraham's faith in the promise of a posterity was reckoned to him as δικαιοσύνη, he was still uncircumcised, Gen. xv. He was only circumcised fourteen years later, Gen. xvii. It was therefore as an uncircumcised man that Abraham was justified, and had his share in the μακαρισμός afterwards uttered by David (vers. 9–10).

(b) *Arg. from the true import of Abraham's circumcision.* His circumcision was (1) a σημεῖον of the covenant. GOD could make no covenant with Abraham before he was justified: Abraham's circumcision was a sign, not an instrument, of his justification. But it was received as (2) a σφραγίς. It was received as an external authentication of the righteousness already obtained by Abraham through faith in the days of his uncircumcision (ver. 11).

(c) *Arg. from the Divine purpose,* εἰς τὸ εἶναι αὐτὸν πατέρα κ.τ.λ. Abraham was to be (i) *spiritual Father of all (uncircumcised) believers in Christ,* who believe in order that to them righteousness may be reckoned as it was to Abraham, and (ii) *spiritual Father of circumcised Jews,* who are not merely circumcised, but who also by believing in Christ follow in the steps of their as yet uncircumcised ancestor (vers. 11–12).

[*Obs.* 1. Order of events in Abraham's life. The question as to the range of the

Dogmatic: ch. IV, vv. 4-25.

μακαρισμός of David's Psalm in ver. 9 is an inference (οὖν) from its connection with what had previously been adduced about Abraham. After περιτομήν supply ἐστί (Meyer; Winer suggests λέγεται, Gr. N. T. p. 734) to complete the structure. The question ver. 9 is supposed to receive the answer, 'This congratulation rests upon the uncircumcised as well as the circumcised.' For this answer a reason follows, (γάρ) 'our assertion is that *faith* was reckoned to Abraham for righteousness'; and this by inference (οὖν) involves the further question, 'Under what circumstances (πῶς;) was it so reckoned?' Was Abraham, at the time, circumcised or uncircumcised? After ἐν ἀκροβυστίᾳ supply ὄντι.]

[*Obs.* 2. Circumcision is said to be (1) a σημεῖον, in Gen. xvii. 11 אוֹת־בְּרִית, a sign of the (already-made) covenant. For covenant S. Paul substitutes the δικαιοσύνη τῆς πίστεως. This was the real content of the בְּרִית with Abraham; what God promised was the Messianic inheritance, Gen. xv. 5-8, which was received by the faith (Gen. xv. 6) which God reckoned as righteousness. Note the difference between circumcision and Christian Baptism. Circumcision is the sign or warrant of a blessing previously received. But the Christian sacraments are 'effectual signs of grace and God's good-will towards us, by the which He *doth work invisibly in us*' (art. 25), and 'Baptism is a sign of Regeneration or new birth, whereby, as *by an instrument,* they that receive Baptism rightly are grafted into the Church' (art. 27). Circumcision is a 'signum merum'; Baptism is a 'signum efficax,' Acts xxii. 16 ἀναστὰς βάπτισαι καὶ ἀπόλουσαι τὰς ἁμαρτίας σου, ἐπικαλεσάμενος τὸ ὄνομα τοῦ Κυρίου: Eph. v. 26 καθαρίσας τῷ λουτρῷ τοῦ ὕδατος ἐν ῥήματι, ἵνα παραστήσῃ αὐτὴν ἑαυτῷ ἔνδοξον: 1 Cor.vi.11 ἀπελούσασθε...ἡγιάσθητε...ἐδικαιώθητε: Tit. iii. 5, 7 ἔσωσεν ἡμᾶς διὰ λουτροῦ παλιγγενεσίας: 1 S. Pet. iii. 21. Circumcision is (2) a σφραγίς or seal,—implying authentication. LXX, for חֹתָם, 'a seal ring,' from חתם, 'to seal,' 'to complete.' Hence it was attached to Jezebel's mandate, 1 Kings xxi. 8. The Corinthians were ἡ σφραγίς μου τῆς ἀποστολῆς to S. Paul, 1 Cor. ix. 2. The words 'The Lord knoweth them that are His' are a σφραγίς of the Church's foundation, 2 Tim. ii. 19. The σφραγὶς τοῦ Θεοῦ occurs in Rev. vii. 2, 3; ix. 4. Confirmation may be traced in 2 Cor. i. 22; Eph. i. 13; iv. 30. Circumcision was the authentication of the previously received δικαιοσύνη τῆς πίστεως which Abraham had received in his uncircumcised days. As a σημεῖον, Circumcision conferred nothing; as a σφραγίς, it implied an authentication from heaven of a gift already received. This gift is (observe the thrice repeated article) the '*already referred to* Righteousness of *that* faith (ver. 3) which existed in *that* state of uncircumcision' (ver. 12).]

[*Obs.* 3. The Divine *aim* of Abraham's σημεῖον ἔλαβε περιτομῆς is expressed in εἰς τὸ εἶναι κ.τ.λ. He was to be (1) the *spiritual father of all uncircumcised believers.* δι' ἀκροβυστίας, with foreskin : διά with gen. loosely used to denote that with which some one is furnished, ii. 27; xiv. 20. Winer, *Gr. N. T.* p. 475. In εἰς τὸ λογισθῆναι, the εἰς is again telic not ecbatic; the persons referred to believe on Jesus Christ in order that to them also righteousness might be reckoned. Abraham was to be also (2) *spiritual father of circumcised believers in Christ.* In πατέρα περιτομῆς observe the absence of the art.; *all* circumcised Jews were not really Abraham's children. He was to be father *to* those who were not merely of the body of circumcised persons, but who also imitated his faith in his uncircumcised days. Thus Abraham's taking the sign of circumcision as a seal of his faith was to have two effects: (1) It made him the spiritual father of all heathen converts to Christ; (2) It excluded *unbelieving* Jews, although circumcised, from the ranks of his spiritual children. τοῖς οὐκ ἐκ περιτομῆς, is a dat. of relation depending on πατέρα: τοῖς ἴχνεσι is a dat. of place, which, though rare in classics, has taken deep root in the New Testament, Winer, *Gr. N. T.* p. 274. For στοιχεῖν, 'to be or move in a line or file,' see Gal. v. 25; vi. 16; Phil. iii. 16. The construction is disturbed by the introduction of τοῖς before στοιχοῦσι, which is parallel to ἐκ περιτομῆς. This is not negligence of expression (Meyer), but a deliberate *oratio variata*, intended to emphasise the idea in στοιχοῦσι, although at the cost of structural regularity. Winer, *Gr. N. T.* p. 722. See Acts xx. 34; Eph. v. 33.]

III. χωρὶς νόμου. Abraham's justification was in no way connected with the gift of the Mosaic Law (13-16 a).

Arg. 1. *from the agency through which the Messianic ἐπαγγελία was given.* That agency was not the Mosaic Law, which as yet had not been proclaimed; it was the δικαιοσύνη πίστεως in Abraham which moved GOD to grant it (ver. 13).

[*Obs.* 1. ver. 13 assigns a reason (γάρ) for the statement that Abraham was to be spiritual father of all the faithful in Christ, circumcised or uncircumcised, and not of the circumcised Jews who rejected Him (ii. 6-12). The reason is that it was not the law, but the righteousness of faith which procured for Abraham and his descendants the promise of possessing the world. By τὸ σπέρμα τοῦ Ἀβραάμ are meant believers in Jesus Christ, the true spiritual posterity of Abraham, ix. 6 sqq.; Gal. iv. 22 sqq., and their Head and King, the seed who is Christ, Gal. iii. 16. The ἐπαγγελία is explained to be τὸ κληρονόμον αὐτὸν εἶναι τοῦ κόσμου. αὐτόν refers to Abraham as representing the σπέρμα. As to the κόσμος, GOD promised to Abraham and his posterity the land of Canaan: Gen. xii. 7; xiii. 14, 15; xv. 18; xvii. 8; xxii. 17; xxvi. 3; Exod. vi. 4. The Jewish doctors already widened this to mean Messianic sovereignty over the world of which Canaan was a type. The New Testament, however, based the world-wide inheritance of Christ, not merely on these passages, but on the explicit statements of the prophets, Ps. xxii, lxxii, &c. So our Lord, S. Matt. v. 5; xix. 28 sqq.; S. Luke xxii. 30; S. Matt. xxv. 21.]

[*Obs.* 2. δικαιοσύνη πίστεως, gen. subj., the righteousness which faith brings, as = δικαιοσύνη ἡ ἐκ πίστεως, Rom. ix. 30; x. 6; Winer, *Gr. N. T.* p. 232, but cf. p. 260, note 2.]

[*Obs.* 3. It is historically noteworthy that the ἐπαγγελία which assured inheritance of the world was given to Abraham before his δικαίωσις, viz. in the plain of Moreh, Gen. xii. 7, and after the parting from Lot, Gen. xiii. 14. But the Apostle is thinking of the more explicit promises, after the making the Covenant, Gen. xv. 18, and at the change of his name, Gen. xvii. 5. If in its earliest forms the ἐπαγγελία was given independently of Abraham's δικαιοσύνη ἐκ πίστεως, the argument that the Mosaic Law from first to last had nothing to do with this gift remains unaffected.]

Arg. 2. (reason, γάρ, for arg. 1) *from the opposition that exists between* νόμος *and* πίστις, *viewed abstractedly.* If the Jewish disciples of the Law inherit the Abrahamic promise, then it follows that (1) faith is rendered inoperative, and (2) the Promise, which is the object of faith, is done away with, i. e. Gen. xv. 6 is meaningless (ver. 14).

1st Reason (γάρ, ver. 15 a). The operation of the Law is entirely opposed to the genius of Faith. Faith looks to the Divine χάρις and to the ἐπαγγελία which is its expression in the human world. The Law placed before man, but disobeyed, produces GOD's wrath (15 a).

2nd Reason (reason γάρ, 15 b for Reason 1). Where there is no Law then transgression of the Law does not exist, to excite the wrath of GOD. Therefore it is the presence of the Law which produces GOD's wrath; and this result of the Law places it in sharp antithesis to πίστις and the promises (15 b).

[*Obs.* 1. The οἱ ἐκ νόμου are the adherents of the Mosaic Law, opposed to οἱ ἐκ πίστεως, Rom. iii. 26; Gal. iii. 7. If the Jewish adherents of Mosaism are right, the faith is emptied of its contents, κεκένωται, and so void and worthless; and the promise is brought to nothing, κατήργηται. The two cannot coexist. This essential opposition between νόμος and ἐπαγγελία is insisted on in Gal. iii. 18.]

[*Obs.* 2. The reason for the opposition between νόμος and πίστις is that the law in question (ὁ νόμος) produces the divine wrath; (while πίστις claims the divine χάρις in its concrete expression the ἐπαγγελία). The wrath of GOD, if not propitiated, takes a penal form, ii. 5 sqq.; iii. 5; ix. 22; Eph. ii. 3; Eph. v. 6.]

[*Obs.* 3. The truth of this κατεργάζεται ὀργήν of the Mosaic Law is found (γάρ) in the fact that when νόμος does not exist, then παράβασις cannot exist. παράβασις is the correlative of νόμος; παράβασις presupposes those limits of conduct which νόμος lays down, and which παράβασις passes over. This is a double argument from *cause to effect*. (1) When the cause, παράβασις, is wanting, then the effect, ὀργή, is wanting; (2) when the cause, νόμος, is wanting, then the effect, παράβασις, is wanting. Therefore (3) when νόμος is wanting, then ὀργή is wanting; in other words it is the νόμος which κατεργάζεται ὀργήν.]

[*Obs.* 4. The Apostle says οὐδὲ παράβασις, in accordance with the doctrine that human ἐπιθυμία is kindled into activity by the power of sin which exists in man, Rom. vii. 7 sqq.; 1 Cor. xv. 56; Gal. iii. 19. But he says here παράβασις not ἁμαρτία. παράβασις is ἁμαρτία relatively to the law: but ἁμαρτία might exist without νόμος, i. e. positive law. Cf. i. 18 sqq.; Eph. ii. 3. Sins against a *law given* are *transgressions*, and so specially provocative of the wrath of the Lawgiver. S. Paul only denies the presence of sin where there is no law, in a *relative* sense; the denial would not be *absolutely* true.]

[*Obs.* 5. With the *à priori* and abstract argument against the possibility that the ἐπαγγελία could have been given to Abraham διὰ νόμου, compare the *à posteriori* historical argument in Gal. iii. 15–22.]

Arg. 3. (inferred from preceding διὰ τοῦτο ver. 16) from the purpose of GOD in making the inheritance of the Messianic ἐπαγγελία depend on πίστις. This is that the κληρονόμοι may be heirs according to the principle of grace, κατὰ χάριν. For this principle there was a twofold reason. It was insisted on

(*a*) that the ἐπαγγελία might be *secure* (βεβαία). Under the νόμος it would have been *sub conditione obedientiae*, and so liable to forfeiture;

(*b*) that the ἐπαγγελία might be secured to the whole spiritual posterity of Abraham, παντὶ τῷ σπέρματι—not only to Christians who are converts from Judaism, but also to Christians who are converts from Heathenism, and whose descent from Abraham is based on their succeeding to Abraham's faith. This Divine purpose made it impossible that Abraham should have received the Messianic ἐπαγγελία through the agency of the Mosaic Law (ver. 16).

[*Obs.* 1. In ver. 16 the structure is incomplete. After διὰ τοῦτο ἐκ πίστεως supply ἐστὶν ἡ κληρονομία, and after ἵνα supply ᾖ. Winer, *Gr. N. T.* p. 747. Ver. 16 is an inference (διὰ τοῦτο) from ver. 15. It follows from the effect of the law in operating wrath, and thus becoming incapable of being the condition of the κληρονομία, that the latter must result from the antithesis of the law, viz. from πίστις. With ἵνα κατὰ χάριν, by way of grace, not merit; cf. ver. 4, where χάρις is contrasted with ὀφείλημα, and iii. 24 δωρεάν. βεβαία only here in S. Paul and 2 Cor. i. 7, where it is applied to ἐλπίς. It means firm under the feet (βαίνω). This security would be imperilled if inheritance of the promise really rested on obedience to the details of the Mosaic Law.]

B. Positive import of Gen. xv. 6 (16 b–25).

I. Qualities which secured to Abraham's faith its justifying power (16 b–22).

1. *Preliminary.* The lofty character of Abraham's faith is implied in the spiritual Fatherhood of all the faithful to which he was appointed, Gen. xvii. 5 (16–17).

[*Obs.* The title πατέρα πάντων ἡμῶν as applied to Abraham is condensed from ver. 11 πατέρα πάντων τῶν πιστευόντων δι' ἀκροβυστίας, and ver. 12 πατέρα περιτομῆς .... τοῖς στοιχοῦσι τοῖς ἴχνεσιν τῆς ἐν τῇ ἀκροβυστίᾳ πίστεως τοῦ πατρὸς ἡμῶν Ἀβραάμ. All believers are through Christ spiritual sons of Abraham, and his heirs, because his sons.]

Gen. xvii. 5 quoted to show that Abraham is the spiritual Father of all believers (ver. 17).

Heb. כִּי אַב־הֲמוֹן גּוֹיִם נְתַתִּיךָ
LXX ὅτι πατέρα πολλῶν ἐθνῶν τέθεικά σε.

[*Obs.* 1. הָמוֹן, 'a multitude,' is somewhat weakened by LXX πολλῶν. This promise gives the reason for the substitution of אַבְרָהָם, 'father of the multitude' (נְרָהָם?=Arab. ruhâm,'multitude') for אַבְרָם, 'high father.' Abraham was to be the ancestor of a multitude of גּוֹיִם, not merely עַמִּים, i. e. of a posterity including Gentile peoples, as well as the tribes of Israel. The promise is understood spiritually by the Apostle ; οὐ κατὰ τὴν φυσικὴν συγγενείαν, ἀλλὰ κατὰ οἰκείωσιν πίστεως S. Chrys. The temporal promise is typical of the spiritual.]

[*Obs.* 2. This promise was given with Abraham's new name and the rite of circumcision fourteen years after the covenant of Gen. xv. 6. God revealed Himself as El Shaddai, God the Mighty One (שָׁדַד, 'to be strong') ; as possessing the power to realise His promises, even when the order of nature gave no prospect of their fulfilment. This name, El Shaddai, is not simply identical with God the Creator ; it refers to God's action in the sphere of salvation, and especially to the miraculous quickening of the physical powers of Abraham, then 99 years old, and of Sarah, so that they became the parents of a numerous posterity. Keil, *in loc.*

2. Specific characteristics of Abraham's faith. It is typical ; and is viewed,

(1) *Relatively to the Divine Omnipotence.* It is, primarily, belief in Him Who quickens the dead, and Who treats the non-existent as if it existed.

[*Obs.* 1. Abraham, as πατὴρ πάντων ἡμῶν, stands in the sacred narrative, Gen. xvii. 5, face to face with God. κατέναντι = class. κατενάντιον, in meaning = κατενώπιον, for לִפְנֵי־יְהוָה. In that solemn moment of his history Abraham, as the father of all Christians, stood before God, before Whom he believed. On the attraction see Winer, *Gr. N. T.* p. 204.]

[*Obs.* 2. God as the object of Abraham's faith is (1) ζωοποιῶν τοὺς νεκρούς. This is a special exercise of the omnipotence of God, 1 Sam. ii. 6 ; Wisd. xvi. 13 ; Deut. xxxii. 39 ; S. John v. 21 ; 2 Cor. i. 9 ; 1 Tim. vi. 13. The expression refers, not to Isaac, but to Abraham's σῶμα ἤδη νενεκρωμένον, and to the νέκρωσις of Sarah's womb. God is also (2) καλῶν τὰ μὴ ὄντα ὡς ὄντα, uttering His controlling word over that which is known not to exist as if it existed. καλεῖν, like קרא, is used of the call of a Ruler addressed to that which is subject to his power, Ps. l. 1 ; Is. xl. 26. In τὰ μὴ ὄντα, God is conceived of as knowing that that which He calls does not exist. The expression refers to Gen. xv. 6 ; when the Lord pointed to the stars and 'said unto him, So shall thy seed be.'

(2) *Relatively to natural probabilities.* It was opposed to anything that could be reasonably expected, παρ' ἐλπίδα. Yet it was based

on hope, ἐπ' ἐλπίδι, i. e. subjective hope. Thus it led Abraham to act with a view to carrying out the purpose of GOD intimated in the promise that his posterity would be as numerous as the stars and the grains of sand, Gen. xv. 5, xiii. 16 (ver. 18).

[*Obs.* That Abraham had no natural grounds for expecting a posterity appears from Gen. xvii. 17 'Then Abraham fell upon his face and laughed, and said in his heart, Shall a child be born unto him that is an hundred years old? and shall Sarah that is ninety years old bear?' In παρ' ἐλπίδα .... ἐπ' ἐλπίδι observe the oxymoron. The clause εἰς τὸ γενέσθαι κ.τ.λ. expressed the divinely intended purpose of Abraham's ἐπίστευσεν;—Abraham's faith led him so to act as to give effect to this purpose.]

Gen. xv. 5 quoted as showing the great range of the promise which was the object of Abraham's faith.

Heb. פֹּה יִהְיֶה זַרְעֶךָ

LXX οὕτως ἔσται τὸ σπέρμα σου.

[*Obs.* οὕτως, viz. ὡς οἱ ἀστέρες τοῦ οὐρανοῦ, not καὶ ἡ ἄμμος τῆς θαλάσσης, which is imported from Gen. xiii. 16. The Apostle supposes his readers to be familiar with the form of οὕτως in such a connection.]

(3) *Relatively to physical obstacles, suggested by the senses.*

(*a*) Abraham's mental attitude towards these obstacles,

(i) *subjective,* μὴ ἀσθενήσας τῇ πίστει. He was not conscious of any weakening in faith.

(ii) *objective,* οὐ κατενόησεν. He did not fix his mind on them (ver. 19 a).

(*b*) What the obstacles were,

(i) the decay of his physical powers, σῶμα νενεκρωμένον:

(ii) his age, approximately (που) 100, really 99, which might well have led him to consider his σῶμα νενεκρωμένον as a decisive difficulty:

(iii) Sarah's νέκρωσις τῆς μήτρας (ver. 19 b).

[*Obs.* 1. The participial clause μὴ ἀσθενήσας κ.τ.λ. explains οὐ κατενόησεν κ.τ.λ. Because Abraham did not feel any weakness of faith, he did not give attention to the physical obstacles which might have impeded it. μή does not stand for οὐ; (Winer. *Gr. N. T.* p. 610, says μὴ ἀσθενήσας represents a conception to be denied, οὐ κατενόησε, a fact to be denied). The οὐ is wanting before κατενόησεν in A.B.C.ℵ, &c. and is omitted by Lachmann and Tischendorf. But it ought probably to be retained, as the omission would have arisen from a desire to harmonize the verse with Gen. xvii. 17. The οὐ κατενόησεν refers to Gen. xv. 5, 6, where after the promise of a posterity as numerous as the stars, Abraham ἐπίστευσεν τῷ Θεῷ. The hesitation of Abraham, fourteen years later, described in Gen. xvii. 17, is well compared by Meyer, al., to the doubts which S. John the Baptist entertained respecting the Messiahship of our Lord (S. Matt. xi. 2 sqq.) after an earlier period of faith. Observe the *meiosis* in μὴ ἀσθενήσας: Abraham's faith was very robust.]

[*Obs.* 2. νενεκρωμένον, like νέκρωσις, is used of the decay and death of the physical powers of procreation and conception; cf. Heb. xi. 12. που implies that ἑκατονταέτης is approximately, but not quite, exact; Abraham was 99, Gen. xvii. 1. 17; xxi. 5. Shem was the last person who had begotten children at 100. Abraham's later children by Keturah (Gen. xxv. 1 sqq.) imply that the physical restoration of his powers continued after the death of Sarah. The οὐ κατενόησεν extends to both the objects of the sentence; καὶ τὴν νέκρωσιν brings the second object under it. νέκρωσις is used as equivalent to θάνατος at 2 Cor. iv. 10: here μήτρα νενεκρωμένη is meant by the expression. Sarah was 90 years of age, Gen. xvii. 17, fourteen years after the incident here referred to; therefore 76 at the time.]

(4) *Relatively to the* ἐπαγγελία τοῦ Θεοῦ,

(i) (negatively described). Absence of indecision (οὐ διεκρίθη) caused by unbelief (τῇ ἀπιστίᾳ, instrumental dat.) (ver. 20).

(ii) (positively described). Invigoration (ἐνεδυναμώθη) through faith (τῇ πίστει, not dat. of exact definition, but of cause) (ver. 20).

This is shown by

(a) Abraham's giving glory to GOD, by recognising His almightiness (ver. 20).

(b) His complete satisfaction respecting GOD's power of making good His Word (ver. 21).

[*Obs.* 1. On the form of εἰς in εἰς δὲ τὴν ἐπαγγελίαν, as = 'with respect to,' see Winer, *Gr. N. T.* 496. The negative statement introduced by δέ (= autem) explains the negative proposition of ver. 19 more fully. With reference to the Divine promise, Abraham did not waver (οὐ διεκρίθη), through unbelief (τῇ ἀπιστίᾳ, dat. of instrumental cause), see Meyer *in loc.* Indecision as to spiritual things has its roots in unbelief: as spiritual vigour is a product of faith. Hence ἐνεδυναμώθη τῇ πίστει. τῇ πίστει seems to glance at τῇ ἀπιστίᾳ and to be like it a *dat. of the cause*, rather than at μὴ ἀσθενήσας τῇ πίστει, ver. 10. Unbelief is not the product of intellectual doubts; but doubts are the result of the loss of faith.]

[*Obs.* 2. The invigoration of Abraham's faith is illustrated in the participial clauses which follow, and which describe actions and states of mind, simultaneous with and not antecedent to the ἐνεδυναμώθη. Abraham 'gave glory' to GOD in the sphere of thought; such 'glory' may be given by words or acts. δόξα is the sum of the attributes or characteristics of GOD.

διδόναι δόξαν is to ascribe to GOD His true character, as the Almighty, the all holy, the all merciful, the all true, as in Josh. vii. 19; 1 Chron. xvi. 29; Is. xlii. 8; S. Luke xvii. 18; S. John ix. 24; Acts xii. 23. The way in which Abraham gave glory to GOD is expressed by πληροφορηθείς, viz. by being fully convinced of GOD'S power to perform His promises. For πληροφορεῖν as applied to *persons*, see xiv. 5; Col. iv. 12, and Dr. Vaughan's note *in loc.* ἐπήγγελται, middle in sense, Winer, *Gr. N. T.* p. 328.]

§ Result of vers. 17–21. Since Abraham's faith was of this character, it was also reckoned to him for righteousness (ver. 22).

[*Obs.* The subject of ἐλογίσθη is the fact that Abraham believed or rather his faith. The justification of the διό lies in the whole negative as well as the positive exposition of Gen. xv. 6 quoted at ver. 3. Abraham's faith involved positively the submission of his understanding to the revelation of GOD (ver. 17 b), and of his will to the Will of GOD (ver. 18), while by implication it rested on One who is not here named by the Apostle expressly, but whose Person and Advent were the contents of the ἐπαγγελία.]

II. Bearing of the Old Testament account of Abraham's justification on the justification of Christians (23–25).

1. *True purpose of the narrative of Gen.* xv. 6. The statement that Abraham's faith was reckoned to him for righteousness (ἐλογίσθη αὐτῷ) was written down, not simply to describe an incident in *his* life (δι' αὐτόν), but also to teach a truth which holds good *of us Christians*, his spiritual children (δι' ἡμᾶς) (ver. 23).

2. Object of the faith which shall be reckoned as righteousness to believing Christians. It is directed towards GOD, as having raised Jesus our Lord from the dead (ver. 24).

§ Reason for the Resurrection of Christ being the object of justifying faith. Christ rose from the dead to make our δικαίωσις possible.

(*a*) He was delivered to death (παρεδόθη) as an ἱλαστήριον, on account of our offences; but this, the objective result of His death, could not have been subjectively appropriated by us, if it had not been followed by some act making this possible. Hence,

(*b*) He was raised again, on account of our δικαίωσις, viz. to make it possible, not merely as warranting faith in the atoning value of his death, but also as making Him, in His Risen Life, a new Life-principle for us, by union with whom our δικαίωσις is secured (ver. 25).

[*Obs*. 1. The statement that Abraham's spiritual history, like his person, has a typical value for all time, is made in Bereschith Rabba 40. 8 'Quicquid scriptum est de Abrahamo, scriptum est de filiis ejus.' Philo Jud. *De Abrahamo*, p. 350, says of the three patriarchs that their virtues have come to be inscribed in (ἐστηλιτεῦσθαι) our sacred books, not in behalf of their own praise but on account of those to whom it should fall to exhort and guide to a zeal for the same. Compare for this principle of the permanent value of Scripture, Rom. xv. 4 ὅσα γὰρ προεγράφη, εἰς τὴν ἡμετέραν διδασκαλίαν ἐγράφη : 1 Cor. ix. 10 ἢ δι' ἡμᾶς πάντως λέγει; δι' ἡμᾶς γὰρ ἐγράφη : 1 Cor. x. 11 ἐγράφη δὲ πρὸς νουθεσίαν ἡμῶν.]

[*Obs*. 2. When faith is said λογίζεσθαι εἰς δικαιοσύνην in the case of Abraham or of Christians, this means that it is imputed or reckoned as righteousness, but it does *not* mean, as is often assumed, that it is imputed or reckoned without being imparted. See above on iv. 6 and cf. with vers. 19-24; S. James ii. 21-23.]

[*Obs*. 3. Abraham's faith corresponds with that of Christians, (1) as to *its Object*, which is (*a*) the omnipotence of GOD, and (*b*) the Messiah, in one case expected, in the other already come; and (2) on its *formal side*; it accepts the quickening, (*a*) in Abraham's case of his σῶμα ἤδη νενεκρωμένον, and (*b*) in our Lord's of His Body in the grave. As Abraham became through the quickening of his bodily powers the ancestor of a numerous posterity; so Christ, by His Resurrection became the father of the family of justified believers in Him.]

[*Obs*. 4. The central object on which justifying faith gazes is the Resurrection of Christ,—and not, as is often popularly stated, Christ's Atoning Death; cf. x. 9 καὶ πιστεύσῃς ἐν τῇ καρδίᾳ σου ὅτι ὁ Θεὸς αὐτὸν ἤγειρεν ἐκ νεκρῶν : 1 S. Pet. i. 21 πιστοὺς εἰς Θεὸν τὸν ἐγείραντα αὐτὸν ἐκ νεκρῶν. Faith in the Resurrection of Jesus 'puts the soul into contact with the whole body of the faith' (Sadler, *Justification*, ed. 2. p. 82); it is the 'doctrine which is most immediate to us, in which Christ most closely approaches us, from which we gain life, and out of which issue our hopes and our duties,' Newman, *Justification*, Lecture IX. p. 222.]

[*Obs*. 5. The word παρεδόθη, implying our Lord's abandonment to death (viii. 32), is taken from Is. liii. 12, and is used sometimes as here and S. Matt. xvii. 22 without reference to an agent, or with reference to the action of Judas (S. Matt. x. 4), the chief priests (S Mark xv. 1), the Jewish people (Acts iii. 13), Pilate (S. Matt. xxvii. 26). The verb is also used of the action of the Eternal Father (viii. 32) ὑπὲρ ἡμῶν πάντων παρέδωκεν αὐτόν, and of our Lord's own act of self-surrender; Eph. v. 2, 25 παρέδωκεν ἑαυτὸν ὑπὲρ ἡμῶν : Gal. ii. 20 παραδόντος ἑαυτὸν ὑπὲρ ἐμοῦ. It implies the surrender of self-control 'which is involved in submission to sufferings and death at the hands of another.' Our Lord voluntarily became ὑπήκοος μέχρι θανάτου Phil. ii. 8.]

[*Obs*. 6. In διὰ τὰ παραπτώματα and διὰ τὴν δικαίωσιν, διά is used in both cases as '*for the sake of*,' but with distinct modifications. 'For the sake of our offences, to take them away. For the sake of our justification, to secure it.' Comp. xiii. 5 οὐ μόνον διὰ τὴν ὀργήν, i. e. to avoid it, ἀλλὰ καὶ διὰ τὴν συνείδησιν, i. e. to keep it in good order. The connection here stated between (1) Christ's death and the forgiveness of offences, and (2) Christ's Resurrection and our δικαίωσις, is not 'an antithesis of words with no antithesis of meaning.' Sin and death, justification and resurrection are cognate terms. Christ died, objectively, to put our sins away, as an ἱλαστήριον, iii. 24 sqq. ; v. 8. But in order to produce in man subjectively the new Life of Righteousness, the Resurrection is necessary, (a) as warranting the value of the atonement and so making faith possible, and (b) as implying the gift of a new and divine principle of life ready to be communicated to any who is willing to receive it. This μερισμός cannot be paralleled with that between δικαιοσύνη and σωτηρία in Rom. x. 10, although there the complete result σωτηρία corresponds with the greater effort. It is well illustrated in Sadler, *Justification*, pp. 79, 80.]

[*Obs.* 7. δικαίωσις, in LXX a sentence in law (= מִשְׁפָּט, Lev. xxiv. 22), and used for a legal claim often in Thucydides, is in the New Testament used in a sense regulated by that of δικαιόω. Hence it means either *acquittal* (as just), or the *making just*. It occurs here and in v. 18, where it is opposed to κατάκριμα.]

D.

Happiness of the justified ἐκ πίστεως (V. 1–11).

I. The Peace towards GOD, in which they live through Our Lord Jesus Christ (ver. 1).

[*Obs.* 1. οὖν, ver. 1, refers to the whole section, iii. 31—iv. 25. The justification dates from (ἐκ) the beginning of the life of faith. Having been justified by faith, Christians possess (ἔχομεν not ἔχωμεν, see Meyer, App. Crit.) peace in relation to GOD. εἰρήνη is here the actual state of reconciliation with GOD, as opposed to the state of enmity with Him (cf. ἐχθροί ver. 10) which preceded it ; cf. εἰρήνη apud Cremer. This meaning of the word implies, but must not be confounded with, *the sense* of being at peace in the man himself, because he is at peace with the author of his life, the εἰρήνη τοῦ Θεοῦ ἡ ὑπερέχουσα πάντα νοῦν Phil. iv. 7 ; Col. iii. 15. For the use of πρός as marking a moral attitude, see Acts ii. 47 χάριν πρὸς ὅλον τὸν λαόν : xxiv. 16 ἀπρόσκοπον συνείδησιν πρὸς τὸν Θεὸν καὶ τοὺς ἀνθρώπους.]

[*Obs.* 2. Our Lord Jesus Christ is the cause of this peace. He is ἡ εἰρήνη ἡμῶν Eph. ii. 14. For ἐλθὼν εὐηγγελίσατο εἰρήνην ὑμῖν τοῖς μακρὰν καὶ εἰρήνην τοῖς ἐγγύς ver. 17. This peace is a result of reconciliation, Eph. ii. 16, 17, effected by Christ.]

II. The state of grace (ver. 2) into which Christ has given the introduction, and in which living Christians remain.

[*Obs.* 1. Probably προσαγωγή is best explained by reference to the usage of courts, whereby approach to the sovereign could only be obtained through a προσαγωγεύς, sequester, admissionalis. Lamprid. *in Alex. Sever.* 4. It means in the New Testament not *power of access*, but *actual leading towards*, a person; Eph. ii. 18; iii. 12. This introduction Christians have had and have, ἐσχήκαμεν, in virtue of their faith (τῇ πίστει).]

[*Obs.* 2. Grace is here conceived of as a sphere or state, with definite frontiers, which are passed when men enter it, or fall from it. The idea of the state of grace is not scholastic; but biblical. Cf. Gal. v. 4 τῆς χάριτος ἐξεπέσατε: 1 Pet. v. 12 ταύτην εἶναι ἀληθῆ χάριν τοῦ Θεοῦ εἰς ἣν ἐστήκατε. Cf. Newman's sermon 'on the State of Grace,' *Par. Serm.* vol. iv. s. 9.]

III. The Hope of future glory, as the ground of religious exultation (ver. 2).

[*Obs.* 1. καυχᾶσθαι with ἐπί alone here in the New Testament. But cf. Prov. xxv. 14; Ecclus. xxx. 2. Generally with ἐν as ver. 3. The word is used, sometimes, in a bad sense, of a proud boasting in something as one's own, sometimes, in a good sense, of thankful rejoicing in GOD's presence or gifts; as here. Cf. 1 Cor. iv. 7 τί καυχᾶσαι ὡς μὴ λαβών; for ἐπ' ἐλπίδι cf. iv. 18.]

[*Obs.* 2. The object of hope is the future δόξα τοῦ Θεοῦ in which the blessed shall hereafter share; 'qualem nobis suo divino munere impertit [Deus] tanquam filiis ad haereditatem adoptatis,' Justiniani. 1 Thess. ii. 12 GOD has called us εἰς τὴν ἑαυτοῦ βασιλείαν καὶ δόξαν: Rom. viii. 17 ἵνα καὶ συνδοξασθῶμεν: viii. 21 εἰς τὴν ἐλευθερίαν τῆς δόξης τῶν τέκνων τοῦ Θεοῦ. In iii. 23 τῆς δόξης τοῦ Θεοῦ means the moral glory of which through grace man is capable in this life.]

[*Obs.* 3. ἐλπίς, which is the basis of exultation in the inner life of the justified, is the subject of vers. 3-10.]

§ Of the ἐλπὶς τῆς δόξης τοῦ Θεοῦ (3-10).

A. *Growth of this ἐλπίς amidst external troubles* (vers. 3-4).

This is introduced by the statement that Christians exult, not merely in the hope of future glory, but in present afflictions.

Reason for this exultation in afflictions. It promotes ἐλπίς by a gradual process, of which the stages are,

(1) θλῖψις, 'outward affliction.' Affliction, borne in faith, which survives and looks beyond the troubles of the hour, works out (ver. 3).

(2) ὑπομονήν, 'persevering endurance.' This in turn achieves (ver. 4),

(3) δοκιμήν, 'proved experience.' Yet, as the Christian is tried, he is thrown forward for support upon the unseen future, and this creates (ver. 4),

(4) ἐλπίδα, which is thus the product of θλῖψις (ver. 4).

[*Obs.* 1. (ver. 3.) For the incomplete structure οὐ μόνον δὲ (καυχώμεθα ἐπ' ἐλπίδι τῆς δόξης) ἀλλὰ καὶ (καυχώμεθα κ.τ.λ.) cf. Winer, *Gr. N. T.* p. 729. Cf. ver. 11; viii. 23; ix. 10; 2 Cor. viii. 19. Observe the ἀπροσδόκητον in passing from the ἐλπὶς τῆς δόξης as a ground of (ἐπί) exultation to θλίψεις as a sphere (ἐν) of exultation. Seneca (*de Prov.* iv. 4) 'gaudent magni viri rebus adversis, non aliter quam fortes milites bellis triumphant.']

[*Obs.* 2. ὑπομονήν, 'endurance,' in the Christian faith and life, ii. 7 ὑπομονὴν ἔργου ἀγαθοῦ : S. Matt. x. 22 ὁ δὲ ὑπομείνας εἰς τέλος, οὗτος σωθήσεται, repeated at xxiv. 13. θλῖψις can only have this effected in the justified whose faith is the governing principle of life; if θλῖψις did not work out ὑπομονή, the failure would imply loss of living faith.]

[*Obs.* 3. δοκιμήν, 'tried experience'; 2 Cor. ii. 9; viii. 2 ἐν πολλῇ δοκιμῇ θλίψεως: xiii. 3 δοκιμὴν ζητεῖτε τοῦ ἐν ἐμοὶ λαλοῦντος Χριστοῦ: Phil. ii. 22. To fail in this is to become ἀδόκιμος—S. James i. 2, 3 corresponds with this passage; τὸ δοκίμιον τῆς πίστεως there answers to S. Paul's θλῖψις, which has a *vim probandi*; thus it κατεργάζεται ὑπομονήν. To the ἔργον τέλειον of ὑπομονή in S. James belong the δοκιμή and ἐλπίς of the present passage.]

[*Obs.* 4. ἐλπίς, i.e. of the future glory, cf. v. 2. Hope does not exist for the first time after the δοκιμή of endurance under affliction; but it gains new strength from such δοκιμή. It is 'the highest subjective blessing' of the justified person.]

B. *Warrant of the reality of the object of* ἐλπίς (5–8).

This hope does not put us to shame (οὐ καταισχύνει) by disappointing us.

(*a*) *Subjective Reason.* The Love of GOD for us is poured out like a stream within our hearts, by the agency of the Holy Spirit, given unto us. The *sense* of GOD's love for us makes us certain that our hope will not fail of its object (ver. 5).

[*Obs.* In ἡ ἀγάπη τοῦ Θεοῦ, the gen. τοῦ Θεοῦ is a *gen. subj.*, cf. τὴν ἑαυτοῦ ἀγάπην ver. 8; S. Chrys. and others. Cf. Winer, *Gr. N. T.* 232, who compares Rom. viii. 35; 2 Cor. v. 14; Eph. iii. 19. But the phrase means the love of man *to* GOD, (*gen. obj.*) in S. John v. 42; 1 S. John ii. 5, 15; iii. 17; 2 Thess. iii. 5. The Holy Spirit is the personified love of GOD; as He is the uncreated bond of love between the Father and the Son, so does He unite the Father to all who through Redemption and Justification are members of the Son. Of the three natural symbols of His action, wind, fire, and water, the verb ἐκχεεῖν belongs to the latter; His descent is like a stream from the skies; cf. Joel ii. 28 ἐκχεῶ ἀπὸ τοῦ Πνεύματός μου: Zech. xii. 10 ἐκχεῶ ἐπὶ τὸν οἶκον Δαυίδ . . . . πνεῦμα χάριτος καὶ οἰκτιρμοῦ: Acts ii. 17, 18, 33; Tit. iii. 5, 6 ἀνακαινώσεως Πνεύματος Ἁγίου, οὗ ἐξέχεεν ἐφ' ἡμᾶς πλουσίως . . . The passage occurs here and Acts x. 45. The sense of GOD's love for us,—which love He has poured into our hearts—assures us that we shall not be disappointed of the object of our hope. Thus the Spirit is the ἀρραβών of the expected δόξα, 2 Cor. i. 22; v. 5.]

(*b*) Objective fact,—independent of our sense of GOD's love for us, and attesting its reality,—viz. that Christ ἀπέθανε. Here are stated,

Dogmatic: ch. V, vv. 1-11.

(i) The *object* and *opportuneness* of Christ's Death (ver. 6).

(a) He died on behalf of us, still weak as we were, and impious, ἔτι ... ἀσθενῶν ... ὑπὲρ ἀσεβῶν (ver. 6).

(b) He died, when the due time had come, κατὰ καιρόν (ver. 6).

[*Obs.* 1. On the misplacement of ἔτι (ver. 6) which belongs to ὄντων see Winer, *Gr. N. T.* p. 652: ('through some inadvertence, or rather because the ancients having only sympathising and intelligent readers in view were not anxious about minute precision'); cf. 1 Cor. xiv. 7; Gal. iii. 15. It is a trace of the change of the originally intended form of a sentence in the process of dictation. γάρ (as in vers. 6 and 7) never stands for the adversative 'but.' In ver. 6 γάρ gives a reason for the ἀγάπη τοῦ Θεοῦ ver. 5; it manifests itself in Christ's dying for sinners. Winer, *Gr. N. T.* p. 568.]

[*Obs.* 2. The *condition* of those, on whose behalf Christ died, is expressed by (1) ἀσθενεῖς, 'without spiritual force.' The sinful condition is thus characterised, in order to account for the pitying interference of GOD's saving Love. (2) ἀσεβῶν (ver. 6) 'without piety towards GOD.' (3) ἁμαρτωλῶν (ver. 8) so acting as to miss the true aim of life. (4) ἐχθροί (ver. 10) 'enemies' to GOD.]

[*Obs.* 3. The *satisfactio vicaria* of Christ's death is implied in, although not distinctly expressed by, ὑπέρ. The general force of ὑπέρ is *in commodum*; not *instead of, loco*; except, possibly, in Gal. iii. 13; 2 Cor. v. 14; 1 Pet. iii. 18. For S. Paul (1) exchanges ὑπέρ with περί, but never uses ἀντί in place of it; and (2) both with ὑπέρ and περί he puts a *genitive* of the thing ἁμαρτιῶν, as well as of the person, viii. 3; 1 Cor. xv. 3, in which case a substitutionary relation is impossible. ὑπέρ expresses the benefit of Christ's death; its vicariousness is taught by the terms ἱλαστήριον iii. 25; θυσία Eph. v. 2; and ἀντίλυτρον 1 Tim. ii. 6. It is, however, to be noted that the later Greeks used περί where the more distinct ἀντί would have been employed in earlier days; cf. Passow, *Lex. s. v.*]

[*Obs.* 4. The *opportuneness* of Christ's death is expressed by κατὰ καιρόν. He died when the hour of man's necessity had struck. The Divine ἀνοχή (iii. 26) had been worn out by the accumulated sins of men. This was the πλήρωμα τῶν καιρῶν Eph. i. 10; Gal. iv. 4. Cf. καιροῖς ἰδίοις 1 Tim. ii. 6; vi. 15.]

(ii) The *moral elevation* of Christ's Death as estimated by comparison with ordinary human generosity (vers. 7, 8).

(a) Scarcely will any one die even of a δίκαιος (ver. 7).

(b) Possibly a case may be found of self-immolation for the ἀγαθός, the man of attractive goodness (ver. 7).

(c) The Love which GOD bears towards us is recommended by Christ's dying for us, when we were yet ἁμαρτωλοί (ver. 8).

[*Obs.* 1. In ver. 7 the first γάρ introduces an illustration which furnishes a reason for the reality of the ἀγάπη τοῦ Θεοῦ. δικαίου (ver. 7) contrasts with ἀσεβῶν (ver. 6). The second γάρ proves the rule, by admitting a possible exception.

For the man of attractive goodness some one may possibly *dare* to die. Tittmann, *Syn. N. T.* p. 19 'In voce ἀγαθός cogitatur bonum seu commodum, quod ex re aut persona bona nascitur; sed δίκαιον est quod tale est, quale esse oportet, nullâ ratione habitâ utrum commodum an malum afferat.' τάχα expresses possibly not without doubt. Ewald compares the rescue of Jonathan by the people when condemned to death by lot for taking the honey, 1 Sam. xiv. 45, and Jonathan's interposition with Saul on behalf of David, 1 Sam. xx. 28.]

[*Obs*. 2. In συνίστησι (GOD proves, cf. iii. 5) remark the lasting effect of our Lord's atoning death, as setting forth the Love of GOD. GOD's own Love, τὴν ἑαυτοῦ ἀγάπην, is authenticated in the death of Christ, for us as sinners. ἁμαρτωλῶν contrasts with ἀγαθοῦ.]

Hence,

C. *Forms which* ἐλπίς *takes in the mind of the justified* (vers. 9, 10).

[*Obs*. Its λογισμός takes the shape of an argument *a majori ad minus*. The logic of Christian hope argues, 'if Christ has already died to save us, and placed us in a state of salvation, *much more* will He complete His work.' πολλῷ μᾶλλον expresses an enhancement of certainty as to that which follows. When Estius and others regard these as arguments *a minori ad majus*, they (1) confine their view to the receiver of Justification, and (2) overlook the force of πολλῷ μᾶλλον.]

(a) *Form* 1. Having been justified in *His* blood, we feel an additional certainty (πολλῷ μᾶλλον) of being saved by *Him* from the Wrath of GOD hereafter (ver. 9).

[*Obs*. 1. He who has done the greater work in giving His Son, will certainly do the less. The greater was the sacrifice of the Son of GOD for sinful men; the less is the completion of that work by the salvation of those for whom the sacrifice was offered. Cf. the argument, viii. 32 ὅς γε τοῦ ἰδίου υἱοῦ οὐκ ἐφείσατο ... πῶς οὐχὶ καὶ σὺν αὐτῷ τὰ πάντα ἡμῖν χαρίσεται; S. Aug. *in psalm.* cxviii (cxix) 'Plus est jam quod fecit Deus quam quod promisit. Quid fecit? Mortuus est pro te. Quid promisit? Ut vivas cum illo.']

[*Obs*. 2. Our justification is contained in (ἐν) the Life Blood of Jesus Christ. In ἀπὸ τῆς ὀργῆς, ὀργή is a technical word as in ii. 5; iii. 5; cf. 1 Thess. i. 10. This σωθησόμεθα is conditioned by the correspondence of our wills to GOD's grace; it is a moral, not a mechanical certainty which the future expresses.]

(b) *Form* 2. (*expansion and justification*, γάρ, *of Form* 1). Having been enemies of GOD, yet reconciled to Him, by the Death of His Son, we have an additional certainty that being reconciled we shall be saved by union with Christ's Glorified Life.

[*Obs*. 1. ἐχθροὶ Θεοῦ, *passive*, 'enemies of GOD'; as θεοστυγεῖς i. 30; τέκνα ὀργῆς Eph. ii. 3, and not merely hostile to GOD; Christ's death removed GOD's enmity against man, and man's enmity against GOD only ceased, as a moral consequence of faith. καταλλαγέντες and κατηλλάγημεν must, therefore, be understood to express, not merely the reconciliation of the moral nature of the Christian with GOD, but the new relation of GOD to man in Christ which made this possible. The argument is, 'If the death of Jesus effected our reconciliation, much more must His Glorified Life complete our deliverance.' The living Jesus cannot leave the work effected by His death incomplete.]

[*Obs.* 2. This second 'form' of ἐλπίς differs from the first in that Christ's Glorified Life, *as well as* His Death, is expressly mentioned as justifying the πολλῷ μᾶλλον of the argumentative inference. For the Life-giving power of Christ's Life in glory, cf. S. John xiv. 19; 2 Cor. iv. 10, 11; Phil. iii. 10, where τὴν δύναμιν τῆς ἀναστάσεως αὐτοῦ refers to the quickening power of His Risen Body.]

IV. Triumphant joy in GOD, through Jesus Christ, by Whose agency we have even in this life received the Reconciliation (ver. 11).

[*Obs.* 1. The construction is best completed thus, οὐ μόνον δὲ καταλλαγέντες ἀλλὰ καὶ καυχώμενοι. The *part.* καυχώμενοι necessarily suggests this. Winer, however, would supply σωθησόμεθα after οὐ μόνον δέ, Gr. N. T. p. 441. διὰ τοῦ Κυρίου. This joy is not merely brought about by Christ, but it is offered through Him. νῦν contrasts not Christian with pre-Christian ages,—but this life with the future beyond the grave.]

[*Obs.* 2. καταλλαγή, κατηλλάγημεν, καταλλαγέντες must be taken passively, not merely or chiefly actively. The reconciliation is accomplished, not only in the hearts of men, but in the Heart of GOD. Men are reconciled with GOD in Christ, in such sense, that GOD, seeing them in union with His Beloved and Perfect Son, abandons His just wrath which their sins have kindled, and admits them to His favour and blessing. This, the constant faith of the Church, was scientifically worked out by S. Anselm of Canterbury in his *Cur Deus homo*. Christ died 'to reconcile His Father to us' (Art. ii). Abelard taught a 'subjective and merely psychological reconciliation,' which Socinianism and some modern schools have insisted on to the exclusion of the truth of an Objective Atonement. They plead that the Eternal and Unchanging Love of GOD needs no reconciliation or atonement; that *only man* has needed to be reconciled, because man does not believe in the Love of GOD; that Christ's death is a token of GOD's enduring love, addressed to the hearts of men, in order to awaken confidence in the Divine Love, and lead men back to the Father. See *Catech. Racov.* pp. 265-268. Now although it is true that the essential nature of GOD is unchangeable Love, yet the living action of GOD's Love in the human world has been hindered and impeded by sin. In reality GOD's Love is identical with His Righteousness. But sin has produced an apparent antithesis between these Attributes. Although GOD eternally and unchangeably loves the world, His actual relation to it is one of opposition, because the Unity of His Attributes is disturbed and the action of His Love *ad extra*, is restrained, by sin. The ὀργὴ τοῦ Θεοῦ is an expression which implies, that in virtue of the Eternal necessities of His being, GOD's relation of Love to the human world is unsatisfied, owing to the agency of sin, since sin contradicts His essential nature. It is not then His Unchangeable Character, but His relation (produced by sin) to the world of men, that is really affected by the καταλλαγή. No mere man could affect that relation by his personal conduct. Jesus Christ, the Eternal Son of God, Who also as the Pattern or Ideal Man represented the whole human race, could, and did, by the consummate expression of His obedience on the Cross, establish a new relation between the active manifestation of the Love of GOD, and all those who by faith are associated with His own supreme self-sacrifice. See Martensen, *Dogmatik*, § 157.]

E.

Parallel between the Redemptive Work of Christ the Second Adam, the Author of the δικαιοσύνη ἐκ πίστεως, and the ruin which resulted from the act of the First Adam (vers. 12–21).

[*Obs.* 1. This parallel between Adam and Christ follows (διὰ τοῦτο ver. 12) upon the preceding allusions to our Lord's Atoning Death and Risen Life, as the ground and substance of our hope (vers. 8–10). Man's Salvation and Life in Christ will be understood by the analogies and contrasts which they present with his fall and death in Adam, the first parent and historic representative of the race.]

[*Obs.* 2. For the doctrine of the Second Adam (הָאָדָם הָאַחֲרוֹן) is a Rabbinical title of Messias; ὁ ἔσχατος Ἀδάμ, of our Lord, 1 Cor. xv. 45: τοῦ μέλλοντος ver. 14), cf. Pabst, *Adam und Christus*, p. 56 sqq.; Wilberforce, *Doctrine of the Incarnation*, pp. 8–82; Sadler, *The Second Adam*; Martensen, *Dogmatik*, §§ 159, 160.]

§ 1. *Work of the First and Second Adam compared* (12–19).

I. *Point of resemblance* (12–14). Each work is effected by a single agent, δι' ἑνός (v. 12).

As From Adam (i) ἁμαρτία   (ii) θάνατος   (iii) εἰς πάντας (actually).
So [From Christ (i) δικαιοσύνη   (ii) ζωή   (iii) εἰς πάντας (in design).]

One man, Adam, introduced sin; sin involved death; and death passed upon all men, because [in Adam] all sinned (ver. 12).

[*Obs.* 1. The apodosis to the sentence beginning ὥσπερ is not completed. S. Paul loses sight of his originally-intended parallel, comp. Tim. i. 3; while proving the truth that in Adam πάντες ἥμαρτον in vers. 13, 14. The clause ὅς ἐστι τύπος τοῦ μέλλοντος is a first substitute for the true apodosis, which would have run thus: οὕτω δι' ἑνὸς ἀνθρώπου (Χριστοῦ) δικαιοσύνη καὶ διὰ τῆς δικαιοσύνης ἡ ζωή κ.τ.λ. It is more nearly reached in ver. 18.]

[*Obs.* 2. The Pelagian theory, that δι' ἑνὸς ἀνθρώπου (ver. 12) refers to Eve (Ecclus. xxv. 24; 2 Cor. xi. 3; 1 Tim. ii. 14), is at issue with ver. 14, where Adam is expressly named, and 1 Cor. xv. 12 sqq. In 1 Tim. ii. 14 the reference is to the relation of the two sexes, not to the race collectively.]

[*Obs.* 3. In ἡ ἁμαρτία conduct is conceived of as self-determination in antagonism to GOD, as a force, as a real power working and manifesting itself in all cases of concrete sin (Meyer). On the connection between sin and physical death, cf. Wisd. ii. 24; S. John viii. 44; 1 Cor. xv. 21; Martensen, *Dogmatik*, § 111. Note too that (1) the remains of 'pre-Adamite' men in strata of an unknown antiquity may well point to ages when this globe was the scene of the probation of earlier races of 'men,'—a probation which was closed by some geological 'catastrophe,' prior to the reconstruction described in Genesis, which made way for our race. (2) The Apostle's argument assumes the organic unity of the present human race; it is inconsistent with any such hypothesis as that of several originally distinct pairs.]

[*Obs.* 4. Sin is described by three words in this passage. As an *act*, it involves (1) overstepping the lines traced round human life by the Divine Law, παράβασις, and so (2) a Fall from GOD, involving recoil into the sphere of self, or of nature (παράπτωμα). As a ruling *principle*, or habitual disposition, it misses the true end of our existence (ἁμαρτία). Considered as his personal act, Adam's sin was a παράβασις in itself, and a παράπτωμα in its immediate consequence; as *the* sin, *per eminentiam*, the source and principle of all later transgressions and falls, in the whole race of men, it was ἁμαρτία (ver. 1).]

[*Obs.* 5. ἐφ' ᾧ = (not, *in quo*, since this would have been ἐν ᾧ, but) ἐπὶ τούτῳ ὅτι, 'in this that,' on the ground that all sinned when through the one man sin entered into the world. The aor. ἥμαρτον refers the sins of all to the act of Adam; it describes a past moment already referred to, 2 Cor. v. 4; Phil. iii. 12; iv. 10. Certainly 'omnes in Adam peccaverunt, quando omnes ille unus homo fuerunt' (S. Aug. *De Bapt. Parv.* i. 10); but this is taught in vers. 13, 14, and must not be reflected back upon ἐφ' ᾧ in ver. 12.]

Subjoined proof of the statement that the (physical) death of all men (ver. 12 b) has its cause in the sin of Adam and in the connexion between that sin and death (vers. 13, 14).

i. Sin was in the world during the whole period which preceded the Mosaic Law. But when law cannot be thought of as existing (μὴ ὄντος), sin is not imputed to man by GOD (ver. 13).

ii. And yet we are met by the fact that the Reign of Death extended from Adam to Moses, even over those who cannot be considered (μή) to have sinned as Adam did, viz. by transgressing *positive* law (ver. 14).

[*Obs.* 1. The Apostle leaves it to the reader to ask, How this intermediate reign of death is to be explained, if in the absence of positive law it cannot be explained by the personal sins of these successive generations of dying men? It must be, by their having all sinned (πάντες ἥμαρτον) *in Adam*, who would naturally have represented the whole human family, and compromised it by his act.]

[*Obs.* 2. In ver. 13 μὴ ὄντος νόμου does not contradict the fact that the Heathen, νόμον μὴ ἔχοντες ἑαυτοῖς εἰσὶ νόμος (ii. 14). The Natural Law not having been given *positively* is not here in question ; and the commands to Noah, and the penal judgments upon Sodom, &c. are not considered, because the Apostle has before his mind only the two great epochs of Divine Legislation in Paradise and on Sinai.]

§ Thus Adam is the historical type of (Christ) the future (Adam) his Antitype (τύπος τοῦ μέλλοντος ver. 14).

[*Obs.* 1. As the whole race of natural men lived and fell in Adam their first parent, to whom they are linked by natural descent ; so the whole race of redeemed men live and are glorified in Christ, their Second Parent, to Whom they are linked by faith on their part, and the gifts of the Spirit and the Sacraments on His. Christ is not to be conceived of as *a* man, but as *The* Man ; not one individual of the race, but its adequate Representative, as realising the perfect Idea of humanity, and so potentially bearing regenerate mankind in Himself, just as Adam bore natural mankind in himself. That our Lord took human nature upon Him at His Incarnation and *not* a new i. e. a human personality, see Hooker, *E. P.* v. 52-3.]

[*Obs.* 2. The moral objections supposed to lie against the doctrine of the transmission of original sin lose sight of the fact, that in nature as in Scripture men are regarded under two aspects, (1) as forming an organic whole, (2) as separate personalities. The transmitted loss of supernatural grace, which is the essence of the Fall, is analogous to the providential 'visiting the sins of the fathers upon the children unto the third and fourth generation' in the entail of loss of property or reputation, or of constitutions impaired by self-indulgence. (See a thoughtful treatise of Bersier on 'Solidarité.') The objections from the point of view of natural justice assume man to be only a person, not a member of an organism, viz. humanity, in the collective destinies of which, for good and evil, the individual man inevitably shares.]

II. *Points of Difference* (15-17).

THESIS. The χάρισμα or *fulness of grace* (ver. 17), *whereof Christians partake in Christ, does not correspond with the* παράπτωμα, *Adam's fall from* GOD *which compromised his descendants* (ver. 15 a).

Contrast 1. In the *nature* and *measure* of their specific effects.

[*Obs.* 1. This difference is expressed in the form of an hypothetical conclusion *a minori ad majus.*]

[*Obs.* 2. (ver. 15.) χάρισμα, Divinae gratiae donum Phil. *Legg. All.* iii. 24. In Rom. i. 11, some one gift, knowledge, piety, virtue ; here, however, not as at xii. 6 ; 1 Cor. xii. 4 sqq. a specific grace, but, as ver. 17 shows, the fulness of grace of which Christians partake in Christ ; παράπτωμα too refers not so much to the actual sin of Adam, as to the resulting condition of all his natural descendants.]

[*Obs.* 3. χάρις and δωρεά are related as cause and effect : as the free love of God, and the gift which results from it. ἐν χάριτι must be taken, not with δωρεά, as this would require ἡ ἐν χάριτι, but with ἐπερίσσευσεν.]

If the effect of Adam's παράπτωμα is the death of all men (οἱ πολλοί), much more (*both* in quantitative measure *and* in logical necessity) the effect of Christ's χάρις is the abundant extension (ἐπερίσσευσε), to all (εἰς τοὺς πολλούς) who will, of the Grace of God, and the Gift (of Justification) which flows from it (ver. 15).

[*Obs.* (i) πολλῷ μᾶλλον seems to express a quantitative *rather* than a logical 'more.' (ii) We should have expected πάντες instead of οἱ πολλοί to describe the sufferers from the παράπτωμα : but the latter expression = πάντες, and is chosen as a natural antithesis to εἷς.]

Contrast 2. In the *number* and *power* of the *causes* which immediately occasioned them : οὐχ ὡς δι' ἑνὸς ἁμαρτήσαντος τὸ δώρημα.

[*Obs.* δι' ἑνὸς ἁμαρτήσαντος indicates the unity of the person and of the accomplished sinful act. Fritzsche supplies after ἁμαρτήσαντος the words τὸ παράπτωμα ἐγένετο.]

1. A single agent by a single act caused the Fall. From (ἐξ) one sinner came the occasion of that judicial sentence (κρῖμα), which led on to condemnation (κατάκριμα). Not so with the δώρημα. Many falls into sin (ἐκ πολλῶν παραπτωμάτων) have moved the Divine Mercy to bestow that great gift of grace (χάρισμα) in Christ, which leads on to a judicial sentence of acquittal (δικαίωμα) from God the Father (ver. 16).

[The contrast here is between
(i) κρῖμα and χάρισμα.
(ii) κατάκριμα and δικαίωμα.
(iii) (especially) ἑνός and πολλῶν.]

2. (Reason for ver. 16). The triumphant certainty of the Reign of Life confirms (γάρ) the τὸ χάρισμα ἐκ πολλῶν παραπτωμάτων εἰς δικαίωμα (in ver. 16). The power of the Second Adam in the direction of salvation *cannot* fall short of the power of the First Adam in the direction of destruction. Rather, if the one παράπτωμα (of the First Man) inaugurated the Reign of Death, much more (πολλῷ μᾶλλον, here a logical and qualitative *plus*) will they who receive τὴν περισσείαν τῆς χάριτος, and its concrete result, τῆς δωρεᾶς τῆς δικαιοσύνης, attain to the Reign of Life, through the instrumentality of the One Jesus Christ (ver. 17).

[*Obs.* 1. This ver. 17 is nearly an expansion of ver. 15, but it is introduced with a different logical object.]

[*Obs.* 2. The antitheses here are,
  1. ἐν ἑνὶ παραπτώματι and οἱ τὴν περισσείαν ... λαμβάνοντες.
  2. ὁ θάνατος ἐβασίλευσεν and ἐν ζωῇ βασιλεύσουσιν.
We should have expected,
  1. ἐν ἑνὶ παραπτώματι and ἐν τῇ περισσείᾳ.
  2. ὁ θάνατος and (nom.) ἡ ζωή.
= 'as through one Fall Death reigned, so much more, through the Abundance of Grace, will Life reign.'
But the change of subject in the two clauses is significant. In pre-Christian times Death, introduced by sin, reigned as a Tyrant; fallen humanity was subject to Death's empire. In Christ the conquered became the conquerors (1 Cor. iv. 8; 2 Tim. ii. 12) believers in Him have overcome death, having already received the seed of a new and endless Life, which ripens at the Resurrection. This Eternal Life is the ἐν ζωῇ of this verse.]

III. *Summary recapitulation of the whole Parallel* (vers. 12–17) *comprehending the points of similarity and unlikeness* (vers. 18, 19).

1. Comparison of the two representative acts, and of their ultimate consequences.

Accordingly then (ἄρα οὖν)

	(1) representative acts.	(2) range in fact or in design.	(3) results *in eternity*.
[ἀπέβη]	{ δι' ἑνὸς παραπτώματος } { δι' ἑνὸς δικαιώματος }	εἰς πάντας ἀνθρώπους	εἰς κατάκριμα / εἰς δικαίωσιν ζωῆς

(ver. 18).

[*Obs.* 1. δικαίωμα here being in antithesis to παράπτωμα must mean an *act of* the Second Adam ('recte factum,' Fritzsche), His moral self-consecration by obedience, as in His Passion preeminently. In ver. 16 it is in antithesis to κατάκριμα, and retains its more natural meaning of a 'justifying sentence.' Meyer understands it of the 'one judicial verdict,' pronounced by the Father on account of our Lord's obedience through His death; but without explaining the antithesis satisfactorily.]

[*Obs.* 2. πάντας refers to our Lord's *intention*, which however is not operative unless corresponded to by the faith of the δικαιούμενοι.]

2. Comparison of the moral dispositions of the two Agents and their more immediate consequences (ver. 19).

(1) moral dispositions of the agents.	(2) range.	(3) more immediate effect *in time*.
{ διὰ τῆς παρακοῆς τοῦ ἑνὸς ἀνθρώπου }	οἱ πολλοί	{ ἁμαρτωλοὶ κατεστάθησαν,
{ διὰ τῆς ὑπακοῆς τοῦ ἑνὸς (Phil. ii. 8; Heb. v. 8.) }		{ δίκαιοι κατασταθήσονται.

Dogmatic: ch. V, vv. 12-21.

[*Obs.* 1. (ver. 19.) Comparing the moral dispositions of the two agents, Adam and Christ, gives the reason (γάρ) for the comparison of their representative acts.]

[*Obs.* 2. καθιστάναι is stronger than εἶναι or ὑπάρχειν Observe its force as implying an actual 'making righteous' (as distinct from *mere* imputation) in the Justification of sinners by Christ.]

[*Obs.* 3. οἱ πολλοί = πάντες, in reality as regards the work of Adam, in intention as regards the work of Christ.]

§ 2. *Function of the νόμος, interposed (alongside of the ἁμαρτία which had already entered the human world) between the First and Second Adam (παρεισῆλθεν)* (vers. 20, 21).

1. It was *immediately* intended (ἵνα) to effect an increase of the Adamic παράπτωμα in humanity (ver. 20).

[*Obs.* This *intervening* aim of the law was essential to the efficacy of the Cure beyond. 'Augetur morbus, crescit molestia; quaeritur medicus, et totum sanatur,' S. Aug. *in Ps.* cii. c. 15. Things had to become worse with the human family, before they could be better. Thus the law was a παιδαγωγὸς εἰς Χριστόν Gal. iii. 24. Compare Gal. iii. 19 τί οὖν ὁ νόμος; τῶν παραβάσεων χάριν προσετέθη, ἄχρις οὗ ἔλθῃ τὸ σπέρμα ᾧ ἐπήγγελται.]

2. This stimulated activity of sin provoked a yet more abounding manifestation of grace (ὑπερεπερίσσευσεν ἡ χάρις), (ver. 20). This manifestation was a *more remote effect* of the interposition of the νόμος (ver. 20).

3. Thus finally (ἵνα of the ultimate purpose of GOD beyond the νόμος and the χάρις) was to be substituted for the reign of Sin in the sphere of death, the Reign of Grace, through righteousness tending towards Eternal Life, through the mediating agency of Jesus Christ our Lord. In this way νόμος realized its original and permanent, as distinct from its incidental, purpose (ver. 21).

[On the functions of the νόμος, as working wrath, see iv. 15; as rousing ἐπιθυμία and so ἁμαρτία into active life, see vii. 8, 9. These are not inconsistent with the fact that it is itself πνευματικός, vii. 14, as being given by the All-holy and revealing His necessary Moral Nature.]

DOGMATIC PORTION OF THE EPISTLE.

Division II. VI—VIII.

MORAL CONSEQUENCES OF ΔΙΚΑΙΟΣΥΝΗ ΘΕΟΥ ΕΚ ΠΙΣΤΕΩΣ.

GENERAL THESIS. *True morality, so far from being imperilled, is actively promoted by this reception of* GOD's δικαιοσύνη *through Faith in Christ.*

[*Obs.* In cc. vi-viii the Apostle seems to be considering two popular Antinomian arguments, which appealed to his own teaching in favour of a lax morality. 1. 'We may sin in order to get grace; because, "where sin hath abounded, grace hath much more abounded"' (ver. 20). This is answered in vi. 2-14 by an analysis of the idea and obligations of Christian Baptism. 2. 'We may sin; because, being in grace, we are emancipated from the law, which forbids sin.' This is answered in vi. 15—viii. (1) by an examination of what is meant by Christian 'freedom'; (2) by a statement of the true office of the Mosaic law; (3) by a description of the Christian περιπατεῖν κατὰ Πνεῦμα.]

A.

Morality not imperilled but promoted by the περισσεία τῆς χάριτος τοῦ Χριστοῦ which results in the gift of δικαιοσύνη Θεοῦ ἐκ πίστεως (vi. 1–14).

Objection.

(Put to himself by the Apostle as if suggested by an Antinomian opponent, and worth consideration.)

> Since οὗ ἐπλεόνασεν ἡ ἁμαρτία ὑπερεπερίσσευσεν ἡ χάρις (v. 20) is a law of GOD's Redemptive Providence, should we, after justification, continue (ἐπιμένωμεν, conj. deliberativus) in our old sinful life, with a view to receiving greater supplies of grace? (ver. 1.)

Resp. I. *From an analysis of the idea of* ἀποθανεῖν τῇ ἁμαρτίᾳ. This is the motto of that life to which Baptism (ver. 3) introduces the Christian. This ἀποθανεῖν has presumably made the Christian as insensible to sin, as a dead man is to the objects of the world of sense. Obviously then the Christian *cannot* live in (ἐν) sin, as if it were the home or sphere of his moral life (ver. 2).

[*Obs.* 1. ζῆν and ἀποθνήσκειν τινί are frequent tropical expressions in S. Paul to describe intimate union with or suspension of all intercourse with a person or object : Gal. ii. 19 ; with ἀπό, Col. ii. 20.]

[*Obs.* 2. Or, if this inference should appear questionable (ἤ), let a second point be considered (ver. 3).]

Resp. II. *From the final moral aim of* (ἵνα ver. 4) *Baptism into the Death of Christ* (vers. 3, 4). To be 'Baptized into Christ' involves,

    a. Baptism εἰς τὸν θάνατον τοῦ Χριστοῦ (not merely into faith in, but) into moral and spiritual communion with His *Death* (ver. 3). Through this βάπτισμα εἰς τὸν θάνατον

    b. there is a consequent (οὖν) spiritual association of the baptized Christian with Christ's *Burial*, συνετάφημεν,

    c. the purpose (ἵνα) of this being, that as Christ rose from the dead (διὰ τῆς δόξης) through the agency of the כָּבוֹד, the collective glories and perfections of the Father ; so the Christian, by means of this new supernatural strength, should walk ἐν καινότητι ζωῆς, in a life the leading feature of which should be innovation upon old habits of sin. How irreconcileable with τὸ ἐπιμένειν τῇ ἁμαρτίᾳ ! (ver. 4.)

[*Obs.* 1. Βαπτίζεσθαι εἰς is not to be explained by 'in reference to,' 'in respect to ' ; but (in accordance with the native force of the preposition εἰς) by 'into.' Christ is the Element into which the βαπτιζόμενος is *immersed*. (Comp. εἰς ἓν σῶμα ἐβαπτίσθημεν 1 Cor. xii. 13.) Hereafter, he is ἐν Χριστῷ: vi. 11 ; vi. 23 ; viii. 1 ; xvi. 11 ; 2 Cor. ii. 14 ; v. 17 ; Gal. i. 22 ; 1 Thess. ii. 14 (on which see Winer, *Gr. N. T.* p. 486, E. T.). The Christian being thus incorporated with Christ, the mysteries of His Life are reproduced in the spiritual life of the Christian. 'Quidquid gestum est in cruce Christi, in sepulturâ, in resurrectione tertio die, in ascensione in caelum in sede ad dexteram Patris, ita gestum est, ut his rebus non mystice tantum dictis sed etiam gestis, configuraretur vita Christiana quae hic geritur.' S. Aug. *Enchir.* cap. 53. Compare Gal. iii. 27 ὅσοι εἰς Χριστὸν ἐβαπτίσθητε, Χριστὸν ἐνεδύσασθε : Col. ii. 12 συνταφέντες αὐτῷ ἐν τῷ βαπτίσματι, ἐν ᾧ καὶ συνηγέρθητε κ.τ.λ. : v. 13 συνεζωοποίησε σὺν αὐτῷ. Cf. Eph. ii. 5, 6 συνεζωοποίησε τῷ Χριστῷ ... καὶ συνήγειρε, καὶ συνεκάθισεν ἐν τοῖς ἐπουρανίοις ἐν Χριστῷ Ἰησοῦ.

[*Obs.* 2. The Baptism of Adults by immersion is present to the Apostle's mind. The (i) descent into the water (κατάδυσις), and (ii) the rising from it (ἀνάδυσις), were the two striking features of the rite, corresponding to (1) the Death, and (2) the Resurrection, of Christ; and so to the Christian's (1) 'Death unto sin,' and (2) 'New Birth unto righteousness.' Between the two comes the moment during which the βαπτιζόμενος is beneath the water; it corresponds to Christ's Burial, and in the Christian's life to the permanent effect of his ἀποθανεῖν τῇ ἁμαρτίᾳ, viz. his insensibility to sin. (For the ancient Rites of Baptism, see Bingham, *Antiq. Chr. Ch.*, book xi. c. 2 sqq.)]

[*Obs.* 3. The δόξα τοῦ Πατρός, the collective perfections of the Father, chiefly His Omnipotence, 1 Cor. vi. 14; 2 Cor. xiii. 4; Eph. i. 19, raised Jesus from the dead. Christ's Resurrection is attributed to the Father in iv. 24; viii. 11; Acts ii. 24-31 sqq. It is understood of our Lord's Own Divine Nature by Theodoret, &c. and Keble, who refers to S. John ii. 19, as showing that Christ's raising Himself is proof of His being very GOD.]

Resp. III. *From the inherent force of that intimate union with* (σύμφυτοι) *Christ's Death* to which Baptism introduces us. It must lead on by an implicit moral necessity to a similar association in His undying Resurrection-life (5-11).

[*Obs.* This is a reason (γάρ ver. 5) for the previous assertion of purpose (ἵνα ὥσπερ ἠγέρθη κ.τ.λ. ver. 4), but it assumes the proportions of a substantive and independent argument.]

1. How this intimate union with Christ's death effected by Baptism is *described* (ver. 5). We are *grown together* with that moral condition which corresponds to the death of Christ in the life of the soul; and this is a moral earnest of our being similarly united to the moral condition which is the counterpart of His Resurrection.

[*Obs.* σύμφυτοι (image from vegetable growth) = '*grown* together with': συμφυής is the usual form, from συμφύω. ('Planted together with' would have been συμφύτευτοι, from συμφυτεύω; cf. Meyer). τῷ ὁμοιώματι, the moral counterpart in us of the objective fact of Christ's Death; it is that in redeemed humanity which is produced by and which answers to the Passion and Death of the Redeemer. For ὁμοίωμα see i. 23; v. 14; viii. 3. It is grammatically possible, but less natural, to make τοῦ θανάτου αὐτοῦ belong to σύμφυτοι, and take τῷ ὁμοιώματι as an interposed instrumental dat., and almost adverbially. ἀλλά emphatically introduces the contrasted clause, which is elliptical, and would, if completed, run thus: ἀλλὰ καὶ τῷ ὁμοιώματι τῆς ἀναστάσεως αὐτοῦ σύμφυτοι ἐσόμεθα. ἐσόμεθα, fut. of *ethical* necessity. Grace is not irresistible; and man's will *may* break away from its directive and impulsive power at any point. But Baptism involves the closest conceivable association with Christ's Death which physical nature can suggest to us, and this *should* involve an equally intimate and a lasting association with His Risen Life (ver. 5.]

2. What this intimate union with Christ's Death *involves* now (vers. 6, 7).

[*Obs.* τοῦτο γινώσκοντες appeals to knowledge as to the effect of the initial sacrament, previously received by oral teaching, and experimentally realized. Compare εἰδότες ver. 9.]

> i. The crucifixion (συνεσταυρώθη) of the old sinful nature (παλαιὸς ἡμῶν ἄνθρωπος) with Christ (ver. 6).

[*Obs.* Comp. Eph. iv. 22; Col. iii. 9 sqq.; not 2 Cor. iv. 16; Rom. vii. 22; Eph. iii. 16; for the distinction between the old and the new nature. Delitzsch, *Bibl. Psychol.* v. 6, pp. 433, ff. E.T.]

> ii. Object of this crucifixion (ἵνα) is the putting out of existence (καταργηθῇ, iii. 3, 31 : 1 Cor. xv. 26) the 'sin-body' (ver. 6).

[*Obs.* The σῶμα τῆς ἁμαρτίας (gen. of remote inner reference, Winer, *Gr. N. T.* p. 235) = τὸ σῶμα τῆς σαρκός : cf. Col. ii. 11. It is the body, so far as it is ruled by sin, not (1) the body in itself, nor (2) the body as the *seat* of concupiscentia which may be controlled, nor (3) sin conceived of as a body which may be crucified, the substance of sin, massa peccati. J. Müller, *Christian Doctrine of Sin,* ii. 2. It corresponds to the σὰρξ σὺν ταῖς παθήμασι καὶ ταῖς ἐπιθυμίαις (cf. Gal. v. 24), and thus in view of its destiny is a σῶμα τοῦ θανάτου Rom. vii. 24.]

> iii. Result of destroying the 'sin-body.' (τοῦ, inf. of purpose, ver. 6.) There can be no more service of the sinful principle (ἁμαρτία). The instrument of such service will have disappeared.
>
> *Reason* (γάρ): this is found even in the generally accepted legal maxim, that a dead man must be acquitted of sins said to have been committed subsequently to the date of his death (ver. 7).

[*Obs.* This 'locus communis' is Rabbinical. Delitzsch, *Hebr. Übersetz.* p. 84.]

> 3. What this intimate union with Christ's Death should *lead on to* (8–11).
>
> i. Fellowship in Christ's Death through Baptism is seen by faith (πιστεύομεν) to involve fellowship in His Resurrection-Life.

[*Obs.* συζήσομεν must be referred mainly to spiritual participation in Christ's Risen Life here, without excluding the fuller communion in it hereafter.]

> ii. (Ground of i). It is a point of Christian knowledge (εἰδότες) that the Risen Christ *dies no more.* If He could do so, there would be no secure ground for πιστεύομεν ὅτι κ.τ.λ. (ver. 8). But death is no longer lord over Him, as was the

case at the Crucifixion (ver. 9). The reason is (γάρ ver. 10) twofold.

    a. The *Death* which He died, He died τῇ ἁμαρτίᾳ (dat. of reference), once for all. Having suffered death on account of human sin, sin has no further power over Him. He cannot die for it again (ver. 10).

    b. The *Life* which He lives, in His glorified humanity, belongs wholly to GOD (ver. 10). He was crucified ἐξ ἀσθενείας, but He lives by Divine power: 2 Cor. xiii. 4.

  iii. Resulting (οὕτω) estimate (λογίζεσθε) of the Life of a Baptized Christian (ver. 11). This governs

his relation to { (i) *Sin*. He is dead to it: for him it does not exist.
(ii) *God*. He lives for Him, as the Object of existence.
(iii) *Christ*. He lives in (ἐν) Him, as the Sphere of his new life. (Since ἐβαπτίσθημεν εἰς Χρ. Ἰησ.)

[*Obs.* For the inconsistency between this culminating description of the effect of Baptism in uniting us with the Passion and Resurrection of Christ, and the ἐπιμένειν ἐν τῇ ἁμαρτίᾳ, cf. vi. 1.]

§ Maxims, based (οὖν ver. 12) on the foregoing argument (12, 13).

  Maxim 1. (On the dominion of ἁμαρτία). *Negative.* Let not the sin-principle (ἁμαρτία) be the *reigning* power in your body, *mortal* (θνητῷ) as it is, (and therefore not worthy to exact the sacrifice of that ζωὴ τῷ Θεῷ (ver. 11) which is yours through Baptism), that you should obey sin in the sphere of bodily ἐπιθυμίαι (ver. 12).

  Maxim 2. (On the employment of the bodily μέλη.) *Negative.* Do not go on placing (παριστάνετε) your bodily members (μέλη) at the disposal of the sinful principle (concupiscentia, ἁμαρτία), to be employed by it as weapons in the warfare against GOD (ὅπλα ἀδικίας) for establishing unrighteousness. *Positive,* (*a*) Place your inmost selves (ἑαυτούς) without delay (παραστήσατε) at the disposal of GOD, as men who share the resurrection-life. (*b*) (Result of foregoing). Surrender to Him your bodily members, to be used as weapons in the cause of righteousness (ὅπλα δικαιοσύνης) and as belonging to GOD (ver. 13).

Dogmatic: ch. VI, *vv.* 15-23.

[*Obs.* 1. ἁμαρτία here = *indulged* concupiscentia. 'Concupiscentia hath of itself the nature of sin,' art. ix. That 'ex peccato est et ad peccatum inclinat' (*Conc. Trid.* sess. v. can. 5) does not go so far: but the art. does not say that it *is* sin. The body is called θνητόν with reference to the contrast it presents to the glorified body (viii. 11), the glories of which are planted within us at our regeneration.]

[*Obs.* 2. ὅπλα is here used like כְּלִי, as 'instruments,' rather than the usual 'weapons.' The imp. aor. παραστήσατε after παριστάνετε marks the peremptoriness of the last command; the pres. imp. being used of an action already commenced, and which is to be continued; the aor. of an action which rapidly passes and should take place at once: S. John ii. 16; 1 Cor. xv. 34; Acts xii. 8; Winer, *Gr. N. T.* p. 394.]

Reason (γάρ) for compliance. Sin will not become lord over you (κυριεύσει, not merely βασιλεύσει), (unless you will it). You are not placed under the law, as a mere outward rule of conduct, but under grace, an invigorating and protecting force (ver. 14).

[*Obs.* 1. The axiom οὐ γάρ ἐστε ὑπὸ νόμον, ἀλλ' ὑπὸ χάριν is of decisive importance, and governs c. vi. 15-23; vii; viii. (i) ὑπὸ νόμον. Aquin. *in loc.* 'Esse sub lege quasi a lege coactus; et sic dicitur esse sub lege, qui non voluntarie ex amore, sed timore cogitur legem observare. . . . Sic igitur quamdiu aliquis sic est sub lege, ut non impleat voluntarie legem, peccatum in eo dominatur, ex quo voluntas hominis inclinatur, ut velit id quod est contrarium legi.' Cf. vii. 5 sqq., 21; viii. 15 πνεῦμα δουλείας εἰς φόβον. Thus in Gal. iii. 22, 23 ὑπὸ ἁμαρτίαν and ὑπὸ νόμον mean practically the same thing. (ii) That χάρις here is not mere favour, but an operative force, invigorating the human soul, and resisting the aggressiveness of ἁμαρτία, is clear from viii. 9 ὑμεῖς οὐκ ἐστὲ ἐν σαρκί, ἀλλ' ἐν πνεύματι, εἴπερ Πνεῦμα Θεοῦ οἰκεῖ ἐν ὑμῖν: Gal. v. 18 εἰ δὲ πνεύματι ἄγεσθε, οὐκ ἐστὲ ὑπὸ νόμον (iii) On the antithesis, comp. S. Aug. *de Continentia*, c. 3 'Non sumus sub lege, bonum quidem jubente, non tamen dante; sed sumus sub gratiâ, quae id quod lex jubet faciens nos amare, potest liberis imperare.' For his summary of man's three successive relations to νόμος, see *De Quibusdam Prop. in Ep. ad Rom.* n. 13 'Ante legem sequimur concupiscentiam carnis; sub lege trahimur ab ea; sub gratiâ nec sequimur eam, nec trahimur ab eâ; in pace nulla est concupiscentia carnis.' Cf. S. John viii. 32 sqq.]

[*Obs.* 2. The relation of this axiom to what follows may be stated thus:—

  (1) What ὑπὸ νόμον does not mean (vi. 13-23).
  (2) What it does mean, with objections and replies (c. vii).
  (3) What ὑπὸ χάριν means (c. viii).]

B.

Morality not imperilled but secured by the relation to the Mosaic Law, which is implied in δικαιοσύνη Θεοῦ ἐκ πίστεως (vi. 15–vii. 25).

§ 1.

What οὐκ ἐστὲ ὑπὸ νόμον *does* NOT *mean. License to sin* (vi. 15-23).

[*Obs.* As in ver. 1 the Apostle puts to himself an Antinomian inference from an axiom which he has just stated, as if it was worth consideration.]

Obj. Does the axiom οὐκ ἐσμὲν ὑπὸ νόμον, ἀλλ' ὑπὸ χάριν leave Christians at liberty to sin by disobeying the Law? (ver. 15).

Answ. Certainly not (vers. 16–23). For the Life of the Justified, so far from being an emancipation with reference to Righteousness, (ἐλευθερία τῇ δικαιοσύνῃ ver. 20) is a new service (δουλεία ver. 16), with its own ineffaceable sense of obligation (vers. 16–18), its own pressing duties (vers. 19, 20), and its own characteristic rewards (vers. 21–23).

[*Obs.* In order to clear the ground by showing what οὐκ εἶναι ὑπὸ νόμον does not mean, the Apostle exhibits the Christian life as the Voluntary Service of an Unseen Master, entered upon at Baptism (vi. 16–23). This representation excludes the Antinomian conception of a life of license.]

THESIS. *The Christian Life, although not* ὑπὸ νόμον, *is really a Service* (δουλεία τῇ δικαιοσύνῃ ver. 18) (vi. 16–23).

I. *Sense of obligation to this Service.* Appeal to the instinct of Christian honour (16–18).

Major prop. Those who voluntarily enter the service of a master, whatever be his character, owe him the debt of obedience (ver. 16).

Minor prop. But Christians, after being the slaves of sin, have entered Christ's service at Baptism, by yielding heartfelt obedience to the τύπος διδαχῆς to which He has given them over to be moulded by it (ver. 17).

Concl. Therefore Christians, although not ὑπὸ νόμον, are yet not free to act in *any* way; they are the slaves of that Righteousness which is their Master's badge and gift (ver. 18).

[*Obs.* 1. In ver. 16 ἤτοι ... ἤ here only in the New Testament. ἤτοι gives special emphasis to the former alternative: *aut sane*. Bauemlein, *Partik*. p. 244. We might have expected Θεοῦ instead of ὑπακοῆς as the antithesis of ἁμαρτίας: but ἁμαρτία suggests as its nearest antithesis a moral disposition, which accordingly is personified as a mistress. It would be natural to expect εἰς ζωὴν αἰώνιον, instead of εἰς δικαιοσύνην, as the antithesis to εἰς θάνατον. But the former is implied in the latter.]

[*Obs.* 2. In ver. 17 τύπος διδαχῆς. 'Form of doctrine' (in the objective sense) into which, as a spiritual mould, Christians were delivered by GOD's providence at their Baptism, to be shaped by it to the outlines of a new life. Comp. κανών Gal. vi. 16; Phil. iii. 16. It is not (1) the impression which Christian doctrine makes on the heart. nor (2) that ideal of moral life which faith in Christ suggests, nor (3) S. Paul's own distinctive manner of

Dogmatic: ch. VI, *vv.* 15–23.

presenting Christian truth, since the Roman Christians had been converted by others. The attraction εἰς ὃν παρεδόθητε τύπον διδαχῆς can be resolved either into ὑπηκούσατε τῷ τύπῳ διδαχῆς εἰς ὃν παρεδόθητε or ὑπηκούσατε εἰς τὸν τύπον διδαχῆς, εἰς ὃν παρεδόθητε. The first is the more natural explanation; the second is quite tenable and it yields the deeper sense. ὑπακούειν εἰς τι is 'to go on obeying up to a certain standard,' 2 Cor. ii. 9. As the *pass.* παρεδόθητε expresses the objective power of Divine Grace, so ὑπηκούσατε ἐκ καρδίας describes the activity of free will. On this inverse attraction, see Winer, *Gr. N. T.* p. 205. On the instruction which preceded and followed Baptism, see Bingham, *Ant.* book x.]

[*Obs.* 3. In ver. 18 the ἐλευθερία of the justified is a δουλεία τῇ δικαιοσύνῃ. There is no intermediate moral condition between the one service and the other. Only as slaves of righteousness, and so free to follow the true law of our being, can we cease to be slaves of sin. 'Deo servire est vera libertas,' S. Aug. 'Whose service is perfect freedom—cui servire regnare est,' Collect for Peace.]

II. *Pressing duties attached to this Service.* Appeal to the instinct of moral enterprise (vers. 19, 20).

[*Obs.* 1. Remembering their moral weakness, ἀσθένεια σαρκός, the Apostle only suggests that which is possible for man to do. Let them do in one direction what they have done in past years in another, viz. place their bodily organs at the disposal of a Governing Influence, as if slaves.]

[*Obs.* 2. For this sense of ἀνθρώπινος comp. πειρασμὸς ἀνθρώπινος, temptation which man can resist: 1 Cor. ii. 13; x. 13. He might have asked for much beyond.]

as they have yielded τὰ μέλη as δοῦλα, so let them yield
{
  1. τῇ ἀκαθαρσίᾳ, moral defilement of the agent *within*;
  2. τῇ ἀνομίᾳ, violation of Divine Law *without*;
  τῇ δικαιοσύνῃ
}
{
  completing the idea of ἁμαρτία, and leading on εἰς τὴν ἀνομίαν—the establishment of God-defying lawlessness as a concrete reality.
  leading on εἰς ἁγιασμόν, the attainment of holiness in thought and act (ver. 19).
}

[*Obs.* μέλη often used in this sense in the Mischna, אברים. Not in Old Testament. A trace of S. Paul's Rabbinical education.]

Reason (γάρ) for this. If the readers object, 'This, after all, is only a new slavery,' let them reflect that they have already tried the *only* alternative condition, the *only* possible ἐλευθερία τῇ δικαιοσύνῃ.

The Epistle to the Romans.

That condition too was, in itself, a slavery,—but τῆς ἁμαρτίας (ver. 20).

[*Obs.* Here, as in ver. 18, (and S. Matth. vi. 24,) the ground-thought is: you must serve one of two lords; there is no intermediate condition of moral suspense between the two services; to escape from the one is to be thereby bound to the other.]

III. *Rewards of this Service.* Appeal to the instinct of prudence. (21–23). (καρπός vers. 21, 22; τέλος vers. 21, 22; ὀψώνια ver. 23; χάρισμα ver. 23).

1. *Test of experience in the past.* What was the moral gain (καρπός) of those past acts on which (ἐφ᾽ οἷς) memory cannot dwell without raising an emotion of shame? Surely, nought. For acts which end in eternal death hereafter cannot bring moral gain *now* (ver. 21).

[*Obs.* Lachmann, Tisch. and many others end the question with τότε, in which case ἐφ᾽ οἷς νῦν ἐπαισχύνεσθε becomes the answer, and τὸ γὰρ τέλος κ.τ.λ. its proof. But the antithesis of καρπόν in ver. 22 shows that in ver. 21 the having of fruit, not its quality, is in question (see Meyer).]

2. *Appeal to present experience.* Having been emancipated from sin and so enslaved to GOD, you possess your *moral gain* (καρπόν), (1) leading on to increasing holiness here (ἁγιασμόν), and (2) ending in ζωὴ αἰώνιος (ver. 22).

3. *General Law of* GOD's *moral government* which is the reason (γάρ) of this experience. (ver. 23.)

$$\begin{cases} \text{τὰ ὀψώνια τῆς ἁμαρτίας} = \text{θάνατος.} \\ \text{τὸ χάρισμα τοῦ Θεοῦ} = \text{ζωὴ αἰώνιος ἐν Χρ. Ἰησ.} \end{cases}$$

[*Obs.* 1. ὀψώνιον, later Greek word, probably whatever is bought to be eaten with bread, specially fish, or meat. As such condiments were given to soldiers instead of pay (Caesar, *B. G.* i. 23. 1 ; Polyb. i. 66. 3) ὀψώνιον came to mean military pay (Polyb. vi. 39. 12), the plural being due to the various goods that constituted the original payments, or to the coins used in the later money wages. Lobeck, *Phryn.* p. 420.]

[*Obs.* 2. θάνατος is not exclusively physical, but the eternal death, cf. ver. 22, where ζωὴ αἰώνιος is its antithesis. S. Paul will not use ὀψώνια of GOD's reward of His free grace to His servants, which is originally a χάρισμα : Origen, *in loc.* On the point common to the two ideas, comp. S. Prosper. *de Vocat. Gent.* ii. 8 'Datur unicuique sine merito, unde tendat ad meritum ; et datur ante ullum laborem, unde quisque mercedem accipiat secundum suum laborem.']

§ 2.

What is meant by οὐκ ἐστέ ὑπὸ νόμον? *Nothing less than a higher degree of Holiness in the emancipated* (vii. 1–6).

THESIS. *The Life of the Baptized, besides being conceived of as a New Service* (vi. 16–23), *is also a Marriage to a Second Husband, the Risen Christ, through Whose grace Christians bring forth good works to* GOD (vii. 1–6).

I. *Legitimacy of this Second Marriage* (vers. 1–4 a).

1. (General Axiom). The authority of the Mosiac Law over a man lasts *during* the man's life-time (ver. 1).

[*Obs.* 1. By ἀδελφοί the Apostle probably means all the readers of his Epistle; and not merely the converts from Judaism, i. 13; viii. 12; x. 1; xi. 25; xii. 1; xv. 14, 30; xvi. 17. This precept was common in the Rabbinical Schools. Schabbath, f. 30. 1 'Homo, postquam mortuus est, cessat a lege.' Talmud. tr. Niddai. cf. Wetstein *in loc.* The Jews thus contrasted the Mosaic Law with human legislation, which might be altered, or suspended, or had only a temporary force. S. Paul is rather thinking of the fact that the jurisdiction of the law does *not* last *beyond* death. As γινώσκοντες τὸν νόμον, converts from Judaism, among his readers, would readily understand the allusion.]

[*Obs.* 2. We must follow S. Augustine in making ἄνθρωπος, and not νόμος, the subject to ζῇ. Comp. vers. 2, 3, 4. The Apostle is not discussing the abrogation of the Mosaic Law, but the relation of Christian converts to it.]

2. (Particular illustration). The Mosaic Marriage-Law bound the married woman to her husband during his life-time. But in the event of his death, she too, in the eye of the law, ceased to exist as wife (κατήργηται). By this her own legal decease she was freed from the Law that bound her to her husband (νόμος τοῦ ἀνδρός). Consequently, a woman who connects herself with another man, during her husband's life-time, takes the formal name of adulteress. But, after the husband's death, as being legally dead, *quâ* wife, she is legally freed from the Law which bound her to him, with the object of her not being deemed an adulteress, although she be married to another man (vers. 2, 3).

[*Obs.* 1. ὕπανδρος γυνή, a phrase implying the 'subjection' of the Hebrew wife = אִשָּׁה תַּחַת אִישָׁהּ Numb. v. 29, LXX. Comp. Gen. iii. 16. On δέδεται cf. Winer, *Gr. N. T.* p. 339, as expressing the life-long obligation of the *vinculum matrimonii* contracted at a past date. With γένηται ἀνδρί comp. הָיוֹת לְאִישׁ Ruth i. 12; Ezek. xvi. 8. For this sense of χρηματίζειν, to take a name from one's business, comp. Acts xi. 26; Joseph. *Ant.* xiii. 11. 3.]

[*Obs.* 2. The Mosaic Law gives the wife no power of divorcing her husband; hence δίδεται. Gen. ii. 24 'they two shall be one flesh'; Eph. v. 31 the man προσκολληθήσεται πρὸς τὴν γυναῖκα αὐτοῦ. The Apostle does not notice the case of a woman *divorced by* her husband: Deut. xxiv. 2; Kiddusch, f. 2. 1 'Mulier possidet se ipsam *per libellum repudii*, et per mortem mariti.' For this permission to divorce a wife *a vinculo matrimonii* had only been given πρὸς τὴν σκληροκαρδίαν of Israel. Our Lord repealed it, thus reverting to the original marriage law of the Creator: S. Matt. xix. 8. (Even adultery (μοιχεία) does not warrant divorce *a vinculo matrimonii*: although concealed sin before marriage (εἰ μὴ ἐπὶ πορνείᾳ) may have vitiated the marriage contract *ab initio*. Cf. Döllinger, *Christenthum und Kirche*, Beit. iii. p. 461.) S. Paul, as writing to Christians, does not notice a legal provision which our Lord had repealed.]

[*Obs.* 3. The illustration has been thought inapposite, because the actually dead person (the husband) and the person released from the law (the wife) are represented as different, so that the axiom of ver. 1 is at first sight inapplicable. This led S. Chrys. to suppose that there is here an inversion of the comparison. But the Apostle's emphasis lies on the legal death of the wife, *quâ* wife (κατήργηται), resulting from the actual death of the husband. The wife is only under the νόμος τοῦ ἀνδρός, so long as she *lives* a wife in the eye of the law—a state of things which ceases with her husband's actual death. Thus the axiom of ver. 1 applies directly.]

3. *Analogous inference from the axiom* (ver. 1) *and its illustration* (2, 3). *Converts to the Church from Judaism may lawfully espouse themselves to Christ* (ver. 4 a).

   1. For they are in the position of the γυνὴ ὕπανδρος after her husband's decease. So far as the Mosaic Law is concerned (τῷ νόμῳ, dat. ref.) they are dead; since they have been put to death (ἐθανατώθητε). This was effected by the Death of the σῶμα τοῦ Χριστοῦ, into which they were at Baptism incorporated. His Death has killed them, as for purposes of sin (Rom. vi. 3 sqq.) so also for their old spouse, the Law (2 Cor. v. 14). They are as if it did not exist (ver. 4 a). Whence,

   2. Under the terms of the axiom in ver. 1 they are at liberty to contract marriage with Another, viz. the Risen One (ver. 4 a).

[*Obs.* 1. Only the Risen Christ can enter into this mystical wedlock with the soul, iv. 24. With εἰς τὸ γενέσθαι ἑτέρῳ connect ἵνα καρποφορήσωμεν κ.τ.λ.]

[*Obs.* 2. γενέσθαι ἑτέρῳ: cf. ver. 3.]

II. *Fruitfulness of this Second Marriage* (vers. 4 b-6).

[*Obs.* Espoused to the ὁ ἐκ νεκρῶν ἐγερθείς, and 'semine gratiae ejus foecundata,' the Christian soul brings forth good works to the honour of GOD. The metaphor of marriage dictates the term καρποφορήσωμεν. Thus, an internal force achieves that which the Law, as an external rule, never could secure.]

Dogmatic: ch. VII, vv. 7–25.

Explanation of ἵνα καρποφορήσωμεν τῷ Θεῷ (vers. 5, 6).

1. Antithesis of this fruitfulness to the status naturae (ἐν τῇ σαρκί) under the rule of the Law. That was marked by

    a. the activity (ἐνηργεῖτο) in the bodily organs of the παθήματα ἁμαρτίας, those movements of passion which result in sin ;

    b. the ultimate καρποφορῆσαι τῷ θανάτῳ. Eternal death is to this legal and natural fruitfulness, what GOD (ver. 4) is to that of the regenerate (ver. 5).

2. Intrinsic character of this fruitfulness. It springs from

    a. freedom from the Law, which had held man in its grasp. Christians are dead to it, through union with Christ's death. Hence they render

    b. a service (δουλεύειν) whose sphere is the new impulse which the Holy Spirit has given from within, and not the old obedience to a literal rule, imposed altogether from without (ver. 6).

§ 3.

Objections to the foregoing account of νόμος considered (vii. 7–25).

Objection I. Does not the foregoing account (οὖν ver. 1) of the relation of the Mosaic Law to Christian Holiness imply that the Law is essentially sin (not ἁμαρτωλός, but ἁμαρτία)? (ver. 7.)

Resp. No: this is so far from being the case, that (ἀλλά) the law actually discharges functions, which, on such a supposition, would be impossible (7–12). The law is really ἅγιος (ver. 12).

[*Obs.* The Apostle cannot be supposed (7–13) to be speaking (1) *simply* of himself, and his own personal experiences before his conversion, nor yet (2) only in the person of the Jewish people as a people, or of human nature. It is a picture of his unregenerate self, at the two stages of χωρὶς νόμου and ὑπὸ νόμον, but widened here and there so as to represent the universal experience.]

Arg. 1. From the *illuminative* office of the Law. The Law brought with it an ἐπίγνωσις ἁμαρτίας. (iii. 20.) It was the Law which threw light upon the existence of the sinful tendency in human nature. It did this by taking the concrete shape of ἐντολή, which revealed ἁμαρτία in the active form of ἐπιθυμία, unregulated desire. [The Law, it is implied, must be essentially different in nature from that which it thus brings to light] (ver. 7).

[*Obs.* The ἐντολή here, οὐκ ἐπιθυμήσεις, is from Ex. xx. 16. The scope of the prohibition is widened by omitting the objects mentioned in the tenth commandment : 'tanquam haec esset vox legis ab omni peccato prohibentis. Neque enim ullum peccatum nisi concupiscendo committitur,' S. Aug.]

Arg. 2. From the (indirectly) *provocative* office of the Law. By means of the precept against concupiscence, the sin-principle, having chosen its occasion, worked out all manner of device after the forbidden. Thus the Law became ἀφορμὴ πάσης ἐπιθυμίας. [The Law, it is implied, must be essentially opposed to the sin-principle, which it only thus irritates into active opposition, by reason of its felt incompatibility] (ver. 8).

Particular description of the Apostle's experience. When as a child he knew nothing of the Law, the sin-principle was dormant, as if dead, νεκρά. In those years (ποτέ) he lived the life of innocence (ἔζων) of any active sin. Then the precept against concupiscence presented itself. The consequence was that the latent sin-principle started up into a second life. This was the tragic moment of conscious spiritual death—ἀπέθανον (ver. 9).

[*Obs.* 1. The dormancy of sin in childhood lasts until the intelligence opens upon the moral Law. 'Peccatum sine lege, tanquam non sit, latet, non apparet, penitus ignoratur; tanquam in nescio quibus ignorantiae tenebris sit sepultum' S. Aug. *Contr. duas Epp. Pelag.* i. 9; 'Hanc legem nescit pueritia, ignorat infantia, et peccans absque mandato, non tenetur lege peccati. Maledicit patri et matri ; parentes verberat ; et quia necdum accepit legem sapientiae, mortuum est in eo peccatum. Cum autem mandatum hoc venerit est tempus intelligentiae appetentis bona et vitantis mala, tunc incipit peccatum reviviscere, et ille mori reusque esse peccati. Atque ita fit ut tempus intelligentiae, quo Dei mandata cognoscimus ut perveniamus ad vitam, operetur in nobis mortem' S. Hieronym. *Ep. ad Algasiam.* qu. 8. S. Aug. explains ἀνέζησεν of the sin of the race in paradise, in which each member has a share; 'vixerat enim [peccatum] aliquando in paradiso'; when the child consciously disobeys 'tunc peccatum quodammodo in notitia nati hominis reviviscet quod in notitia primum facti hominis aliquando jam vixerat' *Contr. duas Epp. Pelag.* i. 9. There is no ground here for the hypothesis of a premundane life, such as that attributed (in Wisd. viii. 20) to the Eternal Wisdom.]

[*Obs.* 2. That man is disposed to regard as a good whatever is prohibited, merely because it is prohibited, was well understood by the heathen. Cato speaks of luxury 'ipsis vinculis, sicut fera bestia, irritata' Liv. xxxiv. 4. Seneca says that 'parricidae cum lege coeperunt' *De Clem.* i. 23. Horace complains that 'Audax omnia perpeti, Gens humana ruit, per vetitum nefas' *Carm.* i. 3. 25. 'Nitimur in vetitum semper' Ov. *Amor.* iii. 4. 17. Comp. Prov. ix. 17.]

Arg. 3. From the *contrast between the actual effect of the Law and its original object*. The precept against concupiscence was originally intended to protect man's moral ζωή. Experience showed (εὑρέθη) this very precept of all others (αὕτη) to tend to promote spiritual death. Like the serpent in paradise, the sinful tendency used the precept to provoke ill-regulated desire: it held out as desirable something intrinsically pernicious, and so ἐξηπάτησε, and accomplished moral murder (ἀπέκτεινεν) (ver. 10–11). *Conclusion* (from vers. 7 b–11). Thus the Law, although misused by sin, remains ἅγιος, as being GOD's unveiling of His moral nature; and the particular concrete ἐντολή is not less ἅγια as coming from GOD, δίκαια, in what it requires of man, and ἀγαθή, in its original and salutary object (vers. 10–12).

[*Obs.* The Apostle, as μέν ver. 12 shows, intended to say further '*but* sin has, through the law, which is itself good, resulted in death to me.' But he has only half completed his inference from the premises (7–11), when (see Winer, *Gr. N. T.* p. 720) there emerges]

Objection II. 'At any rate this amounts to saying that that which is good in itself (the Law) has become a principle of moral death' (ver. 13 a).

Resp. No. Sin it is which really tends to death.

This has been ordered with a two-fold object:

(1) ἵνα φανῇ κ.τ.λ. That sin might be seen in its true colours, as working out the spiritual death of man by its misuse of that which is in itself good. It turns GOD's bounty against Himself, and uses His best blessings to promote man's ruin (ver. 13).

(2) ἵνα γένηται κ.τ.λ. (climatic parallel). That through this misuse of the ἐντολή, sin might become exaggerated, καθ' ὑπερβολὴν ἁμαρτωλός. This would heighten the necessity for a Divine Deliverer, (comp. ch. v. 20) (ver. 13).

§ Proof (not merely of the final purpose of the fact (ver. 13 b) but of the fact (ver. 13 a) that sin, and not the law, really tends to death (14–25).

[*Obs.* 1. This passage (vii. 14–25) was understood by the Greek Fathers, from S. Irenaeus downwards, to apply to man in the *unregenerate state*. So at first by S. Augustine (*Prop.* 45. *in Ep. ad Rom.*; *ad Simplic.* i. 9; *Confess.* vii. 21–27). When the Pelagians, adopting this interpretation, appealed to vers. 17, 18, 22, in proof of their estimate of fallen human nature, Aug. thought that the older interpretation was out of harmony with the general mind of Scripture.

Accordingly, in his later works, he maintained that the ἐγώ of this passage is that of the *regenerate*. (*Retractationes*, i. 23; ii. 7; *contr. duas Epp. Pelag.* i. 10; *contr. Faust.* xv. 8.) The Pelagian controversy had a similar influence upon the judgment of S. Jerome. S. Augustine's later interpretation was followed by S. Anselm, Thomas Aquinas, and in the 16th cent. by the Reformers. The disposition of some among the foreign reformers to treat concupiscence as not merely having 'the *nature* of sin,' but as actually being sin, and also to depreciate the strength and completeness of the regenerate life, led to a re-action against the later Augustinian interpretation. Thus Hammond and Justinian, in the 17th century, already understood it of the *unregenerate* life; and this opinion is, probably, whether among believing or rationalising commentators, the dominant one at the present day, although not always necessarily or chiefly on dogmatic grounds.]

[*Obs.* 2. The reasons for understanding vii. 14-25 of the *regenerate* state *in the phase of struggle*, while viii. 1-11 describes it in *the repose of completed victory*, are as follows: (1) The relation of the νόμος to the unregenerate has been already explained in vii. 7-13. (2) At ver. 14 the *aorists* of vii. 7-13, apparently describing past facts in the Apostle's experience, suddenly cease; and the *presents* of vii. 14-25 would seem to assert facts belonging to an existing spiritual state. (But the change of tense is sufficiently accounted for by the clause ὁ νόμος πνευματικός ἐστιν. The Apostle is confronting the spiritual nature of the law. The paragraph 14-23 describes what is indeed past for him; but he realises it as present; see Meyer.) (3) Throughout vii. 14-25 the inmost self of the writer is on the side of the Divine νόμος: ver. 15 ὃ θέλω, ὃ μισῶ: ver. 16 σύμφημι τῷ νόμῳ: ver. 22 συνήδομαι τῷ νόμῳ τοῦ Θεοῦ: ver. 25 αὐτὸς ἐγώ: and this inmost ἐγώ must not be confounded with the second self which lives ἐν τῇ σαρκί (ver. 18), and has an ἕτερον νόμον of its own (ver. 23), and produces acts which the inmost self condemns (vers. 15, 16, 19, 20). (But this harmonises with the fact that in unregenerate man the moral sense and reason are in sympathy with the Law of God, while the sin-power predominates in the σάρξ so completely as to overbear the inner ἐγώ and to destroy all 'liberum arbitrium in spiritualibus.' This may have been true even of the Jew in Rom. ii. 17-24.) (4) The whole passage seems thus understood to correspond with the account of the Πνεῦμα and the σάρξ in Gal. v. 17 ταῦτα δὲ ἀντίκειται ἀλλήλοις, ἵνα μὴ ἃ ἂν θέλητε, ταῦτα ποιῆτε. (Doubtless that passage does ascribe to the σάρξ a real remaining power in the life of those who are yet regenerate. It warrants the statement of Art. ix. And much of the language which Rom. vii. 14-23 applies to the unregenerate is, as some of the Fathers saw, true of the regenerate also. But the question is to what *does* Rom. vii. 14-23 refer?) (5) 'Non est absurdum ut homo renatus sit simul vetus, ut novus homo operatur malum, et ... pugnam sentiat carnis adversum spiritum' S. Hieron. *Dial. ii. contr. Pelag.* For 'this infection of nature doth remain yea in them which are regenerated, whereby the lust of the flesh ... is not subject to the law of God,' Art. ix. And the ancient Church prayed 'ut nos Unigeniti Tui, nova per carnem nativitas liberet, quos sub peccati jugo vetusta servitus tenet.']

[*Obs.* 3. Reasons for understanding the passage of the *unregenerate* state are given by Meyer, Reithmayr, Tholuck, especially by Julius Müller, *Chr. Doctr. of*

Dogmatic: ch. VII, vv. 7-25.

Sin, b. ii. c. 2. These reasons resolve themselves into two. (1) The difficulty of reconciling the πεπραμένος ὑπὸ τὴν ἁμαρτίαν ver. 14; who does what he would not, ver. 15; in whose σάρξ there is no good discoverable, ver. 18; who is brought into captivity to the νόμος τῆς ἁμαρτίας ἐν τοῖς μέλεσιν ver. 23; who still cries out τίς με ῥύσεται; κ.τ.λ. ver. 24, with the βαπτισθείς who is dead to ἁμαρτία in vi. 3-11; or with Gal. iii. 13; 2 Cor. v. 17; Eph. ii. 10. These passages describe not the *ideal*, but the law, of the regenerate life. (2) The difficulty of supposing that the later Augustinian interpretation of vii. 14-25 can be reconciled with vii. 5, which places the ascendancy of sin within the *status naturae sub lege*; with vii. 6, which places the καινότης πνεύματος within the *status gratiae*; or with viii. 1 sqq. (Tholuck, *in loc.*). This difficulty is apparently insuperable.]

[*Obs.* 4. In the whole passage vii. 7—viii. 1-11, four distinct spiritual states are described. (1) Man χωρὶς νόμου, in the irresponsibility of childhood, vii. 7, 9. (2) Man, ὑπὸ νόμον, when the Law acts (*a*) as an 'index peccati' (S. Ambros.); and (*b*) as (through its misuse by ἁμαρτία) stimulating ἐπιθυμία, vii. 8, 10, 11, 13. (3) Man, οὐκ ὑπὸ νόμον, in internal harmony with the Law. (σύμφημι τῷ νόμῳ ὅτι καλός vii. 16; συνήδομαι τῷ νόμῳ ver. 22.) Yet in conflict with ἁμαρτία,—a conflict which discloses the intrinsic sanctity of νόμος, vii. 14-23. (4) Man, οὐκ ὑπὸ νόμον, and reposing in ascertained victory over ἁμαρτία. ... The question is whether (3) is within or without the frontier of the regenerate state. Looking to the language of Scripture, as well as to actual experience, the difficulties of the *latter* supposition appear to be the more considerable [1].]

Arg. 1. From the intrinsic nature of the Law, which contrasts with that of the Jew, as the spiritual to the carnal (ver. 14 a). Christians know (ὡμολογημένον τοῦτο S. Chrys.) that the Mosaic Law is πνευματικός. In form it is a γράμμα; but in its essence it is the Self-Revelation of the Divine Being, Who is Himself Πνεῦμα (S. John iv. 24) and it is thus fulfilled by the κατὰ Πνεῦμα περιπατοῦντες viii. 4. Whereas the writer knows himself to be σάρκινος, made of flesh.

[*Obs.* 1. The change from the *aorists* in 7-13 which describe the condition of man prior to and under the law to the *presents* in ver. 14 sqq. is determined by the proposition ascribing the spiritual nature of the law, which the unredeemed ἐγώ confronts. The Apostle realizes as present an experience which for himself was long since past.]

[*Obs.* 2. σάρκινος applied to the unredeemed man is not fleshly, but made of flesh, 2 Cor. iii. 3; 1 Cor. iii. 1. Cf. Plat. *Legg.* x. p. 906 C. The word describes the material phenomenal nature of man, in which sin grows apace, and which renders the moral will fruitless.]

---

[1] [This *Obs.* 4 is not in complete harmony with *Obs.* 3. After this Analysis was privately printed Dr. Liddon changed his view on the question under discussion, but did not obliterate the traces of his earlier view altogether.—ED.]

Arg. 2. From the Enslavement of the Jew to the power of sin (ver. 14 b–17).

[*Obs.* πεπραμένος seems to be applicable only to the unregenerate (Dr. Pusey) as it 'implies an entire giving up of self out of one's own power.' The Hebrew הִתְמַכֶּרְךָ, LXX πέπρασαι, used of Ahab by Elijah, 1 Kings xxi. 20, 25; and of the apostate Israelites under Hosea, 2 Kings xvii. 17 ἐπράθησαν τοῦ ποιῆσαι τὸ πονηρὸν ἐν ὀφθαλμοῖς Κυρίου, 1 Macc. i. 15. But disciples of Christ are no longer δοῦλοι τῆς ἁμαρτίας Rom. vi. 17; S. John viii. 34–36.]

This writer feels himself to be σάρκινος, made of flesh, and sold as a slave might be (πεπραμένος) under the dominion of sin (cf. ver. 23). He traces his enslavement—

    a. in his imperfect survey of the field of moral action (ὃ γὰρ κατεργάζομαι, οὐ γινώσκω). A slave must often act without knowing why (ver. 15).

    b. proof of foregoing (γάρ) in his want of decision. His moral activity (πράσσω) is not directed to that which he desires (ὃ θέλω). He actually does (ποιῶ) that which he abhors (ὃ μισῶ) (ver. 15).

Two deductions:

    a. This opposition of his real desires to his actual conduct implies his real concurrence with the *moral excellence of the Law* (σύμφημι τῷ νόμῳ ὅτι καλός) (ver. 16).

    b. It is no longer his true personality (ἐγώ) that works this evil, but the sin-principle, to which his true and better self is enslaved (ver. 17).

[*Obs.* In ver. 17 ἐν ἐμοί does not, like ἐγώ, refer to the self-conscious personality. It is explained in ver. 18 to mean ἐν τῇ σαρκί. This distinction shows that the real ἐγώ, even in the circumstances of vers. 15, 16, may be given to GOD. On the 'empiric ego,' see Delitzsch, *Bibl. Psych.* p. 189.]

Arg. 3. From the experimental sense of the absence of good in the σάρξ, i. e. the phenomenal nature, the home of the sin-principle (vers. 18–20).

This is verified,

    a. by self-introspection. Surveying the inner world, which is open to his view, he sees confronting him (παράκειταί μοι) the θέλειν τὸ καλόν, but he is unable to discover the κατεργάζεσθαι τὸ καλόν. This καλόν=in Greek eyes, the ἀγαθόν, 'quod candore nitet.' He wills, but he does not achieve it.

    b. (Proof of preceding, γάρ) by noting the contrasts between his *actions* and his real *will*.

Dogmatic: ch. VII, *vv.* 7-25.

He wills good, yet does not effect it (ποιῶ).
He does not will evil, yet his moral activity is towards it (πράσσω).

Deduction from (*b*):
This shows that the real agent is not now any longer his true personality, but the indwelling sin-principle (ver. 20).

[*Obs.* The close correspondence between ver. 19 and ver. 15, with, however, the varied use of ποιῶ and πράσσω. Also the repetition of ver. 17 at the end of ver. 20,—not merely a strophical arrangement, but describing a single result which is reached from independent points of consideration.]

Arg. 4. From the resulting perception of a moral dualism in the soul (vers. 21-23).

1. It results (from vers. 14-20, ἄρα) to the writer that while he wills the Divine Law (τὸν νόμον τῷ θέλοντι ἐμοί), in order to do the good (ποιεῖν, inf. of purpose), the evil confronts him (παράκειται) (ver. 21).

2. (Fuller statement, by way of justification (γάρ) of the foregoing.)

   a. His inward man, i.e. his rational and moral nature (νοῦς), is in true sympathy with the Divine Law, in regard of what is good. Its joy (the law being personified) is also his own (ver. 22).

   b. But he sees a law of a different nature (ἕτερον) in his bodily organs, the instruments of the activity of the σάρξ (ver. 23). This law

       a. makes war against the νόμος τοῦ νοός, (local gen.), the law according to which he rejoices inwardly *with* the Divine Law—*not* the Divine Law itself.

       b. makes him prisoner of war (αἰχμαλωτίζοντα) to the law of the sin-principle (= ἕτερος νόμος supr.) in his organs, i.e. to itself (ver. 23).

[*Obs.* 1. The με in ver. 23 is not the νοῦς, or ἔσω ἄνθρωπος, which continues throughout in the service of the Divine Law (ver. 25 αὐτὸς ἐγὼ τῷ μὲν νοῒ δουλεύω νόμῳ Θεοῦ); but the second apparent self which is identified in ver. 18 with the σάρξ, and which is πεπραμένος ὑπὸ τὴν ἁμαρτίαν.]

[*Obs.* 2. In vers. 22, 23 *three* laws are mentioned, not four: (1) the νόμος τοῦ Θεοῦ (gen. auct.), the Law given by God to Moses, ver. 22; (2) the νόμος τοῦ νοός, the Law which brings his inmost self into sympathy with the Divine Law; (3) the ἕτερος νόμος ἐν τοῖς μέλεσιν, which is *not* distinct from, but strictly identical with, the νόμος τῆς ἁμαρτίας (ver. 23). S. Aug. *de Nup. et Concup.* i. 30.]

Arg. 5. From the final crisis and victory (vers. 24, 25).
  1. Cry for aid (ver. 24).
    a. Condition of the suppliant, ταλαίπωρός Rev. iii. 17, (word from Greek tragedy,) weighed upon by the σῶμα τοῦ θανάτου, the body as the seat of this death, as being also the σῶμα τῆς ἁμαρτίας (vi. 6), the seat of that sin-principle which in its triumph is death.

[*Obs.* Delitzsch observes that the very form of this *cry* shows that it proceeds from a person who is regenerate, but it would equally express the anguish of an unregenerate soul, at the crisis of conversion.]

    b. What he needs,—a Deliverer (τίς με ῥύσεται) from the power of sin remaining in him.
  2. The complete Deliverance—termination of the struggle (ver. 25). He thanks GOD, through Jesus Christ, the Mediator both of the deliverance and of his thankfulness for it.

Summary of contents of 14–25 (ἄρα οὖν 25 b). The general result of the foregoing is that in the phase of struggle which terminates at verse 25, the inner self of the regenerate serves with the νοῦς the law of GOD, but with his σάρξ is in the service of the law of sin. This, however, shows the intrinsic holiness of the Law (ver. 12), ver. 25.

C.

Morality not imperilled but secured by the Christian's new Life in Christ through the Holy Spirit (viii. 1–39).

The foregoing (vii. 14–25) leads (ἄρα) on by contrast to the complete victory of the Holy Spirit in the Christian. This victory involves

§ 1.

Freedom of the regenerate life in Christ (viii. 1–11).

I. *Freedom of the regenerate from any sentence of condemnation* (κατάκριμα) *excluding from eternal life* (vers. 1, 2).

[*Obs.* 1. The phrases τοῖς ἐν Χριστῷ Ἰησοῦ, Πνεῦμα Χριστοῦ ἔχειν (ver. 9) and Χριστὸς ἐν ὑμῖν (ver. 10) refer to the same fact. The Spirit unites us to the Divine Humanity of the Son of GOD, so that 'we dwell in Christ and Christ in us, we are one with Christ and Christ with us.' On being 'in' Christ, see Hooker, *Eccl. Pol.* v. 56. 7. The old gloss in the *text. rec.* μὴ κατὰ σάρκα περιπατοῦσι ἀλλὰ κατὰ πνεῦμα is inappositely introduced from ver. 4.]

[*Obs.* 2. κατάκριμα. What faith is represented as effecting in ch. v. 1 is here attributed to the moral freedom granted by the Spirit to the οἱ ἐν Χριστῷ.

Faith then is not merely a receptive faculty, but the motive power of the Divine life in the soul, and inseparably united to love and obedience.]

Arg. This freedom is secured because the law of the Spirit leading to life—the inward power of supernatural grace—has in Christ Jesus (Gal. iv. 31; v. 13; S. John viii. 31) freed the regenerate from the power of the inward law of sin (vii. 23) which leads to death (ver. 2).

[*Obs.* 1. The aor. ἠλευθέρωσεν points to the historic moment of regeneration as that in which the freedom was achieved.]

[*Obs.* 2. The νόμος τῆς ἁμαρτίας is not the Mosaic Moral Law, since that is πνευματικός vii. 14, and ἅγιος vii. 12; but the inward rule of the sin-principle, νόμος ἐν τοῖς μέλεσιν vii. 23, and τῆς ἁμαρτίας ibid. which takes captive (αἰχμαλωτίζει vii. 23) the 'empiric ego.']

[*Obs.* 3. (*Transitional.*) In ver. 3 this ἠλευθέρωσεν (cf. ver. 2) is justified (γάρ) by showing *how* the regenerate Christian is freed from the law of sin. His enfranchisement from the law of death follows in vers. 10, 11.]

II. *Freedom of the regenerate from the νόμος τῆς ἁμαρτίας* (viii. 3-9).

1. Impossibility of this freedom from sin under the Mosaic Law. That the law could not achieve it resulted from man's sinful phenomenal nature, or (σάρξ), which rendered the law impotent for good (cf. vii. 8-12) (ver. 3).

[*Obs.* τὸ ἀδύνατον κ.τ.λ. *nom. absol.* It is a heading or title to what follows. The sentence properly begins with ὁ Θεός. Cf. Meyer, *in loc.*]

2. How is this freedom from sin secured under the Gospel?

Resp. By GOD's Mission of the Eternal Son into the world.

1. *Manner of His Appearance among men.* ἐν ὁμοιώματι σαρκὸς ἁμαρτίας, robed in flesh, which *looked like* sinful flesh (ver. 3).

2. *Occasion of His Appearance among men.* περὶ ἁμαρτίας with reference to sin. That He might both expiate its guilt, and expel it from man's nature, specially the latter (ver. 3).

3. *Effects of His Appearance among men.* He condemned the sin-principle to be deposed from its dominion over human nature. He did this ἐν τῇ σαρκί which He had assumed, and which was representative of all human σάρξ (ver. 3).

4. *Ultimate object of His Appearance among men.* That (ἵνα) the rightful demand (δικαίωμα i. 32; ii. 26) of the Mosaic Moral Law might be fulfilled *in* us who walk not after the rule (κατά) of σάρξ, but after that of Πνεῦμα (ver. 4).

[*Obs.* 1. The Unique Character of Christ's Sonship is implied in ἑαυτοῦ. Compare ἴδιος υἱός ver. 32, and ὁ υἱὸς αὐτοῦ ὁ μονογενής 1 S. John iv. 9. His pre-existence is implied in πέμψας; compare Gal. iv. 4 ἐξαπέστειλεν; while the μορφὴ Θεοῦ of Phil. ii. 6 is indirectly suggested by ἐν ὁμοιώματι κ.τ.λ. The Manifestation of the Eternal Son in a sinless Body, points to His supernatural conception of a Virgin-Mother, which cut off the entail of human sin. (See Origen, *in h. l.*) If this mystery is not expressly mentioned by S. Paul, at least no negative inference can be drawn from his silence.]

[*Obs.* 2. The Docetic Gnostics and Manichaeans appealed to ἐν ὁμοιώματι σαρκὸς ἁμαρτίας to prove that Christ's Human Body was not real, but only apparent. This would have been more justifiable if ἁμαρτίας had been omitted. But σὰρξ ἁμαρτίας, like σῶμα τῆς ἁμαρτίας (vi. 6) is a single conception; it means our phenomenal nature so far as it is the seat of sin. Our Lord's Flesh was real (1 S. John iv. 3; 1 Tim. iii. 16); but it only resembled '*sinful* flesh.' ὁμοίωμα has a negative relation to ἁμαρτίας. Tert. *adv. Marc.* v. 14 'Similitudo ad titulum peccati pertinebit, non ad substantiae mendacium.' ὁμοίωμα in Phil. ii. 7 suggests the contrast between the assumed Humanity and the Pre-existent Person of Christ. For the general subject, see Ullmann on *the Sinlessness of Christ.*]

[*Obs.* 3. The condemnation of sin was achieved by its exclusion from the σάρξ of the Representative Man. (Compare κέκριται in S. John xvi. 11; xii. 31.) By His appearance, it lost its dominion as a universal principle of human nature. In His Sinless Flesh, which He made an offering for sin, sin was condemned and destroyed. All who are truly born again to Him, share this death unto sin by their new birth unto righteousness. As His Death became the Death of all Christians, so His Victory over sin is our common victory, since we are members of His Body, of His Flesh, and of His Bones: Eph. v. 30.]

[*Obs.* 4. περὶ ἁμαρτίας seems to negative the Scotist hypothesis that the Incarnation would have taken place if man had not fallen. Cf. Heb. ii. 14.]

[*Obs.* 5. S. Irenaeus *adv. Haer.* iii. 18. 2 is a clear and beautiful paraphrase of vers. 3, 4. Comp. S. Cyr. Alex. *in Joann.* lib. ix. p. 820, who insists on Χριστὸς ἁγιάζων τὴν τῆς σαρκὸς φύσιν ἐν ἑαυτῷ as the key to the meaning of the passage.]

3. The condition of retaining this freedom from sin is the cooperation of the regenerate will: μὴ κατὰ σάρκα περιπατοῦσιν ἀλλὰ κατὰ Πνεῦμα. (ver. 4.)

[*Obs.* περιπατεῖν, like הָלַךְ Is. xxxviii. 3; Ps. cxix. 1, incedere, vitam instituere. The verb implies *habitual* conformity of outward and inward conduct to a principle. κατά with acc. of the governing rule of life. Compare, however, Gal. v. 16 πνεύματι περιπατεῖτε.]

4. The value of this freedom from sin, shown by the complete antithesis between σάρξ (the seat of the νόμος τῆς ἁμαρτίας) and Πνεῦμα, as rival principles of life (vers. 5–9).

Dogmatic: ch. VIII, vv. 1–11.

[*Obs.* Πνεῦμα here without the art. = the Holy Spirit. It is not 'the higher nature of the regenerate man.' (Harless, &c.) The word does not need the art., being used as a proper name. See Meyer, *in loc.*]

This is seen,

    a. In the difference of their practical interests—

οἱ κατὰ $\begin{Bmatrix} σάρκα \\ Πνεῦμα \end{Bmatrix}$ ὄντες, φρονοῦσι τὰ $\begin{Bmatrix} τῆς σαρκός \\ τοῦ Πνεύματος \end{Bmatrix}$ (ver. 5).

[*Obs.* ὄντες substituted for περιπατοῦντες. Εἶναι κατά describes the fundamental state of the soul; φρονεῖν the development of this state in the inward sphere of thought and will; περιπατεῖν κατά, in the whole life, *outward* as well as inward. φρονεῖν and περιπατεῖν are related to εἶναι, as the branch and flower are to the root. Cf. Gal. v. 25 εἰ ζῶμεν πνεύματι, πνεύματι καὶ στοιχῶμεν, where ζῶμεν corresponds to εἶναι, *h. l.*, and στοιχῶμεν includes φρονεῖν and περιπατεῖν. That φρονεῖν means the concentration of interest upon a subject, and so almost = ζητεῖν, see Col. iii. 1, 2; Phil. iii. 19.]

    b. In the results to which they instinctively tend.

τὸ φρόνημα $\begin{Bmatrix} τῆς σαρκός = θάνατος. \\ τοῦ Πνεύματος = ζωὴ καὶ εἰρήνη \end{Bmatrix}$ (ver. 6).

[*Obs.* In this verse γάρ is explicative of the preceding. For this weakened use, see xi. 24; S. Matt. vi. 32; xviii. 11.]

    c. In their respective relations to GOD, (διότι, reason for ver. 6 a).

φρόνημα τῆς σαρκός is
1. *Hostile.* ἔχθρα εἰς Θεόν: cf. ver. 10; Col. i. 21.
2. *Rebellious.* οὐχ ὑποτάσσεται τῷ νόμῳ τοῦ Θεοῦ.
    [This οὐχ ὑποτάσσεται is the reason (γάρ) of the ἔχθρα ver. 1.]
3. *Incapable of obedience.* οὐδὲ γὰρ δύναται (sc. ὑποτάσσεσθαι), i. e. in its present state (ver. 7).

[*Obs.* οὐδὲ δύναται gives the internal reason (γάρ) for οὐχ ὑποτάσσεται.]

On the other side (δέ), looking at the question in the concrete and practically,

οἱ ἐν σαρκὶ ὄντες $\Big\}$ Θεῷ ἀρέσαι οὐ δύνανται (ver. 8).

[*Obs.* 1. The antithesis between σάρξ and πνεῦμα is not here completed. The reason for ver. 6 b is only introduced in vers. 10, 11, in connection with another group of ideas. But it is here implied that the φρόνημα τοῦ πνεύματος is at peace with GOD, because submissive to His will; and that οἱ ἐν τῷ πνεύματι can and do please Him.]

[*Obs.* 2. The οὐ δύναται, οὐ δύνανται of vers. 7, 8 are only true of the φρόνημα τῆς σαρκός while it lasts. It does not exclude the action of GOD's converting grace upon the subjects of this φρόνημα. The οἱ ἐν σαρκί are in the σάρξ as in the element in which their life exists and moves, and while this is the case they cannot please GOD. οἱ κατὰ σάρκα (ver. 5) are those who make the σάρξ the rule of their life.]

K

5. Relation of the readers to this antithesis ver. 9 (antithetic δέ). They are not ἐν σαρκί, but ἐν πνεύματι since (εἴπερ, cf. S. Chrys. *in loc.*) the Spirit of GOD dwells in them. His dwelling in them implies their living-' in ' Him, as the sphere of their life.

[*Obs* On the ἐνοίκησις of the Holy Spirit, Who thus makes the bodies and souls of men, as well as the collective Church, temples of His and of Christ's Presence, Whose Spirit He is, compare 1 Cor. iii. 16 ; vi. 19 ; Gal. iv. 6.]

6. Bearing of this antithesis on the Christian's relation to Jesus Christ, ver. 9 (antithetic δέ). If any man have not the Πνεῦμα Χριστοῦ (= Πν. Θεοῦ), and so is not ἐν πνεύματι, he does not belong to Christ (ver. 9).

[*Obs.* Πνεῦμα Χριστοῦ is so called because He is sent by Christ, and is the organ of His Presence among men, in the Sacraments and in the heart. Not 'our Lord's Human character,' but the Holy Ghost, the Πνεῦμα Θεοῦ (ver. 9) is here referred to, Phil. i. 19 ; 1 Pet. i. 11 ; and as Πνεῦμα Χριστοῦ in order to emphasise οὐκ ἔστιν αὐτοῦ.]

III. *Freedom of the regenerate from the νόμος τοῦ θανάτου* [cf. viii. 2] (vers. 10, 11).

  1. *Immediate* consequence of the indwelling of the Holy Spirit of Christ in the regenerate (ver. 10).
    1. The *body* is (destined to become) a corpse, on account of sin. It is 'conditioni mortis obstrictum,' S. Aug. *de Pecc. Merit. et Rem.* i. 7. This ἁμαρτία is the original sin transmitted from our first parent. Comp. chap. v. 12. But,
    2. the *personal spirit* (τὸ πνεῦμα) not merely ζῇ, but is ζωή. This is διὰ δικαιοσύνην. The justified spirit of the regenerate is Life, because it bears within itself both Christ, Who is the Life Itself, and His Spirit. The justification which Christ works *in us* through His Spirit is the ground of this ζωή (ver. 10).

  2. *More remote* consequence of the indwelling of the Holy Spirit of Christ in the regenerate (ver. 11).
    1. *The future fact.* The mortal bodies of the regenerate will hereafter be quickened by GOD the Father at the Resurrection (ver. 11).
    2. *Its motive.* These bodies, during life, have been inhabited by the Spirit of Him Who raised up Jesus from the dead. For the honour of that Spirit (διὰ τὸ ἐνοικοῦν Πνεῦμα) He will repeat in the bodies of the οἱ ἐν Χριστῷ the miracle which He wrought in the case of His Son (ver. 11).

Dogmatic: ch. VIII, vv. 12-30.

[*Obs.* 1. In ver. 10 the indwelling of the Holy Spirit in Christians is described by its accompanying effect, Χριστὸς ἐν ὑμῖν. In ver. 11 He is τὸ Πνεῦμα τοῦ ἐγείραντος Ἰησοῦν ἐκ νεκρῶν, as though His Presence pledged the Father to be consistent with His past action in the case of Jesus. This of course does not at all imply that the Spirit's *modus inhabitationis* in Christ and in Christians is identical.]

[*Obs.* 2. In ver. 11 διὰ τὸ ἐνοικοῦν αὐτοῦ Πνεῦμα ἐν ὑμῖν would seem to be a better-supported reading than διὰ τοῦ ἐνοικοῦντος αὐτοῦ Πνεύματος κ.τ.λ. In the last case the Spirit would be the instrument of the ζωοποίησις of Christians, in the first His past indwelling is the reason for it. The latter reading was supported by the Catholic opponents of the Macedonian heresy in the 4th and 5th centuries, probably because it appeared to teach the *personality* of the Holy Ghost more distinctly. But the text must have varied at a much earlier date. Observe ζωοποιήσει, not ἐγερεῖ. The latter will be common to the unregenerate as well as the regenerate (cf. Rom. xiv. 10; 2 Cor. v. 10; S. Matt. xxv. 31, 32; S. John v. 28); but it excludes the *moral* elements of ζωή. On the general subject of the Resurrection of the Body, see Pearson, *On the Creed*, Art. xi.]

[*Obs.* 3. The raising of our Lord from the grave is, as in ver. 11, ascribed to the Father in Gal. i. 1; Eph. i. 20; cf. Acts ii. 32; but also by our Lord to His own agency, S. John ii. 19, 21; S. John x. 17, 18. See Pearson, *On the Creed*, Art. v.]

§ 2.
Obligations of the regenerate life in Christ (viii. 12-30).

I. Duty of the Regenerate stated generally and negatively (12-17).

It follows (ἄρα οὖν ver. 12) from the relation of the Holy Spirit to our θνητὰ σώματα, described in ver. 10, 11, that

THESIS. *Christians are debtors; but they do not owe any debt of obedience to the σάρξ with the view of leading carnal lives* (ver. 12).

[*Obs.* The Apostle is arguing against the assumptions that (1) τὸ κατὰ σάρκα ζῆν is the natural law of human life; and that (2) the *onus probandi* lies with those who would dispute it. He approaches the discussion (ἄρα οὖν ver. 12) from the high vantage ground occupied in ver. 1-11. Christians cannot be bound to obey a law of life, from which it is their happiness to be emancipated.]

Arg. 1. (ex consequentiis.) Life according to the standard of σάρξ leads to death; while mortification of the animal actions of the body, (πράξεις τοῦ σώματος, cf. vii. 23,) by the power of the Holy Spirit, leads to life (ver. 13).

Arg. 2. From the conditions and privileges of the υἱότης Θεοῦ to which Christians are admitted (14-17). For *a*. This υἱότης, although a product of GOD's grace (S. John i. 13), depends for its continuance on man's passive obedience to the leading of the Holy Spirit of GOD (ver. 14).

b. It implies trustful intimacy with a Holy GOD. What Christians have received is (*a*) not such a spirit as might rule a slave, so that they should now again, as under the law, live in terror; but (*b*) the Πνεῦμα υἱοθεσίας, the Spirit that inspires and befits an adopted son. In Him, as in the element of their new life, Christians fervently speak to GOD in prayer, as to their Father (ver. 15).

c. Its reality is concurrently attested on one side by the Spirit speaking from without through Revelation and in the Church, and on the other by the personal conscious spirit of the Christian, who knows that he stands towards GOD in this new relation (ver. 16).

d. It involves the further relation (in accordance with those instincts which are implanted in our nature, and which express themselves in human law) of heirship towards GOD and co-heirship with Christ. This, however, is conditioned; and the condition expresses the *second* obligation of the Regenerate Life, viz. suffering with Christ (ver. 17).

[*Obs*. 1. Connection of thought (vers. 13-17). The attributes of sonship, (1) guidance by the Holy Spirit, (2) intimacy with GOD as a Father in prayer, (3) the inner sense of sonship corresponding to the attestation of the Spirit, and (4) the 'heirship' of GOD and co-heirship with Christ,—all forbid the thought of our being ὀφειλέται τῇ σαρκί. But the exact relation of the verses (14-17) to each other is as follows: ver. 14 supplies a reason (γάρ) for ζήσεσθε in ver. 13, since the future ζωή is destined for the τέκνα Θεοῦ (ver. 17; Gal. iv. 7); ver. 15 explains (γάρ) the applicability of ver. 14 to the readers; ver. 16 is confirmatory of ver. 15; and ver. 17 unfolds the additional fact of κληρονομία which is involved in υἱότης.]

[*Obs*. 2. Although ἄγονται is passive (cf. S. John iii. 8; iv. 14; 2 Tim. iii. 6; 1 Cor. xii. 2; S. Matt. iv. 1; S. Luke iv. 1), it does not compromise the freedom of the human will. The gift of the Spirit restores that freedom by rescuing man from the dominion of sin and nature under which he had fallen. S. Aug. *Serm. de Verb. Apostoli*, clvi. c. 11 'Dicit mihi aliquis, Ergo agimur et non agimus. Immo et agis et ageris; et tunc bene agis, si a bono agaris. Spiritus enim Dei, qui te agit agentibus adjutor est.']

[*Obs*. 3. υἱοὶ Θεοῦ. In the Old Testament the relation of GOD's people to Himself was one of fear. (Ex. xix. 12 sqq.; Heb. xii. 18 sqq.) Kings and single members of the Theocracy were named sons of Jehovah. This external theocratic distinction is, under the Gospel, both in itself spiritualised, and extended to all living members of the Church. As this Christian υἱότης does not belong to man by nature, it is from S. Paul's point of view a υἱοθεσία: but this, as explained by S. John, involves a real second γέννησις, S. John i. 13. υἱοθεσία, only in S. Paul (θέσθαι υἱόν Plat. *Legg.* xi. 929), denotes the assumption into sonship by an act of GOD's grace, as distinct from the sonship which results from birth. Used of (a) Israel's relation to GOD, in contrast with the heathen peoples, Rom. ix. 4, (b) the condition of true Christians as effected by the Holy Spirit (Gal. iv. 5; Eph. i. 5, and *h. l.*) in this life, and (c) the same condition as perfected after Christ's Second Coming, Rom. viii. 23, cf. ver. 19. 'Αββᾶ ὁ πατήρ S. Mark xiv. 36; Gal. iv. 6; ܐܒܐ carefully preserved by Christians, as the very word used by Christ in prayer, and in teaching His disciples to pray. S. Aug. thinks that the two words point to GOD's common fatherhood towards Jews and Gentiles under the Gospel.]

[*Obs.* 4. In ver. 16 is a sharply-drawn distinction between the Absolute and Divine Πνεῦμα, and man's πνεῦμα or conscious personality, the τὸ πνεῦμα τοῦ ἀνθρώπου τὸ ἐν αὐτῷ 1 Cor. ii. 11. These concur, the first speaking from without through revelation, and the second from within in the depths of consciousness; and they witness to the reality of the Christian υἱότης Θεοῦ. Not that this συμμαρτυρεῖν is a single act; the prep. (as in σύμφημι, συνήδομαι, vii. 16, 22) need only point to concurrent although independent action. The passage affords no real support to the theory of a 'fides specialis' or any such particular assurance of justification and sonship, as may be independent of obedience, and due to *physical* temperament. The certainty which results from the συμμαρτυρεῖν is a *moral* one.]

[*Obs.* 5. In ver. 17 καὶ κληρονόμοι. Neither here, nor in Gal. iv. 7, is the Apostle's language based on the *Jewish* law of inheritance, according to which the legitimately-born sons alone (the first-born having a double portion, Deut. xxi. 17) were, as a rule, intestate heirs; but on the *Roman* law, according to which sons and daughters, whether born in marriage or *adopted* children (and the Apostle conceives of Christians as such), were intestate heirs. Cf. Ewald, *Alterth.* p. 238 sqq.; Meyer on Gal. iv. 7. For the full meaning of συγκληρονόμοι δὲ Χρ. cf. S. John xvii. 24; S. Matt. xix. 28; 1 Cor. vi. 2: 2 Tim. ii. 12; S. Aug. *in Ps.* xlix. 2 'Tanta charitas est in illo haerede, ut voluerit habere cohaeredes: haereditas autem, in qua cohaeredes Christi sumus, non minuitur copia possessorum, non fit angustior numerositate cohaeredum; sed tanta est multis quanta paucis, tanta singulis quanta omnibus.']

II. Duty of the regenerate stated positively and specifically (18–30). The Law of suffering with Christ.

§ THESIS. *Christians should gladly share Christ's sufferings, that they may share His glory* (εἴπερ συμπάσχομεν, ἵνα καὶ συνδοξασθῶμεν) (ver. 17 b).

[*Obs.* Those who for the truth's sake accept suffering, S. Matt. x. 38; xvi. 24, suffer with Christ; 1 Pet. iv. 13 κοινωνεῖτε τοῖς τοῦ Χριστοῦ παθήμασιν: S. Matt.

xx. 22 δύνασθε πιεῖν τὸ ποτήριον ὃ ἐγὼ μέλλω πίνειν, καὶ τὸ βάπτισμα ὃ ἐγὼ βαπτίζομαι βαπτισθῆναι; This suffering was a necessary preliminary to a share in Christ's glory (εἴπερ): because it is a mark of real union with Christ suffering and glorified, of true incorporation with His Body Mystical; cf. Acts ix. 4 τί με διώκεις;]

Encouragement to this συμπάσχειν (vers. 18-30).

Reason 1. (for encouragement to suffer with Christ) (vers. 18-25). The revelation of glory which awaits us altogether transcends our present sufferings (ver. 18).

[*Obs.* τὰ παθήματα τοῦ νῦν καιροῦ refers to actual or impending persecutions; δόξα to the irradiation of the bodies and souls of the regenerate hereafter; μέλλουσαν to the αἰὼν μέλλων, the future age of the completed Messianic kingdom, which will date from the Second Coming of Christ, and the general resurrection. Cf. 2 Cor. iv. 17 τὸ γὰρ παραυτίκα ἐλαφρὸν τῆς θλίψεως ἡμῶν καθ᾽ ὑπερβολὴν εἰς ὑπερβολὴν αἰώνιον βάρος δόξης κατεργάζεται ἡμῖν.]

Proof of the reality of this transcendent glory (vers. 19-25). (A) from irrational nature (19-22); (B) from the experience of Christians (23-25).

(A) Proof from irrational nature. (vers. 19-22).

Arg. a. (Warrant (γάρ) of μέλλουσαν ver. 18). From the expectant aspect of nature. The reality of this coming revelation of the glory of the 'sons of GOD' may be inferred from the attitude of expectancy, directed towards an unrealised future, which is observable in the whole irrational creation (ver. 19).

[*Obs.* 1. κτίσις here not the act of creation, but the creature, as S. Mark x. 6; xiii. 19; 2 S. Pet. iii. 4; Wisd. ii. 6: and in a more limited sense, S. Mark xvi. 15; Col. i. 15, 23; Heb. iv. 13. S. Augustine understands by it the perishing element in human life: 'quidquid nunc in homine laborat et corruptioni subjacet.' (*Expos. propos. liii. ex Epist. ad Rom.*) Or unconverted humanity, 'ea, quae tantummodo creatura est, nondum per fidem aggregata numero filiorum Dei.' S. Paul would have named this, not κτίσις, but κόσμος. Theodoret would include even the angels under κτίσις, while S. Chrysostom limits it to inanimate objects. It would seem to mean animate and inanimate nature, in opposition to man; in fact what we generally term 'nature.']

[*Obs.* 2. ἀποκαραδοκία, 'waiting expectation,' from ἀπό, κάρα, and δοκεύω, erecto capite prospicere: S. Chrys. ἡ σφόδρα προσδοκία (tom. ix. p. 581 ed. Ben.), Phil. i. 20. Ascribed by a bold prosopopoeia to nature. For the idea of a coming glorification of nature, see Is. xi. 6 sqq.; Ezek. xxxvii; Is. lxv. 17; lxvi. 1; Ps. cii. 27; Eisenmenger, *Entd. Jud.* ii. p. 367 sqq., 824 sqq.]

[*Obs.* 3. The pessimist philosophy of Schopenhauer dwells constantly, although with a very different drift, on this aspect of nature. 'All human life is essentially suffering,' is his favourite thesis. Cf. *Die Welt als Wille und Vorstellung*, 'Alles Leben Leiden ist,' § 56 (vol. i. p. 356). Cf. 57, 59.]

Dogmatic: ch. VIII, vv. 12-30.

Arg. b. From the grounds of this expectant aspect of nature. The ἀποκαραδοκία of the creature is to be explained by (γάρ ver. 20) its instinctively felt ματαιότης, 'emptiness,' 'nothingness' (ver. 20).

[*Obs.* For ματαιότης see Eph. iv. 17; 2 S. Pet. ii. 18. It seems that ὑποταγῆναι τῇ ματαιότητι here introduces the state described as δουλεία τῆς φθορᾶς in ver. 21. S. Chrysostom paraphrases ver. 20, tom. ix. p. 582, by φθαρτὴ γέγονε, as though ματαιότης and φθορά were practically coincident, although φθορά is developed out of ματαιότης. ματαιότης, corresponding to הֶבֶל in Ecclesiastes, seems to be the felt void, objectlessness, of nature, apart from GOD. ματαιότης is conceived of as a mistress to which nature has been subjected (ὑπετάγη) as a slave.]

Circumstances of this subjection of nature to ματαιότης. It took place

1. at a particular historical epoch (ὑπετάγη, *hist. aor.*), i.e. the Fall. Gen. iii. 17 (ver. 20).
2. through the agency of GOD (really ὁ ὑποτάξας, He did this on account of man's guilt) (ver. 20).
3. on account of GOD (διὰ τὸν ὑποτάξαντα) and in order to satisfy His Will (ver. 20).
4. without the will of nature itself, οὐχ ἑκοῦσα, invitâ et repugnante naturâ (ver. 20).
5. but with the appended condition of a hope, that not merely the children of GOD, but irrational nature as well, would be delivered from the bondage which consists in corruption (*gen. apposit.*) into the freedom which consists (*gen. apposit.*) in the glory of the children of GOD (ver. 21).

[*Obs.* S. Chrys. and others understand Adam by the ὑποτάξας. On man's account and by his act nature was subjected to vanity; nature was originally man's servant, a kind of second and more spacious body to the human spirit. Had man never fallen, nature, like the human body, would have ever realized its true object in subjection to his self-conscious spirit. But with the fall, a separation took place between the spirit of man on one side, and his body and nature on the other; and the latter, no longer sharing the immortality of his spirit, fell under the power of ματαιότης and φθορά. ... We should, however, have expected some expression in the text pointing to Adam as the ὑποτάξας; the text assumes that the ὑποτάξας is well known.]

Arg. c. From the universal and unceasing character of this travail of nature (ver. 22). This condition of nature, which is a point of Christian knowledge, (οἴδαμεν, ii. 2; iii. 19; vii. 14), shows (γάρ ver. 22) that a hope of deliverance (ἐπ' ἐλπίδι ver. 20) is left; had this been otherwise, nature would have ceased, ere now, its συστενάζειν and συνωδίνειν (ver. 22).

(B) Proof from the experience of Christians (23–25).

These sighs are not confined (οὐ μόνον δέ) to irrational nature. They are shared in by Christians, who thus afford a decisive proof of the well-founded character of the ἐλπίς in ver. 20.

Arg. a. Although Christians have received the ἀπαρχὴ τοῦ Πνεύματος, yet they too sigh inwardly, waiting as they do for the complete realisation of their υἱοθεσία, which as yet (ver. 15) they possess only imperfectly, and which the redemption of the body from corruption is necessary to complete. This στενάζειν points to the future ἀποκάλυψις in ver. 19 (ver. 23).

[*Obs* 1. ἀπαρχὴ τοῦ Πνεύματος (*partitive gen.*) possessed by Christians in this life, and in contrast to the full possession of Him in the life to come. Thus it corresponds with ἀρραβὼν τοῦ Πνεύματος 2 Cor. i. 22, cf. Eph. i. 14, where the partial gift of the Spirit here is represented as an earnest of the whole which is to follow. The contrast does not lie with (1) unconverted mankind who had not any such share of the Spirit as to suggest it, or (2) with any lesser gifts of the Spirit in the post-Apostolic age. If a *gen. apposit.*, it must = the Spirit as first-fruits, viz. of a state of glory.]

[*Obs.* 2. The ἀπολύτρωσιν τοῦ σώματος is an epexegetical explanation of the complete υἱοθεσία. By being thus redeemed from the defects of its earthly condition, the body will become a σῶμα ἄφθαρτον, like the body of Jesus glorified. (1 Cor. xv. 51; 2 Cor. v. 2 sqq.; Phil. iii. 21.) Or, in the case of those who die before the Second Advent, it will be raised up as such (1 Cor. xv. 42 sqq.). Not 'redemption from the body,' as Fritzsche and others: ἡμῶν would probably have been added, had σώματος been a *gen. obj.*]

Arg. b. This expectation of the complete υἱοθεσία by Christians is (γάρ) itself in keeping with the conditions under which they had been made partakers of salvation, (ἐσώθημεν). They possessed salvation, not altogether in actual reality, but, so far as the redemption of the body is concerned, *in hope.* Had this object of hope (ἐλπίς) been already seen, it would thereby have ceased to be one; hope has ceased, when we behold its object (ver. 24). Accordingly, Christians patiently look out for a future which they do not see, but for which they hope (ver. 25). This future is the ἀποκάλυψις τῶν υἱῶν τοῦ Θεοῦ ver. 19.

[*Obs.* For the objective sense of ἐλπίς in ver. 24, comp. Col. i. 5 ἐλπὶς ἀποκειμένη: 1 Tim. i. 1; Heb. vi. 18.]

Reason 2. (for encouragement to suffer with Christ), (vers. 26, 27). The Holy Ghost assists Christians.

[Corresponding to *our* waiting with patience (ὡσαύτως) is the assistance, on GOD'S side, of the Holy Spirit, (ver. 26).]

In this assistance of the Holy Spirit, note

1. *Its general character.* By this assistance He cooperates, actively, with our weakness (ver. 26).

[*Obs.* The activity of the Divine Πνεῦμα is here again, as in vers. 16, 23, distinguished clearly from the subjective consciousness of the soul. The Spirit συναντιλαμ-βάνεται τῇ ἀσθενείᾳ : He joins His activity to that natural weakness in us, which makes ὑπομονή (ver. 25) so difficult. Observe the idea of concurrence in συν-.]

The Reason for this assistance (γάρ) is to be discovered in one particular want, viz. our ignorance of what to pray for, according to certain circumstances (καθὸ δεῖ). This is relieved by the Holy Spirit, in whose assistance note further

2. *Its specific character.* By this assistance He interposes, on our behalf, with GOD in prayer, which takes the shape of sighs whose meaning no words can convey (ver. 26).

[*Obs.* 1. So S. Paul himself had prayed ὑπὲρ τοῦ σκόλοπος, but in vain ; S. Chrys. : cf. 2 Cor. xii. 8, 9.]

[*Obs.* 2. ὑπερεντυγχάνει (ἅπ. λεγ.) = ἐντυγχάνει ὑπὲρ ἡμῶν, scil. τῷ Θεῷ. Cf. vers. 27, 34 ; Heb. vii. 25. The στεναγμοὶ ἀλάλητοι, our sighs, the full meaning of which cannot be expressed in human speech. That these sighs may be expressed, as sighs, outwardly, is possible ; like the charisma of γλώσσαις λαλεῖν 1 Cor. xiv. 2-4, 13 sqq. S. Aug. *Tr. vi. in Joann.* 2 'Non ergo Spiritus Sanctus in semetipso, apud semetipsum, in illâ Trinitate, in illâ beatitudine, in illâ aeternitate substantiae gemit, sed in nobis gemit, quia gemere nos facit. Nec parva res est, quod nos docet Spiritus S. gemere ; insinuat enim nobis quia peregrinamur, et docet nos in patriam suspirare, et ipso desiderio gemimus.' Origen. *Expos. in loc.* (vol. iv. p. 602 Ben.) 'Non verbis offerre dicitur Spiritus interpellationem pro sanctis, sed gemitibus, et non communibus istis gemitibus, sed inenarrabilibus. Quomodo enim enarrari potest, quod Spiritus Dei loquitur Deo, cum interdum nec ipse quidem noster Spiritus quod sentit et intelligit sermone possit exponere?' Note here (1) the dogmatic bearing of this verse on the personality of the Holy Ghost, Who is clearly distinguished as an agent (*a*) from GOD the Father Whose Spirit He is, and (*b*) from the human spirit within which He sighs ; and (2) its relation to the higher and supernatural kind of mental prayer, described by Tauler and other Christian Mystics, in which the collective powers of the soul are stilled, and the Divine Spirit alone is active. It is no longer, as in the lower form of mental prayer, man who prays, but the Holy Ghost Who prays in him : in such prayer man is lost to himself in GOD.]

3. *Its real value.* It is understood by Him to Whom it is addressed.

Obj. It is impossible to say what value there is in prayer which takes the form of ἀλάλητοι στεναγμοί.

Resp. True ; if man were addressed in prayer. But untrue in fact. For

(1) this prayer is addressed to GOD, the Searcher of hearts.

(2) He knows that the specific φρόνημα of the interceding Spirit is (i.e. what the Spirit intends in prayer), viz. to make intercession (*a*) for Christians, (*b*) according to the Divine Will (ver. 27).

[*Obs.* The title ἐρευνῶν τὰς καρδίας, applied to GOD, is of peculiar solemnity; 1 Sam. xvi. 7 ; 1 Kings viii. 39 ; Psalm vii. 10 ; Jer. xvii. 9 sqq. The לֵב, or καρδία, is the central chamber of self-conscious life in the personal spirit of man. Delitzsch, *Bibl. Psychol.* pp. 292 ff.]

Reason 3. (for encouragement to suffer with Christ), (28-30). All things (including suffering) cooperate with those who love GOD to promote their good (ver. 28).

[*Obs.* 1. This is a Christian conviction (οἴδαμεν), which is set off against (δέ) the στενάζομεν of the regenerate in ver. 23 sqq. The πάντα include the παθήματα τοῦ νῦν καιροῦ (ver. 18). The συνεργεῖν refers not to the concurrence of all circumstances, but to the cooperation of all with the ἀγαπῶντες τὸν Θεόν. (Cf. Mark xvi. 20 ; 2 Cor. vi. 1 ; S. James ii. 22.) The ἀγαθόν is purposely indefinite, because so inclusive.]

[*Obs.* 2. πάντα here does not appear to include sinful acts, into which the regenerate may fall ; the regenerate *as such* sinneth not. 1 S. John iii. 9 ; iv. 7. It is only as ruled by the old nature that he sins. S. Chrys. limits πάντα to the sum of hindrances and sufferings which Christians experience in serving GOD. Yet S. Aug. takes in their *falls* as well : 'adeo prorsus *omnia*, ut si etiam qui eorum deviant, et exorbitant, etiam hoc ipsum eis faciat proficere in bonum, quia humiliores redeunt atque doctiores,' *De Corrept. et Grat.* cap. 9.]

Arg. 1. Those who do love GOD are κατὰ πρόθεσιν κλητοί, [and, as such, are natural objects of His loving care, Who has thus from all eternity proposed to call them to Himself] (ver. 28).

[*Obs.* 1. πρόθεσις is understood by S. Chrysostom of the resolve of the called to obey GOD's voice : οὐχ ἡ κλῆσις μόνον, ἀλλὰ καὶ ἡ πρόθεσις τῶν καλουμένων τὴν σωτηρίαν εἰργάσατο. And this human πρόθεσις is mentioned in Acts xi. 23 ; 2 Tim. iii. 10. But the whole connection shows that the πρόθεσις here is that which has existed from eternity in the Divine Mind ; cf. Rom. ix. 11

πρόθεσις τοῦ Θεοῦ: Eph. i. 11 προορισθέντες κατὰ πρόθεσιν τοῦ τὰ πάντα ἐνεργοῦντος κατὰ τὴν βουλὴν τοῦ θελήματος αὐτοῦ: Eph. iii. 11 κατὰ πρόθεσιν τῶν αἰώνων ἣν ἐποίησεν ἐν τῷ Χριστῷ Ἰησοῦ. The opposite account of the motive of the κλῆσις is rejected in 2 Tim. i. 9 καλέσαντος ἡμᾶς κλήσει ἁγίᾳ οὐ κατὰ τὰ ἔργα ἡμῶν, ἀλλὰ κατὰ ἰδίαν πρόθεσιν καὶ χάριν τὴν δοθεῖσαν ἡμῖν ἐν Χρ. Ἰ. πρὸ χρόνων αἰωνίων. This πρόθεσις is dictated by His Eternal Love; it is εὐδοκία ἣν προέθετο ἐν αὐτῷ Eph. i. 9.]

[Obs. 2. The Divine κλῆσις emerges into time and history in the preaching of the Gospel; and, in the widest sense of the expression, all are said to be κλητοί who are reached by it. But of these the many are contrasted by our Lord with the ἄξιοι (S. Matt. xxii. 8), and with the ἐκλεκτοί (S. Matt. xx. 16), who are comparatively few. These last are κλητοί in a narrower sense; they hear and obey. Rom. i. 7; 1 Cor. i. 2, 24. They are the last class described in the Parable of the Sower (S. Luke viii. 8, 15), and thus correspond to the τετηρημένοι κλητοί of S. Jude 1, and to the κατὰ πρόθεσιν κλητοί of this passage.]

Arg. 2. That all things must cooperate with those who love GOD for good becomes clearer, if the successive stages of GOD'S κατὰ πρόθεσιν κλῆσις in its majestic development through eternity and time are considered (vers. 29, 30).

§ *Five points are distinguishable in this* κατὰ πρόθεσιν κλῆσις (vers. 29, 30).

1. The Divine Foreknowledge (οὓς προέγνω). GOD foreknew the ἀγαπῶντες τὸν Θεόν (ver. 29).

[Obs. This προέγνω is strictly an act of the Divine Intelligence: novit suos antequam vocaret. It has been understood to mean a creative knowledge,— a knowledge which includes affection and choice; and is thus an *actus voluntatis* as well as an *actus intellectus*. So Origen, iv. p. 604 'Cognovisse suos dicitur, hoc est, in dilectione habuisse sibique sociâsse.' But the New Testament use of the word does not sanction this (not even in Rom. xi. 2; 1 S. Pet. i. 20), or any other meaning than *to know beforehand*. Acts xxvi. 5; 2 S. Pet. iii. 17. For γιγνώσκειν, see S. John ii. 24, 25; x. 14, 27; 2 Tim. ii. 19; and especially S. John vi. 69 for the general sense.]

2. The Divine Fore-ordaining (προώρισεν). GOD predestined the foreknown to be like His Son (ver. 29).

[Obs. To say that the προορισμός, following the πρόγνωσις is *propter praevisa merita*, would be semi-pelagian; it is not even *post praevisa merita*. For the προορισμός includes the gifts of grace, as well as the glory of the world to come. 'Sub praedestinatione cadit omne beneficium salutare, quod est homini ab aeterno divinitus praeparatum. Unde eadem ratione, omnia beneficia quae nobis confert ex tempore, praeparavit nobis ab aeterno. Unde ponere quod aliquod meritum ex parte nostrâ praesupponatur, *cujus praescientia sit ratio praedestinationis*, nihil est aliud quam gratiam ponere dari ex meritis nostris, et quod principium bonorum operum est ex nobis, et consummatio est ex Deo,' Aquin. *in loc.*]

a. *Form of this Predestination.* Our conformity to the Image of His Son (a) in suffering, perhaps, (συμπάσχειν ver. 17). but chiefly (b) in glory (υἱοθεσίαν, τὴν ἀπολύτρωσιν τοῦ σώματος ver. 23) (ver. 29).

[*Obs.* συμμόρφους τῆς εἰκόνος, *gen. of dependence*, where we should have expected a *dat.* after a word compounded with σύν. In Christ our Lord, according to Phil. ii. 6, 7, there is a two-fold μορφή. As being in the μορφὴ Θεοῦ, He is the Image of the Invisible God : Col. i. 15. In the μορφὴ δούλου He has so entered into the conditions of our nature that we can be σύμμορφοι with Him. Especially is conformity with His Glorified Manhood the form to which true Christians are predestined : 1 Cor. xv. 49 ; Phil. iii. 21 εἰς τὸ γενέσθαι αὐτὸ (sc. our body of humiliation) σύμμορφον τῷ σώματι τῆς δόξης αὐτοῦ.]

b. *Final Aim* (εἰς τό) *of this Predestination.* That Christ might be the πρωτότοκος ἐν πολλοῖς ἀδελφοῖς. His glory is the Final Cause of that of His members (ver. 29).

[*Obs.* While our Lord, in his Eternal Relation to the Father, is the μονογενής, the One and only Son of GOD, He is the πρωτότοκος relatively to the adopted υἱοὶ Θεοῦ, whose conformity to His Image is thus essential to His fully entering upon this relation towards them, while it has its basis in the communication of His new nature by Grace. As the πρωτότοκος He addresses His brethren in S. John xx. 17, and rises from the dead, Col. i. 18. See on this subject, S. Cyr. Alex. *Thesaur. Assert.* 25, p. 236.]

3. **The Divine Call to the Predestined** (ἐκάλεσε). Here the Divine πρόθεσις takes shape in time (ver. 30).

[*Obs.* The κλῆσις is partly external, through the preaching of the Gospel ; partly internal, as being the appeal of the Divine Spirit to the heart. Cf. S. John x. 27 ; Acts xiii. 48 ; 2 Tim. i. 9. They who obey the κλῆσις are emphatically the κλητοί and they obey because they are προωρισμένοι.]

4. **The Divine Justification of the Called** (ἐδικαίωσεν) (ver. 30).

[Cf. iii. 26 ; iv. 5, 25 ; v. 19 ; viii. 4.]

5. **The Divine Glorification of the Justified** (ἐδόξασεν) (ver. 30).

[*Obs.* 1. On the close connection between Justification and Glory, see ii. 7 ; vers. 9, 17, 21 ; vi. 23 ; viii. 10–17.]

[*Obs.* 2. ἐδόξασε is not an *aor.* used for a *fut.* Each of these acts is viewed as already historically accomplished in the Divine Mind ; the last not less than the first. There is no *succession* in GOD's thoughts and resolves ; all that was and is and is to come is seen at once, as present in its completeness to the Infinite Mind, which sees all at a glance.]

[Obs. 3.

The κλῆσις κατὰ πρό- θεσιν,

{ (i) as an eternal act of GOD, independent of our cooperation or *praevisa merita*, is } { i. { in the Divine Intelligence } πρόγνωσις. ii. in the Divine Will, προορισμός. }

{ (ii) as emerging into time, and implying the cooperation of the predestinated, which, however, is invariable, is } { iii. { in its approach to the soul } κλῆσις. iv. { in its work upon the soul } δικαίωσις. v. in its final results, δοξασμός.] }

[Obs. 4. On the general subject, see Bp. Browne, *Articles*, Art. xvii. sect. 1. History : Martensen's *Dogmatik*, §§ 210-224 ; Petavius, *de Deo Deique proprietatibus*, Libri ix x ; Weiss, *Biblische Theologie des N. T.* p. 144 sqq.]

§ 3.

Permanence of the regenerate life in Christ (viii. 31–39).

This permanence is warranted by three arguments.

Arg. 1. From the relation of the οἱ ἐν Χριστῷ to GOD the Father (31–34 a).

[Obs. In ver. 31 οὖν shows the logical relation between vers. 29, 30, and 31 sqq. It is in view of the foregoing description of the predestination of the saints (πρὸς ταῦτα) that the Apostle *does* say in the name of the οἱ ἐν Χριστῷ what follows (vers. 31-39).]

    a. GOD is their *Guardian* (ὑπὲρ ἡμῶν). With such protection, an attack from any quarter must fail (ver. 31).

[Obs. 1. The question τί οὖν ἐροῦμεν ; asked in the name of the elect, is answered by another question, which contains the beginning of *what the elect do say*, εἰ ὁ Θεός, κ.τ.λ. Resolved into an affirmative proposition it would be, Since GOD guards us, none can harm us. On the opposition between ὑπέρ and κατά, cf. 2 Cor. xiii. 8.]

[Obs. 2. ὑπὲρ ἡμῶν is a summary of vers. 29, 30. The thought is that of Ps. xxvii. 1 ; S. John x. 28 sqq.]

[Obs. 3. *Transitional.* ὑπὲρ ἡμῶν is justified also by ver. 32. ὅς γε used for ὅτι as a causal particle. He who in deed, etc.]

    b. GOD is their *Benefactor*, therefore they will want nothing. His Bounty

        (i) *in the past* is seen in the astonishing surrender even of His Own Son to death (ὑπὲρ ἡμῶν πάντων).

        (ii) *in the future* may be expected freely to bestow all things necessary to Salvation in and with this transcendent gift of His Son (ver. 32).

[*Obs.* 1. The arg. (cf. ver. 32) is *a majori ad minus*: the greater implies the less. The surrender of the Everlasting Son to sufferings and death must carry with it all the blessings and graces which are needed to secure the regenerate life in Christians. The greatness of the gift is implied (1) by the use of ἰδίου, His own Son by nature, (cf. ver. 3 τὸν ἑαυτοῦ υἱόν;) (2) by οὐκ ἐφείσατο (xi. 21; 2 Cor. xiii. 2; 2 S. Pet. ii. 4, 5), which implies that the Father's Eternal Love did a certain violence to Itself in the surrender of His Son; (3) by the juxta-position of the negative and positive phrases (οὐκ ἐφείσατο . . . ἀλλὰ παρέδωκεν), enhancing the significance of the surrender, (παρέδωκεν, sc. εἰς θάνατον, iv. 25). What can be refused after this gift of gifts? what that is necessary to a Christian is not, by anticipation, included in it?]

[*Obs.* 2. In ἐφείσατο there is a clear reference to Abraham, Gen. xxii. 16 οὐκ ἐφείσω τοῦ υἱοῦ σου τοῦ ἀγαπητοῦ. ἰδίου is here substituted as the stronger word, ὑπὲρ πάντων ἡμῶν. On the effect of the death of Christ cf. Rom. v. 6-11; 1 Tim. i. 15; 1 S. John iv. 9, 10, 14; 1 S. Pet. ii. 24.]

    c. GOD is their *Justifier* (ὁ δικαιῶν); they have no accuser to fear.

    Qu. Who shall make accusation against the elect of GOD?

    Ans. There is no one to condemn, because GOD is the Justifier: consequently the accusation would be without result (ver. 33).

[*Obs.* 1. In ver. 33, as in 31, 32, the question is answered by a counter question. τίς ὁ κατακρίνων; really = the *neg. prop.* οὐκ ἐστὶν ὁ κατακρίνων. The words Χριστὸς ὁ ἀποθανών introduce a second answer to τίς ἐγκαλέσει;]

[*Obs.* 2. ἐκλεκτοὶ Θεοῦ are identical with the κατὰ πρόθεσιν κλητοί, ver. 28, cf. S. Matt. xxii. 14; 1 Tim. v. 21. Those whom GOD has chosen out of the κόσμος (S. John xvii. 6) to be members of His Church, and blessed for Christ's sake eternally, Eph. i. 4. This is the Christian transfiguration of the Old Testament national, external, theocratic conception of ἐκλεκτοί. (Ps. civ. 43; cv. 5; Is. xlii. 1; lxv. 9; Wisd. iii. 9.)]

    Arg. 2. From the relation of οἱ ἐν Χριστῷ to Jesus Christ, Whose past and present acts for us are the warrant of His love (ver. 34).

    (a) in the past
(i) He is ἀποθανών. 'Greater love hath no man than this, that a man lay down his life for his friends.' Rom. v. 6; Eph. iii. 18 sqq. (ver. 34).

(ii) Yet more, He is ὁ ἐγερθείς. This διὰ τὴν δικαίωσιν ἡμῶν Rom. iv. 25: cf. also Rom. v. 10; 1 Cor. xv. 20-23; S. John xxi. 14 (ver. 34).

Dogmatic: ch. VIII, *vv.* 31-39.

b. { at the present moment, }

(iii) ἔστιν ἐν δεξιᾷ τοῦ Θεοῦ. Ps. cx. 1 ; S. Matt. xxii. 44 ; S. Mark xvi. 19 ; Eph. i. 20 ; Acts ii. 34, 35, 36 ; Heb. i. 13 ; 1 S. Pet. iii. 22 (ver. 34).

[*Obs.* The Right Hand of GOD signifies (1) the great power of GOD, (2) the place of honour in heaven (1 Kings ii. 19), (3) the place of perfect happiness: Ps. xvi. 11. Cf. Pearson *on the Creed*, Art. 6.]

(iv) ἐντυγχάνει ὑπὲρ ἡμῶν. Although the σύνθρονος of the Father, He intercedes for us ; being present with the Father in His glorified Humanity, He continuously presents His finished ἱλαστήριον on our behalf (1 S. John ii. 2), and as our High Priest : Heb. vii. 26 ; ix. 24 (ver. 34).

[*Obs.* This passage is fatal to the theory that on His Ascension our Lord made one act of Intercession, and then ceased. It is a present and continuous action, which is described by ἐντυγχάνει ; (and it is the warrant of the continuous intercessions of His members, whether on earth or in Paradise). On the *omnipotentia supplex* of the Ascended Mediator, see Pearson, *On the Creed*, Art. 6.]

Arg. 3. From the relation of the οἱ ἐν Χριστῷ to all possible trials, states, unseen beings, or conditions of being (35-39).

    a. No *trials* in this life can of themselves separate us from the Love of Christ for us (35-37).

[*Obs.* The ἀγάπη τοῦ Χριστοῦ here, as in Rom. v. 5, is *gen. subj.* His acts of love are enumerated in ver. 34; He is called ὁ ἀγαπήσας ἡμᾶς in ver. 37, and the expression is paraphrased by ἀγάπη τοῦ Θεοῦ ἡ ἐν Χριστῷ in ver. 39 ; cf. Winer, *Gr. N. T.* p. 232.]

    (1) Seven representative forms of earthly trials which cannot sever us from the ἀγάπη τοῦ Χριστοῦ (ver. 35).

Trials,
- *a.* generic,
  - oppression, θλίψις.
  - straitened circumstances, στενοχωρία.
  - persecution, διωγμός.
- *b.* specific,
  - through want of means
    - hunger, λιμός.
    - nakedness, γυμνότης.
  - through risks from without
    - danger of violent death, κίνδυνος.
    - contact with violent death, μάχαιρα.

[*Obs.* 1. θλῖψις and στενοχωρία are coupled in ii. 9. The former corresponds in LXX to צָרָה and צַר. The latter is the stronger word; it is opposed to εὐροχωρία, and means loss of liberty, straitened circumstances, or worse: 2 Cor. vi. 4; xii. 10. διωγμός, lit. 'persecution': S. Matt. xiii. 21; S. Mark iv. 17; Acts viii. 1; xiii. 50; plural, S. Mark x. 30; 2 Cor. xii. 10; 2 Thess. i. 4; 2 Tim. iii. 11.]

[*Obs.* 2. λιμός and γυμνότης are coupled in S. Paul's description of the trials of the Apostles, 1 Cor. iv. 11, and of his own, 2 Cor. xi. 27. For κίνδυνος, see 2 Cor. xi. 26 κινδύνοις ποταμῶν, κινδύνοις λῃστῶν and 1 Cor. xv. 30 κινδυνεύομεν πᾶσαν ὥραν: μάχαιρα Heb. xi. 34, 37.]

(2) Of these, the last suggests the persecutions undergone by the Jews,—persecutions which had a typical value for the Christian ages (ver. 36).

Ps. xliv. 23, quoted (καθὼς γέγραπται) as describing by anticipation the sufferings of persecuted Christians.

Heb. כִּי־עָלֶיךָ הֹרַגְנוּ כָל־הַיּוֹם
נֶחְשַׁבְנוּ כְּצֹאן טִבְחָה

[*Obs.* 1. The quotation from the LXX is exact. In the Heb. the emphasis lies on עָלֶיךָ, which is used as in Psalm lxix. 7. By καθὼς γέγραπται the Apostle treats the verse — not as an historical coincidence,—but as a Divine utterance in an earlier age, which corresponds prophetically to the sufferings of the Church of Christ. It forms, in fact, a motto for the Church in time of persecution, and σοῦ is naturally referred to the Church's Lord.]

[*Obs.* 2. Delitzsch gives reasons for referring this Psalm to the reign of David, under the events which resulted from the Syro-Ammonitic war. While David was engaged with the Syrians, the Edomites swept down upon the country as being denuded of troops, and caused great bloodshed: 1 Kings xi. 15. The lofty sense of loyalty to GOD which pervades this Psalm best befits the age of David; no other Psalm contains any like expression of the consciousness of innocence. It may therefore have been composed by a sufferer under the Edomite invasion. The only satisfactory alternative is to place it in the times succeeding the exile, when the nation had been free from the taint of idolatry for some years, but before the Maccabaean period, when the Psalm had already acquired a kind of liturgical or popular use. See Delitzsch on Psalm xliv.]

[*Obs.* 3. This is intended to describe the present or impending persecution of Christians in the Apostolic age. 1. The *motive* of such persecutions was hatred of GOD and His truth, ἕνεκεν σοῦ. 2. Their relentless character is shown in that they went on from morning to night, ὅλην τὴν ἡμέραν. 3. The estimate of their victims formed by the persecutors, ἐλογίσθημεν ὡς πρόβατα σφαγῆς.]

(3) In all these (vers. 35, 36) Christians do more than conquer (ὑπερνικῶμεν), because they are helped by Christ Who has loved them so well (ver. 37).

Dogmatic: ch. VIII, vv. 31-39.

[*Obs.* 1. ὑπερνικῶμεν, not found in ancient Greek. Coined to express the Christian sense of jubilant triumph. It is used by late writers to mean pushing a victory too far: Socr. *H. E.* iii. 21.]

[*Obs.* 2. The ἀγαπήσας is Christ, whose Atoning Death—the consummate proof of His love—is glanced at by the *historic aorist*: Rom. v. 6; Gal. ii. 20; Eph. v. 2, 25. (Compare ver. 35.) For διὰ τοῦ ἀγ. cf. 2 Cor. xii. 9 ἵνα ἐπισκηνώσῃ ἐπ' ἐμὲ ἡ δύναμις τοῦ Χριστοῦ. The power which our Lord supplies is love, 2 Cor. v. 14 ἡ γὰρ ἀγάπη τοῦ Χριστοῦ (*gen. object.* here) συνέχει ἡμᾶς. So Thomas à Kempis, *De imit.* iii. 5 Amor onus sine onere portat, et omne amarum dulce ac sapidum efficit.' And S. Cyprian says of the Martyrs of his day: 'Certamini suo adfuit [Christus]; proeliatores atque assertores sui nominis erexit, corroboravit, animavit. Et qui pro nobis mortem semel vicit, semper vincit in nobis.... Ipse luctatur in nobis, ipse congreditur, ipse in certamine agonis nostri et coronat pariter et coronatur' *Epist.* x. 3. 4.]

[*Obs.* 3. By πέπεισμαι the Apostle expresses his strong personal conviction that what is true of earthly persecutions will hold equally good of all beyond the range of sense and time.]

  b. The Love of Christ for us is that from which we can be parted neither by dying nor by continuing to live: οὔτε θάνατος, οὔτε ζωή. Cf. Phil. i. 21. (ver. 38.)

[*Obs. Transitional.* In verses 38, 39 there are four groups of words, the two former pairs, the two latter threes. The third term in each of the two latter is a general one, having no immediate relation to the preceding antithesis.

{ θάνατος, ζωή, } the two possible conditions of human existence.

{ ἄγγελοι, ἀρχαί, } invisible personal beings, or orders of such beings.

{ ἐνεστῶτα, μέλλοντα, δυνάμεις, } anything in time, however powerful.

{ ὕψωμα, βάθος, τις κτίσις ἑτέρα, } anything in space, anything that comes from the Hand of the Creator.]

  c. The Love of Christ for us is that from which we cannot be parted

  (1) by any invisible beings, such as the ἄγγελοι and ἀρχαί of the heavenly hierarchy, or among fallen spirits (ver. 38);

  (2) by any circumstances of present or future time, ἐνεστῶτα οὔτε μέλλοντα: or by any powers—personal or impersonal—δυνάμεις—of any kind (ver. 38);

  (3) by any conceivable variations of space, ὕψωμα οὔτε βάθος: or indeed by anything else in the shape of a created thing, οὔτε τις κτίσις ἑτέρα (ver. 39).

[*Obs.* 1. In ver. 38 δυνάμεις must (see *apparatus criticus*) be placed after μέλλοντα, and consequently has not necessarily the definite meaning of an order of angelic beings, as have ἄγγελοι and ἀρχαί. (For lists of angelic beings, cf. 1 Cor. xv. 24; Col. i. 16; ii. 15; Eph. i. 21; vi. 12.) St. Paul's teaching on this subject belongs chiefly to the Epistles of the first imprisonment. For the Jewish traditions, see Eisenmenger, *Entd. Jud.*, II. p. 370 sqq.]

[*Obs.* 2. In ver. 39 the 'Love of Christ' for us is resolved into 'the Love of God which is in Christ Jesus.' Our Lord's Human Love is traced to its source in the Divine Nature.]

[*Obs.* 3. This passage (31–39) does not afford countenance to that theory of the Final Perseverance of the Saints which makes their salvation independent of responsibility and free-will. That forfeiture of Grace, which God the Father and our Lord never will, and which no external power or circumstance ever can effect, may be brought about by the free-will of the Christian himself. So S. Bernard, *Ser. de dupl. Bapt.* (qu. by Just.) 'Attende quanta enumeravit Apostolus, ejus enim verba sunt, minime tamen adjiciens, *nec nos ipsi*. Nimirum haec est libertas quâ Christus nos liberavit, ut nulla penitus creatura avellero nos aut vim facere possit. Solum id deserere possumus propriâ voluntate abstracti, et illecti a propriâ concupiscentiâ: praeter hanc enim nihil est quod timeamus.' And S. Ambrose: 'Nemo tibi Christum potest auferre, nisi te Illi ipse auferas.' Comp. Rev. ii. 4 τὴν ἀγάπην σου τὴν πρώτην ἀφῆκας: 1 Cor. x. 12 ὁ δοκῶν ἑστάναι, βλεπέτω μὴ πέσῃ: 1 Cor. ix. 27 μήπως ἄλλοις κηρύξας, αὐτὸς ἀδόκιμος γένωμαι.]

[*Obs.* 4. In *De Doctr. Christ.* iv. 20, S. Aug. refers to this whole passage (31–39) as an example of the 'grande dicendi genus' which, he says, 'non tam verborum ornatibus comtum est quam violentum animi affectibus.' He compares 2 Cor. vi. 20 sqq. and Gal. iv. 10. It is, in fact, a passage of lyrical beauty, like 1 Cor. xiii; but the elevation of feeling does not oblige us to ignore the sequence of thought.]

DOGMATIC PORTION OF THE EPISTLE.

DIVISION III. IX—XI.

RELATION OF THE JEWISH PEOPLE TO ΔΙΚΑΙΟΣΎΝΗ ΘΕΟΥ ΕΚ ΠΙΣΤΕΩΣ.

[*Obs.* 1. The problems discussed in chapters ix, x, xi arise inevitably out of the earlier argument of the Epistle. On the one hand, the Gospel was intended to be a δύναμις Θεοῦ εἰς σωτηρίαν, in the first instance, to the Jews (i. 16). On the other hand, this σωτηρία could only be gained by those who believed the Gospel. And, as the whole Jewish people, with the exception of a small body of converts, deliberately rejected the Gospel, their case presented a contradiction between the actual fact and the original Divine intention, which needed explanation on abstract grounds, and which appealed most closely to the sympathetic nature of S. Paul. Chapters ix, x, xi are best regarded as an historico-theological Appendix to the dogmatic portion of the Epistle.]

[*Obs.* 2. The opinion that chapters ix, x, xi form the germ of the Epistle to which i. 17-viii are merely introductory (Baur, *Paulus*, ii. 3) is untenable, (1) as assuming that the Jewish Christians are addressed throughout the Epistle and that they formed the predominant element in the Roman Church ; cf. ch. xvi; and (2) as obliging Baur, when analyzing the first eight chapters, to overlook the most important elements of the argument, and to thrust incidental features into unnatural prominence. At the same time, the Jewish converts are addressed in ch. ix-xi, except when the Apostle turns to the converts from heathenism, xi. 13-36 ; cf. vers. 28, 30, 31.]

A.

INTRODUCTION (ix. 1–5).

Sorrow of the Apostle at the ἀποβολή of Israel.

[*Obs.* The blessedness of the οἱ ἐν Χριστῷ, so exultingly celebrated in viii. 32-39, makes the actual condition (ἀποβολή xi. 5) of the majority of the Apostle's countrymen all the more painful by contrast. Hence the burst of passionate sorrow, ix. 1-5. Compare x. 1 ; xi. 1 sqq.; 14 sqq. : as also iii. 1 sqq. ; xv. 8 for like expressions of feeling.]

1. *Sincerity* of the Apostle's feeling (ix. 1). This sincerity is

   a. affirmed both positively and negatively, ἀλήθειαν λέγω ... οὐ ψεύδομαι.

b. witnessed to by conscience, συμμαρτυρούσης μοι τῆς συνειδήσεως.

c. hallowed by Christ, the element in which his mental life moves (ἐν Χριστῷ); and by the Holy Spirit, within whose encompassing Presence the report of his conscience is given (ver. 1).

[*Obs.* 1. For instances of the negation following and strengthening the affirmation, see S. John i. 20; Eph. iv. 25; 1 Tim. ii. 7.]

[*Obs.* 2. As the positive ἀλήθειαν λέγω has received its solemn guarantee by the added words ἐν Χριστῷ, so the negative οὐ ψεύδομαι is concurrently attested by conscience, ἐν Πνεύματι ἁγίῳ. For ἐν Χριστῷ, see 2 Cor. xi. 17; xii. 19; 1 Thess. iv. 1; Eph. iv. 17. It cannot = *per Christum*. An adjuration '*by Christ*' would have required πρός with the gen.]

[*Obs.* 3. On συνείδησις as the knowledge which man has with himself of a Divine law established in his heart (the ethical side of the general sense of truth); related to that law as prophecy was in Israel to the Thorah, proclaiming it, and judging acts and motives with reference to it, cf. Delitzsch, *Bibl. Psychol.* p. 159 and Rom. ii. 15; xiii. 5; 1 Cor. viii. 7; x. 28; 2 Cor. i. 12; iv. 2; v. 11; Heb. ix. 14; 1 Tim. iv. 2; Tit. i. 15 : βροτοῖς ἅπασιν ἡ συνείδησις Θεός Menander, *Gnom. Monostich.* 654. The law which conscience recognises is in a heathen often darkened. In a Christian it is illuminated by the Holy Spirit.]

2. *Intensity* of the Apostle's feeling (introduced by ὅτι), (vers. 2, 3 a).

a. described in terms which mark

{ i. its greatness, λύπη μεγάλη.
ii. its continuance, ἀδιάλειπτος ὀδύνη.
iii. its depth, τῇ καρδίᾳ (not on the soul's surface, but at its centre (ver. 2).

[*Obs.* λύπη, 'sadness,' opposed to χαρά, S. John xvi. 20; Heb. xii. 11. ὀδύνη has a more positive character of mental pain. This sorrow may coexist with perfect sincerity with the joy described in viii. sub fin. : the motives of the two feelings being perfectly distinct. From delicacy the Apostle does not name the cause of the sorrow : he leaves it to be gathered from what follows.]

b. Justification (γάρ) of this description. This feeling has taken shape in a definite prayer.

He wished, if it could be so, to be himself Anathema (and so separate) from Christ, instead of his kinsmen (ver. 3).

[*Obs.* 1. For *construction* of ηὐχόμην without ἄν, see Gal. iv. 20; Acts xxv. 22; and Winer, *Gram. N. T.* p. 353. I was wishing, if it were practicable. The thought of its being fulfilled or not is in the background of his mind. But the wish is represented as continuing. The 'imp. marks an action that does not attain to accomplishment, but would do so on certain conditions:' Kühner. ηὐχόμην ἄν would mean 'I should wish, if the wish were possible; but the wish is not possible, therefore I do not wish.']

[*Obs.* 2. *Substance* of the ηὐχόμην. ἀνάθεμα (Att. ἀνάθημα) originally something consecrated, or something accursed. For the two meanings, see Lev. xxvii. 28, 29, LXX. Gradually, however, ἀνάθημα was appropriated to expressing the idea of something consecrated; ἀνάθεμα that of something accursed, devoted to destruction. So, of Jericho, Josh. vi. 17 הָעִיר חֵרֶם הִיא, ἔσται ἡ πόλις ἀνάθεμα. This sense of being devoted to destruction appears in Acts xxiii. 14 ἀναθέματι ἀνεθεματίσαμεν ἑαυτούς: 1 Cor. xii. 3 λέγει Ἀνάθεμα Ἰησοῦν : xvi. 22 εἴ τις οὐ φιλεῖ τὸν Κύριον . . . ἤτω ἀνάθεμα : Gal. i. 8, 9 ἀνάθεμα ἔστω. Only here with ἀπὸ τοῦ Χριστοῦ. The construction is pregnant; and some verb denoting *separation* (καὶ χωρίζεσθαι) is implied, as involved in the eternal ἀπώλεια. αὐτὸς ἐγώ here describes his own single personality, as in contrast with his fellow-countrymen, τῶν ἀδελφῶν μου. But in vii. 25 his true personality is contrasted with his σάρξ, which during the stage of struggle is in the service of ἁμαρτία.]

[*Obs.* 3. 'Lawfulness' of the wish. It is formed on Ex. xxxii. 32 'Yet now, if thou wilt forgive their sin; and if not, blot me, I pray thee, out of Thy book which Thou hast written.' It expresses an emotion of unmeasured devotedness, which however is controlled by the sense of GOD's known will. If the Apostle could take the place (ὑπέρ here = ἀντί) of his countrymen, he would do so, fearful as would be the eternal loss. It is unselfishness of feeling carried to a point which is unintelligible to selfish calculations.]

3. *Grounds* of the Apostle's feeling.

(*a*) *Natural.* The tie of blood : τῶν ἀδελφῶν μου, τῶν συγγενῶν μου κατὰ σάρκα (ver. 3).

[*Obs.* 1. The expression συγγενῶν κατὰ σάρκα contrasts with ἀδελφοῖς ἐν Κυρίῳ Phil. i. 14 : ἁγίοις ἀδελφοῖς 1 Thess. v. 27 ; cf. Heb. iii. 1 ; Col. i. 2. Compare Phil. ver. 16, where Onesimus the slave is described as ἀδελφὸς ἀγαπητὸς καὶ ἐν σαρκὶ καὶ ἐν Κυρίῳ. The distinction between natural and spiritual relationships is familiar to the Apostle.]

[*Obs.* 2. Natural relationships are here recognised as warranting some of the strongest feelings of the soul. Cf. Eph. v. 29 οὐδεὶς γάρ ποτε τὴν ἑαυτοῦ σάρκα ἐμίσησεν. The claims of nature, which is itself from GOD, are not really in conflict with those of the kingdom of grace, or such evangelical counsels as S. Luke xiv. 26. On the duties which natural ties imperatively prescribe, see 1 Tim. v. 8.]

(*b*) *Theocratic.* Prerogatives of the covenant-people (vers. 4, 5).

[*Obs.* οἵτινες gives a further and stronger motive for what is said in ver. 3, 'quippe qui.' But this does not imply that, if the natural bond of ἀδελφοί and συγγενεῖς had *alone* existed, the Apostle would not have felt grief at Israel's fall.]

They are
'Ισραηλῖται,
(ancient
valued
theocratic
name):
Gen. xxxii. 28;
S. Matt. ii. 6;
S. Luke ii. 32;
S. John i. 48;
Rom. xi. 1;
2 Cor. xi. 22;
Phil. iii. 5.
(ver. 4.)

I.
ὧν,
who as
such
enjoyed
six
special
marks
of the
Divine
favour.

1. ἡ υἱοθεσία, the adoption of this people by God into the place of children, in the national, theocratic sense: Ex. iv. 22 sqq.; Deut. xiv. 1; xxxii. 6; Hos. xi. 1. (ver. 4.)

2. ἡ δόξα, the Glory, not of Israel but of Jehovah, the Shekinah of the Rabbis, כְּבוֹד יְהוָה, Ex. xvi. 10; xxiv. 16; xl. 34, 35. Cf. 1 Sam. iv. 22 ἀπῴκισται δόξα 'Ισραήλ: 1 Kings viii. 11. (ver. 4.)

3. αἱ διαθῆκαι (not here the Jewish and Christian, but) the Covenants made by GOD with the Patriarchs since Abraham. Gen. xvii. 7; Ex. xix. 5; Deut. xix. 1; Wisd. xviii. 22; Ecclus. xliv. 11. (ver. 4.)

4. ἡ νομοθεσία, the Sinaitic legislation, (not = νόμος). Israel was distinguished as the people to which GOD had revealed His moral Nature in the Mosaic Law. Cf. Ps. cxlvii. 19, 20; Deut. iv. 7–14; Acts vii. 53; Gal. iii. 19; Heb. ii. 2 sqq.; xii. 18 sqq.

5. ἡ λατρεία, the עֲבֹדָה, Ex. xxxv. 24; xxxix. 42, the solemn cultus of the true GOD, as ordered by Himself: Heb. ix. 6. (ver. 4.)

6. αἱ ἐπαγγελίαι, specially the Messianic promises made to Abraham: Rom. iv. 13; xv. 8; Gal. iii. 16, 21; Heb. vi. 12; vii. 6; xi. 13, 17, 33. (ver. 4.)

II.
ὧν, and
were the
race who
could
claim the
Patriarchs.

οἱ πατέρες. The Patriarchs, as saintly ancestors, belong to all the generations of Israel: Ex. iii. 13, 15; iv. 5; Acts iii. 13; vii. 32. The word πατήρ is applied to Abraham, S. John viii. 39; S. Luke i. 55; Isaac, Rom. ix. 10; Jacob, S. John iv. 12; and David, S. Luke i. 32, 55; Acts ii. 29. (ver. 5.)

III.
ἐξ ὧν,
and of
whose
blood
came the
Divine
Messiah.

ὁ Χριστός. So far as His assumed Humanity is concerned, τὸ κατὰ σάρκα, while, in His Eternal Person, He is (ὁ ὤν)

i. over all, ἐπὶ πάντων.
ii. God, Θεός.
iii. blessed for ever, εὐλογητὸς εἰς τοὺς αἰῶνας (ver. 5).

Dogmatic: ch. IX, *vv.* 1–5.   151

[*Obs.* 1. Israel was the name given to the Patriarch Jacob, who had struggled with GOD (אֵל and שָׂרָה), Gen. xxxii. 28, and Jacob had prayed that his descendants might be named after himself and his fathers, Gen. xlviii. 16; Is. xlviii. 1. Along with this name the promise and hope of Jacob passed to his posterity; the people, like the patriarch, had power with GOD. The spiritual dignity of the nation was wrapped up in this name; which however finds its chief fulfilment in the Church of Christ.]

[*Obs.* 2. This υἱοθεσία is not to be confounded with its antitype—the Christian υἱοθεσία of viii. 15. 'The Old Testament exhibits man at the beginning of his sonship, but under the discipline of the Law; the New Testament in the completeness of his sonship, as one of full age.' But the Jews are referred to by our Lord as τέκνα Matt. xv. 26. Comp. 'the generation of Thy children,' Ps. lxxiii. 15; and cp. Gen. vi. 2. In Wisdom the use of πατήρ with reference to GOD and υἱὸς Θεοῦ of the devout Jew, approaches the New Testament account.]

[*Obs.* 3. The Gentiles had a natural νόμος but no νομοθεσία. Israel was the people of Revelation.

[*Obs.* 4. The Doxology (ver. 5 ὁ ὢν κ.τ.λ.) has been dealt with in three principal ways.

  (1) Referred *to Christ our Lord*, with a comma after σάρκα.

  (2) Treated as an independent doxology *to God the Father*, by placing a full stop after σάρκα. [With Codd. C. L. 5. 47; Lach., Tisch.]

  (3) Broken up, by placing a full stop after πάντων with Cod. 71. In this case ὁ ὢν ἐπὶ πάντων is referred to Christ; and what follows is a doxology to the Father. (Erasmus, &c.)

  Of these, (3) has few defenders, (a) ὁ ὢν ἐπὶ πάντων is abrupt: cf. Acts x. 36; Rom. x. 12, (b) no explanation can be given of the position of εὐλογητός after Θεός, not even that of an 'emphasis in view,' (c) while such a punctuation implies a contrast between ἐπὶ πάντων and Θεός, and thus tends to an indirect disparagement of the Person and Glory of Christ, a result which, no one can suppose, was intended by the writer.

  The real question lies between (1) and (2).]

[*Obs.* 5. The authority of Christian antiquity is on the side of (1).
S. Irenaeus, *adv. Haer.* iii. 16. n. 3 (vol. i. p. 506, ed. Stieren).
Tertullian, *adv. Prax.* c. 13, 15 (vol. ii. pp. 669, 673, ed. Oehler).
Conc. Ant. A.D. 269, ap. Routh, *Rel. Sacr.* iii. 292 (ed. 1846).
Novatian, *de Trinitate*, c. 13, 30 (pp. 43, 118, ed. Welchman).
S. Athanasius, *contr. Arian. Orat.* i. 10; *Orat.* iv. 1 sub in. (vol. i. p. 415, ed. Ben.).
    ,,   *Epist. ad Epictetum* (vol. i. pt. ii. p. 908, ed. Ben.).
S. Epiphanius, *Haer.* 57. 2, p. 483; 76, conf. 30 (p. 978).
S. Hilarius, *De Trinitate*, viii. c. 37, 38 (p. 970, ed. Ben.).
S. Ambrosius, *De Spiritu Sancto*, i. 3. 46 (vol. ii. p. 609, ed. Ben.).
S. Gregorius Nyss., *contra Eunom. Orat.* x. (vol. iii. p. 695, ed. Paris, 1638).
S. Augustinus, *De Trinitate*, ii. 13. n. 23 (vol. viii. p. 786, ed. Ben.).
    ,,   *Contra Faustum*, iii. c. 6 (vol. viii. p. 192, ed. Ben.).
S. Hieronymus, *Ep. ad Algas.* Qu. ix. (vol. iv. p. 204, ed. Ben. Par.).

The passages which Wetstein has adduced from the Fathers in favour of (2) are allowed by Fritzsche (*in loc.*) and Meyer (*in loc.*) to be inapposite: Meyer himself only produces two quotations, which can imply a non-reference to Christ. Of these that in *Pseudo-Ign. ad Tars.* 5 is only an indirect implication; while Diodorus of Tarsus (ap. Cramer, *Catena*, Oxon p. 162) was in other ways rationalizing. The passage was not used in the earlier controversy against Arianism, probably because Sabellianism was still too recent and too powerful to allow the Catholics generally to appeal to it, without being supposed to 'confound the Persons' of the Son and the Father. (See Reiche, *Comm.* vol. ii. p. 268, note.) At a later stage it was constantly referred to by Catholic opponents of Arianism, as by Oecumenius *in loc.* ἐνταῦθα λαμπρότατα Θεὸν τὸν Χριστὸν ὀνομάζει ὁ ἀπόστολος· Αἰσχύνθητι τρισάθλιε 'Αρεῖε, ἀκούων παρὰ Παύλου δοξολούμενον τὸν Χριστὸν Θεὸν ἀληθινόν. The Arians do not appear to have challenged the reference. Later Arians, Whitby, Crell, &c. endeavoured to escape its force by reading ὧν ὁ instead of ὁ ὤν, in defiance of MSS. and of good sense. When Julian the Apostate sarcastically observed that τὸν γοῦν Ἰησοῦν οὔτε Παῦλος ἐτόλμησεν εἰπεῖν Θεόν, nor yet the three earlier Evangelists, but only ὁ χρηστὸς Ἰωάννης, S. Cyril Alex. replied by pointing to this passage, ἰδοὺ τὸν κατὰ σάρκα ἐξ Ἰουδαίων, τούτεσσι Χριστόν, καὶ Θεὸν ἐπὶ πάντων, κ.τ.λ., *c. Julian.* x. p. 328. The early Socinians did not question the reference to Christ, but explained Θεός away: *Catech. Racov.* 159 sqq. Among writers of note Erasmus first innovated on the traditional judgment and sense of the Church, and he has been largely followed since Wetstein.]

[*Obs.* 6. The *structure of the passage* lends itself naturally to (1). Observe (*a*) that there is no adequate reason for the abrupt transition which occurs, if a full stop is placed after σάρκα, unless, indeed, it be assumed that the Apostle *could* not predicate ἐπὶ πάντων Θεός of Christ : (*b*) that in detached doxologies εὐλογητός always stands at the beginning, as in thirty places of the LXX following the Hebrew use of בָּרוּךְ, מְבֹרָךְ, Gen. ix. 26 ; 1 Sam. xxvi. 25 ; 2 Sam. xviii. 28, &c. The only *apparent* exception is Ps. lxviii. 20. LXX (Κύριος ὁ Θεὸς εὐλογητός, εὐλογητὸς Κύριος ἡμέραν καθ' ἡμέραν, Hebrew only בָּרוּךְ אֲדֹנָי יוֹם יוֹם) where the first clause ending in εὐλογητός would seem to be interpolated, or the LXX is a free paraphrase with a designed rhetorical emphasis (with the inverted order of words, the doubled εὐλογητός, the stronger form of blessing following the weaker one). Winer would arbitrarily account for the exceptional position here of εὐλογητός, by suggesting that 'the subject of the doxology is antithetical to another subject,' *Gr. N. T.* p. 690, thus begging the question. Εὐλογητὸς εἰς τοὺς αἰῶνας is used elsewhere twice by S. Paul, and each time as an assertion respecting the subject of the sentence, not in a *detached* ascription of praise : Rom. i. 25 τὸν κτίσαντα, ὅς ἐστιν εὐλογητὸς εἰς τοὺς αἰῶνας: 2 Cor. xi. 31 ὁ Θεὸς καὶ Πατὴρ . . . ὁ ὢν εὐλογητὸς εἰς τοὺς αἰῶνας. Wherever it does not occur in a relative clause, εὐλογητός, εὐλογημένος stands at the beginning of a doxology, S. Matt. xxi. 9 ; Luke i. 68 ; 2 Cor. i. 3 ; Eph. i. 3 ; 1 S. Pet. i. 3. It is, therefore, in its *natural* position, as a predicate of Χριστός. (*c*) That τὸ κατὰ σάρκα, *of itself,* implies that Christ was not altogether sprung from the race of Israel, but that He had another and higher Nature. It suggests as its antithesis some positive ascription of Divinity which would satisfy the suppressed τὸ κατὰ

Πνεῦμα. Compare Rom. i. 3. The suppression of the antithesis to τὸ κατὰ σάρκα that it may be supplied in thought (2 Cor. xi. 18; Col. iii. 22; 1 Cor. i. 26) cannot take place where, as here, the thesis only exists for the sake of the antithesis. Without ὁ ὢν ἐπὶ πάντων Θεός the words τὸ κατὰ σάρκα would imply a diminution of the prerogative of Israel. Of themselves they weaken the passage. That Christ springs from the Jews does the Jews more honour than that Christ springs from them merely after the flesh. But what privilege can compare with theirs from whom He springs after the flesh Who is over all, God blessed for ever? (d) That ὤν is altogether superfluous, if (2) be adopted, while in (1) it vividly expresses the present momentous fact that Christ is God. Comp. S. John i. 18; iii. 13; xii. 17; and especially 2 Cor. xi. 31, where it = ὅς ἐστιν.]

[Obs. 7. The passage is in harmony with the *teaching of S. Paul and the New Testament* on the subject of Christ's Person, if (1) be adopted. To take Meyer's objections: I. 'Paul never uses Θεός of Christ.' But see Eph. v. 5 ἐν τῇ βασιλείᾳ τοῦ Χριστοῦ καὶ Θεοῦ, i. e. the kingdom of Him Who is Christ and God, as is implied in the connection by means of the same article. Cf. also the true reading Col. ii. 2 τοῦ Θεοῦ Χριστοῦ, Lachmann. Probably Tit. i. 3 κατ᾽ ἐπιταγὴν τοῦ σωτῆρος ἡμῶν Θεοῦ. Certainly ii. 13 ἐπιφάνειαν τῆς δόξης τοῦ μεγάλου Θεοῦ καὶ σωτῆρος ἡμῶν Ἰησοῦ Χριστοῦ: iii. 4 ἡ χρηστότης καὶ ἡ φιλανθρωπία ἐπεφάνη τοῦ σωτῆρος ἡμῶν Θεοῦ: if 1 Tim. iii. 16 be not adduced. To predicate Θεός of Christ is not inconsistent in a writer who speaks of Him as ἐν μορφῇ Θεοῦ ὑπάρχων Phil. ii. 6; and asserts that ἐν αὐτῷ κατοικεῖ πᾶν τὸ πλήρωμα τῆς θεότητος σωματικῶς Col. ii. 9. If the Apostle thinks of Christ as God, it is natural that he should call Christ God, in a passage where it was important to express the complete antithetical relation of His Higher Nature to His Manhood. And he attributes to Christ eternity, Col. i. 15, 17; and omnipresence, Eph. i. 23; the creation and upholding in being of the world, Col. i. 16, 17; and the award of judgment, Rom. xiv. 10; 2 Cor. v. 10; 2 Thess. i. 7-10. Christ is the author of grace, Rom. i. 7; 1 Cor. i. 3; and the object of worship, Rom. x. 13; Phil. ii. 10, 11. Even if Θεός as a predicate of Christ in Rom. ix. 5 were a ἅπ. λεγ. this does not, of itself, show that the construction of the passage which makes it such is untenable, unless the expression be really in advance of the modes of thought about our Lord which are observable in other passages. And Meyer admits that 'Paul agrees essentially *in substance* with the Christology of John, and might have affirmed just as appropriately as the latter (S. John i. 1) the predicative Θεός of Christ.' But, then, II. 'Paul has not adopted, like John, the Alexandrian form of conceiving and stating the Divine essence of Christ, but has adhered to the popular, concrete, strictly monotheistic terminology.' But that S. Paul had Alexandrian thought in view in his use of εἰκών (a favourite word with Philo) and πρωτότοκος, as applied to our Lord, is more than probable; and his 'monotheism' must have led him to include Christ within the One Divine essence, unless such passages as Col. i. 15-17 are unmeaning rhetoric. III. 'Paul always accurately distinguishes God and Christ.' This is true, if it be meant that the Apostle does not anticipate the Sabellian heresy by 'confounding the Persons.' But it is inaccurate, if it be intended to suggest that, according to S. Paul, Christ is something else or less than God. When Meyer says that S. Paul sharply and clearly distinguishes Christ as the Κύριος from Θεός in Rom. x. 9 ; 1 Cor. xii. 3, the question arises, What did S. Paul mean to say of Him by terming Him Κύριος? What place was there in the belief of so serious a Monotheist as S. Paul for such a Being, confessedly superhuman, yet not literally Divine? In 1 Cor. viii. 6 εἷς Θεὸς ὁ Πατήρ is merely opposed to the πολλοῖς θεοῖς of the heathen, and the εἷς Κύριος Ἰησοῦς Χριστός to their πολλοῖς κυρίοις, and the κυριότης, which especially belongs to Christ as the Revealer of the Hidden Deity, and Lord of the kingdom of souls, just as little excludes the θεότης as the θεότης does the κυριότης. In 1 Cor. xv. 22-29 it is the human as well as the Divine Nature of Christ that is in question, and especially the former. When the Redemption of the species is complete, Christ, as the Mediator, delivers up His kingdom to the Father, but, says S. Aug. *De Trin.* I. c. x 'Christus in quantum Deus est, cum illo nos subjectos habet, in quantum sacerdos nobiscum illi subjectus est.' As for Meyer's assertion, that 'there runs through the whole New Testament a delicate line of separation between the Father and the Son,' this is recognised, so far as it is true, by the Catholic doctrine of the Subordination of the Son ; but the Arianising drift of the remark is excluded by the passages which Meyer quotes, S. John i. 1 ; xx. 28 ; and 1 S. John v. 20. IV. 'In the properly Apostolical writings we meet no doxologies to Christ.' Here Meyer begins by observing that Heb. xiii. 21 ; 2 Pet. iii. 18, do not belong to these writings! He reluctantly admits that 2 Tim. iv. 8 certainly refers to Christ ; but leaves us in doubt as to his inference respecting the Pastoral Epistles. Yet 1 Pet. iv. 11 ; Rev. i. 5, 6 ; and Rev. v. 12-14 ; vii. 10 (where He is associated with the Father), as well as Rom. xvi. 27, are doxologies of this kind, while their principle is justified in 2 Thess. i. 12 ὅπως ἐνδοξασθῇ τὸ ὄνομα τοῦ Κυρίου ἡμῶν Ἰησοῦ Χριστοῦ ἐν ὑμῖν. Consider S. John v. 23. V. 'The insuperable difficulty is that Christ is ἐπὶ πάντων Θεός,' if (1) be adopted. But why insuperable? The relation to the Universe implied in ἐπὶ πάντων is already involved in what is said of Christ in Col. i. 15-17. The Universe was created ἐν αὐτῷ, δι' αὐτοῦ, εἰς αὐτόν : He ἐστὶ (not ἐκτίσθη) πρὸ πάντων, and τὰ πάντα ἐν αὐτῷ συνέστηκεν. After this it is little to say that He is ἐπὶ πάντων, although this is predicated of the Father (Eph. iv. 6 , Who, it *ought* to be unnecessary to add, cannot be included in the πάντα : 1 Cor. xv. 27. Christ is ἐπὶ πάντων Θεός, not ὁ ἐπὶ πάντων Θεός, as if He were αὐτόθεος ; and for this preeminence see Rom. x. 12 ; Acts x. 36. The absence of the article proves nothing ; Θεός is predicate, and the object is to affirm Christ Θεὸν εἶναι, not τὸν Θεὸν εἶναι. He is not ὁ Θεός, i. e. the Triune God, but God ; cf. S. John i. 1 καὶ Θεὸς ἦν ὁ λόγος. Εὐλογητός seems to be sustained by εὐλογημένος, applied to Christ in S. Matt. xxi. 9 ; S. Luke xix. 38. Meyer well observes that 'if Christ is here referred to, we need not shrink from acknowledging that He is not *nuncupative*, but *naturaliter*, God.']

B.

Israel's general failure to attain δικαιοσύνη Θεοῦ ἐκ πίστεως considered in the light of the Divine Attributes (ix. 6–29).

[*Obs.* 1. The first section of this treatise belongs to what would now be called Theodicea. This word as now commonly used to describe such efforts of

Dogmatic: ch. IX, vv. 6-29.

Theological Science as are devoted to explaining and justifying GOD's government of the world, in those particulars which present the greatest difficulty to the moral sense or the understanding of man, only dates from the end of the 17th or the beginning of the 18th century. But the effort is as old as, or older than, Christianity. The Book of Job in the Old Testament, and this passage in the New Testament (Rom. ix. 6-29), are its chief Biblical examples. The distribution of pain presents as many difficulties to human thought as the mysteriousness of the kingdom of grace. In Christian antiquity S. Augustine's Treatise *de Civitate Dei* represents an attempt of Christian thought to answer objections to the idea of a Divine Government of the world, which arose out of the miseries that prevailed at the destruction of the Roman Empire. When at the close of the 17th century men were distracted between Spinoza's absorption of all free-wills into a single substance and Bayle's proclamation of a modified dualism, Leibnitz published his *Essai de Théodicée, sur la bonté de Dieu, la liberté de l'homme, et l'origine du mal*, 1710. An entire literature has sprung from or been modelled on this book; and the word Theodicea has been since appropriated in ordinary theological language to that department of Christian Apologetics which vindicates the attributes of GOD, against the objections which appeal to the existence of evil, moral and physical, and to the 'clouds and darkness' which surround certain districts of GOD's action upon the world and humanity. Considering GOD's promises to Israel, the rejection of the mass of the Israelites presented difficulties which required explanation.]

[*Obs.* 2. The situation which made the following discussion necessary is thus described by Baur, *Paulus*, ii. 3 'After many years of the Apostle's ministry great numbers of heathen had embraced the Christian faith, while the number of Jews who were converted formed a very trifling proportion of the nation as a whole: and thus the very condition on which the Messianic faith of the Jewish Christians was based, namely that the fulfilment of the old promises made to Israel had come about in Jesus, appeared not to have been fulfilled. How could Jesus be the Messiah of the nation if the nation did not believe in Him, nor seem at all likely to do so, and if the respective proportions of Gentile and Jewish Christianity made it clear that the blessings which Messiah was to bring had, so far, gone much more to the Gentiles than to the Jews? . . . Either this glaring disproportion, which so conflicted, as the Jewish converts thought, with the old promises, must lead them to renounce their faith in Jesus as the Messiah altogether, or they must have serious scruples as to the mode in which the Gentiles had been called to Christianity.' That such scruples were justified S. Paul could on no account admit: he had replied to them by anticipation in his whole account of δικαιοσύνη ἐκ πίστεως. He must therefore address himself to the task of showing that the Jewish Christians misunderstood the real drift and import of the promises made to Israel, and that there was no such contradiction between the circumstances of their day, and the faithfulness and pledged word of GOD, as they were disposed to imagine.]

Prop. I.

(Concerning GOD's veracity). GOD's promise has not been violated by the reprobation of the Jewish people (ix. 6-13).

Jewish objection (kept in view by S. Paul). The ἀποβολή of Israel implies that the Messianic promise made to Israel had failed (ver. 6).

[The λόγος τοῦ Θεοῦ refers to Gen. xii. 3, and the ἐξ ὧν ὁ Χριστὸς τὸ κατὰ σάρκα of ver. 5. It means God's word of promise to Israel, specially the promise of salvation through the Messiah. This λόγος might seem to have fallen out of its place (ἐκπέπτωκεν) in the order of Providence, when the great majority of the people to whom it belonged were altogether unaffected by it, at least for good.]

Resp. No. It is not a matter of such a nature as the ἐκπίπτειν of the Divine word which has caused the grief of the Apostle in ix. 1–5. For

[Obs. 1. οὐχ οἶον ὅτι is a solecism mixing up two modes of expression, (1) οὐχ οἶον with a finite tense ἐκπέπτωκεν, and (2) οὐχ ὅτι = οὐκ ἐρῶ ὅτι. As it stands the phrase in full is οὐ τοῖον λέγω, οἶον ὅτι, 'I do not speak of such a kind of thing as (that is) that.' Cf. Meyer *in loc.*]

[Obs. 2. ἐκπίπτειν is here used like נָפַל in Joshua xxi. 43 (Heb.), διαπίπτειν, xxiii. 14, πίπτειν, of sayings which are not fulfilled. The sense of 'to fall out of position' satisfies the various uses of the word in the New Testament. S. Mark xiii. 25; Acts xii. 7; 1 Cor. xiii. 8; Gal. v. 4; S. James i. 11; 1 S. Pet. i. 24; Rev. ii. 5. Cf. the classical ἐκβάλλεσθαι. Opposed to this is μένειν ver. 11.]

Thesis. God's *Promise to Israel, instead of having failed, has been fulfilled* (6 b–13).

Arg. The reason why (γάρ) the Promise of God to Israel has not failed is that *all* who spring from Israel are not Israel's true children. Of those who are by natural descent Israelites, only a certain number really correspond to the import of the name. To these the Divine promise was really made; and with them it has been kept (ver. 6 a).

[Obs. 1. The distinction between the true Israel and the merely natural Israel is implied in ἀληθῶς Ἰσραηλίτης S. John i. 48; ἐν τῷ κρυπτῷ Ἰουδαῖος Rom. ii. 28, 29; Ἰσραὴλ κατὰ πνεῦμα Gal. iv. 29; Ἰσραὴλ τοῦ Θεοῦ Gal. vi. 16. The spiritual Israel was at once narrower and wider than the natural Israel: narrower in that it included only a minority of the nation, and wider in that it was to embrace, as τέκνα τῆς ἐπαγγελίας and τέκνα τοῦ Θεοῦ, men of all races, within the Catholic Church of Christ.]

[Obs. 2. Does οἱ ἐξ Ἰσραήλ mean those who have sprung from the Patriarch Jacob, or from the People? Probably the latter. The Apostle distinguishes between the natural Israel and the Israel chosen by God, before he proceeds to justify this distinction by the history of the Patriarchal families. Among Jacob's posterity there was no such distinction as that between the children of Abraham and of Isaac. None of the twelve sons of Jacob were excluded from the theocratic body.]

This restriction of the true spiritual Israel to a limited number of born Israelites is referred to a general law, obtaining throughout the Patriarchal Age, by which the τέκνα τῆς ἐπαγγελίας are always only a portion of the τέκνα τῆς σαρκός (7–13).

(A) *Case of the children of Abraham* (7–9). Here the prerogative title of σπέρμα Ἀβραάμ—implying true descent from Abraham—so far from being extended to Ishmael, is limited by the express word of GOD to Isaac. If, therefore, the Jews were by descent σπέρμα Ἀβραάμ, it did not follow that they were also τέκνα, i. e. true children (ver. 7).

[*Obs.* σπέρμα here means mere natural offspring: in ver. 8 it means spiritual descendants.]

a. Gen. xxi. 12 (being the promise to Abraham, at the expulsion of Ishmael) *quoted* in order to show that the spiritual prerogatives of the chosen race were limited to a portion of the family of Abraham (7 b).

Heb. כִּי בְיִצְחָק יִקָּרֵא לְךָ זָרַע

LXX ὅτι ἐν Ἰσαὰκ κληθήσεταί σοι σπέρμα.

[*Obs.* 1. 'In the person of Isaac posterity shall be named to thee'; i. e. Isaac's children will pass as thy descendants; Ishmael's are tacitly excluded. It is the reason given to Abraham warranting compliance with Sarah's demand for the expulsion of Ishmael. But (see ver. 9) the Apostle limits the saying to *the person of Isaac* himself, Isaac being Abraham's *promised* child, and thus representing in himself Abraham's true posterity. For all Israelites were descendants of Isaac; and they could not therefore be treated by the Apostle, as the type of the true sonship of Abraham, in an argument, by which the claim to that sonship which rests upon bodily descent is withdrawn.]

[*Obs.* 2. This saying, being well known, is introduced immediately without καθὼς γέγραπται : Gal. iii. 11, 12; 1 Cor. xv. 27.]

b. Gen. xxi. 12 *explained* as illustrating a general law (ver. 8). This expresses the idea (τοῦτ' ἔστιν) that (1) it is not all the physical progeny of a saintly Patriarch who are as such necessarily GOD's children, but (2) that those children of Abraham who, like Isaac, are made his sons by the creative virtue of a Divine Promise, are accounted by GOD to be Abraham's true posterity, (λογίζεται εἰς σπέρμα) (ver. 8).

[*Obs.* Gentile converts to the Church cannot *here* be included under the τέκνα τῆς ἐπαγγελίας without ignoring the context. Abraham's race is alone in question; all his natural descendants are not considered by GOD to belong to it. Yet in another connection the Apostle writes to heathen converts, Gal. iv. 28 ἡμεῖς δέ, ἀδελφοί, κατὰ Ἰσαὰκ ἐπαγγελίας τέκνα ἐσμέν. For λογίζεται, see Rom. iv. 3, 5.]

c. The explanation *justified* (γάρ ver. 9) by an appeal to the words spoken by Jehovah at Mamre in Gen. xviii. 10, and Gen. xviii. 14 (ver. 9).

Gen. xviii. 10 and 14, blended and quoted to show (γάρ) that Isaac was the child (not of nature) but of Promise (ver. 9).

Gen. xviii. 10.
Heb.   שׁוֹב אָשׁוּב אֵלֶיךָ כָּעֵת חַיָּה וְהִנֵּה־בֵן
          לְשָׂרָה אִשְׁתֶּךָ

LXX ἐπαναστρέφων ἥξω πρὸς σὲ κατὰ τὸν καιρὸν τοῦτον εἰς ὥρας, καὶ ἕξει υἱὸν Σάρρα ἡ γυνή σου.

Gen. xviii. 14.
Heb.   אָשׁוּב אֵלֶיךָ כָּעֵת חַיָּה וּלְשָׂרָה בֵן

LXX εἰς τὸν καιρὸν τοῦτον ἀναστρέψω πρὸς σὲ εἰς ὥρας καὶ ἔσται τῇ Σάρρᾳ υἱός.

[*Obs.* 1. In the text, as quoted by S. Paul, κατὰ τὸν καιρὸν τοῦτον is taken from ver. 10, and καὶ ἔσται τῇ Σάρρᾳ υἱός from ver. 14, while ἐλεύσομαι is substituted for ἥξω. The words of the Divine Speaker in the grove of Mamre, before Sarah's laughing, are combined with His repeated promise which occurs in the reproof afterwards.]

[*Obs.* 2. The blended quotation is *a word of promise*. τέκνα τῆς ἐπαγγελίας means that Isaac was born *by virtue of* the Divine promise, not simply that he realised it, Gal. iv. 23 : ἡ τῆς ἐπαγγελίας ἰσχὺς ἔτεκε τὸ παιδίον S. Chrys. Sarah's child was a child not of nature, but of the ἐπαγγελία. κατὰ τὸν καιρὸν τοῦτον ver. 10 represents כָּעֵת חַיָּה, i.e. as the time revives, i.e. when the present season lives again (next year).]

(B) *Case of the children of Isaac* (vers. 10–13).

[*Obs.* 1. οὐ μόνον δέ (Σάρρα λόγον Θεοῦ, or ἐπαγγελίαν, εἶχεν). Abraham's family is not the strongest case. For it might be objected that Ishmael's rejection was to be explained by his being illegitimate. But the same distinction between *the natural child* and *the child of promise* reappears in the sons of Isaac, who were not merely both legitimate, but twins. The more definite idea of promise which governs the argument of vers. 8, 9 is here exchanged for the more general one of Divine appointment.]

[*Obs.* 2. We should have expected that Abraham with the two sons from two wives, so unequal in their positions, would have been followed by Isaac with his two sons from the one lawful wife. But the mention of Sarah in the composite quotation in ver. 9, and still more the fact that the Divine declaration in ver. 12 was made, not to Isaac but to Rebecca, leads S. Paul to state the contrast between the mothers, ver. 10.]

The *Prediction to Rebecca* (vers. 10–13).

1. *Circumstances* under which the Prediction to Rebecca was given (vers. 10, 11 a).

   a. Rebecca was ἐξ ἑνὸς κοίτην ἔχουσα, namely, by our father Isaac (ver. 10).

[*Obs.* 1. After ἀλλὰ καὶ 'Ρεβέκκα supply συμμαρτυρεῖ ἡμῖν or παράδειγμα παρέχει. ἐξ ἑνός does not simply affirm Rebecca's conjugal faithfulness. It proves the worthlessness of mere bodily descent in the transmission of the ἐπαγγελία. Rebecca was to be a mother of twins by *one* man, yet how different would be their religious destiny! κοίτην (used like εὐνή and λέχος) as in Heb. xiii. 4; Lev. xv. 18; xviii. 20; Wisd. iii. 13.]

[*Obs.* 2. The arg. is strengthened by the solemn title τοῦ πατρὸς ἡμῶν given to Isaac. Lawful descent from the most venerable ancestors does not carry with it heirship to the ἐπαγγελία. For πατήρ, see Rom. iv. 1.]

   b. As GOD indeed knew, Rebecca's twins were yet unborn, and had done nothing, whether good or bad (ver. 11 a).

[*Obs.* μήπω, not οὔπω. The subjective negative relation is insisted on. Not only were the twins unborn in fact, but this fact was before the Divine Mind. Winer, *Gr. N. T.* p. 608.]

2. *Purpose* (ἵνα) with which the Prediction to Rebecca was given (ver. 11 b).

   That the ἡ κατ' ἐκλογὴν πρόθεσις (the Divine purpose which was so formed that in it an election was made) might have its unchangeable character (μένῃ), not as a result of any works which those whom it concerned would perform, but as the outcome of His agency, Who calls nations and souls to His Kingdom and Service (cf. viii. 28, 30).

[*Obs.* 1. ἵνα κ.τ.λ. ver. 11 specifies the purpose with which the Divine πρόθεσις respecting Rebecca's children was declared before their birth. For other examples of a sentence expressing purpose, being thus placed before a governing verb, cf. S. Matt. xvii. 27; S. John xix. 28, 31; Acts xxiv. 4.]

[*Obs.* 2. With ἡ κατ' ἐκλογὴν πρόθεσις compare xi. 5 κατ' ἐκλογὴν χάριτος, and, as parallel phrases, Heb. xi. 7 ἡ κατὰ πίστιν δικαιοσύνη, Rom. xi. 21 οἱ κατὰ φύσιν κλάδοι: ἐκ τοῦ καλοῦντος = χάριτι, or ἐκ χάριτος, xi. 6; Eph. ii. 8, 9; 2 Tim. i. 9 τοῦ καλέσαντος (ἡμᾶς) κλήσει ἁγίᾳ, οὐ κατὰ τὰ ἔργα ἡμῶν, ἀλλὰ κατ' ἰδίαν πρόθεσιν καὶ χάριν.]

[*Obs.* 3. GOD's purpose expressing itself in the election of a minority of the Jews, corresponding to Jacob, and in the ἀποβολή of the majority, corresponding to Esau, is not the result of the presence or absence of conduct in conformity with the law, moral or ceremonial, but has its ground in the will of GOD. It is οὐκ ἐξ ἔργων, ἀλλ' ἐκ τοῦ καλοῦντος. But it does not from this follow that the Divine πρόθεσις, the free self-determination of GOD with respect to His creatures, is in itself a mere arbitrary caprice. It must, on the contrary, be in strict harmony with the Eternal Moral Laws of GOD's Nature, with that unerring Justice and Love which is GOD. This is not indeed here stated by S. Paul; but it is not denied. S. Paul merely says that the ἐκλογή in which the Divine πρόθεσις takes form is *not* determined by the ἔργα of the person or nation which is its object. He *may* mean that it is determined by πίστις: but he does not say so here. See, however, iii. 22 εἰς πάντας καὶ ἐπὶ πάντας τοὺς πιστεύοντας.]

3. *Substance* of the Prediction to Rebecca (ἐρρήθη αὐτῇ), (ver. 12).

Gen. xxv. 23, quoted to show that GOD had foretold very different destinies for the two children of Rebecca.

Heb. וְרַב יַעֲבֹד צָעִיר

LXX ὁ μείζων δουλεύσει τῷ ἐλάσσονι.

[*Obs*. μείζων and ἐλάσσων mean the greater and the less, not the first born and second born. The prediction refers to the 'two *nations* in the womb' of Rebecca, of which one was greater than the other, and yet was to serve it. It was fulfilled by David's conquest of Edom (2 Sam. viii. 14); by the later conquests under Amaziah (2 Kings xiv. 7; 2 Chron. xxv. 11) and Uzziah (2 Kings xiv. 22; 2 Chron. xxvi. 2); and under John Hyrcanus (Jos. *Ant.* xiii. 9. 1). S. Paul is thinking, however, not of the nations, but of the brothers; and as to these, the prediction was justified by Isaac's blessing, Gen. xxvii. 29 γίνου κύριος τοῦ ἀδελφοῦ σου cf. 37, 40.]

4. *Illustration* of the Prediction to Rebecca by GOD's later declaration, through Malachi, of His eternal love for Jacob, and hatred of Esau (ver. 13).

Mal. i. 2, 3, quoted to show that the Prediction to Rebecca respecting GOD's relations with Jacob and Esau, was borne out by history (ver. 13).

Heb. וָאֹהַב אֶת־יַעֲקֹב וְאֶת־עֵשָׂו שָׂנֵאתִי

LXX καὶ ἠγάπησα τὸν Ἰακώβ τὸν δὲ Ἡσαῦ ἐμίσησα.

[*Obs*. 1. The passage occurs in Malachi's opening reproach to Israel for ingratitude: Mal. i. 2, 3 'I have loved you, saith the Lord. Yet ye say, Wherein hast thou loved us? Was not Esau Jacob's brother? saith the Lord: yet I loved Jacob and I hated Esau, and laid his mountains and his heritage waste for the dragons of the wilderness.' Thus, that Israel had been exalted and Edom destroyed, was a practical illustration in history of this ἠγάπησα and ἐμίσησα. But in the Apostle's sense the aorists are to be referred not to GOD's practical dealings with the nations in history, but to the Divine πρόθεσις which preceded the birth of the brothers. Yet, as Petavius observes, the saying of Malachi does not touch upon the eternal weal or loss of the two brothers, personally, but only on their *typical* relationships to the ἐπαγγελία. It seems otherwise with Isaac and Ishmael. Pet. *de Dogm. Theol.* t. 1. lib. 10. c. 1. n. 7.]

[*Obs.* 2. ἐμίσησα (1) may be used in the privative sense of *not to love*, or *to love less*, See S. Jerome *on Mal.* i. Aq. *Summ. Th.* p. 1. qu. 23. art. 3. ad. 1 'In quantum Deus quibusdam non vult hoc bonum quod est vita aeterna, dicitur cos odio habere.' As ἀγαπᾶν sometimes = εὐλογεῖν, καλῶς ποιεῖν, so μισεῖν has this *privative* sense in Eph. v. 29 οὐδεὶς γάρ ποτε τὴν ἑαυτοῦ σάρκα ἐμίσησεν, ἀλλ' ἐκτρέφει καὶ θάλπει αὐτήν. Comp. S. John xii. 25. The word has been taken to describe conduct which would imply in man arbitrary hatred. Since God is love, 'He hateth nothing that He has made'; but He acts sometimes towards men, as men would act, they think, if they felt hatred. μισεῖν thus describes not an emotion in God but an effect of an emotion, anthropopathically attributed to Him: Gen. xxix. 30, 31; Deut. xxi. 15 sqq.; Prov. xiii. 24; S. Matt. vi. 24 &c. In the present case μισεῖν expressed itself in, or was recognized in, Esau's rejection : ἀγαπᾶν in the ἐκλογή of ob.

[*Obs.* 3. This failure of natural descent to secure the ἐπαγγελία, which the Apostle traces in the earliest history of the theocracy, shows the fundamental unity of the O. T. and N. T. on the question of man's Salvation, and is the ground of that necessity for a new Birth which our Lord and His Apostles insist upon : S. John i. 13; iii. 3-6; 1 S. Pet. i. 23. Comp. Eph. ii. 5.]

Prop. II.

(Concerning God's justice.) That God is just when He freely chooses a small number of Jews to be members of the Church of Christ, while the great majority are rejected, can be shown from the language of the Jewish Scriptures themselves (14–18).

Jewish obj. (suggested by vers. 11-13). Is not the restriction of the promises (*a*) to Jacob to the exclusion of Esau, and (*b*) to converted Jews to the exclusion of the majority of Jews, suggestive of capricious injustice on the part of God? (ver. 14).

[*Obs.* μὴ ἀδικία παρὰ τῷ Θεῷ; 'Is there not unrighteousness with God?' S. Paul's anticipation of the Jewish Christian inference from 11-13, which he negatives by μὴ γένοιτο. The stress lies on ἀδικία. For παρά with *dat.* in order to express qualities or attributes, see Winer, *Gr. N. T.* p. 492. The presumed ἀδικία of God would consist in His choosing Jacob, without reference to any human claims, since the idea of δίκη implies, apparently, reward for meritorious effort.]

Resp. No. According to the Jewish Scriptures themselves, God Himself so asserts His free choice in the exercise both of Mercy and of Severity, as to silence the suggestion (15-18).

[*Obs.* This is an *ad hominem* arg. as against a Jewish controversialist, who would be bound to accept those representations of the Divine character and conduct which are put forward in the Hebrew Scriptures. Though these representations have an equally binding authority for Christians, and may be illustrated by independent moral considerations, yet this is not immediately in question.]

(A) The Jewish Scriptures represent GOD as acting with perfect freedom in His exercise of Compassion (15, 16).

[*Obs.* The quotation in ver. 15 is a reason (γάρ) for μὴ γένοιτο (ver. 14). Only Moses, the venerated *recipient* of the word, is named; Θεός is understood before λέγει from ver. 14.]

   a. Proof from Ex. xxxiii. 19. GOD's word to Moses in the vision before the giving of the Law, quoted to show that GOD's mercy is not conditioned by any human right or title (ver. 15).

Heb. וְחַנֹּתִי אֶת־אֲשֶׁר אָחֹן וְרִחַמְתִּי אֶת־
אֲשֶׁר אֲרַחֵם׃

LXX καὶ ἐλεήσω ὃν ἂν ἐλεῶ, καὶ οἰκτειρήσω ὃν ἂν οἰκτείρω.

[*Obs.* 1. The Hebrew, 'I am gracious to whom I will be gracious,' &c. LXX 'I will be gracious to whomsoever I am gracious,' &c. But the sense is the same.]

[*Obs.* 2. Moses had prayed, 'Suffer me, I pray Thee, to see Thy glory.' The request was granted; and the quotation assigns a reason for the promise which precedes: 'I will make all thy goodness pass before thee, and I will proclaim the Name of the Lord before thee.' But the *axiomatic* form of this reason enables S. Paul to detach it from its immediate context, as a general statement of the law that GOD's Mercy is exercised in accordance with His Free-will.]

[*Obs.* 3. οἰκτείρω expresses more strongly the exercise of mercy than ἐλεῶ. In the LXX ἐλεεῖν represents חָנַן = gratiâ seu favore prosequi; and οἰκτείρειν stands for רָחַם = clemens esse. Probably the Hebr. leads Tittmann (*Syn.* p. 69 sqq.) to distinguish ἐλεεῖν GOD's active mercy, from οἰκτείρειν His pitying loving-kindness.]

[*Obs.* 4. It may be said that the charge of ἀδικία παρὰ τῷ Θεῷ which S. Paul is here repelling is aggravated rather than met by the contents of the citation in ver. 15. But for the disputant with whom the Apostle conceives himself to be arguing, who takes his stand on the Jewish Scriptures, and accuses GOD of being unjust to the majority of Israel in the Apostolic age, the reply is sufficient. It lies in the fact that the citation is from the Hebrew Scriptures; that it is an authority which the objector must own to have a binding force. If S. Paul argues as he does from the histories of the children of Abraham and Isaac, his inference is borne out by GOD's words about Himself in the Jewish Law; and no good Jew, or Jewish Christian, can doubt that what GOD says about Himself in his own Law, must be in

Dogmatic: ch. IX, *vv.* 6-29. 163

harmony with this absolute Righteousness. Further than this it is not necessary for the Apostle to go, at the present stage of his argument.]

 b. Inference (ἄρα οὖν) from the Divine saying to Moses (just quoted), as to the causality of Redemption (ver. 16).

Man's share in the saving ἔλεος and οἰκτιρμός of God is due	not	to any (inward) earnest longings for salvation (Phil. ii. 13), οὐ τοῦ θέλοντος : to any active (outward) efforts to serve God, οὐδὲ τοῦ τρέχοντος : but to God's (free) compassion, τοῦ ἐλεοῦντος Θεοῦ.

[*Obs.* 1. The *gen.* θέλοντος, τρέχοντος, ἐλεοῦντος expresses the Lat. *penes.* τρέχειν means active effort; the figure is borrowed from the public games : 1 Cor. ix. 24, 26 ; Gal. v. 7 ; Phil. ii. 16. It is equivalent to διώκειν δικαιοσύνην in ix. 30, and τὴν ἰδίαν δικαιοσύνην ζητεῖν στῆσαι in x. 3. It seems very doubtful whether τρέχειν has any reference to Esau's fruitless running in from the chase ; or θέλειν to Abraham's wish to make Ishmael, or Isaac's wish to make Esau, heir of the ἐπαγγελία.]

[*Obs.* 2. The idea of ver. 16 is more fully expanded in ix. 30–33, and x. 1–3. It is simply, but adequately, expressed as follows : 'Salus hominis non debetur alicui per aliquam ejus voluntatem, vel exteriorem operationem, sed procedit ex solâ Dei misericordia,' Aquin. *in loc.* The τρέχων, in the strength of grace received, only acts conformably to the ἡ κατ' ἐκλογὴν πρόθεσις : and yet, viewed from the side of human experience, he acts freely ; and hence the Apostle bids him τρέχειν in 1 Cor. ix. 24.]

(B) The Jewish Scriptures represent God as acting with perfect freedom in His exercise of severity (17, 18).

[*Obs.* In ver. 17 γάρ is explained as implying that the case of Pharaoh affords a reason *e contrario* for the proposition stated in ver. 16. The Divine σκληρύνειν is the counterpart of the Divine ἐλεεῖν. ἡ γραφή is said to speak, because God speaks in it : Gal. iii. 8, 22. Pharaoh is the chosen contemporaneous historical antithesis of Moses : the Divine rejection is contrasted with the Divine election. Pharaoh, like the rejected majority of the Jewish people, stood on his rights. He claimed to have a right to the continued possession of Israel ; and he asserted this right against the Will of God, as proclaimed through Moses. So the Jews of the Apostolic age appealed to the position secured to them, as they thought by the Mosaic Law, as against the Will of God revealed by Christ and His Apostle.]

 a. Proof from Ex. ix. 16. (Message to Pharaoh, in announcing the Plague of Hail). Quoted to show that God is not less free in His exercise of severity, than in His showing compassion (ver. 17).

Heb. וְאוּלָם בַּעֲבוּר זֹאת הֶעֱמַדְתִּיךָ בַּעֲבוּר הַרְאֹתְךָ
אֶת־כֹּחִי וּלְמַעַן סַפֵּר שְׁמִי בְּכָל־הָאָרֶץ׃

LXX καὶ ἕνεκεν τούτου διετηρήθης, ἵνα ἐνδείξωμαι ἐν σοὶ τὴν ἰσχύν μου, καὶ ὅπως διαγγελῇ τὸ ὄνομά μου ἐν πάσῃ τῇ γῇ.

{
  i. εἰς αὐτὸ τοῦτο ἐξήγειρά σε.
  ii. ὅπως ἐνδείξωμαι ἐν σοὶ τὴν δύναμίν μου.
  iii. καὶ ὅπως διαγγελῇ τὸ ὄνομά μου ἐν πάσῃ τῇ γῇ.
}

i. Act of GOD. Assigning to Pharaoh his place in human history : ἐξήγειρά σε.

ii. Its *immediate* purpose. The manifestation of GOD's punitive power : ὅπως ἐνδείξωμαι, κ.τ.λ.

iii. Its *more remote* purpose. The world-wide publication of the Divine Name : καὶ ὅπως διαγγελῇ τὸ ὄνομα, κ.τ.λ.

[Obs. 1. *God's act.* ἐξήγειρά σε Heb. הֶעֱמַדְתִּיךָ. 'I have made thee stand up,' 1 Kings xv. 4; Prov. xxix. 4. The reference to the pestilence (Ex. ix. 15) led the LXX to translate freely by διετηρήθης (see Hexapla), *thou hast been preserved alive*. Chald. Paraph. קַיָּמְתָּךְ. S. Paul's ἐξήγειρα, while referring immediately to the historical incident (comp. S. James v. 15), suggests the whole appearance of Pharaoh on the scene of history. He had been raised up for *this*. So ἐγείρειν is used in this sense : S. Matt. xi. 11; xxiv. 11; S. John vii. 52; Ecclus. x. 4; 1 Macc. iii. 49. εἰς αὐτὸ τοῦτο, stronger than LXX ἕνεκεν τούτου, for זֹאת בַּעֲבוּר. Attention concentrated on ὅπως, κ.τ.λ.]

[Obs. 2. *Immediate purpose.* ὅπως ἐνδείξωμαι ἐν σοὶ τὴν δύναμίν μου. A various reading of the LXX which stands ἵνα ἐνδείξωμαι ἐν σοὶ τὴν ἰσχύν μου. The Divine Power (δύναμις) exhibited partly in the successive plagues of Egypt, and chiefly in the destruction of the Egyptian hosts and their king (ἐν σοί). On ἐνδείκνυσθαι, see ii. 15; iii. 25; Eph. ii. 7; 1 Tim. i. 16. GOD would cause His power to be recognised. ὅπως here expresses not GOD's *antecedent* will respecting any creature of His Hand, but His *consequent* will,—consequent, that is, on Pharaoh's becoming what GOD eternally foreknew that he would be. 'Non Deus auctor fuit malitiae Pharaonis, sed cum destitutus Divinae Gratiae praesidiis, multis sese sceleribus inquinârit, divinae potentiae illustrandae materiam praebuit,' (Just. *in loc.*). GOD could not *positively* and *directly* contribute to Pharaoh's wickedness, without doing violence to His own Sanctity ; but He did *privatively* contribute to it by gradually withdrawing from Pharaoh such grace and opportunities as might have saved him, when Pharaoh's repeated sin had made this penal privation just. This is all that S. Augustine means in paraphrasing the passage, 'Excitavi te, ut contumacius resisteres imperio meo, non tantum permittendo, sed multa etiam tam intus quam foris operando.']

[Obs. 3. *More remote purpose.* καὶ ὅπως, κ.τ.λ. The world-wide (ἐν πάσῃ τῇ γῇ) publication (διαγγελῇ) of the Name of GOD as the Judge and Punisher of

Pharaoh was to follow in all coming time. The Egyptian wonders, and especially the destruction of the Egyptian host, produced a great effect on the mind of the heathen world. In the Song of Moses, the effect upon the Cannanites, Edomites and Moabites is anticipated: 'The people shall hear and be afraid: sorrow shall take hold of the inhabitants of Palestina. Then the dukes of Edom shall be amazed; the mighty men of Moab, trembling shall take hold upon them; all the inhabitants of Canaan shall melt away' Ex. xv. 14, 15. Compare the prayer of the Levites in Neh. ix. 10. The destruction of Pharaoh is often mentioned in the Koran.]

b. Inference (ἄρα οὖν) from the Divine saying to Pharaoh, (just quoted,) as to GOD's free-agency in the exercise of severity, as well as of mercy (ver. 18).

ὃν θέλει { ἐλεεῖ. / σκληρύνει.

[*Obs.* 1. The subject to θέλει, viz. ὁ Θεός, is suppressed from a feeling of awe, and because every reader could easily supply it. Winer, *Gr. N. T.* p. 736, E. T. By θέλει is denoted the action, not of a capricious, but of a perfectly Holy Will. The ultimate reason for man's salvation (ἐλεεῖ) lies not in his will but in that of GOD, Who is ὁ ἐνεργῶν ἐν ὑμῖν καὶ τὸ θέλειν καὶ τὸ ἐνεργεῖν ὑπὲρ τῆς εὐδοκίας Phil. ii. 13. ἐλεεῖ summarises vers. 15, 16.]

[*Obs.* 2. σκληρύνει Acts xix. 9; Heb. iii. 8, 13, 15. Cf. Ex. iv. 21, LXX ἐγὼ δὲ σκληρυνῶ αὐτοῦ τὴν καρδίαν: vii. 3; ix. 12; x. 20, 27; xi. 10; xiv. 4, 8, 17. σκληρύνειν, from σκληρός (σκέλλω σκλῆναι) durus, asper, rigidus, LXX for קָשָׁה, Hiph. הִקְשָׁה, 'to make *hard*.' It cannot be here 'to treat harshly,' (on the ground that in ver. 17, the subject is not the hardening, but the overthrow of Pharaoh), because this would do violence to the language. Akin to σκληρύνειν is βαρύνειν = Heb. הִכְבִּיד ingravare; 'to make *heavy*.' Cf. Ex. viii. 15, 32. The two metaphors make up the idea of moral insensibility. Yet (1) this hardening is also said to be Pharaoh's own act; Ex. viii. 15, 32 ἐβάρυνεν Φαραὼ τὴν καρδίαν αὐτοῦ: Ex. ix. 34; xiii. 15 ἐσκλήρυνεν Φαραὼ ἐξαποστεῖλαι ἡμᾶς. Compare 1 Sam. vi. 6. Elsewhere, (2) such hardening is represented as a punishment sent by GOD: Ex. ix. 12; x. 20, 27; Is. vi. 9 sqq. GOD has given man a moral nature, which may surrender itself to evil, until it reaches a point at which return has become impracticable. GOD is said Himself to do that which results from a misuse of the laws of the nature which He has given; and yet, so far as GOD is concerned, this result is always a judgment for man's neglect of GOD's merciful calls and warnings. 'Man first closes his own heart and then his heart is closed.' So even Christ is 'a stone of stumbling and a rock of offence to them who stumble at the word, being disobedient,' 1 Pet. ii. 7, 8. In theological language, when man neglects *gratia sufficiens* which GOD gives to all, GOD withholds His *gratia efficax*. In this privation consists the σκληρύνειν, which however is here, consistently with his present point of view, regarded by the Apostle as exclusively the product of GOD's Holy and Absolute Will (ὃν δὲ θέλει), and irrespectively of those conditions of human responsibility which he elsewhere recognizes. Cf. S. Aug. *de div. Quaestt. ad Simplic.* 1. Qu. 2. 15 'obduratio Dei ... nolle misereri, ut non ab illo irrogetur aliquid quo sit homo deterior, sed tantum quo sit melior non erogetur.' But see the exhaustive discussion of σκληρύνειν considered as evidencing the testing power of GOD's Revelations, Müller, *Chr. Doctr. of Sin,* Bk. v. 3 (vol. ii. p. 465, E. T.); Is. vi. 10 sqq.; S. Matt. xiii. 12. And observe how the ἀτιμάζεσθαι and πάθη ἀτιμίας of Rom. i. 24, 26 were punishments of the Heathen for refusing to retain GOD in their knowledge, when revealed in Nature and Conscience.]

Prop. III.

(Concerning GOD's Justice.) Man is not in a position which enables him to criticize the Justice of GOD's dealings with sinners (vers. 19-21).

Jewish obj. (suggested by ver. 18 ὃν δὲ θέλει σκληρύνει, to which οὖν (ver. 19) refers). How can GOD reproach hardened sinners, since it is asserted that they have been hardened by the Divine Will Itself, to which no created will offers successful opposition? (ver. 19).

[*Obs.* 1. The Apostle does not make himself in any way responsible for the objection, when he says ἐρεῖς οὖν: cf. Rom. xi. 19; ἐρεῖ τις 1 Cor. xv. 35; S. James ii. 18. When he feels sympathy with some element in an objection, he asks, τί οὖν ἐροῦμεν; iii. 5; vi. 1; vii. 7; ix. 14, 30. The insolence of the antagonist is further implied in μενοῦνγε, ὦ ἄνθρωπε.]

[*Obs.* 2. βούλημα = the thing willed; a ἅπ. λεγ. in S. Paul. We might have expected θελήματι (ver. 18 ὃν δὲ θέλει), but the word is purposely varied; consilium, not merely voluntas. ἀνθέστηκε, perf. pres. Winer, *Gk. N. T.* p. 342, implies the ever resistless character of GOD's Will. The objector does not mean that GOD *could* have nothing in *any* one to censure, because nobody could resist His predestinating Will; but he asks, *how* GOD's censure of the σκληρυνόμενοι can be at all explained. 'The question is partly impious, partly tragic.']

a. Resp. Man is in no position which entitles him thus to reply by way of opposition to the Divine Judgment of sinners (ver. 20 a).

[*Obs.* 1. μενοῦνγε (Rom. x. 18; S. Luke xi. 28) denotes an objection, and is slightly ironical; τίς concentrates attention on the nothingness of man, face to face with his Creator. ἀνταποκρινόμενος describes putting the question τί ἔτι . . . . ἀνθέστηκε, which is a reply by way of opposition to GOD's μέμφεται of hardened sinners. The verb ἀνταποκρίνεσθαι is used by the LXX to translate אָמַר הֵשִׁיב and עָנָה, and means to give a contradictory or gainsaying reply: S. Luke xiv. 6. S. Chrys. paraphrases by ἀντιλέγων, ἐναντιούμενος.]

[*Obs.* 2. A direct answer to the objection would have been that the objector misunderstood the nature of the σκληρύνειν in ver. 19, which cannot be imagined to be a *positive* process urged forward by the Will of GOD, without blasphemy. But the Apostle replies, not to the question of the objector, but to the disposition from which it issued. Apart from its misconception of the sense of σκληρύνειν, the question implied a total forgetfulness of the real relations of man to his Creator. So our Lord often ignored the point of a question put to Him, and addressed Himself to the temper which prompted it : S. Matt. viii. 20, 22 ; xix. 17 ; S. John iii. 3 ; vi. 65 ; S. Matt. xxii. 29, 31. Even had the case been as the objector supposed, how could a man presume to make the objection ? That it was not so, is implied in the δέ of ver. 22.]

b. Justification of *Resp.* from the Old Testament simile of the potter and the clay, which sets the Divine Power, as contrasted with man's insignificance, in the strongest light (vers. 20 b–21).

[*Obs.* The simile occurs in Is. xxix. 16 ; xlv. 9 ; lxiv. 8 ; Jer. xviii. 6 ; Ecclus. xxxiii. 13 ; Wisd. xv. 7. In ver. 20 the Apostle has in view Is. xlv. 9 ; in ver. 21, as it seems, Wisd. xv. 7 'For the potter, tempering soft earth, fashioneth every vessel with much labour for our service ; yea of the same clay he maketh both the vessels that serve for clean uses, and likewise also all such as serve to the contrary ; but what is the use of either sort the potter himself is the judge.']

The simile suggests,

(1) The *absurdity* of man's remonstrating with GOD for His conduct in Creation and Providence. GOD is the potter: man the clay (ver. 20).

(2) The *power* of GOD (ἐξουσία) to make out of the same mass of human nature (πηλός, φύραμα) some who would become children of glory, and some children of shame (ver. 21).

[*Obs.* 1. The simile forms an *a minori ad majus* arg. If not even in the case of a plastic image can the question, Why hast thou made me thus? be conceived as being put ; how much less in the case of man, who is so much further removed from the Creator, than any created matter from a human artist !]

[*Obs.* 2. The point suggested by the simile is not GOD's freedom to create beings with different capacities, but to mould beings, already created, (φύραμα, πηλός,) to different destinies. 'Ἐποίησας οὕτω must be explained by τῷ πλάσαντι, which implies an already existing material, ver. 20.]

[*Obs.* 3. σκεῦος εἰς τιμήν, εἰς ἀτιμίαν. εἰς of destination, a vessel destined for a noble, and a base use. Philo, *de Vit. Contempl.* ed. Mangey, ii. 472, explains it thus. In 2 Tim. ii. 20, the being a σκεῦος εἰς τιμήν depends on ἐὰν ἐκκαθάρῃ ἑαυτόν. Here the Divine order is alone in view.]

[*Obs.* 4. The problem respecting the Justice of GOD is not solved in vers. 20, 21. The objection is only silenced by reference to the unconditional power of the Creator. 'One abstraction is set against another.' As the objector puts forward claims on GOD's justice, which rest on human rights, and leave GOD's unlimited supremacy out of account, so the Apostle puts forward this unlimited supremacy of GOD, without, at the moment, referring to the Love and Sanctity which regulate its exercise. The pride of the objector must be humbled, by contemplating the utter insignificance of man before his

Maker, as taught in the Jewish Scriptures, before he can hope to understand the true account of GOD's dealings with Israel. With this object in view the Apostle will not qualify his assertion of the Absolute Supremacy of GOD.]

Prop. IV.

(Concerning GOD's Mercy.) The action and purpose of GOD in bearing with sinners who deserve punishment should silence the cavils of man (vers. 22-29).

1. The *fact* of His bearing with the σκεύη ὀργῆς (ver. 22).

[*Obs.* The aor. ἤνεγκεν, although primarily glancing at the case of Pharaoh (S. Chrys.), includes all hardened sinners until the Advent. For φέρειν in the sense of 'to endure,' cf. Deut. i. 12; Jer. xliv. 22; Heb. xii. 20. When GOD is said to endure the σκεύη ὀργῆς, it is implied that His penal σκληρύνειν did not positively form them for destruction.]

2. The *difficulty* of His bearing with the σκεύη ὀργῆς (ver. 22) seen in

    a. His will (θέλων) to manifest His ὀργή against that which provokes it (ver. 22).
    b. His will to make known τὸ δυνατὸν αὐτοῦ, i. e. what He can do to repress it (ver. 22).
    c. The condition of the σκεύη ὀργῆς as already κατηρτισμένα εἰς ἀπώλειαν (ver. 22).

[*Obs.* On ὀργή cf. S. Aug. *Civ. Dei,* xv. 25 'Ira Dei non perturbatio animi ejus est, sed judicium quo irrogatur poena peccato.' τὸ δυνατὸν αὐτοῦ glances at δύναμις, ver. 17. But GOD's righteous indignation and His Power are represented as *held in check* by His long-suffering for sinners, and His designs of boundless munificence for His elect. θέλων = καίπερ θέλων.]

3. The *motives* of His bearing with the σκεύη ὀργῆς (vers. 22, 23).

    a. His abundant long-suffering (πολλὴ μακροθυμία) is the attribute within (ἐν) which this takes place (ver. 22 b).
    b. (Secondary or accessory (καί) motive.) His purpose (ἵνα) of making known the wealth of His moral glories to be shed upon the σκεύη ἐλέους, whom He had previously fashioned for glory. This required delay (ver. 23).

4. The *concrete* result to the readers of His bearing with the σκεύη ὀργῆς (ver. 24).

Dogmatic: ch. IX, *vv.* 6-29.

> *a.* He has called them, as σκεύη ἐλέους, to a state of salvation (ver. 24).
> *b.* He thus has taken them, (i) not only from among the Jews, who might (however erroneously) deem themselves hereditary σκεύη ἐλέους, but (ii) from among the heathen nations, who might have been considered beyond the range of the Divine compassion (ver. 24).

[*Obs.* 1. In vers. 22, 23, the different constructions which have been given turn upon the words in ver. 22, with which καὶ ἵνα γνωρίσῃ (ver. 23) is connected.

καὶ ἵνα γνωρίσῃ
ver. 23.

> (1) connected with ἤνεγκεν ver. 22. In this case καὶ ἵνα γνωρίσῃ gives a second motive, over and above that supplied by the Divine Attribute of μακροθυμία, for God's bearing with the σκεύη ὀργῆς. It was that He might make known what He had done for the σκεύη ἐλέους. (Meyer.)
> (2) connected with κατηρτισμένα εἰς ἀπώλειαν (ver. 22). In this case καὶ ἵνα γνωρίσῃ would express the purpose with which the σκεύη ὀργῆς are made ready for destruction.
> (3) connected with (as coordinate with) θέλων ὁ Θεὸς ἐνδείξασθαι. In this case εἰ must be repeated again before ἵνα γνωρίσῃ, and the verb depending on εἰ is not actually inserted. There are then two coordinate clauses.
>
> A. But if God,
>   (1) although willing to show His Wrath, and to make known His Power,
>   (2) endured with great long-suffering the vessels of wrath fitted to destruction.
>
> B. And if God,
>   (1) in order that He might make known the wealth of His Glory upon the vessels of mercy, whom He had before prepared unto glory,
>   (2) [did all that was needful to conduct these vessels to the glory prepared for them, by calling and justifying them, viii. 30],
>
> [what room is there for gainsaying after the manner of the objector in ver. 19?]

The most perfect meaning is yielded by (3), but in addition to the suppression of the apodosis of the whole sentence, we have to suppose the additional suppression of a *most important* clause B (2), upon which ἵνα γνωρίσῃ really depends. This is taking too great a liberty with the text. In (2) the last chief thought is made to depend quite subordinately on the secondary qualification κατηρτισμένα εἰς ἀπώλειαν. We therefore fall back on (1) as presenting fewest difficulties.]

[*Obs.* 2. The *apodosis* of the question in vers. 22, 23 is not expressed. The question introduced by εἰ δέ—'But how if'—is not completed; the *aposiopesis* being even more expressive than the completed sentence. 'But how if God, although willing to manifest His anger on sinners and to show what He can do against sin, has nevertheless hitherto, in His abounding tenderness, endured sinners, fitted though they are for everlasting destruction, with the further object of making known, during this period of deferred judgment, His wealth of glorious perfections in respect of the objects of His mercy, whom by His grace He has fashioned for eternal glory,'—how in view of GOD's long-suffering towards the one class, and His purposes of mercy towards the other, must not any desire to dispute with Him be at once extinguished?]

[*Obs.* 3. σκεύη used like כלים. σκεῦος ὀργῆς (ver. 22) corresponds to σκεῦος εἰς ἀτιμίαν (ver. 21), and σκεῦος ἐλέους (ver. 23) to σκεῦος εἰς τιμήν (ver. 21); ἀτιμία being the effect of the ὀργή, τιμή of the ἔλεος. Compare the Rabbinical use of כלי and in Is. xiii. 5. In σκεῦος ὀργῆς—ἐλέους—the *gen.* is of the object, 'destined to experience GOD's wrath' or mercy; σκεῦος ἐκλογῆς (Acts ix. 15) must be taken actively. The 'vessels of wrath' are κατηρτισμένα εἰς ἀπώλειαν, the *passive* verb being dictated by a motive of piety which for the moment veils the Divine Agent, and suggests the responsibility of the wicked in making themselves what they become, (contrast the προητοίμασεν (ver. 23) of the *aeterna electio* of the saved, cf. Eph. ii. 10,) although the simile of the potter (ver. 21) makes it impossible not also to think of GOD as the καταρτίζων, so far as withholding His *gratia efficax* is concerned. Compare Acts xiii. 48 ὅσοι ἦσαν τεταγμένοι: S. Jude 4 οἱ προγεγραμμένοι εἰς τοῦτο τὸ κρίμα: 2 Tim. ii. 21 σκεῦος ἡτοιμασμένον. Observe that προετοιμάζειν implies the communication of certain qualities which καταρτίζειν does not: 1 Cor. ii. 9; Eph. ii. 10; S. Matt. iii. 3; S. Luke i. 17.]

[*Obs.* 4. Vers. 22, 23 are apparently moulded on Wisd. xii. 20, 21 'For if Thou didst punish the enemies of Thy children, and the condemned to death with such deliberation, giving them time and place whereby they might be delivered from their malice; with how great circumspection didst Thou judge Thine own sons, unto whose fathers Thou hast sworn and made covenant of good promises!' S. Augustine paraphrases the motive, καὶ ἵνα γνωρίσῃ κ.τ.λ. in Ep. 186 *ad Paulinum*, § 24 'Pertulit in multa patientia vasa irae aptata in interitum, non quod illi essent necessaria, . . . sed ne se (vasa misericordiae) in bonis operibus tanquam de propriis extollerent viribus, sed humiliter intelligerent nisi illis Dei gratia, non debita, sed gratuita, subveniret, id fuisse reddendum meritis suis, quod aliis in eadem massa redditum cernerent.']

[*Obs.* 5. In ver. 24 the Apostle recurs to the starting-point of the discussion in ver. 6, viz. the exclusion of the majority of Israelites from the Christian Church, and the admission of heathen converts in their place. In οὓς καὶ ἐκάλεσεν the relative is attracted in gender by the following ἡμᾶς—'as which, viz. as σκεύη ἐλέους ἃ προητοίμασεν εἰς δόξαν, He also called us,' &c., Winer, *Gr. N. T.* p. 662.]

§ *Appendix* on the *Witness of Prophecy* to the call of the σκεύη ἐλέους out of Heathendom, and to the fact that the great

Dogmatic: ch. IX, vv. 6-29.

majority of the Jewish people, in their unbelieving rejection of Jesus Christ, were σκεύη ὀργῆς (vers. 25–29).

[*Obs.* The statement of ver. 24 was too paradoxical to pass without some justification. Certainly ἐξ 'Ιουδαίων required no confirmation. But ἐξ ἐθνῶν seemed to involve repudiation of God's Covenant with Israel. And ἐξ 'Ιουδαίων implied that the mass of God's ancient people were left in unbelief. Did Jewish prophecy anticipate this state of things, which placed Gentiles and Jews, religiously speaking, each in a new position?]

(A) *Prophetic Witness* to the vocation of the σκεύη ἐλέους out of Heathendom into the Church of Christ (vers. 25, 26).

[*Obs.* The two passages which illustrate this are both taken from Hosea,—the 'Prophet of the Divine Tenderness.']

a. Hosea ii. 23, quoted to show that heathens would be God's people and objects of His Love (ver. 25).

Heb. וְרִחַמְתִּי אֶת־לֹא רֻחָמָה
וְאָמַרְתִּי לְלֹא־עַמִּי עַמִּי־אָתָּה

'I will have mercy upon her who had not obtained mercy;
And I will say to them which were not my people, Thou art my people.'

LXX καὶ ἐλεήσω τὴν οὐκ ἠλεημένην (B. καὶ ἀγαπήσω τὴν οὐκ ἠγαπημένην)
καὶ ἐρῶ τῷ οὐ λαῷ μου·
Λαός μου εἶ σύ.

[*Obs.* 1. The Apostle's rendering varies both from the LXX and Heb.
καλέσω τὸν οὐ λαόν μου, λαόν μου·
καὶ τὴν οὐκ ἠγαπημένην, ἠγαπημένην.]

[*Obs.* 2. In the Hebrew the reference is to the symbolical names of the prophet's son לֹא עַמִּי and daughter לֹא רֻחָמָה, given in token of the rejection of Israel, Hos. i. 6-9. It was not the heathen, but the idolatrous people of the ten tribes, whose pardon and renewed adoption was thus announced. S. Paul applies the prophet's words to the case of the Gentile converts to Christ, because Israel had fallen to the level of the idolatrous heathen and had sinned against greater light and knowledge. Israel's pardon was therefore typical of God's mercies to the heathen: and S. Paul changes ἐρῶ τῷ οὐ λαῷ into καλέσω τὸν οὐ λαόν κ.τ.λ. because the true Messianic fulfilment of the words is already present to his mind. S. Peter similarly applies Hosea's language to the heathen; 1 S. Pet. ii. 10.]

b. Hosea i. 10, quoted to show that heathen lands would be the home of many of God's true children (ver. 26).

Heb. וְהָיָה בִּמְקוֹם אֲשֶׁר יֵאָמֵר לָהֶם
לֹא־עַמִּי אַתֶּם
יֵאָמֵר לָהֶם בְּנֵי אֵל־חָי

LXX καὶ ἔσται ἐν τῷ τόπῳ οὗ ἐρρέθη αὐτοῖς
   οὐ λαός μου ὑμεῖς,
   ἐκεῖ κληθήσονται υἱοὶ Θεοῦ ζῶντος.

[*Obs.* Hos. i. 10; (*in Heb.* ii. 1) 'And it shall come to pass, that in the place where it was said unto them, Ye are not my people, there it shall be said unto them, Ye are the sons of the living GOD.' Here again the reference is to the ten tribes, who would be restored and united with Judah after their dispersion. Hence בִּמְקוֹם refers, in the prophet, not to the place of the exile, but to Palestine,—the scene of their restoration as of their sin. S. Paul sees the *antitypical* fulfilment of the promise in the Call of the Gentiles, who, after being 'not-GOD's-people' for long ages, will now be called 'the sons of the living GOD.' Hence τόπος οὗ ἐρρέθη αὐτοῖς is, in the sense of the Apostle, all the countries of Heathendom. S. Peter understands the passage (1 S. Pet. i. 1) of converts to the Church of Christ from among the dispersed ten tribes.]

(B) *Prophetic Witness* to the eventual salvation of a mere remnant of the natural Israel,—the great majority, in their rejection of Jesus Christ, being σκεύη ὀργῆς (vers. 27–29).

[*Obs.* The two passages which illustrate this are both taken from Isaiah,—the great Prophet of Israel's future, and of the Messianic age. Of these utterances, respectively, the *impassioned* character is noted by κράζει (which = the Rabbinical צוח הנביא) ver. 27, and the *predictive* by προείρηκεν ver. 29.]

a. Isaiah x. 22, 23, quoted to show that only a remnant of the natural Israel would be saved by conversion to Christ, the great majority being destined to destruction (vers. 27, 28).

[*Obs.* 1. The citation varies from the LXX most remarkably in substituting ὁ ἀριθμὸς τῶν υἱῶν Ἰσραήλ for ὁ λαὸς Ἰσραήλ, to express the point of the great *number* of the people at large in contrast with the κατάλειμμα, which varies from the Hebrew considerably.

Heb.   כִּי אִם־יִהְיֶה עַמְּךָ יִשְׂרָאֵל כְּחוֹל הַיָּם
   שְׁאָר יָשׁוּב בּוֹ
   כִּלָּיוֹן חָרוּץ שׁוֹטֵף צְדָקָה׃
   כִּי כָלָה וְנֶחֱרָצָה
   אֲדֹנָי יְהוִה צְבָאוֹת עֹשֶׂה בְּקֶרֶב כָּל־הָאָרֶץ׃

Translation of Hebrew:—
   'For though thy people, O Israel, shall be as the sand of the sea,
   A remnant of them only shall return :
   Destruction is decreed, it brings in as with a flood penal justice ;
   For the destruction, and that which is decreed,
   Doth Jehovah, the Lord of Hosts, accomplish in the midst of the whole earth.'

LXX καὶ ἐὰν γένηται ὁ λαὸς Ἰσραὴλ ὡς ἡ ἄμμος τῆς θαλάσσης, τὸ κατάλειμμα αὐτῶν σωθήσεται· λόγον συντελῶν καὶ συντέμνων ἐν δικαιοσύνῃ, ὅτι λόγον συντετμημένον Κύριος ποιήσει ἐν τῇ οἰκουμένῃ ὅλῃ.

Dogmatic: ch. IX, vv. 6–29.

(Citation.) ἐὰν ᾖ ὁ ἀριθμὸς τῶν υἱῶν Ἰσραὴλ ὡς ἡ ἄμμος τῆς θαλάσσης τὸ ὑπόλειμμα σωθήσεται· λόγον γὰρ συντελῶν καὶ συντέμνων ποιήσει Κύριος ἐπὶ τῆς γῆς.

[*Obs.* 1. שְׁאָר is emphatically accentuated—only a remnant will turn to GOD. σωθήσεται, which the LXX understood of a return to Palestine, is retained by S. Paul in its Christian sense. The LXX translation of the third line of the Hebrew is apparently incorrect. The LXX sometimes render חָרַץ (rad. 'to cut') by συντέμνειν Is. xxviii. 22. And, the voices being, as often, changed, συντέμνων represents חָרוּץ, while כִּלָּיוֹן, prop. 'wasting away,' is translated by λόγον in the sense of decree, although 'utterance' (see Meyer) is a better rendering. But how is συντελῶν to be accounted for? Possibly, as an attempt to exhaust the idea of כִּלָּיוֹן, so imperfectly represented by λόγον. שׁוֹטֵף however is wholly untranslated; unless the LXX be supposed to have read שׁוֹפֵט. The LXX may have thought that the sense was sufficiently expressed in συντέμνων and συντελῶν. The Apostle however keeps to the LXX since, equally with the original, it prophetically illustrates the destiny of the great mass of the people of Israel. 'For accomplishing His utterance [is He] and cutting short (delay) in penal justice, for a summary utterance of punishment will the Lord bring to pass upon the earth.' See Lowth on Isaiah, p. 94; Meyer *in loc.*]

[*Obs.* 2. The prophecy probably belongs to the first three years of the reign of Ahaz, and to the period which preceded the destruction of the two allies by Tiglath-pileser. To the small remnant that would escape of the all-destroying host of Assyria (ver. 19) corresponds the small remnant that alone would turn to GOD, under this penal visitation, even though the numbers of Israel were the highest that had been promised to the Patriarchs. With regard to the majority, destruction was irrevocably determined; and this destruction in its onward sweep would carry out the penal righteousness of GOD. It would embrace, if not every single individual, at any rate the great majority—all the land and all the people. Antitypical to this was the spiritual situation of Israel at the date of the first promulgation of the Gospel; cf. Delitzsch on Is. x.]

b. Isaiah i. 9, quoted to show that the remnant of Jewish Converts to the Faith of Christ alone saves Israel from spiritual annihilation (ver. 29).

Heb. לוּלֵי יְהוָה צְבָאוֹת הוֹתִיר לָנוּ
שָׂרִיד
כִּמְעַט כִּסְדֹם הָיִינוּ לַעֲמֹרָה דָּמִינוּ

LXX καὶ εἰ μὴ Κύριος Σαβαὼθ ἐγκατέλιπεν ἡμῖν σπέρμα
ὡς Σόδομα ἂν ἐγενήθημεν
καὶ ὡς Γόμορρα ἂν ὡμοιώθημεν.

[*Obs.* 1. The citation closes the first paragraph of the opening address in Isaiah respecting GOD'S dealings with His ungrateful people. But for His Compassion, all must have been destroyed. And His Omnipotence (glanced at in the title, 'Jehovah (GOD) of the hosts of heaven') set His Compassion in motion to save the remnant. From Sodom four human beings only escaped: Gomorrah was absolutely annihilated.]

[*Obs*. 2. In the expression Κύριος Σαβαώθ, which occurs fifty times in the LXX of Isaiah, and may be illustrated from 1 Kings xxii. 19, צְבָאוֹת is a dependent gen., and not an independent name of GOD as the Absolute. שָׂרִיד, paraphrastically translated by the LXX σπέρμα, means a survivor, one escaped from a great slaughter (see Ges.), who so may be the parent of others. In Job xx. 21, a survival, after general destruction. In Deut. ii. 34, without כִּמְעָט = 'a remnant which was but a mere trifle.' In ὡς Σ. ἂν ἐγενήθημεν and ὡς Γ. ἂν ὡμοιώθημεν, two modes of conceiving the relation of likeness are intermixed: Hos. iv. 6; Ez. xxxiv. 2.]

[*Obs*. 3. Throughout this section (ix. 6-29) no attempt is made by the Apostle to harmonize the absolute Freedom and Omnipotence of GOD with man's self-determination and responsibility. For the moment, the former truth is stated with such imperious force, that the latter appears to be quite lost sight of: and the necessity for this 'one-sidedness' of statement lay in the presumption entertained by the Jews, that in virtue of their theocratic position GOD *must* be gracious to them. Without attempting to determine the relation of interdependence which exists between Divine and human freedom, (secured by the truth that the former is ruled by GOD's essential Sanctity and is consequently conditioned by moral facts on the side of man), S. Paul passes on to consider the other side of the phenomenon before him, viz. the responsibility of the Jews themselves for their failure to attain the δικαιοσύνη Θεοῦ. On the general subject of Predestination, see Bishop Browne on Art. xvii; Mozley on *the Augustinian Doctrine of Predestination* (who however perhaps states S. Augustine's position somewhat one-sidedly); and, for the difference between the teaching of S. Augustine and Calvin on the subject, Petavius, *de Dogm. Theol.* vol. i. lib. x. c. 7 sqq. *de Predestinatione*.]

C.

Israel's failure to attain δικαιοσύνη Θεοῦ ἐκ πίστεως considered in the light of human responsibility (ix. 30—x. 21).

[*Obs*. The preceding prophecies (vers. 25-29) lead (οὖν) to the historical result stated in ver. 30, as an answer to the question τί οὖν ἐροῦμεν; This is, that)

i. [Some] Heathens, whose efforts were not directed (μή) to becoming righteous, have, at their conversion, obtained that righteousness which proceeds from faith (ver. 30).

[*Obs*. The Heathen had no revelation, and did not observe the moral law. In this sense they were μὴ διώκοντα δικαιοσύνην, and yet they had moral aspirations which faith in Christ satisfied. On the use of διώκειν, καταλαμβάνειν of competitors in the Greek Games, see 1 Cor. ix. 24; Phil. iii. 12-14; 1 Tim. vi. 11, 12.]

ii. [Most] Israelites pursuing the [ideal] law of righteousness have not attained it, because they set out from their own outward acts, not from a divinely-given inward disposition (vers. 31, 32).

Dogmatic: ch. IX, *v.* 30—X, *v.* 21. 175

[*Obs*. 1. The νόμος δικαιοσύνης is not legal righteousness, but the Law which confers righteousness. This is not simply the Mosaic Law, but that ideal law which the Jew vainly endeavoured to reach by literal obedience to the Mosaic ordinances. οὐκ ἔφθασε εἰς in ver. 31 corresponds by contrast to κατέλαβε in ver. 30.]

[*Obs*. 2. In ὡς ἐξ ἔργων [νόμου] ver. 32, ὡς used to be explained by reference to the Hebrew *Caph veritatis* (see Gesenius on Is. i. 7), as involving a comparison with all objects of the same species. See S. John i. 14; vii. 10; Phil. ii. 12. But it is better (Winer, *Gr. N. T.* p. 771) to understand it as contrasting the *imaginary* rule ἐξ ἔργων with the objectively-true one ἐκ πίστεως. ὡς introduces the subjective conception and implies that nothing true in the objective sense, answered to it. Omit νόμου which here, as in iv. 2, was added by the glossarists; although it is justified by iii. 20; Gal. ii. 16.]

[*Obs*. 3. The contrast may be thus exhibited :—

In the ἔθνη observe
 (i) The effort (negative), μὴ διώκοντα δικαιοσύνην (ver. 30).
 (ii) The result (positive), κατέλαβε δικαιοσύνην (ver. 30).
 (iii) The reason for this, [ὅτι] ἐκ πίστεως (ver. 30).

In Israel observe
 (i) The effort (positive), διώκων νόμον δικαιοσύνης (ver. 31).
 (ii) The result (negative), εἰς νόμον δικαιοσύνης οὐκ ἔφθασεν (ver. 31).
 (iii) The reason for this, ὅτι οὐκ ἐκ πίστεως ἀλλ᾽ ὡς ἐξ ἔργων νόμου (ver. 32).]

[*Obs*. 4. Thus this contrast introduces the subject of the section, (ix. 32 b–x. 21), viz. the failure of Israel to attain δικαιοσύνη Θεοῦ ἐκ πίστεως, and his responsibility and guilt on account of this failure. The whole section is an expansion of the clause ὅτι οὐκ ἐκ πίστεως, ἀλλ᾽ ὡς ἐξ ἔργων νόμου.]

Guilt of Israel (ix. 32 b–x. 21).

§ 1.

First evidence of Israel's Guilt. Their rejection of the Messiah, prophesied in their own Scriptures (ix. 32 b, 33).

 a. The fact. They stumbled at the true historical λίθος προσκόμματος, i. e. the Messiah, by not believing in Him when He came (ver. 33).

[*Obs*. It is the quotations in ver. 33 which lead the Apostle to select the title λίθος προσκόμματος for our Lord here; but the title well suits the metaphor implied in διώκειν, φθάνειν, καταλαμβάνειν (vers. 30, 31). It was, as crucified, that our Lord especially became a σκάνδαλον and a πρόσκομμα to the Jews. In Himself He was θεμέλιος καὶ ἑδραίωμα (Theophyl.); cf. S. Matt. xxi. 44 ὁ πεσὼν ἐπὶ τὸν λίθον τοῦτον συνθλασθήσεται, ἐφ᾽ ὃν δ᾽ ἂν πέσῃ λικμήσει αὐτόν.]

 b. The prophecies which should have saved them (Is. xxviii. 16, and viii. 14, blended into one) are quoted to show that

Israel had been warned that Messiah would be rejected by His own people.

1. Is. xxviii. 16.
Heb.

הִנְנִי יִסַּד בְּצִיּוֹן | אָבֶן
אֶבֶן בֹּחַן | פִּנַּת יִקְרַת מוּסָד מוּסָּד |
הַמַּאֲמִין לֹא יָחִישׁ:

'Behold, I am He who hath laid in Sion
A stone, a stone of trial,
A precious corner stone, of well-founded founding:
Whosoever believes shall not have to move.'

LXX ἰδοὺ ἐγὼ ἐμβάλλω εἰς τὰ θεμέλια Σιὼν λίθον πολυτελῆ, ἐκλεκτόν, ἀκρογωνιαῖον, ἔντιμον, εἰς τὰ θεμέλια αὐτῆς, καὶ ὁ πιστεύων ἐπ' αὐτῷ οὐ μὴ καταισχυνθῇ.

2. Is. viii. 14.
Heb.

וְהָיָה לְמִקְדָּשׁ | וּלְאֶבֶן נֶגֶף
וּלְצוּר מִכְשׁוֹל | לִשְׁנֵי בָתֵּי יִשְׂרָאֵל
לְפַח וּלְמוֹקֵשׁ לְיוֹשֵׁב יְרוּשָׁלָםִ:

'So will He become a sanctuary,
But a stone of stumbling and a rock of offence
To both the houses of Israel,
A snare and trap to the inhabitants of Jerusalem.'

LXX ἔσται σοι εἰς ἁγίασμα, καὶ οὐχ ὡς λίθου προσκόμματι συναντήσεσθε αὐτῷ, οὐδὲ ὡς πέτρας πτώματι.

[Obs. 1. (Citation.) ἰδοὺ τίθημι ἐν Σιὼν λίθον προσκόμματος καὶ πέτραν σκανδάλου· καὶ πᾶς ὁ πιστεύων ἐπ' αὐτῷ οὐ καταισχυνθήσεται.

Speaking generally, the Apostle has composed his citation by inserting the description of the Stone and Rock in c. viii as λίθος προσκόμματος and πέτρα σκανδάλου into the place occupied by that of the λίθος in c. xxviii, viz. λίθος πολυτελής, ἐκλεκτός, ἔντιμος. Compare especially 1 S. Pet. ii. 6 8, where the same two passages are referred to, with the same variations from the LXX but kept distinct, the passage in Ps. cxviii. 22 being inserted between them. S. Paul keeps closer to the Hebrew in c. viii לְאֶבֶן נֶגֶף וּלְצוּר מִכְשׁוֹל. The LXX usually render מִכְשׁוֹל by σκάνδαλον, which S. Paul here puts into the citation; while the LXX have πτῶμα. The LXX καταισχυνθῇ stands for יָחִישׁ, 'flee quickly': they may have read יָבוּשׁ, or more probably paraphrased יָחִישׁ by giving its motive or moral accompaniment.]

[Obs. 2. Is. xxviii. 16 belongs to the Book of Woes or Discourses relating to Assyria and the Egyptian alliance: Is. xxviii–xxxiii. An irreligious popular faction desired to enter into alliance with Egypt against Assyria. In opposition to this, GOD announces by His Prophet, that for all His true subjects He had laid in Sion a Foundation-stone which was more firmly set than all human schemes. This Stone is the theocracy centering in the future theocratic King Messias. The prophetic praeterite יִסַּד is no objection to this: the Stone is not actually laid in the young King Hezekiah,

Dogmatic: ch. IX, *v.* 30—X, *v.* 2.   177

but only contemplated as laid in the future King Messiah. See Schöttgen, *Horae Talm.* vol. ii. pp. 170, 290, for the Jewish interpretation. Compare Ps. cxviii. 22, for the prophecy of the Corner-Stone, which our Lord (S. Matt. xxi. 42, 44; S. Luke xx. 17) applied to Himself, and He is followed by His Apostles (Acts iv. 11; 1 S. Pet. ii. 7). The second passage (Is. viii. 14) occurs in the consolations of Emmanuel in the midst of the Assyrian oppressions, cc. vii-xii. It is addressed by the prophet, in the Name of Jehovah, to subjects of the kingdom of Judah, who were tempted to distrust His aid against Israel and Syria. GOD offers Himself to all who trust Him as a מִקְדָּשׁ or sure sanctuary, but, on the other hand, to the mass of those who opposed Him in Israel and Judah as a Stone of Offence and Fall. Thus Simeon says of the Infant Jesus, οὗτος κεῖται εἰς πτῶσιν καὶ ἀνάστασιν πολλῶν ἐν τῷ Ἰσραήλ: S. Luke ii. 34; 1 S. Pet. ii. 7, 8. In Is. xxviii the theocracy centering in a Monarch is the Stone laid by GOD; in Is. viii GOD Himself is the Stone of Stumbling and Rock of Offence to His enemies. Both meet in the Messianic interpretation, and are accordingly blended into one passage by the Apostle.]

[*Obs.* 3. The rejection of the Messiah by Israel is taught in Zech. xi. 12; Is. liii. 1; in several Psalms, and in express terms by the author of the Midrasch.]

[*Obs.* 4. πιστεύων ἐπ' αὐτῷ, viz. our Lord Jesus Christ. πιστεύειν ἐπί τινι describes faith resting on its Object as on a foundation; in πιστεύειν εἰς τινα, it moves towards its Object as a goal or end; cf. x. 11; 1 Tim. i 16 πιστεύειν ἐπ' αὐτῷ εἰς ζωὴν αἰώνιον: 1 S. Pet. ii. 6; S. Luke xxiv. 25 πιστεύειν ἐπὶ πᾶσιν οἷς ἐλάλησαν οἱ προφῆται. The contrasted expression προσκόπτειν τινὶ implies that what ought to be rested on by faith, is for the non-believing soul an obstacle in the path of thought and life, at which it stumbles.]

Interposed assurance of the Apostle's deep personal interest in his readers (x. 1, 2).

I.
This interest measured by
- *a.* his inward disposition (εὐδοκία τῆς καρδίας) of heart-felt good-will, passing into wish, longing.
- *b.* its practical result, δέησις πρὸς τὸν Θεόν for those who were its objects.
- *c.* its purpose, viz. that of promoting (εἰς) their salvation (x. 1).

II.
For this interest in Israel the reason is, that
- *a.* Israel has *zeal for* GOD (gen. obj.).
- *b.* (reserve in stating the above (*a*)), Israel's zeal is not according to the measure of accurate spiritual knowledge (οὐ κατ' ἐπίγνωσιν) (ver. 2).

[*Obs.* 1. This protestation of heartfelt interest in the spiritual condition of Israel corresponds to the introduction to this entire section of the Epistle (ix. 1-5). *There* the Apostle bases his sympathy on the divinely given privileges accorded to Israel: here on Israel's zeal, mistaken as it was, for GOD and His law. The protestation is rendered necessary, because the Apostle is about to make his severest criticisms on the conduct of the Jews when confronted by the true Messiah : μέλλει πάλιν αὐτῶν καθάπτεσθαι σφοδρότερον ἢ πρότερον· διὸ πάλιν ἀναιρεῖ πάσης ἀπεχθείας ὑπόνοιαν (S. Chrys. ix. p. 621.)]

[*Obs.* 2. ἀδελφοί, as at vii. 1, is a tender appeal to affection. εὐδοκία = רָצוֹן : Ecclus. xviii. 31 εὐδοκία ἐπιθυμίας : 2 Thess. i. 11 εὐδοκία ἀγαθωσύνης. It implies here taking personal pleasure in an object, S. Matt. xi. 26; S. Luke ii. 14; x. 21; 2 Thess. i. 11, rather than good-will, Eph. i. 5, 9; Phil. i. 15; ii. 13, because the latter would involve an inappropriate self-commendation. There is no δέ to correspond with μέν, ver. 1. Cf. Winer, *Gr. N. T.* p. 719.]

[*Obs.* 3. On Israel's zeal for GOD, compare the vivid description of Philo Judaeus, ii. 562, *Legat. ad Caium*, p. 1008 (ἔθνος) εἰωθὸς ἑκουσίους ἀναδέχεσθαι θανάτους ὥσπερ ἀθανασίαν, ὑπὲρ τοῦ μηδὲν τῶν πατρίων περιϊδεῖν ἀναιρούμενον, εἰ καὶ βραχύτατον εἴη : Ibid. ii. 577, p. 1022; Josephus, *contra Apion.* ii. 20; *de Bell. Jud.* ii. 17, &c. Hecataeus of Abdera mentions the Jewish ἰσχυρογνωμοσύνη, cf. Rom. ii. 17. S. Paul was, before his conversion, ζηλωτὴς τοῦ νόμου Acts xxii. 3 : and indeed περισσοτέρως ζηλωτὴς ὑπάρχων τῶν πατρικῶν παραδόσεων Gal. i. 14 : and accordingly κατὰ ζῆλον διώκων τὴν ἐκκλησίαν Phil. iii. 6. Even Jewish converts were ζηλωταὶ τοῦ νόμου Acts xxi. 20 ; cf. 1 Macc. ii. 58. It is the intensity, not the precise objects, or moral flavour, of Jewish zeal to which the Apostle bears witness. See Newman, *Par. Serm.* vol. iii. 13, Jewish Zeal a Pattern to Christians.]

[*Obs.* 4. That vital spiritual knowledge was not the measure of Israel's zeal, is shown in the second evidence of Israel's guilt (ver. 3), which is accordingly a reason (γάρ) for the clause οὐ κατ' ἐπίγνωσιν. With οὐ κατ' ἐπίγνωσιν compare Acts iii. 17 κατ' ἄγνοιαν ἐπράξατε.]

§ 2.

Second evidence of Israel's guilt. The attempt to substitute purely human efforts after Righteousness for submission to the gift of Righteousness by GOD, in spite of the clear warnings of the Jewish Law itself (x. 3-13).

[*Obs.* 1. This (ver. 3) is introduced as a reason (γάρ ver. 3) for the statement, ver. 2, that the Jewish zeal for GOD was οὐ κατ' ἐπίγνωσιν. It does this by explaining in what the οὐ κατ' ἐπίγνωσιν consists. They were ignorant of the real character of ἡ τοῦ Θεοῦ δικαιοσ νη. This ἄγνοια is not here branded as wilful, as in Eph. iv. 18; 1 S. Pet. i. 14.]

[*Obs.* 2. In ver. 3 ἡ τοῦ Θεοῦ δικαιοσύνη is the Righteousness which GOD gives through His Son, in contrast with the ἰδία δικαιοσύνη, or self-achieved righteousness of Israel. Of the first the Jews were ignorant (ἀγνοοῦντες) ; how far culpably, is not here explained. But this ignorance proves their zeal for GOD to have been οὐ κατ' ἐπίγνωσιν. Their own private righteousness (ἰδία δικαιοσύνη) they endeavoured to make valid (στῆσαι) by obedience to the law; thus constructing, each one for himself, an ἐμὴν δικαιοσύνην τὴν ἐκ νόμου, in contrast with the ἡ διὰ πίστεως Χριστοῦ, ἡ ἐκ Θεοῦ δικαιοσύνη ἐπὶ τῇ πίστει Phil. iii. 9; see i. 17. This effort prevented their *submission* by faith (ὑπετάγησαν) to GOD's gift of Righteousness. On the use of the pass. with middle force, see viii. 7; xiii. 1.]

[*Obs.* 3. ὑπετάγησαν suggests as its correlative the Will rather than the Righteousness of GOD. But GOD's Righteousness is here conceived of as the expression of His Will, and so requiring the obedience of faith, i. 5; x. 16; and He has willed to give us the ἐντολή, ἵνα πιστεύσωμεν τῷ ὀνόματι τοῦ Υἱοῦ αὐτοῦ 1 S. John iii. 23].

[*Obs.* 4.
In the Jews consider
    i. their *ignorance* (ἀγνοοῦντες) of δικαιοσύνη Θεοῦ.
    ii. their *effort* after (ζητοῦντες στῆσαι) their ἰδία δικαιοσύνη.
    iii. their *failure* to submit themselves (οὐχ ὑπετάγησαν) to GOD's gift of Righteousness in His Blessed Son.]

Reason for οὐχ ὑπετάγησαν (ver. 3). The law, as an instrument for attaining righteousness, has ended in Christ. Christ, in Whom the law ends, enables every believer in Him to partake of righteousness (ver. 4).

[*Obs.* 1. The reason which is given for the statement that the Jews did not submit to GOD's righteousness is that they did submit to the Mosaic law and not to Christ. And the law as an instrument for attaining righteousness has ended in Christ.]

[*Obs.* 2. τέλος is not (i) the *fulfilment* (τελείωσις or πλήρωμα) of the law in the sense that the types of the ritual law were realized in our Lord, while He fulfilled the moral law by His perfect obedience. That this is true is asserted in Heb. x. 1; S. Matt. vi. 17; Heb. vii. 18: but τέλος will not bear this meaning, even in 1 Tim. i. 5. Nor is it (ii) here, the *aim and intention* of the law (S. Chrys. and others), considered as the παιδαγωγὸς εἰς Χριστόν Gal. iii. 24, by making man aware of his profound moral deficiencies, and of his helplessness, and so leading him to Christ, because this signification does not harmonize with the context; but (iii) it is the *termination* of the law, in accordance with the natural sense of the word and drift of the passage. The law has come to an end, in that, in place of its requirement of external effort, the inward act of faith is the condition of receiving righteousness, vii. 1–6. The ritual law ended altogether in Christ, Who was its Antitype. And although the moral law is eternal, yet under the Gospel it loses its form of *external law*, and becomes an internal principle of life: Col. ii. 14; Eph. ii. 15. Cf. ὁ νόμος καὶ οἱ προφῆται ἕως Ἰωάννου S. Luke xvi. 16.]

(A) Proof of the *Reason* (ver. 4) for the second evidence of Israel's guilt (ver. 3) from the Mosaic Law itself (vers. 5–10).

[*Obs.* In vers. 5-10 δικαιοσύνη ἡ ἐκ τοῦ νόμου and ἡ ἐκ πίστεως δικαιοσύνη are personified. Moses describes the first by the fundamental rule of Lev. xviii. 5. The second describes herself by her use of Deut. xxx. 11, 12, 14.]

The law, by obedience to which ἰδία δικαιοσύνη is supposed to be worked out, itself points to the Gospel as putting an end to its own validity, that is, so far as the law is understood to represent a system supposed to be capable of securing δικαιοσύνη (vers. 5–10).

a. By a description of ἡ ἐκ τοῦ νόμου δικαιοσύνη which confines the promise of its own blessings to those who really fulfil its precepts (ver. 5).

Lev. xviii. 5 (almost after LXX), quoted. The man who shall have done the προστάγματα Θεοῦ shall live through their being fulfilled (ἐν αὐτοῖς). 'Ye shall therefore keep My statutes and My judgments, which if a man do (יַעֲשֶׂה אֹתָם) he shall live in them' (ver. 5).

Lev. xviii. 5.
Heb.   אֲשֶׁר יַעֲשֶׂה אֹתָם הָאָדָם
        וָחַי בָּהֶם

LXX ὁ ποιήσας αὐτὰ ἄνθρωπος ζήσεται ἐν αὐτοῖς.

[*Obs.* 1. This Law is repeated in Ezek. xx 21; Neh. ix. 29; cf. S. Luke x. 28 τοῦτο ποίει καὶ ζήσῃ: S. Matt. xix. 16 τί ἀγαθὸν ποιήσω, ἵνα ἔχω ζωὴν αἰώνιον; comp. Gal. iii. 11, 12, where Lev. xviii. 5 is quoted in contrast to Hab. ii. 4 ὁ δίκαιος ἐκ πίστεως ζήσεται, to show that ἐν νόμῳ οὐδεὶς δικαιοῦται παρὰ τῷ Θεῷ. Ζῆν, like the Hebrew חָיָה, means 'to be happy in existence.' The later Jews understood that the ζωή promised by Moses referred not merely to happy and prosperous life in Palestine, but to the ζωὴ αἰώνιος. Onkelos translates: 'Whosoever keeps these commandments shall thereby live in the life eternal.']

[*Obs.* 2. The emphatic word is ποιήσας, which characterises Moses' description of the production of δικαιοσύνη ἡ ἐκ τοῦ νόμου. If ὅτι be read before τὴν δικαιοσύνην, the latter depends on ὁ ποιήσας. For ποιεῖν τὴν δικαιοσύνην, cf. 1 S. John ii. 29; Rev. xxii. 11. On the difficulty of fulfilling the legal precepts, see Rom. ii. 21–24; iii. 19, 20. The difficulty of fulfilling the law is suggested by the statement that life is promised (only) to the man who has fulfilled it.]

b. By supplying language which is appropriate in the mouth of ἡ ἐκ Θεοῦ δικαιοσύνη and which insists on the facility with which the true righteousness which God gives is attained by man (vers. 6–8).

Deut. xxx. 12–14, quoted (with variations from the LXX and the Heb.) in order to show that the evangelical ῥῆμα τῆς πίστεως, in embracing which the soul acquires the δικαιοσύνη τοῦ Θεοῦ, is unlike the δικαιοσύνη τοῦ νόμου in its easy accessibility to every believing Christian (vers. 6-8).

Deut. xxx. 12-14.
Heb.

12. לֹא בַשָּׁמַיִם הִוא
לֵאמֹר מִי יַעֲלֶה־לָּנוּ הַשָּׁמַיְמָה
וְיִקָּחֶהָ לָּנוּ וְיַשְׁמִעֵנוּ אֹתָהּ וְנַעֲשֶׂנָּה׃

13. וְלֹא־מֵעֵבֶר לַיָּם הִוא
לֵאמֹר מִי יַעֲבָר־לָנוּ אֶל־עֵבֶר הַיָּם
וְיִקָּחֶהָ לָּנוּ וְיַשְׁמִעֵנוּ אֹתָהּ וְנַעֲשֶׂנָּה׃

14. כִּי־קָרוֹב אֵלֶיךָ הַדָּבָר מְאֹד
בְּפִיךָ וּבִלְבָבְךָ לַעֲשֹׂתוֹ׃

LXX Deut. xxx. 11-14 ἡ [ἐντολὴ αὕτη, ἣν ἐγὼ ἐντέλλομαί σοι σήμερον, οὐχ ὑπέρογκός ἐστιν οὐδὲ μακρὰν ἀπὸ σοῦ ἐστιν. 12. οὐκ ἐν τῷ οὐρανῷ ἄνω ἐστί,] λέγων· τίς ἀναβήσεται ἡμῖν εἰς τὸν οὐρανὸν [καὶ λήψεται ἡμῖν αὐτήν, καὶ ἀκούσαντες αὐτὴν ποιήσομεν; 13. οὐδὲ πέραν τῆς θαλάσσης ἐστί,] λέγων, τίς διαπεράσει ἡμῖν εἰς τὸ πέραν τῆς θαλάσσης, [καὶ λήψεται ἡμῖν αὐτήν, καὶ ἀκούσαντες αὐτὴν ποιήσομεν;] 14. ἐγγύς σού ἐστι τὸ ῥῆμα [σφόδρα] ἐν τῷ στόματί σου καὶ ἐν τῇ καρδίᾳ σου [καὶ ἐν ταῖς χερσίν σου] ποιεῖν αὐτό.

[*Obs.* 1. The citation differs from the LXX, of which only parts of verses 12, 13, and 14 are given, (1) by expanding (ver. 12) λέγων LXX, Heb. לֵאמֹר into μὴ εἴπῃς ἐν τῇ καρδίᾳ σου. The original indirect sense of forbidding is widened thus into the direct, with the addition ἐν τῇ καρδίᾳ, because unbelief has its seat in the heart, where unholy thoughts and feelings are the moral equivalent of language, Ps. xiv. 1; S. Mark iii. 5; (2) by omitting ἡμῖν and all after οὐρανόν in ver. 12; (3) by reading (in ver. 13) τίς καταβήσεται εἰς τὴν ἄβυσσον; instead of τίς διαπεράσει ἡμῖν εἰς τὸ πέραν τῆς θαλάσσης; and omitting all that follows. This change is probably to be explained as a paraphrase giving the sense in which the typical force of the original was fulfilled. Εἰς τὸ πέραν τῆς θαλάσσης conveyed on the surface of the language no typical reference to Christ; but in Holy Scripture the sea is often termed ἄβυσσος (Job xli. 23), and this noun would suggest a change of the accompanying verb to express sounding the depths of the sea, rather than traversing its surface. (4) In ver. 14 σφόδρα, ἐν ταῖς χερσίν σου (which is not found in the Hebrew, but is in Philo) and ποιεῖν αὐτό, are omitted.]

[*Obs.* 2. In the original text Moses is speaking of GOD's command to Israel to fulfil His law. 'This commandment,' he says, 'is not beyond the reach of accomplishment, nor out of the range of man's moral and mental life (Deut. xxx. 11). It is not up in heaven, nor is it beyond (S. Paul substitutes "beneath") the sea; so that a man must mount to the one or traverse (or sound) the other, in order to fetch it. On the contrary, Israel repeats this commandment in every-day talk, and it is stamped upon Israel's heart (in its written form it is in his hands, LXX), in order that he may accomplish it (vers. 12-14).' For S. Paul, this language really describes the facility of faith in Christ more accurately than that of obedience to the Mosaic Law, the difficulty of which elsewhere is recognised by the Law itself. The Apostle sees in this aspect of the Old Law something typical of the New—a virtual prophecy of the δικαιοσύνη ἐκ πίστεως. He adapts the quotation from the passage to its ultimate and deepest sense, partly by alteration, and partly by omission of that which was non-relevant (cf. ver. 14 לְעָשׂתוֹ). S. Paul puts the quotation in the mouth of ἡ ἐκ πίστεως δικαιοσύνη (ver. 6), which is boldly personified, as forbidding questions that imply unbelief in the Incarnation and Resurrection of Christ, and as directing men to the Word of Faith, i. e. the Gospel Revelation as a whole, which is deposited in man's very heart and mouth by the preaching of the Apostles.]

[*Obs.* 3. The method of quotation in vers. 6-8, with interspersed commentary, is that of the Midrasch, as in Rom. ix. 8; Gal. iii. 16; iv. 23, 24. Jewish methods of exegesis, like Rabbinical opinions, or quotations from Greek poets, are consecrated when they are adopted by an inspired Apostle; but this consecration of a selected extract does not by any means involve a sanction of the entire exegetical system, or class of opinions, or literature, of which the extract forms a part. By τοῦτ' ἐστι, which is thrice repeated, (=scilicet), the Apostle by an inserted comment decides the sense in which the passage is used by the personified ἡ ἐκ πίστεως δικαιοσύνη. Each clause introduced by τοῦτ' ἐστι should be bracketed.]

The Gospel, using the language of the Law, but with far greater appropriateness (vers. 6-8),

> (1) Warns against the unbelieving thought that Christ has still to be fetched down from heaven, in order to become an Object of faith; since His Incarnation is already a fact (ver. 6).
>
> (2) Warns against the unbelieving thought that, in order to be possessed by faith, Christ has to be recovered from that place of departed spirits into which His Human Soul entered after His Crucifixion; since His Resurrection from the dead is already a fact (ver. 7).
>
> (3) Bids the Christian know that the ῥῆμα πίστεως—the Gospel-Revelation addressed to faith—is here, ready to be professed and believed by Christians; since it is the very subject of the Apostolic preaching (κηρύσσομεν) (ver. 8).

[*Obs.* 1. The first unbelieving question against which the Christian is warned (in ver. 6) cannot refer to Christ's Session at the Right Hand of God, since this sense gives no explanation of καταγαγεῖν (which corresponds to καταβαίνειν, S. John iii. 13; vi. 33, 38). The second unbelieving question must refer to the Descent into Hades, which is called ἄβυσσος here, in accordance with the *typical* employment of the word in Jonah ii. 5; ᾅδης, in Ps. xvi.

Dogmatic: ch. X, *vv.* 3-13.

10; φυλακή, in 1 S. Pet. iii. 19; τὰ κατώτερα τῆς γῆς, in Eph. iv. 9. Elsewhere in the New Testament ἄβυσσος is the place of torment: S. Luke viii. 31; Rev. ix. 1, 11; xi. 7; xvii. 8; cf. Vaughan *in loc.*]

[*Obs.* 2. τὸ ῥῆμα τῆς πίστεως, the (definite) word or 'spoken-fact,' which has to be believed (gen. obj.) as reality. It is the Gospel κήρυγμα, and corresponds to what we generally mean by Revelation, or the Creed of a Christian. It is that body of objective truth, which is warranted by GOD'S authority, and is addressed to faith. It centres in our Lord's Person and Work; cf. 1 Tim. iv. 6 λόγος πίστεως.]

§ Appended discussion of the foregoing (vers. 6-8) argument from the evangelical sense of Deut. xxx. 12-14 (vers. 9, 10).

Proof (ὅτι ver. 9) of correspondence between the τὸ ῥῆμα of Deut. xxx. 14, and the τὸ ῥῆμα τῆς πίστεως as actually proclaimed by the Apostles (vers. 9, 10).

Arg. 1. Corresponding to the ἐν τῷ στόματί σου καὶ ἐν τῇ καρδίᾳ σου of Deut. xxx. 14, are the Gospel requirements of outward public confession (ἐν τῷ στόματι) of the Κυριότης of Jesus, and internal assent (ἐν τῇ καρδίᾳ) to the truth of His Resurrection from the dead through Divine Power (ver. 9).

Arg. 2. (Reason for (γάρ) these requirements on the part of the Gospel). Internal assent, by faith, to revealed truth, specially to the doctrine of a Risen Christ, leads to δικαιοσύνη τοῦ Θεοῦ. Outward confession of Christ's Divinity before men leads to σωτηρία (ver. 10).

[*Obs.* 1. In ver. 9 S. Paul mentions ὁμολογῆσαι ἐν τῷ στόματι and πιστεῦσαι ἐν τῇ καρδίᾳ in the order suggested by the passage from Deut. cited in ver. 8. In ver. 10 he is no longer under the influence of this quotation, and accordingly inverts the order, following that of the spiritual fact. 'I believed and therefore will I speak.' The heart first yields internal assent to the truth revealed by GOD, and then 'the fire kindles,' and with the mouth confession is made unto salvation.]

[*Obs.* 2. ὁμολογία τῷ στόματι is the fruit of πίστις ἐν τῇ καρδίᾳ. Faith unites the soul to the Crucified One, Living because Risen, and true faith cannot but own Him as the soul's Κύριος before men. The necessity of an outward profession of the truths to which we yield internal assent is taught by our Lord, S. Matt. x. 32 sqq.; S. John ix. 22; 1 S. John iv. 2; and especially in the fragment of an Apostolic Hymn quoted at 2 Tim. ii. 12 εἰ δὲ ἀρνούμεθα, κἀκεῖνος ἀρνήσεται ἡμᾶς. Not merely in conversation and example, but in creeds, in worship, if need be at the cost of suffering, must this ὁμολογία be made. In an age of persecution, like the Apostolic, it chiefly takes the form of ὑπομονή, Rom. viii. 17, 25; 2 Tim. iv. 7, 8; Rev. iii. 10, &c. Cf. Origen, vol. i. p. 277, *Exhortat. ad Martyr.* cap. 5 ἑαυτοὺς γὰρ ἀπατῶσιν οἱ νομίζοντες ἀρκεῖν πρὸς τὸ τυχεῖν ἐν Χριστῷ τέλους τὸ "καρδίᾳ γὰρ πιστεύεται εἰς δικαιοσύνην," κἂν μὴ προσῇ τὸ "στόματι δὲ ὁμολογεῖται εἰς σωτηρίαν." Καὶ ἐστί γε εἰπεῖν, ὅτι μᾶλλόν ἐστι τοῖς χείλεσι τιμᾷν τὴν καρδίαν πόρρω ἔχοντα ἀπὸ Θεοῦ, ἤπερ τῇ καρδίᾳ τιμᾷν αὐτόν, τοῦ στόματος μὴ ὁμολογοῦντος εἰς σωτηρίαν. See too S. Irenaeus, *Haer.* iv. 33. n. 9 ; and Tertullian's vigorous treatise *Scorpiace*, in which he examines some current sophistical reasons against the duty of confessing Christ when Martyrdom was the consequence.]

[*Obs.* 3. The confession before the world of the Κυριότης of Jesus (ver. 9), while acknowledging His *present* relation to the πιστεύων and to the Church (1 Cor. xii. 3; viii. 6; Phil. ii. 11), also glances back at His Pre-existent, as yet Un-incarnate, Person ; (Rom. viii. 3; Gal. iv. 4; Phil. ii. 6). He is the eternal Κύριος, as the 'Son of God'; and this is powerfully proclaimed to the world by His Resurrection (Rom. i. 4). The Resurrection is especially the object of Christian πίστις, as warranting belief in the entire Work and in the Divine Person of Jesus Christ, so that Christian faith as a whole depends on its being believed, 1 Cor. xv. 17, 18. As the true Divinity of the Incarnate Jesus is suggested by the unbelieving question rebuked in ver. 6 ; so the reality of His Resurrection from Death is suggested by the unbelieving question rebuked in ver. 7.]

[*Obs.* 4. The question why S. Paul connects δικαιοσύνη with the faith of the heart, and σωτηρία with the confession of the lips in ver. 10, is to be answered (as at Rom. iv. 25), at least in part, by reference to the parallelism of Hebrew poetry, the rhythm of which sometimes shapes the Apostle's prose. And yet the distribution of his thought is not wholly or chiefly to be accounted for thus. He conceives of a δικαιοσύνη which may not issue in σωτηρία, since δικαιοσύνη may be itself forfeited by the moral cowardice of the πιστεύων, who does not venture to avow his faith before men. If πίστις does not grow into ὁμολογεῖσθαι, it dies back, first into mere 'opinion,' and then into unbelief.]

(B) Proof of the *Reason* παντὶ τῷ πιστεύοντι ver. 4, for the second evidence of Israel's guilt (ver. 3) from the previously-quoted (ix. 33) language of prophecy (vers. 11–13).

Is. xxviii. 16, quoted to show that *every* (true) believer in Messiah would escape the shame of rejection from His Kingdom, by securing the δικαιοσύνη τοῦ Θεοῦ ἐκ πίστεως (ver. 11).

Heb. הַמַּאֲמִין לֹא יָחִישׁ:

LXX ὁ πιστεύων ἐπ' αὐτῷ οὐ μὴ καταισχυνθῇ.

[*Obs.* πᾶς is significantly added before ὁ πιστεύων. It is found neither in the LXX nor in the Hebrew, but is suggested, perhaps by Joel ii. 32, but much more by the unlimited character of ὁ πιστεύων in Is. xxviii. 16, and the practical interpretation which the growth of a *Catholic* Church was already putting upon the prophet's language. Hence there follows a comment on the]

    a. significance of πᾶς, in Is. xxviii. 16. It is warranted (γάρ) by the fact that *no* difference is made between heathens and

Jews in respect of the bestowal of the blessing of δικαιοσύνη on the believing (ver. 12 a).

[*Obs.* Generally S. Paul insists on this equality of Jew and Gentile, in order to show that the believing heathen are called into the Church of Christ equally with believing Jews. Here, as he is insisting on the responsibility of the *Jews*, he means that the promise is for their encouragement, as well as for that of believing heathen.]

b. The reason (γάρ ver. 12 b) for this perfect equality of all believers in respect of the blessings promised to faith is, that the same Lord of all (Jesus Christ) is rich in His bestowal of grace and salvation on all who pray to Him (ver. 12 b).

[*Obs.* 1. That Κύριος here is Christ, (and not the Eternal Father,) is clear both from the whole context in ver. 4, and from the meaning of αὐτῷ in ver. 11. It is in harmony with the Messianic reference of the citation from Joel in ver. 13, and especially with ver. 14. If the Father were meant, it would be necessary to supply the hiatus of meaning by 'GOD in Christ.' Jesus Christ is πάντων Κύριος Acts x. 36; He died, and rose, and revived, ἵνα καὶ νεκρῶν καὶ ζώντων κυριεύσῃ, Rom. xiv. 9; and the final object of His exaltation is that every tongue should confess ὅτι Κύριος Ἰησοῦς Χριστός Phil. ii. 11; cf. Rom. ix. 5. This Κυριότης πάντων, a Lordship of the Universe and of Humanity, is, however, ultimately grounded on the fact that all originally owe existence to Him: S. John i. 9-11; 1 Cor. viii. 6; Col. i. 16 sqq. Hence the divisions of mankind are ended in Him (Eph. ii. 13-17); all races, stations, even the sexes, find in Him their point of unity, Gal. iii. 28; Col. iii. 11. And as He is Lord of all without distinction, so the wealth of His compassion and grace is for all. πλουτῶν εἰς πάντας is the correlative of Κύριος πάντων.]

[*Obs.* 2. The ἐπίκλησις of Christ is not to be identified with the ὁμολογία that is made before man, vers. 9, 10. For instances of such ἐπίκλησις, see Acts ii. 21; vii. 59; ix. 14, 21; xxii. 16; 1 Cor. i. 2; 2 Tim. ii. 22. This ἐπικαλεῖσθαι, or calling upon Jesus Christ for grace and help, cannot be deemed (with Meyer, who here arbitrarily imports an Origenizing gloss, quite unwarranted by the text) only a *relative* worship, and as such distinct from the *absolute* worship paid to the Eternal Father. See Waterland's dissection of the Arianizing hypothesis of 'an inferior worship' offered to Christ, *Works*, iii. p. 363 (Oxford, 1823), 'Second Defence of some Queries,' qu. xvii: 'Where do you find two different worships, more than two different natures [i.e. in the Son and the Father]? Only the worship, as the Nature, being One, is considered primarily in the Father, and secondarily in the Son. . . . You will never prove anything of inferior worship, unless you can first prove the nature of the Son to be inferior to the Father.' Again, worship, he observes, whether addressed to the Father or the Son, 'terminates in the Divine Nature considered primarily in the Father and derivatively in the Son.' (*1b*) On the Scriptural authority for the worship of our Lord Jesus Christ, and on the usage of the Primitive Church, see Waterland, *Works*, v. pp. 379-386, 'Remarks upon Dr. Clarke's Exposition of the Church Catechism.']

c. The ground (γάρ ver. 13) for predicating πλουτῶν εἰς πάντας τοὺς ἐπικαλουμένους αὐτόν (ver. 12) of our Lord Jesus Christ is furnished by Jewish prophecy (ver. 13).

Heb.   כֹּל אֲשֶׁר־יִקְרָא בְּשֵׁם יְהֹוָה יִמָּלֵט

LXX πᾶς ὃς ἂν ἐπικαλέσηται τὸ ὄνομα Κυρίου, σωθήσεται.

Joel ii. 32 (iii. 5, Heb.), quoted to show that Jesus Christ will save all who pray to Him (ver. 13).

[*Obs*. 1. The expression קָרָא בְּשֵׁם יְהֹוָה means to worship the Lord as He is. His Name reveals His Nature or mode of existence; for in inspired language there is no felt distinction between the name and the Reality. To call upon *the Name* of the Lord implies right faith about Him, as the Object of worship. (See Pusey, *Minor Prophets in loc.* pp. 130, 131.) Of the LXX renderings, (1) ἐπικαλεῖσθαι τὸ ὄνομα Κυρίου Gen. iv. 26, to call on the Lord as being what He is. (2) ἐπικαλεῖσθαι ἐπὶ τῷ ὀνόματι Κυρίου Gen. xii. 8, to make His Name, as a revelation of His Nature, the ground of calling on Him. (3) ἐπικαλεῖσθαι ἐν ὀνόματι Κυρίου 1 Kings xviii. 24, to call upon Him, within the revealed conditions of His Nature expressed in His Name. (4) ἐπικαλεῖσθαι τὸν Θεὸν Ἰσραήλ Gen. xxxiii. 20, includes all the foregoing, which, indeed, give different senses of the Hebrew expression.]

[*Obs*. 2. This passage is Messianic: it describes the deliverance which would be found in the Kingdom of Messiah, before the Great Day of the Lord, by the שְׂרִידִים, the escaped ones, whom the Lord would call. The deliverance would be obtained by prayer to the Lord, and, considering the Messianic import of the passage, S. Paul understands this of Jesus Christ. S. Peter quoted the whole passage, Joel ii. 28-32, (excepting ver. 32 b,) after the outpouring of the Holy Spirit at Pentecost, as having been fulfilled by that great miracle (Acts ii. 17-21). And he adds with reference to it, in addressing the first Christians, 'For the promise is unto you and to your children, and to all that are afar off, and even as many as the Lord our God shall call' (Acts ii. 39). Jarchi and Kimchi understand the whole passage of the times of the Messiah. See Keil *in loc.*; Hengstenberg, *Christology*, i. pp. 345, 346, E. T.]

§ 3.

Third evidence of Israel's Guilt. Deliberate neglect of great opportunities for attaining the πίστις upon which δικαιοσύνη Θεοῦ depends (x. 14-21).

[*Obs*. Knowledge being an element of responsibility, (S. John xv. 22 'If I had not come and spoken to them, they had not had sin;' Arist. *Nic. Eth.* iii. 1. 13 sqq.) S. Paul proceeds to admit, or rather to assert, this general principle (in vers. 14, 15), before insisting on the responsibility of Israel for the advantages they had actually enjoyed.]

I. Necessity of adequate opportunities for hearing the Faith, in order to full responsibility for believing or rejecting it (vers. 14, 15).

> *Prop.* If Salvation, through ἐπικαλεῖσθαι τὸ ὄνομα Κυρίου (ver. 13), is to be attained, a Divinely-commissioned Teacher is necessary (vers. 14, 15).
>
> *Arg.* 1. From the nature of the case (vers. 14, 15 a).
>
>> In order to pray, men must believe in Him to Whom prayer is addressed:
>> In order to believe in Him, men must have heard Him:
>> In order to hear Him, men must have listened to a preacher through whom He speaks (ver. 14).
>
> But, In order to speak for Him in preaching, men must be commissioned by GOD (ver. 15 a).
>
>> Therefore, if men are to attain σωτηρία by prayer to Jesus Christ, an Apostolate is indispensable (vers. 14, 15 a).

[*Obs.* 1. The arg. of ver. 14 is a 'reversed sorites,' thrown into a series of four questions, each introduced by πῶς. By οὖν the Apostle glances backwards at the ἐπικαλεῖσθαι of the quotation in ver. 13. ἐπικαλέσονται, fut. of ethical possibility: Winer, *Gr. N. T.* p. 348. The future converts to Christ, whether heathen or Jews, are the *subjects* to the first three verbs—ἐπικαλέσονται, πιστεύσουσι, ἀκούσουσι: the Apostles to the last two—κηρύξουσι, ἀποσταλῶσι. οὗ before οὐκ ἤκουσαν refers to Christ *speaking in His envoys* (cf. Eph. ii. 17); not to Christ as the great subject of Apostolic preaching, which would probably be ὅν, Eph. iv. 21; nor yet to Christ as Him, *de quo* they would hear (since New Testament usage does not sanction this); still less is it the adv. of place, 'where,' which would break up the symmetry of the passage: Meyer, *in loc.*]

[*Obs.* 2. κηρύξουσι ver. 15, 'discharge the duty of heralds.' The word implies (i) that the Gospel message, consisting as it does of divinely-attested facts respecting the Person and Work of Jesus Christ, must *come to man from without him.* Being objective historical matter of fact, it cannot be 'evolved from man's consciousness by reflexion'; it must be brought to him from without himself, and he must first *hear* of it in order to believe it. Instead of being a human 'speculation about GOD,' it is a message from GOD, transmitted through His herald. Hence the word implies (ii) that the Christian teacher must have *Mission,* and this, not from those to whom he delivers his message, but from the Divine Monarch Whose herald he is. Hence the value placed by S. Paul on his title ἀπόστολος, Rom. i. 1; Gal. i. 1, 12, 16; ii. 7 sqq.; Tit. i. 1, &c. This ἀποστολή from GOD is transmitted through the Apostles and their successors to the end of time: its absence is much more serious than 'an ecclesiastical irregularity.' Cf. οἷς οὐ διεστειλάμεθα in the Apostolic Letter, Acts xv. 24.]

Arg. 2. From the welcome given in Isaiah, by anticipation, to the arrival of the Apostles of σωτηρία among men (ver. 15).

Is. lii. 7, quoted to illustrate the welcome accorded to an Apostolic ministry, which satisfies the great needs of humanity by announcing the joyful tidings of salvation (ver. 15).

Heb.   מַה־נָּאווּ עַל־הֶהָרִים
רַגְלֵי מְבַשֵּׂר מַשְׁמִיעַ שָׁלוֹם
מְבַשֵּׂר טוֹב

'How lovely upon the mountains
Are the feet of them that bring good tidings, that publish peace;
That bring tidings of good.'

LXX πάρειμι ὡς ὥρα ἐπὶ τῶν ὀρέων, ὡς πόδες εὐαγγελιζομένου ἀκοὴν εἰρήνης, ὡς εὐαγγελιζόμενος ἀγαθά.]

[*Obs.* 1. (*Citation.*) ὡς ὡραῖοι οἱ πόδες τῶν εὐαγγελιζομένων [εἰρήνην, τῶν εὐαγγελιζομένων] τὰ ἀγαθά.

The citation follows neither the Hebrew nor the LXX, though keeping more closely to the former, while omitting ἐπὶ τῶν ὀρέων as of local reference; cf. Nahum i. 15. Καθὼς γέγραπται states the correspondence between the last question, insisting on the need of a κῆρυξ ἀποσταλείς, and the Old Testament anticipations of Messiah's Kingdom.]

[*Obs.* 2. The prophet sees in vision the redemption of Jewish prisoners consequent on the fall of Babylon. The tidings are being carried to Jerusalem, over the mountains to the north of the City; in his ecstasy the prophet exclaims that the feet of the messengers (מְבַשֵּׂר is collective) are lovely, from their swiftness, as they approach. Cf. Cant. ii. 17; viii. 14. It is the message which makes the arrival so welcome: they announce שָׁלוֹם, peace as involved in theocratic deliverance from the heathen power; and טוֹב, all good in the future to which Israel is heir, through the promises. The Rabbins understood this of the days of the Messiah; and S. Paul applies the exclamation to the appearance of the Apostles of Christ upon the scene of history. Their feet are ὡραῖοι (beautiful, like fruit in its maturity, S. Matt. xxiii. 27) in his eyes, as they announce the end of the captivity of sin, and publish εἰρήνη (Eph. vi. 15 τὸ εὐαγγέλιον τῆς εἰρήνης), made by Christ, through the Blood of His Cross, between God and man, between earth and heaven (2 Cor. v. 18-20; Eph. ii. 17; Col. i. 20); and all the blessings of goodness (τὰ ἀγαθά) which God in Christ bestows on the redeemed, especially δικαιοσύνη.]

II. The historical fact, however, is that the majority of the Jews have heard and rejected the Apostolical teaching (vers. 16, 17).

Dogmatic: ch. X, *vv.* 14-21.

a. The fact stated. Notwithstanding the commission and labours of the Apostles (ἀλλά), the Jews have not, all of them, *obeyed* the good news of Messiah and His Kingdom (ver. 16).

[*Obs.* οὐ πάντες is a tragic *litotes*; the fact being that an enormous majority refused obedience; cf. iii. 3 ἠπίστησάν τινες. With ὑπήκουσαν compare ὑπετάγησαν ver. 3, as indicating the attitude of submission which becomes man when in presence either of God's Truth or His Grace.]

b. The fact prophetically anticipated in Isaiah (ver. 16).

Is. liii 1, quoted to show that history repeats itself, since the rejection of the prophet's teaching was singularly typical of Israel's rejection of the Gospel in the Apostolic age (ver. 16).

Is. liii. 1.

Heb. מִי הֶאֱמִין לִשְׁמֻעָתֵנוּ

LXX Κύριε, τίς ἐπίστευσεν τῇ ἀκοῇ ἡμῶν;

[*Obs.* Delitzsch assigns the question 'Who hath believed our preaching?' to Israel, (not to the prophet,) as the connection between Is. lii. 13-15 and Is. liii. 1 implies. The nation acknowledges with penitence, how shamefully it has mistaken its own Saviour. 'Who hath believed our preaching, i. e. the preaching that was commonly heard among us?' The Hebrew מִי הֶאֱמִין לִשְׁמֻעָתֵנוּ is without any equivalent to Κύριε in the citation, or to Κύριος in LXX. שְׁמוּעָה, the hearing = the tidings, especially the announcement in Is. xxviii. 9, of the exaltation of the Servant of God from deep degradation. ἀκοή similarly has an *objective* meaning, that which is heard, tidings. Meyer understands the prophetic preaching, not its contents, see Gal. iii. 2. Compare the application of Is. liii. 1, by S. John xii. 38, to the unbelief of the Jews after witnessing our Lord's miracles.]

c. Inference (ἄρα) from this prophecy, in confirmation of what has been said (ver. 14) as to the conditions required for the growth of πίστις (ver. 17).

(i) πίστις is ἐξ ἀκοῆς. It originates in the preaching, whether of Prophets or Apostles (ver. 17).

(ii) ἀκοή, the Apostolic preaching is made possible by the Revealed Word of God (διὰ ῥήματος Θεοῦ), which furnishes an Apostle both with his message and his credentials (ver. 17).

[*Obs.* 1. This inference is a parenthetical confirmation, suggested by the quotation in ver. 16 of the earlier assertion, in ver. 14, of the necessity of Apostolic preaching, and an Apostolic mission, in order to the genesis of faith and worship.]

[*Obs*. 2. ῥῆμα Θεοῦ referring to ῥῆμα τῆς πίστεως ver. 8. The revealed Word of GOD (answering to דְּבַר יְהוָֹה, the substance of the prophetic proclamation) as taught by the Apostles. So at S. Luke iii. 2; iv. 4; S. John iii. 34; viii. 47; Eph. vi. 17; Heb. vi. 5; xi. 3; 1 Pet. i. 25. Not the command of GOD only which gives the Apostle his commission, although this is included.]

III. Possible excuses for the conduct of the Jews considered (vers. 18–21).

Excuse I. (Put by the Apostle to himself.) 'Surely it cannot be that Israel has not heard the Apostolic preaching?' (ver. 18).

[*Obs*. The question is introduced by an ἀλλά of 'objection, whether proposed by the speaker or by some one else.' In μὴ οὐκ ἤκουσαν; the interrogative μή anticipates that οὐκ ἤκουσαν will be negatived. Winer, *Gr. N. T.* p. 642. οὐ μή would be only a strengthened form of the simple negative. The subject of ἤκουσαν is οὐ πάντες (ver. 16), the unbelieving Jews; its object is τὴν ἀκοήν (ver. 17).]

Resp. The excuse is dismissed by a quotation from the Psalter, which describes the world-embracing scope of the Apostolical preaching (ver. 18).

[*Obs*. μενοῦνγε, 'immo vero,' with a slight touch of irony, warranted by the fact that the spread of the Gospel, as described in the quotation, was much greater than was necessary to give Israel the required opportunity; cf. ix. 20.]

Ps. xix. 4, quoted to show that the Apostolic ἀκοή had been sufficiently wide-spread to afford an opportunity of hearing it to all Jews, whether in Palestine, or among the two Dispersions (ver. 18).

Heb. בְּכָל־הָאָרֶץ יָצָא קַוָּם
וּבִקְצֵה תֵבֵל מִלֵּיהֶם

'Into all lands is gone forth their line,
And to the end of the world their utterances.'

[*Obs*. 1. The citation exactly follows the LXX. ὁ φθόγγος αὐτῶν corresponds to קַוָּם, i. e. the measuring-line of the heavens. The parallel מִלֵּיהֶם shows that this line was traced by them as heralds of GOD, and this may explain the paraphrastic translation φθόγγος. קַו however might mean a harpstring, as being a cord in tension, and then, like τόνος, a sound, which would lead more easily to the LXX ὁ φθόγγος, and Symm. ὁ ἦχος: although the LXX may have read קוֹלָם.]

[*Obs*. 2. Ps. xix is Davidic. It places side by side the glory of GOD in Nature (vers. 1-6) with the mercy of GOD in His Law (vers. 7-14). Nature too is an organ whereby GOD reveals to man His Power, Magnificence, Wisdom, Bounty, and this Revelation penetrates everywhere. And thus 'the measuring-line of the heavens,' as interpreted by the LXX, suggests to the

Apostle, as to Jewish teachers, (Sohar, Genes. ii) the spread of the Gospel by the Apostolic ministry throughout the earth. The *praeconium caelorum* is a figure of the all-penetrating *praeconium Evangelii*, as the argument of the Psalm itself suggests. This is independent of, but not inconsistent with, the ancient allegorical exposition, which makes the heavens a figure of the Church, and the sun, of Jesus Christ or the Gospel.]

[*Obs.* 3. Perhaps it was on account of his own share in it that S. Paul shrank from describing the spread of the Gospel in language of his own. The verse which he quotes is in its meaning at once historical and prophetic. Historically, it states that the Apostolic teaching had already penetrated, εἰς πᾶσαν τὴν γῆν and εἰς τὰ πέρατα τῆς οἰκουμένης, sufficiently to reach the great mass of the Jewish population wherever dispersed. As yet the Apostle had not preached in Spain, xv. 20, 24, 28, and it was only later that S. Clement Romanus describes S. Paul as δικαιοσύνην διδάξας ὅλον τὸν κόσμον 1. *ad Cor.* v. 7. Although in Col. i. 6, 23 ; Rom. i. 8, the dissemination of the Faith throughout at least the civilized and Roman world is referred to as achieved. The quotation refers to a proclamation of the faith which was accomplishing itself, and which had been already sufficiently achieved to make the Jewish people responsible for the possession of sufficient knowledge to secure their conversion. Prophetically understood, it pictures the spread of the Church into all the countries of the world ; but it does not oblige us to suppose that in the Apostolic age itself Christian Missionaries had reached America or Australia.]

Excuse II. (Put by the Apostle to himself.) 'Surely it cannot be that Israel was ignorant of the (universal destination and consequent) world-wide proclamation that was to characterize the Messianic good-tidings?' (ver. 19).

[*Obs.* μὴ 'Ισραὴλ οὐκ ἔγνω ; is parallel to μὴ οὐκ ἤκουσαν ; ver. 18 : but the object of ἔγνω is not (like that of ἤκουσαν) the Apostolic ἀκοή, but the universal diffusion of the Gospel as suggested by the quotation, Ps. xix. 4. Was it the case that Israel did not know that Christianity was destined for every human being, and was universally preached ?]

Resp. The excuse is set aside by two quotations from Moses and Isaiah, which are prophecies even of the conversion of the heathen among whom therefore the Gospel must previously have been proclaimed, (vers. 19, 20); and by a third from Isaiah, which rebukes the Jews for the moral temper of disobedient opposition, when confronted with Christ Crucified, Who it is thus implied was preached to them also (ver. 21).

> *a*. Deut. xxxii. 21, quoted to show how the heathen would be admitted to share in the communion of GOD's people, whereby the jealousy and anger of the Jews would be excited (ver. 19).

[*Obs.* πρῶτος, here not = πρότερος, as in S. John i. 15, but 'first in order of the Sacred Writers.' Of the many later testimonies which might have been quoted, the Apostle contents himself with one from Isaiah.]

Deut. xxxii. 21.

    Heb.   וַאֲנִי אַקְנִיאֵם בְּלֹא־עָם
                    בְּגוֹי נָבָל אַכְעִיסֵם

    'And I will provoke you to jealousy by a no-people,
    And by a foolish nation will I anger you.']

[*Obs.* 1. The citation closely follows the LXX: it substitutes ὑμᾶς twice for αὐτούς.

[*Obs.* 2. The passage occurs in the Song of Moses. παραζηλώσω, Heb. אַקְנִיא, implies the conjugal relation in which GOD stands to His ancient people; His jealousy is the effect of His love. Even in the Mosaic age, Israel provoked GOD by unbelief and idolatry. בְּלֹא־עָם, ἐπ' οὐκ ἔθνει, in respect to a 'not-people'; οὐκ ἔθνος forming a single negative notion. By οὐκ ἔθνος and ἔθνος ἀσύνετον, Canaan primarily, and afterwards every heathen nation is meant. One people only in the ancient world corresponded to the Divine Idea of a people; the rest, in GOD's eyes, were non-existent. Yet, if Israel would serve gods which were 'not-gods,' GOD would move them to jealousy by showing mercy to a people which, theocratically speaking, had no existence; cf. ix. 25; 1 S. Pet. ii. 10. On the connection of οὐ with a noun, cancelling its notion altogether, see Winer, *Gr. N. T.* p. 597. ἔθνος ἀσύνετον, i. e. in not seeking or asking after GOD (Eph. iv. 17). The expressions in Deut. xxxii. 21 are explained by Is. lxv. 1. As Israel did fall into idolatry, the conditional menace became a fulfilled prophecy, and as such is appealed to here.]

    b. Isaiah lxv. 1, quoted to show how GOD would become known to and found even by Heathens, who during long ages had neither sought nor asked for Him (ver. 20).

[*Obs.* ἀποτολμᾷ is not merely a Hebraizing way of expressing the adv. 'boldly.' Apart from his words, Isaiah is bold in confronting the men of his own day, and the historical prejudices of Israel. The *present* tenses represent him (as Moses in ver. 19) as still present through his writings in the Apostolic age.]

Is. lxv. 1.

    Heb.   נִדְרַשְׁתִּי לְלוֹא שָׁאָלוּ
                   נִמְצֵאתִי לְלֹא בִקְשֻׁנִי

    'I was to be discerned by those who did not enquire,
    I was to be discovered by those who did not seek me.'

    LXX   ἐμφανὴς ἐγενόμην τοῖς ἐμὲ μὴ ἐπερωτῶσι,
              εὑρέθην τοῖς ἐμὲ μὴ ζητοῦσιν.

    Citation.   εὑρέθην τοῖς ἐμὲ μὴ ζητοῦσιν,
                   ἐμφανὴς ἐγενόμην τοῖς ἐμὲ μὴ ἐπερωτῶσι.

[*Obs.* 1. The LXX follows the order of clauses in the Hebrew, which S. Paul transposes, possibly with a view to the order of the ideas.]

s. 2. The passage refers originally to *Jews* who had apostatized from GOD through sin and idolatry. The prophet has begged for grace on their behalf. And, in reply, he is reminded how GOD had given Himself to be found, and had revealed Himself to a people which asked no questions, and did not seek Him. נִדְרַשְׁתִּי is not 'I have become manifest,' but (niphal tolerativum) 'I allowed myself to be found out.' So נִמְצֵאתִי, 'I let myself be found.' Israel did not trouble itself about GOD ; yet GOD would be known to and found by Israel ; cf. Is. lv. 6. In its idolatrous apostasy Israel had actually become גּוֹי לֹא־קֹרָא בִשְׁמִי, a nation in which the Lord's Name was not invoked : its thorough heathenism is expressed by the substitution of גּוֹי (LXX ἔθνος) for עַם (LXX λαός). This apostate condition of Israel made it in S. Paul's eyes typical of the heathen world, which did not concern itself about GOD (Eph. ii. 12 ἄθεοι ἐν τῷ κόσμῳ,) but to which GOD has given Himself to be found in the Gospel. The Gentiles have accepted GOD's mercy ; Israel has resisted it : hence in ver. 21 S. Paul applies Is. lxv. 2, exclusively to Israel. Hosea ii. 23, and i. 10, are quoted on a similar principle in Rom. ix. 25, 26, with reference to the Gentiles, although the idolatrous Israelites were, originally, in both cases alluded to.]

    c. Isaiah lxv. 2, quoted to show that Israel too had had the largest opportunities of hearing the ἀκοή, but that Israel's own disobedience and gainsaying was the real reason of its not having been converted as a people to the Faith of Christ (ver. 21).

s. πρός used figuratively of mental direction (Heb. i. 7 ; S. Mark xii. 12). Turning to Israel, Isaiah says, in the Name of GOD, the words in c. lxv. 2.]

Is. lxv. 2.   Heb.   פֵּרַשְׂתִּי יָדַי כָּל־הַיּוֹם
                                     אֶל־עַם סוֹרֵר

                'I spread out My Hands all the day
                 To a refractory people.'

s. 1. The citation follows the LXX, except that in the latter and the Hebrew ὅλην τὴν ἡμέραν follows χεῖράς μου. LXX ἀπειθοῦντα καὶ ἀντιλέγοντα are an expanded rendering of סוֹרֵר, being stubborn, סרר is used of refractory beasts. The present part. denotes the continuance of the disobedience and contradiction.]

s. 2. It may at first sight seem arbitrary, that while Is. lxv. 1, originally applicable to the Jews, is applied by S. Paul to the heathen, Is. lxv. 2, in the immediate context, should be restricted in its application (cf. πρός ver. 10) to the Jews. In truth apostate Israel's indifference to GOD was on a level with that of the heathen : and so far a similarity of moral circumstances justified the application of the text. But, on the other hand, Israel's persistent disobedience and contradiction were without any parallel in heathen history ; since the heathen never had the light and grace which alone made this sharp antagonism to GOD possible. And GOD's love for Israel was unique. Though Israel was as estranged from GOD as were the heathen, yet GOD, in His exhaustless love, turned towards Israel again and

o

again during the long day of its chequered history, and conspicuously at the climax of that history when His Son appeared among men. The outstretched hands of GOD are a symbol of His immense, persevering, all-embracing Love; of the tender, patient, incessant invitations whereby He sought to draw to His heart the people of His choice, which remained fixed in rebellion and contradiction (Acts vii. 51; xiii. 45; xix. 9). Israel lacked not opportunities for knowledge; the heart of Israel was at fault, not its means of acquiring necessary religious information. As S. Augustine says, 'nemo credit, nisi volens'; and a rebellious will is not forced to faith even by the Infinite Love of GOD.]

[*Obs.* 3. In ἐξεπέτασα τὰς χεῖράς μου, Origen, S. Augustine, and S. Jerome (on Is. lxv) see a prophetic anticipation of Christ Crucified, while hanging on the Cross. S. Jerome, 'Significant expansae manus parentis clementiam suos filios in sinum recipere gestientis.' On ἀπειθοῦντα, see S. Matt. xxiii. 37. ἀντιλέγειν (cf. ἀντιλογία Heb. xii. 3) means contradiction *in words* (Meyer), not general opposition (Winer, *Gr. N. T.* p. 23). Of the Jewish ἀντιλογία to our Lord, the sayings, that He was a Samaritan and had a devil; that He cast out devils through Beelzebub the prince of the devils; that He was not from GOD because He kept not the Sabbath day; that being a man He made Himself GOD, were instances.]

D.

Israel's failure to attain δικαιοσύνη Θεοῦ ἐκ πίστεως considered with reference to some consolations and encouragements which qualify the sterner aspects of the fact (xi. 1–32).

[*Obs.* These consolations are, (i) that the whole nation of Israel has not failed to secure δικαιοσύνη Θεοῦ: (ii) that the failure of the majority is closely connected with the conversion of Heathendom, which will in turn promote that of Israel: (iii) that a bright future is in store for Israel itself.]

Consolation I.

Israel, as a people, has not wholly failed to attain δικαιοσύνη Θεοῦ ἐκ πίστεως (xi. 1–10).

[*Obs.* This general proposition is established by the consideration of a question arising out of (οὖν) those which have been already asked and answered to himself by the Apostle in x. 18–21. These questions and answers might have seemed to imply that the *whole* nation, conjointly and severally, had been shut out from the Kingdom of Messiah. Hence the Apostle asks,]

Question. Surely GOD has not *cast away* His own people? (ver. 1).

[*Obs.* The question expects a negative answer. The emphatic ἀπώσατο is placed first, and implies *entire* rejection: the retention of τὸν λαὸν αὐτοῦ to designate Israel implies that the enquiry could only be answered in one way. ἀπώσατο and τὸν λαὸν αὐτοῦ are mutually exclusive notions. The question seems

Dogmatic: ch. XI, *vv.* 1–10.

formed on Ps. xciv. 14 ὅτι οὐκ ἀπώσεται Κύριος τὸν λαὸν αὐτοῦ, καὶ τὴν κληρονομίαν αὐτοῦ οὐκ ἐγκαταλείψει.]

Resp. μὴ γένοιτο. No. The very thought of ἀπώσατο is horrible.

Proof that GOD has not rejected Israel as a whole (vers. 1–10).

Arg. 1. From the Apostle's own case. S. Paul himself is an instance of a Jew who had not been rejected by GOD. And he is a representative Jew, both as not being a proselyte (ἐκ σπέρματος Ἀβραάμ), and as belonging to a tribe which, together with that of Judah, was the theocratic centre of the nation (ἐκ φυλῆς Βενϊαμίν). Hence, to say the least, οὐκ ἀπώσατο ὁ Θεός every member of His people (ver. 1).

[*Obs.* 1. καὶ ἐγώ is a reason (γάρ) for μὴ γένοιτο. Meyer understands the Apostle to refer only to his own sentiment as 'a true Israelite of patriotic feeling whose theocratic self-esteem would not allow him to admit the ἀπώσατο,' mainly on the ground that the proof proper does not begin until ver. 20. Certainly the first argument is only a prelude to others which are to follow; as if the Apostle said, 'To begin with, I am a case in point,' which shows that ἀπώσατο cannot be pressed in the full force of the words. But it *is* an argument; and surely S. Paul had parted with his 'theocratic self-esteem' at his conversion. See Phil. iii. 7.]

[*Obs.* 2. On ἐκ σπέρματος Ἀβραάμ, no mere proselyte, see Phil. iii. 5; Rom. ix 7. On Benjamin, Acts xiii. 21. On the separation of the State into two kingdoms, Benjamin was attached to the tribe of Judah, and with it constituted the kingdom of Judah, 1 Kings xii. 21. After the captivity, these two tribes formed the heart of the Jewish colony in Palestine. See Ezra iv. 1; ix. 9.]

Arg. 2. From the Divine foreknowledge. GOD foreknew His people as being such from all eternity; but if He could have been supposed to have thrust Israel altogether away from Him, His foreknowledge of His own actions towards His people would have been at fault. This is inconceivable (ver. 2 a).

[*Obs.* 1. In introducing this argument, the proposition which is being proved in xi. 1–5, and which negatives the question in ver. 1, is stated, οὐκ ἀπώσατο ὁ Θεὸς τὸν λαὸν αὐτοῦ. As in ver. 1 the emphasis lies on ἀπώσατο and αὐτοῦ.]

[*Obs.* 2. προέγνω, as in viii. 29, precedes προορίζειν, not chronologically and in the Divine mind, but in the order of our apprehension. GOD foreknew His people as being what they were to be, when as yet creation was not. The ἀμετάθετον τῆς βουλῆς αὐτοῦ (Heb. vi. 17) makes it impossible that His πρόγνωσις could have been at fault, since his βουλή is based upon it. Nor does the πρόγνωσις, as here conceived, include the sins and apostasies of Israel, since this πρόγνωσις of Israel's sin could not have been the basis of the Divine προορισμός. ὃν προέγνω is not a limiting definition; as meaning *that part of GOD'S people which* He foreknew, as predestined to Salvation in Christ; because λαὸς αὐτοῦ here as in ver. 1 must mean the entire nation.]

Arg. 3. From historical analogy. The spiritual situation of Israel in the days of Elijah corresponded to that of the Apostolic period (2 b–4).

[*Obs.* ἐν Ἠλίᾳ—in the passage of Holy Scripture treating of Elijah—as often in LXX and Rabb., S. Mark xii. 26 ἐν τῇ βίβλῳ Μωσέως: S. Luke xx. 37 Μωσῆς ἐμήνυσεν. ἢ οὐκ οἴδατε κ.τ.λ. ;=or (if you do not agree that GOD has not rejected the people of His foreknowledge) is it the case that you do not know what Scripture says in respect of Elijah?]

1 Kings xix. 10, 14, 18, quoted to show that general national apostasy does not always involve total and unconditional national rejection; but that it is, on the contrary, consistent with the existence of a 'remnant' which by its presence proves that GOD οὐκ ἀπώσατο τὸν λαὸν αὐτοῦ (vers. 3, 4).

a. Elijah's intercession in accusation of (κατά) Israel : 1 Kings xix. 10 (ver. 3).

Heb. קַנֹּא קִנֵּאתִי לַיהוָה אֱלֹהֵי צְבָאוֹת
כִּי־עָזְבוּ בְרִיתְךָ בְּנֵי יִשְׂרָאֵל
אֶת־מִזְבְּחֹתֶיךָ הָרָסוּ וְאֶת־נְבִיאֶיךָ
הָרְגוּ בֶחָרֶב וָאִוָּתֵר אֲנִי לְבַדִּי
וַיְבַקְשׁוּ אֶת־נַפְשִׁי לְקַחְתָּהּ :

LXX ζηλῶν ἐζήλωκα τῷ Κυρίῳ παντοκράτορι, ὅτι ἐγκατέλιπόν σε οἱ υἱοὶ Ἰσραήλ· τὰ θυσιαστήριά σου κατέσκαψαν, καὶ τοὺς προφήτας σου ἀπέκτειναν ἐν ῥομφαίᾳ, καὶ ὑπελείφθην ἐγὼ μονώτατος, καὶ ζητοῦσι τὴν ψυχήν μου λαβεῖν αὐτήν.

[*Obs.* 1. This prayer is repeated in 1 Kings xix. 14 (after the question of the φωνὴ αὔρας λεπτῆς), with the substitution of τὴν διαθήκην σου for σε, and of ὑπολέλειμμαι for ὑπελείφθην. In the Hebrew, however, בְּרִיתְךָ and וָאִוָּתֵר are found alike in ver. 10 and ver. 14, which entirely correspond.]

[*Obs.* 2. The Apostolic citation varies from the LXX freely. It omits the reference to the covenant, and inverts the order of the slaughter of the prophets and the destruction of the altars, probably because the slaying of the prophets was a much graver sign of national apostasy than the destruction of the altars. For μονώτατος it has only μόνος : and, as if showing that it was made with a view to conciseness, ἐν ῥομφαίᾳ and λαβεῖν αὐτήν, which both occur in the Hebrew, are left out.]

[*Obs.* 3. The Israelites, under Ahab, were the murderers (ἀπέκτειναν) of the prophets : 1 Kings xviii. 4. 13, 22. They utterly razed the altars of Jehovah, i.e. those which, since the separation of the ten tribes, had been erected on the high places throughout Israel. These altars were indeed forbidden by the law (Lev. xvii. 8, 9 ; Deut. xii. 13, 14); and Hezekiah and Josiah, Kings of Judah, were praised for destroying them. In Judah they were wholly out of place ; but they stood on a somewhat different footing in

Dogmatic: ch. XI, vv. 1–10.

Israel, as the devout worshippers of the Lord Jehovah were not allowed to go to the Temple at Jerusalem, and erected these altars, not out of disobedience, but in order to offer such worship as was possible, under the circumstances of the schism. Accordingly these altars were destroyed in Israel under Ahab, from a purely irreligious motive—not because they violated the precepts of the law, but—because they were suggestive of the worship of the God of Israel. Hence Elijah's complaint. μόνος, in Elijah's sense, among the *prophets*; in S. Paul's, among the *people*. For ζητεῖν τὴν ψυχήν, 'seeks to destroy life,' see 1 Sam. xxii. 23 בַּקֵּשׁ אֶת־נֶפֶשׁ, S. Matt. ii. 20. For the parallel between the two religious situations, see S. Matt. xxiii. 29 sqq.; Acts vii. 52; 1 Thess. ii. 14 sqq.]

b. The Divine response (χρηματισμός) to Elijah: 1 Kings xix. 18 (ver. 4).

Heb.   וְהִשְׁאַרְתִּי בְיִשְׂרָאֵל שִׁבְעַת אֲלָפִים
        כָּל־הַבִּרְכַּיִם אֲשֶׁר לֹא־כָרְעוּ לַבַּעַל
        [וְכָל־הַפֶּה אֲשֶׁר לֹא־נָשַׁק לוֹ׃]

'Yet I have (marg. will leave) left Me seven thousand in Israel,
All the knees which have not bowed unto Baal,
[And every mouth that hath not kissed him.']

LXX καὶ καταλείψω [καταλείψεις] ἐν Ἰσραὴλ ἑπτὰ χιλιάδας ἀνδρῶν, πάντα τὰ γόνατα ἃ οὐκ ἔκαμψαν [ὤκλασαν] τῷ [τῇ] Βάαλ, [καὶ πᾶν στόμα ὃ οὐ προσεκύνησεν αὐτῷ].

[*Obs.* 1. The citation gives κατέλιπον ἐμαυτῷ [Hebrew וְהִשְׁאַרְתִּי] for καταλείψω ἐν Ἰσραήλ: ἑπτακισχιλίους ἄνδρας for ἑπτὰ χιλιάδας ἀνδρῶν: οἵτινες for πάντα τὰ γόνατα ἅ: τῇ Βάαλ (see App. Crit.) for τῷ Βάαλ.]

[*Obs.* 2. This sentence is termed by S. Paul ὁ χρηματισμός, the Divine response, or oracle, a ἅπ. λεγ. here in N. T. as=a special revelation; but found in 2 Macc. ii. 4; xi. 17. χρηματίζω means (actively) 'to transact business, decide, ordain'; here *passively* 'to assume a title, office, character.' For χρηματίζω in the *passive*, see S. Matt. ii. 12, 22; S. Luke ii. 26; Acts x. 22; Rom. vii. 3; Heb. viii. 5; xi. 7; the *active*, often of God in Josephus: and of His representatives, Jer. xxxiii. 2; xxxvi. 23; Heb. xii. 25. It is a word, which after doing heathen work has been consecrated by Revelation, like λειτουργία, ἐκκλησία, &c.]

[*Obs.* 3. κατέλιπον ἐμαυτῷ. God had left remaining to Himself, and as His own property, seven thousand men who were not slaughtered with the rest, yet had not worshipped Baal. These were concealed from view; to the prophet the apostasy seemed universal. As in the days of Noah, and in the wilderness, so now the faithful remnant were a minority. Jezebel had introduced the cultus of the Phoenician בַּעַל, also known as מֶלֶךְ, the Punic Μόλοχ. For his worship, see Lev. xviii. 21; 1 Kings xi. 5, 7, 33; 2 Kings xxiii. 10; Jer. xxxii. 35; Acts vii. 43. The fem. τῇ Βάαλ (the LXX reads τῷ) is probably to be explained by the popular conception of this god as androgynous. Movers (*Phoenic.* i. 178 sqq.) shows that this Tyrian Baal, as the sun-god, is substantially identical with the Babylonian and Syrian Baal, and with the Greek Heracles. In Phoenicia, a rude physiological materialism had been early digested into a formal idolatry, which worshipped the productive powers of nature in personified conceptions; and this worship centred in that of the sun, who was regarded as the chief fertilizing power in nature: Creuzer, *Symbol.* ii. 266 sqq.; Winer, *Bibl. Real-Woerterbuch*, s. v. Baal. The form of the worship seems to have been to kneel before the idol of Baal, and kiss the right hand to it.]

Arg. 4. From the actual fact that a remnant of Jews were Christian. As in the days of Elijah, so (οὕτως) now in the Apostolic age, and in order to make vers. 3, 4 applicable (οὖν), there was a λεῖμμα κατ' ἐκλογὴν χάριτος, a chosen remnant of Jews whose conversion to the Faith of Christ proved that οὐκ ἀπώσατο ὁ Θεὸς τὸν λαὸν αὐτοῦ (ver. 5).

[*Obs.* The converts to Christ of Jewish descent correspond to the seven thousand of Elijah's day: they are termed λεῖμμα κατὰ τὴν ἐκλογὴν χάριτος. The expression is immediately suggested by κατέλιπον ἐμαυτῷ ver. 4. λεῖμμα, a term from Isaiah (cf. Rom. ix. 27, 29), means the remainder from a whole of which the larger part has been removed. But in Elijah's day and in S. Paul's the λεῖμμα seemed insignificant when compared with the perishing or unbelieving majority; and yet, in the Apostolic age, the Christian λεῖμμα of the natural Israel was, in point of numbers, considerable. Cf. Acts xxi. 20, for the representation of the πρεσβύτεροι to S. Paul, πόσαι μυριάδες εἰσὶν Ἰουδαίων τῶν πεπιστευκότων: also Acts ii. 41. Rev. vii. 4 makes the mystical number of the Jews predestined to salvation through Christ 144,000. This λεῖμμα was taken from the rest of Israel, not in consequence of meritorious service, but through GOD's free choice, dictated by His compassion, κατ' ἐκλογὴν χάριτος.]

§ (*Transitional.*) Negative import of the production of the λεῖμμα in the way of ἐκλογὴ χάριτος (ver. 6). It excludes ἔργα as entitling to a place in the λεῖμμα, on the ground that, if this were otherwise, grace would cease to be grace; it would give up its specific character of gratuity by being conditioned (ver. 6).

[*Obs.* 1. The *logical* οὐκέτι, as at vii. 17. The idea is epigrammatically expressed by S. Augustine: 'Gratia, nisi gratis sit, non est gratia.' It is not purely parenthetical, since, besides explaining the negative import of the principle on which the λεῖμμα (ver. 5) was constructed, it accounts by anticipation for the failure of Israel's ἐπιζητεῖν (τὴν δικαιοσύνην) ἐξ ἔργων in ver. 7.]

[*Obs.* 2. The clause εἰ δὲ ἐξ ἔργων, οὐκ ἔτι ἐστὶ χάρις· ἐπεὶ τὸ ἔργον οὐκ ἔτι ἐστὶν ἔργον, although occurring in B. C. ℵ³ Syr. S. Chrys., is probably an old interpolation intended to complete the argument. See App. Crit.]

Arg. 5. From the true account of the failure of the majority of Israelites, and of the salvation of the minority which thus (οὖν) presents itself (vers. 5–10).

Dogmatic: ch. XI, vv. 1–10.

(A) The failure of the majority of Israelites to obtain δικαιοσύνη, viewed *on the side of human responsibility*, and as the result of vers. 5, 6 (ver. 7 a).

> *a*. Israel, in the mass, did not obtain even τοῦτο, the δικαιοσύνη which it sought, ἐξ ἔργων (ver. 7 a).
> *b*. The converted minority, or ἐκλογή, did obtain δικαιοσύνη, scil. ἐκ πίστεως (ver. 7 a).
> Hence, what occurred cannot be described as ἀπώσατο ὁ Θεὸς τὸν λαὸν αὐτοῦ, since the cause lay in Israel itself.

[*Obs.* To this it might be objected that the reference to Pharaoh in ix. 17 suggests that GOD did in some sense reject Israel: ὃν δὲ θέλει σκληρύνει. Hence follows,]

(B) The failure of the majority of Israelites to obtain δικαιοσύνη, viewed *on the Divine side* (vers. 7 b–10).

> *a*. This failure applies only to that portion of Israel which remains after the deduction of the Christian λεῖμμα, viz. οἱ λοιποί, the unbelieving majority (ver. 7 b).
> *b*. The internal cause which brought this failure to pass is described by ἐπωρώθησαν. The intellect and will of the majority were hardened by the withdrawal of GOD's grace, so as to be irreceptive of faith in Christ. Such a process differs from the summary rejection implied by ἀπώσατο, in being gradual, as well as in being the penal result of their own misconduct (ver. 7 b).
> *c*. This account of the failure corresponds with the typical language (καθὼς γέγραπται) of the O.T. which describes a like process in the days of Moses, David, and Isaiah (vers. 8–10).

[*Obs.* The πώρωσις of ver. 7, although describing the same general moral fact as the τὸ σκληρύνεσθαι of ix. 18, is perhaps stronger in its import. The metaphor implies not merely the stiffening of the existing soul and character, but the outgrowth of a new feature, which obscures while it hardens, by an outer coating of mental habit. πώρωσις differs from σκληρύνεσθαι by the idea of a *new outgrowth* of mental obduracy. πῶρος, the tufa-stone, is specially used of a callus or substance exuding from fractured bones and joining their extremities as it hardens: hence πωρόω, 'to petrify,' 'form a bony substance,' and so *metaph*. 'to harden.' The word is not to be identified with πωρόω = πηρόω, 'to make blind,' although ver. 8 has suggested this; indeed in S. John xii. 40 it is contrasted with τυφλόω. This πώρωσις produced permanent bluntness and insensibility in the intelligence (2 Cor. iii. 14 κάλυμμα ἐπὶ τῇ ἀναγνώσει τῆς παλαιᾶς διαθήκης μένει): but it was especially (as among the brutalized heathen) a πώρωσις τῆς καρδίας Eph. iv. 18, issuing in the spiritual blindness, described in S. Matt. xiii. 13 sqq.; in σκληροκαρδία: in the being σκληροτράχηλοι καὶ ἀπερίτμητοι τῇ καρδίᾳ καὶ τοῖς ὠσίν Acts vii. 51. As in earlier ages, so in the Apostolic, this πώρωσις, viewed from the human side, was a penal judgment for prolonged indifference to grace and light.]

a. Isaiah xxix. 10, blended with Deut. xxix. 3, quoted to show that this πώρωσις of the majority of Jews in the Apostolic age corresponded with that of the people of Israel in the days of Moses and Isaiah,—a hardening which was typical of that which characterized the Jews of the Messianic period (ver. 8).

(i.) Is. xxix. 10.
Heb. כִּי־נָסַךְ עֲלֵיכֶם יְהוָה
רוּחַ תַּרְדֵּמָה

'For He hath poured on you, hath Jehovah,
A spirit of deep sleep.'

LXX ὅτι πεπότικεν ὑμᾶς Κύριος πνεύματι κατανύξεως.

Citation. ἔδωκεν αὐτοῖς ὁ Θεὸς πνεῦμα κατανύξεως.

(ii.) Deut. xxix. 3.
Heb. וְלֹא־נָתַן יְהוָה לָכֶם לֵב לָדַעַת
וְעֵינַיִם לִרְאוֹת וְאָזְנַיִם לִשְׁמֹעַ
עַד הַיּוֹם הַזֶּה

'Yet the Lord hath not given unto you an heart to perceive
And eyes to see, and ears to hear,
Unto this day.'

LXX καὶ ἔδωκε Κύριος ὁ Θεὸς ὑμῖν [καρδίαν εἰδέναι καὶ] ὀφθαλμοὺς βλέπειν, καὶ ὦτα ἀκούειν ἕως τῆς ἡμέρας ταύτης.

Citation. ὀφθαλμοὺς τοῦ μὴ βλέπειν, καὶ ὦτα τοῦ μὴ ἀκούειν, ἕως τῆς σήμερον ἡμέρας.]

[*Obs.* 1. Is. xxix. 10 is a line in the Book of Woes (ch. xxviii–xxxii on Assyria and the projected alliance with Egypt). Woe II. On the Oppression and Deliverance of 'Ariel' (chap. xxix). The prophet has traced the humiliation of 'Ariel' (vers. 1–4) and its wonderful deliverance (vers. 5–8); but in order to understand the depths and heights of their history, the nation wanted faith. All was lost on the obtuseness of the mass. The self-induced indifference of the people becomes a judicial sentence of obduracy (ch. xxix. 9 b–12). All the members of the nation, even its eyes and heads, were possessed by a רוּחַ תַּרְדֵּמָה, a passive state of complete spiritual impotence and insensibility. תַּרְדֵּמָה (from רדם) is deep sleep, Gen. ii. 21; xv. 12; 1 Sam. xxvi. 12: and the word is used of a corresponding spiritua condition, Prov. xix. 15, and here. It is variously translated by the LXX according to the connection; as by ἔκστασις, at Gen. ii. 21; by θάμβος, at 1 Sam. xxvi. 12; by ἀνδρόγυνον, at Prov. xix. 15. Here the LXX render by πνεῦμα κατανύξεως, a spirit that induces stupefaction. Calvin, and other critics, following the etymology of κατάνυξις, render 'spiritus compunctionis'; but this severs the Greek word altogether from the meaning of תַּרְדֵּמָה, which it was intended to represent. On the other hand, it is impossible to derive the noun κατάνυξις from κατανυστάζω, which would yield κατανυσταγμός—νύσταγμα: or from κατα-νύω (if it was ever used), since this would form κατάνυσις. It is derived from κατά and νύσσω, properly 'to prick,' then 'to wound' (Hom. Il. μ. 395; S. John xix. 34), finally 'to strike.' The compound verb κατανύσσω is rarely found in its proper signification of 'compungere'; it is used, especially in the middle and passive, of passing under the overwhelming influence of fear, dejection, and the like (Gen. xxxiv. 7; Ps. iv. 5; cix. 16, &c.). Hence it comes to mean, to be mentally overwhelmed—struck dumb (Is. vi. 5; Lev. x. 3). Although the substantive κατάνυξις generally denotes some mental disturbance produced by grief, compassion, or fear, it may mean simple *stupor*. Thus in Ps. lx. 5 the LXX translates יַיִן תַּרְעֵלָה by οἶνον κατανύξεως, lit. 'wine of reeling,' i. e. producing the stupefaction which makes a man reel. So in Is. xxix. 10 ὅτι πεπότικεν ὑμᾶς ὁ Κύριος πνεύματι κατανύξεως: 'bibendum vobis Dominus dedit spiritum, *qui torpidos vos* faceret.' See the Excursus in Fritzsche, *Ep. Rom.* ii. p. 558 sqq. That S. Paul understood by πνεῦμα κατανύξεως, not a mere moral state, but an evil personal being or daemon, producing spiritual insensibility, might be gathered from 2 Cor. iv. 4 ἐν οἷς ὁ θεὸς τοῦ αἰῶνος τούτου ἐτύφλωσε τὰ νοήματα, or Eph. ii. 2, where heathen life is κατὰ τὸν ἄρχοντα τῆς ἐξουσίας τοῦ ἀέρος, τοῦ πνεύματος τοῦ νῦν ἐνεργοῦντος ἐν τοῖς υἱοῖς τῆς ἀπειθείας.]

[*Obs. 2.* Deut. xxix. 3 occurs in Moses' parting exhortation to obey the Law: it refers immediately to the insensibility of Israel to the real import of the plagues of Egypt. τοῦ μὴ βλέπειν (gen. of the aim) is 'eyes, that they may not see'; a fatal oxymoron. Cf. Is. vi. 9, 10; S. John xii. 40; Acts xxviii. 27.]

[*Obs. 3.* The general sense of these passages is as follows:—The majority of the Jewish people in the time of Christ and His Apostles act like men drunk, or in a dream. Their eyes are open, but they see no one object clearly; sounds fall on their ears, but no ideas are conveyed. The Eternal Truth, to Whom their whole history points, presents Himself before them; yet they cannot recognise Him. How can this obtuseness be anything less than a penal visitation? God must have deserted them; or rather He must have deprived them altogether of His illuminating grace; and as the last influences of the πνεῦμα ἅγιον depart, the πνεῦμα κατανύξεως supervenes. The πώρωσις is then complete.]

    b. Psalm lxix. 23, 24, quoted to show that the curse denounced by David, whether as prophet or type of the Messiah, had been fulfilled in the πώρωσις of the majority of the Jews, who, in the Apostolic age, had rejected the true Messiah (vers. 9, 10).

Heb.
יְהִי שֻׁלְחָנָם לִפְנֵיהֶם
לְפָח וְלִשְׁלוֹמִים לְמוֹקֵשׁ:
תֶּחְשַׁכְנָה עֵינֵיהֶם מֵרְאוֹת
וּמָתְנֵיהֶם תָּמִיד הַמְעַד:

'Let their table before them become a snare
And to the unconcerned a trap.
Let their eyes be darkened that they see not,
And make their loins continually to shake.'

LXX γενηθήτω ἡ τράπεζα αὐτῶν ἐνώπιον αὐτῶν εἰς παγίδα καὶ εἰς ἀνταπόδοσιν καὶ εἰς σκάνδαλον. Σκοτισθήτωσαν οἱ ὀφθαλμοὶ αὐτῶν τοῦ μὴ
βλέπειν, καὶ τὸν νῶτον αὐτῶν διαπαντὸς σύγκαμψον.

[*Obs.* 1. The citation differs from the LXX in omitting ἐνώπιον αὐτῶν after τράπεζα
αὐτῶν: in inserting καὶ εἰς θήραν after παγίδα: in substituting ἀνταπόδομα for
ἀνταπόδοσιν, and transposing it with σκάνδαλον. The LXX rendering εἰς
ἀνταπόδοσιν is only a comment on, not a translation of, וְלִשְׁלוֹמִים (= the
carnally secure, who enjoy peace without solid grounds); and σύγκαμψον,
'bend together,' is an effect of הַמְעַד, imp. Hiph. 'make them to shake.']

[*Obs.* 2. Ps. lxix according to the inscription is *David's*, and belongs, like Ps.
xl, which it most nearly resembles, to the period of his persecution by
Saul. Delitzsch follows Hitzig in ascribing it to Jeremiah, but against
S. Paul, as well as the inscription, and upon internal grounds which do not
appear to be convincing. It is not altogether a typically-prophetic Psalm;
David here, as in Ps. xxii (which with Ps. lxix is most frequently quoted
in the New Testament with reference to Christ's sufferings), loses his own
individuality in that of the Ideal Holy Man under persecution who became
concrete in Christ. As such David identifies himself in vers. 23, 24 with
the Divine Mind in respect of his persecutors; and he utters the curse,
which Absolute Justice, as distinct from any private feelings of revenge,
would prescribe. In this, as in Ps. cix and Ps. cxxxix. 21 'Do not I hate
them, O Lord, that hate Thee?' the Psalmist regards the enemies of the
Theocracy as his own, and his own enemies as enemies only so far as they
fought against the Divine order of the world. The imprecations, therefore,
are only the form which 'Thy Will be done' necessarily assumes in the
presence of aggressive evil. They are a prayer that the Divine Justice
might be revealed in action for the protection of the cause of Truth and
Righteousness against its enemies. So far are they from being 'peculiar to
the moral standard of Judaism,' that they are, as here, deliberately adopted
by the inspired teachers of Christianity. Were they indeed the language
of mere human passion, they would be very alien from the Christian
spirit; but, in truth, they rank with the sterner sentences of our Lord and
His Apostles, as utterances of the penal Justice of God. Cf. Gal. i. 8, 9, &c.]

[*Obs.* 3. The persecutors of the Sufferer, who in ver. 20 have given Him gall, and
vinegar, fall in ver. 23 under His prophetic imprecations. Their table,
which was abundantly supplied with the good things, is to be turned into
a snare; they will be slain while sitting at the feast. In their carnal

security (שְׁלוֹמִים) they little heed the coming ruin. Those eyes, which gloated on the sufferings of the Righteous One, are to be closed to spiritual truth. Those loins, so full of self-confident defiance, must shake with fear. (הַמְעַד). The Apostle in quoting the passage, contemplates the ruin which ἡ τράπεζα αὐτῶν was, according to the prophetic imprecation, to bring upon Israel. This well-furnished table was in S. Paul's sense either God's earlier Revelation, or the Jewish Scriptures; 'on which table,' says Origen, 'any who wished to feed on the Word of God was nourished with the discourses of the Law and the prophets.' And, as our Lord said to the Jews, ὑμεῖς δοκεῖτε ἐν αὐταῖς ζωὴν αἰώνιον ἔχειν (S. John v. 39). Yet the same spirit which rejected the true Messiah obscured the true meaning of the Scriptures which spoke of Him. The Jews (δόξαν παρὰ ἀλλήλων λαμβάνοντες S. John v. 44; cf. xii. 43) glided into a false exegesis, based on self-love and self-flattery, until the true tendency of the Law and the moral elevation of the prophets were lost sight of, and the sources of Divine Truth were overlaid with profitless controversy and logomachy. In this way their Scriptures became 'snares' and 'traps' to Israel, nay, an enemy chasing them to their destruction, and 'repaying' them for their treatment of the Messiah. Under the dark shadow of this false exegesis, the Jewish Scriptures have been the fertile source of the miseries of Israel, from the days of the destruction of Jerusalem until now. And at the root of this is the spiritual blindness, which sees not that the Law ended when the true Messiah came; and the spiritual servitude to sin personal and national, which lasts, because the one possible Deliverer has been rejected.]

[*Obs.* 4. The πώρωσις lies, not in ἡ τράπεζα αὐτῶν, the well-spread board, at which Israel feasted on the dainties of the ancient Scriptures; but in γενηθήτω εἰς παγίδα, as ver. 10 more precisely explains. For καὶ εἰς θήραν there is no equivalent in the Heb. or LXX; the Apostle expands the thought suggested by παγὶς: θήρα can only mean 'the chase by which they are captured.' σκάνδαλον = σκανδάληθρον, the stick set in a trap, often used in the LXX for מוֹקֵשׁ, 'a snare.' ἀνταπόδομα, not classical; but often in the LXX εἰς ἀνταπόδομα is added to suggest that all the instruments of the downfall of Israel have the character of being a retribution. καὶ εἰς ἀνταπόδομα, 'and thus a retribution.' Cf. S. Luke xiv. 12. νῶτος (Att., νῶτον), here masc. Lobeck, *Phryn.* p. 290. The bending down of the back of Israel was a figure of its spiritual bondage under the law.]

Consolation II.

The failure of the majority of Israel to attain through Christ δικαιοσύνη Θεοῦ ἐκ πίστεως is intended to promote the salvation of Heathendom: while the conversion of the Heathen will in turn bring about the restoration of Israel (xi. 11-24).

I. Divinely-intended results of Israel's offence in rejecting Christ (vers. 11-16).

[*Obs.* These results are stated in four theses (ver. 11-16).]

THESIS 1. (*Negative.*) It is not to be imagined (μὴ γένοιτο) that the offence taken at the claims of Christ on the part of the majority of Israel involves permanent spiritual ruin (ver. 11).

[*Obs.* ἔπταισαν (ver. 11) refers (οὖν ver. 11) to οἱ δὲ λοιποὶ ἐπωρώθησαν (ver. 7) for its occasion. The antithesis lies between ἔπταισαν and πέσωσι. πταίειν is a figurative expression for taking such offence at the claims or Person of Christ, as to refuse faith in Him. The expression is chosen with reference to our Lord's title λίθος προσκόμματος ix. 32, possibly to σκάνδαλον ver. 9. For moral stumbling, see S. James ii. 10; iii. 2; S. Pet. i. 10. πίπτειν here implies a fall into unending destruction: Heb. iv. 11. S. Paul denies that there was any Divine purpose (ἵνα) of an irrecoverable fall in Israel's stumbling at the claims of Christ. He does this by indignantly answering his own question in the negative.]

THESIS 2. (*Positive.*) The offence (παράπτωμα) of Israel in rejecting Salvation through Christ has led to the acceptance of this Salvation by the heathen, and this tends to make (εἰς) the Jews (in a good sense) emulate the heathen, who have succeeded to their leadership in religious privilege (ver. 11 b).

[*Obs.* 1. παράπτωμα refers to ἔπταισαν, not to πέσωσι: παράπτωμα gives the moral import of an act, which, viewed historically, and with sympathy for the unhappy agent, is described as πταῖσμα. For the ellipse of γέγονεν after τοῖς ἔθνεσιν, see Winer, *Gr. N. T.* p. 733. For the fact that the Christian Faith was addressed to the heathen world in consequence of its rejection by the Jews, see S. Matt. xxi. 43 ἀρθήσεται ἀφ' ὑμῶν ἡ βασιλεία τοῦ Θεοῦ καὶ δοθήσεται ἔθνει ποιοῦντι τοὺς καρποὺς αὐτῆς : Id. xxii. 9 πορεύεσθε οὖν εἰς τὰς διεξόδους τῶν ὁδῶν καὶ ὅσους ἂν εὕρητε, καλέσατε εἰς τοὺς γάμους. Acts xiii. 46 (S. Paul to the Jews in the Pisidian Antioch) ὑμῖν ἦν ἀναγκαῖον πρῶτον λαληθῆναι τὸν λόγον τοῦ Θεοῦ· ἐπειδὴ δὲ ἀπωθεῖσθε αὐτὸν καὶ οὐκ ἀξίους κρίνετε ἑαυτοὺς τῆς αἰωνίου ζωῆς, ἰδοὺ στρεφόμεθα εἰς τὰ ἔθνη : Id. xxviii. 28 (at Rome) γνωστὸν οὖν ἔστω ὑμῖν, ὅτι τοῖς ἔθνεσιν ἀπεστάλη τὸ σωτήριον τοῦ Θεοῦ, αὐτοὶ καὶ ἀκούσονται. But the ultimate intention and drift of this admission of the heathen was εἰς τὸ παραζηλῶσαι αὐτούς, namely the Jews;—here is the antithesis to ἵνα πέσωσι in the question put to himself by the Apostle.]

[*Obs.* 2. On εἰς τὸ παραζηλῶσαι αὐτούς, comp. Deut. xxxii. 21, quoted in x. 19. GOD desired, by tokens of His love towards the Canaanites, to stir up His Own people to jealousy. 'Sicuti uxorem a marito sua culpa rejectam accendit aemulatio, ut se reconciliare studeat, ita nunc fieri posse dicit, ut Judaei, quum viderint Gentes in locum suum subrogatas, repudii sui dolore tacti ad reconciliationem aspirent.' Calv.]

THESIS 3. If so much spiritual advantage has resulted to mankind at large from the failure of Israel in the mass to attain δικαιοσύνη τοῦ Θεοῦ, much more may be expected to result from Israel's entire conversion to Christ (vers. 12–15).

Dogmatic: ch. XI, vv. 11-24.

[*Obs*. 1. This may be described as an inference 'a felici effectu causae pejoris ad feliciorem effectum causae melioris.' As drawn out by Aquinas it runs thus : 'Bonum est potentius ad utilitatem inferendam quam malum ; sed malum Judaeorum magnam utilitatem gentibus contulit ; ergo, multo majorem conferet mundo eorum bonum.']

[*Obs*. 2. The paragraph (vers. 12-15) contains three parallel statements of the same argument, with a passage practically parenthetical (vers. 13, 14), although closely connected with that which precedes and follows it, inserted between the second (ver. 12) and third (ver. 15). Thus,

εἰ $\begin{Bmatrix} τὸ\ παράπτωμα \\ τὸ\ ἥττημα \\ ἡ\ ἀποβολὴ \end{Bmatrix}$ αὐτῶν $\begin{Bmatrix} πλοῦτος\ κόσμου \\ πλοῦτος\ ἐθνῶν \\ καταλλαγὴ\ κόσμου \end{Bmatrix}$ $\begin{Bmatrix} πόσῳ\ μᾶλλον \\ τίς \end{Bmatrix}$

$\begin{Bmatrix} τὸ\ πλήρωμα \\ ἡ\ πρόσλημψις \end{Bmatrix}$ αὐτῶν $\begin{Bmatrix} \text{[scil. πλοῦτος κόσμου, καὶ ἐθνῶν], (ver. 12).} \\ εἰ\ μὴ\ ζωὴ\ ἐκ\ νεκρῶν\ \text{(ver. 15).} \end{Bmatrix}$

Although in ver. 12 the logical force of the argument is expressed verbally by πόσῳ μᾶλλον, it lies equally in τίς εἰ μή (ver. 15) ; since in ver. 15 the Apostle argues, not merely that the conversion of the Jews will at least be as beneficial to the world at large as their failure to attain δικαιοσύνη, but also that it will produce an effect as much greater as ζωὴ ἐκ νεκρῶν is than καταλλαγὴ κόσμου.]

§ The argument is threefold in its mode of presentation.

a. If the 'offence' (παράπτωμα) of (the majority of) Israel in rejecting the Gospel has enriched the world, how much more must the restoration of Israel to its full number of faithful [πλήρωμα] enrich it ! (ver. 12).

[*Obs*. 1. In ver. 12, δέ is transitional. Israel's offence became the πλοῦτος κόσμου because in consequence of it the Christian σωτηρία was offered to, and accepted by, the converted portion of Heathendom. The πλήρωμα of Israel means the fully restored number of faithful Israelites, through the conversion of the unbelieving οἱ λοιποί (ver. 7) to the Christian Faith. On the word, see Fritzsche, *Ep. Rom.* ii. p. 469.]

[*Obs*. 2. πλήρωμα, here 'the complement of Jews filling up the gap in God's kingdom.' Fritzsche has shown, *in loc.*, that the passive meaning of the word is the most common in the New Testament, πλήρωμα means, (1) that with which a thing is filled up, (2) that which is filled up, (3) *actively*, the action of filling up. Fritzsche only adduces Rom. xiii. 10, for the active sense, πλήρωμα νόμου ἡ ἀγάπη, yet this may be taken passively thus ; love is that by which the Law, conceived of as an outline of duty, is filled up, 1 Cor. x. 26 τὸ πλήρωμα τῆς γῆς, that by which the earth is filled by the processes of nature ; so S. Matt. ix. 16 ; Mark ii. 21 ; Eph. iii. 19 ; iv. 13 ; Col. i. 19 ; ii. 9. πλήρωμα τοῦ Θεοῦ and τοῦ Χριστοῦ is the sum of perfections with which God, or Christ is filled. The Church is Eph. i. 23 τὸ πλήρωμα τοῦ τὰ πάντα ἐν πᾶσιν πληρουμένου, the fulness with which Christ is filled and which also fills the Church. In ver. 25 πλήρωμα τοῦ ἐθνῶν cannot mean that with which the Gentiles are filled up, the sum of qualities or characteristics which makes them to be what they are ; but the complement which the Gentiles supply to fill up the gap in the βασιλεία τοῦ Θεοῦ created by the apostasy of the Jewish majority. It is a *gen. apposit.*; as in Cant. v. 12 πληρώματα ὑδάτων, i. e. the waters by which the river-bed is filled. And πλήρωμα means here what it means in ver. 25, and is in antithesis to ἥττημα : viz. the full number of Jews by which the apostasy of the majority will be repaired ; see Philippi *in loc.*]

b. If the 'overthrow' (ἥττημα) of Israel, through the loss of the unbelieving majority, has enriched the heathen nations, how much more must the restoration in Israel of its full number of faithful enrich them! (ver. 12).

[*Obs.* 1. ἥττημα (1 Cor. vi. 7 ; Is. xxxi. 9) is not classical. It = ἧττα. The Apostle conceives of Israel as an army, which has experienced defeat through the loss of a majority of its men.]

[*Obs.* 2. At this point, before the third statement of his position in ver. 15, the Apostle becomes conscious that his ex-heathen readers will think his enthusiasm on behalf of Israel inconsistent with his office. To meet this latent objection he interposes a parenthetical explanation (ver. 13, 14).]

§ Parenthetical explanation addressed to converts from Heathenism, in justification of the inferences of ver. 12, and in preparation for that of ver. 15 (vers. 13, 14).

Supposed Objection of the ex-heathen Christians. ' As the ἐθνῶν ἀπόστολος S. Paul has no concern with the future conversion and πλήρωμα (ver. 12) of Israel' (ver. 13).

Resp. (1) So far as he is ἐθνῶν ἀπόστολος, he magnifies his office. He claims all honour for it, and he practically illustrates its importance by his work (ver. 13).

(2) But in doing this, he admits, he has an object beyond. His work for Heathendom is in reality work for Israel. Israel, he hopes, will be stirred to a holy emulation at the sight of heathen conversions to Christ, and thus at any rate *some* Jews may be rescued from their unbelief (ver. 15).

[*Obs.* 1. S. Paul's title ἐθνῶν ἀπόστολος, Doctor Gentium, seems to have been already fixed; and it is treated as involving corresponding obligations. Our Lord gave it Himself, Acts xxii. 21 ἐγὼ εἰς ἔθνη μακρὰν ἐξαποστελῶ σε. As contrasted with the ἀποστολὴ τῆς περιτομῆς of SS. Peter, James, and John, it was an ἀποστολὴ εἰς τὰ ἔθνη, corresponding to the εὐαγγέλιον τῆς ἀκροβυστίας, Gal. ii. 7-9. In discharging this apostolate S. Paul naturally became (1 Tim. ii. 7) a διδάσκαλος ἐθνῶν : and he says accordingly, 2 Tim. i. 11 εἰς ὃ

Dogmatic: *ch*. XI, *vv*. 11-24.   207

ἐτέθην ἐγὼ κήρυξ καὶ ἀπόστολος καὶ διδάσκαλος ἐθνῶν. The διακονία which he magnifies consisted in διαμαρτύρασθαι τὸ εὐαγγέλιον τῆς χάριτος τοῦ Θεοῦ Acts xx. 24; 2 Cor. iv. 1.]

[*Obs*. 2. S. Paul's affection for Israel appears (1) in the use of μου τὴν σάρκα, cf. ix. 3 τῶν συγγενῶν μου κατὰ σάρκα : 2 Sam. xix. 12, 13 ; (2) in παραζηλώσω, the language of injured love ; (3) in σώσω τινάς. He did not venture to expect *all* or *many*, at least yet. Cf. 1 Cor. ix. 22 ἵνα πάντως τινὰς σώσω. He ascribes σώζειν to himself, because he administers the Gospel which is δύναμις εἰς σωτηρίαν i. 16 ; 1 Cor. vii. 16 ; ix. 22 ; 1 Tim. iv. 16.]

[*Obs*. 3. The argument suspended at the end of ver. 12 is resumed in ver. 15, and as a reason (γάρ ver. 15) for the hope expressed in εἴ πως παραζηλώσω.]

   c. If the 'loss' (ἀποβολή) of the majority of Israel has issued in the reconciliation of (so many converts from) the world, what will the reception (πρόσλημψις) of Israel back to GOD's favour be but the final ζωὴ ἐκ νεκρῶν? (ver. 15).

[*Obs*. ἀποβολή (see Acts xxvii. 22 with ψυχῆς) explains ἥττημα in ver. 12. For καταλλαγή, see Rom. v. 10 ; πρόσλημψις only here ; but προσλαμβάνεσθαι often, cf. Rom. xiv. 3 ; xv. 7. ζωὴ ἐκ νεκρῶν may be taken, (1) as the Resurrection of the dead to eternal life, since the conversion of the Jews (ver. 25) will coincide with the end of time (Origen, S. Chrys.) ; (2) as the Resurrection of the whole world from the death of sin to newness of life (S. Ambr.) ; (3) as a proverbial expression. The entrance of the converted Jews into the Church will quicken Christendom with so powerful a moral impulse, that it will seem as if the world had risen from death to life. Of these, (1) which makes ζωή = ἀνάστασις is most probable. See Col. iii. 3, 4 ; 1 Thess. iv. 14, &c.]

THESIS 4. The spiritual glories of the Patriarchs of Israel are an earnest of the future which awaits the race (ver. 16).

[*Obs*. This is a corroboration of the hopes of Israel's πρόσλημψις (ver. 15) and is introduced by the metabatic δέ, ver. 16. It also supplies a ground for the threefold warning afterwards addressed to the converts from Heathendom (17-24).]

   Analogy 1. From the *legal* symbolism of the first-fruits and lump of the dough in Numb. xv. 19-21. When the dough was kneaded, a portion was set aside, and a cake of it baked for the priests. This ἀπαρχή had the effect of consecrating the remainder of the lump, φύραμα. This ἀπαρχή symbolizes the Patriarchs, the historical ἀπαρχή of the mass of Israel, from whom the collective people (φύραμα) received an indelible character of theocratic consecration (in the external sense) to GOD (ver. 16).

[*Obs.* 1. Numb. xv. 20 ἀπαρχὴ τοῦ φυράματος = רֵאשִׁית עֲרִסֹתֵיכֶם. The word עֲרִסָה, (only found in pl. from עָרֵס 'to pound up') is coarse meal, polenta. Vulg. *pulmentum*. In Neh. x. 38, Ezek. xliv. 30, rendered by σῖτος, which however cannot be understood here, since φύραμα always means a kneaded mass, dough: 1 Cor. v. 6, 7; Gal. v. 9.]

[*Obs.* 2. ἁγία is here used 'non de actuali sanctitate, sed de potentiali,' Aquinas. Like קדוש it means 'something separate from common use.' So in 1 Cor. vii. 14 the children of believing parents are said to be, not personally, but theocratically, ἅγιοι: and in the Creed, the Catholic Church is 'Holy.' 'Non ergo sanctum vocat Judaicum populum Paulus, quod sanctitatem in se habeat; sed quia habet unde sanctificetur, tanquam massa ex primitiis, et rami ex radice, ut proinde sanctus dici possit in spe, et causa probabili, et in quadam praeparatione, quam Scriptura non raro sanctificationem vocat.' Estius.]

Analogy 2. From the *natural* symbolism of the root and branches of a tree. The root communicates its qualities to the branches. The Patriarchs, the ῥίζα of Israel, impart theocratic consecration to the branches of the race which springs from them (ver. 16).

[*Obs.* 1. The second figure, borrowed from nature, teaches the same truth as did the first, borrowed from legal prescriptions. The image of a tree is used for the theocracy in Neh. viii. 15; Jer. xi. 16; Hos. xiv. 6; Zech. iv. 11: its root was in the Patriarchs, of whom κατὰ σάρκα came the Messiah. By rejecting Him, the majority of the Jews severed themselves from the Root, i. e. from the Patriarchs, to whom He was promised as the ripe product of their race,—and so became broken-off branches: S. John viii. 37, 39, 40. Our Lord adapted this image of the vine to teaching the necessity of union with Himself: S. John xv. 1–8.]

[*Obs.* 2. ver. 16, although constituting a distinct thesis, stands in the relation of an argument to the teleology of vers. 11, 12, 15. The belief that the conversion of Heathendom, itself resulting from the fall of Israel, would yet work out Israel's good by provoking emulation, is based on the Apostle's faith in all that is involved in the calling of the Patriarchs, as the ἀπαρχή and ῥίζα of the race. See ver. 29.]

II. Warnings to converts from heathenism against certain errors to which they might be prone in their words and thoughts respecting Israel (vers. 17–24).

[*Obs.* The metaphor of the ῥίζα and κλάδοι, as applied to the Patriarchs and their descendants (in ver. 16), shapes the entire section vers. 17–24.]

Warning I. Against indulging in boastful and triumphant language over Israel's fall (μὴ κατακαυχῶ τῶν κλάδων), (vers. 17, 18).

a. Circumstances under which the ex-heathen convert is tempted to triumph over Israel (ver. 17).

1. *Some* 'branches' of Israel have been severed from the ῥίζα of the Patriarchs (ver. 17).

[*Obs.* τινές, as at iii. 3, is a *litotes*; the great number of these 'branches' is not mentioned, in order not to encourage self-exaltation among the ex-heathen converts. Young twigs, κλάδοι, so called, because broken off on account of unfitness for bearing.]

2. The convert from heathenism (σύ), himself originally from the wild-olive-tree, has been grafted in among the Israelitic 'branches' which spring from the old ῥίζα, and so has become a fellow-partaker with these Judaeo-Christians in fellowship with the Patriarchs, and in the πιότης, or rich blessings of the Evangelical promises which the Church of Christ inherits from them (ver. 17).

[*Obs.* 1. ἀγριέλαιος (an adjective) = ἐκ τῆς ἀγριελαίου ver. 24. Each convert from heathenism is addressed individually by σύ, which cannot impersonate Heathendom as a whole, since the heathen converts were only grafted into the Tree of the Church, one by one. For the πιότης τῆς ἐλαίας, see Judges ix. 9. S. Paul chooses the olive, (not the vine,) because its πιότης was symbolical of the spiritual fulness of Israel. For the ritual use of oil, as a symbol of the Spirit, see Ex. xxv. 6; xxx. 31; xxxvii. 29. And for the beauty and productiveness of the tree, see Ps. lii. 10. ἐν, 'among' (Theodoret); rather than 'in the place of' the branches. (S. Chrys.)]

[*Obs.* 2. In antiquity, scions of the wild olive were grafted into old trees, in order to renew their fertility (Columella, *De re rustica*, v. 9, 11, &c.; but this practice is not in S. Paul's view in the present passage. In the garden, the young shoot was grafted upon the decrepit stem, in order to invigorate its life; in the spiritual world, the heathen convert was grafted into the Tree of the Church, which had its roots in the Patriarchs, and its stem in Christ, not for the sake of the tree, but for his own.]

[*Obs.* 3. The insertion or ingrafting into Christ which ἐνεκεντρίσθης implies, is explained by S. Cyril of Jerusalem of Baptism, *Catech. Myst.* ii. 3. That ex-heathen Christians become 'very members incorporate in the mystical body' of the Son of GOD, is taught in Ep. iii. 6 εἶναι τὰ ἔθνη συγκληρονόμα, καὶ σύσσωμα, καὶ συμμέτοχα τῆς ἐπαγγελίας αὐτοῦ ἐν τῷ Χριστῷ διὰ τοῦ εὐαγγελίου: Eph. v. 30. The metaphors of the Tree and the Body both imply the organic life of the Church; but the former lends itself to the idea of insertion from without (as through Baptism) more readily than the latter.]

[*Obs.* 4. The convert from heathenism then had no reason for triumphing over Israel to which, indirectly at least, he owed all that made him what he was as a member of Christ.]

b. Precept to the converted heathen against triumphing boastfully over Israel (μὴ κατακαυχῶ τῶν κλάδων) (ver. 18).

[*Obs.* The κλάδοι are not merely the broken-off branches, that is, Jews who, by rejecting the apostolical preaching, had been severed from true communion with the Patriarchs; but also converts from Judaism to the Church, who were still living 'branches' of the Patriarchal Tree, and indeed first in honour among them, but to whom the unbelief of the mass of their countrymen was imputed as a degradation by heathen converts.]

  c. Absurdity in the conduct of a heathen convert who triumphs boastfully over Israel (ver. 18).

  If he does it (the possibility is expressed at vers. 21, 22), the fact remains that it is not he who bears the Patriarchal ῥίζα, (as his boastfulness might seem to imply), but the ῥίζα which bears him as one of its branches (ver. 18).

[*Obs.* For the form κατακαυχᾶσαι, cf. Rom. ii. 17, 23; ὀδυνᾶσαι S. Luke xvi. 25. The position of heathen converts in the Church afforded even less ground for καύχησις than did that of Jewish converts. As our Lord said to the Samaritan woman, 'Salvation is of the Jews,' S. John iv. 22. The Jew was already in a sense growing out of the root of the Patriarchs. The heathen was altogether a graft from without, inserted upon conditions, and had no ground whatever for self-exaltation.]

Warning II. Against self-exalting thoughts, (μὴ ὑψηλοφρόνει ver. 20), which misapprehend the true purpose and lessons of the Divine Judgments on Israel (vers. 19–21).

[*Obs.* Rejoinder of the converted heathen, which he will therefore (οὖν ver. 19 make, because the remark ἡ ῥίζα σὲ βαστάζει stops his καύχησις, ver. 18.]

  a. Anticipated Objection from the converted heathen: 'The Jewish branches were broken off the Patriarchal Tree with the express object of my being grafted into it' (ver. 19).

[*Obs.* ἵνα ἐγώ has the tone of arrogant self-esteem. The heathen convert might appeal to the Apostle's own statement in ver. 11. And he insists on his rhetorical advantage in a purely selfish spirit.]

  Resp. (1) The fact is admitted (καλῶς), (ver. 20).

  (2) The fact is explained by its immediate causes. Unbelief caused the ἐξεκλάσθησαν of the Jews; faith is the condition of the perseverance of the converted heathen in his present position (ver. 20).

[*Obs.* τῇ ἀπιστίᾳ, τῇ πίστει are datives of the ground or reason, Gal. vi. 12; Col. i. 21; Winer, *Gr. N. T.* p. 270, E. T. Their position, each before the verb which describes the consequent effect, gives them the emphasis of solemn warning. ἕστηκας refers, (1) to the position of the ingrafted branch upon the tree, and (2) to the Christian life of grace, Rom. v. 2; 1 Cor. x. 12; as opposed to πίπτειν, xi. 11, 12; xiv. 4.]

b. *Precept.* (To the converted heathen) forbidding conceited thoughts about himself, and suggesting humble anxiety as to his real position (μὴ ὑψηλοφρόνει, ἀλλὰ φοβοῦ) (ver. 20).

[*Obs.* 1. ὑψηλοφρονεῖν xii. 16; 1 Tim. vi. 17; cf. ὑπερφρονεῖν xii. 3; 1 S. Pet. v. 5. Opposed to ταπεινοφρονεῖν, Ps. cxxxi. 1, 2. In classical Greek the verb is not found, only μεγαλοφρονεῖν: but the adj. ὑψηλόφρων is used in the *good* sense of high-spirited. On the subject of humility, Heathen and Christian ethics differed fundamentally; and accordingly their terminology differs.]

[*Obs.* 2. The fear, here prescribed, is the antithesis of false security, and is not therefore that servile apprehension of evil which is cast out by ἡ τελεία ἀγάπη 1 S. John iv. 18.]

c. Reasons (γάρ) for the precept ἀλλὰ φοβοῦ (ver. 21).

1. (Implied reason.) The converted heathen too *may* lose faith.

2. He, a mere παρὰ φύσιν κλάδος, has, in that case, the more reason to dread the Divine Judgment, since GOD has so severely punished the κατὰ φύσιν κλάδοι (ver. 21).

[*Obs.* 1. The κατὰ φύσιν κλάδοι are opposed to the ingrafted κλάδοι. μή πως οὐδὲ σοῦ φείσεται (not φείσηται), 'it is to be feared lest He will not also (as a matter of fact) spare thee.' The fut. ind. is more definite and certain than the conj. On the other hand, μή πως softens down οὐδὲ σοῦ φείσεται from a pure matter of fact, into one of mental apprehension. (See Winer, *Gr. N. T.* p. 595, E. T.)]

[*Obs.* 2. The argument suggested is an *a fortiori* one. The κατὰ φύσιν κλάδοι of the καλλιέλαιος (ver. 24), the 'natural' members of the Church of GOD rooted in the Patriarchs, had been cast off for their lack of faith in Christ. Much more would the παρὰ φύσιν κλάδοι, the heathen converts ingrafted into the Church, be cut off, if they lost hold on faith,—a grace which might easily be forfeited.]

Warning III. To contemplate the Divine Attributes of Goodness and Severity in their bearing upon present circumstances, and upon the possible changes of the future (vers. 22-24).

[*Obs.* The precept of ver. 22 is inferred (οὖν) from ver. 21, and corresponds to the precept μὴ ὑψηλοφρόνει, ἀλλὰ φοβοῦ in ver. 20.]

(I.) The two Divine Attributes to be contemplated (ἴδε), (ver. 22).

a. χρηστότης. Eternal Loving-kindness passing into beneficence towards created beings (ver. 22).

[*Obs.* On χρηστότης, see Rom. ii. 4 τοῦ πλούτου τῆς χρηστότητος αὐτοῦ: 1 S. Pet. ii. 3, quoting Ps. xxxiv. 9 LXX γεύσασθε καὶ ἴδετε ὅτι χρηστὸς ὁ Κύριος: S. Luke vi. 35 χρηστός ἐστιν ἐπὶ τοὺς ἀχαρίστους καὶ πονηρούς. The LXX use it often for טוֹב, Ps. lxxxv. 13: cxix. 68; cxlv. 9. On the distinction between the 'bonitas Dei' which impels GOD to surround Himself with creation, and the 'benignitas' which leads Him to confer His benefits on the creatures of His Hand, see Bp. Pearson, *Minor Theol. Works*, vol. i. pp. 73–75. The Incarnation was the Supreme Manifestation of this Attribute, Tit. iii. 4 ἡ χρηστότης καὶ ἡ φιλανθρωπία ἐπεφάνη τοῦ Σωτῆρος ἡμῶν Θεοῦ. See especially Tertullian, *adv. Marcion.* ii. c. 4; Lessius, *De Perfectionibus Moribusque Divinis*, lib. xii; Martensen, *Dogmatik*, § 50 sub fin.; Grimm, *Inst. Theol. Dogm. Ev.* p. 210.]

b. ἀποτομία, the penal severity of GOD's Justice (ver. 22).

[*Obs.* ἀποτομία, 'pars justitiae, quae ita scelera ulciscitur, ut nihil de supplicio remittat, sed resecet atque exigat omnia ad vivum,' Justinian. The subst. only here. Wisd. v. 21 ἀπότομος ὀργή: 2 Cor. xiii. 10 ἀποτόμως χρήσωμαι: Tit. i. 13 ἔλεγχε αὐτοὺς ἀποτόμως. On the severity of the Divine Justice, guarded by Wisdom and Goodness, see Martensen, *Dogmatik*, § 50; Butler, *Analogy*, part i. c. 2; Lessius, *De Perfect. Mor. Div.* lib. xiii. cc. 13, 14; Grimm, *Inst. Theol. Dogm. Ev.* p. 208; Newman, *Univ. Sermons*, Ser. 5, 'On Justice as a principle of Divine Governance.']

(II.) Present operation of these Attributes (ver. 22).

  a. Of Divine Severity, ἐπὶ τοὺς πεσόντας, on the unbelieving Israelites (ver. 22).

[*Obs.* 1. ἐπί is here used of the direction of will and aim, the Attributes being really the Divine Will under particular aspects. See Winer, *Gr. N. T.* p. 509.]

[*Obs.* 2. The unbelieving Israelites are here called πεσόντες, although (ver. 11) they did not stumble ἵνα πέσωσι. πίπτειν is here used, not of a final lapse from GOD, as when opposed to πταίειν, but, in view of the metaphor of the falling branch which has been severed, as describing that which inevitably followed on the ἀποβολή, ver. 15.]

  b. Of Divine Goodness, ἐπί σε, i. e. on the converted heathen (ver. 22).

[*Obs.* The order of the Attributes is here reversed, but with the words ἐὰν ἐπιμείνῃς (ver. 22) the Apostle's thought turns back again to its original order.]

(III.) Future and contingent operation of these Attributes (vers. 22 b–24).

  a. In the case of the converted heathen, χρηστότης may give place to ἀποτομία (ver. 22 b).

Dogmatic: ch. XI, vv. 11-24.

1. All depends on the convert's resolution ἐπιμένειν ἐν τῇ χρηστότητι,—to rest by faith, and obedience, in the encompassing Benevolence of GOD (ver. 22 b).

[*Obs.* χρηστότης here does not mean human good conduct, but Divine Goodness, as the context requires. The mode of abiding in the Divine Goodness is faith, which apprehends It. Clement. Alex. *Paedag.* I. 8. p. 140 τοῦτ' ἔστι τῇ εἰς Χριστὸν πίστει. ἐπιμένειν is generally used thus with reference to a human grace, virtue, or habit, or quality, rather than to a Divine attribute. Cf. Acts xiii. 43 ἐπιμένειν τῇ χάριτι: Rom. vi. 1 τῇ ἁμαρτίᾳ: Col. i. 23 τῇ πίστει. The Divine χρηστότης is here conceived of as a sphere of being in which man *may* rest, while he also *may* wilfully plunge out of it by a sinful or unbelieving act.]

2. If the convert from heathenism does sever himself by unbelief or by sin from the goodness of GOD, then he also will be cut off (from the sacred Tree), (ver. 22 b).

[*Obs.* 1. ἐπεί, 'since, if otherwise, then,' &c. The threatening character of the discourse suggests the stronger term ἐκκοπήσῃ, as an act of the Divine ἀποτομία. The unfaithful convert will no longer be living in the sphere of the Divine χρηστότης.]

[*Obs.* 2. ἐπεὶ καὶ σὺ ἐκκοπήσῃ. This is a *dictum probans* for the possibility of the loss of grace by the regenerate. The assumption that such loss is only possible when there was a feigned or hypocritical faith, is at issue with the fact that the heathen convert who is addressed, had at his conversion and baptism been actually grafted into the spiritual olive tree; cf. 1 Cor. ix. 27.]

b. In the case of the unbelieving Israelite, ἀποτομία may give place to χρηστότης (vers. 23, 24).

Prop. If the Israelites do not remain fixed in unbelief, they will be grafted into the Tree of the Church (ver. 23 a).

Arg. 1. From the Omnipotence of GOD, (γάρ ver. 23). If the cause, ἀπιστίᾳ, on account of which GOD broke off these branches, has ceased to exist, His power to restore them to their old places cannot be questioned (ver. 23 b).

[*Obs.* 1. πάλιν is not redundant; it suggests that the ἐγκέντρισις will restore the believing Israelites to their previous place of honour on the Tree of the Patriarchs. With δυνατὸς γάρ ἐστιν ὁ Θεός, comp. iv. 21; xiv. 4; 2 Cor. ix. 8; 2 Tim. i. 12; Heb. xi. 19.]

[*Obs.* 2. This whole passage shows, (1) that grace is not indefectible, since man may fall from it; (2) that, having been forfeited, it may be recovered; (3) that, viewed from the human side, and in each particular case, predestination is not to be deemed absolute.]

Arg. 2. A minori ad majus. The restoration of converted Jews to the Patriarchal communion must from the nature of the case be more natural than the conversion of the heathen (ver. 24).

[*Obs.* 1. γάρ (ver. 24) introduces a further explanation of the argument in ver. 23 b. The argument is, that Omnipotence would find less to do in promoting the conversion of the Jews; since, unlike the conversion of the heathen, it is only a recurrence to an order of things which has already existed. πόσῳ μᾶλλον does not so much suggest what is done *more easily* than another; as what follows, in the course of things and logically, *more surely* or *more probably*: cf. ver. 12; S. Matt. vii. 11; x. 25; S. Luke xii. 24, 28; Philem. 16; Heb. ix. 14. So πόλλῳ μᾶλλον Rom. v. 9, 10, 15, 17; 1 Cor. xii. 22; 2 Cor. iii. 9, 11; Phil. ii. 12. This completes the reason for ἐγκεντρισθήσονται ver. 23.]

[*Obs.* 2. The contrasts are as follows:—

If the heathen convert $\begin{cases} \text{ἐκ τῆς} \\ \text{κατὰ} \\ \text{φύσιν} \\ \text{ἀγριελαίου} \end{cases}$ $\Big\}$ ἐξεκόπη καὶ $\begin{cases} \text{παρὰ} \\ \text{φύσιν} \\ \text{εἰς} \\ \text{καλλιέλαιον} \end{cases}$ $\Big\}$ ἐνεκεντρίσθη

πόσῳ μᾶλλον shall converted Jews (οὗτοι) $\begin{cases} \text{οἱ κατὰ} \\ \text{φύσιν} \\ \text{(ἐκ τῆς} \\ \text{καλλι-} \\ \text{ελαίου)} \end{cases}$ [ὄντες] $\begin{cases} \text{τῇ ἰδίᾳ} \\ \text{ἐλαίᾳ} \end{cases}$ $\Big\}$ ἐγκεντρισθήσονται.

The heathen who is converted to Christ has, (1) to be cut off from the wild tree of heathen life (ἐξεκόπη), and (2) to be grafted *praeter naturam* on the Tree of the People of Revelation, with which he has no previous affinities. Neither of these efforts of grace has to be made in the case of the Jewish convert to Christianity. He has not to be violently separated from an irreligious human society, since by descent he already belongs to the People of Revelation; and his conversion, and insertion into the Church of Christ, is so far from involving anything 'unnatural,' that it only replaces him in the position for which he was already destined by his theocratic antecedents.]

[*Obs.* 3. Observe the sustained contrast between κατὰ φύσιν and παρὰ φύσιν. The Tree of the Patriarchs, now become the Catholic Church of Christ, is the ἰδία ἐλαία of the unbelieving Jews. They have grown upon it; and they have been cut off from it. It is still their own, if they only knew it.]

Consolation III.

A bright future is yet in store for Israel, (πᾶς 'Ισραὴλ σωθήσεται ver. 26), notwithstanding the present failure of the majority to attain δικαιοσύνη Θεοῦ ἐκ πίστεως (vers. 25–32).

Dogmatic: ch. XI, vv. 25-32.

Prop. The πώρωσις of the majority of Israelites will only last until the full number of the heathen have by conversion entered the Church of GOD, after which the whole of Israel will be saved (ver. 26).

In this prop. remark

(1) its *importance*: the heathen converts in Rome must not be ignorant of it (ver. 25).

[*Obs.* Although it appears as a corroboration (γάρ) οἱ ἐγκεντρισθήσονται (ver. 24), the prop. is introduced by the Apostle's accustomed formula of peculiar solemnity, οὐ θέλω ὑμᾶς ἀγνοεῖν (cf. i. 13; 1 Cor. x. 1; xii. 1; 2 Cor. i. 8; 1 Thess. iv. 13), reinforced by the fervent address, ἀδελφοί.]

(2) its *character*: it is a μυστήριον (ver. 25).

[*Obs.* μυστήριον properly an adj. Μύω, 'to close,' and 'to be shut,' especially of the lips or eyes; whence μύστης, 'initiatus,' the man who will not improperly disclose the secrets entrusted to him. Μυστήριον is that which is so made known to the μύστης, while it is hidden from mankind at large. This sense of the word is *essentially* that which is found in the Christian Fathers. S. Chrys. *in loc.* (ix. p. 651) μυστήριον = τὸ ἀγνοούμενον καὶ ἀπόρρητον, καὶ πολὺ μὲν τὸ θαῦμα, πολὺ δὲ τὸ παράδοξον ἔχον: and Theodoret, μυστήριόν ἐστι τὸ μὴ πᾶσι γνωριμόν, ἀλλὰ μόνοις τοῖς θεωρουμένοις. Practically the New Testament use of the word agrees with this; since μυστήριον means in the New Testament that which having been from all eternity known only to GOD, and hidden from all created intelligences, and so inaccessible to man's natural reason, is now graciously disclosed to the Apostles, and through them to Christians, while it is still withheld from all outside this circle,—from the world and the worldly wise. The μυστήριον is ἀποκεκρυμμένον ἀπὸ τῶν αἰώνων, Eph. iii. 9; Col. i. 26. The σοφία which it contains is still (1 Cor. ii. 7, 8) ἡ ἀποκεκρυμμένη . . . ἣν οὐδεὶς τῶν ἀρχόντων τοῦ αἰῶνος τούτου ἔγνωκεν. Cf. S. Matt. xi. 25 sqq. Yet ἡμῖν ὁ Θεὸς ἀπεκάλυψε διὰ τοῦ πνεύματος αὐτοῦ is the language of Apostles, 1 Cor. ii. 10; the Holy Spirit is the Initiator; the Apostles are μύσται, as having τὴν σύνεσιν ἐν τῷ μυστηρίῳ τοῦ Χριστοῦ, Eph. iii. 4-9. The New Testament μυστήριον then is something which natural understanding does not discover, and which is made known to the chosen band of faithful by a positive revelation of the Holy Spirit. The great truths of Christianity are μυστήρια, 1 Cor. xiii. 12: cf. μυστήρια τῆς βασιλείας τῶν οὐρανῶν S. Matt. xiii. 11; S. Mark iv. 11; S. Luke viii. 10. Among such μυστήρια are the nature and development of the work of Christ in the Divine kingdom, S. Matt. xiii. 11; the incorporation of the heathen into the Church of Christ, Eph. iii. 4 sqq.; the spiritual union of Christ with His Church, Eph. v. 32; the change which will pass upon the bodies of those who are still alive at the second coming of Christ, 1 Cor. xv. 51 sqq.; especially μέγα τὸ τῆς εὐσεβείας μυστήριον, that is, the Incarnation and Glorification of the Son of GOD, 1 Tim. iii. 16, &c. Unless the Sacraments are included under μυστήρια Θεοῦ in 1 Cor. iv. 1, they do not seem to be called mysteries in the New Testament. But the word was naturally applied to them on account of their restriction to those who were admitted to the fellowship of Christian faith, and with reference to their 'inward and spiritual grace,' the reality of which was only known to Christians. μυστήριον is used of the Eucharist by S. Greg. Naz. *Or.* 41. p. 740 (ed. Par. 1778); Conc. Laod. *Can.* 7, &c. The Eucharistic μυστήρια are said by S. Chrys. to be θαυμαστά, φρικτά, ἅγια, θεῖα, τελεστικά. See Suicer *in voc.* Observe that the original character of 'mystery,' as 'something originally hidden, comprehended only by the initiated, and concealed from the profane,' is not forfeited by the Divine ἀποκάλυψις to the Apostles; the ἀποκάλυψις does not *ipso facto* destroy the 'mystery,' by putting the Christian Apostles and Church in possession of it. For (1) the Christian believer receives the truth contained in the μυστήριον as a μύστης, (2) while this truth is hidden from the uninitiated world, and (3) is itself still in some respects incomprehensible and inconceivable to those who apprehend it, since it reaches away into spheres beyond their range of mental vision. In the popular use of the word this specific element of surviving incomprehensibleness is dwelt upon more particularly than the other elements of 'mystery,' and so far the proportions, rather than the constituent features, of the Scriptural conception are lost sight of. Here, as in 1 Cor. xv. 51, S. Paul is conscious of having received a special μυστήριον, which he forthwith announces. The prop. which follows is ἀποκάλυψις μυστηρίου Rom. xvi. 25; 1 Cor. ii. 7–10. The account of μυστήριον given by Toland, *Christianity not Mysterious,* sect. 3. chaps. 2, 3, by Meyer *in loc.* and others, ignores the real continuity of signification in the classical and Christian uses of the word.]

(3) Its *intention*: to suppress a false-conceit of knowledge in the heathen converts (ἵνα μὴ ἦτε παρ' ἑαυτοῖς φρόνιμοι), (ver. 25).

[*Obs.* παρ' ἑαυτοῖς φρόνιμοι here (as at xii. 16; Prov. iii. 7 LXX) means possession of the contracted wisdom which never passes the frontier of mere natural subjective reflection and experimental knowledge. It corresponds to חָכָם בְּעֵינֶיךָ Prov. iii. 7. 'Insultare lapsis ... non fit per Dei sapientiam, sed per humanam,' Origen, iv. p. 639. On παρά with dat. *of opinion,* see Winer, *Gr. N. T.* p. 493.]

(4) Its *contents* (vers. 25 b, 26 a).

[*Obs.* ὅτι (ver. 25) introduces the contents of the μυστήριον which is contained in the words πώρωσις ... σωθήσεται. It does not end at γέγονεν.]

ὅτι {
(i) A πώρωσις has befallen Israel, (*a*) ἀπὸ μέρους partially and (*b*) for a predetermined period (ver. 25).
(ii) The πώρωσις of Israel will cease, when the full number of the heathen shall enter [the Church of GOD], (ver. 25).
(iii) Correspondingly with which consummation all Israel will be saved (ver. 26).
}

[*Obs.* 1. ἀπὸ μέρους (ver. 25) is connected with γέγονεν (compare τινές ver. 17): it recognises the fact that many Israelites were not victims to the πώρωσις,

Dogmatic: ch. XI, vv. 25-32.

since they were already converts to Christ. For γέγονεν, see ver. 8 ἔδωκεν αὐτοῖς ὁ Θεός: cf. ver. 20. The πώρωσις as a penal visitation from GOD, 2 Cor. iii. 14.]

[*Obs.* 2. ἄχρις οὗ εἰσέλθῃ (ver. 25), usque dum intraverit. In εἰσέλθῃ the metaphor of the Olive Tree is dropped, and the Church which it symbolises has taken its place in the Apostle's thought. The word, like עַל and בָּא in the Rabbinical writers, has a recognised sense when used absolutely, as in S. Matt. vii. 13; xxiii. 14; S. Luke xiii. 24 εἰς τὴν βασιλείαν, εἰς τὴν ζωήν or εἰς τὴν χαράν, being understood. Here every reader would understand εἰς τὴν βασιλείαν τοῦ Θεοῦ. τὸ πλήρωμα τῶν ἐθνῶν = πάντες οἱ προεγνωσμένοι ἐθνικοί, (Theodoret,) i. e. the full complement, as fixed in the Divine foreknowledge. Had every single individual heathen been meant, the expression would have been stronger. In ver. 12 πλήρωμα as here = that by which completeness is secured, as in S. Matt. ix. 16; Rom. xiii. 10; xv. 29; and even Eph. i. 23; Col. i. 19. On the preaching of the Gospel to all nations, see S. Matt. xxiv. 14; S. Mark xiii. 10.]

[*Obs.* 3. καὶ οὕτω does not = καὶ τότε: but it expresses the relation of causality between the conversion of Jews and that of the heathens, already referred to in ver. 11. Whenever a time arrives at which all the heathen nations of the world have entered within the Church of GOD, the Jews too, seeing themselves cut off from a Religion in which all others have found happiness and blessing, will finally come to Christ for salvation. The intermediate period is described in Hos. iii. 4, 5 'The children of Israel shall abide many days without a king, and without a prince, and without a sacrifice, and without an image, and without an ephod, and without teraphim : afterward shall the children of Israel return, and seek the Lord their GOD.' See Pusey, *Minor Prophets*, p. 24 *in loc.* The period preceding Israel's conversion is the καιροὶ ἐθνῶν S. Luke xxi. 24. That πᾶς Ἰσραήλ means the whole Jewish nation appears from πλήρωμα αὐτῶν (ver. 12), and the antithetical expression ἀπὸ μέρους (ver. 25). For the Christian tradition that Elijah will be the instrument of the conversion of his countrymen, see Theodoret *in loc.*; S. Aug. *de Civ. Dei*, xx. 29; S. Justin Martyr, *Dial. cum Tryph.* c. 49.]

[*Obs.* 4. πᾶς Ἰσραήλ is understood of the *Spiritual* Israel (Gal. vi. 16), composed of elect heathen as well as Jews, by Theod.; S. Aug. *Ep. ad Paulin.* cxlix. cap. ii. 19; as later by Luther, who denies the possibility of converting Jews (*Werke*, ed. Walch. Th. xx. p. 2529, 'Ein Jude, oder Jüdisch Herz ist so stock-stein-eisen-teufelhart, das mit keiner Weise zu bewegen ist'); and the Reformers generally. But the *context* requires the *literal* Israel; considering, (i) what is meant by πλήρωμα αὐτῶν, ver. 12; (ii) the subject of ἐὰν μὴ ἐπιμείνωσι τῇ ἀπιστίᾳ, ἐγκεντρισθήσονται ver. 23; (iii) the parallel instituted between the Jews and the Heathen in vers. 30, 31; and (iv) ἵνα τοὺς πάντας ἐλεήσῃ ver. 32. Israel's entrance as a nation into the Church of Christ, although contrary to all present probabilities, is a climax of the μυστήριον disclosed by the Apostle in vers. 25, 26. So Origen, S. Chrys., S. Ambr., and (in *de Civ. Dei*, xx. 29; *Quaest. Evang.* ii. 33) S. Augustine; S. Jerome, while on one occasion treating this interpretation as judaizing, (*Comm. in Is.* xi) more often adopts it (in Hos. iii. 5; in Hab. iii. 17).]

Considerations which illustrate the closing statement of the μυστήριον, viz. that eventually πᾶς Ἰσραὴλ σωθήσεται (vers. 25 b–32).

[This proposition, that 'all Israel will be saved' by Christ, is not so much *established* by argument, (since it is part of the μυστήριον disclosed to the Apostle ἐν ἀποκαλύψει,) as shown to harmonize with facts and prophecies which have an immediate bearing on its subject-matter (vers. 25 b–32).]

Arg. 1. That 'all Israel will be saved' in harmony with prophecy (καθὼς γέγραπται), (vers. 26, 27).

Isaiah lix. 20, 21, blended with Is. xxvii. 9, and quoted to show that those who reject Messiah will be converted and pardoned, and that thus, as a consequence, the Messianic σωτηρία will be extended to all Israel (vers. 26, 27).

Heb. Is. lix. 20, 21.   וּבָא לְצִיּוֹן גּוֹאֵל
                            וּלְשָׁבֵי פֶשַׁע בְּיַעֲקֹב
                            נְאֻם יְהוָה :

'And there comes for Zion a Redeemer,
And for those who turn from apostasy in Jacob,
Saith Jehovah.

                            וַאֲנִי זֹאת בְּרִיתִי אוֹתָם
                            אָמַר יְהוָה

And I, this is My Covenant with them,
Saith Jehovah.

Is. xxvii. 9.   לָכֵן בְּזֹאת יְכֻפַּר עֲוֹן־יַעֲקֹב
                            וְזֶה כָּל־פְּרִי הָסִר חַטָּאתוֹ

'Therefore in this will be purged the guilt of Jacob,
And this [is] all the fruit of the taking-away his sin.'

LXX Is. lix. 20, 21 καὶ ἥξει ἕνεκεν Σιὼν ὁ ῥυόμενος, καὶ ἀποστρέψει ἀσεβείας ἀπὸ Ἰακώβ· καὶ αὕτη αὐτοῖς ἡ παρ' ἐμοῦ διαθήκη, εἶπε Κύριος κ.τ.λ.

Is. xxvii. 9 (διὰ τοῦτο ἀφαιρεθήσεται ἀνομία Ἰακώβ, καὶ τοῦτό ἐστιν ἡ εὐλογία αὐτοῦ,) ὅταν ἀφέλωμαι τὴν ἁμαρτίαν αὐτοῦ κ.τ.λ.

[*Obs* 1. Citation.   ἥξει ἐκ Σιὼν ὁ ῥυόμενος,
                     (καὶ) ἀποστρέψει ἀσεβείας ἀπὸ Ἰακώβ·
                     καὶ αὕτη αὐτοῖς ἡ παρ' ἐμοῦ διαθήκη,
                     ὅταν ἀφέλωμαι τὰς ἁμαρτίας αὐτῶν.

Here (1) ἐκ Σιών in the citation corresponds to לְצִיּוֹן and LXX ἕνεκεν Σιών. The change of proposition is probably an intentional variation from the (LXX and Heb.) text of Isaiah, suggested by Ps. xiv. 7, liii. 6, in order to bring into stronger relief the promises made to the Jewish people. (2) ἀποστρέψει ἀσεβείας ἀπὸ Ἰακώβ (cit. and LXX) corresponds to וּלְשָׁבֵי פֶשַׁע בְּיַעֲקֹב, 'and unto them that turn from transgression in Jacob.' The LXX may have read וְיָשׁוּב פֶּשַׁע מִיַּעֲקֹב. The Syr. reads וְהֵשִׁיב for לְשָׁבֵי. (3) αὕτη, pointing to the following clause in the LXX (Is. lix. 21), refers to the words of the covenant, τὸ πνεῦμα τὸ ἐμὸν οὐ μὴ ἐκλίπῃ ἐκ τοῦ στόματος κ.τ.λ.; but in the citation, it refers to the words substituted from Isaiah xxvii. 9 ὅταν ἀφέλωμαι κ.τ.λ. The fundamental unity of Revelation deprives this substitution of any real arbitrariness.]

[*Obs.* 2. Is. lix. 20, 21 follows Isaiah's statement of the sins which retarded Israel's Redemption. The subject of וּבָא is Jehovah. He comes for Zion, as a Redeemer, and those who turn away from apostasy, שָׁבֵי פֶשַׁע. A double object of redemption is specified: (1) Zion, the Church which has remained true, and more especially, (2) those who turn again from their previous apostasy. See Delitzsch *in loc.* Is. xxvii. 9 occurs almost at the end of the last portion of The Great Catastrophe (chaps. xxiv-xxvii), where the Prophet is describing the chastisement and salvation of Israel, xxvii. 7-13. Israel's punishment would cease as soon as its purpose was secured; it would cease at once, if Israel would renounce its sin, especially idolatry. In the original of Is. xxvii. 9 the final conversion of Israel is not alluded to, and yet the language would only receive its complete fulfilment at that event.]

[*Obs.* 3. ὁ ῥυόμενος, the Messiah: גֹּאֵל. Christ self-revealed in His teaching Church (Eph. ii. 17) will convert Israel. גֹּאֵל is used of GOD, redeeming Israel from Egypt, Ex. iv. 6; from Babylon, Is. xliii. 1; xliv. 22; xlviii. 20; xlix. 7; and absolutely of Messiah, Ps. lxxii. 14; Is. li. 10; Job xix. 25.]

[*Obs.* 4. ἡ παρ' ἐμοῦ διαθήκη does not = ἡ ἐμὴ διαθήκη, but = the covenant *which proceeded from* Me. αὕτη refers to ὅταν ἀφέλωμαι, where ὅταν is not temporal, but a particle of definition. 'In eo testamentum hoc implebitur quod auferam,' &c. Closely connected with this passage is Jer. xxxi. 33, 34. The New Covenant was to consist not in the bestowal of a new outward Law, but in the forgiveness of transgressions, preceding the gift of the Spirit, Who would enforce the Evangelical Law as an inward principle.]

Arg. 2. That 'all Israel *will* be saved' is not inconsistent with existing facts. For Israel has a double aspect. Israelites are

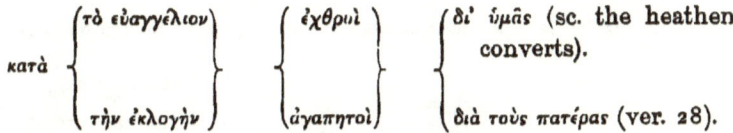

$$\kappa\alpha\tau\grave{\alpha} \begin{Bmatrix} \tau\grave{o}\ \epsilon\dot{v}\alpha\gamma\gamma\acute{\epsilon}\lambda\iota o\nu \\ \\ \tau\grave{\eta}\nu\ \dot{\epsilon}\kappa\lambda o\gamma\grave{\eta}\nu \end{Bmatrix} \begin{Bmatrix} \dot{\epsilon}\chi\theta\rho o\acute{\iota} \\ \\ \dot{\alpha}\gamma\alpha\pi\eta\tau o\acute{\iota} \end{Bmatrix} \begin{Bmatrix} \delta\iota'\ \dot{v}\mu\hat{\alpha}s\ \text{(sc. the heathen converts).} \\ \\ \delta\iota\grave{\alpha}\ \tau o\grave{v}s\ \pi\alpha\tau\acute{\epsilon}\rho\alpha s\ \text{(ver. 28).} \end{Bmatrix}$$

[*Obs.* In respect of the Gospel Message, which they rejected, the majority of Israelites are under GOD's wrath (ἐχθροί), since they have refused the means of attaining δικαιοσύνη Θεοῦ, and this was (in the design of Providence) for the sake of the heathen (δι' ὑμᾶς), who were thus enabled to attain to σωτηρία (ver. 11). But in respect of the elect remnant (ἐκλογή = λεῖμμα, see vers. 5, 7), the minority of Israelites, with whom was lodged the promise of the future, Israel is beloved by GOD for the sake of the Patriarchs, whose faithfulness and privileges this remnant shared. (S. Luke i. 54, 55.) The existence of this minority shows that the preceding prophecy (vers. 26 b, 27) and μυστήριον were on the road to fulfilment.]

Arg. 3. That 'all Israel will be saved' is in accordance with that rule of the Divine government of the world, which makes GOD's gifts to, and calling of, men irrevocable (ver. 29).

[*Obs.* 1. This (ver. 39) is immediately a reason (γάρ) for the preceding statement (ver. 28) that Israelites, so far as the elect-remnant is concerned, are still beloved of GOD, for the sake of the Patriarchs. The κλῆσις τοῦ Θεοῦ can, in connection with what precedes, only refer to the calling of the people of Israel in the person of the Patriarchs to the salvation through Messiah, that formed the main purport of the Divine covenant-promise. This call, as it cannot be retracted, must yet be realized. It might have been suggested that the Divine Gifts and Calls vouchsafed to the Patriarchs were now altogether things of the past. But to this the Apostle replies practically, that there is no Past for the Eternal Mind, before which the Past and Future are spread out as an illimitable present; and, therefore, that the anthropomorphic conceptions of forgetfulness or change of purpose are wholly irrelevant. GOD, having once made Israel the recipient of His Gifts, and having called it to salvation through His Son, will not now leave it to itself. That He has done so much, is an earnest that He will do more. On ἀμεταμέλητα, see 2 Cor. vii. 10. God would not recall gifts which He could not repent of having given.]

[*Obs.* 2. The axiom ἀμεταμέλητα τὰ χαρίσματα καὶ ἡ κλῆσις τοῦ Θεοῦ is not inconsistent with the fact that Divine Gifts are withdrawn, and Divine Calls neglected and wasted. 'Et tamen ipsum temporale Dei donum et temporalis vocatio non irritatur per mutationem Dei, quasi poenitentis, sed per mutationem hominis qui gratiam Dei abjicit.' (Aquin.) On the Immutability of GOD, in virtue of which 'non potest ita mutari ut aliquid velit, quod prius nollet; ut aliquid nolit, quod prius vellet,' see Pearson, *Min. Theol. Works*, i. pp. 93, 94; Petavius, *De Deo, Deique prop.* lib. iii. cap. 2.]

Arg. 4. That 'all Israel will be saved' is suggested by the case of the converts from heathenism (vers. 30, 31).

[*Obs.* This parallel is introduced as a sensible proof (γάρ) of the truth of the axiom stated in ver. 29.]

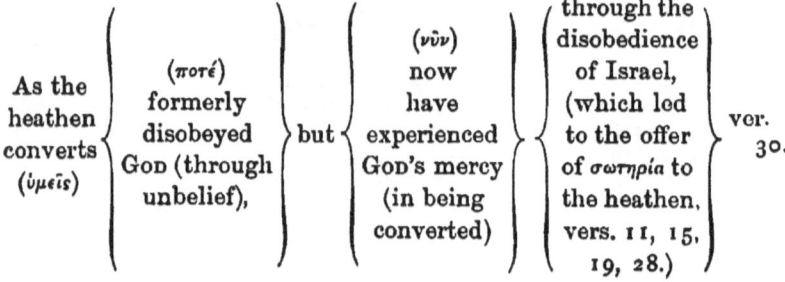

Dogmatic : ch. XI, *vv.* 33-36.   221

| So the unconverted Jews (οὗτοι) | have disobeyed GOD (by rejecting the Gospel), | but | in order that they too should experience GOD's mercy (in being converted) | through the mercy that was shown to the heathen (as in ver. 12) and which will stimulate them. | ver. 31. |

[*Obs.* τῷ ὑμετέρῳ ἐλέει is emphatically placed before ἵνα for the sake of emphasis (see 1 Cor. ix. 15; 2 Cor. ii. 4; Gal. ii. 10; Winer, *Gr. N. T.* p. 688), and the comma must be placed after ἠπείθησαν, not after ἐλέει. On the objective force of ὑμετέρῳ, the mercy shown *to* you, see Winer, *Gr. N. T.* p. 191. ἵνα (ver. 31) introduces the Divine purpose with which ἠπείθησαν was permitted.]

Arg. 5. That 'all Israel will be saved' is involved in the universal method of GOD's government, namely, that He has given over all to unbelief at one period, that He may, at a later period, have mercy upon all by bringing them to the True Faith (ver. 32).

[*Obs.* 1. ver. 32 is given as the general principle which warrants (γάρ) the specific historical statement about the heathen converts to Christ in ver. 30, and consequently the inference respecting the now disobedient and unbelieving majority of Israel in ver. 31.]

[*Obs.* 2. συγκλείειν εἰς = הִסְגִּיר בְּיַד with either לְ or אֶל, as in Ps. xxxi. 9; lxxviii. 50. So in later Greek, (Diod. Sic. xix. 19 εἰς τοιαύτην ἀμηχανίαν συγκλεισθεὶς Ἀντίγονος μετεμέλετο,) it = 'to hand over to or put under the power of.' Thus it expresses the same idea as παρέδωκε Rom. i. 24. In Deut. xxxii. 30; Job xvi. 11, הִסְגִּיר is rendered by παραδίδωμι. The best parallel is Gal. iii. 22 συνέκλεισεν ἡ γραφὴ τὰ πάντα ὑφ' ἁμαρτίαν. See S. Luke v. 6. συνέκλεισε is not merely permissive; it describes a penal visitation after unfaithfulness to whatever degree of light and grace. This visitation consists in the privation of GOD's assistance, whereby fallen man is shut up into the sphere of his own downward tendencies. The context obliges us to understand τοὺς πάντας not of all human beings collectively, but of all *peoples*, specially Jews and heathens. Origen attempts to appropriate the passage in the interests of his theory of a general ἀποκατάστασις.]

E.

Concluding Doxology (vers. 33-36).

[*Obs.* At the close of the Doctrinal portion of the Epistle, the Apostle is moved to offer to GOD an enraptured expression of praise (vers. 33-36), before he passes to the hortatory and ethical part of the Epistle. Especially this is prompted by the immediately preceding description of the slow and intricate processes whereby the Divine Will is accomplished in history, and above all by the final statement (ver. 32) how evil is overruled by and made subservient to the purposes of good.]

I. Adoring wonder at contemplating the three Divine Attributes, which are chiefly observable in the foregoing discussion, chap. ix. 1 to xi. 32 (ver. 33 a).

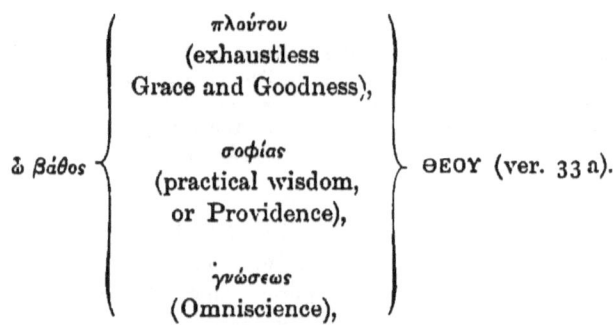

[*Obs*. 1. βάθος expresses the felt unfathomableness of the Attributes of the Infinite Being, when contemplated by a created intelligence. S. Chrys. ix. p. 653 θαυμάζοντός ἐστιν ἡ ῥῆσις, οὐκ εἰδότος τὸ πᾶν. On the use of βάθος, βαθύς, to suggest great fulness and abundance, see the reff. in Meyer, *in loc.* That πλούτου, σοφίας, and γνώσεως must be co-ordinated as all depending *immediately* on βάθος (S. Chrys., Theodor., Theophyl.), instead of treating βάθος πλούτου as = βαθὺς πλοῦτος, and σοφίας, γνώσεως, as the treasures which constitute the πλοῦτος (S. Aug., Ambr., &c.), see Winer, *Gr. N. T.* p. 238.]

[*Obs*. 2. Of the three Attributes, (1) πλοῦτος is the superabundant wealth of the Divine Resources, as shown especially in GOD'S saving φιλανθρωπία and χρηστότης, abounding to the happiness of all, ver. 32. πλοῦτος stands independently in Phil. iv. 19 as a Divine Attribute; in Rom. xi. 12, for human endowments; cf. Eph. iii. 8 ἀνεξιχνίαστος πλοῦτος Χριστοῦ : and Rom. ii. 4; x. 12; Eph. i. 7; ii. 4, 7; Tit. iii. 6. (2) σοφία, prudential wisdom (Rom. xvi. 27; Eph. iii. 10), disposing everything in the best way, and with a view to its final purpose; as shown in the abandonment of the heathen and election of the Jews, then in the rejection of the Jews and the conversion of the heathen, which finally leads to the conversion of the Jews. (3 γνῶσις, GOD'S knowledge. especially directed towards events still future to and unknown by man, as here the conversion of the majority of the Jews. Thus σοφία is less purely intellectual than γνῶσις : in man σοφία is practical wisdom, as opposed to higher theoretical knowledge, γνῶσις : 1 Cor. xii. 8; Eph. v. 15. Even in Col. ii. 3 the distinction is not lost. In GOD σοφία and γνῶσις are nearly contrasted as Providence with Omniscience; cf. 1 Cor. i. 21 and 2 Cor. x. 5, where τοῦ Θεοῦ is gen. subj. Each Attribute is here viewed by the Apostle in its relation to the Divine Government of the

Dogmatic: ch. XI, vv. 33-36.

world and the Oeconomy of Salvation. On the Providence of God, see Pearson, *Min. Theol. Works*, vol. i. pp. 232-242; Petavius, *De Deo*, lib. viii. c. 4. On the Knowledge of God, see Pearson, *ubi supra*, pp. 149-205; Petavius, *De Deo*, lib. iv. c. 1-7; Martensen, *Dogmatik*, §§ 49, 50.]

II. Expansion of the contemplation of the Three Attributes (vers. 33 b-36).

[*Obs.* The order of 33 a is varied. Instead of πλοῦτος, σοφία, γνῶσις, we have σοφία, γνῶσις, πλοῦτος.]

1. βάθος σοφίας. This is contemplated in the ἀνεξερεύνητα κρίματα of God. His secret resolves or decisions, according to which His action upon the world is governed, elude all human efforts to discover the causes or reasons which shape them (ver. 33 b).

[*Obs.* Compare Ps. xix. 6; xxxvi. 7: מִשְׁפָּטֶיךָ תְּהוֹם רַבָּה. The Divine judgments are as difficult to explore as the depths of the ocean. For ἀνεξερεύνητα, see Prov. xxv. 3, Symm.; Jer. xvii. 9; ἅπ. λεγ. in New Testament. It is the depth of the σοφία of God, which makes His decisions unsearchable by man. The κρῖμα especially in view of the Apostle is that in ver. 32, viz. that all should be disobedient, in order that all might find mercy.]

2. βάθος γνώσεως. This is contemplated in the ἀνεξιχνίαστοι ὁδοί of God. His modes of procedure, whereby He carries His decisions into effect, can be tracked out by no human discoverer, since they are known only to His Omniscience (ver. 33 b).

[*Obs.* 1. ὁδοί, used of the methods pursued by God in His dealings with man, (αἱ οἰκονομίαι S. Chrys.): Heb. iii. 10; Acts xiii. 10; cf. the metaphorical use of ὁδοί in classical Greek, and of the Heb. דֶּרֶךְ. For ἀνεξιχνίαστοι, see Eph. iii. 8, where the epithet is applied to the πλοῦτος Χριστοῦ. Only the illimitable γνῶσις of God can track out the measures which He takes in His dealings with man; for man, when he would explore them, μηδ' ἴχνος ἐστὶν εὑρεῖν—there are no foot-marks to guide him.]

[*Obs.* 2. On the general subject of the Divine Incomprehensibility, see Job v. 9; ix. 10; xi. 7; Eccles. iii. 11; S. Aug. *Serm.* 117. iii. 5 'De Deo loquimur; quid mirum si non comprehendis? Si enim comprehendis, non est Deus ... Attingere aliquantum mente Deum magna beatitudo est; comprehendere autem omnino impossibile.' On ἀνεξερεύνητα, S. Chrys. argues, *in loc.* (p. 653) εἰ δὲ ἐρευνηθῆναι ἀδύνατον, πολλῷ μᾶλλον καταληφθῆναι ἀδυνατώτερον. See Pearson, *Min. Theol. Works*, i. pp. 128-134.]

3. Confirmation (γάρ) of the two foregoing contemplations from the words of Isaiah (ver. 34).

Is. xl. 13, quoted in illustration of the truth that GOD's Knowledge and His Providence are alike beyond the reach of human efforts to comprehend them (ver. 34).

Is. xl. 13.

Heb. מִי־תִכֵּן אֶת־רוּחַ יְהוָה
וְאִישׁ עֲצָתוֹ יוֹדִיעֶנּוּ׃

Transl. of Heb.
'Who brought the Spirit of Jehovah into conformity with rule? And (who) instructed Him as His Counsellor?'

LXX τίς ἔγνω νοῦν Κυρίου ;
καὶ τίς σύμβουλος αὐτοῦ ἐγένετο ;

[*Obs.* 1. The citation reads ἤ for καί in the LXX. ἔγνω expresses the cause of תִכֵּן—Who knew enough to regulate the mind of Jehovah?]

[*Obs.* 2. The quotation occurs among the questions which succeed the Prologue (xl. 1-11) to the second great division of Isaiah's Prophecy. The Prologue had announced the coming Redemption, and the incomparable Exaltation of Him Who was to redeem His people. The questions which follow are designed to rouse among the exiles this sense of the exaltation of the Lord; first as the Creator (vers. 12-14), and then as Governor of the world (vers. 15-17). Throughout these questions the antithesis presented by the popular idolatry is present to the writer's mind.]

[*Obs.* 3. In the quotation, the first line refers to the βάθος γνώσεως τοῦ Θεοῦ, the second to the βάθος σοφίας. Left to himself man cannot be privy as σύμβουλος to GOD's Providential decisions, nor can he discern the means which the Uncreated νοῦς knows to be the best for giving them effect. νοῦς, in GOD, is the 'Absolute Intelligence,' to which all ideas and the essence of things are eternally present. Here are τὰ βάθη τοῦ Θεοῦ 1 Cor. ii. 10. No created mind can penetrate these depths; GOD only can reveal any part of them: 1 Cor. ii. 7-15.]

[*Obs.* 4. For the sense of the quotation, compare Wisdom ix. 17; Ecclus. xviii. 2-5; Xen. *Mem.* i. 4. 17; Hesiod, *Fragm.* 196. The passage is quoted at 1 Cor. ii. 16, but with the purpose, not of suggesting the Incomprehensibleness of the Divine γνῶσις, but of asking a question, which is answered by an appeal to the gift of the Holy Spirit to the Apostles and Church of Christ.]

3. βάθος πλούτου. This Attribute is contemplated in the relation of the entire universe to GOD as His property. None can lay Him under obligations; since everything proceeds from Him, is sustained in existence by Him, and exists for His glory (vers. 35 b-36).

[*Obs.* In the case of this Attribute, the method pursued in the two preceding is inverted. The Old Testament quotation precedes the statement of facts in which the Attribute is to be contemplated.]

a. Job xli. 3, quoted to show that no man is in the position of receiving a recompense for any real gift or favour conferred by himself upon GOD; since we receive nothing but *grace*, and He has given us all that we are and have (ver. 35 b).

Heb.   מִי הִקְדִּימַנִי וַאֲשַׁלֵּם

Transl. of Heb.
'Who hath prevented me that I should repay him?'

LXX τίς ἀντιστήσεταί μοι καὶ ὑπομενεῖ;

[*Obs*. Citation. τίς προέδωκεν αὐτῷ, καὶ ἀνταποδοθήσεται αὐτῷ;

Here the LXX appears to represent some lost Hebrew text; while S. Paul follows, with a change of person, the existing Hebrew text closely. The words of the citation are found in the LXX Cod. A and ℵ at Is. xl. 14, close after those quoted in ver. 35. Ewald thinks that they may have existed there in the Apostle's copy of the LXX; but they are probably an interpolation in the LXX text from this passage in the Epistle.]

b. Reason for (ὅτι) the inevitable answer to the question asked in the words of Job. No one has been beforehand with GOD in conferring any kind of benefit, because the universe was already in the most absolute sense GOD's property, being related to Him as (i) its Creator, (ii) its Preserver, and (iii) its Last End (ver. 36).

[*Obs*. 1. The βάθος πλούτου is illustrated by this exhaustive account of the relation of all created beings to GOD. For εἰς αὐτόν, GOD as the Last End of all creatures, see Lessius, *de Div. Perfect.* lib. xiv.

τὰ πάντα {
  ἐξ αὐτοῦ, proceed from GOD the Creator as the source of being.
  δι' αὐτοῦ, are upheld in being by the instrumentality of GOD's continuous operation, without which they would relapse into nothingness.
  εἰς αὐτόν, are destined to promote His will and glory, since He is the Object and End of their existence.]

[*Obs*. 2. For these prepositions, cf. 1 Cor. viii. 6, where ἐξ and εἰς are used of the Father, διά of the Son; Col. i. 16, where δι' αὐτοῦ, εἰς αὐτόν, and ἐν αὐτῷ are used of Christ in His relation to the universe; Heb. ii. 10 δι' ὃν τὰ πάντα καὶ δι' οὗ τὰ πάντα is said of the Father; and Eph. iv. 6 ἐπὶ πάντων, διὰ πάντων, ἐν πᾶσιν, of GOD.]

[*Obs*. 3. The doctrine of the Holy Trinity is recognised in ver. 36 by Origen *in loc.*; S. Aug. *de Trin.* i. 6; S. Hilar. *de Trin.* viii. 38. Origen also finds it in ver. 33, referring πλοῦτος to the Father, σοφία to the Son, and γνῶσις to the Holy Ghost. In ver. 36 it is adumbrated by the language without being taught, since the drift of the passage is to describe not those Eternal Subsistences within the Divine Being Which are revealed to us, but His threefold relation to the universe. Yet ἐξ οὗ does describe the Father's relation to all created beings as their *original* source, and δι' οὗ the Son's work as *Organ* of creation (1 Cor. viii. 6; Col. i. 16), while εἰς ὅν may refer to the Holy Spirit, although this is rather suggested by its place in the clause than by intrinsic considerations.

The New Testament frequently expresses the
- (a) Father's
- (b) Son's
- (c) Holy Ghost's

relation to created things by

- (a) { ἐκ, as their source.
       { ἐπί, as governing them.
- (b) { διά, as the instrument of their creation and preservation.
- (c) { ἐν, as the element within
       { εἰς, as furnishing the ideal towards } which all things move.

Of these prepositions, however, ἐπί and εἰς are equally applicable to Each of the Divine Persons. And, indeed, ἐν and εἰς are used of the Son in Col. i. 16, and διά of the Father in Heb. ii. 10. All that can be maintained is that *upon the whole* the more restricted use of the prepositions is traceable.]

Ὦ
ἡ δόξα
εἰς τοὺς αἰῶνας.

[*Obs.* On ἡ δόξα, see xvi. 27; Gal. i. 5. *The* glory which befits GOD, and which cannot be given to any created being, is here ascribed to Him. The word is connected with ἔπαινος, Phil. i. 11; 1 S. Pet. i. 7; with τιμή, 1 Tim. i. 17; Heb. ii. 7, 9; 2 S. Pet. i. 17; Rev. iv. 11; with τιμή and εὐλογία, Rev. v. 12. It means the recognition of GOD as being what He is. The כְּבוֹד יְהוָה comprises all the Divine Perfections. See Cremer's *Biblico-Theol. Lexic.* s. v.]

PRACTICAL PORTION OF THE EPISTLE.

(XII. 1—XV. 13.)

[*Obs.* 1. The distribution of this, as of other Epistles of S. Paul, into a doctrinal and an ethical part is only a rough approximation to the truth. For as S. Paul's dogmatic teaching is constantly suggestive of practical consequences, so his moral and spiritual exhortations are continually based on dogma. Cf. xii. 4, 5; xiv. 9, 10; xv. 8-12 sqq.]

[*Obs.* 2. This practical part of the Epistle consists, (1) of a positive statement of the law and obligations of Christian Holiness (xi, xiii), and (2) of a discussion of questions of conscience respecting private observances, which were warmly agitated in the Roman Church (xiv. 1-xv. 12).]

Division I.

THE OBLIGATIONS OF CHRISTIAN MORALITY (xii, xiii).

[*Obs.* 1. These obligations are traced,

(A) in their application
- (i) to the natural being of the Christian, bodily and mental (xii. 1, 2).
- (ii) to the Christian, as a supernaturally-endowed member of the Body of Christ (xii. 3-8).
- (iii) to the Christian, as having various social relations both with fellow-believers and with heathens (xii. 9-21).
- (iv) to the Christian, as living under a (pagan) civil government (xiii. 1-7).

(B) to their animating principles
- (i) to the unlimited obligations of ἀγάπη (xiii. 8-10).
- (ii) to the never-ceasing lapse of time, and nearer approach of the eternal world (xiii. 11-14).]

[*Obs.* 2. On the relations between Christian Holiness and Christian Doctrine, see especially the Series of Sermons, Nos. 90-103, in Bishop Beveridge's *Works*, vol. v. pp. 20-257 (London, 1824).]

A.

Obligations of Christian Morality in various spheres of life and duty (xii. 1—xiii. 7).

§ 1.

Obligations of Christian Morality for the Christian, as possessing σῶμα *and* νοῦς (xii. 1, 2).

1. Consecration of the Christian's σῶμα to GOD (ver. 1).

   a. Its *importance*, shown by the terms of the Apostolic exhortation (παρακαλῶ ... διὰ τῶν οἰκτιρμῶν τοῦ Θεοῦ) (ver. 1).

   b. Its *character*. The body should be presented *in sacrifice* to GOD (ver. 1).

   This θυσία of the body is to be
   { ζῶσα (not *slain*, like the O. T. sacrifices).
   { ἁγία (like תמים, free from defects).
   { εὐάρεστος τῷ Θεῷ (Eph. v. 2).

   c. Its *rationale*. This sacrificial consecration of the body to the service of GOD is the rational λατρεία which the Christian offers Him (ver. 1).

[*Obs.* 1. The moral obligations of the Christian are an inference (οὖν) *immediately* from the undeserved and *abundant* mercy of GOD (xi. 35, 36), and *more remotely* from the entire dogmatic teaching of the Epistle (i. 16-xi. 36). Yet the Apostle says παρακαλῶ, not ἐπιτάσσω. 'Moses jubet: Apostolus hortatur,' Beng.; Philem. 8; 2 Cor. v. 20.]

[*Obs.* 2. The Divine Compassions furnish the impulsive motive to Christian thankfulness, expressing itself in a life consecrated to GOD's service. On διά with gen. of the motive *through* which the writer hopes to succeed in his appeal, see 1 Cor. i. 10; 2 Cor. x. 1; Winer, *Gr. N. T.* p. 477. The plur. form οἰκτιρμοί is shaped by רחמים, which the LXX often thus translates: but it accords with the Greek use of the plur. for abstract nouns, Phil. ii. 1; 2 Cor. i. 3. In using the word the Apostle is probably thinking more especially of iii. 24; v. 6-11; viii. 3, 31-39.]

[*Obs.* 3. The oblation of *the body* as an offering to GOD has been already enjoined under another image in vi. 23 παραστήσατε τὰ μέλη ὅπλα δικαιοσύνης τῷ Θεῷ: ib. ver. 19 δοῦλα τῇ δικαιοσύνῃ εἰς ἁγιασμόν. For the sacrificial sense of παριστάναι, see Xen. *Anab.* vi. 1, 22; Polyb. xvi. 25. 7 θύματα τοῖς βωμοῖς παραστήσαντες: Virg. *Aen.* xii. 171 'admovitque pecus flagrantibus aris': S. Luke ii. 22; Lev. xvi. 10. That σώματα ὑμῶν means not 'yourselves,' but 'your *bodies*,' is clear from the antithesis of νοῦς in ver. 2. The 'body,' with all its limbs, powers, and faculties, although νεκρὸν δι' ἁμαρτίαν viii. 10, is yet so quickened by Christ's indwelling as to become a θυσία ζῶσα: cf. vi. 11;

1 S. Pet. ii. 5; 1 Cor. vi. 15 τὰ σώματα ὑμῶν μέλη Χριστοῦ ἐστίν: ib. ver. 19 τὸ σῶμα ὑμῶν ναὸς τοῦ ἐν ὑμῖν Πνεύματος Ἁγίου ἐστίν: ib. ver. 20 δοξάσατε τὸν Θεὸν ἐν τῷ σώματι ὑμῶν. For the sacrificial act, cf. 1 Cor. ix. 27 ὑπωπιάζω μου τὸ σῶμα καὶ δουλαγωγῶ: Col. iii. 5 νεκρώσατε τὰ μέλη ὑμῶν. The Christian estimate of the body is equally removed from heathenish contempt of the body, and from heathenish worship of the body and bodily objects, cf. Harless, *Christ. Eth.* iii. § 44. Note here, in opposition to a false 'spiritualism,' the *religious* significance of the body in relation, (1) to ethics, (2) to Christian worship, (3) and (through the Resurrection) to the eternal future. Cf. Tertull. *de Res. Carnis*, c. 47, where he argues from this precept for the Resurrection of the Body. If it perished at death, how could it be such a θυσία as the Apostle describes?]

[*Obs.* 4. θυσία, properly 'mactatio,' then = θῦμα, the victim sacrificed, as זֶבַח Lev. iii. 6, 9; S. Mark ix. 49; and in a wider sense any other offering. Here the word is used in the strict sense. United with the Redeemer in Baptism the Christian is crucified with Him, vi. 6; vii. 4; viii. 3. Communion with His Life implies fellowship in His Sufferings, 2 Cor. iv. 10. The body is the instrument which the Christian soul employs at will: the victim which the soul, as a priest, offers to GOD. The Christian offers his body in union with the Sacrifice of Calvary. The victim which he offers should be 'living' with Christ's Life; and 'holy,' ἅγιος (ἄμωμος, תָּמִים), because sanctified by the Holy Spirit (xv. 16; 1 Cor. iii. 16; vi. 19), and consequently εὐάρεστος τῷ Θεῷ, which the Old Testament sacrifices frequently were not; cf. Ps. l. 13.]

[*Obs.* 5. The clause τὴν λατρείαν λογικὴν ὑμῶν is in apposition not with θυσίαν, but with the whole sentence, παραστῆσαι κ.τ.λ.: cf. Winer, *Gr. N. T.* p. 669. This λατρεία, or cultus, is offered to GOD by every Christian, who, as such, is a priest, and, says S. Chrys., ἱερεὺς τοῦ οἰκείου σώματος. On λατρεία, cf. ix. 4, compared with i. 9 and S. John xvi. 2. The heathen, and to a great extent the Jewish, λατρεία, was of an external, material, mechanical character. The Christian λατρεία is λογική, that is, offered by the active effort of the soul or reason, λόγος, and so contrasted with the external ceremonial of the Jewish and heathen cultus. So 1 S. Pet. ii. 2 speaks of the λογικὸν γάλα of Christian doctrine, i.e. 'quod ratione ac mente gustatur,' Justiniani. The *Testament of the XII Patriarchs*, Levi, c. 3, calls the sacrifice of the angels ὀσμὴν εὐωδίας λογικήν, καὶ ἀναίμακτον προσφοράν. Cf. Athenagoras, *Legat. pro Christ.* c. 13; S. John iv. 24; Phil. iii. 3; 1 S. Pet. ii. 5 πνευματικαὶ θυσίαι εὐπρόσδεκτοι.]

2. Renewal of the Christian's mental life (ver. 2).

   a. (*Negative duty.*) Not to take a mental shape conformably with the type prevalent in the αἰὼν οὗτος.

   b. (*Positive duty.*) Mental transformation through the renewal of the thinking faculty (ἀνακαίνωσις τοῦ νοός).

   c. (*Aim of this* ἀνακαίνωσις.) A personal testing, by the continuous experience and activity of conscience, of what *is* willed by

God, as being, in itself, that which is good, and so acceptable to Him, and so ideally perfect.

[*Obs.* 1. For the readings συσχηματίζεσθαι, μεταμορφοῦσθαι (instead of imper.) see App. Crit. These infinitives depend on παρακαλῶ ver. 1. The aor. παραστῆσαι shows that the Christian offers his body once for all: the present inf. συσχηματίζεσθαι, μεταμορφοῦσθαι point to continuous acts. The verbs are distinguished chiefly by the prepositions; although μορφή is more internal than σχῆμα: μορφή organic form, σχῆμα external form. Cf. Lightfoot on Phil. ii. 7 for a complete history of the words. Christians are to avoid *even* the appearance of moral assimilation to the life of the world, and are to be really and inwardly changed to a new moral type by the ἀνακαίνωσις τοῦ νοός. The αἰὼν οὗτος is the Rabbinical עוֹלָם הַזֶּה, the pre-Messianic period, as contrasted with the αἰὼν μέλλων, עוֹלָם הַבָּא, the days of Messiah. The Apostolic Christians spoke of the non-Christian world as αἰὼν οὗτος: the αἰὼν μέλλων being that which had become partaker in the Messianic Redemption. Thus the phrase lost its chronological significance, and acquired a purely moral or religious one. With οὗτος, αἰών, like κόσμος, acquired a bad ethical association, cf. Gal. i. 4 ἐκ τοῦ ἐνεστῶτος αἰῶνος πονηροῦ, Eph. ii. 2; 2 Cor. iv. 4.]

[*Obs.* 2. The μεταμορφοῦσθαι is the immediate effect of τῇ ἀνακαινώσει, dat. *instrument.* not dat. *modi*, since the νοῦς does not cover all the ground in which a change of μορφή is required. The νοῦς, the ἀνακαίνωσις of which will be the instrument of the contemplated transformation, is the practical reason; it wills as well as thinks, Delitzsch, *Bibl. Psychol.* p. 211. The predominance of ἁμαρτία in the σάρξ of fallen man has darkened and enfeebled his practical reason or νοῦς, making it a νοῦς τῆς σαρκός Col. ii. 18; or even a νοῦς ἀδόκιμος Rom. i. 28. Hence the νοῦς of fallen man needs ἀνακαίνωσις: and even the baptized and regenerate man must work for it, on account of the struggle in which he is still engaged, viii. 3, 4; Gal. v. 16-18. Of this ἀνακαίνωσις, the original principle is the Holy Spirit, given to the Christian in Baptism (Tit. iii. 5 διὰ λουτροῦ παλιγγενεσίας καὶ ἀνακαινώσεως Πνεύματος ἁγίου): while the scene of its activity is the πνεῦμα τοῦ νοός, or spiritual element in the mind, and its effect complete investiture with the new nature of the Son of Man (Eph. iv. 23, 24). It is by faith, which makes the unseen realities perpetually present to the νοῦς, that the ἀνακαίνωσις is pushed forward (Phil. iii. 10-14), bringing it to pass at last; κατὰ τὸν πλοῦτον τῆς δόξης αὐτοῦ, δυνάμει κραταιωθῆναι διὰ τοῦ Πνεύματος αὐτοῦ εἰς τὸν ἔσω ἄνθρωπον, κατοικῆσαι τὸν Χριστὸν διὰ τῆς πίστεως ἐν ταῖς καρδίαις Eph. iii. 16, 17; 2 Cor. v. 17.]

[*Obs.* 3. τὸ ἀγαθὸν καὶ εὐάρεστον καὶ τέλειον are substantival adjectives, in apposition with τὸ θέλημα τοῦ Θεοῦ, which here means not God's action of willing, but that which He wills, ii. 18; 1 Thess. iv. 3. The art. is omitted before εὐάρεστον and τέλειον, because the three words form parts of one whole. The Christian, whose νοῦς has been renewed, tests the reality and power of moral truth by actual experience; to others it is a region of phrase and fancy. Eph. v. 10 δοκιμάζοντες τί ἐστιν εὐάρεστον τῷ Κυρίῳ: Phil. i. 10 εἰς τὸ δοκιμάζειν ὑμᾶς τὰ διαφέροντα: Heb. v. 14 διὰ τὴν ἕξιν τὰ αἰσθητήρια γεγυμνασμένα ἐχόντων πρὸς διάκρισιν καλοῦ τε καὶ κακοῦ. His ὀφθαλμοὶ τῆς διανοίας (Eph. i. 18) are farsighted to discern the Divine will: he has put on τὸν νέον ἄνθρωπον, τὸν ἀνακαινούμενον εἰς ἐπίγνωσιν. Not merely τὸ ἀγαθόν, ii. 10; vii. 18; xii. 9; but εὐάρεστον, Heb. xiii. 21; good, as being well-pleasing to GOD, and attaining ideal perfection, τέλειον, S. Matt. v. 48; 1 Cor. xiii. 10, is his aim.]

§ 2.

Obligations of Christian Morality for the Christian as a member of the Body of Christ (ἐν σῶμά ἐσμεν ἐν Χριστῷ ver. 5), (vers. 3–8).

[*Obs.* The governing idea of this paragraph (vers. 4, 5) is introduced incidentally as a reason for the precept μὴ ὑπερφρονεῖν (in ver. 3), while it is the ground of the successive precepts which follow (vers. 6-8).]

A. General duty. (Humility.) Every Christian should form an accurate, and therefore a humble, estimate of his own importance to the Church (ver. 3).

In this general precept note

(i) its significance.
  (a) It is promulgated by a distinct exercise of the Apostolic authority committed to S. Paul (διὰ τῆς χάριτος τῆς δοθείσης μοι ver. 3).
  (b) It is addressed to every single Christian, the lowest and the highest, the most gifted and the least (παντὶ τῷ ὄντι ἐν ὑμῖν ver. 3).

(ii) its contents.
  (a) *Negative*; = not to think lofty thoughts (μὴ ὑπερφρονεῖν) about self, going beyond ὃ δεῖ φρονεῖν, i.e. the kind of thoughts which are in keeping with Christian duty (ver. 3).
  (b) *Positive*; = to think such thoughts as tend to (εἰς) a sober discretion, as their aim (τὸ σωφρονεῖν ver. 3).
  (c) *Regulative standard*; = the μέτρον πίστεως, or degree of faith, which GOD has given to each (ver. 3).

[*Obs.* 1. This exhortation to humility in ver. 3 is confirmatory of, and, in this sense, a reason (γάρ) for, the more general one to ἀνακαίνωσις τοῦ νοός (ver. 2) which precedes it.]

[*Obs.* 2. That the χάρις δοθεῖσα (ver. 3) refers not to any private grace, but to S. Paul's public apostolate of the nations, is clear from the subjoined μοι. He shared it with none of his readers. Cf. 1 Cor. iii. 10; xv. 9, 10, 15; Eph. iii. 7, 8; Gal. i. 15, 16; ii. 9. It was the possession of this divinely-given authority which relieved the Apostle's didactic attitude of any immodesty. The jurisdiction of the Apostolate being universal, S. Paul speaks παντὶ τῷ ὄντι ἐν ὑμῖν.]

[*Obs.* 3. Of the three infinitives ὑπερφρονεῖν, φρονεῖν, and σωφρονεῖν (other paronomasiai in S. Paul, 1 Cor. xi. 31, 32; xiii. 6, 7, 13), the generic idea is given by φρονεῖν, which, as at 1 Cor. iv. 6, means here 'to form judgments about oneself'; (although it more often means to judge rightly, as = הֵבִין Is. xliv. 18; cf. 1 Cor. xiii. 11; Phil. ii. 5). ὑπερφρονεῖν then = to form an exaggerated estimate of oneself; and σωφρονεῖν, to form a sober or accurate estimate, the rule of which is given presently: ἑκάστῳ ὡς ὁ Θεός κ.τ.λ.]

[*Obs.* 4. The μέτρον πίστεως is not the measure supplied by the true Christian Faith (objectively taken), but that which is supplied by the grace of faith as measured out by the Holy Spirit to the individual Christian. This μέτρον may differ, in different cases, both as to quality and as to intensity; see 1 Cor. xiii. 2. And since it is faith which receives and appropriates other graces, 'per quam quis gratiam capit' (Origen *in loc.*) a man's faith is presumably the true measure of his general spiritual capacity (Theodoret *in loc.*). Thus practically the χάρισμα given to each Christian is the measure of his faith. προφητεία is the μέτρον πίστεως of the προφήτης, &c. The precept is directed against a man's thinking himself capable of a higher work or office in the Church than his μέτρον πίστεως warrants. Only in Christ, the Head of the Church is grace *unmeasured*, S. John i. 14-16; iii. 34; Col. i. 19: of His servants the most gifted receive only a limited μέτρον, whether more or less, from the ὁ μερίσας ἑκάστῳ. Origen sees in the expression a reference to the heathen converts—grafts from the wild olive tree, inserted in the Tree of the Patriarchs.]

[*Obs.* 5. For the hyperbaton of ἑκάστῳ before ὡς, cf. 1 Cor. iii. 5; vii. 17; Winer, *Gr. N. T.* p. 688.]

§ Dogmatic Reason (γάρ ver. 4) for the General Duty of Humility (ver. 3); namely, the relation of Christians to one another in the Church or Body of Christ (vers. 4, 5, 6 a).

1. Simile (καθάπερ ver. 4) of the natural organised body (ver. 4).

   { a. Each human body has many members (ver. 4).
   { b. The members, all of them, have different functions (ver. 4).

2. Corresponding Spiritual Reality (οὕτως) in the Church of Christ (vers. 5, 6 a).

Practical : ch. XII, vv. 3-8.

(a) The many [Christians] are a single body (ver. 5).
  (i) relation to Christ (the ground of this organic unity). They are ἐν Χριστῷ (ver. 5).
  (ii) relation to each other (the consequence of this organic unity). They are ἀλλήλων μέλη (ver. 5).

(b) They possess however individually χαρίσματα, which differ κατὰ τὴν χάριν τὴν δοθεῖσαν to each (ver. 6 a).

[Obs. 1. The comparison between the human body and the body social or politic was familiar to the ancient Roman world. For the discourse of Menenius Agrippa, cf. Liv. ii. 32. Cf. also Cicero, *de Officiis*, iii. 5; Seneca, *de Ira*, ii. § 31. S. Paul adapts the metaphor to a higher purpose by substituting the Church or Body of Christ for the 'corpus sociale'; this comparison is most carefully elaborated in 1 Cor. xii. 12-30. The Christian Church is sometimes called simply σῶμα, 1 Cor. x. 17; xii. 13; xv. 20; Eph. iv. 4; Col. i. 18; iii. 15 : sometimes σῶμα τοῦ Χριστοῦ 1 Cor. xii. 27; Eph. i. 23; iv. 12; v. 23; the faithful μέλη Χριστοῦ and μέλη τοῦ σώματος αὐτοῦ 1 Cor. vi. 15; Eph. v. 30 : Christ is elsewhere especially the κεφαλή, Eph. i. 22; iv. 15; v. 23; Col. i. 18; ii. 19, the figure being slightly changed : the Church conceived of as an organism complete in itself but only living when associated with Christ. Once the Church is called simply ὁ Χριστός 1 Cor. xii. 12. Other metaphors in the New Testament which teach the nature of the Christian Church are βασιλεία, πόλις, οἶκος, ναός, ἐλαία.]

[Obs. 2. πρᾶξις, as at Ecclus. xi. 10, 'function.' S. Ambr. 'officium.' οἱ πολλοί, 'the (well-known) many who compose the Church,' Winer, *Gr. N. T.* p. 137. For ἐν Χριστῷ, see Hooker, *E. P.* v. 56. 7 'The Church is in Christ, as Eve was in Adam. Yea, by grace we are, every one of us, in Christ and in His Church, as by nature we are in those our first parents'; Wilberforce, *Doctr. of Incarnation*, c. xi. p. 257, 4th ed. τὸ δὲ καθ' εἷς, a popular solecism in later Greek, instead of καθ' ἕνα, S. Mark xiv. 19; S. John viii. 9; 3 Macc. v. 34. The regular form occurs in 1 Cor. xiv. 31 καθ' ἕνα πάντες : Eph. v. 33 ὑμεῖς οἱ καθ' ἕνα. The transition to the irregular idiom εἷς καθ' εἷς, &c. was probably suggested by the neut. ἐν καθ' ἕν Rev. iv. 8. The κατά lost its government, and served merely as an adverb. Here = in what concerns the individual relation. Christians are ἀλλήλων μέλη, because each limb belongs not merely to the body as a whole, but to every member that composes it. The Apostle had meant to say we are all μέλη τοῦ Χριστοῦ or τοῦ σώματος τοῦ Χριστοῦ. But the figure is departed from in the interest of the truth which is being taught. The idea of ἀλλήλων μέλη forbids ὑπερφρονεῖν.]

[Obs. 3. Ver. 6 a probably begins a new construction, while, as to the idea, it corresponds to τὰ δὲ μέλη οὐ τὴν αὐτὴν ἔχει πρᾶξιν of the simile in ver. 4. ἔχοντες (ver. 6 a) *may* depend on ἐσμέν (ver. 5), but is better taken as introducing a new and highly elliptical paragraph, as δέ would of itself imply. The χαρίσματα, supernaturally imparted faculties for advancing the life of the Church (1 Cor. xiv. 1 πνευματικά), are concrete products of the χάρις to which they owe their existence.]

B. *Specific* duties. Each Christian should make the best possible use of the particular χάρισμα which he has actually received in his capacity of member of the Holy Body of Christ (vers. 6 b–8).

[*Obs.* 1. χάρις is the vital force of the σῶμα τοῦ Χριστοῦ, which flows from Christ through all its living members; χάρισμα, a special determination of this force to enable a particular μέλος to do its part towards the whole σῶμα. The talent of natural social life becomes the χάρισμα of the higher life of the Holy Body; the natural endowment is often the raw material of the spiritual. S. Paul here enumerates or implies *seven* χαρίσματα: he gives *nine* at 1 Cor. xii. 1–12, 28–30; *five* at Eph. iv. 11.]

[*Obs.* 2. The χαρίσματα referred to may be thus arranged:—

Seven χαρίσματα in the exercise of which τὸ σωφρονεῖν (ver. 3) consists,

(i) in observing the proportion imposed by an external standard;
 1. προφητεία, which must be κατὰ τὴν ἀναλογίαν τῆς πίστεως.

or,

(ii) in undistracted attention to the implied duties;
 2. διακονία
 3. διδασκαλία   ἐν αὐτῇ ἔστω.
 4. παράκλησις

or,

(iii) in the assistance afforded by an additional grace or virtue.
 5. ὁ μεταδιδούς needs ἁπλότης (χάρισμα of ἀντίληψις, 1 Cor. xii).
 6. ὁ προϊστάμενος needs σπουδή (χάρισμα of κυβέρνησις, 1 Cor. xii).
 7. ὁ ἐλεῶν needs ἱλαρότης (χάρισμα ἰαμάτων 1 Cor. xii).]

1. προφητεία. The χάρισμα of 'inspired discourse' presupposing ἀποκάλυψις from GOD. This gift is to be exercised according to the proportion of the Faith (ver. 6).

[*Obs.* 1. The New Testament προφήτης, 'qui praedicit, Dei interpres apud homines,' corresponds generally to the Old Testament נביא. In the sphere of their action, and in the measure of their endowment, the προφῆται ranked next to the Apostles, 1 Cor. xii. 28; Eph. iv. 11. A very high value was therefore set upon προφητεία (1 Cor. xiv. 1, 39). The προφήτης could unveil the future, Rev. i. 3; xxii. 7, 10; Acts xi. 28; xxi. 10, 11. Especially the προφήτης had a knowledge of undisclosed μυστήρια, and of Christianity as a γνῶσις, 1 Cor. xiii. 2. He could even lay bare τὰ κρυπτὰ τῆς καρδίας 1 Cor. xiv. 25; he administered οἰκοδομὴν καὶ παράκλησιν καὶ παραμυθίαν 1 Cor. xiv. 3; and was thus an instrument of building up the Church, 1 Cor. xiv. 4. His *sphere of operation* was accordingly nearly that of the Christian preacher whom S. Chrysostom identifies with him, although his gift was transcendent; the Apostolic rule about προφῆται (1 Cor. xiv. 24) was in S. Chrysostom's time still observed as to preachers, two or three of whom might address a single congregation (*Hom.* 26 *in* 1

Cor. c. 4. tom. x. p. 338). The very ancient liturgical response of the people, 'Et cum Spiritu tuo,' probably greeted the Christian προφήτης on his appearance with a 'Dominus vobiscum,' in the assembly of the faithful.]

[*Obs.* 2. Corinth was the Church most richly endowed with χαρίσματα of the unusual kind : Rome more sparingly. προφητεία alone of *these* charisms is mentioned.]

[*Obs.* 3. The προφήτης must speak κατὰ τὴν ἀναλογίαν τῆς πίστεως. The majestic proportion of the (objective) Faith is before him, and, keeping his eye on it, he avoids private crotchets and wild fanaticisms, which exaggerate the relative importance of particular truths to the neglect of others. Observe the distinction between μέτρον πίστεως (subjective), ver. 3 ; and ἀναλογία τῆς πίστεως (objective), ver. 6. ἀναλογία in classical Greek is used as a mathematical expression, Plat. *Pol.* p. 257 B, &c. With the Latin Fathers we must understand πίστις *objectively* of the *fides quae creditur*, as the rule or standard of the προφητεία (the Greeks take it *subjectively*, as the *fides quâ creditur*, the intensity or direction of which must determine the range of the prophetic utterances). The act of believing furnishes no standard for the προφητεία, no safeguard against confusions and fluctuations of thought. κατὰ τὴν ἀναλογίαν = pro congruentiâ cum [veritate fidei]. See Fritzsche's defence of the objective sense of πίστις in Rom. i. 5 εἰς ὑπακοὴν πίστεως : cf. Gal. i. 23 ; iii. 23, 25 ; Eph. iv. 5 ; 2 Pet. i. 1.]

2. διακονία. This gift, including all the duties that further the service of the Church, is to be exercised without looking beyond it for distinction or reward (ver. 7).

[*Obs.* 1. διακονία is here used generically, as in διαιρέσεις διακονιῶν (1 Cor. xii. 5), of *any* place in the *ministerium ecclesiasticum*, not only of the order of the diaconate, as in Acts vi. 3 ; Phil. i. 1 ; 1 Tim. iii. 8, 12 ; 1 S. Pet. iv. 11. In 1 Cor. xii. 28 the functions of the diaconate proper are termed ἀντιλήψεις.]

3. διδασκαλία. The man who gives Christian instruction is to find his satisfaction in, and not beyond, this work (ver. 7).

[*Obs.* 1. The abstract words προφητεία, διακονία are here exchanged for concretes, ὁ διδάσκων, ὁ παρακαλῶν, &c. *because* the corresponding abstract words διδασκαλία, παράκλησις would not combine with ἔχοντες (ver. 6 b), on which the two former depend. They are less endowments than duties which presuppose endowments.]

[*Obs.* 2. The difference between the προφήτης and the διδάσκων is stated by S. Chrys. *Hom.* 22 *in* 1 *Cor.* c. 1. tom. x. p. 286 ὁ μὲν γὰρ προφητεύων πάντα ἀπὸ τοῦ πνεύματος φθέγγεται· ὁ δὲ διδάσκων ἐστὶν ὅπου καὶ ἐξ οἰκείας διανοίας διαλέγεται. Thus the two would differ as a man speaking when inspired from a man using his natural understanding ; and accordingly the same person might be at different times a προφήτης and a διδάσκων. The difference would in some respects correspond to that which now separates Christian preaching, understood in its highest sense, from the work of the Catechist or Christian instructor. The διδάσκαλος was also a definite Church official, (ἐπίσκοπος or πρεσβύτερος) who was as such a teacher, Eph. iv. 11 ; 1 Tim. iii. 2 ; 2 Tim. ii. 2 ; Tit. i. 9.]

[*Obs.* 3. The διδάσκαλος occupies the third place after Apostles and Prophets in 1 Cor. xii. 28, the fifth in Eph. iv. 11. Had the Church been only a school of philosophy, he must have been always first.]

4. παράκλησις. The man who exhorts, encourages to action or suffering, or consoles, is to find his satisfaction in, and not beyond, his work (ver. 8).

[*Obs.* This χάρισμα was addressed to the heart and will of those whom it benefited; as διδασκαλία was to their intelligence. It seems in Israel to have been connected with the public reading of Scripture, as by our Lord in the Synagogue of Nazareth, Luke iv. 20, 21, so afterwards by S. Paul at Antioch in Pisidia, Acts xiii. 15, where the ἀρχισυνάγωγος asked for a λόγος παρακλήσεως. It was exercised by the προφῆται as well as by the usual Church teachers, Acts xiii. 15; 1 Cor. xiv. 3, 31. S. Timothy was to give heed to παράκλησις, as well as to διδασκαλία, 1 Tim. iv. 13. This very passage commences with παράκλησις (xii. 1 παρακαλῶ). It required a capacity for spiritual sympathy, but was not a distinct ministerial service. S. Chrys. speaks of it as exercised by Ministers of the Church. Instances are given at Acts iv. 36; xi. 23, 24.]

5. ὁ μεταδιδούς. The Almoner. He who exercises the χάρισμα of ἀντίληψις (1 Cor. xii. 28), *by imparting* his wealth to the poor, should do it from a simply religious, as distinct from a mixed or selfish, motive (ver. 8).

[*Obs.* 1. In these last three examples (ver. 8), the χάρισμα no longer appears except by implication, in the initial participles. They describe forms of Christian effort which imply the presence of spiritual endowments. The form of the precept changes also: distinct graces or virtues—ἁπλότης, σπουδή, ἱλαρότης—are to characterize these efforts, over and above the duty of not looking beyond the work.]

[*Obs.* 2. The μεταδιδούς distributed that which was his own, Luke iii. 11 ὁ ἔχων δύο χιτῶνας μεταδότω τῷ μὴ ἔχοντι. Eph. iv. 28, the repentant thief is to work with his hands, ἵνα ἔχῃ μεταδιδόναι τῷ χρείαν ἔχοντι. 1 Tim. vi. 18, the wealthy are to be taught to be εὐμετάδοτοι. On the other hand of the common fund of the Church it was said διεδίδοτο ἑκάστῳ καθότι ἄν τις χρείαν εἶχεν Acts iv. 35. Thus the deacon distributing public Church funds as in Acts vi. 1 would have been termed ὁ διαδιδούς. There is more need of ἁπλότης in private than in public or official charity: because the *tendency* to ostentation or some sort of selfish seeking for a return is greater. Cf. S. Matt. vi. 2 ὅταν ποιῇς ἐλεημοσύνην, μὴ σαλπίσῃς ἔμπροσθέν σου. ἁπλότης would exclude a desire for human praise, as well as all sorts of favoritism towards the persons relieved, &c.]

6. ὁ προϊστάμενος. The Church-ruler, of whatever grade. He who presides in the Church, exercising the χάρισμα of κυβέρνησις (1 Cor. xii. 28), is to do it in an earnest spirit (ver. 8).

[*Obs.* 1. προϊστάμενος, as a generic word, might apply to ἀπόστολος, προφήτης, or διδάσκαλος. In 1 Thess. v. 12 ; 1 Tim. v. 17 (οἱ καλῶς προεστῶτες πρεσβύτεροι), iii. 4, 5, it means the presiding Minister in the Church, Bishop or Presbyter. It apparently corresponds with the προεστώς of S. Justin Martyr (*Apol.* i. 67), with the προκαθήμενος of the Ignatian Epistles, with the ἡγούμενος of the Epistle to the Hebrews, and of S. Clem. Rom. It implies the gift of guiding and overseeing the faithful, as by ποιμένες Eph. iv. 11 ; and ἐπίσκοποι Acts xx. 28. To understand by ὁ προϊστάμενος, the 'patron of strangers,' in accordance with the Greek προστάτης, patron of the μέτοικοι, and προστάτις Rom. xvi. 2, a transient (ἐγενήθη) occupation of Phoebe, is against New Testament usage. It is no objection that high office in the Church is thus ranged side by side with humble forms of Church work. There is no classification here of χαρίσματα, and no distinction between them and mere offices. (See the same neglect of classification in 1 Cor. xii. 28 ; Eph. iv. 11.) The promiscuous enumeration of gifts and offices of very different value was a reminder that each Christian was a μέλος τοῦ σώματος and a warning against ὑπερφρονεῖν.]

[*Obs.* 2. The appropriate virtue for a ruler in the Church is σπουδή: cf. S. Paul's own μέριμνα 2 Cor. xi. 28. Cf. 2 Tim. iv. 5 τὴν διακονίαν σου πληροφόρησον : 1 S. Pet. v. 2 ἐπισκοποῦντες μὴ ἀναγκαστῶς, ἀλλὰ ἑκουσίως, μηδὲ αἰσχροκερδῶς ἀλλὰ προθύμως : S. Ignat. ad *Polyc.* cc. 1–3.]

7. ὁ ἐλεῶν. The 'Hospitaller,' having the χάρισμα τῶν ἰαμάτων, 1 Cor. xii. 28. He who takes charge of the sick and suffering is to do so with a bright cheerful temper and manner (ver. 8).

[*Obs.* It is probable that ὁ ἐλεῶν exercised the χάρισμα ἰαμάτων, S. Matt. xxv. 36 ; 1 Cor. xii. 28. This was to be done ἐν ἱλαρότητι, which is nowhere more necessary than in a sick room, where a gloomy or constrained manner is very depressing to the patient. Yet, on the other hand, constant brightness, after the fatigue of long nursing, is often very difficult. As to the meaning of the word, see 2 Cor. ix. 7, where the ἱλαρὸς δότης, whom GOD loves, is contrasted with the man who gives ἐκ λύπης ἢ ἐξ ἀνάγκης. So S. Paul will do nothing for Onesimus without Philemon's permission, ἵνα μὴ ὡς κατὰ ἀνάγκην τὸ ἀγαθόν σου ᾖ, ἀλλὰ κατὰ ἑκούσιον Philem. 14.]

§ 3.

Obligations of Christian Morality for the Christian as a member of human society (vers. 9–21).

[*Obs.* 1. Like the precept on Humility (ver. 3), and in contrast to the seven precepts addressed to possessors of particular χαρίσματα (ver. 6 b-8), the rules which follow (vers. 9-21) are binding on every Christian. They refer to the duties of Christians, (1) in the spheres of the Christian life and Church (vers. 9-13), and (2) in the sphere of general human society, Pagan as well as Christian (vers. 14-21.]

[*Obs.* 2. The construction in this paragraph is very elliptical ; only the main words which suggest a duty are jotted hastily down, the sentences being left incomplete. The imperative of the substantive verb (ἔστω ver. 1, ἔστε generally) must be supplied after each participle and adjective; δεῖ after the infinitives in ver. 15. Compare Heb. xiii. 5.]

A. Rules for the Christian in his personal life and conduct, *within the Church* (vers. 9–13).

1. Concerning ἀγάπη, the Love of God and man (vers. 9–11).

Christian conduct in *ordinary circumstances* within the Church (energy of ἀγάπη).

    a. It must be in reality what it professes to be in words (ver. 9).

    b. It implies earnest hatred of and shrinking from moral evil, as well as determined adhesion to moral good (ver. 9).

    c. As existing between brethren in Christ (φιλαδελφία), love should resemble natural affection between members of a family (ver. 10).

    d. In readiness to do honour to merit in others, love should make a Christian take the lead and encourage others by his example (ver. 10).

    e. Love is enthusiasm. *Negatively*, it is inconsistent with sloth (ὄκνος), where there should be zeal (σπουδή) for the cause of Christ. *Positively*, it implies fervour (ζέσις) in the spirit or soul of man. But it is always service, rendered to an unseen Lord (ver. 11).

[*Obs.* 1. The datives are continued from ver. 9 to ver. 13, but with very various force, and for the sake of structural uniformity. Cf. Winer, *Gr. N. T.* p. 271.]

[*Obs.* 2. ἡ ἀγάπη, absolutely, of God, and, for His sake, of men, is to be ἀνυπόκριτος, without outward pretence, or self-seeking. ἀνυπόκριτος is not classical; but it is used of κρίσις, Wisd. v. 19; of ἐπιταγὴ τοῦ Θεοῦ, xviii. 16; of πίστις, 1 Tim. i. 5; 2 Tim. i. 5; of σοφία, S. James iii. 17; of φιλαδελφία, 1 S. Pet. i. 22; of ἀγάπη, 2 Cor. vi. 6. The ὑποκρίτης says one thing in public, but feels another; love is untheatrical by the terms of its essence, which consists in the gift of *self*, ἐκ καθαρᾶς καρδίας, καὶ συνειδήσεως ἀγαθῆς, καὶ πίστεως ἀνυποκρίτου. Here, as in 1 Cor. xiii. 1 sqq.; Eph. iv. 15, ἀγάπη is represented as the greatest virtue of the Christian life; and here too, as in 1 Cor. xii. 31; xiii. 1 sqq., the Apostle passes from describing the manifold χαρίσματα of Christ to that which is higher than them all, ἀγάπη.]

[*Obs.* 3. In ἀποστυγοῦντες (ver. 9) remark the idea of shrinking which the compound (ἀπό) adds to the radical idea of hatred. So in Hdt. ii. 47. It is not enough to keep clear of (ἀπέχεσθαι) moral evil; the Christian must shrink from it with hatred; this hatred being a necessary correlative of his love of God, the Absolute Good. κολλᾶσθαι, Heb. דָּבַק, 'agglutinare' (used of metals, Is. xli. 7; of the marriage tie, Gen. ii. 24; S. Matt. xix. 5; of the adhesion of a girdle to the body round which it is bound, Jer. xiii. 11; of keeping one's seat in a chariot, Acts viii. 29) implies the closest union. Cf. 1 Cor.

vi. 16, 17, for the contrast between ὁ κολλώμενος τῇ πόρνῃ and ὁ κολλώμενος τῷ Κυρίῳ; cf. 1 Thess. v. 21, 22.]

[*Obs.* 4. φιλαδελφίᾳ, (dat. modalis,) love towards brethren in Christ. Through their Second Birth of the Holy Ghost, Christians are made members of an ἀδελφότης, (1 S. Pet. ii. 17; v. 9) or family of brothers. GOD is the Father of this family, and Christ is the πρωτότοκος ἐν πολλοῖς ἀδελφοῖς viii. 29. 'Fratres dicuntur et habentur, qui unum Patrem Deum agnoverunt, qui unum Spiritum biberunt sanctitatis' Tert. *Apolog.* c. 39. Hence the affection which they mutually feel, and which binds them to each other, is 'brother's love,' 1 Thess. iv. 9; Heb. xiii. 1; in accordance with the Elder Brother's precept, 'that ye love one another, as I have loved you,' S. John xv. 12. This love should have the freedom and strength of natural affection (φιλόστοργοι). στέργειν = θερμῶς φιλεῖν. (S. Chrys.) Indeed, στοργή generally means the love of parents and children; the affection of Christian brothers should rival this *strongest* form of natural affection.]

[*Obs.* 5. προηγεῖσθαι (in ver. 10) cannot = ἡγεῖσθαι ἄλλους ὑπερέχοντας ἑαυτῶν (Phil. ii. 3) consistently with usage, but 'to go first and lead the way,' Hdt. ii. 48, generally with a dat. Love makes a man lead others by the example of showing respect to worth or saintliness. Compare our Lord's words, S. John xiii. 14; S. Luke xiv. 17.]

[*Obs.* 6. τῇ σπουδῇ μὴ ὀκνηροί and τῷ πνεύματι ζέοντες are the negative and positive sides of a single precept. Love forbids the thought (μή) of sloth in zeal for the good of others, because 'propter abundantiam divinae dilectionis totus homo fervet in Deum,' Aquin. For ὀκνηρός, see S. Matt. xxv. 26. πνεῦμα is here the spirit of man penetrated by the Holy Spirit of GOD, who, as Fire, illuminates man's understanding by the gift of faith, and enkindles his heart by the gift of charity. Apollos was ζέων τῷ πνεύματι Acts xviii. 25; S. Luke xii. 49.]

[*Obs.* 7. In ver. 11 τῷ Κυρίῳ (A.B.D** ℵ, most minor vss. and Greek Fathers, Tisch., Lachm., Tregelles) has the weight of *external* evidence in its favour; καιρῷ (D* F. G. 5, Lat. Fathers; Meyer, obs. Fritzsche, Olshausen). δουλεύειν τῷ Κυρίῳ is a phrase familiar to S. Paul, Rom. xiv. 18; xvi. 18; Eph. vi. 7; Col. iii. 24; Acts xx. 19. So general a precept as τῷ Κυρίῳ δουλεύειν occurring in the midst of specific precepts is to be accounted for as giving the scope and limits of the two preceding exhortations. The service of the Lord guards glowing zeal against the fanaticism which becomes only too easy where self is the real object of work. See the warnings against man-service in Eph. vi. 6; Col. iii. 22. Those who read καιρῷ understand the Apostle to mean that the circumstances of their age may and should, *within limits*, influence the action of Christians; that different duties are imposed by different circumstances, stages of civilisation, &c., see Phil. iv. 12, 13; 1 Cor. iv. 11 sqq.; viii. 13; Acts xvi. 3; xx. 35; xxi. 23 sqq. But δουλεύειν seems to express something more than this, and is hardly to be justified by 'tempori servire': Cic. *Tusc. Disp.* iii. 27; *Epp. ad Div.* ix. 17. S. Paul would have said τηρεῖν τὸν καιρόν: he does say ἐξαγοράζειν τὸν καιρόν. He reserves δουλεύειν—in describing Christian duty—to express man's relation to GOD or to our Lord or to δικαιοσύνη (Rom. vi. 18). But the Christian may not be a δοῦλος ἀνθρώπων (1 Cor. vii. 23; Gal. i. 10 ἤρεσκον,) and would hardly have been desired by S. Paul to be a δοῦλος καιροῦ. Assuming Κυρίῳ to be the true reading on external grounds, the precept assigns the motive which imparts steadiness and reverence to, while it sustains spiritual fervour in, the δοῦλος Χριστοῦ: cf. xiv. 7, 8; xvi. 18. It supplies a caution against the subtle selfishness which often enters into religious enthusiasm.]

2. Concerning ἐλπίς and works of ἀγάπη.

Conduct in troublous times within the Church. Energy of ἐλπίς and ἀγάπη.

1. (The) *hope* (of future Blessedness), (ver. 12).
   - (1) *Active effect on the soul.* Joy (ver. 12).
   - (2) *Passive effect.* Patience in tribulation (ver. 12).
   - (3) *Practical result.* Perseverance in prayer (ver. 12.)

   [*Obs.* τῇ ἐλπίδι, dat. of motive, v. 2 καυχώμεθα ἐπ' ἐλπίδι τῆς δόξης τοῦ Θεοῦ: Phil. iv. 4. On ὑπομονή, see viii. 25 with vers. 3–5; S. James i. 2 sqq. The sight of the endless future which Hope enjoys, fills the Christian heart with καύχησις and χαρά, and makes ὑπομονή easy. On the other hand, Hope expresses and strengthens itself in persevering prayer, Col. iv. 2; προσκαρτερεῖτε 1 Thess. v. 17; ἀδιαλείπτως 2 Thess. iii. 1; 1 S. Pet. iv. 7, &c.]

2. Concerning works of charity (ver. 13).
   - I. *Generic.* Share in the needs of fellow-Christians (ver. 13).
   - II. *Specific.* Specially seek occasions for φιλοξενία (ver. 13).

[*Obs.* 1. The reading μνείαις (S. Ambr., Hil.), instead of χρείαις, is traceable to the use of this passage in a Church lesson, Acts xx. 34; Tit. iii. 14. For κοινωνεῖν, see Phil. iv. 15; Gal. vi. 6. Not almsgiving, so much as actively sh—ing the wants of the ἅγιοι,—'censum nostrum cum ipsis quodammodo habere communem,' Orig. (iv. p. 652).]

[*Obs.* 2. Φιλοξενία was of peculiar importance in the early days of the Church. Christians when travelling were, as a rule, unbefriended. Cf. the suggestive definition of ξένοι ὦν ξένα τὰ κοσμικά Clem. Alex. *Strom.* ii. 9. p. 450; hence the duty of giving them bed and board. It was to be discharged ἄνευ γογγυσμῶν 1 S. Pet. iv. 9; and with the hopes inspired by recollecting that διὰ ταύτης ἔλαθόν τινες ξενίσαντες ἀγγέλους Heb. xiii. 2; S. Clem. Rom. 1 *Cor.* c. 10 sq. S. Paul insists that a Bishop must be φιλόξενος, 1 Tim. iii. 2; Tit. i. 8. On which passage S. Jerome observes: 'Domus Episcopi omnium debet esse commune hospitium. Laicus enim unum aut duos aut paucos recipiens implebit hospitalitatis officium; episcopus nisi omnes receperit, inhumanus est' (*Comm.* in Tit. i. 8). διώκοντες implies that φιλοξενία is not merely to be exercised when opportunities present themselves, but that 'sectemur et perquiramus ubique hospites,' Orig. *in loc.* Φιλοξενία is a modified application of the principle of community of goods (Acts iv. 34), which had for its result that οὐδὲ ... ἐνδεής τις ὑπῆρχεν ἐν αὐτοῖς. On the hospitality of the Clergy of the Primitive Church, see Bingham, *Antiquities*, book vi. c. 2. sect. 7. It was destined for the poor, not for the noble or the rich. *Ibid.* sect. 8.]

Practical: ch. XII, vv. 9-21.

B. Rules for the Christian in his daily intercourse with general *society around him*, being chiefly *Pagan* (vers. 14-21).

		Persons and circumstances.		Right conduct.
	I.	I. persecutors (ver. 14),	let *words* be	I. blessings and prayers (ver. 14).
In reference to	II.	II. the joyful and the sad (ver. 15),	let *thoughts and feelings* be	II. sympathetic in each case (ver. 15).
		III. fellow-Christians (ver. 16),		III. harmonious (with a view to effect on heathens), (ver. 16).
		IV. the occurrence of splendid or of humble circumstances (ver. 16),		IV. not aiming at τὰ ὑψηλά, but attracted by τὰ ταπεινά (ver. 16).
		V. your own opinions on general subjects (ver. 16),		V. not self-confident (ver. 16).
	III.	VI. any man who has done you (κακόν) an ill turn (ver. 17),	let your *rule of action* be	VI. not to punish him by retaliating (ver. 17).
		VII. the public opinion of the day (ver. 17 b),		VII. to consult its prejudices *within certain limits* suggested by natural morality (ver. 17 b).
		VIII. general heathen society, although hostile (ver. 18),		VIII. *if possible*, to live at peace with it (ver. 18).
		IX. those who have injured you (cf. vi), (ver. 19),		IX. not to vindicate personal rights, but to leave wrongdoers to God's ὀργή (ver. 19).
		X. an enemy (ver. 20),		X. to win them by persistent kindness (ver. 20).
		XI. evil in the abstract (ver. 21),		XI. to conquer it by active good (ver. 21).

[*Obs.* 1. *On blessing persecutors* (ver. 14). The διώκοντες are heathens, emperors, proconsuls, &c. εὐλογεῖτε is repeated twice on account of its importance; the second time it is followed by the (implied) negative μὴ καταρᾶσθε, a redundancy which the ordinary lower instincts of human nature make necessary. S. Paul is thinking of our Lord's precept, S. Matt. v. 44, where προσεύχεσθαι ὑπέρ implies εὐλογεῖν. This language towards persecutors is not 'conventional or artificial,' but is based on the ground stated at 1 S. Pet. iii. 9, viz. that Christians are called ἵνα εὐλογίαν κληρονομήσητε :—an inheritance which is secured by suffering, and which therefore entitles those who inflict it to the gratitude of the sufferers; cf. S. Matt. v. 10-12. Besides which this εὐλογεῖν may win the persecutor to the truth which he is opposing. Cf. S. Chrys. *in loc.*; S. Clem. Alex. *Strom.* iv. c. 11; Acts vii. 60; 1 Cor. iv. 12; 1 S. Pet. ii. 23. That the *love* of enemies is a precept of the Gospel is certain; whether εὐλογεῖν is an evangelical counsel or a precept is discussed by S. Aug. *de Mendac.* c. 15; *Enchir.* c. 73.]

[*Obs.* 2. *On sympathy with the joyous and the sad* (ver. 15). χαίρειν is considered an ex. of the imperatival use of the inf. as Phil. iii. 16. But cf. Winer, *Gr. N. T.* p. 397, and supply δεῖ. S. Chrys. observes that to rejoice with others is harder than to weep with them.]

[*Obs.* 3. *On unity of thought and feeling* (ver. 16). τὸ αὐτὸ φρονεῖν means, not to have the same mind (as that above mentioned) in your relations with each other, but to be of one mind, 2 Cor. xiii. 11; Phil. ii. 2; iv. 2; Rom. xv. 5. The occurrence of a precept insisting upon Christian unity in *this* connection is to be accounted for by the effect of such unity upon the heathen world, and by the effect of its absence. εἰς ἀλλήλους, generally ἐν ἀλλήλοις : S. Mark ix. 50; S. John xiii. 35; Rom. xv. 5. εἰς marks the direction of φρονεῖν, ἐν its sphere : the practical result is the same; but the former preposition implies the transit of the Apostle's thought in this verse from the heathen world (in ver. 15) to the Christian Church.]

[*Obs.* 4. *On unambitious aims and tastes* (ver. 16). τὰ ὑψηλά, high positions, a distinguished career, &c.; cf. xi. 20. τὰ ταπεινά, humble tasks, interests, relations in life. These should have an attractive force for the Christian, and carry him away with them. συναπάγεσθαι has a bad sense in Gal. ii. 13; 2 S. Pet. iii. 17, through the context : not here. The dogmatic reason for this precept is given at Phil. ii. 5 sqq. as the self-humiliation of the Eternal Son at His Incarnation ; He Himself connected the duty with His own example, S. Matt. xx. 26-28.]

[*Obs.* 5. *On Self-distrust* (ver. 16). For φρόνιμοι παρ' ἑαυτοῖς, see xi. 25. On a great many questions heathens may be better informed than Christians ; a man's being a Christian does not justify him in affecting a tone of self-confident indifference to what others may say. The moral self-sufficiency which leads a man to despise the opinion or feeling *of others* is here specially meant : Is. v. 21 ; Prov. iii. 5, 7. 'Non potest veram sapientiam Dei scire, qui suam stultitiam quasi sapientiam colit ' Orig. (iv. p. 653).]

[*Obs.* 6. *On non-retaliation* (ver. 17). μηδενί includes non-Christian as well as Christian, S. Matt. v. 38 sqq. ; 1 S. Pet. iii. 9 ; 1 Thess. v. 15. This precept is opposed to the Hellenic ἀδικεῖν τῷ ἀδικοῦντι, as well as to the Pharisaic glosses in favour of retaliation. It applies to Christians in their *private* capacity. When charged with public interests, whether in Church or State, they *may* be bound to punish evil, as being done (not against themselves, but) against GOD, or the Body of Christ, or natural society. The civil government is Θεοῦ διάκονος, ἔκδικος εἰς ὀργὴν τῷ τὸ κακὸν πράσσοντι Rom. xiii. 4; and of such a government a Christian may be a member. And as to Church censures, the punishment of Ananias and Sapphira by S. Peter, of Elymas and the incestuous Corinthian by S. Paul, are in point.]

[*Obs.* 7. *On a respect (within limits) for public opinion* (ver. 17). This precept is traceable to Prov. iii. 4 προνοοῦ καλὰ ἐνώπιον Κυρίου καὶ ἀνθρώπων: cf. 2 Cor. viii. 21 προνοούμενοι καλὰ οὐ μόνον ἐνώπιον Κυρίου ἀλλὰ καὶ ἐνώπιον ἀνθρώπων. The word πάντων shows that even the pagan public had claims upon Christian πρόνοια: such claims as are supplied by the possession of a certain common moral sense or judgment as to τὰ καλά, which enables it to appreciate conduct higher than its own. When indeed this public opinion was in conflict with truth or goodness, the Christian would disregard it, since it does not furnish him with his true standard in faith or morals. The precept, says Theophylact, is not intended to encourage κενοδοξία, but is given ἵνα μὴ παρέχωμεν καθ' ἡμῶν ἀφορμὰς τοῖς βουλομένοις. On avoiding the *appearance* of evil, for the sake of non-Christians, see 1 Cor. x. 32 ἀπρόσκοποι γίνεσθε καὶ Ἰουδαίοις καὶ Ἕλλησι: 1 Thess. iv. 12 περιπατῆτε εὐσχημόνως πρὸς τοὺς ἔξω, 1 S. Pet. ii. 12.]

[*Obs.* 8. *On living peaceably (if possible) with all men* (ver. 18). τὸ ἐξ ὑμῶν used adverbially, as i. 15. The seventh Beatitude is awarded to the εἰρηνοποιοί, S. Matt. v. 9; but while the Christian must desire, on his part, μετὰ πάντων εἰρηνεύειν, his duty to truth may make this quite impossible. Then the words apply (S. Matt. x. 34) οὐκ ἦλθον βαλεῖν εἰρήνην ἀλλὰ μάχαιραν. Hence, εἰ δυνατόν. Pagan hostility to Revealed Faith and Morals might make 'peace' with Christians impracticable; Christians were concerned to see that peace is not forfeited by their own faults of temper or judgment; τὸ ἐξ ὑμῶν.]

§ Precepts as to conduct under a sense of injury (ver. 19-21).

[*Obs.* 1. On account of the practical difficulty and high importance of right action in this department of Christian duty, the Apostle abandons the concise style of vers. 9-18, completes his constructions, and enforces his moral teaching by arguments (vers. 19-21). The tender epithet ἀγαπητοί (ver. 19) marks a new attitude towards his readers. He is no longer merely teaching, but appealing to their affections, while recommending portions of the law of Jesus Christ which present the greatest difficulties to human nature.]

[*Obs.* 2. These precepts are three.
  (1) (*Passive duty.*) What *not to do* when wronged (ver. 19).
  (2) (*Active duty.*) What *to do* when wronged (ver. 20).
  (3) (*General duty.*) Think of the evil done to you as an enemy to be vanquished by charity (ver. 21).]

Precept I. (*Passive* duty.) What *not to do*, when injured (ver. 19).

(i) Do not insist on taking vengeance by legal processes against those who injure *you*, but

(ii) let the Divine ὀργή have its course. The All-just will deal with them in His own time and way. Give place to Him (ver. 19).

[*Obs.* 1. ἐκδικεῖν here means to *avenge*, as in Rev. vi. 10; xix. 2; S. Luke xviii. 3; and not to *punish*, as 2 Cor. x. 6. The emphatic word is ἑαυτούς. The precept is like that in ver. 17 against retaliation; but is directed against a different motive for punishing one who has injured us. In ver. 17 the thought of making *an adversary suffer* an equivalent, while here, that of *avenging self*, is condemned.]

[*Obs.* 2. ἡ ὀργή here, as in iii. 5; v. 9; 1 Thess. i. 10; ii. 16, is a 'dogmatic technical term,' the Divine wrath. (Winer, *Gr. N. T.* p. 743.) So ἡ χάρις, τὸ θέλημα, Rom. ii. 18. τόπον διδόναι = to make place for another, S. Luke xiv. 9; and so inferentially, to give him time and opportunity to act. That ἡ ὀργή does not mean, (1) the Christian's *own wrath* at being injured, which might pass away, if time were given it (cf. Livy viii. 32 *irae spatium dare*, but τόπον διδόναι in Greek does *not* mean this, but to give room for indulgence, Plut. *De irâ cohibendâ*, p. 462); or (2) the wrath of the man who inflicts the injury, and before which it might be prudent to retreat, is clear from the quotation. The latter would be a maxim of worldly, as distinct from Christian, prudence.]

Reason for (ii). In Deut. xxxii. 35 GOD claims to punish injuries, in virtue of His moral prerogatives; and He also undertakes to punish them (ver. 19).

Heb. לִי נָקָם וְשִׁלֵּם

'To Me [belongs] revenge and recompense.'
LXX. ἐν ἡμέρᾳ ἐκδικήσεως ἀνταποδώσω.

[*Obs.* 1. Deut. xxxii. 35 is quoted to show that the right and duty of punishing those who are guilty of injustice is reserved by GOD for Himself. The LXX departs from the Hebrew, to which S. Paul keeps more closely, using however the words of the LXX and adding λέγει Κύριος. The citation reappears exactly in Heb. x. 30, and in the paraphrase of Onkelos. Meyer suggests that the saying had become proverbial as a 'formula of warning,' and thus influenced both S. Paul and the paraphrase of Onkelos.]

[*Obs.* 2. Does this precept make it wrong to prosecute for burglary or assault? It would do so, if these offences could only affect the individual. They are prosecuted, however, not as wrongs done to the individual, but as crimes against GOD and society. If the individual only were affected, such prosecutions would be un-Christian. On the Stoic conception of forgiveness of injuries, see Seneca, *de Irâ*, ii. 32, 33; iii. c. 5. On the patience of the Christian populations under the stress of Pagan persecution, see Tertull. *Apolog.* c. 37 'Cui bello non idonei, non prompti fuissemus, etiam impares copiis, qui tam libenter trucidamur si non apud istam disciplinam (scil. Christianam) magis occidi liceret quam occidere?' cf. too *contra Marcion.* ii. c. 18. Cf. S. Matt. v. 39.]

Precept II. (*Active* duty.) What *to do*, when injured. Be energetically kind to the man who has done the wrong (ver. 20).

{ (1) If he is hungry, feed him thyself (ver. 20).
  (2) If he is thirsty, give him drink (ver. 20).

Reason for the precept.

In doing this, thou wilt bring him to remorse and shame for his conduct. Thy large-hearted kindness will heap up on him the 'glowing coals of fire'—the pain of remorse (ver. 20).

[*Obs.* 1. ψωμίζειν (ψωμός), give morsels, as if with thine own hand. The expression is affectionate, 1 Sam. xxviii. 22, LXX; 1 Cor. xiii. 3; Deut. viii. 16.]

[*Obs.* 2. Verse 20 is a quotation from Prov. xxv. 21, 22 :—

אִם־רָעֵב שֹׂנַאֲךָ הַאֲכִילֵהוּ לָחֶם
וְאִם־צָמֵא הַשְׁקֵהוּ מָיִם:
כִּי גֶחָלִים אַתָּה חֹתֶה עַל־רֹאשׁוֹ:

The LXX corresponds with S. Paul's text, except that cod. A. reads τρέφε for ψώμιζε, and omits πυρός after ἄνθρακας. The expression σωρεύειν ἄνθρακας ἐπὶ τὴν κεφαλήν = to heap up pain that clings to a man. 'Glowing coals' are used as a metaphor for 'pain that strikes deep and cleaves.' The Rabb. phrase 'to give any one coals and lightning' is formed on Ps. xi. 6; xviii. 8. 'Coals of the wise' mean, cutting remarks that give pain. *Pirqe Aboth*, ii. 14. In 2 Esdr. xvi. 53 the burning fiery coals on the head is an image of painful punishment, sent by GOD; but the context *there* makes it necessary, while it suggests another sense in the present passage. That enemies should be benefited, in order to secure their severer punishment hereafter is as far as possible from the Apostle's mind. S. Jerome, *contra Pelag.* lib. i. p. 840 'Non in maledictum et condemnationem, ut plerique existimant, sed in correctionem, ut superatus beneficiis, excoctus fervore, inimicus esse desistat': S. Aug. *de Catechiz. rudibus* 'Nulla est major ad amandum provocatio quam praevenire amando': *De Doct. Christ.* iii. 16, where the ἄνθρακας πυρός are explained as 'urentes poenitentiae gemitus.']

Precept III. (*General* duty.) Be not vanquished by the evil which an enemy does against thee, but conquer it in the power of the good which thou doest in return (ver. 21).

[*Obs.* On this, see Seneca, *de Benef.* vii. 31 'Vincit malos pertinax bonitas.']

§ 4.

Obligations of Christian Morality for the Christian as living under a (pagan) civil government (xiii. 1–7).

[*Obs.* 1. The necessity for this section is traceable to the widespread feeling of irritation against the Roman government among the Jewish populations. To the Jew the theocracy seemed to be the only legitimate form of government: Deut. xvii. 15 'Thou mayest not set a stranger over thee, which is not thy brother.' The Messianic promise, as understood by the Jews, was hostile to the claims of any pagan government. Notwithstanding the Roman conquests, the Jews still debated whether ἔξεστι δοῦναι κῆνσον Καίσαρι, ἢ οὔ (S. Matt. xxii. 17), and maintained that οὐδενὶ δεδουλεύκαμεν πώποτε (S. John viii. 33). Judas the Gaulonite had founded a sect which held that it was unlawful to obey earthly rulers (Joseph. *Ant.* xviii. 1. 1; Acts v. 37); and the enterprise of Theudas (Joseph. *Ant.* xx. 51) and the speech of Eleazar at Maseda (Joseph. *de Bell. Jud.* vii. 8. 6) are equally illustrative of the prevailing temper. Indeed Rome itself had recently been the scene of Jewish insubordination, Suetonius, *vit. Claudii*, c. 25; Acts xviii. 2; Dio Cassius, *Hist. Rom.* lx. c. 5. The heathens did not yet distinguish between Jews and Christians; and some converts from Judaism may have brought with them their revolutionary sympathies and projects into the Church of Christ. On the revolutionary temper imputed to the Christians by Jewish agitators, see Acts xvii. 6, 7; and by Pagan orators, see Acts xxiv. 5, 6.]

[*Obs.* 2. But probably the reason for the paragraph is to be found more precisely in the Ebionite conception that the power which governs the world, and acts through the civil magistracy is devilish. This belonged to the dualistic tendency in Ebionitism; cf. Epiph. *Haer.* xxx. 16. So the author of the Clementine Homilies (xv. 7) says, 'The True Prophet says that GOD the Creator of all things assigned two realms to two beings, the one good, the other evil. To the evil being he gave the lordship of the present world, with the proviso, that he should punish those that do evil: to the good being, the future eternal world ... The children of the future world are while they remain in this one, in the hostile realm of a foreign king.' This antagonist position enables us to understand the Apostle's passing over the many questions that might be raised as to the relation of the governed to the government, and insisting on what might seem at first a truism, οὐκ ἔστιν ἐξουσία εἰ μὴ ἀπὸ τοῦ Θεοῦ: cf. Baur, *Paulus d. Apostel*, ii. 3.]

[*Obs.* 3. S. Peter insists, with equal earnestness, on the duty of obedience to civil governments (1 S. Pet. ii. 13–17; comp. 2 S. Pet. ii. 19). There is no reason for supposing that he had S. Paul's language in view, or that S. Paul had his.]

A. *Duty* I. Every Christian should *submit* (ὑποτασσέσθω) to the imperial government (xiii. 1).

Proved (xiii. 1–6).

[*Obs.* 1. πᾶσα ψυχή, כָּל־נֶפֶשׁ, yet not a mere Hebraistic paraphrase, for the personal pronoun. ψυχή, like נֶפֶשׁ, is never entirely without meaning. It here means man, conceived of as feeling pleasure or displeasure, attraction or repugnance: in Rom. ii. 9, man as feeling punishment. For other shades of meaning, see S. Matt. xxvi. 38; Acts ii. 43; iii. 23; Heb. xiii. 17; 1 S. Pet. ii. 25.]

[*Obs.* 2. The ἐξουσίαι ὑπερέχουσαι, magistracies of commanding position, include all the high offices of the empire. For ἐξουσίαι, in the sense of earthly authorities, see S. Luke xii. 11; Tit. iii. 1. In Eph. iii. 10; vi. 12; Col. ii. 15; 1 S. Pet. iii. 22, it refers to an order of spiritual beings, whether angels or demons. The abstract term ἐξουσίαι (without the article) is (as in ver. 3 ἄρχοντες sqq.) elsewhere rendered into concrete equivalents; cf. 1 S. Pet. ii. 13, where after the emperor (βασιλεὺς ὡς ὑπερέχων), are specified the legati (ἡγεμόνες), or other high officials who represent him. So 1 Tim. ii. 2, the Church is to offer intercessions, ὑπὲρ βασιλέων καὶ πάντων τῶν ἐν ὑπεροχῇ ὄντων. The emperor, who in the West was princeps or imperator, never rex, was bluntly termed βασιλεύς in the eastern provinces.]

[*Obs.* 3. In ὑπερεχούσαις and ὑποτασσέσθω, ὑπέρ and ὑπό are correlative. Preeminence implies submission.]

Arg. 1. From the *Divine origin* of civil government (vers. 1 b, 2).

1. General theses.
    a. No magistracy exists which is not ἀπὸ Θεοῦ (ver. 1 b).
    b. The *de facto* magistracies are appointed ὑπὸ τοῦ Θεοῦ (ver. 1 b).

2. Inferences (ὥστε) from these theses.
    a. Resistance to the magistracy is resistance to GOD's διαταγή (ver. 2 a).
    b. Those who do resist will to their own hurt (ἑαυτοῖς, *dat. incommodi*) receive a penal judgment (κρίμα), (ver. 2 b).

[*Obs.* 1. In ver. 1 b, ἀπό and ὑπό are not arbitrarily interchanged. Civil government derives its authority from GOD (ἀπό), and He, by His providence, establishes it among men (ὑπό). The objection that whatever might be said about the abstract origin of civil government, *de facto* governments (αἱ οὖσα ἐξουσίαι) are too bad to be obeyed, is met by the fact that GOD has given them their lease of power.]

[*Obs.* 2. Civil government being ἡ τοῦ Θεοῦ διαταγή, resistance to it is resistance to Him, and the κρίμα which punishes it, though inflicted by man, is really His. It is clear from ver. 3 that the Apostle is thinking of penalties inflicted by the ἄρχοντες. This applies not only or chiefly to hereditary monarchies, but to all regularly-constituted governments, whether monarchical or republican. All that is requisite to cultivate the obligation of obedience to a government is that it is οὖσα. With the origin of a government, or its political form the Apostle does not concern himself; nor does he enter upon the question at what point during a period of revolutionary change a given government is to be considered as οὖσα, or as non-existent; and when a government, originally illegitimate, acquires a prescriptive right. The imperial authority was too old, and too firm to make these questions practical; and the Apostle gives the precepts which are required by the circumstances of his readers. The Roman ἐξουσίαι combined the forms of a republic with the reality of a despotism. See Merivale, *Romans under the Empire*, vol. iv. c. 32. The imperial authority was, as regards the Romans, an usurpation; as regards the provincials, the result of war and conquest. Yet it was ἡ οὖσα ἐξουσία, and, as such, was from GOD.]

Arg. 2. From the *providential and beneficial purpose* of civil government (vers. 3, 4).

[*Obs.* The prop. that οἱ ἄρχοντες οὐκ εἰσὶ φόβος τῷ ἀγαθῷ ἔργῳ in ver. 3 is introduced as a reason (γάρ) for the immediately preceding statement that a Divine judgment will fall upon rebels.]

The providential purpose of a Ruler is to inspire fear, not into those who do good, but into those who do wrong (ver. 3 a).

Hence,

    a. Those who act rightly need not fear government: government will show them some mark of its approbation (ἔπαινος), since it is after all GOD's minister, intended by Him to promote the cause of good (vers. 3 b, 4 a).

    b. Those who act criminally ought to fear government. It is armed with the power of life and death for a serious purpose. It is GOD's minister, designed by Him to punish the evil-doer (ver. 4 b).

[*Obs.* 1. The abstract ἐξουσία here becomes concrete οἱ ἄρχοντες, but the term is still general. φόβος, 'a terror' (used like timor), for φοβεροί, 'metonymia rei pro rei causa.' So τὸ ἀγαθὸν ἔργον (see App. Crit.) and τὸ κακὸν ἔργον are personified; the ἄρχων has only to deal with the ἔργον. Of the intention he knows nothing. The ἔπαινος which government bestows is not a reward, but only its approbation. The reason (γάρ) for expecting this lies in the Divine mission of government, which is Θεοῦ διάκονος. The μάχαιρα which government bears is not the παραξιφίς or dagger worn by the emperor and others as the symbol of the *jus vitae et necis*, but, as always in the New Testament, the curved sword, which used to be borne by, or before, the Greek magistrates. φορεῖν marks the *continued* habit, and so means more than φέρειν.]

[*Obs.* 2. The expression φόβος τῷ κακῷ ἔργῳ is the key to the feeling about the Pagan Imperial Despotism which prevailed in the early Church. S. Irenaeus (*Haer.* v. 24. 2) traces the necessity for such a government to the fall of man. Since the fall human nature has been avaricious and cruel ; and, accordingly, 'ad utilitatem gentilium terrenum regnum positum est a Deo, ... ut timentes regnum hominum non se alterutrum homines vice piscium consumant.... Cujus jussu homines nascuntur, ejus jussu et reges constituuntur, apti his qui illo tempore ab ipsis regnantur.' This view of despotic government, as a safe-guard provided for fallen human nature against the effects of its own selfish vices, might seem to be inconsistent with the heathen cruelty and levity of some of the Roman emperors ; but S. Irenaeus ascribes such abuse of absolute power to God's just judgment of a guilty world. The duty of submission had nothing to do with the faith or character of the reigning emperor. S. Aug. *de Civ. Dei*, v. 21 'Qui dedit imperium Constantino Christiano, Ipse Apostatae Juliano.']

[*Obs.* 3. The description of government as Θεοῦ διάκονος, which is twice repeated, and as εἰς τὸ ἀγαθόν (ver. 4 a) and ἔκδικος εἰς ὀργὴν τῷ τὸ κακὸν πράσσοντι (ver. 4 b), applies to it as designed by Providence, not always as existing in fact. But as yet it was the earlier and happier period of Nero's reign, when ἔπαινος might be sometimes accorded to virtue. Cf. Merivale, *Romans under the Empire*, vol. vi. c. 52 : Seneca, *de Clementia*, i. 1. For the atrocities and degradation of Nero's later years, see Tacitus, *Ann.* xvi. 1-16.]

Arg. 3. (Subjective inference from preceding arguments.) From the double moral necessity (ἀνάγκη) for submission, which thus (διό) presents itself (ver. 5).

This necessity is
- i) partly, but not chiefly, political : διὰ τὴν ὀργήν. To refuse submission is to incur the vengeance of the government (ver. 5).
- (ii) partly, and more especially, moral : διὰ τὴν συνείδησιν. To refuse submission is to disobey the commands of the Christian conscience (ver. 5).

[*Obs.* 1. ἀνάγκη means a moral necessity in 1 Cor. ix. 16. The Jews knew of no motive of submission to the government of the Empire, save their dread of its vengeance. Christians were compelled to submit by their conscientious conviction that, amid all its degradations, it wielded a power which came from God. For διὰ τὴν συνείδησιν, compare διὰ τὸν Κύριον, 1 S. Peter ii. 13 and 1 Cor. x. 25-29.]

[*Obs.* 2. συνείδησις here, not consciousness, as Heb. x. 2 τῶν ἁμαρτιῶν συνείδησις, but, as generally, conscience, i. e. the moral faculty distinguishing good from evil, praising the one and blaming the other: cf. Rom. ii. 15 ; ix. 1 ; 1 Cor. viii. 7, 10, 12 ; x. 29 ; 2 Cor. 1. 12 ; iv. 2 ; v. 11 ; Heb. ix. 14.]

[*Obs.* 3. Conscience recognizes as a general law the duty of submission to the civil government. There are however grave questions, which S. Paul does not here raise, but which in later times have had to be answered : e. g. (i) What is a Christian's duty during a revolution, when political power is changing hands, and it is doubtful where ἡ οὖσα ἐξουσία is to be found ? On this, see Tertullian, *Apolog.* 30-37. In *ad Scapulam*, c. 1 he observes that Christians were accused of disloyalty : ' tamen nunquam Albiniani, nec Nigriani, vel Cassiani inveniri potuerunt Christiani.' (ii) What is a Christian's duty if the government enjoins that which is contrary to the Law of God? The rule is given Acts v. 29 πειθαρχεῖν δεῖ Θεῷ μᾶλλον ἢ ἀνθρώποις. The admitted jurisdiction of the civil government in matters of earthly concern cannot be pleaded as a reason for submitting to it when it usurps the duties of ministers of religion, still less when it prescribes idolatry or religious error. Tertullian notices the use which was made of this passage by those who shrank from martyrdom, and wanted a good reason for submitting to government when it insisted on apostasy: *Scorpiace*, c. 14 'Non in occasione frustrandi martyrii, jubet te subjici potestatibus, sed in provocatione bene vivendi, etiam sub illarum respectu, quasi adjutricum justitiae.' So in his *de Idol.* 15. It is the duty of Christians to be 'subditos magistratibus, et principibus, et potestatibus, sed intra limites disciplinae quousque ab idololatria separamur.' He then cites the cases of the Three Children and Daniel, who were absolutely obedient to the commands of the kings, until the law of God was imperilled. The modern misconstructions of S. Paul's language arise from a neglect of limitations to its scope which Scripture elsewhere supplies. Cf. Harless, *Christian Ethics*, iii. 54.]

Arg. 4. From consistency, the Principle implied by the existing practice of the Apostle's readers who already paid taxes to the civil government (ver. 6).

[*Obs.* 1. The fact that Christians pay taxes to the civil government is a reason (γάρ) confirmatory of the ἀνάγκη stated in ver. 5. διὰ τοῦτο marks the ground of such payment; taxes are paid because government is from God, and submission to it a Christian duty. οὖν, in ver. 7, must prevent one considering τελεῖτε an imperative. The Apostle is arguing from the *practice* of Christians to the principle it implies. If submission to government was wrong, they ought not to recognize and support government by paying taxes.]

[*Obs.* 2. On the payment of taxes to the Imperial officers, cf. Tert. *Apol.* 42 'Sed caetera vectigalia [i. e. other than those paid to keep up the temples] gratias Christianis agent ex fide dependentibus debitum, qua alieno fraudando abstinemus, ut si ineatur quantum vectigalibus pereat fraude et mendacio vestrarum professionum, facile ratio haberi possit, unius speciei querela compensata pro commodo caeterarum rationum.' What was withdrawn from the temples was more than made up to the revenue in other ways. Cf. S. Justin. *Apol.* i. 17 φόρους δὲ καὶ εἰσφορὰς τοῖς ἐφ' ὑμῶν τεταγμένοις πειρώμεθα φέρειν, ὡς ἐδιδάχθημεν παρ' αὐτοῦ.]

§ Justification of διὰ τοῦτο. The rulers of the State (οἱ ἄρχοντες) have a certain priestly or sacrificial character in Christian eyes. As the ἐξουσία is Θεοῦ διάκονος (ver. 4), so its representatives are λειτουργοὶ Θεοῦ. It is for this very object, εἰς αὐτὸ τοῦτο, viz. τὸ λειτουργεῖν τῷ Θεῷ, that they labour so perseveringly; and they are supported in this high function by the proceeds of taxation (ver. 6 b).

[*Obs.* 1. The sacredness of the civil magistracy which had been indicated in Θεοῦ διάκονος (twice repeated, vor. 4) minister of a justice which is really GOD's, is here enhanced by λειτουργοὶ Θεοῦ, entrusted by GOD with a public service, that of collecting the taxes which acknowledge the sanctity and rights of government. λειτουργεῖν, λειτουργία, λειτουργός, all had a classical use: referring especially to public duties or services at Athens undertaken by a citizen at his own expense: Plat. *Laws*, xii. p. 949 C. So in Lysias, Isocrates, Theophrastus. The verb was used by the LXX (to render שָׁרַת, 'to wait upon,' Numb. xviii. 2; Ex. xxviii. 31, 39; xxix. 30 sqq. &c. and עָבַד, Numb. iv. 38; xvi. 9; xviii. 6 sqq.) of the sacred duties of Priests and Levites. So S. Paul calls himself λειτουργὸς Ἰησοῦ Χριστοῦ Rom. xv. 16; and Christian worship is described as λειτουργεῖν τῷ Θεῷ Acts xiii. 2. The word λειτουργός is used of heathen priests by Dion. Halicarn. *Ant.* ii. 73, of Jewish priests, cf. Neh. x. 39; Ecclus. vii. 31; Heb. viii. 2; x. 11. It is already applied to royal officers and servants, 1 Kings x. 5; Ecclus. x. 2. Here in a sense which partakes of its classical and sacred associations. The adjective λειτουργικός does not occur except in LXX and N. T., used of σκεύη, Numb. iv. 28; στολαί, Ex. xxxi. 10; πνεύματα, Heb. i. 14, &c.]

[*Obs.* 2. In εἰς αὐτὸ τοῦτο, εἰς defines the aim of προσκαρτεροῦντες. αὐτὸ τοῦτο would have no adequate motive, if it referred only to taxation.]

B. Duty II. Every Christian should contribute money and moral support to the government (ver. 7).

[*Obs.* This precept is *suggested* by the fact just (ver. 6) noticed, that Christians do pay taxes. It is a moral *inference* (οὖν) from the now-established claims of government as Θεοῦ διάκονος (ver. 4). The construction is elliptical; supply after τῷ φόρον, τέλος, κ.τ.λ. ἀπαιτοῦντι.]

ἀπόδοτε
πᾶσι
τὰς ὀφειλάς.

(i) φόρον.   *Taxes* on persons and property: *tributum*; (so κῆνσος), (ver. 7).
(ii) τέλος.   *Customs* on goods: *vectigal*; (ver. 7).
(iii) φόβον.   *The profound veneration* due to the *highest* persons in the State (ver. 7).
(iv) τιμήν.   *The honour* and respect due to all who hold public offices (ver. 7).

[*Obs.* 1. The Jews had scruples about paying taxes to the Pagan Government. Judas of Gamala taught τὴν ἀποτίμησιν οὐδὲν ἄλλο, ἢ ἀντικρὺς δουλείαν ἐπιφέρειν, Josephus, *Ant.* xviii. 1. 1. Our Lord was asked whether it was *lawful* to pay tribute, S. Matt. xxii. 17. Moreover, the character of the τελῶναι for peculation was proverbial: the taxes were embezzled throughout the empire. On Nero's proposal to abolish the *vectigalia*,—probably only in Italy and the Coloniae,—see Tacitus, *Ann.* xiii. 50. The duty of Christians was not affected by any abuses in the administration, or by political considerations.]

[*Obs.* 2. On ver. 7 b, see Tatian, *contra Graecos*, c. 4, who insists that he is ready to discharge the duties of a subject; but reserves φόβος for GOD: τὸν μὲν γὰρ ἄνθρωπον ἀνθρωπίνως τιμητέον, φοβητέον δὲ μόνον τὸν Θεόν. Cf. 1 S. Pet. ii. 17 τὸν Θεὸν φοβεῖσθε, τὸν βασιλέα τιμᾶτε. S. Paul used φόβος in a restricted sense: he implies that there are high State-officers to whom it is due.]

B.

Animating motives of Christian Morality (xiii. 8–14).

Motive I. *The Love of* God, *and, for His sake, of man, considered as a debt which can never be paid off* (vers. 8–10).

[*Obs.* The precept in ver. 8 is a *more general* statement of that in ver. 7. The duty of Christians towards the officers of the State (ver. 7) is widened, so as to include all obligations that may be due to any human being. One debt alone can never be paid off, because no external acts or sacrifices exhaust its claim—the debt of ἀγάπη. ἀγάπη remains, eluding all efforts to discharge its obligations; being as it is the inspiring creative force to all Christian excellence. Cf. S. Aug. *Ep.* cxcii. 1. *ad Celest.* 'Semper autem debeo caritatem quae sola etiam reddita semper detinet debitorem. Redditur enim cum impenditur, debetur autem etiam si reddita fuerit, quia nullum est tempus quando impendenda jam non sit, nec cum redditur amittitur, sed potius reddendo multiplicatur.']

Precept. After paying off all other debts, continue to pay the inexhaustible debt of ἀγάπη (ver. 8 a).

§ *Reasons* for this Precept, drawn from the significance of ἀγάπη (vers. 8 b, 9).

Arg. 1. (γάρ ver. 8 b.) From the inherent moral force of ἀγάπη. The man who really loves his neighbour (τὸν ἕτερον), already, in doing so, has implicitly fulfilled the Second Table of the Law (ver. 8 b).

[*Obs.* In τὸν ἕτερον, any other human being with whom ὁ ἀγαπῶν has to do is brought definitely before the mind's eye (Rom. ii. 1, 21; 1 Cor. iv. 6; vi. 1, &c.). πεπλήρωκε, as in ii. 25, present of the completed action: in the act of ἀγαπᾶν the precepts of the law have been fulfilled: Gal. v. 14; S. Matt. xxii. 39, 40; 1 Tim. i. 5; S. James ii. 8. Although νόμον without the *art.* may mean 'abstract law,' the context (ver. 9) points to the Mosaic Law here as a proper name.]

Arg. 2. (γάρ ver. 9; reason for πεπλήρωκε ver. 8 b.) From the language of the Mosaic Law. In Leviticus xix. 18 the previously enumerated commandments respecting a man's duty to his neighbour are repeated and summarized in the precept to 'love him as thyself' (ver. 9).

Lev. xix. 18. Heb. וְאָהַבְתָּ לְרֵעֲךָ כָּמוֹךָ
LXX ἀγαπήσεις τὸν πλησίον σου ὡς σεαυτόν.

[*Obs.* 1. In Lev. xix the preceding precepts referred to by the Apostle (ver. 9) are not only or all the commandments of the Second Table. But all duties of a man to his neighbour are dictated by ἀγάπη.]

[*Obs.* 2. The *sixth* commandment here follows the *seventh*, as in S. Mark x. 19; S. Luke xviii. 20; S. James ii. 11; Philo, *de Decalogo*; S. Clem. Alex. *Strom.* vi. 16. S. Paul followed copies of the LXX which had the same order, as codex B. Deut. ver. 17. The fifth commandment is not given; the ninth, οὐ ψευδομαρτυρήσεις, has been added by a copyist for the sake of completeness. For this ἀνακεφαλαίωσις of the Second Table in Lev. xix. 18, see S. Matt. xxii. 39; S. Mark xii. 31; S. Luke x. 27; Gal. v. 14: νόμος βασιλικός S. James ii. 8.]

Arg. 3. From the negative force of ἀγάπη. It refrains from working ill to a neighbour. Hence the conclusion (οὖν) that, since the seventh, sixth, tenth, and other commandments of the Second Table (except the fifth) forbid such ill in detail, ἀγάπη is the πλήρωμα νόμου. Through ἀγάπη the spirit of the Law has already been fulfilled (ver. 10).

[*Obs.* For the negative, repressive power of ἀγάπη, see 1 Cor. xiii. 4 b-6). It is this, rather than its active and productive force, which makes it πλήρωμα νόμου, the νόμος being chiefly prohibitory. ἀγάπη is the πλήρωμα νόμου, that in which its fulfilment really consists; not merely πλήρωσις, the process of achieving this fulfilment. Cf. Gal. v. 14, where however the positive as well as the negative force of ἀγάπη is insisted on as making it fulfil the law. On the subject-matter, see Newman, *Par. Serm.* v. 23 'Love the one thing needful.']

Motive II. *The nearness of the Second Advent of Christ* (vers. 11-14).

A. The period (καιρός) characterized, in accordance with the (instructed) knowledge (εἰδότες) of the Roman Christians (ver. 11).

[*Obs.* ver. 11 is introduced as yielding a motive for the precept in ver. 8 καὶ τοῦτο, and for this, viz. μηδενὶ μηδὲν ὀφείλετε εἰ μὴ τὸ ἀλλήλους ἀγαπᾶν, no supplement like ποιεῖτε is required, Winer, *Gr. N. T.* p. 717; 1 Cor. vi. 6, 8; Eph. ii. 8; Phil. i. 28.]

a. It is ὥρα ἐξ ὕπνου ἐγερθῆναι — high time for awaking out of moral and spiritual slumber (ver. 11).

b. (Reason (γάρ) for ὥρα, κ.τ.λ.) The completed salvation (ἡ σωτηρία) to follow upon Christ's Second Coming is much nearer now (νῦν *objective*) than at the date of the conversion of the Roman Christians, or of the Apostle (ver. 11).

c. The period preceding the Second Advent—the *night* of time—is far advanced in its course. The period following the Second Advent—the *day* of Eternity—is at hand (ver. 11).

[*Obs.* 1. For the same motive, see Heb. x. 25, 37; 1 Cor. vii. 29; 1 S. Pet. iv. 7. Καιρός, the appointed measure of time, S. Matt. xxiv. 45; S. John vii. 6. It refers to the period between the present and the Second Coming. This καιρός was continually becoming shorter. The Apostles felt that the Second Coming *might* occur at any moment (Phil. iv. 5; 1 Thess. v. 6; Rev. xxii. 12); our Lord having desired them to be always prepared for it (S. Matt. xxiv. 42; xxv. 13; S. Luke xxi. 34-36); as indeed fast approaching 'S. Matt. xxiv. 29'. But that they were mistaken in their anticipations, or disappointed at the result, is an unwarranted assumption: see 2 S. Pet. iii. 8 for their real mind.]

[*Obs.* 2. ὕπνος and νύξ are often used as figures of the life without Christ, 1 Cor. xv. 34; Eph. v. 14; 1 Thess. v. 6. Christ's disciples at their conversion have come from darkness into the light, Eph. v. 8, 11; 1 S. Pet. ii. 9; S. John iii. 20, 21. Here however (ver. 12) νύξ means the period before the Second Advent, and ὕπνος, which corresponds to it (ver. 11), here indicates a condition of the regenerate, in which full moral and spiritual activity is slumbering, owing to the remaining power of sin. The Christian therefore needs awakening from time to time.]

[*Obs.* 3. ὅτε ἐπιστεύσαμεν, the historic moment of conversion to the Faith. For πιστεύειν, see 1 Cor. iii. 5; xv. 2; Gal. ii. 16; 2 Thess. ii. 11; S. John i. 7. 12. ἡ σωτηρία ἡμῶν, the complete salvation into which Christians enter at the Second Advent, 1 S. Pet. i. 5, 9; Rom. i. 16; v. 9; viii. 23.]

B. Practical results of this knowledge. The ἐγερθέντες ἐξ ὕπνου should live as children of the Day which is already dawning (vers. 12-14).

1. *Change* in the moral clothing (ἀποθώμεθα, ἐνδυσώμεθα) of the soul, as befits the break of 'day' (ver. 12).

   a. Put off (like night-clothes) the ἔργα τοῦ σκότους, works which belong to moral darkness, as the sphere in which they are wrought: Eph. v. 11 (ver. 12).

   b. Put on (like a soldier's day attire) the ὅπλα τοῦ φωτός, principles and methods of action which belong to the sphere of spiritual light (ver. 12).

[*Obs.* The Christian is awaking from sleep. His first duty is to change the garments of the night for those of the day. The ἔργα τοῦ σκότους are regarded as night-clothes, which the sleeper has had on; σκότος is the robe of which the ἔργα are appropriate decorations. The ὅπλα τοῦ φωτός become the Christian as a warrior for Christ, and are 'put on' like garments, Eph. vi. 11; 1 Thess. v. 8. Here σκότος and φῶς correspond to νύξ and ἡμέρα: ὅπλα is the designed antithesis to ἔργα, since in the Christian new principles are the best safeguard against old acts of sin.]

2. *Conduct* (περιπατήσωμεν) which befits the '*day*' (ver. 13).

   1. *Positive* characteristic (εὐσχημόνως). Moral *decorum* (ver. 13 a).
   2. *Negative* characteristic. It is incompatible with (ver. 13 b),

Practical: ch. XIII, *vv.* 8 14. 255

> *a.* Sins of gluttony and their occasions (ver. 13 b)—
>   κώμοις, revellings : Gal. v. 21.
>   μέθαις, carousals.
> *b.* Sins of impurity (ver. 13 b)—
>   κοίταις : ix. 10 ; Wisd. iii. 13.
>   ἀσελγείαις : 2 Cor. xii. 21 ; Eph. iv. 19 ; 1 S. Pet. iv.
>   3. 'Protervitas et petulantia, non obscaenitas libidinis,' Tittman, *Syn.* p. 151. Except 2 S. Pet. ii. 18.
> *c.* Sins of temper (ver. 13 b)—
>   ἔριδι : 2 Cor. xii. 20 ; Gal. v. 20.
>   ζήλῳ, jealousy : 1 Cor. i. 11 ; iii. 3.

[*Obs.* 1. These sins commonly grow in the order given by the Apostle. Excess at the table leads to impurity, and this to strife and jealousy. On the fatal oscillation of fallen human nature between θυμός and ἐπιθυμία until completely rescued by Christ, see J. Müller, *Ch. Doctr. of Sin*, ii. 5 sub fin.]

[*Obs.* 2. This verse is historically of great interest, as having determined the conversion of S. Augustine. Cf. *Confessions*, viii. 12. 28 sqq.]

3. *Fundamental principles* of the life which befits the '*day*' (ver. 14).

a. Positive. Put on the Lord Jesus Christ (ver. 14 a).

[*Obs.* The phrase ἐνδύσασθε τὸν Κύριον Ἰ. Χ., expressing intimate union with Jesus Christ, may be compared with לבש בגדי שכינה of the Synagogue. By putting on the clothes of the Shekinah, it is meant that man's sin must be 'covered' by Divine glory (Delitzsch, *Hebr. Uebersetz. in loc.*). This ἐνδύσασθαι τὸν Κ. Ἰ. Χ. is the secret of ἐνδύεσθαι τὰ ὅπλα τοῦ φωτός and of εὐσχημόνως περιπατεῖν. Real moral renovation is impossible, unless there be intimate union with the New Manhood of the Second Adam. ἐνδύεσθαι is often used metaphorically with a quality ; Job xxix. 14 ἐνδύνειν δικαιοσύνην: Hom. *Il.* xix. 36 δύσεο δ' ἀλκήν. But the 'praesens efficacia' of Christ makes the metaphor mean much more than the adoption of His modes of feeling and action, which would be its natural meaning in the case of a dead exemplar. The use of לבשׁ in a figurative sense, which means 'to be wholly filled with' some person or thing, probably governs S. Paul's use of ἐνδύεσθαι (see above). This investiture with the New Humanity of Christ first takes place in Baptism: Gal. iii. 27 ὅσοι γὰρ εἰς Χριστὸν ἐβαπτίσθητε, Χριστὸν ἐνεδύσασθε : but each revival or advance of the spiritual life is a new putting on of Christ ; hence the precept, Eph. iv. 24 ἐνδύσασθε τὸν καινὸν ἄνθρωπον τὸν κατὰ Θεὸν κτισθέντα ἐν δικαιοσύνῃ καὶ ὁσιότητι τῆς ἀληθείας. In Col. iii. 12 this is further expanded. See Wilberforce, *Incarn.* chap. xiii.]

b. Negative. Not to take such care for the σάρξ as to stimulate the ἐπιθυμίαι, which have their seat in it (ver. 14 b).

[*Obs.* σάρξ does not here exactly = σῶμα : but it is the material of the σῶμα, the animal nature of man, considered as the source of sensuous and sinful desires, in contrast to πνεῦμα. It is not, on the other hand, the sinful principle in man, as at Gal. v. 16-21, because *this* σάρξ is to be crucified (Gal. v. 24 ; Rom. viii. 6, 7, 13 ; Col. ii. 13, 14', as utterly intolerable to a Christian, as belonging to the past unconverted life (Rom. vii. 5 , and having no claims whatever on him now (Rom. viii. 12'. πρόνοιαν μὴ ποιεῖσθε would be advice altogether unequal to the occasion, if the Apostle were alluding to a deadly enemy of the spiritual life. This precept against taking too much care of the σάρξ is not inconsistent with the Apostle's condemnation of the false asceticism, ἀφειδία σώματος, at Colossae (ii. 23', which differs from the true in its principle and motive, rather than in its outward form.]

PRACTICAL PORTION OF THE EPISTLE.

Division II.

CHRISTIAN DUTIES WITH RESPECT TO EXISTING SCRUPLES ABOUT PRIVATE RELIGIOUS OBSERVANCES (xiv. 1 – xv. 13).

[*Obs.* 1. The questions discussed in this section originated in scruples entertained by converts from Judaism in the Church of Rome. These converts could not make up their minds to abandon the private observance of (1) such ascetic rules as (*a*) to eat *no* flesh (ver. 2), and (*b*) to drink *no* wine (ver. 21); or of (2) the Jewish feasts and fasts, or some of them (ver. 5). They seem to have judged somewhat hardly the Gentile Christians, who did not at all share their scruples (vers. 3, 10), and to have been treated in turn with a contemptuous disregard for their scruples (vers. 3, 10, 15, 16). These Jewish converts, forming the minority, are termed ἀσθενοῦντες τῇ πίστει (xiv. 1, 2), οἱ μὴ ἐσθίοντες (ver. 3), οἱ φρονοῦντες τὰς ἡμέρας (ver. 6), οἱ διακρινόμενοι (ver. 23), οἱ ἀδύνατοι (xv. 1). The majority, consisting of converts from Heathendom, are οἱ ἐσθίοντες (ver. 3), οἱ μὴ φρονοῦντες τὰς ἡμέρας (ver. 6), οἱ δυνατοί (xv. 1).]

[*Obs.* 2. The ἀσθενοῦντες (xiv. 2) are not to be confounded, (1) with the pure Judaizers of the Epistle to the Galatians. For in eating *no* flesh and drinking *no* wine, they observed a rule different from and stricter than that of the Mosaic Law. They do not seem, moreover, to have insisted on circumcision; and, instead of saying that through their adhesion to Jewish forms Christ would profit them nothing (Gal. v. 2), S. Paul pleads for toleration of their scruples. Nor, (2) with the cabalistic theosophists of the Epistle to the Colossians. Nothing is said here about a philosophical basis for the asceticism practised at Rome; and S. Paul does not condemn the Roman ascetics for presumption (Col. ii. 18), or ἐθελοθρησκεία (*ib.* ver. 23), or 'not holding the Head' (*ib.* ver. 19). Nor, (3) with the ἀσθενεῖς at Corinth (1 Cor. viii), who were scandalized at the use of εἰδωλόθυτα for Christian food, and whose case is treated very similarly to the present. There is however no trace of any such motive for abstinence from flesh and wine on the part of the Roman Christians. They seem to have followed a private rule, possibly of Essenic origin, like many Jews of that period (Philo in Eus. *Praep. Ev.* 8 fin.), and to have shrunk from abandoning it on their conversion to the Church. Banus, the pious and ascetic master of

Josephus, lived on vegetables (in *vit. Josephi*, c. 2); and there were pious priests who lived on figs and dates (in *vit. Josephi*, c. 3). Compare S. John the Baptist, S. Luke i. 15; vii. 33; S. Matt. iii. 4. For the ascetic life of S. Matthew, see S. Clem. Alex. *Paedagog.* i. 16. p. 174; of S. James, Eus. *Hist. Eccl.* ii. 23. There were Christian ascetics of this kind, contemporaries of Origen, *Contra Cels.* v. 49. The apostolical Canons condemn those Clergy who considered the use of flesh and wine actually sinful, but not those who abstained from them for ascetic and disciplinary reasons (Can. 43 (51)). Read the account of the Christian ascetic and martyr Alcibiades under Marcus Aurelius, Eus. *Hist. Eccl.* v. 3. The Pythagorean asceticism was an instance of a corresponding moral temper in Heathendom; but it would not have in any degree influenced the ascetic converts from Judaism to Rome. Cf. Tholuck *in loc.*]

[*Obs.* 3. The section may be analyzed as follows:—

§ 1. Statement of the points in controversy, with appended encouragements and warnings (xiv. 1–5).

§ 2. Principles to be kept in view when dealing with these questions (xiv. 6–xv. 13).

  i. The risk involved in passing judgment on others (xiv. 6–13 *a*).
  ii. The danger of injuring or wounding weak consciences (xiv. 13 b–xv. 4).
  iii. The duty of mutual forbearance and union within the Church, based on Christ's relation both to Jews and Heathen (xv. 5–13).]

A.

Statement of the points in controversy, with appended encouragements and warnings (xiv. 1–5).

General duty of the majority of the Roman Church (δυνατοὶ τῇ πίστει) towards the minority (ἀσθενεῖς τῇ πίστει) which entertains scruples in favour of certain private observances. This duty is twofold: (1) to give it a welcome (προσλαμβάνεσθε), and (2) to avoid judgments on the thoughts and motives which have shaped its scruples (ver. 1).

[*Obs.* By προσλαμβάνεσθαι is meant a cordial welcome to all the intimacy and privileges of a common church-life, xv. 7; Acts xviii. 26; Philemon 17. Opposed to it is ἐκκλεῖσαι θέλειν Gal. iv. 17. The ἀσθενοῦντες were already in the communion of the Church; but the majority of δυνατοί were indisposed to cooperate with them, except on the condition of constantly making unfavourable criticisms on the motives which actuated them. The ἀσθένεια τῇ πίστει consisted, not in a defective hold upon the Object-matter of faith, but in a failure to understand what it involved in respect of freedom from the rules of earlier or human systems. Eἰs may express 'intention' or 'result' (Winer, *Gr. N. T.* p. 496). διάκρισις, 'discrimination between,' as in Heb. v. 14; 1 Cor. xii. 10. διαλογισμοί, as Rom. i. 21; 1 Cor. iii. 20: as also S. Matt. xv. 19; S. Mark vii. 21; S. Luke ix. 46; xxiv. 38. In Phil. ii. 14; 1 Tim. ii. 8, 'outspoken arguments.']

A. *First point in controversy.* Whether it be right to insist upon abstaining from all animal food (ver. 2).

{ (i) The δυνατός is convinced that he may eat anything, without restriction (ver. 2).
(ii) The ἀσθενής eats only vegetables (λάχανα), (ver. 2).

[*Obs.* 1. The Neo-Pythagoreans were vegetarians, Seneca, *Ep.* cviii. 17-20; Porphyr. *de abst.* quoted by Meyer; but this cannot have determined the rule of the Roman ἀσθενεῖς. Yet this rule undoubtedly excluded (legally) 'clean' meats as well as 'unclean'; and meat not offered in sacrifice to idols as well as εἰδωλόθυτα. It was probably a variety of Essenic discipline.]

[*Obs.* 2. When Jovinian compared the private rules observed by the ἀσθενεῖς at Rome with those enjoined for Christian edification by common Church authority, S. Jerome observed, after quoting this verse, that the Apostle, 'non inter jejunia et saturitatem aequalia merita dispensat; sed contra eos loquitur, qui in Christum credentes, adhuc judaizabant,' *Contr. Jovinian.* ii. 16, tom. ii. p. 351. c. ed. Vallars.]

§ Apostolic cautions (vers. 3, 4).

Caution 1. (To the δυνατοί.) The Christian who eats all food indiscriminately is not to be *contemptuous* (μὴ ἐξουθενείτω) towards the vegetarian (ver. 3).

Caution 2. (To the ἀσθενεῖς.) The Christian who only eats vegetables is not to be *censorious* (μὴ κρινέτω) towards the man who observes no restrictions (ver. 3).

[*Obs.* This tendency on the part of the ἀσθενεῖς to form narrow and hard judgments of the δυνατοί required more notice than did the ἐξουθένησις of the latter towards their 'weak' brethren. It was in fact more religious, and therefore more likely to win approval from misinformed consciences. Accordingly the Apostle contents himself with showing the evil of such narrow judgments.]

Arg. 1. (γάρ ver. 3.) GOD *has* accepted (προσελάβετο) the man who eats food of all kinds (viz. by admitting him into the Church). It is not then for men to condemn him (ver. 3).

Arg. 2. Such condemnation pronounced on the δυνατοί by the ἀσθενεῖς is *intrusive* and *erroneous* (ver. 4).

    a. Intrusive, because the person who eats food of all kinds is after all ἀλλότριος οἰκέτης—a servant in the House (not of his critic, but) of Jesus Christ. Whether he perseveres in grace or falls from it, is a matter which concerns, not the critic, but his real Master, Christ (ver. 4).
    b. Erroneous, because charity must presume that such a person will persevere, σταθήσεται. GOD'S power *can* effect this (ver. 4).

[*Obs.* That στήκει ἢ πίπτει, σταθήσεται are to be explained, not of *acquittal* or *condemnation* at the Judgment, but of *perseverance in* or *falling from* grace appears from δυνατεῖ γάρ, κ.τ.λ. Cf. 1 Cor. x. 12 τῷ ἰδίῳ Κυρίῳ, *dat. of relation.*]

B. *Second point in controversy.* Whether particular days ought to be privately observed as feasts and fasts (ver. 5).

    (i) The ἀσθενής sets an especial value on particular days (ver. 5).
    (ii) The δυνατός treats all days as alike (ver. 5).

§ Apostolic caution for both (ver. 5 b).

Let every one be satisfied in his own practical reason with the motives of his action, and independently of the judgment of others (ver. 5 b).

[*Obs.* 1. The Jewish observance of days is here in question; as Gal. iv. 10 ἡμέρας παρατηρεῖσθε, καὶ μῆνας, καὶ καιροὺς καὶ ἐνιαυτούς: Col. ii. 16 μὴ οὖν τις ὑμᾶς κρινέτω ἐν βρώσει καὶ ἐν πόσει, ἢ ἐν μέρει ἑορτῆς ἢ νουμηνίας ἢ σαββάτων. In the Galatian and Colossian Churches such observance was connected with errors condemned. Not so at Rome. The Jewish Sabbath and other sacred days were *privately* observed by a section of the Roman Christians, without dishonouring the work of Christ.]

[*Obs.* 2. On πληροφορείσθω, see iv. 21; Col. iv. 12. πληροφορία, Col. ii. 2; 1 Thess. i. 5; Heb. vi. 11; x. 22. Whether these days are observed or not, Christians should be satisfied, each in *his own* mind, that they are doing GOD'S Will. This purely subjective standard of conduct only applies in cases like the present where nothing is clearly laid down by Revelation or Church-authority. To apply it to the Christian Lord's Day, or to other Holy days which the Church prescribes for observance in the Prayer Book, is to assume an analogy between the cases which does not exist. On the observance of Festival Days, see Hooker, *Eccl. Pol.* v. 69-71. On Fasts, public and private, *Ibid.* v. 72.]

B.

Principles to be kept in view when dealing with these questions (xiv. 6—xv. 13).

Principle I.

Much risk is involved in passing judgment on the private religious life of others (xiv. 7–13 a).

Arg. 1. The observances of the ἀσθενεῖς, and the neglect of these observances by the δυνατοί, have *a common motive*, namely, the desire to please our Lord Jesus Christ (ver. 6). [In view of this sacred motive, criticism on outward details should be silenced.]

a. This is true of private distinctions of days, according to the Jewish Calendar (ver. 6 a).

$$\left\{ \begin{array}{l} 1.\ \text{The}\ \dot{a}\sigma\theta\epsilon\nu\dot{\eta}s \left\{ \begin{array}{l} \dot{o}\ \phi\rho\rho\nu\hat{\omega}\nu \\ \tau\dot{\eta}\nu\ \dot{\eta}\mu\dot{\epsilon}\rho a\nu \end{array} \right\} \\ 2.\ \text{The}\ \delta\nu\nu a\tau\dot{o}s \left\{ \begin{array}{l} [\dot{o}\ \mu\dot{\eta}\ \phi\rho\rho\nu\hat{\omega}\nu \\ \tau\dot{\eta}\nu\ \dot{\eta}\mu\dot{\epsilon}\rho a\nu \end{array} \right\} \end{array} \right\} K\upsilon\rho\iota\hat{\omega} \left\{ \begin{array}{l} \phi\rho o\nu\epsilon\hat{\iota}. \\ \\ o\dot{\upsilon}\ \phi\rho o\nu\epsilon\hat{\iota}.] \end{array} \right.$$

b. This is also true of private abstinence [or non-abstinence] from animal food (ver. 6 b).

$$\left\{ \begin{array}{l} 1.\ \text{The}\ \delta\nu\nu a\tau\dot{o}s \left\{ \begin{array}{l} \dot{o} \\ \dot{\epsilon}\sigma\theta\iota\omega\nu \end{array} \right\} \\ 2.\ \text{The}\ \dot{a}\sigma\theta\epsilon\nu\dot{\eta}s \left\{ \begin{array}{l} \dot{o}\ \mu\dot{\eta} \\ \dot{\epsilon}\sigma\theta\iota\omega\nu \end{array} \right\} \end{array} \right\} K\upsilon\rho\iota\hat{\omega} \left\{ \begin{array}{l} \dot{\epsilon}\sigma\theta\iota\epsilon\iota \\ \\ o\dot{\upsilon}\kappa \\ \dot{\epsilon}\sigma\theta\iota\epsilon\iota \end{array} \right\} \left\{ \begin{array}{l} \text{proved}\ (\gamma\acute{a}\rho)\ \text{by his} \\ \text{thanksgiving.} \\ \text{proved also by his} \\ \text{thanksgiving.} \end{array} \right.$$

[*Obs.* 1. The Κύριος of this verse is our Lord Jesus Christ: see ver. 9. *Obs.* the *dat. commodi* Κυρίῳ, in Whose interest both parties to the controversy act, as belonging to Him. φρονεῖν means giving careful thought to an object. Cf. viii. 5; xii. 3.]

[*Obs.* 2. The clause ὁ μὴ φρονῶν τὴν ἡμέραν Κυρίῳ οὐ φρονεῖ is wanting in A. B. ℵ. C*. D. E. F. G. al. Vulg. It. Lat. Fathers.]

[*Obs.* 3. The εὐχαριστία, or grace, implies that the ἀσθενής and the δυνατός were alike willing to consecrate what they did by invoking the Name of God. For the εὐχαριστία before meals; cf. S. Matt. xv. 36, our Lord blessed the seven loaves and two fishes; Acts xxvii. 35, S. Paul during the voyage to Malta; 1 Cor. x. 30 τί βλασφημοῦμαι ὑπὲρ οὗ ἐγὼ εὐχαριστῶ; 1 Tim. iv. 4 πᾶν κτίσμα Θεοῦ καλὸν .... μετὰ εὐχαριστίας λαμβανόμενον.]

[*Obs.* 4. In the second part of ver. 6 the Apostle returns to the first point of controversy, namely, about abstinence from meat; and the second point, about private observance of days, is not again discussed. From this we may infer that the former occupied a much larger share of attention in the Church of Rome, although the principles appealed to by the Apostle are equally applicable to both.]

§ Proof of *Arg.* 1 (vers. 7-9).

Reason I. (γάρ ver. 7). From *the subjective direction of the true Christian's life.* The Christian, whether living or dying, *feels* that he owes himself unreservedly to Christ (vers. 7, 8).

1. Stated *negatively* (ver. 7).

{ οὐδεὶς ἡμῶν ἑαυτῷ ζῇ,
  οὐδεὶς ἑαυτῷ ἀποθνήσκει (ver. 7).

[*Obs.* ἑαυτῷ, like τῷ Κυρίῳ (ver. 1), is a dat. of the moral aim. The *subjective* direction of the Christian's life and death is described negatively; the Christian is conscious that he neither dies nor lives for *himself*. ἑαυτῷ ἀποθνήσκειν means to welcome or seek death, as a relief from the troubles of life. Of this selfishness in death, suicide is the highest expression.]

2. Stated *positively*, (so as to justify (γάρ ver. 8) the preceding (ver. 7) *negative* statement), (ver. 8 a).

ἐάν τε { ζῶμεν / ἀποθνήσκωμεν } τῷ Κυρίῳ { ζῶμεν / ἀποθνήσκομεν (ver. 8 a).

[*Obs.* 1. Here the subjective direction of the Christian's life and death is described positively. Whether living or dying, he knows that he owes himself, and therefore he gives himself, by a conscious act, to Christ. In the expression τῷ Κυρίῳ ἀποθνήσκειν, death is conceived of—not as a collapse of vital force, but as a moral act, wherein, by a conscious effort of will, the Christian surrenders his soul into the hands of the Redeemer. It is the final act of a life which has been deliberately given to an Unseen Master. Cf. ἐν Κυρίῳ ἀποθνήσκειν Rev. xiv. 13; Phil. i. 20; Christ will be magnified in my body whether by life or death: Rom. viii. 38; S. John xxi. 19.]

[*Obs.* 2. That Jesus Christ is the Person to whom the Christian, renouncing self, consecrates his life, is plain from ver. 9, which fixes the meaning of τῷ Κυρίῳ in ver. 8, as of Κυρίῳ (used as a proper name without the art.) in ver. 6. This self-consecration in life and death would be idolatry, unless He Who is its Object were truly GOD.]

3. Consequence (οὖν ver. 8 b) of 1 and 2. Whether in life or death, the Christian knows himself to be Christ's property (ver. 8 b).

Practical: chs. XIV, v. 6–XV, v. 13.

$$ἐάν τε \begin{cases} ζῶμεν \\ ἀποθνήσκωμεν \end{cases} τοῦ Κυρίου ἐσμέν \text{ (ver. 8 b).}$$

[*Obs.* in ver 8 the threefold Κύριος, as implying the Majesty of Christ, to Whom the Christian is consciously surrendered in life and death.]

Reason II. (γάρ ver. 9. Ground of the foregoing *subjective* relation of the Christian to Christ.) From the purpose of the *objective* historical fact of Christ's Death and Resurrection Life— ἀπέθανε καὶ ἔζησεν. (ver. 9 a.)

[*Obs.* 1. ἀπέθανε καὶ ἔζησεν is probably the original text, to which ἀνέστη was first added marginally as a gloss upon ἔζησεν, and then crept into the text itself, thus accounting for the variations; see Moyer. ἔζησεν, 'became alive'; the *hist. aor.* marking the commencement of His Risen Life after His Passion. There is no reference here to our Lord's earthly life before His Passion.]

[*Obs* 2. On the use of ζωή, ζῆν for the Resurrection Life of Christ, cf. Rom. v. 10; 2 Cor. iv. 10; Rev. ii. 8; xx. 4, 5. It was as dying and living after death that our Lord warranted the self-consecration of the Christian to Himself both in life and death : Rom. viii. 34; Phil. ii. 8, 9; S. Matt. xxviii. 18; S. Luke xxiv. 26.]

§ The Purpose (εἰς τοῦτο ... ἵνα) of the Death and Resurrection Life of Christ (ver. 9 b), was to establish His κυριότης over the dead and the living. By His descent into hell, He claimed rule over the dead (Phil. ii. 10); and by His Risen Life in Heaven, over the living (ver. 9).

[*Obs.* The unusual order of the words νεκρῶν καὶ ζώντων corresponds to that of Christ's Death and Risen Life. Cf. Winer, *Gr. N. T.* p. 691.]

Arg. 2. From the *Divine prerogative* of judgment, which it is not for man to usurp (vers. 10–13 a).

§ Both parties are reproved; the ἀσθενεῖς for their harsh judgments of the majority, and the δυνατοί for their contemptuousness towards the ἀσθενεῖς. The error of such κρίσις and ἐξουθένησις is shown (vers. 10 b–12).

[*Obs.* In ver. 10 σὺ δὲ τί κρίνεις is an *arg. ad verecundiam*, based on the contrast presented by the personality of the ἀσθενής who is thus addressed, to the κυριότης (ver. 9) of Jesus Christ. καὶ σὺ τί ἐξουθενεῖς is a still stronger *arg. ad verecundiam*, based on the contrast presented by the δυνατός who is thus addressed, to the Lord Jesus Christ. Compare ver. 3.]

Arg. 1. (γάρ ver. 10 b.) There is ONE tribunal of judgment—the βῆμα τοῦ Θεοῦ—before which all will present themselves (ver. 10 b).

[*Obs.* βῆμα occurs in the sense of *tribunal* in S. Matt. xxvii. 19; S. John xix. 13; Acts xii. 21; xviii. 12, 16, 17; xxv. 6, 10, 17. With this compare 2 Cor. v. 10 φανερωθῆναι δεῖ ἔμπροσθεν τοῦ βήματος τοῦ Χριστοῦ, where φανερωθῆναι expresses the consequence of παραστησόμεθα in this passage. That βῆμα τοῦ Θεοῦ (not Χριστοῦ) is the true reading, see Meyer. Christ as man will sit upon the βῆμα (S. Matt. xxv. 31; 2 Cor. v. 10) as the Divinely-appointed Judge (Acts x. 42; xvii. 31; Rom. ii. 16); and hence, as also on account of Christ's Divine Nature, it is βῆμα τοῦ Θεοῦ. On the Final Judgment, see Pearson *on the Creed,* Art. vii.]

Arg. 2. (γάρ ver. 11, in proof of Arg. 1, ver. 10 b.) From the language of prophecy respecting a future universal acknowledgment of GOD (ver. 11).

Is. xlv. 23, quoted to show that *all* human beings (πᾶν γόνυ καὶ πᾶσα γλῶσσα) will acknowledge GOD's supremacy at the Judgment of the World (ver. 11).

Heb.   בִּי נִשְׁבַּעְתִּי
יָצָא מִפִּי צְדָקָה דָּבָר
וְלֹא יָשׁוּב
כִּי־לִי תִּכְרַע כָּל־בֶּרֶךְ
תִּשָּׁבַע כָּל־לָשׁוֹן׃

'By Myself have I sworn,
There has gone forth from a-mouth-of-righteousness a word,
And it will not return;—
That to Me shall bend—every knee,
Shall swear—every tongue.'

LXX (Tisch.) κατ' ἐμαυτοῦ ὀμνύω, εἰ μὴ ἐξελεύσεται ἐκ τοῦ στόματός μου δικαιοσύνη, οἱ λόγοι μου οὐκ ἀποστραφήσονται, ὅτι ἐμοὶ κάμψει πᾶν γόνυ καὶ ὀμεῖται πᾶσα γλῶσσα τὸν Θεόν.

[*Obs.* 1. In the citation, the Apostle renders the oath by ζῶ ἐγώ, omits the two clauses εἰ μὴ ἐξελεύσεται .... ἀποστραφήσονται, paraphrases ὀμεῖται by ἐξομολογήσεται, and accordingly substitutes τῷ Θεῷ for τὸν Θεόν.]

[*Obs.* 2. The verse occurs at the close of the Prophecy on Cyrus, the Deliverer of Israel (Is. xliv. 24—xlv). It is a Messianic prediction of the final and universal triumph of the Theocracy. The Apostle sees a *complete* satisfaction of the Prophet's words in a still future event, viz. the Last Judgment, to which he accordingly applies them. The last Judgment presupposes all that the words more immediately foretell.]

[*Obs.* 3. In the words בִּי נִשְׁבַּעְתִּי GOD, swearing by Himself, pledges what He swears with His own life; hence the Apostolic ζῶ ἐγώ (instead of κατ' ἐμαυτοῦ ὀμνύω LXX), following חַי אָנִי, Numb. xiv. 21, 28; Deut. xxxii. 40, &c. λέγει Κύριος (cf. xii. 19) is added in accordance with the usual O. T. formula. The LXX ὀμεῖται follows the Heb. The reading ἐξομολογήσεται in Cod. Alex. is probably introduced from the N.T. הִשָּׁבַע may be used, as in 2 Chron. xv. 14, of swearing allegiance to GOD; Is. xix. 18; Zeph. i. 5. ἐξομολογεῖσθαι with the dat. means *to praise*: S. Matt. xi. 25; S. Luke x. 21; used absolutely 'to promise,' S. Luke xxii. 6; Rom. xv. 9; it requires an accusative of the object when it means *to confess* sins, S. James v. 16.]

Conclusion (οὖν ver. 12) *from the two preceding arguments.* Every one individually must give an account of himself to GOD (ver. 12).

[*Obs.* The emphasis lies on ἕκαστος, which is warranted by πᾶν and πᾶσα in the quotation, ver. 11. The logical inference is, that since every one without exception will give an account περὶ ἑαυτοῦ to GOD, the κρίσις of the ἀσθενεῖς and the ἐξουθένησις of the δυνατοί are superfluous and unwarrantable. The practical inference is stated in ver. 13.]

Practical Rule. Let neither class pass judgments, whether harsh or contemptuous, on the other (ver. 13 a).

[*Obs.* κρίνωμεν here, as ἀλλήλους shows, includes the ἐξουθένησις of the δυνατοί, as well as the narrow and harsh judgments of the ἀσθενεῖς. Observe the *antanaclasis* in κρίνατε. For this figure *antanaclasis*, see Bengel, *Gnomon Index term Tech.* s. v. In the first case the verb = 'to pass a judicial decision.' In the second 'to form a moral judgment.' To the *unchristian* κρίνωμεν is opposed, with this new sense, the *Christian* κρίνατε. What the judgment of Christians ought to be, the Apostle proceeds to state.]

Principle II.

The danger of injuring weak consciences (xiv. 13 b–xv. 4).

[*Obs.* This section is addressed throughout to the δυνατοί, who were disposed to insist upon Christian freedom from [private] rules of life, without any consideration for the conscientious difficulties of the ἀσθενεῖς on the subject.]

Precept addressed to the δυνατοί. Do not put moral difficulties in the way of a brother in Christ (ver. 13 b).

[*Obs.* πρόσκομμα is a stone against which a man stumbles in walking; σκάνδαλον a trap into which he falls: Rom. ix. 32, 33; xi. 9; Lev. xix. 14. The two words are combined here to describe the complete effect on the conscience of a cause of moral offence.]

§ *Arguments enforcing the precept on the* δυνατοὶ τῇ πίστει (xiv. 14 –xv. 4).

Arg. 1. The spiritual mischief done by wounding the consciences of the ἀσθενεῖς is much greater than the spiritual advantages which may be secured by insisting on freedom from their ascetic rules (vers. 14–20 a).

A. Concession to the case of the δυνατοί. They are quite right in supposing that the idea of κοινόν, as attaching to any species of food, is purely *subjective*. There is no such thing as a κοινὸν δι' ἑαυτοῦ. But there is a κοινὸν τῷ λογιζομένῳ, and this has to be kept in view in deciding the question before us (ver. 14).

[*Obs.* 1. οἶδα is more precisely defined by πέπεισμαι ἐν Κυρίῳ Ἰησοῦ. S. Paul's indwelling in Christ was the source of his spiritual knowledge. Our Lord had taught that it is not τὸ εἰσπορευόμενον εἰς τὸ στόμα which κοινεῖ τὸν ἄνθρωπον S. Matt. xv. 17, 18, and S. Peter was bidden ἃ ὁ Θεὸς ἐκαθάρισε σὺ μὴ κοίνου Acts x. 15. Cf. 1 Cor. viii. 4-6; x. 26; 1 Tim. iv. 4, 5. For καὶ πέπεισμαι, cf. viii. 38, warranted by Col i. 19; ii. 3, 17; Eph. i. 22. Christ is the source of true spiritual knowledge. His knowledge of the inherent nature of things is implied in His relation to the universe, as stated in Col. i. 16 sqq.]

[*Obs.* 2. If, for δι' ἑαυτοῦ, δι' αὐτοῦ be read, the reference is to Christ: S. Paul is persuaded that He has not made anything κοινόν by His teaching, or that nothing is unclean in consequence of His redemptive work. But the reading ἑαυτοῦ is to be preferred. The ordinary Jewish distinction between 'clean' and 'unclean' has no ground in objective fact. In this passage the modern distinction between *objective* (δι' ἑαυτοῦ) and *subjective* (τῷ λογιζομένῳ) is applied to κοινότης. The Apostle allows only a *subjective* τὸ κοινόν. δι' αὐτοῦ = φύσει, S. Chrys.; 'natura sua immundum,' Orig. κοινόν should be compared with ἀκάθαρτον Acts x. 14; ἀπόβλητον 1 Tim. iv. 4; and ποιῶν βδέλυγμα, 'abominabile,' Rev. xxi. 27, corresponding to נִדָּה. For the account of the word, cf. S. Jerome, *Comm. in S. Matt.* xv. 11 'Populus Judaeorum, partem Dei esse se jactitans, *communes* cibos vocat, quibus omnes utuntur homines, v. g. suillam carnem, lepores, &c. ... Commune ergo, quod caeteris hominibus patet, quasi non de parte Dei, pro immundo appellatur.' κοινόν does not presuppose any inherent evil in particular kinds of food; but the Roman ἀσθενεῖς, following some Essenic teaching, extended the idea of the word (restricted by the Jews to particular kinds of meat) to all animal food whatever. Yet—ἐκείνῳ κοινόν—the uncleanness is really *subjective*; it exists only for the individual ἀσθενής, in consequence of the condition of his conscience. For ἐκείνῳ, cf. S. Mark vii. 15, 20; 2 Cor. x. 18.]

B. Reasons why the δυνατοί should not do violence to the scruples of the ἀσθενεῖς (vers. 15-18).

Reason 1. (γάρ, not δέ, ver. 15.) *The rule of charity*: κατὰ ἀγάπην περιπατεῖς. This will no longer be observed, if the δυνατοί insist on eating everything indiscriminately. For, in seeing them violate rules which he thinks sacred, the ἀσθενής cannot but experience some moral perplexity and distress (λυπεῖται). No particular kind of food can be really worth the infliction on others of serious moral pain (ver. 15 a).

Reason 2. *The Redemptive effect of Christ's death.* There is real risk lest the δυνατοί, by insisting on their freedom, should *destroy souls for which Christ has died*. The meat which they insist on eating *will* effect this destruction. It cannot be worth such a price (ver. 15 b).

[*Obs.* The construction changes from the indicative to the imperative, from the form of argument to that of deprecation. ἀπόλλυε is the result of λυπεῖται: it is to be understood of the eternal ἀπωλεία, from which Christ redeemed men by His death. Into this ἀπωλεία the ἀσθενής might fall, by being tempted to disregard his conscience, although, on this particular point, it was misinformed. Christ's Life, (the Apostle argues,) given for the ἀσθενής, ought to be more precious to the δυνατός than insistance on eating flesh-meat.]

Reason 3. *Influence on the surrounding heathen.* The result (οὖν) of violating charity and destroying souls, for such a poor object as freedom to eat anything, would be to *draw down upon the Kingdom of Christ* (ὑμῶν τὸ ἀγαθόν) *the calumnies of the heathen*, who will say that Christians hope to get to heaven by virtue of insisting on eating everything (ver. 16).

[*Obs.* In ver. 16 οὖν implies that heathen calumnies would be a natural consequence of the evils referred to in ver. 15. For βλασφημεῖν, i. e. βλάπτειν τὴν φήμην, bringing [holy things] into dishonour, cf. Rom. ii. 24; iii. 8; Tit. ii. 5. ὑμῶν τὸ ἀγαθόν is understood of (1) Christian faith, S. Chrys. and S. Ambrose; (2) Christian hope; (3) Christian ἐλευθερία, as represented by the δυνατοί themselves, 1 Cor. x. 29, 30; cf. 1 Cor. viii. 4; x. 25; but more probably (4) of the Kingdom or Church of Christ (see ver. 17); the Jewel or Treasure which the Christian purchases at his conversion, by the sacrifice of everything else (S. Matt. xiii. 44-46), and in which he finds all the μέλλοντα ἀγαθά Heb. ix. 11; x. 1. It was not any sectional interest, but the influence and character of the whole Body of Christ, which was the true ὑμῶν τὸ ἀγαθόν of the δυνατοί (as well as of others), and which was now imperilled. The Church would be calumniated, if the δυνατοί insisted on their inconsiderate neglect of the prejudices of the ἀσθενεῖς.]

§ Two *subordinate reasons* for μὴ βλασφημείσθω ὑμῶν τὸ ἀγαθόν. There *are* objects to secure which a Christian will turn a deaf ear to heathen criticism. But insistance upon freedom to eat everything is not such an object (vers. 17, 18).

Reason (*a*), (γάρ ver. 17). The essential characteristic of GOD's Kingdom *does not* consist in the principle of eating and drinking everything indiscriminately. It *does* consist in righteousness, peace, and spiritual joy. [If then the δυνατοί respect the prejudices of the ἀσθενεῖς, they will not thereby forfeit anything essential to a share in the Kingdom, while they will illustrate those supernatural graces which are its distinguishing characteristics], (ver. 17).

[*Obs.* 1. The βασιλεία τοῦ Θεοῦ here, as in 1 Cor. iv. 20; S. Luke xvii. 21, is viewed on its *subjective* side, Aquin. 'Regnum Dei dicitur id, per quod Deus regnat in nobis, et per quod ad regnum ipsius pervenimus.' It does not consist in *the act of eating or drinking* (βρῶσις and πόσις, not βρῶμα and πόμα) this or that, 1 Cor. viii. 4; 2 Cor. ix. 10; Col. ii. 16. Observe that the false idea here combated by the Apostle, is *not* the supposed necessity of abstinence from particular kinds of food, *but* the supposed necessity of making no distinctions between different kinds of food under any circumstances.]

[*Obs.* 2. The βασιλεία τοῦ Θεοῦ is apprehended subjectively by means of three graces in particular:—

(a) δικαιοσύνη, S. Matt. vi. 33, *first* before God, and *next*, as the context would suggest (ver. 18), *moral uprightness* in dealing with Christian brethren.

(b) εἰρήνη, *first* with God, and *next* with other men, especially Christians, xii. 18; σύνδεσμος εἰρήνης Eph. iv. 3; the third fruit of the Spirit, Gal. v. 22.

(c) χαρά, *first* rising towards God, out of faith and hope, xii. 12; ver. 3; and *next*, illuminating all acts of intercourse with Christian brethren. 'Gaudium referendum est ad modum, quo sunt justitiae opera perficienda,' Aquinas. Its sphere is the Holy Ghost, 1 Thess. i. 6 χαρὰ Πνεύματος ἁγίου: Phil. iii. 1. χαίρειν ἐν πνεύματι, in opposition to natural high spirits, Phil. iv. 4.]

Reason (b), (γάρ ver. 18, confirmatory of Reason (a), ver. 17 b). The man who serves Christ in the sphere of δικαιοσύνη, εἰρήνη, and χαρά is (a) well-pleasing (εὐάρεστος) to God, and (b) approved (δόκιμος) by the higher moral judgment of his fellow-men. [This should determine the course of the δυνατοί towards the ἀσθενεῖς], (ver. 18).

[*Obs.* 1. ἐν τούτοις (although ἐν τούτῳ is better supported, but see Meyer, App. Crit.), sc. δικαιοσύνη, εἰρήνη and χαρά. It denotes the life element; the sphere in which the Christian lives and works.]

[*Obs.* 2. For εὐάρεστος τῷ Θεῷ, cf. 1 Cor. viii. 3 βρῶμα δὲ ἡμᾶς οὐ παρίστησι τῷ Θεῷ: for δόκιμος τοῖς ἀνθρώποις, whose highest interests are forwarded by the Christian self-denial of others, 1 Cor. ix. 19 sqq.; x. 24. Observe that the service of *Christ* is the root of this, xii. 11; Phil. i. 20.]

Practical conclusion (ἄρα οὖν) from vers. 17, 18 (vers. 19, 20 a).

i. *Positive* (ver. 19).

διώκωμεν { τὰ τῆς εἰρήνης (ver. 19), all that promotes peace.
τὰ τῆς οἰκοδομῆς τῆς εἰς ἀλλήλους (ver. 19), all that promotes Christian perfection in others.

ii. *Negative* (ver. 20 a).

μὴ ἕνεκεν βρώματος κατάλυε τὸ ἔργον τοῦ Θεοῦ (ver. 20 a).

[*Obs.* 1. τὰ τῆς εἰρήνης, everything that can promote peace in the Church : here especially consideration for the prejudices of the ἀσθενεῖς about food and Jewish days. τὰ τῆς οἰκοδομῆς, everything that can build up the life of faith and love in souls, and in the Church at large. οἰκοδομή is used sometimes of the *process of building*, sometimes of *the edifice itself*. For the latter, cf. 1 Cor. iii. 9 ; Eph. ii. 21 : for the former, or all that promotes it, cf. Rom. xv. 2 ; 2 Cor. x. 8 ; xiii. 10 ; 1 Thess. v. 11. That it is here used in the sense of active edification, the addition τῆς εἰς ἀλλήλων shows. διώκειν, as implying earnest moral effort, has for objects φιλοξενίαν Rom. xii. 13 ; ἀγάπην 1 Cor. xiv. 1 ; δικαιοσύνην 1 Tim. vi. 11.]

[*Obs.* 2. By the ἔργον τοῦ Θεοῦ is here meant the state of grace in which the ἀσθενής is—the καινὴ κτίσις of Eph. ii. 10 ; 2 Cor. v. 17 ; Gal. vi. 15 ; 1 Cor. iii. 9, which cost so dear a price, 1 Cor. viii. 11, 12. This might be destroyed, if the example of the δυνατοί led the ἀσθενεῖς to imitate them, while doing violence to their consciences. καταλύειν is the reverse process to οἰκοδομεῖν, S. Matt. xxvi. 61 ; 2 Cor. v. 1 ; Gal. ii. 18. Observe the antithesis of τὸ ἔργον τοῦ Θεοῦ in the soul, and—βρῶμα.]

Arg. 2. The pleas insisted on by the δυνατοί do not warrant them in wounding the consciences of the ἀσθενεῖς by doing violence to their prejudices (xiv. 20 b-23).

Plea I. 'πάντα καθαρά, all kinds of food are in themselves really pure ; and it is of importance to proclaim this, in the face of the error which denies it' (ver. 20 b).

[*Obs.* This is the same position as the Apostle himself has already conceded, οὐδὲν κοινὸν δι' ἑαυτοῦ ver. 14. He admits it here by μέν, but proceeds to show its irrelevancy as bearing on the practical question.]

§ *Answer to Plea* I (ἀλλά ver. 20 b). Two *moral* considerations (20 b, 21).

Ans. 1. It is *sinful* (κακόν) for the ἀσθενής to eat [that which is intrinsically καθαρόν, but] διὰ προσκόμματος, while giving offence to his sense of right. [And to this he *may* be urged by the conduct of the δυνατοί], (ver. 20 b).

[*Obs.* The reference of τῷ ἀνθρώπῳ τῷ διὰ προσκόμματος ἐσθίοντι to the ἀσθενής is suggested by vers. 13, 14. If προσκόμματος referred to the offence given by the βρῶσις of the δυνατοί, 1 Cor. viii. 10 would exactly illustrate it. For the relaxed use of διά, cf. Winer, *Gr. N. T.* p. 475, as ii. 17.]

Ans. 2. It would be morally *noble* (καλόν) for the δυνατός to eat *no* animal food whatever, and to drink *no* wine, (in accordance with the Essenic rule of the Judaeo-Roman ἀσθενεῖς), and indeed to do nothing which could occasion spiritual offence or scandal or weakness to a brother in Christ (ver. 21).

[*Obs.* 1. For the absolute use of προσκόπτειν, cf. Ecclus. xxxiv. 17; xiii. 23; S. John xi. 9, 10.]

[*Obs.* 2. To the καθαρά of the plea, are opposed the κακόν (ver. 20 b) and καλόν (ver. 21) of the reply. These words represent much weightier *moral* considerations; and the plea must therefore be set aside.]

[*Obs.* 3. (ver. 21.) ἢ σκανδαλίζεται ἢ ἀσθενεῖ must be retained. The threefold description of a single disastrous moral result is to be explained by the Apostle's strong sense of the extreme and varied character of the disaster. ἀσθενεῖ here '*is* weak,' not 'becomes weak.' That the ἀσθενεῖς drank no wine is here only intimated.]

Plea II. The δυνατός urges that he 'has a firm "faith" [in Christ], which leads him to treat the scruples and observances of the ἀσθενεῖς with pardonable impatience' (ver. 22 a).

§ *Answer to Plea* II (vers. 22, 23).

Ans. 1. It should suffice the δυνατός that he may cherish *this* 'faith' in respect of himself alone [κατὰ σεαυτόν] before God [ἐνώπιον τοῦ Θεοῦ], (ver. 23 a).

[*Obs.* S. Chrys. paraphrases: ἀρκείτω σου τὸ συνειδός. God knows of this moral confidence of the δυνατός, and He will approve it the better, if it is not made a ground for wounding the consciences of other men.]

§ Reason for κατὰ σεαυτὸν ἔχε (ver. 22 a).

a. The δυνατός himself already μακάριος in being free from any self-condemnatory judgment on the score of conduct which he approves. [Thus he can afford to be considerate and generous to others.]

[*Obs.* 1. The implied argument is that the strong can afford to be generous and considerate towards the weak. ἐν ᾧ δοκιμάζει,—in that which he approves as the right course of action, 2 Macc. iv. 3.]

[*Obs.* 2. The maxim μακάριος κ.τ.λ. *may* be applied to the ἀσθενής also. In that case it is a warning to the δυνατός not to disturb his μακαριότης. Probably therefore it is best taken generally, with however a more immediate application to the case of the δυνατός.]

Ans. 2. The ἀσθενής, on the other hand, if he eats, doubting whether such eating is right or not, falls under the penal judgment of GOD (ver. 23). This κατακέκριται is proved, ὅτι οὐκ κ.τ.λ.

[*Obs.* κατακέκριται is proved by a syllogism.
{ In a Christian, all action which does not spring from the moral confidence of faith is sinful:
But indiscriminate eating on the part of the ἀσθενής would not spring from the moral confidence of faith:
Therefore it would be sinful.
These premises are stated in the reverse order of the reasoning.]

(i) (*Minor premiss.*) Because he eats not ἐκ πίστεως, i.e. with that moral confidence in the general rightfulness of his conduct with which Faith in Christ endows *a Christian* in all those matters as to which the Will of GOD is not clearly revealed (ver. 23).

(ii) (*Major premiss.*) Because *in a Christian* all which does not thus spring ἐκ πίστεως, (from the moral confidence which faith implies), is *sin* (ver. 23).

[*Obs.* 1. The conclusion is that the δυνατός, by his inconsiderately insisting on the plea of πίστις for himself, may become, in whatever degree, responsible for the *sin* against conscience and so for the condemnation of the ἀσθενής.]

[*Obs.* 2. The principle πᾶν ὃ οὐκ ἐκ πίστεως ἁμαρτία ἐστίν, is only applied by S. Paul to the *Christian* life. To infer from it that all the virtues and works of unbelievers are sins, is to reason 'a dicto secundum quid ad dictum simpliciter.' Cf S. Aug. *contra Julian.* iv. c. 3; *de Gratiâ Christi*, c. 26; *de Adult. conjug.* i. c. 18; S. Prosper. *de vit. Contempl.* iii. c. 1. So especially Calvin, *Institut.* ii. 3. n. 3, 4; iii. 15. n. 6. Art. xiii says that works before Justification 'cum ex fide Jesu Christi non prodeant minimè Deo grata sunt,' and that 'peccati *rationem* habere non dubitamus.' The Council of Trent, sess. 6, can. 7, condemns those who say that works done before Justification are sins—which, as Bp. H. Browne says, does not positively contradict the Art. S. Paul does not say πᾶν ὃ ἐκ πίστεως δίκαιόν ἐστιν. There are such sins as sins of ignorance, and their guilt is proportioned to the responsibility of the agent for the ignorance. But, says S. Chrys. (ix. 715) ταῦτα πάντα περὶ τῆς προκειμένης ὑποθέσεως εἴρηται τῷ Παύλῳ, οὐ περὶ πάντων. Against the error that subjective conviction warrants any action whatever, thus denying that the objective Will of GOD is the standard of our conduct, cf. Delitzsch, *Bibl. Psych.* iii. § 4; Julius Müller, *Chr. Doct. of Sin*, i. 2. § 1.]

[*Obs.* 3. On *the relation of chapters* xv, xvi *to the rest of the Epistle* there are, speaking broadly, three theories. (i) That these chapters are to be considered a sort of appendix to the Epistle written by S. Paul in separate fragments, with the exception of xvi. 25-27, which properly follows xiv. 23, and closes the Epistle. (ii) That these chapters were written by S. Paul, but did not originally belong to the Epistle to the Romans at all. (iii) That these chapters were not written by the Apostle, but at a later period, and by an inferior hand (Baur).

The arguments for (i) and (ii) are based, (a) on Marcion's having ignored these chapters. But Origen expressly says (on xvi. 25), that Marcion cut them out. (b) On Tertullian's (*contra Marcion.* v. 14) saying that xiv. 10, on the 'tribunal Christi,' is found *in clausulâ* of the Epistle. But Tertullian is plainly referring to Marcion's copy. (c) On the difficulty of supposing that S. Paul had, *as yet*, so many acquaintances in Rome, as c. xvi implies, since he had never visited it. But Rome was the 'colluvies gentium': everybody went there sooner or later; and the Apostle need not have known *by face* all of those whom he mentions. (d) On the difficulty of supposing that Aquila and Priscilla (xvi. 3) were now in Rome, since shortly before (1 Cor. xvi. 19), and some years after (2 Tim. iv. 19), they were living at Ephesus. But they might easily have migrated, after the date of 1 Cor., from Ephesus to Rome; and their change of home would be known to the Apostle; while there is still less difficulty in supposing that they went back, at a later date, to their old home in Ephesus. (e) On the *repeated* formulae of conclusion (xv. 33; xvi. 20, 24), before the close of the Epistle. But this is naturally accounted for by the occurrence of fresh matter, which suggested successive postscripts to what had been already written. Meanwhile observe the intimate relation between xiv. 23 and xv. 1.

Baur (iii) attacks the Pauline authorship of cc. xv, xvi on various grounds of detail (*Paulus*, ii. 3), but chiefly because the advances to the Jewish Christians in xv. 3, 8, 14, and the drift of the quotations in xv. 9-12, are in conflict with Gal. i, ii. It may be replied that they are not more so than Rom. xiv to which Baur does not object, and to which they are a natural sequence. The circumstances of the Jewish converts at Rome, and of the Galatian Judaizers, were so entirely different, as to relieve the Apostle of any reproach of inconsistency.]

Arg. 3. The δυνατοί are under an obligation (ὀφείλομεν)

{ *a. Specifically*; to bear the infirmities (ἀσθενήματα) of their weaker brethren (xv. 1).

b. Generally; to avoid self-pleasing in religious matters (xv. 1).

[*Obs.* This obligation is immediately contrasted (δέ) with the preceding warning as to those perilous consequences to the ἀσθενεῖς which a reckless insistance on their privileges by the δυνατοί might involve (xiv. 23). The ἀσθενεῖς are here termed the ἀδύνατοι (a gentler expression), in contrast with the δυνατοί (more precisely defined as τῇ πίστει), with whom the Apostle classes himself (ἡμεῖς). The ἀσθενήματα (ἅπ. λεγ.) are the concrete manifestations of the ἀσθένεια, little prejudices and scruples, 'imbecillitates,' which to S. Paul appear burdensome (Gal. vi. 2 τὰ βάρη), and which the δυνατοί should bear with (βαστάζειν), for the sake of the ἀσθενεῖς, in a spirit of charity, sympathy, and patience. But this can only be done if the latter courageously determine not to make their own wishes and satisfaction in religious matters a first consideration. ἀρέσκειν ἑαυτῷ = to live so as to please self. On ἀρέσκειν, see viii. 8; 1 Cor. vii. 32.

Thus (a) and (b) are the *specific* and *general*, the *positive* and *negative* aspects of a single duty—namely, religious unselfishness: 1 Cor. x. 33 καθὼς κἀγὼ πάντα πᾶσιν ἀρέσκω, μὴ ζητῶν τὸ ἐμαυτοῦ σύμφερον, ἀλλὰ τὸ τῶν πολλῶν, ἵνα σωθῶσι: 1 Thess. ii. 4 οὕτω λαλοῦμεν οὐχ ὡς ἀνθρώποις ἀρέσκοντες, ἀλλὰ τῷ Θεῷ τῷ δοκιμάζοντι τὰς καρδίας ἡμῶν.]

Precept. The ὀφειλή, thus insisted on, is now thrown into the form of a general and positive rule of life: viz. that every Christian should please his neighbour, with a view to promoting his highest and eternal good (ver. 2). In this observe

(1) its *universal obligation* among Christians (ἕκαστος ἡμῶν):
(2) its *substance*; to win the approval of others (ἀρέσκειν τῷ πλησίον):
(3) its *intention*; { *generally*, to promote good (εἰς τὸ ἀγαθόν):
{ *specifically*, to build up in others the perfect Christian life (πρὸς οἰκοδομήν), (ver. 2).

[*Obs.* γάρ (ver. 2) is to be erased; see Tisch. App. Crit. The sphere within which ἀρέσκειν τῷ πλησίον is possible is defined by the general purpose which should govern it, εἰς τὸ ἀγαθόν. This excludes all mere worldly flattery, and sinful complaisance with human error. Of this the Apostle says, Gal. i. 10 εἰ ἔτι ἀνθρώποις ἤρεσκον, Χριστοῦ δοῦλος οὐκ ἂν ἤμην. εἰς τὸ ἀγαθόν marks the general tendency (εἰς), which is more specifically explained by the immediate aim πρὸς οἰκοδομήν: and this may be compared with τὸ σύμφερον τῶν πολλῶν 1 Cor. x. 33: cf. Rom. xiv. 19. In this sense S. Paul says, ἐγενόμην τοῖς ἀσθενέσιν ὡς ἀσθενής, ἵνα τοὺς ἀσθενεῖς κερδήσω. See the whole passage, 1 Cor. ix. 20-23.]

Reason 1 for the Precept, ver. 2 and ver. 1 b. (γάρ ver. 3.) Our Lord's example. Even Christ pleased not Himself; He lived conformably to Ps. lxix. 9, which describes prophetically the spirit of His Life (ver. 3).

Psalm lxix. 9, quoted to show that Jesus Christ renounced all self-pleasing, by exposing Himself to the reproaches of the enemies of the Eternal Father (ver. 3).

Heb. וְחֶרְפּוֹת חוֹרְפֶיךָ נָפְלוּ עָלָי׃

LXX οἱ ὀνειδισμοὶ τῶν ὀνειδιζόντων σε ἐπέπεσον ἐπ' ἐμέ.

[*Obs.* 1. The citation follows the LXX.]

[*Obs.* 2. This Psalm (vers. 23, 24) has been already quoted at Rom. xi. 9 sqq. with reference to the rejection of Israel. It is a Psalm of David when persecuted by Saul, and is throughout typically prophetic of the sufferings of Christ. The following verses are quoted in the New Testament.

ver. 4. Of the hatred of Christ's enemies, S. John xv. 25.

9 a. Of His driving the buyers and sellers from the Temple, S. John ii. 17.

9 b. Of His bearing the reproaches of God's enemies, Rom. xv. 3.

12. Of the mockery by the soldiers in the praetorium, S. Matt. xxvii. 27–30.

21. Of the offer of vinegar mingled with gall before the Crucifixion, S. Matt. xxvii. 34; and of the sponge dipped in vinegar afterwards, S. John xix. 29.

22 sq. Of the present rejection of Israel, Rom. xi. 9.

25 a. Of the deposition of Judas, Acts i. 20.]

[*Obs.* 3. That the reproaches of God's enemies fell on our Lord Jesus Christ, shows that Christ's will was not to please Himself: S. Luke vii. 39; S. Mark ii. 16; S. Matt. ix. 11; S. John viii. 49. For He took these indignities and sufferings upon Him voluntarily, Phil. ii. 6–8; Heb. xii. 2, 3. The quotation indeed speaks of devotion to *the cause of God*, while the context insists upon self-renunciation *for the spiritual interests of man*. There is no contradiction; the second object is implied in any adequate conception of the first. Our Lord gave Himself for His brethren in surrendering Himself perfectly to the Father's will.]

[*Obs.* 4. Our Lord, whether in action or in suffering, is the example of Christians, as being the Ideal or Archetypal Man. S. John xiii. 15 ὑπόδειγμα ἔδωκα ὑμῖν: 1 S. John ii. 6 ὁ λέγων ἐν αὐτῷ μένειν ὀφείλει καθὼς ἐκεῖνος περιεπάτησε καὶ αὐτὸς οὕτως περιπατεῖν: cf. Wilberforce, *Incarn.* c. iii. 'Christ the Pattern Man by Nature.']

Reason 2 (γάρ ver. 4) for the appropriateness of the preceding quotation in ver. 3. From the purpose of the O. T. Scriptures. Observe here —

i. The *description* of the O. T. (ὅσα προεγράφη), as the Sacred Writings of ages which preceded the Apostolic (ver. 4).

ii. The *general* purpose of the O. T. (εἰς τὴν ἡμετέραν διδασκαλίαν). Christian Instruction (ver. 4).

iii. The *more specific* (ἵνα) and *moral* purpose of the O. T. is the firm maintenance of the Christian *Hope* in the Eternal Future (ἵνα τὴν ἐλπίδα ἔχωμεν ver. 4). This is secured by two particular effects of the O. T.

ἡ
ἐλπίς
fostered
{
a. by ἡ ὑπομονή, the patience which is so peculiarly Christian, but of which the O. T. gives such bright examples (ver. 4).
b. by ἡ παράκλησις, *the* encouragement which the O. T. affords by promises as well as examples (ver. 4).
}

[*Obs.* 1. The Old Testament is not merely archaeologically precious as a record of the past, but has *enduring* and *spiritual* value: it is destined εἰς ἡμετέραν διδασκαλίαν: cf. Art. vii 'Of the Old Testament.' It is 'not contrary to the New, for both in the Old and New Testament everlasting life is offered to mankind by Christ.' (Marcion denied this in his *Antitheses*, a work in which there were passages from the Law and the Gospel contrasted in order to show that they did not proceed from the same author; cf. Tertullian, *adv. Marcion.* lib. 4. So the Manichaeans, Aug. *de Haeres.* 46; Socr. *H. E.* i. 22, and probably the Manichaean sects of Bulgarians, Cathari, &c. in the Middle Ages; Mosh. *Eccl. Hist.* cent. xi. pt. 2, 5. §§ 2, 3.) It was indeed the manual of Christian διδασκαλία in the Apostolic age, ὠφέλιμος πρὸς διδασκαλίαν 2 Tim. iii. 16: and διδασκαλία, as has been seen (xii. 7), was itself a χάρισμα. This general purpose of the Old Testament is more specifically described as enabling Christians to cling to their hope of an Eternal Future.]

[*Obs.* 2. ἡ ἐλπίς, the (specifically) Christian Hope. This may be (*a*) (*subjective*), the virtue by which the Christian looks forward to the promised future. Rom. v. 6; 1 S. Pet. iii. 15: or (*b*) (*objective*), the future to which he looks forward, Rom. viii. 24 sq. The Old Testament warrants (*b*), and so strengthens (*a*); but διὰ τῆς ὑπομονῆς καὶ παρακλήσεως seems to show that (*a*) is here meant. τῶν γραφῶν (*gen. auctoris*: Winer, *Gr. N. T.* p. 236) belongs to τῆς ὑπομονῆς as well as τῆς παρακλήσεως.]

[*Obs.* 3. The particular lesson of patience and encouragement in the Apostle's mind is that afforded by our Lord's example in His voluntary acceptance of the reproaches of the Jews, as prophetically described centuries before (προεγράφη) in Ps. lxix. 9.]

[*Obs.* 4. In the Collect for 2nd Sunday in Advent what is here said of the Old Testament is applied to the New Testament as well, and the idea of παράκλησις is determined into 'comfort.']

Principle III.

The duty of mutual forbearance and union (τὸ αὐτὸ φρονεῖν) incumbent upon the ἀσθενεῖς and δυνατοί alike, and based on Christ's double relation to the Jews and the Heathen (xv. 5–13).

Benediction. (Suggested by ver. 4), (vers. 5, 6).

1. The *source* of the Blessing.

ὁ Θεὸς { τῆς ὑπομονῆς καὶ / τῆς παρακλήσεως } δῴη ὑμῖν (ver. 5).

2. The *substance* of the Blessing.

τὸ αὐτὸ φρονεῖν : { (i) *Sphere* of this φρονεῖν = ἐν ἀλλήλοις (ver. 5).
(ii) *Standard* of this φρονεῖν = κατὰ Χριστὸν Ἰησοῦν. The *Will* of Christ (ver. 5). }

3. The *purpose* of the Blessing.

Unity { (i) of mind, ὁμοθυμαδόν, (ii) and voice, ἐν ἑνὶ στόματι, } in glorifying the Eternal Father of our Lord Jesus Christ (ver. 6).

[*Obs.* 1. The words τῆς ὑπομονῆς καὶ τῆς παρακλήσεως (gen. of quality, Winer, *Gr. N. T.* p. 231, Theophyl. αἰτίαν καὶ δοτῆρα ὀνομάζει Θεόν), are suggested by ver. 4; but the Benediction which they introduce consists in τὸ αὐτὸ φρονεῖν, which cannot exist, unless men are taught forbearance, and are consoled by GOD. GOD unites these in His Essence, which is Love, and imparts them to those who ask Him, Rom. viii. 37. On this subject, see S. Cyprian's Treatise, *De Bono Patientiae*. For analogous titles, cf. xv. 13 ὁ Θεὸς τῆς ἐλπίδος, Phil. iv. 9 ὁ Θεὸς τῆς εἰρήνης, see Rom. xv. 33; 1 Thess. v. 23; Heb. xiii. 20.]

[*Obs.* 2. δῴη, a late form of δοίη. Lobeck, *Phryn.* p. 346; cf. Eph. i. 17; iii. 16; 2 Thess. iii. 16; 2 Tim. i. 16, 18. The gift is Unity.]

[*Obs.* 3. Essence of this unity. τὸ αὐτὸ φρονεῖν = ἡ καρδία καὶ ἡ ψυχὴ μία Acts iv. 32; σύμψυχοι Phil. ii. 2. Of this Unity our Lord's Will is the standard (κατά), and Christians, as mutually related to each other, the sphere (ἐν).]

[*Obs.* 4. Result of this unity (ἵνα). Unanimous acknowledgment of the Father: ἐν ἑνὶ στόματι (instrumental). The inner unity naturally shows itself in unity of creed, of public prayer, of places and forms of worship.]

[*Obs.* 5. τοῦ Κυρίου Ἰησοῦ Χριστοῦ belongs *only* to πατέρα, *not* to the preceding τὸν Θεόν. καὶ (epexegetic) defines τὸν Θεόν more precisely as πατέρα Ἰησοῦ Χριστοῦ. Theodoret: ἡμῶν Θεὸν ἐκάλεσε τὸν Θεόν, τοῦ δὲ Κυρίου Ἰησοῦ πατέρα. So in 2 Cor. i. 3; xi. 31; Eph. i. 3; Col. i. 3; 1 S. Pet. i. 3. That πατέρα is thus related to Θεόν appears more clearly, where the two words occur without the appended Ἰησοῦ Χριστοῦ: 1 Cor. xv. 24; Eph. v. 20; Col. iii. 17; S. James i. 27; iii. 9. Meyer, *in loc.*]

§ *Precept* (suggested (διό) by the foregoing Benediction, with a view to attaining its object, τὸ αὐτὸ φρονεῖν κ.τ.λ.).

Let both parties (the δυνατοί and ἀσθενεῖς) welcome each other to full communion of heart and life (προσλαμβάνεσθε ἀλλήλους), (ver. 7 a).

Practical: chs. XIV, v. 6—XV, v. 13.

[*Obs.* That this precept is addressed not to the δυνατοί only, but to the ἀσθενεῖς also, is clear from ἀλλήλους, ver. 7 a, and ὑμᾶς (not ἡμᾶς), ver. 7 b.]

§ *Reason* for the Precept. Christ's example (καθώς). He *has* received into fellowship with Himself *both Jewish and Heathen converts* (ὑμᾶς addressed to *all*), that GOD might be glorified in this association of the human family with His Son (ver. 7 b).

[*Obs.* εἰς δόξαν Θεοῦ seems to depend, not on προσλαμβάνεσθε, but on the immediately preceding προσελάβετο, cf. v. 8, 9. προσελάβετο is predicated of Θεός, xiv. 3. That Θεοῦ is *gen. obj.*, not *gen. subj.*, results from vers. 6, 8, 12.]

§ *Proof* (γάρ, not δέ, ver. 8) of the *Reason* (ver. 7 b) from the relation of our Lord Jesus Christ to Jews and Heathens (vers. 8–12).

Christ became διάκονος περιτομῆς at His Incarnation,
{
1. (generally) on behalf of the Truth of GOD (ὑπὲρ ἀληθείας Θεοῦ). The Father was pledged to the promises which His Son thus realized (ver. 8 a).

2. (specifically)
{
a. with the *proximate* design of confirming the *promises* made to the Patriarchs (by fulfilling them in His own Person) (ver. 8 b).

b. but with the *more remote* design that the Gentiles should praise GOD on account of His mercy (ver. 9 a).
}
}

[*Obs.* 1. λέγω γάρ—' I mean,' in order to explain προσελάβετο (ver. 7 b), according to Meyer. δοξάσαι is parallel to the preceding βεβαιῶσαι, and depends (not on λέγω), but on εἰς τό. ὑπὲρ ἐλέους is only partly in contrast to ὑπὲρ ἀληθείας. Christ came ' to perform the promises made unto the Fathers, and to remember the Holy Covenant.' But when the Jews refused the message of salvation, He brought mercy to the heathen, on account of which they would praise GOD, as Jewish prophecy itself anticipated. It is common to make δοξάσαι depend—not on εἰς τό, but on λέγω, and to account for the retention of the aorist δοξάσαι, as pointing to the historical fact that the Gentiles had already been received into the Church, and had praised GOD for His mercy. Perhaps, if the thought favours this construction, the structure of the language suggests the other.]

[*Obs.* 2. The heathen converts had to remember, (1) that Christ was διάκονος περιτομῆς, Himself a circumcised Jew, and the Minister of the circumcised people, to whom, as Messiah, He devoted Himself: S. Matt. xv. 24 οὐκ ἀπεστάλην εἰ μὴ εἰς τὰ πρόβατα τὰ ἀπολωλότα οἴκου Ἰσραήλ. For διάκονος, see

S. Matt. xx. 28. He came not διακονηθῆναι ἀλλὰ διακονῆσαι. And (2) that the Jews could appeal to GOD's Promises, which Christ came to make good. On the other hand, the Jewish converts must not forget that, if the Gentiles would praise GOD for His unmerited mercy (ὑπὲρ ἐλέους), Jewish prophecy itself had said that they would do so, and thus GOD's ἀλήθεια was pledged to them also, and that for them too, although more remotely, Christ became incarnate.]

§ Predictions in the O. T. of the praise which converted heathen peoples would offer to GOD (vers. 9 b–12).

[*Obs.* καθὼς γέγραπται. The praises for the mercy offered to GOD by the heathen world are in correspondence with Psalm xviii. 50. In ver. 10 ἡ γραφή is the subject of λέγει, and is suggested by γέγραπται. In ver. 11 ἡ γραφὴ λέγει is repeated after πάλιν.]

Prediction 1. Psalm xviii. 50, quoted as prophetically expressing, in the language of Jesus Christ, the praise which He, with His brethren converted from Heathendom, would offer to the Father (ver. 9).

Heb. עַל־כֵּן אוֹדְךָ בַגּוֹיִם יְהוָה
וּלְשִׁמְךָ אֲזַמֵּרָה׃

LXX (Tisch.) διὰ τοῦτο ἐξομολογήσομαί σοι ἐν ἔθνεσι, Κύριε, καὶ τῷ ὀνόματί σου ψαλῶ.

[*Obs.* 1. The citation corresponds with the LXX, except in the omission of Κύριε.]

[*Obs.* 2. Psalm xviii is certainly Davidic. It is given in 2 Sam. xxii; and the inscription is justified by vers. 5–20, which must refer to the persecution by Saul. As David is a type of Christ, his language is typically-prophetic; David, when among the heathen, will praise GOD for deliverance; Christ, present among the converted heathen, will, *in union with them*, praise GOD for His mercy. That is to say, the heathen, in union with and through Jesus Christ, will offer this tribute of praise, εὐχαριστοῦντες τῷ Θεῷ καὶ Πατρὶ δι' αὐτοῦ Col. iii. 17.]

Prediction 2. Deut. xxxii. 43, quoted as a summons addressed by Moses to the heathen, bidding them join Israel in the joyous praise of GOD, when, in a distant future, Israel's deliverance and triumph should be complete (ver. 10).

Heb. הַרְנִינוּ גוֹיִם עַמּוֹ

LXX (Tisch.) εὐφράνθητε ἔθνη μετὰ τοῦ λαοῦ αὐτοῦ.

[*Obs.* 1. The citation follows the LXX, which differs from the Heb. In the latter, there is at present nothing to explain μετά. The LXX may have read אֶת־עַמּוֹ (Kennicott). The Hiphil הַרְנִינוּ may mean either, 'to cause to shout for joy,' Ps. lxv. 9, Job xxix. 13; or 'to shout for joy,' 'to rejoice,' followed by לְ, Ps. lxxxi. 2; or may be used absolutely, Ps. xxxii. 11. Render accordingly: 'Shout for joy, ye heathen, (who are now) His people.' (Aquila, Theodorus), or (Hengstenberg), 'Shout for joy, ye heathen, [let] His people [shout].' The double subject being rendered by μετὰ τοῦ λαοῦ. Wogue translates, *Nations, félicitez son peuple*: Vulg. *Laudate, gentes, populum ejus*: De Wette, 'Rejoice, ye tribes (!), His people.']

[*Obs*. 2. In Deut. xxxii 'Israel reads its past, present and future, and indeed in one sense the future of humanity.' See Siphra, *Deuteron*. p. 932 (in Ugolini, *Thesaur. Antiq. Sacr.* Venet. 1753). The LXX and the Apostle saw that Israel's future triumph involved the association of converted heathen with the covenant people in the work of praise.]

Prediction 3. Psalm cxvii. 1, quoted as containing a twofold summons to the praise of God, addressed to all the peoples of Heathendom (ver. 11).

Heb.   הַלְלוּ אֶת־יְהוָה כָּל־גּוֹיִם
             שַׁבְּחוּהוּ כָּל־הָאֻמִּים׃

LXX (Tisch.) αἰνεῖτε τὸν Κύριον πάντα τὰ ἔθνη ἐπαινέσατε αὐτὸν πάντες οἱ λαοί.

[*Obs*. 1. The citation follows the LXX, except in adding καί. A.B.C.D.E.א. S. Chrys. read ἐπαινεσάτωσαν for ἐπαινέσατε.]

[*Obs*. 2. Ps. cxvii, the shortest of all the Psalms, is a later Hallelujah addressed to the heathen world, inviting its peoples to come into the Kingdom of God. אֻמִּים occurs here only in the Old Testament Hebrew; the word elsewhere means Ishmaelites, or Midianitish tribes. כל־גוים, all peoples without distinction; כל־האמים, all nations without exception.]

Prediction 4. Isaiah xi. 10, quoted to show that the King Messiah, Who was to descend from David, would reign over the heathen, and be the Object of their hope (ver. 12).

Heb.   וְהָיָה בַּיּוֹם הַהוּא
       שֹׁרֶשׁ יִשַׁי אֲשֶׁר עֹמֵד לְנֵס עַמִּים
         אֵלָיו גּוֹיִם יִדְרֹשׁוּ

'And it shall come to pass in that day,
The Root of Jesse, which stands as a Banner of peoples,
For It will the nations ask.'

LXX (Tisch.) καὶ ἔσται ἐν τῇ ἡμέρᾳ ἐκείνῃ ῥίζα τοῦ Ἰεσσαί, καὶ ὁ ἀνιστάμενος ἄρχειν ἐθνῶν ἐπ' αὐτῷ ἔθνη ἐλπιοῦσι.

[*Obs*. 1. The citation follows the LXX, except in omitting ἐν τῇ ἡμέρᾳ ἐκείνῃ. But the LXX differs from the Hebrew. אֲשֶׁר עֹמֵד לְנֵס עַמִּים is paraphrased by its concrete historical meaning, ὁ ἀνιστάμενος ἄρχειν ἐθνῶν: and ἐλπιοῦσι represents the spiritual impulse which results in or from the act described by יִדְרֹשׁוּ.]

[*Obs.* 2. The citation occurs in the last of the poems designed to console Israel under the Assyrian oppressions (c. vii-xii); and it describes the destruction of the world-empire, and the rise of the Kingdom of the Lord in Messiah (x. 5-xii). The tree of David's sovereignty has been hewn down: the root alone remains. Out of this root, however, springs up שֹׁרֶשׁ יִשַׁי, the root-sprout of Jesse, Who is, also, the Root itself, as being of its substance, and as having preserved it from utter decay. In Him the root of Jesse recovers a second youth; He is exalted into a Banner, which summons the nations to gather round it, לְנֵס עַמִּים, and they ask for Him as the new Object of their hope. The passage is strictly Messianic, Delitzsch *in loc.* S. Paul traces the fulfilment of this יִדְרֹשׁוּ in the praises offered to GOD for His mercy by the converted heathen.]

[*Obs.* 3. ἡ ῥίζα τοῦ Ἰεσσαί, Radix Jesse, ἡ ῥίζα Δαβίδ, applied to our Lord in Rev. v. 5; xxii. 16. Its full sense is given in Is. xi. 1 ἐξελεύσεται ῥάβδος ἐκ τῆς ῥίζης Ἰεσσαί, καὶ ἄνθος ἐκ τῆς ῥίζης ἀναβήσεται. חֹטֶר, 'a rod' Prov. xiv. 3. נֵצֶר (ἄνθος), 'a sprout,' 'shoot'; from נצר, (1) 'to shine,' (2) 'to flower,' שֹׁרֶשׁ, 'a root,' שֵׁרֵשׁ (Pi.) 'to root out.']

[*Obs.* 4. ἐπ' αὐτῷ ἐλπιοῦσι. ἐπί, of the object on which Hope rests, 1 Tim. iv. 10; vi. 17. It is similarly used of the object of Faith: πιστεύειν ἐπ' αὐτῷ Rom. ix. 33; x. 11. Observe the bearing of ἐπ' αὐτῷ on the Divinity of Christ.]

§ *Concluding Benediction* (ver. 13).

[*Obs.* This Benediction is suggested by the preceding citation; ὁ Θεὸς τῆς ἐλπίδος by ἐλπιοῦσι, just as that in ver. 5 is suggested by ver. 4. This section ends, as it began, with a Benediction.]

1. *Author* of the Blessing.

    ὁ Θεὸς τῆς ἐλπίδος (*gen. auctoris*), cf. ver. 5 (ver. 13).

2. *Substance* of the Blessing.

    πληρῶσαι ὑμᾶς πάσης { χαρᾶς καὶ εἰρήνης } ἐν τῷ πιστεύειν (ver. 13).

3. *Aim* of the Blessing (to be secured ἐν δυνάμει Πνεύματος ἁγίου). The abundance of Hope: εἰς τὸ περισσεύειν ὑμᾶς ἐν τῇ ἐλπίδι (ver. 13).

[*Obs.* 1. The Blessing begins and ends with ἐλπίς, without which χαρά and εἰρήνη cannot fill the soul. When, in the life of faith, they do fill the soul, they react upon the ἐλπίς which produces them, εἰς τὸ περισσεύειν.]

[*Obs.* 2. Baur's objection (*Studien*, 1836. n. 3) to the Pauline origin of xv. 1-13, turns chiefly upon the expression διάκονος περιτομῆς (xv. 8), which he considers unlike the Apostle, and inconsistent in the author of Gal. i, ii. But this strong and condensed expression is intentionally chosen to remind the Gentiles of the high honour which had been put upon Israel by the Birth and early Ministry of Jesus Christ. That διάκονος harmonizes with S. Matt. xv. 24; xx. 28, has been observed already. But that Christ was, primarily, διάκονος περιτομῆς is implied in Rom. i. 16 (πρῶτον), and in ix. 5; xi. 16, 28. Certainly in xv. 8 the Apostle represents our Lord's relation to the Jews as in some sense the payment of a debt, by the expression ὑπὲρ ἀληθείας Θεοῦ (ver. 8), while His relation to the heathen was purely one of compassion (ὑπὲρ ἐλέους ver. 9): and at first sight this might seem to be in conflict with the argument of ch. x, in which he will not allow that GOD owed the Jews anything. In reality there is no contradiction; since what GOD did not owe to the Jews, He may be represented, κατ' ἄνθρωπον, as having owed to Himself. S. Paul lays stress upon this aspect of religious history, with a view to correcting the Gentile ἐξουθένησις of everything Jewish.]

EPILOGUE.

XV. 14-33.

Tone of parts of the Epistle justified.

[*Obs.* This Epilogue should be compared with the Introduction, ch. i. 8-16, to which it corresponds in several respects. It may be analyzed briefly as follows:—

The Apostle justifies the frank tone he has assumed (τολμηρότερον ver. 15) in writing to a Church which so entirely enjoys his confidence as the Roman (vers. 14, 15), by reference to

1. his calling to be the λειτουργὸς Ἰησοῦ Χριστοῦ εἰς τὰ ἔθνη (ver. 16).
2. his past labours among the heathen nations (vers. 17-21).
3. his plans, past and present, for visiting Rome: (proof of interest), (vers. 23-29).
4. his anxiety to be assisted by the prayers of the Church of Rome under these circumstances; (proof of confidence), (vers. 30-33).]

§ *General Statement* (vers. 14, 15). The Apostle, although himself *persuaded* (not less than others) that the Roman Christians are

eminently gifted in
- *a.* general excellence—μεστοὶ ἀγαθωσύνης (ver. 14).
- *b.* knowledge of Christian truth—πεπληρωμένοι πάσης γνώσεως (ver. 14).
- *c.* power of giving good spiritual advice—δυνάμενοι ἀλλήλους νουθετεῖν (ver. 14).

Yet has *written* to the Romans —

(ἔγραψα)
- *a.* more 'boldly' (τολμηρότερον) than such an estimate (as that in ver. 1) would seem to warrant (ver. 15).
- *b.* *in parts* of his Epistle (ἀπὸ μέρους) (ver. 15).
  [Cf. vi. 12 sq., 19; viii. 9; xi. 17 sq.; xii. 3; xiii. 3 sqq., 13, 14; xiv. 3, 4, 10, 13, 15, 20; xv. 1-8.]
- *c.* in the *manner* of one who again reminds them of truths which they knew before (ὡς ἐπαναμιμνήσκων) (ver. 15).

[*Obs.* 1. The three qualities predicated of the Romans, ἀγαθωσύνη, γνῶσις, νουθετεῖν, advance from the general to the particular. ἀγαθωσύνη, 'general excellence,' wider than χρηστότης (S. Chrys. ix. p. 729 ὁλόκληρον τὴν ἀρετὴν οὕτω καλεῖ), Gal. v. 22; Eph. v. 9; 2 Thess. i. 11. γνῶσις, here of Christian truth, 1 Cor. i. 5; viii. 1, 7. νουθετεῖν Acts xx. 31; 1 Cor. iv. 14; Eph. vi. 4; Col. i. 28; iii. 16. The expressions μεστοί, πεπληρωμένοι must be understood *relatively*; and not of individuals, but of the whole Church. There was still room therefore for the πνευματικὸν χάρισμα which the Apostle says at i. 11, he was anxious to communicate to them and which Baur (*Paulus*, ii. c. 3) refers to as disproving the Pauline authorship of c. xv. The Apostle is not inconsistent with any of his former language: still less is he 'writing insincerely.' The Roman Church, as a whole, was what he here says. Cf. i. 8.]

[*Obs.* 2. τολμηρότερον (cf. Winer, *Gr. N. T.* p. 304). This expression is not 'too apologetic to be apostolical,' since it refers to the manner, not to the matter, of parts of the Epistle; and courtesy is an Apostolic grace. ἔγραψα, not the epistolary use, like *scripsi*; since the Apostle refers not to the whole letter (which his readers would think of), but to particular parts of it. (Winer, *Gr. N. T.* p. 347.) In ἐπαναμιμνήσκων remark the reference to the previous teaching which the Romans had enjoyed, and the Apostolic modesty which limits the scope of the Epistle so considerably. S. Chrys. τουτέστιν μικρόν τι. Cf. 2 S. Pet. i. 12. Observe the ἐπι- in ἐπαναμιμνήσκων.]

§ Justification of the Apostle's frankness in addressing the Romans. It is in keeping with his whole relation towards the Romans and the Church at large (vers. 16-33).

Reason I. The Apostle's 'boldness' is justified by the high grace which he had received to be the priest (λειτουργὸν ... ἱερουργοῦντα) of Jesus Christ towards the heathen (ver. 16).

In the grace of S. Paul's Apostolic office observe
{
1. Its *source*. ἡ χάρις ἡ δοθεῖσα ὑπὸ τοῦ Θεοῦ (ver. 16).
2. Its *effect* on the Apostle: εἰς τὸ εἶναί με.
   {
   (*Character*), λειτουργὸν Ἰησοῦ Χριστοῦ, priest of Jesus Christ (ver. 16).
   (*Field of work*), εἰς τὰ ἔθνη, the heathen (ver. 16).
   (*Description of work*), ἱερουργοῦντα, doing priestly work (in respect of), (ver. 16).
   (*Subject matter*), τὸ εὐαγγέλιον τοῦ Θεοῦ, the Gospel message (ver. 16).
   }
3. Its *purpose*, that (ἵνα) the oblation of the converted heathen might be acceptable to the Father, being ἡγιασμένη ἐν Πνεύματι ἁγίῳ (ver. 16).
}

[*Obs.* 1. That λειτουργός here means, not a public οἰκόνομος nor a διάκονος, but specifically a *priest* (cf. Acts xiii. 2; Phil. ii. 17), deriving his authority from Jesus Christ (Rom. i. 5), is clear from the explanatory ἱερουργοῦντα which follows. ἱερουργεῖν = 'sacra facere,' as a priest; often *intrans.* but here *transit.*, like ἐργάζεσθαι and ἐμπορεύεσθαι, cf. Winer, *Gr. N. T.* p. 279, with τὸ εὐαγγέλιον: which however is not the προσφορά (the ἔθνη are the προσφορά), but the system or doctrine which is administered. Ἱερουργοῦντα is rendered 'sacrificans' by Rufinus, 'consecrans' by S. Augustine, 'sanctificans' by the Vulgate. For this use of ἱερουργεῖν, see Joseph. *Ant.* vi. 6. 2.]

[*Obs.* 2. ἡ προσφορὰ τῶν ἐθνῶν (*gen. apposition*, Winer, *Gr. N. T.* p. 666), a more solemn word than παριστάνειν (2 Cor. iv. 14; xi. 2; Col. i. 22, 28). See Heb. x. 10 προσφορὰ τοῦ σώματος Ἰησοῦ Χριστοῦ: Ep. v. 2. In order that the converted Gentiles, consecrated by the Holy Spirit to be God's, may be an offering acceptable [to the Father, and] made by the Apostle as the priest of Christ, it is necessary that the offering must be pure (Rom. xii. 1). Hence ἡγιασμένη.]

[*Obs.* 3. ἡγιασμένη ἐν Πνεύματι ἁγίῳ is in contrast to the purely external consecration of the Levitical Sacrifices. ἁγιάζειν means to consecrate as an offering (S. John xvii. 19), like קָדַשׁ Ex. xiii. 2. This consecration of the converted ἔθνη takes place in Baptism (Gal. iii. 27; Tit. iii. 5; Eph. v. 26).]

[*Obs.* 4. The cast of the phraseology of this passage is very remarkably liturgical. Without directly mentioning the Eucharist, it seems already to take for granted those ways of referring to it, which we find in the early Fathers; see Hickes, on *The Christian Priesthood*, vol. ii. pp. 93–100 (Oxf. 1847): Keble, *Sermons Academical and Occasional*, p. 366, note.]

Reason II. The Apostle's 'boldness' is justified by his past labours (vers. 17–21).

[*Obs.* This is introduced by a proposition which follows from ver. 16, but is connected still more closely with ver. 18.]

§ Inference (οὖν ver. 17) from the foregoing. The καύχησις of the Apostle (the warrant of his attitude towards the Roman Church) (ver. 15) properly belongs to him (ἔχω); since it is wholly unconnected with self, as being, (1) ἐν Χριστῷ Ἰησοῦ, in Christ, Whose λειτουργός he is; and (2) as dealing with τὰ πρὸς τὸν Θεόν, Whose Gospel he administers as a priest. He therefore proceeds to the proof of καύχησιν ἔχω (ver. 17), (vers. 18–21).

Arg. 1. (*Negative confirmation.*) (*Limits of the work referred to.*) The Apostle makes *no* reference to the labours of others for the propagation of the Faith (vers. 18, 19 a).

[*Obs.* 1. The words οὐ κατειργάσατο are emphatic. The καύχησις, he implies, would be forfeited, if he were claiming as his own the labours of other Apostles.

Epilogue: ch. XV, vv. 14-33.

Rendered affirmatively, ver. 18 runs: 'I will venture to let myself be heard only as to those things which Christ has brought about by my agency towards making the heathen obedient to Him.']

[*Obs.* 2. Remark the Apostolic conception of a mission to the heathen.

1. The real Converter is Christ, Χριστὸς κατειργάσατο.
2. The instrument is His Apostle, δι' ἐμοῦ.
3. The purpose in view is that the heathen should *obey* Jesus Christ, by faith and good works, εἰς ὑπακοὴν ἐθνῶν Rom. i. 5 ; xvi. 26.
4. The means employed are

{ 1. natural agencies.
  { a. λόγῳ, preaching the Gospel.
  { b. ἔργῳ, active efforts, journeys, organizations, &c.

  2. supernatural agencies.
  { a. *power* which goes forth from (gen. deriv.) *miracles.*
    { (i) σημεῖα, אֹתוֹת, tokens of GOD's near Presence.
    { (ii) τέρατα, מֹפְתִים, as producing astonishment.
  { b. *power* which goes forth from the Holy Spirit into the minds of men, ἐν δυνάμει Πνεύματος ἁγίου.]

[*Obs.* 3. For a complete account of the words τέρας, σημεῖον, as also δύναμις and ἔργον, see Archbishop Trench, *Miracles of our Lord*, pp. 2-8. σημεῖα and τέρατα both refer to the *significant* aspect of miracles; but of the two, σημεῖον is the more ethical. The usual order of the words follows in Heb. אֹתוֹת וּמֹפְתִים: exceptions are in Acts ii. 22, 43 ; vi. 8 ; vii. 36.]

Arg. 2. (*Range of previous labours.*) (Result (ὥστε) of vers. 18, 19 a.) The Apostle had fully published the Gospel of Christ between Jerusalem and Illyria, besides making a circuit (κύκλῳ) in Arabia and Syria (ver. 19 b).

[*Obs.* 1. Although S. Paul had *begun* to preach at Damascus, and having made a retreat in Arabia did not go to Jerusalem until three years after his conversion (Gal. i. 17, 18) ; yet he entered the Apostolic fellowship first at Jerusalem, Acts ix. 26, and made it the *terminus a quo* of later efforts, Acts xviii. 22 ; xx. 16. Jerusalem was the centre of the Apostolic Church : Is. ii. 3 was fulfilled in its relation to the Gospel. S. Paul writes Ἱεροσόλυμα only at Gal. i. 17, 18 ; ii. 1.]

[*Obs.* 2. καὶ κύκλῳ negatives the idea of working *directly* between Jerusalem and Illyria. S. Chrys. and others understand it to describe the course of his journey through Syria, Asia Minor, Troas, and Macedonia, — a course which was inevitable, unless the Apostle had gone to Greece by sea. Κύκλῳ means 'in the arc of a circle,' and καί shows that it refers to a journey over and above the nearest land route between Jerusalem and Illyria. It thus glances at the facts of Gal. i. 17, 18.]

[*Obs.* 3. Μέχρι, like ἄχρι, is used alike of place and time. To understand by μέχρι that the Apostle only reached the Illyrian frontier during a Macedonian excursion, is inconsistent with ver. 23 ; although of itself μέχρι decides nothing, since it sometimes includes and sometimes excludes the point attained to. Cf. Rom. v. 14; S. Matt. xiii. 30; Phil. ii. 30, and S. Matt. xi. 23; Phil. ii. 8. Probably the Illyrian Mission is to be referred to the μῆνας τρεῖς of Acts xx. 3; the silence of the Acts is no reason against it. The intention to visit Nicopolis, referred to at Tit. iii. 12, would have been at a much later date.]

[*Obs.* 4. The phrase πληροῦν τὸ εὐαγγέλιον, 'fulfil the Gospel,' implies preaching it so that it is received. Cf. Col. i. 25 πληρῶσαι τὸν λόγον τοῦ Θεοῦ. Compare S. Luke vii. 1 with S. Matt. vii. 28.]

Arg. 3. (*Method of action.*) The Apostle had made it a point of honour to preach, not in districts where Christ had been already named by preachers and confessors of the faith, but (in accordance with the spirit of Is. lii. 15) where He was as yet entirely unknown (ver. 20, 21).

[*Obs.* 1. By the word φιλοτιμούμενον, the Apostle means that he followed as a point of honour the rule which he proceeds (οὕτω) to state in preaching the Gospel. On φιλοτιμεῖσθαι, see 2 Cor. v. 9; 1 Thess. iv. 11.]

[*Obs.* 2. Of this rule the *negative* side is, *not* to preach where others had founded Churches previously. His *motive* was (ἵνα μή κ.τ.λ.) to avoid continuing the work of conversion which others had already begun. Compare 2 Cor. x. 14 b–16 ἄχρι γὰρ καὶ ὑμῶν ἐφθάσαμεν ἐν τῷ εὐαγγελίῳ τοῦ Χριστοῦ· οὐκ εἰς τὰ ἄμετρα καυχώμενοι ἐν ἀλλοτρίοις κόποις, ἐλπίδα δὲ ἔχοντες, αὐξανομένης τῆς πίστεως ὑμῶν, ἐν ὑμῖν μεγαλυνθῆναι, κατὰ τὸν κανόνα ἡμῶν εἰς περισσείαν, εἰς τὰ ὑπερέκεινα ὑμῶν εὐαγγελίσασθαι, οὐκ ἐν ἀλλοτρίῳ κανόνι εἰς τὰ ἕτοιμα καυχήσασθαι. It is a mistake to suppose that S. Paul followed this rule in order to avoid controversies with those who had preceded him. For him the Apostolic office was first in labour as first in honour; and he confined himself to the work of *founding* Churches, as being the most difficult. His rule did not prevent him from *writing* to Churches which others had founded, as, e.g., to the Colossians and the Romans; he only avoided such work as implied personal residence in these places. Thus, he only contemplated passing through (διαπορευόμενος ver. 24) Rome; his later residence there was compulsory—as a prisoner.]

§ Is. lii. 15 quoted in illustration of the Apostle's rule to confine his labours to those heathens who had not received the Faith of Christ from others (ver. 21).

Heb.   כִּי אֲשֶׁר לֹא־סֻפַּר לָהֶם רָאוּ
             וַאֲשֶׁר לֹא־שָׁמְעוּ הִתְבּוֹנָנוּ׃

'For what has not been told unto them they see,
And what they have not heard they discover.'

LXX (Tisch.) οἷς οὐκ ἀνηγγέλη περὶ αὐτοῦ ὄψονται, καὶ οἳ οὐκ ἀκηκόασι συνήσουσι.

Epilogue: ch. XV, vv. 14–33.

[*Obs.* 1. The citation follows the LXX, who took אֲשֶׁר in each line as masc., and added περὶ αὐτοῦ.]

[*Obs.* 2. The lines occur at the beginning of the prophecy of the exaltation of the Servant of the Lord out of deep degradation (Is. lii. 13-liii. 12). In the Hebrew the kings, who shut their mouths in amazement at the exaltation of the Servant, are the subjects of רָאוּ and הִתְבּוֹנָנוּ. But the Apostle here substitutes the heathen-nations to whom the true Servant of the Lord is not yet made known, on the ground that together with and as represented by the 'kings' (in the prophecy) their people also must see His glory. Cf. especially S. Matt. xiii. 23; xv. 10. The Apostle deduces a rule for his own work from a law of God's Providence.]

Reason III. The Apostle's 'boldness' is warranted by the practical interest in the Roman Church which his past and present plans for visiting Rome have consistently implied (vers. 22–29).

1. *Past* schemes for *visiting Rome*. These have resulted in nothing, because (διό ver. 22) the Apostle's mode of working has obliged him to confine himself to the districts mentioned in vers. 19, 20 (ver. 22).

[*Obs.* ver. 22 is an answer to a tacit objection. 'If you have felt such interest in us as to write as you do, why have you not paid us a visit before now?' ἐνεκοπτόμην need not be explained of external hindrances: the Apostle's sense of duty has prevented the journey. Τὰ πολλά: in *most* cases, 'plerumque.' The Apostle will not say that this motive *entirely* accounts for his continued absence.]

2. *Present* anticipations of *visiting Rome* (vers. 23–29).

(A) General hopes of *visiting Rome* (vers. 23, 24). Their warrant.

[*Obs.* νυνὶ δέ (ver. 23) introduces a contrast to ἐνεκοπτόμην ver. 22.]

    a. The Apostle has no longer scope (τόπον) for founding new Churches in the κλίματα between Jerusalem and Illyria (ver. 23 a).

[*Obs.* κλίμα, 'region,' (from the apparent declension of the sky to the horizon): 2 Cor. xi. 10; Gal. i. 21.]

    b. The Apostle's ἐπιποθία to visit the Romans is now of many years' standing (ver. 23 b).

[*Obs.* ἐπιποθία only here. 2 Cor. vii. 7, 11 ἐπιπόθησις. Phil. iv. 1 ἐπιπόθητος. On the subject, see ch. i. 11, 13.]

c. The Apostle hopes, whenever he carries out his projected journey into Spain, to pass through Rome, and have a sight (θεάσασθαι) of the Roman Christians. After *partially* satisfying his longing to see them, he hopes to be sent forth by them on his Spanish journey, with escort and provisions (ver. 24).

[*Obs.* 1. The words ἐλεύσομαι πρὸς ὑμᾶς in the text. rec. are doubtful. The construction is broken; ἐλπίζω [γάρ] begins a new sentence, and the sentence, which is thus interrupted, beginning at ὡς ἐὰν πορεύωμαι, is not resumed. The implied sense is given in ver. 28 ἀπελεύσομαι δι' ὑμῶν εἰς Σπανίαν.]

[*Obs.* 2. S. Paul only contemplated passing through Rome (διαπορευόμενος ver. 24; δι' ὑμῶν ver. 28), and remaining just long enough to see the several members of the Church there. θεᾶσθαι here only in S. Paul. It was in accordance with the Apostolic rule, stated in ver. 20, that he would thus hasten on to Spain, where as yet no Church had been founded. Σπανία, generally in Greek Ἰβηρία, Hdt. i. 163; Strabo, iii. 4. 16: but also Ἰσπανία 1 Macc. viii. 3.]

[*Obs.* 3. προπεμφθῆναι. This solemn act by which an Apostle was sent forth on his work, accompanied by an escort of Christian friends, is most fully described in Acts xxi. 5. Cf. Acts xv. 3; xx. 38; 1 Cor. xvi. 6, 11; 2 Cor. i. 16. From these two last passages it seems that provision for the journey was often made. ἐκεῖ (by attraction for ἐκεῖσε, S. Matt. ii. 22; xvii. 20; S. John xviii. 3) seems to show that S. Paul hoped to be accompanied, all the way, by members of the Church of Rome; probably too, *provisions* would be given him for the whole journey: Tit. iii. 13; 3 S. John 6, 7.]

[*Obs.* 4. By ἀπὸ μέρους the Apostle implies that he cannot hope within so short a time for perfect spiritual satisfaction (ἐμπλησθῶ) through intercourse with the Roman Church. They had more to give than he could expect to receive. Observe the *gen.* of the person after ἐμπλησθῶ.]

(B) Engagement in the immediate future, which (only) postpones his *visit to Rome* (vers. 25–28).

[*Obs.* νυνὶ δέ here introduces a contrast with the future sketched out in ver. 24, just as νυνὶ δέ in ver. 23 introduced a contrast with ἐνεκοπτόμην. The Apostle has to account for not being able to act *immediately* in the spirit of ver. 24; and his reasons follow.]

(1) He is on his way to Jerusalem, in the service of the Christians who live there (διακονῶν τοῖς ἁγίοις), (ver. 25).

[*Obs.* By the pres. part. διακονῶν the Apostle implies that the journey itself was part of the service, Winer, *Gr. N. T.* p. 429.]

§ Explanation (γάρ ver. 26) of his phrase διακονῶν τοῖς ἁγίοις (vers. 26, 27).

a. The *fact* which this phrase presupposes. [The Churches of] Macedonia and Achaia have been pleased to make some collection for those members of the Church of Jerusalem who are poor (τοὺς πτωχοὺς τῶν ἁγίων), (ver. 26).

[*Obs.* 1. κοινωνία is used for almsgiving, because true *fellowship* on the part of the wealthy with the poor, implies a *communication* of some part of their substance. Hence the word acquires its *active* meaning. For κοινωνίαν ποιήσασθαι, see 2 Cor. viii. 4; ix. 13: also cf. Rom. xii. 13, which explains the expression, ταῖς χρείαις τῶν ἁγίων κοινωνοῦντες. By εὐδόκησαν the spontaneous character of the effort is marked; the reason of the εὐδοκία follows in ver. 27.]

[*Obs.* 2. 'Macedonia' and 'Achaia' were the two provinces into which Greece was divided by the Romans. The names of the territorial districts are used for the Christians who inhabit them. The Church has already a presentiment of empire.]

[*Obs.* 3. The journey here alluded to is that to which 1 Cor. xvi. 1–4; Acts xix. 21 refer. For the collection in Macedonia, see 2 Cor. viii. 1; ix. 2 sqq.; for that in Achaia, see 1 Cor. xvi. 1 sqq. (comp. Gal. vi. 6 sq.). By τινά the Apostle hints at his ignorance of the amount collected: the moral value of the collection was in his eyes of much greater importance than the exact sum.]

b. The motive for this collection. The Greek Churches were spiritually debtors to the Church of Jerusalem, from which the Gospel had gone forth. The claim of the Church of Jerusalem upon the charity of the Greek Churches takes the form of an *arg. a majori ad minus* :—

If the converted heathen had shared in the *spiritual privileges* of the Jewish Christians, the converted heathen ought to make a sacrifice, in the matter of *their worldly goods*, for the Jewish Christians (ver. 27).

[*Obs.* καὶ ὀφειλέται adds a new element to the repeated ηὐδόκησαν. The collection was a matter of free-will; and yet the Greek Churches were *in the debt* of the Church of Jerusalem. By τὰ πνευματικά all the blessings of the Gospel considered as gifts of the Holy Spirit are meant. Antioch, the first heathen Church, was founded from Jerusalem, Acts xi. 19, 20. The least the heathen could do was (λειτουργῆσαι) to make a sacrificial service of τὰ σαρκικά (their possessions belonging to the world of sense) for the benefit of the poor Christians in Jerusalem. λειτουργῆσαι, as at xiii. 6; xv. 16; cf. Phil. iv. 18.]

(2) (*Practical inference,* οὖν ver 28.) When he has done his work [for the Greeks who commission him, and] for the Jewish

Christians at Jerusalem, he will set out on another journey (ἀπελεύσομαι) for Spain, and will pass through Rome (δι' ὑμῶν) (ver. 28).

[*Obs.* 1. τοῦτο refers to the duty suggested by the circumstances described in vers. 26, 27. For ἐπιτελεῖν, 'to complete,' see 2 Cor. vii. 1; viii. 6, 11. σφραγισάμενος, 'having secured, as by affixing a seal to a document,' this fruit of charity to the Jewish Christians. By handing over to the Church of Jerusalem the alms which were sent from Greece, the Apostle assured these alms to that Church as its property. αὐτοῖς, like αὐτῶν and αὐτοῖς in ver. 27, refers to the Christians in Jerusalem, rather than the Greek Christians.]

[*Obs.* 2. It is clear that S. Paul subsequently abandoned for awhile the hope of visiting Spain: cf. Acts xx. 25. During his first imprisonment at Rome, he looked forward to visiting Philippi (Phil. ii. 24), and Colossae (Philem. 22). This anticipation, however, is not inconsistent with his having actually made a western journey before his second imprisonment. S. Clement of Rome says expressly that he went ἐπὶ τὸ τέρμα τῆς δύσεως (1 *ad Cor.* c. v, on which see the note in Lightfoot's ed.). Cf. Muratorian Fragment apud Westcott, *Hist. Canon,* pp. 525 ff.: and among later authorities, S. Jerome, *De Vir. Illust.* c. 5; *Comm. in Amos,* v. 8: S. Epiphanius, *Haer.* xxvii. n. 6; Theodoret, *Comm. in 2 Tim.* iv. 17. Cf. Neander, *Pflanzung d. Kirche,* i. p. 390.]

(C) Encouraging conviction about his *visit to Rome* (οἶδα ver. 29), He knows that it will be accompanied by a full measure of Christ's Blessing (ver. 29).

[*Obs.* 1. τοῦ εὐαγγελίου, text. rec. is not found in A. B. C. D. E. F. G. Clem. Alex. Orig. Copt. al.]

[*Obs.* 2. This expression of confidence in the Blessing from Christ which would attend his visit forms a natural transition to the exhortation which follows (vers. 30–32).]

Reason IV. The Apostle's 'boldness' is warranted by the affectionate proof of confidence in the Roman Church which he gives by asking to be personally remembered in its intercessions (vers. 30–32).

1. *Motives* to this intercession (ver. 30).

  { *a.* Our Lord Jesus Christ (ver. 30).
  { *b.* ἡ ἀγάπη τοῦ Πνεύματος (ver. 30).

[*Obs.* 1. διά belongs to παρακαλῶ. It is *by referring to* our Lord Jesus, and to the Love of the Spirit, that the Apostle desires to move his Roman readers to pray for him. Cf. Winer, *Gr. N. T.* p. 477.]

[*Obs.* 2. The ἀγάπη τοῦ Πνεύματος may mean, (1) the Love of the Spirit whereby He is the eternal Bond between the Father and the Son, or (2) the Love which He inspires, Gal. v. 22.]

2. *Description* of this intercession,—

1. its *generic character*. It will occur among (ἐν) the προσευχαὶ ὑπὲρ ἐμοῦ πρὸς τὸν Θεόν, which (he takes it for granted) are offered by the Roman Church, (ver. 30).
2. its *specific character*. It is to be an earnest struggle, concerted between the Apostle and his readers (συναγωνίζεσθαι), (ver. 30).

[*Obs.* On συναγωνίζεσθαι, see Col. ii. 1 ἀγῶνα περὶ ὑμῶν : Col. iv 12 ἀγωνιζόμενος ὑπὲρ ὑμῶν. Prayer is often an earnest struggle, as with Jacob, Gen. xxxii. 24 ; and our Lord in Gethsemane, S. Matt. xxvi. 37-44 ; S. Luke xxii. 40-44. Cf. S. Clem. Rom. 1 *ad Cor.* c. 2 ἀγὼν ἦν ὑμῖν ἡμέρας τε καὶ νυκτὸς ὑπὲρ πάσης τῆς ἀδελφότητος.]

3. *Particular aims* of this intercession (vers. 31, 32).

(1) That the Apostle might be delivered, during his approaching journey, from the unbelieving Jews (ver. 31).

[*Obs.* The ἀπειθοῦντες are those Jews who refuse to give to Jesus Christ the ὑπακοὴ πίστεως, and therefore they are *not* the Judaeo-Christians, Rom. xi. 30, 31 ; Acts xiv. 2. S. Paul anticipated persecution from this quarter, Acts xx. 22, 23. This prayer was not fulfilled (Acts xxi. 27), because Christ had another destiny (Acts ix. 16) in store for His servant.]

(2) That the Apostle's service, destined for Jerusalem, might prove acceptable to the poor Christians living there (ver. 31 b).

[*Obs.* S. Paul might have felt doubtful as to the reception *he* (Rom. xi. 14 ; Acts xx. 21 seq.) would meet, when bringing the alms of Greek Churches to the Christians of Jerusalem. It could not be taken for granted that he would be welcome, as representing the Greek Churches.]

(3) That the Apostle, by GOD's will, might carry out his plan of visiting Rome, ἐν χαρᾷ (ver. 32).

[*Obs.* He *was* led to Rome, διὰ θελήματος Θεοῦ. *But* as a prisoner, Acts xxvii. For διὰ θελήματος Θεοῦ, cf. Rom. i. 10 ; 1 Cor. i. 1 ; 2 Cor. i. 1, &c.]

(4) That the Apostle might *refresh* himself by spiritual intercourse with the members of the Roman Church (ver. 32).

[*Obs.* With συναναπαύσωμαι compare συμπαρακληθῆναι, i. 12. The interchange of spiritual thoughts and sympathies would bring rest to the Apostle. συναναπαύεσθαι corresponds to συναγωνίζεσθαι.]

§ Benediction. $\begin{cases} source. & \text{GOD the Author of Peace } (\text{ὁ Θεὸς τῆς εἰρήνης}), \\ & \text{(ver. 33).} \\ Substance. & \text{GOD's presence } (\mu\epsilon\tau\acute{\alpha}), \text{ (ver. 33).} \\ Range. & \text{All members of the Roman Church } (\pi\acute{\alpha}\nu\tau\omega\nu \\ & \dot{\upsilon}\mu\hat{\omega}\nu), \text{ (ver. 33).} \end{cases}$

[*Obs.* χάρις is generally found, as in xvi. 20, 24. Probably the context suggested εἰρήνη : GOD is the author of the Blessing for which he asked the Romans to pray.]

CONCLUSION.

Ch. XVI.

[*Obs.* 1. Recommendation of the Deaconess Phoebe to the care of the Church of Rome (xvi. 1, 2).
2. Christians, and groups of Christians, at Rome to whom greetings and messages are sent (vers. 3-16).
3. Warnings against schismatics and false teachers (vers. 17-20).
4. Christians who join the Apostle in sending greetings to the Church of Rome (vers. 21-24).
5. Solemn concluding doxology (vers. 25-27).]

§ 1.

Commendation of the Deaconess Phoebe, bearer of the Epistle, to the care of the Church of Rome (xvi. 1, 2).

Phoebe is recommended to the Roman Church,—

1. (*description*) as being,
    - *a. generally*, a sister in Christ (ver. 1).
    - *b. specifically*, a Deaconess of the Church in Cenchreae (ver. 1).
2. (*purpose*, ἵνα ver. 2),
    - *a.* that the Roman Church should receive her,
        (1) from a sense of fellowship with our Lord (ἐν Κυρίῳ), and so (2) in a manner worthy of Christians who realize this (ver. 2 a).
    - *b.* that it should assist her in any respect wherein she might need assistance (ver. 2 a).
3. *Especial reason*, καὶ γάρ (ver. 2 b)—
    - *a.* she has been a προστάτις πολλῶν (ver. 2 b):
    - *b.* and indeed of the Apostle himself (ver. 2 b).

[*Obs.* 1. συνίστημι. Cf. 2 Cor. v. 12 ἑαυτοὺς συνιστάνομεν. For the three kinds of 'literae formatae' in the ancient Church, 'commendatoriae,' 'communicatoriae,' and 'dimissoriae,' see Bingham, *Antiq.* i. p. 100. book ii. c. 4. § 5 'Strangers travelling without commendatory letters might partake of the Church's charity, but not of the communion of the altar'; *Ib.* vi. p. 366, book xvii. c. 3. § 7.]

[*Obs.* 2. ἀδελφή, as a member of the *family* of Christ, cf. φιλόστοργοι xii. 10. διάκονος, in later Greek διακόνισσα, also πρεσβῦτις, probably also χήρα. In later times the χῆραι were an order, at least at Ephesus, of women who had only married once, and were sixty years of age, 1 Tim. v. 9. The πρεσβύτιδες, besides moral qualifications, were to be καλοδιδάσκαλοι Tit. ii. 4. Pliny speaks of putting two Christian 'ministrae' to the torture, *Lib.* x. *Ep.* 97. For a full account of deaconesses in the Primitive Church, see Bingham, *Antiq.* vol. i. p. 332 sq. book ii. c. 22.]

[*Obs.* 3. Cenchreae was 70 stadia from Corinth, and its eastern port on the Saronic gulf; cf. Acts xviii. 18. The expression καὶ αὐτοῦ ἐμοῦ (ver. 2) might seem to imply that the Apostle had been ill at Cenchreae, and had been nursed by Phoebe.]

[*Obs.* 4. Observe the play on παραστῆτε and προστάτις. παραστάτις would have corresponded with παραστῆτε, but προστάτις, 'patroness,' 'protectress,' answered better to the official and personal eminence of Phoebe.]

§ 2.

Thirty-one names, or groups, of Christians at Rome, to whom the Apostle sends messages or greetings (vers. 3–16).

1. Prisca (ver. 3).

2. Aquila (ver. 3).

   a. They have worked with the Apostle, συνεργοὶ ἐν Χριστῷ (ver. 3).

   b. They volunteered to suffer death, in order to save him (ver. 4).

   c. They have thus earned the gratitude of all the Gentile Churches, as well as his own (ver. 4).

[*Obs.* 1. Prisca, 2 Tim. iv. 19, is Priscilla, Acts xviii. 2; 1 Cor. xvi. 19. When addressed or referred to she is named first, probably as being the stronger and more decided character, Acts xviii. 18; 2 Tim. iv. 19: not in 1 Cor. xvi. 19, where both *salute*. Aquila was a native of Pontus, who had settled with his wife at Rome, when he was expelled by the Decree of Claudius Caesar (Merivale, *Romans under the Empire,* vi. p. 263, ed. 1858). On reaching Corinth they met S. Paul, and their conversion followed. They thence went to Ephesus (Acts xviii. 18, 26; 1 Cor. xvi. 19), and had again, before the date of this Epistle, returned to Rome. At the close of S. Paul's life (2 Tim. iv. 19) they were again living at Ephesus.]

[*Obs.* 2. Of the epithet συνεργοί, the instruction in Christian doctrine which Aquila and his wife gave to the learned Alexandrian Apollos is a conspicuous illustration, Acts xviii. 26. They (τράχηλον ὑπέθηκαν) placed their own necks under the axe of the executioner ; i. e. invited death, in order to save the Apostle's life. This may have occurred during the Jewish riots at Corinth, Acts xviii. 12 ; or in the pagan τάραχος οὐκ ὀλίγος at Ephesus, Acts xix. 23.]

3. The ἐκκλησία in the house of Prisca and Aquila (ver. 5).

[*Obs.* τὴν κατ' οἶκον αὐτῶν ἐκκλησίαν probably means the Christians who were accustomed to meet at the house of Aquila and Prisca, rather than the members of their household, which would have been very small. Aquila and Prisca used their house at Ephesus for a similar purpose, 1 Cor. xvi. 19. Nymphas had a κατ' οἶκον ἐκκλησία at Laodicea (Col. iv. 15) ; so had Philemon at Colossae (Philem. 2).]

4. Epaenetus (ver. 5).

> *a.* Beloved by the Apostle, ἀγαπητός μου (ver. 5).
> *b.* The first convert from the western portion of Asia Minor (ἀπαρχὴ τῆς 'Ασίας), (ver. 5).

[*Obs.* 1. Instead of 'Αχαίας text. rec., read 'Ασίας with A. B. ℵ. C. D*. F. G. It. Copt. aeth. etc. 'Αχαίας is at issue with 1 Cor. xvi. 15, where Stephanas is said to be ἀπαρχὴ τῆς 'Αχαίας, unless, (1) ἀπαρχή be *a* first-fruit, or (2) Epaenetus was an inmate of the household of Stephanas, and baptized at the same time. Dorotheus, quoted by Justiniani, makes Epaenetus subsequently Bishop of Carthage.]

[*Obs.* 2. Asia is here used not as 'Asia proconsularis,' or 'cis Taurum,' but in the narrowest of its three senses, as when it is contrasted with Pontus (Acts ii. 9) or Cilicia (Acts vi. 9) ; or described as lying in the Apostle's journey between Phrygia and Galatia on the one hand, and Mysia on the other (Acts xvi. 6) ; or distinguished from Cappadocia and Bithynia, as well as Pontus and Galatia (1 S. Pet. i. 1) ; or referred to as the district within which the Seven Churches of the Apocalypse were situated (Rev. i. 4, 11).]

5. Mary (Μαριάμ), a Jewess by birth (ver. 6). At some past time she had toiled much with a view to helping (εἰς) the Romans (ὑμᾶς) (ver. 6).

[*Obs.* 1. The aorist ἐκοπίασε points to some past date well known to the readers of the Epistle. Probably she was a deaconess. The work of this Mary would not have included *public* teaching, see 1 Cor. xiv. 34, 35 ; but very probably private instruction in Christian doctrine. See S. Chrys. *in loc.*]

[*Obs.* 2. There seems no sufficient reason for εἰς ἡμᾶς.]

6. Andronicus (ver. 7).

[*Obs.* He is said by Dorotheus to have become a bishop in Pannonia. Such traditions are probably of later growth.]

7. **Junias, or Junianus,** 'Ιουνιᾶς (ver. 7).

[*Obs.* S. Chrys. and others, with the A. V. accentuate 'Ιουνίαν as *feminine*, and understand the sister or wife of Andronicus. ἐπίσημοι ἐν τοῖς ἀποστόλοις (ver. 7) is not decisive. Cf. συνεργοί (ver. 3) of Prisca.]

§ Andronicus and Junias characterized (ver. 7)—

(1) as *kinsmen* of the Apostle (συγγενεῖς), (ver. 7).

(2) as having been *fellow-prisoners* with him (συναιχμάλωτοι), (ver. 7).

(3) as enjoying *great consideration* (ἐπίσημοι) among the Apostles (ver. 7).

(4) as having been 'members of Christ' (ἐν Χριστῷ) *before* the Apostle himself (ver. 7).

[*Obs.* 1. συγγενεῖς may mean only Israelites (ix. 3). But when the context does not require this, the narrower meaning of 'relations' is more natural (S. Mark vi. 4; Acts x. 24), as also implying a distinction which Jewish birth alone would hardly give. The Apostle had a sister and a nephew, Acts xxiii. 16. In vers. 11, 21 the designation is applied to Herodion, Lucius, Jason, and Sosipater. We know too little of the Apostle's family to indulge in conjectures as to the degree of kin in which these persons stood to him: probably it would have been a distant one.]

[*Obs.* 2. συναιχμαλώτους refers to some unrecorded imprisonment of the Apostle: we know that he was imprisoned seven times, S. Clem. Rom. 1 *Ep. ad Cor.* 5; cf. 2 Cor. vi. 5. The word is based on the metaphor of captivity *in war*, vii. 23; 2 Cor. x. 5; Eph. iv. 8.]

[*Obs.* 3. For ἐπίσημοι ἐν ἀποστόλοις, highly esteemed by the Apostles, cf. Eur. *Hippol.* 103 ἐπίσημος ἐν βροτοῖς, &c. In 1 Cor. xv. 7 ἀπόστολος is used by S. Paul in the *generic* sense, but even then including the twelve. Meyer will not allow this wider reference elsewhere. But see 2 Cor. viii. 23; compare Acts xiv. 4, 14. Origen, S. Chrys. understand 'distinguished among Apostles,' i. e. distinguished Apostles; and S. Chrys. expresses his wonder at the distinction thus conferred upon a woman, as he reads Junia (*in loc.*).]

[*Obs.* 4. Obs. the expression ἐν Χριστῷ εἶναι, for being a Christian; ἐν Χριστῷ γίνεσθαι, for conversion. The Christian life is conceived of, not simply as an assent to the doctrine of Christ, but as incorporation with —existence in—Christ, as the sphere of the New Life. An earlier date of conversion than his own was in S. Paul's eyes a great distinction. Comp. Acts xxi. 16 ἀρχαίῳ μαθητῇ.]

8. **Amplias,** ἀγαπητός μου ἐν Κυρίῳ (ver. 8).

[*Obs.* Amplias, abbreviated for Ampliatus, a common name in the imperial household: Gruter, *Inscr. Rom. Corp.* p. 62. 10; Lightfoot, *Philippians*, p. 174, 'Caesar's household.' Tradition (pseudo-Hippolytus quoted by Justiniani) makes him subsequently Bishop of Odessa.]

9. Urbanus, συνεργὸς ἡμῶν ἐν Χριστῷ (ver. 9).

[*Obs.* Also common in the imperial household: Lightfoot, p. 174. Said by pseudo-Hippolytus, in his 'history of the Seventy disciples' quoted by Justiniani, to have become a Bishop in Macedonia. Nothing about him is certainly known; but the prep. ἡμῶν seems to show that Urbanus had helped, not the Apostle (who uses μου when referring to himself), but the Roman Church, at some earlier time, in propagating the Faith.]

10. Stachys, ἀγαπητός μου (ver. 9).

[*Obs.* Possibly a court-physician mentioned in an inscription: Lightfoot, *ubi supra*. The Roman Martyrology makes him Bishop of Byzantium.]

11. Apelles, ὁ δόκιμος ἐν Χριστῷ (ver. 10).

[*Obs.* The name of a well-known Jew of the previous generation: Hor. *Sat.* i. 5. 100. And of a court-tragedian, who belonged to Ascalon under Caligula (Lightfoot). He is not to be confounded with Apollos.]

12. Some of the slaves of Aristobulus, οἱ ἐκ τῶν Ἀριστοβούλου (ver. 10).

[*Obs.* Possibly Aristobulus the younger, grandson of Herod the Great. He died at Rome, and may have left his slaves to the Emperor Claudius: Joseph. *Bell. Jud.* ii. 11. 6; Lightfoot, p. 175.]

13. Herodion, a kinsman of the Apostle (ver. 11).

[*Obs.* Possibly a freedman of the Herodian family, one of the Aristobuliani.]

14. Some of the slaves of Narcissus, οἱ ἐκ τῶν Ναρκίσσου, ὄντες ἐν Κυρίῳ (ver. 11).

[*Obs.* Narcissus *may* have been the powerful libertus of the Emperor Claudius: Suet. *Claudius*, 37; *Vesp.* 4; Tac. *Ann.* xi. 29 sqq.; xii. 57. Although his death occurred in the first year of Nero, A.D. 54: Tac. *Ann.* xiii. 1, his household would have been kept together, and have continued to bear his name, after passing into the hands of the Emperor. On his enormous fortune, see Juv. xiv. 329; Neander, *Planting and Training*, i. p. 279, note 1, E. T.]

15. Tryphaena (ver. 12), } κοπιῶσαι ἐν Κυρίῳ (ver. 12).
16. Tryphosa (ver. 12),

17. Persis, ἡ ἀγαπητή, ἥτις πολλὰ ἐκοπίασεν ἐν Κυρίῳ (ver. 12).

[*Obs.* For the occurrence of these names in inscriptions referring to the imperial household, see Lightfoot, p. 173. These women were probably deaconesses: Persis evidently stood highest in the estimate of the Apostle. A rich widow, Tryphaena of Iconium, is mentioned in the *Acts of Thecla*, c. 9.]

18. Rufus, ὁ ἐκλεκτὸς ἐν Κυρίῳ (ver. 13).

[*Obs.* He may have been the son of Simon of Cyrene, and brother of Alexander, S. Mark xv. 21. S. Mark, who probably wrote in Rome, assumes that Rufus was well known. ἐκλεκτὸς ἐν Κυρίῳ, 'a choice Christian,' not merely chosen to be a Christian, which would imply nothing distinctive. Cf. 1 Tim. v. 21; 1 S. Pet. ii. 4; 2 S. John i. 13; Wisd. iii. 14.]

19. The mother of Rufus, who by her tender charity made herself a mother to the Apostle (ver. 13).

[*Obs.* For an earlier acknowledgment of *personal* indebtedness, see ver. 2. Also 1 Cor. xvi. 18; Philem. 11. The circumstances referred to are quite unknown.]

20. Asyncritus (ver. 14).

[*Obs.* With Asyncritus, the laudatory epithets cease. S. Chrys. thinks that the names which follow are those of Christians of less eminence for sanctity or labour. The order of names Ἑρμῆν, Πατρόβαν, Ἑρμᾶν, according to A. B. C. D.* F. G. P. ℵ.]

21. Phlegon (ver. 14).

22. Hermes (ver. 14).

[*Obs.* A very common name in inscriptions of the household.]

23. Patrobas (ver. 14).

[*Obs.* Perhaps a dependent of Patrobius, the freedman of Nero, who was killed by Galba: Tac. *Hist.* i. 49; ii. 95.]

24. Hermas (ver. 14).

[*Obs.* Origen (*in loc.*) makes this Hermas the author of the book ὁ ποιμήν: so Eus. *Eccl. Hist.* iii. 3, on which however see the note of Valesius, *Annotat. Var.* i. p. 90, ed. Cantab. 1720. According to the Muratorian Fragment, the writer of the ποιμήν was a brother to Pius I, Bishop of Rome, and would therefore have lived in the middle of the second century.]

25. Christians associated with the five persons who are last named (ver. 14).

[*Obs.* These 'brethren' were probably members of κατ' οἶκον ἐκκλησίαι, gathered round each of the above-named Christians, who, Olshausen suggests, may have been presbyters.]

26. Philologus (ver. 15).

[*Obs.* The name is found in inscriptions connected with the imperial household.]

27. Julia, probably wife of Philologus (ver. 15).

[*Obs.* This name would belong to a dependent of the court.]

Conclusion: ch. XVI.

28. Nereus (ver. 15).

29. The Sister of Nereus (ver. 15).

[*Obs.* Nereis was a member of the household about this time.]

30. Olympas (ver. 15).

31. Christians associated with the five persons who are last named (ver. 15).

[*Obs.* The names in vers. 14, 15 occur in Gruter. On the general subject of these names, see Lightfoot's account of inscriptions in Columbaria at Rome (*Journal of Classical Philology*, No. x. p. 57), used as receptacles for the ashes of slaves and freedmen of the imperial family. Some of the names, as Hermas and Nereis, are connected with the Claudian gens; others, as Tryphaena and Tryphosa, with the Valerian (that of Messalina); others, as Philologus and Ampliatus, occur independently. Cf. Merivale, *Romans under the Emp.* vi. 259, note 3. See the note 'Caesar's Household' in Lightfoot, *Philippians*, pp. 171-177.]

§ *Precept.* The Roman Christians are to salute each other with the φίλημα ἅγιον (ver. 16 a).

[*Obs.* The ancient eastern and especially Jewish custom of marking a greeting with a kiss led to the Christian ceremony of the φίλημα ἅγιον 1 Cor. xvi. 20; 2 Cor. xiii. 12; 1 Thess. v. 26: φίλημα ἀγάπης 1 S. Pet. v. 14; *Const. Ap.* ii. 57. 12 τὸ ἐν Κυρίῳ φίλημα: Tert. *de Orat.* 18 'osculum pacis.' On the moral meaning of the ceremony, see the beautiful words of S. Chrysostom. *Hom. in* 2 *Cor.* viii. 12. So S. Cyr. Hierosol. *Cat. Myst.* v. 3 [τοῦτο τὸ φίλημα] ἀνακίρνησι τὰς ψυχὰς ἀλλήλαις, καὶ πᾶσαν ἀμνησικακίαν αὐταῖς μνηστεύεται. Σημεῖον τοίνυν ἐστὶ τὸ φίλημα, τοῦ ἀνακραθῆναι τὰς ψυχάς, καὶ πᾶσαν ἐξορίζειν μνησικακίαν. The Kiss of Peace was a feature of the Eucharistic Service of the Primitive Church; but in the East, in accordance with S. Matt. v. 24, it took place at the Oblation of the Elements, (S. Cyr. Hierosol. *Catech. Mystagog.* v. 3; S. Chrys. *de Compunct. Cord.* i. 3; perhaps too S. Justin Martyr, *Apol.* i. 65); while in the West, it was after the Consecration and the Lord's Prayer, 'inter ipsa Sacramenta'; S. Aug. *contr. lit. Petiliani*, ii. 53; *Serm. de tempore*, ccxxvii; especially, Innocentii I, *Ep.* xxv. *ad Decentium*, c. 1 'Pacis osculum dandum esse post confecta mysteria, ut appareat populum ad omnia, quae in mysteriis aguntur, atque in ecclesia celebrantur, praebuisse consensum.']

§ Greetings sent to the Church of Rome from *all* the Churches of Christ (ver. 16 b).

[*Obs.* The evidence for πᾶσαι (ver. 16 b), omitted by *text. rec.*, is decisive. It does not follow that all the Churches had actually entrusted the Apostle with their greetings to the Church of Rome; but 'quoniam cognovit omnium erga Romanos studium, omnium nomine salutat.' It seems difficult to restrict πᾶσαι to (1) all the Greek Churches, or (2) all the Churches in and about Corinth, without arbitrariness.]

§ 3.

Warnings against false teachers who might be expected to introduce error and division into the Church of Rome (vers. 17–20).

[*Obs.* 1. If the false teachers had actually appeared in Rome when S. Paul wrote, he would probably have treated of the dangers which they brought with them at length, and in the body of the Epistle. This supplementary treatment shows that a hint of a possibly impending danger was all that was needed.]

[*Obs.* 2. It would seem from ver. 17 that Judaizing teachers are meant: Gal. ii. 6. 11 sq.; Phil. iii. 2 sqq. 18, 19; 2 Cor. xi. 13 sqq.]

§ *Precept.* Mark and avoid false teachers (ver. 17).

(1) The *persons* referred to are characterized by two notes (ver. 17).
- *a.* They cause διχοστασίαι and σκάνδαλα (ver. 17).
- *b.* They act παρὰ τὴν διδαχὴν ἣν ἐμάθετε (ver. 17).

[*Obs.* 1. The expression διχοστασίαι finds its foil and explanation in the Apostle's fervent language about Church Unity in xv. 6 sq. as κατὰ Ἰησοῦν Χριστόν and designed to glorify GOD the Father. διχοστασίαι would include any separations which break up the religious intercommunion of souls: they characterise the σαρκικοί 1 Cor. iii. 3, and form the twelfth ἔργον τῆς σαρκός Gal. v. 20. For σκάνδαλα, see xiv. 13. It is here used, perhaps, in a wider sense.]

[*Obs.* 2. In παρὰ τὴν διδαχὴν ἣν ἐμάθετε, παρά means 'opposition as implied in going beyond' the received Revelation. The principle of Divine Revelation is opposed, when anything is added on *human* authority. For the use of παρά, see Rom. i. 25; iv. 18; xii. 3; Gal. i. 8. This canon of truth is stated more strongly at Gal. i. 8, and is also found in 1 S. John ii. 20–27; 2 S. John 9; S. Jude 3. It is the principle of Catholic prescription, as worked out by S. Irenaeus and Tertullian in the second and third centuries; and it is equally opposed to all denials and all accretive developments of the original deposit of Christian Doctrine committed to the Church of Christ.]

2. The *conduct* towards them prescribed by the Apostle is,

- *a.* σκοπεῖν, keep them in view (in order to guard against them), (ver. 17).

  [*Obs.* σκοπεῖν = 'speculari.' Cf. Phil. iii. 2 βλέπετε.]

- *b.* ἐκκλίνατε ἀπ' αὐτῶν, 'turn away from them' (ver. 17).

  [*Obs.* This *rule*, ἐκκλίνατε κ.τ.λ., is not for the Rulers of the Church who might be bound to excommunicate such offenders; but for private Christians. It is a specific application of the general principle ἐκκλίνειν ἀπὸ κακοῦ 1 S. Pet. iii. 11. Compare περιίστασο, Tit. iii. 9 and 2 S. John 10. S. Timothy as a Bishop was desired ἐν πραΰτητι παιδεύειν τοὺς ἀντιδιατιθεμένους 2 Tim. ii. 25. Cf. ver. 14, and Titus, αἱρετικὸν ἄνθρωπον μετὰ μίαν καὶ δευτέραν νουθεσίαν παραιτοῦ iii. 10.]

Conclusion: ch. XVI.

Arg. 1. From the *character* and *proceedings* of these teachers (ver. 18).

a. The *Master* whom they *serve* (δουλεύουσι) is, (ver. 18),
{ (negative) *not* our Lord Jesus Christ (ver. 18),
{ (positive) *but* τῇ ἑαυτῶν κοιλίᾳ (ver. 18).

b. The *nature* of their efforts (ver. 18)—

{ (their *teaching*); deception (ἐξαπατῶσιν), (ver. 18).
{ (*sphere* in which they work); the affections of the simple (αἱ καρδίαι τῶν ἀκάκων), (ver. 18).
{ (*means* which they employ); speeches reassuring as to substance, and well-expressed (χρηστολογία and εὐλογία), (ver. 18).

[*Obs.* 1. The *sensual* trait implied in τῇ κοιλίᾳ αὐτῶν corresponds to the description of the Judaizing ἐχθροὶ τοῦ σταυροῦ in Phil. iii. 18. The phrases τῇ κοιλίᾳ δουλεύειν, τῇ γαστρὶ δουλεύειν, 'abdomini servire' (Seneca, *de Benef.* vii. 26), describe the particular form of selfishness to which the teachers in question were enslaved, and which their influence and popularity enabled them to gratify. Cf. 2 Cor. xi. 20 εἴ τις κατεσθίει.]

[*Obs.* 2. The *deceitfulness* of these teachers corresponds with that ascribed to the Corinthian Judaizers: 2 Cor. xi. 13 ψευδαπόστολοι, ἐργάται δόλιοι, μετασχηματιζόμενοι εἰς ἀποστόλους Χριστοῦ κ.τ.λ. The heretics of the Pastoral Epistles too νομίζουσι πορισμὸν εἶναι τὴν εὐσέβειαν 1 Tim. vi. 5. They are φρεναπάται μάλιστα οἱ ἐκ τῆς περιτομῆς, and διδάσκοντες ἃ μὴ δεῖ αἰσχροῦ κέρδους χάριν (Tit. i. 10, 11). The πλάνη τοῦ Βαλαὰμ μισθοῦ S. Jude 11; 2 S. Pet. ii. 15; Rev. ii. 14. Cf. ib. ver. 9 βλασφημία τῶν λεγόντων Ἰουδαίους εἶναι ἑαυτοὺς καὶ οὐκ εἰσί are analogous, but distinct, as belonging to a later Antinomianism which caricatured S. Paul's doctrines on the Subject of Grace.]

[*Obs.* 3. *Machinery of deception.* χρηστολογία differs from εὐλογία as the substance of what is said from its form. The false teachers said admirable things and expressed themselves well. *Julius Capitolinus* referring to Pertinax, c. 13 'Chrestologum eum appellantes, qui bene loqueretur et male faceret.' So S. Chrys. *in loc.* The classical λόγοι χρηστοί is equivalent. εὐλογία here rather 'fine phraseology' (Plat. *Rep.* 400 D) than, according to the more ordinary signification, 'praise,' 'blessing.' The ἄκακοι (Heb. vii. 26) neither do, nor suspect others of, evil.]

Arg. 2. From the Apostle's (i) *delight* in, and (ii) *wishes* respecting the Roman Christians (ver. 19).

[*Obs.* γάρ (ver. 19) apparently assigns a new reason for παρακαλῶ κ. τ. λ. ver. 17. Meyer will not allow that the use of a second *coordinated* γάρ is to be found in the N. T., and he refers γάρ here to τὰς καρδίας τῶν ἀκάκων ver. 18, as justifying that phrase. But cf. Winer, *Gr. N. T.* p. 560. This is hardly an 'explicative' γάρ.]

i. The obedience of the Romans to the Faith is a matter of general notoriety in the Church; and on this very account (οὖν ver. 19) the Apostle delights in them. Surely they would not belie their character! (ver. 19).

[*Obs.* ὑπακοή here = πίστις. Rom. i. 8 ἡ πίστις ὑμῶν καταγγέλλεται ἐν ὅλῳ τῷ κόσμῳ. For the reputation of the Thessalonians, cf. 1 Thess. i. 4; and Corinthians, cf. 2 Cor. vii. 14. There is no sufficient authority for τό before ἐφ' in text. rec. A.B. al. read ἐφ' ὑμῖν οὖν χαίρω.]

ii. But (δέ, adversat.) the Apostle wishes them to be—

{ *a.* practically wise in the pursuit of good (ver. 19).
{ *b.* undefiled (ἀκεραίους) in the direction of evil (ver. 19).

This will only be possible, if they resolve to keep away from (ἐκκλίνειν ἀπό) the teachers referred to in ver. 17.

[*Obs.* Compare with the Apostolic θέλω our Lord's precept, S. Matt. x. 16 γίνεσθε φρόνιμοι ὡς οἱ ὄφεις, καὶ ἀκέραιοι ὡς αἱ περιστεραί. The Apostle uses σοφός as practically equivalent to φρόνιμος. Cf. xi. 33. ἀκέραιος, lit. *unmixed*; not from κέρας, κεραΐζειν (Reithmayr). Obs. εἰς, as = with reference to, in the direction of. The abstract words ἀγαθόν, κακόν, mean respectively the Apostolic Faith, and the error of the Judaizing teachers.]

Arg. 3. From encouraging *promise of victory;* (δέ contrasts with the apprehensions of ver. 20). The GOD of Peace will bruise Satan under the feet of the Roman Church shortly. [Let it not forfeit victory by sinful concessions.] (ver. 20).

[*Obs.* 1. The name Satan הַשָּׂטָן (enemy. LXX transl. διάβολος) occurs in 1 Chron. xxi. 1; Job i. 6; Zech. iii. 1, &c. In N. T. thirty-five times. On the personality of the Evil One, see Martensen, *Dogmatik*, § 101, E. T. p. 188. The Christian belief in the Devil as 'a superhuman yet created spirit, who originally was good, but fell from his station, and in pride became the enemy of GOD, involves the clearest contrast and opposition to the dualism of heathendom, which either makes two fundamentally distinct existences, as in the Persian religion; or makes evil the dark and mysterious source from which good developes itself, and which existence conquers, the view adopted by the Greek and Northern mythologies.' See the whole section.]

[*Obs.* 2. When naming Satan, S. Paul thinks of the ministers or organs through whom Satan works, namely, the Judaizing teachers. Cf. 2 Cor. xi. 15. The bruising Satan takes place only in the might of GOD's power. GOD is said to be τῆς εἰρήνης in contrast to the ποιοῦντες τὰς διχοστασίας ver. 17. συντρίψει is an allusion to Gen. iii. 15.]

§ Benediction (ver. 20) conveys—

Conclusion: ch. XVI. 303

ἡ χάρις   { a. *source* (τοῦ Κ. 'Ι. Χ.) is Jesus Christ (ver. 20 b).
of which   { b. *recipients* (μεθ' ὑμῶν) are the readers of the Epistle
the   (ver. 20 b).

§ 4.

Eight Christians who unite with the Apostle in sending greetings to the Roman Church (vers. 21–23).

1. Timotheus, ὁ συνεργός μου (ver. 21).

[*Obs.* On the history of S. Timothy, see the materials in Winer's *Rehlwoerterbuch*. s. v. Besides the two Epistles addressed to him by the Apostle, see especially Acts xvi. 1–3; Phil. ii. 19 sqq. His name is associated with that of S. Paul as a joint writer of 2 Cor.; Phil.; Col.; 1 Thess.; 2 Thess.; Philemon; and, as he was in Corinth when the Epistle to the Romans was written, surprise may be felt at the omission of his name at the beginning of this Epistle. It is possible that, (1) he did not arrive in Corinth until the Epistle was partly composed, or (2) that S. Paul was unwilling to associate any one of less than Apostolic authority with himself when addressing the Roman Church.]

2. Lucius,
3. Jason,   } οἱ συγγενεῖς μου (ver. 21).
4. Sosipater,

[*Obs.* 1. Lucius is identified with S. Luke the Evangelist by Origen, and some moderns. He is probably Lucius of Cyrene, a teacher in the Church of Antioch, Acts xiii. 1, who, according to *Const. Apost.* vii. 46, was made Bishop of Cenchreae by S. Paul, although a distinct tradition places him at Laodicea.]

[*Obs.* 2. Jason is probably the Thessalonian Christian of that name, with whom S. Paul lodged in his Second Missionary Journey, Acts xvii. 5 sqq., and who would have been likely to attach himself to the Apostle. Tradition makes him Bishop of Tarsus, Fabricius, *Lux Evangelii*, p. 91.]

[*Obs.* 3. Sosipater, probably (although not certainly) Sopater of Beroea in Macedonia, whom in his Third Missionary Journey the Apostle took with him from Greece to Asia, Acts xx. 4. According to tradition, Bishop of Iconium. All three were συγγενεῖς of the Apostle, but how nearly related it is impossible to conjecture.]

5. Tertius, the Amanuensis.

{ a. His *claim*, ὁ γράψας τὴν ἐπιστολήν (ver. 22).
{ b. His *message*, ἀσπάζομαι ἐν Κυρίῳ (ver. 22).

[*Obs.* 1. Tertius was probably an Italian merchant at Corinth, well known to members of the Roman Church: he too is traditionally represented as becoming a Bishop of Iconium; Fabricius, *Lux Evangelii*, p. 117. The opinions, (1) that the Apostle's own name was Tertius Paulus (Roloff, *de tribus Pauli nomin.* 1731), and (2) that Tertius was the same person as Silas, as being the Latin rendering of שְׁלִישׁ or שְׁלִישִׁי (Burmann al.), are only *curiosa*. Silas was not with S. Paul at this time, but in Antioch, Acts xv. 34: and there does not seem to have been any such Hebrew proper name as שְׁלִישִׁי. Tertius was a common name; cf. Gruter.]

[*Obs.* 2. Tertius, as ὑπογραφεύς, is allowed by the Apostle to send a greeting in his own name, and in the first person. This is what would have occurred naturally: S. Paul resumes his dictation in ver. 23. There is no ground for the theory of Grotius, that Tertius merely copied S. Paul's MS., and placed this personal greeting in the margin. For the Apostle's custom of dictating his Epistles, see 1 Cor. xvi. 21; Gal. vi. 11; Col. iv. 18; 2 Thess. iii. 17.]

6. Gaius, the host (ξένος), (ver. 23)—
{   *a.* of the Apostle (μου), (ver. 23).
    b. of all Christians who claim hospitality from him (καὶ τῆς ἐκκλησίας ὅλης), (ver. 23).

[*Obs.* This Gaius must be identified with Gaius of Corinth, who was baptized by the Apostle, 1 Cor. i. 14. The phrase καὶ τῆς ἐκκλησίας ὅλης is better explained by his hospitality to all Christians visiting Corinth (Meyer), than by his opening his house for prayer. When S. Paul first arrived at Corinth, he stayed with Aquila and Priscilla, Acts xviii. 1 sqq. He preached, but did not lodge, in the house of Justus, Acts xviii. 7. This Gaius of Corinth *may* be also Gaius of Derbe, Acts xx. 4; Derbe being his real birthplace: but he cannot also be identified with Gaius of Thessalonica, Acts xix. 29. He has also been identified with the Gaius of 3 Ep. S. John: this is possible, if he is the same person as Gaius of Derbe. (See Michaelis, *Einl. N. T.* ii. 1279 sq.)]

7. Erastus, οἰκόνομος τῆς πόλεως (Arcarius civitatis), (ver. 23).

[*Obs.* There seems to be no adequate reason for rejecting the identity of this Erastus with the person named in Acts xix. 22, and 2 Tim. iv. 20, as he would probably have given up his civil position, in order to devote himself to the Apostle, and is called οἰκόνομος τῆς πόλεως, as having occupied that office in former years. Neander, *Pflanzung*, i. 394, however, will not allow this supposition, and denies the identity. In the *Menolog. Graecum* (i. 179) he is described as subsequently Oeconomus of the Church at Jerusalem, and Bishop of Paneas. He must have been a person of high consideration at Corinth. See 1 Cor. i. 26 sqq.]

8. Quartus, ὁ ἀδελφός (ver. 23).

[*Obs.* ἀδελφός = a Christian. The absence of αὐτοῦ (see ver. 15) is fatal to the supposition that he was a brother of Erastus.]

Conclusion: ch. XVI.

§ Benediction (repeated from ver. 20 b), (ver. 24).

[*Obs.* This benediction, repeated from ver. 20, is an Apostolic equivalent to the Latin 'vale iterum,' and is wanting in A. B. C. ℵ. Copt. Aeth. Vulg. etc. But the repetition, of itself, would have led the copyists to omit it, cf. Meyer. Wolf says, 'Apostoli mos ita fert ut eandem salutandi formulam aliquoties repetat.' Vide 2 Thess. iii. 16 and 18.]

§ 5.

Concluding Doxology (vers. 25–27).

[*Obs.* 1. *Genuineness of the Doxology.* This has been disputed on the grounds of (1) 'the unsuitableness of its position, whether at the end of c. xiv. or after xvi. 23.' It is unsuitable in the former, but not in the latter position, where, after all the closing messages have been delivered, it gathers up the main thoughts of the Epistle into an ascription of praise to GOD. (2) 'Its "unpauline" want of simplicity.' It is more elaborate, certainly, than any other doxology in S. Paul; it much resembles S. Jude 24, 25, which is, not impossibly, modelled on it. But its unique position, at the close of an Epistle so full of the deepest thought, will account for its fervid language and broken structure—evidences of the strong, over-mastering feelings of the writer. (3) 'The unusual and obscure character of some of its language.' But when examined in detail, this is found to represent in a concentrated form the leading truths of the Epistle, and to be especially characteristic of S. Paul. The suggestion that χρόνοις αἰωνίοις, σεσιγημένου, αἰωνίου Θεοῦ, γνωρισθέντος, belong to the 'gnosticising' phraseology of a later period, is a mistake which rests on a very partial and clearly accidental coincidence of expression.]

[*Obs.* 2. *Position of the Doxology.* It is placed—

(1) *After* xvi. 24, by B. C. D. E. ℵ. Syr. Copt. Aeth. Vulg. Lat. Fathers.

(2) *After* xiv. 23 by L. most min. Syr. Chrys. Theod. Oecum. Theophyl. etc.

(3) *Both after* xiv. 23 *and* xvi. 23 by A. P. al.

(4) *Nowhere.* D.*** F. G. Marcion al.

The weight of evidence is in favour of (1). The *early* witnesses in favour of (2) may be easily accounted for (*a*) by the uniqueness of a doxological conclusion in a Pauline Epistle; (*b*) by the apparent reference of ὑμᾶς στηρίξαι to the case of the ἀσθενεῖς in c. xiv, which would have led early copyists to place it after xiv. 23. (3) The repetition of the doxology represents uncertainty in early times as to its real position, an uncertainty produced by the mistake of the copyists just referred to. (4) The total omission of the doxology by Marcion is explained by ver. 26 διά τε γραφῶν προφητικῶν. In modern times the omission has been due to 'an old precarious criticism' which inferred from the uncertainty of the position the conclusion that it could not be genuine. See Meyer, *App. Crit.*]

x

[*Obs.* 3. *Analysis of the Doxology.*

I. τῷ δὲ δυναμένῳ ὑμᾶς—

στηρίξαι
{
  i. κατὰ { τὸ εὐαγγέλιόν μου, καὶ
           { τὸ κήρυγμα Ἰησοῦ Χριστοῦ (ver. 25).

  ii. κατὰ ἀποκάλυψιν μυστηρίου
{
    a. χρόνοις αἰωνίοις σεσιγημένου (ver. 25).
    b. φανερωθέντος δὲ νῦν (ver. 26).
    c. γνωρισθέντος {
      a. διὰ γραφῶν προφητικῶν,
      b. κατ' ἐπιταγὴν τοῦ αἰωνίου Θεοῦ,
      c. εἰς ὑπακοὴν πίστεως,
      d. εἰς πάντα τὰ ἔθνη (ver. 26).
}

II. Θεῷ { *a.* μόνῳ σοφῷ,
      b. διὰ Ἰησοῦ Χριστοῦ, *Ω*
      c. [εἴη δόξα].
      { *a.* ἡ δόξα
        b. εἰς τοὺς αἰῶνας (ver. 27).

[*Obs.* 4. *Incomplete Structure of the Doxology.* In the rapid pressure of the thoughts of vers. 25, 26 τῷ δὲ δυναμένῳ is left without any governing verb; the Apostle would probably have added ἡ δόξα εἴη. With a view to doing this, he resumes μόνῳ σοφῷ Θεῷ διὰ Ἰησοῦ Χριστοῦ in ver. 27. But the mention of Jesus Christ, Whose appearance among men enables them to glorify the σοφία of GOD, again creates an anacoluthon, by diverting the doxology to Jesus Christ Himself; so that μόνῳ σοφῷ Θεῷ is also without government.]

§ *Ascription* I (vers. 25, 26).

1. Subject of the Doxology—GOD's *power* to confirm the faithful.

To GOD, as to Him Who is able to keep you steadfast (στηρίξαι) —[be glory], (ver. 25).

[*Obs.* 1. The construction is incomplete: the dat. τῷ δυναμένῳ being without government. Olshausen's conjecture συνίστημι is entirely without basis in MSS.]

[*Obs.* 2. For στηρίξαι, see i. 11 στηριχθῆναι. It is used of human agency, S. Luke xxii. 32; 1 Thess. iii. 2; S. James v. 8: or of Divine, as here, 1 Thess. iii. 13; 2 Thess. ii. 17; iii. 3; 1 S. Pet. v. 10. Perseverance is an especial grace of GOD.]

2. *Reference* of στηρίξαι. It was in respect of (κατά) adhesion to *the* GOSPEL, which is characterised, in two ways (ver. 25).

I. (*Ratione subjecti*) as
{
  a. The Gospel, which had been entrusted to *the Apostle* to preach (τὸ εὐαγγέλιόν μου) (ver. 25).
  b. The Gospel which *Christ Himself* preached (by means of the Apostle), (κήρυγμα Ἰησοῦ Χριστοῦ), (ver. 25).
}

[*Obs.* 1. κατά here of *reference*; not apparently, (1) of the standard or rule, 'according to the rule of my Gospel'; nor (2) of the mode or character, 'after the manner of my Gospel,' cf. Meyer. It is to be explained by his anxieties about a Judaizing mission in Rome (vers. 17-19).]

[*Obs.* 2. τὸ εὐαγγέλιόν μου. Cf. Rom. ii. 16 'the Gospel as revealed to me' (1 Cor. xv. 1), in contradistinction here to the Gospel as corrupted by the Judaizers. But, after all, this εὐαγγέλιον was not only the Apostle's own belief; it was, he thankfully adds, nothing less than the truth preached through his agency by Christ Himself.]

[*Obs.* 3. κήρυγμα Ἰησοῦ Χριστοῦ. Origen and Theodoret regard Ἰησοῦ Χριστοῦ as a *gen. object.*, in which case it = Χριστὸς ἐσταυρωμένος, 1 Cor. i. 23; ii. 2. Christ, His Person and Redemptive work, being the subject-matter of the Apostle's preaching. But as a clause, designed to explain the preceding, κήρυγμα is better taken as = ὃ Χριστὸς ἐκήρυξε (S. Chrys.); i. e. through S. Paul as His organ. Cf. Rom. xv. 18 κατειργάσατο Χριστὸς δι' ἐμοῦ: Eph. ii. 17; 2 Cor. xiii. 3. For this use of κήρυγμα, see S. Matt. xii. 41; S. Luke xi. 32; 1 Cor. i. 21; xv. 14; 2 Tim. iv. 17; Tit. i. 3.]

II. (*Ratione objecti*) as the unveiling of the mystery of Redemption.

1. *A mystery*, kept in silence during eternal ages (χρόνοις αἰωνίοις σεσιγημένου), (ver. 25).

2. *A mystery*, made manifest in the *present* time (φανερωθέντος δὲ νῦν), (ver. 26).

3. *A mystery*, made an object of human knowledge (γνωρισθέντος),

   1. (διά) by *means* of the Old Testament prophetic writings, which were its proof and confirmation, διὰ γραφῶν προφητικῶν (ver. 26).

   2. (κατά) in *accordance* with the *command* of GOD, the Eternal, Who commissioned the Apostles to proclaim it (ver. 26).

   3. (εἰς, of *purpose*). In *order to* produce *obedience* to the Faith (ver. 26).

   4. (εἰς, of the *range* of destination.) Among *all the heathen* peoples (ver. 26).

[*Obs.* 1. κατὰ ἀποκάλυψιν is in apposition with κατὰ τὸ εὐαγγέλιόν μου. S. Paul's Gospel was considered, with reference to its contents, as the uncovering of a mystery. That mystery was the whole plan or work of human salvation, perfected through Christ. The appearance of Christ in the world of sense and time was the ἀποκάλυψις μυστηρίου,—and this ἀποκάλυψις was carried forward by the preaching of the Apostles. On μυστήριον, see Rom. xi. 25.]

[*Obs.* 2. The μυστήριον, consisting in the Divine plan of man's Redemption through Jesus Christ, had been kept in silence through the whole duration of a past eternity. χρόνοις αἰωνίοις, dat. of *a space of time* ; so S. John ii. 20 ; Acts viii. 11 ; xiii. 20 ; Eph. iii. 5. It is practically equivalent to the expression πρὸ χρόνων αἰωνίων, although this is stronger in point of form. No human being, of himself, could anticipate GOD's method of redeeming His creatures, Col. i. 26 ; ii. 2 ; Eph. vi. 19 ; 1 S. Pet. i. 20. Even the Prophets, though assisted by the Holy Ghost, only discerned this μυστήριον in a shadowy way, συνεσκιασμένως (Theod.). Comp. 1 S. Pet. i. 10.]

[*Obs.* 3. The Incarnation of the Son of GOD was the φανέρωσις or ἀποκάλυψις μυστηρίου. φανερωθέντος is in contrast (obs. δέ, ver. 26) with σεσιγημένου (ver. 25) ; and νῦν marks the period which has set in since the historic act of φανέρωσις. Cf. Col. i. 26 τὸ μυστήριον τὸ ἀποκεκρυμμένον ἀπὸ τῶν αἰώνων καὶ ἀπὸ τῶν γενεῶν, νῦν δὲ ἐφανερώθη : 2 Tim. i. 9, 10 φανερωθεῖσαν δὲ νῦν : Tit. i. 2, 3 ἐφανέρωσε δὲ καιροῖς ἰδίοις : 1 S. Pet. i. 20 φανερωθέντος δὲ ἐπ' ἐσχάτου τῶν χρόνων : cf. 2 Tim. i. 10 διὰ τῆς ἐπιφανείας. The result of this φανερωθέντος is expressed by γνωρισθέντος : having become manifest in Christ, the Eternal Secret becomes a matter of human knowledge, Rom. iii. 21 ; Col. iv. 4.]

[*Obs.* 4. The γραφαὶ προφητικαί of the Old Testament are the instrument (διά) for propagating a knowledge of the μυστήριον : cf. Rom. i. 2. They supply proof and confirmation of the Gospel-account of Redemption. For their use by our Lord, see S. Matt. v. 17 ; S. Luke xxiv. 27, 44 ; S. John v. 39 : by the Apostles, see Acts xvii. 11 ; 1 S. Pet. i. 11, &c. Prophecy was already ancient ; Christ and His Apostles had only to appeal to it as an anticipation of their teaching.]

[*Obs.* 5. It is in accordance with a command of the Eternal God, that the μυστήριον of Human Redemption, so long kept in silence, thus becomes an object of human knowledge. The predicate αἰωνίου belongs to Him Who disposes of the χρόνοι αἰώνιοι, and of their μυστήρια. But it also enhances the significance of the ἐπιταγή, and the responsibility and dignity of those who, like the Apostles, give it effect, Rom. i. 9 ; 1 Cor. iv. 1 : also Rom. x. 14-16 ; xv. 18 ; 1 Tim. ii. 7 ; Tit. i. 3.]

[*Obs.* 6. The knowledge of the secret Plan of Redemption was intended to produce (εἰς) *obedience* of faith. Cf. Rom. i. 5 ; not to gratify mere human curiosity. And this effect was to extend (εἰς) throughout all the peoples of heathendom, εἰς πάντα τὰ ἔθνη. See Rom. i. 5 ; x. 12, 13 ; Col. i. 6, 23, 26 ; 1 Tim. iii. 16. For this use of εἰς, see S. John viii. 26 λέγω εἰς τὸν κόσμον.]

§ *Ascription* II (ver. 27).

1. *Subject* of the (resumed) Doxology.   GOD's Absolute Wisdom. (μόνῳ σοφῷ) (ver. 27).

[*Obs.* μόνος σοφός = the absolutely wise ; cf. 1 Tim. vi. 15 sq. μόνος δυνάστης, μόνος ἔχων ἀθανασίαν. In Christ, too, are πάντες οἱ θησαυροὶ τῆς σοφίας ... ἀπόκρυφοι, Col. ii. 3, since, according to His Higher Nature, He is one with the μόνος σοφός. Of the σοφία, or practical wisdom of GOD, especially in His dealings with man, the whole Epistle to the Romans is a lengthened exposition: and GOD is therefore, at its close, fittingly glorified in the Attribute, which is so present to the mind of the Apostle and his readers.]

2. *Offerer* of the Doxology (διὰ Ἰησοῦ Χριστοῦ). Jesus Christ (ver. 27).

[*Obs.* Meyer would connect διὰ Ἰησοῦ Χριστοῦ with μόνῳ σοφῷ, 'To GOD only wise through Jesus Christ'; Christ's appearance in the world having been the instrument of exhibiting to man GOD's absolute wisdom. The position of Θεῷ appears to interfere with this: it is more natural to understand εἴη δόξα after Ἰησοῦ Χριστοῦ. Only through Jesus Christ the One Mediator, because He is both GOD and Man, can praise or prayer be offered to the Most High.]

3. Appended Doxology to Jesus Christ Himself (ver. 27).

Ἰ. Χ.

ᾯ

ἡ δόξα

εἰς τοὺς αἰῶνας. ἀμήν

(ver. 27).

[*Obs.* There is no doubt that ᾧ must be retained in the text (see Tisch. *App. Crit.*) and, if so, it is most naturally referred to Jesus Christ. Winer, *Gr. N. T.* p. 710, says, that instead of simply adding ἡ δόξα εἰς τοὺς αἰῶνας the Apostle expresses the substance of the Doxology by a relative clause, just as if Θεῷ had concluded the sentence: and he compares Acts xxiv. 5, 6. So also Meyer *in loc.* and Buttmann, *Neutest. Gr.* p. 252. But this forced manner of construing the sentence is apparently due to an unwillingness to recognise any Apostolic Doxologies addressed to Jesus Christ. Cf. Rom. ix. 5; 2 Tim. iv. 18; Heb. xiii. 21; Rev. i. 6.]

THE END.

www.ingramcontent.com/pod-product-compliance
Lightning Source LLC
Chambersburg PA
CBHW030810230426
43667CB00008B/1143